THE OXFORD HANDBOOK OF

PUBLIC MANAGEMENT

Edited by
EWAN FERLIE
LAURENCE E. LYNN, JR.
and
CHRISTOPHER POLLITT

OXFORD

UNIVERSITY PRESS

OXFORD

UNIVERSITY PRESS

Great Clarendon Street, Oxford OX2 6DP

Oxford University Press is a department of the University of Oxford.
It furthers the University's objective of excellence in research, scholarship,
and education by publishing worldwide in

Oxford New York

Auckland Cape Town Dar es Salaam Hong Kong Karachi
Kuala Lumpur Madrid Melbourne Mexico City Nairobi
New Delhi Shanghai Taipei Toronto

With offices in

Argentina Austria Brazil Chile Czech Republic France Greece
Guatemala Hungary Italy Japan Poland Portugal Singapore
South Korea Switzerland Thailand Turkey Ukraine Vietnam

Oxford is a registered trade mark of Oxford University Press
in the UK and in certain other countries

Published in the United States
by Oxford University Press Inc., New York

British Library Cataloguing in Publication Data

Data available

Library of Congress Cataloguing in Publication Data

Data available

Typeset by SPI Publisher Services, Pondicherry, India
Printed in Great Britain
on acid-free paper by
Antony Rowe Ltd, Chippenham, Wiltshire

ISBN 0-19-925977-1   978-0-19-925977-9

1 3 5 7 9 10 8 6 4 2

Contents

SECTION 3: EXPLORING CURRENT PUBLIC POLICY AND MANAGEMENT THEMES

SECTION 4: FUNCTIONAL AREAS

SECTION 5: NATIONAL AND INTERNATIONAL COMPARISONS

List of Figures

LIST OF TABLES

LIST OF BOXES

LIST OF CONTRIBUTORS

Anthony Bertelli Assistant Professor, Department of Public Administration and Policy, School of Public and International Affairs, University of Georgia, Athens, Georgia, USA

Peter Bogason Professor of Public Administration, Department of Social Sciences, Roskilde University, Roskilde, Denmark

Mark Bovens Professor of Public Administration, Utrecht School of Governance, University of Utrecht, Utrecht, the Netherlands

Young Han Chun Professor, Department of Public Administration Yonsei University, Seoul, Korea

Peter Dahler-Larsen Professor of Evaluation, Dept of Political Science and Public Management, University of Southern Denmark, Odense M, Denmark

Linda deLeon Associate Professor, Department of Public Administration, Graduate School of Public Affairs, University of Colorado at Denver and Health Services Center, Denver, Colorado, USA

Jean-Louis Denis Professeur titulaire, Département d'administration de la santé, Université de Montréal, Montréal, Canada

Robert Dingwall Professor, Institute for the Study of Genetics, University of Nottingham, Nottingham, UK

J. Patrick Dobel Professor, Evans School of Public Affairs, University of Washington, Seattle, Washington, USA

Ewan Ferlie Professor, Centre for Public Services Organisations, School of Management, Royal Holloway University of London, Egham, Surrey, UK

H. George Frederickson Edwin O. Stene Distinguished Professor of Public Administration, Department of Public Administration, The University of Kansas Lawrence, Kansas, USA.

Keith J. Geraghty Centre for Public Services Organizations, School of Management, Royal Holloway University of London, Egham, Surrey, UK

Gregory C. Hill Department of Political Science, Texas A and M University, College Station, Texas, USA

Christopher Hood Gladstone Professor and Fellow of All Souls College, University of Oxford, Oxford, UK

Joanne Kelly Senior Lecturer in Public Budgeting, Government and International Relations, The University of Sydney, Sydney, Australia

Erik-Hans Klijn Professor, Centre for Public Management, Faculty of Social Sciences Erasmus University, Rotterdam, the Netherlands

Patricia W. Ingraham Distinguished Professor of Public Administration, Maxwell School of Citizenship and Public Affairs, Syracuse University, Syracuse, New York, USA

Ann Langley Professeure titulaire, Department of Management, HEC-Montréal, Montréal, Canada

Laurence E. Lynn, Jr. George H. W. Bush Chair and Professor of Public Affairs, George Bush School of Government and Public Service, Texas A and M University, College Station, Texas, USA

Helen Margetts Professor of Society and the Internet, Oxford Internet Institute, University of Oxford, Oxford, UK

David Mathiasen Fellow, National Academy of Public Administration, Washington DC, USA.

Kenneth J. Meier Professor, Department of Political Science, Texas A and M University, College Station, Texas, USA

John Øvretveit Director of Research, The Karolinska Institute Medical Management Centre, Stockholm; Professor of Health Management, The Nordic School of Public Health, Gothenberg and Bergen University Faculty of Medicine, Norway

Christopher Pollitt Professor, Centre for Public Management, Faculty of Social Sciences, Erasmus University, Rotterdam, the Netherlands

Michael Power Professor of Accounting, London School of Economics, London

Isabella Proeller Lecturer, Institute for Public Services and Tourism, University of St Gallen, Switzerland

Hal G. Rainey Alumni Foundation Distinguished Professor, School of Public and International Affairs, University of Georgia, Athens, Georgia, USA

Linda Rouleau Associate Professor, Department of Management, HEC-Montréal, Québec, Canada

Irene S. Rubin Professor Emerita, Department of Political Science, Public Administration Division, Northern Illinois University, USA

Denis Saint Martin Professeur Agrégé, Departement de science politique, Université de Montréal, Montréal, Canada

Kuno Schedler Professor, Institute for Public Services and Tourism, University of St Gallen, Switzerland

Chris Skelcher Professor, School of Public Policy, Institute of Local Government Studies, The University of Birmingham, Birmingham, UK

Steven Rathgeb Smith Professor of Public Affairs, Director, Nancy Bell Evans Center for Nonprofit Leadership, Daniel J. Evans School of Public Affairs, University of Washington, Seattle, Washington, USA

Ignace Snellen Professor, Centre for Public Management, Faculty for Social Sciences Erasmus University, Rotterdam, the Netherlands

Tim Strangleman Senior Research Fellow, Working Lives Research Institute, London Metropolitan University, London, UK

Colin Talbot Director, Nottingham Policy Centre, Law and Social Sciences, University of Nottingham, Nottingham, UK

Aidan R. Vining CNABS Professor of Business and Government Relations, Faculty of Business Administration, Simon Fraser University, Burnaby, Canada

David L. Weimer Professor, LaFollette School of Public Affairs, University of Wisconsin at Madison, Madison, Wisconson, USA

INTRODUCTORY REMARKS

EWAN FERLIE
LAURENCE E. LYNN, JR.
CHRISTOPHER POLLITT

THE organization and management of public services is moving through an intriguing and even disorientating period across the world. Governments have been launching major public sector "reform" programs now for over twenty years. Long-standing "taken for granted" assumptions and orthodoxies no longer hold. Traditional public sectors are under pressure to change and seem to be evolving—but into what? How are we to understand what is really going on and move from immersion in short-term events and parochial perspectives so as to recognize underlying patterns and enduring trends?

The editors and authors of this Handbook have sought to rise above detail and generate a big picture of the current state of the field, taking stock of how the recent generation of public management reforming has changed the way we think about and practice public management. In the 1970s, one normally talked of "public administration." In the 1980s came the move to "new public management," embraced by some and criticized by others. (Some of our authors refer to "public management" or "new public management"; others to "public administration"—the editors left the choice of terminology to authorial discretion!) These changes have had the effect of attracting additional academic disciplines (such as management and economics) to the study of "reformed" public management. More recently some have argued that there is a further shift from a "new public management" perspective to a "governance" perspective. Is the NPM itself becoming old and passé? Or is the NPM more than a policy fad, having had a more enduring impact than its early critics supposed? Are the same NPM based trends in public management reform evident globally or are reforms better seen as nationally specific and differentiated?

Communication between the three editors, which began soon after our receiving this commission from Oxford University Press, generated an editorial consensus that the Handbook should aim to provide a wide-ranging, authoritative, and internationally focused overview of major themes and key debates within the current field(s) of public management and administration. While we wanted an authoritative collection of essays, we also wanted one which, to the greatest extent possible, featured diverse disciplinary and methodological perspectives and authorial attributes such as age, sex, and nationality.

First of all, we wanted well-written, authoritative essays that discussed the important developments both in public policy and in relevant scholarship. The use of the word "authoritative" is deliberate. The editors have been fortunate in attracting distinguished authors who are recognized experts in their fields. In order to promote the authoritative nature of the chapters, authors were given a generous word length for their chapters so that they had the opportunity to develop sustained and subtle arguments. We negotiated an overall brief with our authors but gave them considerable latitude to develop their subjects as they saw fit (they were the subject experts, after all). We encouraged originality, preferring provocative ideas and arguments and strong individual voices over bland, encyclopaedic summaries. Authors were also encouraged to explicate the theoretical and analytical foundations of their topics, identifying as far as possible where theoretical and applied frontiers lie. We wanted fully developed, engaging, and stylish chapters even if these qualities were achieved at the cost of our commissioning fewer chapters than otherwise would have been the case.

Second, we wanted to ensure strong international coverage across the chapters. The three editors are based in three different geographic locations: the UK (Ferlie); the USA (Lynn) and continental Europe (Pollitt) and brought with them the different perspectives of their surrounding intellectual communities. We deliberately sought to recruit a similar mix of contributors.. In reading their essays, the rather different preoccupations of the British, continental European, and American scholars become evident. At the same time, sensing that even greater geographical diversity would pose editorial challenges, we did not cast our net wider. Should there ever be a second edition of the Handbook, we would wish to commission more authors from the developing world, thereby raising additional opportunities to explore the diffusion of managerial reform ideas and their "translation" into non-western, as well as the fascinating subject—largely unexplored in the Anglophone literature—of "home-grown" reforms in these contexts.

Our preference for authors who were fluent in English may have excluded non-Anglophone authors and affected the resulting balance. We are light, for instance, on French and Spanish authors but stronger on Dutch and Scandinavian authors who more often write in English. In sum, continental European scholarship is certainly represented in this book, but not to its full breadth or depth.

Third, the editors sought to encourage different perspectives rather than orthodoxy. The Handbook displays a colourful mix of different disciplines and theories: the old charge that public administration is a parochial, empiricist, and a-theoretical field divorced from a social science base has never been less accurate. Management academics follow democratic theorists; postmodernists rub shoulders with public choice economists; constructivists alternate with positivists. Intellectual polycentrism in public management scholarship seems to be here to stay, and any attempt to impose "one best way" would be strongly resisted. However, extreme diversity in any scholarly field presents some novel challenges of its own. Will the field disintegrate into a plethora of non-communicating subfields? What are the indicators of "quality" in each subfield and do they vary? How does the well-informed but general reader navigate the many academic tribes and boundaries and make sense of a greater whole? These are questions that need to be addressed if (as seems likely) conditions of high scholarly diversity within the study of public management persist.

Fourth, without sacrificing authoritativeness, we sought to achieve diversity across the population of authors, paying attention to issues of sex (women as well as men) and seniority (promising younger scholars as well as established senior writers). In the end, however, the shift in the mix we achieved was only moderate—perhaps we could not overcome the underlying diversity problems of the profession. Some more senior scholars have co-written their essays with younger colleagues, but this may be a field where the authority we wanted tends to be associated with some maturity of judgement and experience.

We encountered other limitations and difficulties. For a variety of reasons, important subjects that belonged in the Handbook could not be included. It was difficult for authors to be authoritative about some national literatures with which they were initially unfamiliar, although the editors' comments on first drafts often emphasized the importance of greater international coverage. There are more comparativists and internationalists in the field than a generation ago, but the majority of public management scholars are still overwhelmingly focused on their own country.

We have grouped the essays into five sections to make the journey through the Handbook inviting for the reader. Our intention is to move from the more general to the more particular, and then to return to the general at the end. Section 1 orientates the reader by exploring basic frameworks, background, and key current controversies at a high level of generality. This is followed by a set of chapters in Section 2 which explore alternative theoretical and disciplinary perspectives on public management. Section 3 covers a number of current public policy and management themes, albeit from a scholarly and social-science-based point of view. The chapters in Section 4 consider developments in particular functional areas, such as Human Resource Management. This is followed by a Section 5 which explicitly considers the international and comparative dimensions of public management reforming. The final chapter by the editors considers emerging overall themes across the set of chapters and outlines possible future directions.

We hope that readers' interest in understanding more about the current state of the field will be invigorated by this Handbook. It is intended to be useful to faculty, reflective practitioners, research students, and international public management institutions. Those looking for consensus will be disappointed; those who relish debate will be stimulated. Despite our reservations indicated above, we feel that we have accomplished much of what we originally intended: a handbook that is current, lively, original, and deserving of a wide and international readership. The Handbook is neither an encyclopaedia nor a survey but an intellectual whole which is greater than the sum of its parts in that it reveals both enduring and emerging trends, both durable and fresh ideas, and locates areas of consensus and controversy.

The debates addressed in the Handbook will improve our understanding of major contemporary developments in public management. While the public domain may be changing, the view characteristic of the 1980s that it would "wither away" has proved inaccurate: government still very much matters, albeit in altered forms. Linked to these policy developments, the study of public management is going through a fresh and exciting period, evidence of which awaits the reader of this Handbook.

SECTION I

BASIC FRAMEWORKS

CHAPTER 1

PUBLIC MANAGEMENT

THE WORD, THE MOVEMENT, THE SCIENCE

CHRISTOPHER HOOD

1.1 INTRODUCTION

DIVINITIES—and devilries—by their nature tend to be mystical in essence. Public management, which over the past few decades has tended to excite quasi-religious fervor and denunciation in almost equal measure, is no exception. Hyperbolic statement (or forthright denial) of what public management can achieve has been "often combined with under-explanation of what it is and of precisely how it is to achieve the outcome expected" (Keeling 1972: 18). It is tempting to explain that combination by suggesting—perhaps paradoxically—that in a supposedly post-religious age in the "first world," liberal democracy has become a secular religion and the organization of government has become one of the main theological issues in politics. But the fact is that "religious wars" over the terminology and content of public management are not a new phenomenon.

This observation may seem provocative, because on the face of it, there is no great mystery about what public management means. Though authors vary in the detailed definitions of the term that they offer, most of the standard definitions of public management amount to some variant on "the study and practice of design and operation of arrangements for the provision of public services and executive government," while management itself is conventionally defined as direction of resources or human effort towards the achievement of desired goals. And it is often observed that organization—and the willingness to be organized—is as important, if not more so, as money and other resources for the effective conduct of warfare, welfare, and many other kinds of public activity (see Hood 1976). So if the design and operation of public projects, services, and organizations forms the heart of public management, the subject might seem straightforward—even humdrum—enough. "So far, so bland," as Lewis Gunn (1987: 35) once put it, reviewing one of the early texts of the recent generation of public management literature.

But it is when we go beyond such utilitarian and innocent-seeming catch-all formulations to try to clarify (*inter alia*) what precisely is the relationship between public administration and public management, between public management and "managerialism," between government management and public management, and between public and private management, that those mysteries of essence and the corresponding theological issues start to emerge. The issue of what exactly is signified by the "public" and "management" and whether the stress goes on the first word of the phrase or the second (ibid.) can provoke the same kind of highly charged doctrinal debates that surrounded church government in sixteenth- and seventeenth-century Europe, and indeed many of the fundamental issues about organization are not so different.

1.2 THE WORD: WHAT'S IN A NAME?

As with divinities, etymological analysis can provide perspective, but not resolution of such matters, because each of the two words in the term has a range of meanings. Management is a word that seems to have originally come into English in the sixteenth century from the Italian verb *maneggiare*, meaning to train or ride a horse with skill (OED), and is indeed to be found in the plays of Shakespeare and the King James Bible. Long before it came to acquire its main contemporary meaning, denoting the running of companies and business administration, the word management was commonly used for the conduct of wars and other public affairs, and was often used in the eighteenth century to mean political manipulation. For example, the British government had a "Scottish Manager" after the 1745

Jacobite rebellion to exchange government patronage for political support (Kellas 1980: 88).

Indeed, the word management was commonly used to denote the conduct of public affairs in more than a casual sense in the eighteenth and early nineteenth century. And, just as the dating of points of origin is often uncertain for religious events, the *fons et origo* of the modern public management tradition is elusive. Though most US textbooks locate both the development of "public administration" and the founding fathers of management science in the late nineteenth century, there are other and earlier possible candidates for those inclined to ancestor-worship. For example, Vincent Ostrom (1973) prefers to follow the founding fathers of the US constitution, who (he claims) developed at least a proto-theory of "democratic" public administration a century or so before Woodrow Wilson looked to the Continental European police-science tradition for a modern American science of bureaucracy. In similar vein, Leslie Hume (1981) argues that Jeremy Bentham developed a coherent theory of management in the public sector almost a century before the supposed founding of modern management science. (Though, as Andrew Dunsire (1973: 8) points out, much of Bentham's detailed work on administration was not available to his contemporaries, and some has still not been published.)

Not only did Bentham apply the term management to the delivery of public services and offer a well-worked-out theory of management to underlie that usage, but he also placed the management of public services in a broader intellectual frame comprising an elaborate general philosophy of rewards and punishments. In a famous encyclopaedic table of the arts and sciences that sets out the different branches of "chrestomathic" or useful knowledge, one of the branches of deontology (Bentham's term for the science of what ought to be) is "aneunomoethicoscopic" knowledge. That term (also coined by Bentham) denotes "government-other-than-by-legis knowledge" (see Bentham 1983), and, ponderous as it may be, it is essentially the definition of public management given by most contemporary authors today.

However, the Benthamite gospel of "work and save" and the associated management principles and terminology that were taken up by early nineteenth-century utilitarians such as Sir Edwin Chadwick (see Finer 1952), has largely disappeared from sight in modern public management. That represents a notable contrast with the position of Adam Smith as the patron saint of modern economics, and is perhaps more like the disappearance of the cameralistic "state science" tradition in Germany in the mid-nineteenth century (Maier 1966). Instead, in the nineteenth century the word "administration" (from the Latin *ministrare*, to serve) became commonly used in the English-speaking countries to denote the operational work of executive government. That usage is also long-standing (e.g., Jonathan Swift in *Gulliver's Travels*, published in 1726, calls for projects in "public administration"). But "administration" may have been favored because in an age of democratization, rule-of-law constitutionalism and developing parliamentary government, it better conveyed the notion of subordination to constitutional authority and rule-governed institutional activity than the word drawn from the half-dead horse-mastering metaphor. "Public administration" became the commonest term for the academic study of executive government in the English-speaking countries from the late nineteenth century, and became the approved label for the various journals, professorial chairs, degree and diploma courses, and professional organizations—the conventional apparatus of institutionalized knowledge—that started to develop from that time (see Hood 1999).

However, the term "management" did not disappear completely. In fact, it came to be widely used in the late nineteenth century to connote the conduct of public affairs, in conjunction with the development of the modern managerial movement. In the USA, "city managers" were central to the progressive movement, with its faith in autonomous and high-minded professionals and scientists rather than political machine bosses (see, e.g., Stone et al. 1940). The movement reflected an ideal of politics-free conduct of government and public services by public-spirited professionals according to pre-set guidelines or shared understandings of good practice rather than the manipulation and string-pulling implied in the title of "Scottish manager" as mentioned earlier. And the development of "management science" in the late nineteenth century, albeit claimed by Hume to have been anticipated by Bentham by almost a century, also brought a new terminology and approach to government, notably in Frederick Winslow Taylor's (1911) well-known but controversial doctrines of management control (originating in a paper on individualized incentive payment systems and later branded as "scientific management").

Treading a middle path between "administration" and "management," the 1937 Brownlow Commission appointed by US President Franklin Roosevelt coined the famous—and perhaps doubly ambiguous—terminological hybrid of "administrative management," to denote the design and operation of executive government. Indeed, during and after the Second World War, explicitly "management" ideas and terminology were widely applied to government, from the developing science of operational research (distantly descended from "scientific management") to techniques for selecting and handling staff that formed the origin of the later "competency" movement. Those ideas came to be reflected in academic writing about the operation of executive government, such as John Millett's (1954) *Management in the Public Service.* There was much discussion of management in public enterprises, developing countries and local government in the 1960s and 1970s, and to a lesser extent central or federal government, as reflected for instance in Desmond Keeling's (1972) *Management in Government,* as mentioned earlier.

But it was the introduction of "public management" into the curriculum of the new graduate schools of public policy that developed in the USA in the 1960s and 1970s (particularly Harvard's Kennedy School of Government) that brought the term into general currency in its modern sense and introduced a new academic

movement. The movement distinguished itself from the schools of public administration that had grown up in an earlier generation and from the orthodox
political and social science approaches of the universities, rather as the protestant
churches of the fifteenth and sixteenth century distinguished themselves from the
older church establishments (for an account of the development of public management in the public policy schools, see Lynn 1996). By the 1980s the term "public
management" had become established to denote both an activity and a field of
study, though its distinctiveness from public administration on the one hand and
general management science on the other tended to be elusive. And public management as a term, like public administration before it, became institutionalized in
that it was built into the names of schools and courses, journals and books
(following early developments such as Perry and Kraemer 1983) and a conference
circuit. How far it acquired the attributes of "institutionalization" identified by
Samuel Huntington (1968: 12–24) and Nelson Polsby (1990)—in the sense of
coherence, organizational complexity and autonomy—is debatable, but the same
could certainly be said of public administration.

During the same decade, "public management," or variants of it, became a
fashionable term for numerous official bodies at national and international level.
The New Zealand Treasury produced a landmark document called *Government
Management* in 1984, reflecting the application of institutional-economics ideas
linked with ideas drawn from business management, and thereafter a flood of
official documents appeared under the label of public (or government) management rather than public administration. But after a point of high academic and
official fashion in the "New Right" 1980s, public management in turn started to
lose some ground in the "Third Way" 1990s, at least in the terminology of
international bodies such as the World Bank and the OECD. One of the terms
that started to supplant it was the word "governance," drawn from another half-
dead metaphor, the Greek verb to steer a boat—perhaps because the softer term,
with its network-of-organizations view of public service delivery, fitted the "third
way" mood of the times, like public administration in the nineteenth century (see
Chapter 12 on "governance" by George Frederickson). Others used "governance" as
a more general and neutral term for control and guidance systems in general. But
public management nevertheless remains a well-established term that has succeeded in becoming embedded into government and academic institutions.

How much significance should be read into these various terminological shifts
over time? Is there some platonic essence of public management, irrespective of the
particular terms that are deemed politically correct at any one time—as some
theologians claim for the deity, whatever the various names by which it is called?
Or, to the contrary, are the various labels central to the story, and is the subject
better studied as an essentially linguistic phenomenon, rather like the way the now-
defunct "Oxford school" studied philosophical issues in the 1950s? Or—mixing the
first and the second possibilities—may there be less to the different terms for the

operational activity of executive government than meets the eye? That is, is the terminological ambiguity and linguistic change merely the product of a need by politicians and bureaucracies to find mealy-mouthed euphemisms for politics, rather as politics was commonly discussed in the language of religion and through the institutions of the church in the days of monarchical government in Europe?

The answer is probably somewhere between all and none of the above. The platonic essence view cannot be altogether dismissed. After all, whatever particular terms are used to denote it, there is an important difference between a focus on the "production engineering" side of executive government activity or on the activity of leaders and "change agents", and a preoccupation with broader issues of bureaucratic design and operation. As noted earlier, such themes have arguably been in tension in the analysis of executive government for a century and more. So the 1980s were by no means the only "public management moment" when production-engineering and choice-of-instrument concerns were asserted against other approaches, such as the preoccupation with the politics–administration dichotomy in US public administration, or with the politics of accountability in UK public administration.

There is probably something in the "euphemism for politics" view as well, particularly since supposedly technocratic international institutions like the World Bank and Asian Development Bank (and domestic bodies such as audit organizations) are precluded by their charters from engaging in "politics" and therefore have to deal with political issues tangentially in an ostensibly depoliti-cized and therefore managerial language. But the parallel with things that polite-ness (or political prudence) dictates should not be named too directly is not exact, because the terminological changes in the various words used to denote executive government and public services seem to be bound up with both ideological and analytic shifts, and not just with finding new names for the same old thing, to pep a dullish subject up and inject new life into tired doctrines and approaches.

Indeed, it is difficult to dismiss changing fashions in terminology in this field, because "logomachy"—the battle for theologically-correct power-words—is central to the world of government and bureaucracy (see Kiggundu 1998: 161). So linguistic change takes place for a reason and typically reflects struggles for power. "Public management" can be considered as a movement as well as an intellectual perspec-tive, and it is to the idea of public management as a movement that we now turn.

1.3 PUBLIC MANAGEMENT AS A MOVEMENT

In a landmark contribution to the analysis of public management, Laurence Lynn (1996) considered three possible images of public management, as art, science, and profession. Broadly, by "art" Lynn means creative activity by practitioners that cannot be learned by numbers; by "science" he means the systematic analysis of cases using the orthodox canons of interpretation and explanation; and by "profession" he means a group dedicated to a particular calling.

There is no doubt that each of these images captures an important part of what some have claimed to be the essence or public management, and that they have different implications or entailments for the way the subject is to be approached and for who is to be the ultimate arbiter or controller of knowledge about it. One interpretation of the "art" perspective is the idea that the views of master practitioners should determine what is considered to be "best practice" (though it could equally well be argued that art critics or "posterity" might be the true arbiters of such matters), and that issue has been central to the debate about the foundations of "best" or "smart" practice research, as Lynn shows (see also Frederickson 2003). As that example indicates, the three views may be difficult to reconcile, although there are different possible visions of each of those three perspectives, dependent on what view one takes of "art," "science," or "profession."

However, those three images, powerful and important as they undoubtedly are, do not necessarily exhaust the possible ways of looking at public management as a body of ideas and practices. A slightly different image, to be considered here, is that of public management as a social and perhaps quasi-religious movement, arguably part of a broader "managerial" movement. Such movements typically have a number of characteristics: they develop in antagonism to one or more alternative or established approaches, engender antagonism in their turn, represent a mixture of ideas and interests, and comprise a particular worldview and a characteristic style of rhetoric.

All of those features can be detected in contemporary public management. But before briefly exploring them, it is worth noting at the outset that the public management movement of the 1980s and 1990s had at least some partial historical parallels. The cameralist movement that developed from the sixteenth century in the German states (and later moved to Sweden, Russia, and to some extent even Japan) was built on the notion of rule by a middle class of college-trained state managers rather than landed aristocrats loyal to the crown by ties of blood. And from the late eighteenth century, Jeremy Bentham attempted to build a movement to manage the state based on utilitarian logic and grounded in "useful knowledge" rather than the university staples of his day.

How successful Bentham was in building utilitarianism into a broad public management movement is debatable; Shirley Letwin (1995) argues that the movement got diverted into philosophical aridity under James Mill. But, to hark back to our earlier theme, there was a distinct quasi-religious dimension to Bentham's program for public management. Charles Bahmueller (1981: 197–200), in a discussion of Bentham's attempt "to co-opt religious habit and even the church itself to the Utilitarian cause" (p. 197), notes Bentham's idea that workhouse managers ought to be given sinecure positions in the established church (of England), that the reading of reports on pauper management—and associated homilies on good practice, of course—be directly incorporated into the liturgy of the church, and that churches themselves should double as public banks after Sunday services. If that is not a recipe for turning public management into a religion, it comes pretty close.

A third possible specimen, mentioned in the previous section, is Frederick Winslow Taylor's "scientific management" movement that developed from the early twentieth century. That movement too had quasi-religious overtones, since Taylor advanced his management doctrines with "driving moralism" and saw science as a moral system that would replace what he saw as moribund conventional religion (see Merkle 1980: 40–1). Taylor (1916) certainly saw government and public services as a prime site for the application of his principles of monitoring and incentivation.

Accordingly, the public management movement that developed from the 1970s was not without some historical precedents. And like those earlier cases, the public management movement of the last two decades developed in antagonism to earlier or established approaches. The cameralists aspired to professional "state science" in reaction to the conduct of executive government by members of the landed classes trained in feudal law. Bentham aspired to government by reason by those schooled in "chrestomathic" skills in antagonism to the aristocratic and custom-bound government of his day. Taylor sought to transform both government and industry by manager-engineers trained in methodical observation and rational incentive systems, reacting against rule-of-thumb management and shirking by workers. The public management movement of the 1980s and 1990s was a reaction against those in public law and public administration who put the focus on constitutional and institutional design of the machinery of government. It stressed production engineering and managerial leadership, rather than rule-bound bureaucracy, as the essence of executive government.

Arguably, that focus had strong antecedents within the public administration tradition itself. For instance, as long ago as 1954, John Millett (1954: vii–viii) had distinguished two kinds of "problems" in executive government, one comprising "the politics of public administration" (the constitutional and institutional politics of accountability) and the other comprising "problems of management," which he described as "the more prosaic matters . . . of getting work done." Richard Chapman and Andrew Dunsire (1971: 17) later made a similar claim, reflecting on recurrent genres of writing about executive government in Britain. They argued, "There have always been two styles, two traditions . . . a Benthamite and Taylorite . . . tradition, as well as a Macaulayite and Bridges tradition." Rather than a wholly new departure, the public management movement of the 1980s and 1990s can be construed in some ways as a relabeling of what Millett had called the "prosaic matters . . . of getting work done" and Chapman and Dunsire had termed the "Benthamite and Taylorite" tradition.

Further, like its earlier counterparts, the public management movement of the 1980s and 1990s in turn engendered antagonism in the form of anti-managerial reactions of several kinds. The cameralists were opposed by a new generation of jurists who successfully argued after 1848 that the rule of law regime that succeeded absolutism required executive government to be staffed by lawyers rather than managers. The utilitarian management movement that Bentham and Chadwick sought to develop was outflanked by a move towards Chinese-type mandarinism in the British civil service, favoring rule by lay scholar-gentry rather than those trained in Bentham's vision of "useful knowledge". Taylorism also attracted the mixture of quasi-religious fervor and denunciation that we noted at the outset as commonly surrounding the idea of public management. While scientific management was applied to various parts of US state and local government, including schools, and became an article of faith for the communist regime in the USSR (following Lenin's enthusiasm for Taylorism as part of the recipe for socialism), the gospel of managerial monitoring and payment by results in the state's services was far from unopposed. Public service labour unions mounted a holy war against scientific management that led the stopwatch and elements of the "Taylor system" to be banned by Congress from the US federal government after 1912 (Merkle 1980: 29 and 271).

The public management movement of the 1980s and 1990s displayed a similar mix of management evangelism and counter-evangelism. For example, in Britain a senior government minister (Michael Heseltine) declared in 1980 that "the management ethos must run right through our national life" (quoted in Protherough and Pick 2002: 15-6) and one of the more gung-ho management reformers of the 1980s and 1990s (Sir Peter Kemp, who directed a much-publicized program for hiving off semi-independent executive agencies for the operational work of British central government departments) refused to use the term "public administration" at all, seeing it as an unacceptably old-fashioned and passive label for the operations of executive government. On the other side of the theological divide, "management" and managerialism became a term of abuse on the left in several countries, and towards the end of those religious wars, at least one English local authority actually banned the use of the term "management" in the 1990s.

Indeed, the public management movement of recent decades has attracted various kinds of anti-managerial reaction from jurists, labor unions and professional organizations (particularly in education and health), advocates of a Weberian vision of rule-governed bureaucracy who argued that the public management school downplayed accountability and *Beamtenethos*, and various scholars and intellectuals who saw the expansion of the scope of management in government as the problem rather than the solution. One example of the latter kind of heretic was Shan Martin (1983), who offered a recipe of "managing without managers" for many kinds of front-line public services (arguing that cutbacks should be disproportionately directed towards managers and cooperative group working should be encouraged instead). Another was Walter Kickert (1997), who denounced what he saw as an "Anglo-American" approach to public management that he claimed was alien to the law-centered continental European approach to executive government and public services. A third example was Robert Protherough and John Pick (2002), who equated "managerialism" with the spread of bureaucracy and attempts to control the media and public opinion. Protherough and Pick (p. 199) saw managerial thinking as a "psychological plague" affecting modern societies and argued, on the basis of selective and colorful examples (p. 197) that "modern management systems corrode and destroy the enterprises they ostensibly support"—though their definition of "managerialism" was very wide, they selected on the dependent variable (like many proponents of "best practice" in management) and they focused mainly on language, jargon, and overpaid Armani-suited managers.

Such anti-managerial reactions, though widespread, seem to have been (to date, at least) fairly diffuse and incoherent, rarely progressing beyond the vein of ill-tempered letters to the editor complaining about the spread of business jargon and consisting of different preferred alternatives to "managerialism" (including the individualist idea of turning everything into a spot market and the collectivist idea of turning everything into a matter of group solidarity). But arguably, as in the nineteenth century, it is legalism and juridification that constitute the most substantial "anti-managerialist" movement in modern developed states. They introduce pressure to reduce any discretion managers may win by "bonfires of controls" from the center by a compensating increase in process rules and protocols introduced in the name of minimizing legal liability or litigation risk—one of the major growth points in government and organizations generally over the past decade or so.

The third feature of social or quasi-religious movements that was noted earlier is the combination of ideas and interests. The doctrines, according to an early commentator on the public management reform movement of the 1980s and 1990s, Peter Aucoin (1990) comprised a mixture of institutional-economics ideas and corporate-management ideas, and their novelty and coherence has been much debated. As for the "interests" side of the equation, managerialism as a movement reflecting the interests and ideals of managers as a group has been discussed at least since James Burnham's *Managerial Revolution* of 1941. Burnham, a former Marxist, argued that a managerial class was emerging as a new power-holding elite in capitalist countries in the mid-twentieth century, transforming an older style of capitalism. The same theme has appeared in work about contemporary managerialism, for instance, Michael Pusey's (1991) "new class" interpretation of the generation of senior public servants who spearheaded the new religion of "economic rationalism" in Australian government in the 1980s.

Though the debate about managers as an interest group is far from new, one of the features that does seem to distinguish the most recent public management movement from its earlier counterparts is the extent of the "new public management industry" that grew up with the movement. Apart from the new generation of public policy and management schools that has already been referred to, that industry also comprised the major international consulting and accountancy firms as they moved increasingly into public-sector work in the 1980s. The linked development of the new world of information technology consultancy and distribution changed the context too (see Margetts 1999). Indeed, it might be argued that a modified form of Burnham's prophecies about managers as a group asserting rights to state power (a process he expected to be complete by the 1960s) came true in at least some countries in the 1980s and 1990s, as significant new corporate and professional players allied with forces within government to challenge or bypass older forms of professional knowledge about executive government. From Burnham's perspective, such an alliance might be argued to have significantly changed the "means of production" of public services through outsourcing and information technology and to have exposed executive government and bureaucracy to a relatively new cognitive world of expensively acquired and rapidly changing management jargon.

The fourth feature of social movements that was mentioned earlier was the presence of a characteristic style of rhetoric and a distinctive ideology or universal worldview that links etiology, politics, and prophylaxis. The rhetorical dimension of managerial argument has been much explored by authors such as Hood and Jackson (1991) and Huczynski (1993), using classical tools of rhetorical analysis, and Patrick Dobel (1992: 147) saw in some of the modern US public management literature "an ongoing effort to create a new 'myth' for public management," in the sense of a focus on saints and heroes rather than institutional design. Indeed management can be seen as a field where rhetorical analysis is particularly appropriate, because the heart of management is the power to persuade and shape impressions (as Sun Tzu (1985: 11) long ago claimed for the art of war). As soon as the analysis of management goes beyond the tautologies of mathematicized decision science it is centrally concerned with situations where action has to be taken in the absence of incontrovertible proof that one approach will work better than another (another feature that it shares with religion). However, to date most rhetorical analyses of management have focused on the activity of "gurus" or government reports, and as yet there is no close parallel to the work of scholars like McCloskey (1985) or Edmondson (1984) in exploring the rhetorical features of the scholarly literature in public management that has appeared in the 1980s and 1990s.

To identify rhetoric as a dimension of a social movement is not quite the same as to see such movements as reflecting a worldview or ideology. An ideology can be justified by more than one form of rhetoric and a rhetorical argument need not necessarily be ideological. But some have certainly considered managerialism to be an ideology (in the sense of a body of beliefs that gives a comprehensive view of the world which is not falsifiable by any particular events), comparable to fields like feminism or environmentalism, which also comprise social and quasi-religious movements as well as fields of study. For example, Judith Merkle (1980) has expounded this view, tracing the development of the idea of management as a cure-all, worldview, way of life and new form of religion.

While Merkle's analysis is concerned with management in general, Christopher Pollitt (1990) has also identified ideological features of managerialism in public service provision. If militarism is an ideology that sees "war and the preparation for war as a normal and desirable social activity" (in Michael Mann's (1988: 124) well-known definition), the corresponding features of public management as an ideology might be considered to be the long-standing belief that to be effective and modern, all activities of government and public service need to involve a clear division of work into operational and supervisory or leadership activity and that the latter kind of work should be performed by a special group of functionaries trained or encouraged to think in a particular way (Martin 1983). While it seems more plausible to argue that there are multiple and contradictory cultural biases in the modern public management movement (see Hood 1998), that ideology is certainly one of the common specimens.

Ideology is also often defined as a worldview that is not readily "disprovable" by facts and events, because after every apparent failure the true believers can argue that the problem (whatever it was) arose because their preferred approach was not applied vigorously enough, rather than that it was tried and failed. Downs and Larkey (1986) have argued that the recurring idea of modeling public management on business organization in the USA has had something of that character over more than a century, and Ingraham (1993) has shown how the idea of performance-related pay keeps re-emerging as a recipe for better public-sector performance in spite of repeated evidence about the negative effects of performance pay schemes.

If contemporary public management has something of the character of a social and quasi-religious movement, some of those features also seem to apply to public management movements of earlier generations, three of which were briefly mentioned above. Each of them developed as a challenge to earlier or established approaches, comprised a particular worldview and deployed a characteristic style of rhetoric. But it is at least possible that the current generation may have been different in the rather more diffuse antagonism that it generated and in the breadth and depth of the interests—in the form of the "new public management industry"—that linked up with the ideas during the information age. If so, it remains to be seen whether those features will serve to create instability or to buttress the current public management movement to a greater extent than its forebears.

1.4 PUBLIC MANAGEMENT AS SCIENCE

Out of Lynn's trio of "art, science and profession," public management as a science, subject or type of analysis deserves particular attention, because there is much debate about what exactly counts as the core of that subject, what if anything constitutes its distinct form of analysis or ABC, and where it fits relative to the management sciences on the one hand and public administration on the other.

If public management is a "science", up to now it has largely been so at best in the German sense of *Wissenschaft*—systematic study—rather than in the conventional English sense of knowledge founded on strict experimental method and rigorous logical reasoning. Some, notably Michael Barzelay (2001), have argued that public management needs to get closer to the second sense of science through greater formalization of its propositions and more precision in its narrative analysis. And certainly public management has a long way to go before it approaches the status of a "normal science" in the Kuhnian sense (Kuhn 1961), with a generally accepted analytic ABC and method of working. As with management science more generally, there is a striking range of analytic starting points and methods in play.

At one end of the spectrum is what Andrez Huczynski (1993) terms "guru theory," which includes some of the most fervently "religious" texts (and indeed Huczynski draws explicit parallels with religious evangelism). Much of the guru literature comprises the large body of writing by management consultants, but there is also writing that straddles the boundary between "guru theory" and more conventional academic literature, including Osborne and Gaebler's (1992) bestseller *Reinventing Government* and much of the "best practice" literature (see Frederickson 2003). At the other end of the spectrum is analysis based on variations of Popperian method, using orthodox canons of scientific reasoning and evidence—a "conventional science" approach represented in the US by the Public Management Research Association. A further widely used body of literature on the subject that does not quite fit into either the "guru theory" or "conventional science" comprises what can be broadly termed "social constructivist" approaches of various kinds, including the works of March and Olsen (1989) and Nils Brunsson (1989; 2000). This wide range of methods and approaches also appears in related subjects, such as town planning, social policy and indeed in public administration itself, which was once famously described by Dwight Waldo (1968: 2) as "a subject-matter in search of a discipline."

But even the subject matter of public management is not generally agreed. Is it primarily centered on individual managers, on "management" as the collectivity of individuals who exercise formal authority in public organizations, on reform strategies, on broader patterns of discourse—or all of the above? Some of the leading academic exponents of contemporary public management, following a classic article by Graham Allison (1979), focus on the strategic activity of particular managers or leaders and the "best" or "smart" practices they promote. One of the bolder examples of that approach is Eugene Bardach's notion of "craftsmanship theory" (Bardach 1998). This approach clearly fits with the Benthamite notion of public management as a branch of deontology, though the "craft theory" and "best practice" approach propounded by scholars such as Bardach puts considerably more faith in the ability of practitioner-leaders to make reliable, impartial and valid judgments about "best practice" than Bentham and the utilitarians ever did, and pays little attention to the "rule of law" perspective of structural design that was central to Bentham's ideas about public management. And in contrast to the craft-theory, manager-centered approach are numerous studies (particularly by European scholars such as Christopher Pollitt and Geert Bouckhaert (2000)) that pursue more detached analyses of broad institutional design arrangements rather than individual manager strategies.

It could be argued that science in the sense of systematic analysis involves at least three related types of activity. One is the cartographic work of trying to better describe and characterize the phenomena it embraces. In social science as in history, it is common to draw a distinction between explanation and description, and description is often looked down on by those who aspire to be "theoreticians." But mapping and categorization is fundamental to any systematic field of study, the distinction between description and explanation is often challengeable, and good descriptive methods are particularly important for elucidating the "how" questions that some claim to be more analytically tractable than "why" questions (see Fischer 1971). A second is the collection and analysis of "hard data" in the sense of comparative datasets—not necessarily quantitative—that enable variables to take the place of proper names in part or whole (see Przeworksi and Teune 1970 on this approach to comparison). A third is the identification of anomalies, surprises and counter-intuitive observations that challenge received theory or ways of looking at the world.

The development of the analysis of "new public management" from the late 1980s reveals each of these approaches. One, closely related to the traditional preoccupations of public administration, comprises the difficult but necessary task of conceptualizing and analyzing institutional developments, identifying the design principles underlying them and evaluating their efficacy and normative value. Much of the "early" writings on New Public Management from the late 1980s were in this vein, since much of that literature consisted of attempts to identify the main traits in the design principles for government reform that were developing across several countries at that time, and to distinguish those principles from those that had held sway in an earlier era (see Hood 1989 and 1991; Flynn 1990; Pollitt 1990). And much attention was given to normative and analytic critiques of the new generation of public sector managerialism that was emerging at that time. Such work remains important—it has been a staple of public administration for over a century, and for good reasons—and it was to some extent reinvigorated with the "third way" debates in politics in the 1990s.

An analogous intellectual concern, reflecting a theme more closely associated with management science, has been the identification and discussion of alternative forms of control. Beyond particular topics such as marketing, strategy or management accounting, it might be argued that what public management has in common with management science more generally is a preoccupation with control, in its broadest sense meaning the ability to keep or move the state of particular systems within some desired subset of all their possible states. In recent decades, the most common intellectual perspective for analyzing control in management has been through the lens of institutional economics, in the search for a way of aligning incentives among different strategic actors. That is an intellectual tradition that has greatly developed since the 1960s, for instance in the development of "optimal reward theory" building out of the preoccupation with X-inefficiency in economics that is associated with the modern theory of the firm in economics (see, e.g., Leibenstein 1976). It has also been an important theme in thinking about public management, particularly in the preoccupation with developing output- or outcome-based controls to supplement or replace input- or throughput-based controls (see, e.g., New Zealand Treasury 1987; Thompson 1993).

Influential though it may be, the institutional-economics approach is not the only generic way of analyzing control. Another, notably unfashionable at present, is cybernetics, the science of general control systems, which was much developed in the 1960s and 1970s in management (see, e.g., Beer 1966) and in the sociology of law and other fields since then (see Teubner 1987). The central proposition of cybernetic theory is its iron law of requisite variety (the proposition that complex systems can only be controlled by equally complex systems, formulated by Ross Ashby in 1957), its preoccupation with autopoiesis (self-closure and self-referentiality in complex systems) and the logics of indirect control systems that derive from the requisite variety theorem. And distinct from both the institutional-economics and cybernetic approaches is the analysis of control through human group dynamics in general and culture in particular—which became fashionable at a popular level in the "corporate culture" literature of the 1980s and also generated considerable analytic work. Indeed, one way of thinking about what distinguishes public management as a science from the management sciences more generally is to conceive it as a way of working out the scope and limits of control in executive government and public services by applying such generic modes of analysis to particular institutional arrangements and cultures.

The second strain associated with scientific inquiry that was mentioned earlier—the collection of systematic data—has also been a developing theme in public management. The early "trait" approach to public management in the early 1990s has been developed and refined with the identification of different ages, stages, and variants of public-management initiatives (see Ferlie et al. 1996), the elaboration of methods of conceptual and narrative analysis (e.g. in the work of Barzelay 2001) and more systematic cross-national studies of public management changes. Examples of the latter include Spencer Zifcak's (1994) comparison of administrative reform in Whitehall and Canberra, Donald Savoie's (1995) comparison of Thatcher, Reagan and Mulroney in their approaches to central government bureaucracy, Peter Aucoin's (1995) comparison of a number of Westminster-model cases, and Pollitt and Bouckaert's (2000) comparison of public management reforms in ten countries.

The third strain—the identification of anomalies, surprises and counter-intuitive observations that challenge received theory or ways of looking at the world—is not sharply distinguishable from the first two. But from the late 1990s numerous scholars of public management rediscovered the ironies of social intervention and highlighted paradoxes and surprises in public-management reforms (e.g., Hood 1998; Christensen and Laegreid 2001; Hesse, Hood, and Peters 2003). One example is Robert Gregory's (1995) "production paradox," namely the claim that the extension of what he calls the "production" approach into realms where activities or results or both are not readily observable produces several unintended effects, including a blurring rather than the intended clarification of management responsibilities within executive government. A second is Moshe Maor's (1999) "managerial" paradox, the claim that public management reforms in parliamentary countries produce more politicization in the form of intervention by elected politicians rather than the intended aim of improving public service quality by "depoliticizing" operational work in government. A third is the "Tocquevillian paradox" (that more, not less, regulation, oversight, and process control has often been the unintended outcome of reforms ostensibly intended to "free" managers from such controls) that has been identified by scholars such as Light (1993), Jones and Thompson (1999), Hood et al. (1999), and Hoggett (1996). A fourth is Frederickson's (2003: 27–8) paradox that the vogue for benchmarking and comparative ratings that developed in public management in the 1990s unintendedly promotes uniformity and conformity rather than radical innovation. As in philosophy (for which John Austin (1962: 2) once said that the discovery of new kinds of nonsense had done the subject nothing but good) the identification of surprise and paradox signifies a point at which a field of study can no longer be dismissed as merely a collection of proverbs linked to anecdotes or statements of the obvious that can easily be recognized by any casual observer (see Brams 1976: xv; Quinn and Cameron 1988).

1.5 A FINAL WORD

"Religiosity" can have unexpected effects. After all, the great sociologist Robert Merton made his reputation in the 1930s by arguing that in seventeenth-century England ascetic Protestantism unintendedly helped to legitimize the emergence of modern science, and the associated development of skepticism that is said to have undermined religious faith (see Merton 1936; 1998). It is possible that something similar might happen with public management. But it seems unlikely that "religiosity" will disappear altogether from the field, because matters of organization and direction generate strong and contradictory world-views (see Hood 1998). Religious wars can be damaging and dangerous for scholarship if they mean intolerance of diversity, narrow sectarianism and disregard of evidence, and the discovery of anomalies and paradoxes can often be the point at which heretics are excommunicated and bitter schisms develop. But the point at which soft theory meets hard cases is also the opportunity for the development of genuinely counterintuitive ideas, if the stultifying effects of religious wars can be kept in check.

REFERENCES

ALLISON, G. T. (1979), "Public and Private Management: Are They Fundamentally Alike in All Unimportant Respects?" *Proceedings of the Public Management Research Conference*, Washington, DC, Office of Personnel Management.

ASHBY, W. R. (1957), *An Introduction to Cybernetics*, London: Chapman and Hall.

AUCOIN, P. (1990), "Administrative Reform in Public Management: Paradigms, Principles, Paradoxes and Pendulums" *Governance* 3 (2): 115–37.

—— (1995), *The New Public Management: Canada in Comparative Perspective*, Québec: Ashgate: IRPP Governance.

AUSTIN, J. (1962), *Sense and Sensibilia*, Oxford: Clarendon.

BAHMUELLER, C. (1981), *The National Charity Company*, Berkeley, University of California Press.

BARDACH, E. (1998), *Getting Agencies to Work Together*, Washington, DC: Brookings Institution.

BARZELAY, M. (2001), *The New Public Management*, Berkeley: University of California Press.

BEER, S. (1966), *Decision and Control*, New York: Wiley.

BENTHAM, J. (1983; orig. 1817), ed. M. J. Smith and W. H. Burston, *Chrestomathia*, Oxford: Clarendon.

BRAMS, S. J. (1976), *Paradoxes in Politics*, New York: Free Press.

BRUNSSON, N. (1989), *The Organization of Hypocrisy*, tr. N. Adler, Chichester: Wiley.

—— (2000), *The Irrational Organization*, 2nd edn., Bergen: Fagbokforlaget.

BURNHAM, J. (1941), *The Managerial Revolution*, New York: John Day.

CHAPMAN, R. A., and DUNSIRE, A. (eds.) (1971), *Style in Administration*, London: Allen and Unwin.

CHRISTENSEN, T., and LAEGREID, P. (eds.) (2001), *The New Public Management*, Aldershot: Ashgate.

DOBEL, J. P. (1992), Review of *Impossible Jobs in Public Management*, in *Journal of Policy Analysis and Management* 11 (1): 144–7.

DOWNS, G. W., and LARKEY, P. D. (1986), *The Search for Government Efficiency*, Philadelphia: Temple University Press.

DUNSIRE, A. (1971), *Administration*, Oxford: Martin Robertson.

EDMONDSON, R. (1984), *Rhetoric in Sociology*, London: Macmillan.

FERLIE, E., PETTIGREW, A., ASHBURNER, L., and FITZGERALD, L. (1996), *The New Public Management in Action*, Oxford: Oxford University Press.

FINER, S. E. (1952), *The Life and Times of Sir Edwin Chadwick*, London: Methuen.

FISCHER, D. H. (1971), *Historians' Fallacies*, London: Routledge and Kegan Paul.

FLYNN, N. (1990), *Public Sector Management*, Brighton: Harvester.

FREDERICKSON, H. G. (2003), "Easy Innovation and the Iron Cage: Best Practice, Benchmarking, Ranking and the Management of Organizational Creativity," Kettering Foundation Occasional Paper, Dayton, Ohio, June 2003.

GREGORY, R. (1995), "Accountability, Responsibility and Corruption: Managing the 'Public Production Process,'" in J. Boston (ed.), *The State under Contract*, Wellington: Bridget Williams Books.

GUNN, L. A. (1987), "Perspectives on Public Management," in J. Kooiman and K. A. Eliasson (eds.), *Managing Public Organizations*, London: Sage.

HESSE, J. J., HOOD, C. C., and PETERS, B. G. (eds.) (2003), *Paradoxes in Public Sector Reform: An International Comparison*, Berlin: Duncker and Humblot.

HOOD, C. (1976), *The Limits of Administration*, London: Wiley.

—— (1989), "Public Administration and Public Policy: Intellectual Challenges for the 1990s," *Australian Journal of Public Administration* 48 (4): 346–58.

—— (1991), "A Public Management for All Seasons?" *Public Administration* 69 (1): 3–19.

—— (1998), *The Art of the State*, Oxford: Clarendon.

—— (1999), "British Public Administration: Dodo, Phoenix or Chameleon?" in J. E. S. Hayward, B. Barry, and A. Brown (eds.), *The British Study of Politics in the Twentieth Century*, Oxford: British Academy/Oxford University Press.

—— and JACKSON, M. (1991), *Administrative Argument*, Aldershot: Dartmouth.

—— SCOTT, C., JAMES, O., JONES, G. W., and TRAVERS, T. (1999), *Regulation Inside Government*, Oxford: Oxford University Press.

HOGGETT, P. (1996), "New Modes of Control in the Public Service," *Public Administration* 74: 9–32.

HUME, L. J. (1981), *Bentham on Bureaucracy*, Cambridge: Cambridge University Press.

HUNTINGTON, S. (1968), *Political Order in Changing Societies*, New Haven: Yale University Press.

HUCYZNSKI, A. (1993), *Management Gurus*, London: Routledge.

INGRAHAM, P. (1993), "Of Pigs in Pokes and Policy Diffusion: Another Look at Pay for Performance," *Public Administration Review* 53 (4): 348–56.

JONES, L. R., and THOMPSON, F. (1999), *Public Management*, Stanford, CT: Elsevier-JAI Press.

KEELING, D. (1972), *Management in Government*, London: Allen and Unwin.

KELLAS, J. G. (1980), *Modern Scotland*, London: Allen and Unwin.

KICKERT, W. (1997), "Public Management in the United States and Europe," in W. Kickert (ed.), *Public Management and Administrative Reform in Western Europe*, Cheltenham: Edward Elgar.

KIGGUNDU, M. N. (1998), "Civil Service Reform: Limping into the Twenty-First Century," in M. Minogue, C. Polidano, and D. Hulme (eds.), *Beyond the New Public Management*, Cheltenham: Edward Elgar, 155–71.

KUHN, T. (1961), *The Structure of Scientific Revolutions*, Chicago: Chicago University Press.

LEIBENSTEIN, H. (1976), *Beyond Economic Man*, Cambridge, MA: Harvard University Press.

LETWIN, S. R. (1965), *The Pursuit of Certainty*, Cambridge: Cambridge University Press.

LIGHT, P. (1993), *Monitoring Government*, Washington, DC: Brookings Institution.

LYNN, L. E. (1996), *Public Management as Art, Science and Profession*, Chatham, NJ: Chatham House Publishers.

MCCLOSKEY, D. N. (1985), *The Rhetoric of Economics*, Madison: Wisconsin University Press.

MAIER, H. (1966), *Die ältere deutsche Staats-und Verwaltungslehre*, Munich: C. H. Beck'sche Verlagsbuchhandlung.

MANN, M. (1988), *States, War and Capitalism*, Oxford: Blackwell.

MAOR, M. (1999), "The Paradox of Managerialism," *Public Administration Review* 59 (1): 5–18.

MARCH, J. G., and OLSEN, J. P. (1989), *Rediscovering Institutions*, New York. Free Press.

MARGETTS, H. Z. (1999), *Information Technology in Government*, London: Routledge.

MARTIN, S. (1983), *Managing without Managers*, Beverly Hills: Sage.

MERKLE, J. A. (1980), *Management and Ideology*, Berkeley, CA: University of California Press.

MERTON, R. K. (1936), "The Unintended Consequences of Purposive Social Action," *American Sociological Review* 1: 894–904.

—— (1998), "Afterword: Unanticipated Consequences and Kindred Sociological Ideas: A Personal Gloss," in G. Mongardine and S. Tabboni (eds.), *Robert K Merton and Contemporary Sociology*, New Brunswick: Transaction Publishers, 295–318.

MILLETT, J. D. (1954), *Management in the Public Service*, New York: McGraw-Hill.

New Zealand Treasury (1987) *Government Management*, Wellington: Government Printer.

OSBORNE, D., and GAEBLER, E. (1992), *Reinventing Government*, Reading, MA: Addison-Wesley.

OSTROM, V. (1973), *The Intellectual Crisis in American Public Administration*, Alabama: Alabama University Press.

PERRY, J. L., and KRAEMER, K. L. (eds.) (1983), *Public Management*, Palo Alto, CA: Mayfield Publishing.

POLLITT, C. (1990), *Managerialism and the Public Services*, Oxford: Blackwell.

—— and BOUCKHAERT, G. (2000), *Public Management Reform*, Oxford: Oxford University Press.

POLSBY, N. (1990; orig. 1975), "Legislatures," in P. Norton (ed.), *Legislatures*, Oxford: Oxford University Press, 138–41.

PROTHEROUGH, R., and PICK, J. (2002), *Managing Britannia*, Denton: Brynmill Press.

PRZEWORSKI, A., and TEUNE, H. (1970), *The Logic of Comparative Social Inquiry*, Malabar: Krieger.

PUSEY, M. (1991), *Economic Rationalism in Canberra*, Cambridge: Cambridge University Press.

QUINN, R. E., and CAMERON, K. S. (eds.) (1988), *Paradox and Transformation*, Cambridge, MA: Ballinger.

SAVOIE, D. (1995), *Thatcher, Reagan, Mulroney*, Pittsburgh, PA: Pittsburgh University Press.

STONE, H. A., PRICE, D. K., and STONE, K. H. (1940), *City Manager Government in the United States*, Chicago: published for the Committee of Public Administration of the Social Science Research Council by Public Administration Service.

SUN TZU (1985, orig. *c.*500 BC), *The Art of War*, ed J. Clavell, New York: Delta.

TAYLOR, F. W. (1911), *The Principles of Scientific Management*, New York: Harper.

—— (1916), "Government Efficiency," *Bulletin of the Taylor Society* December 1916: 7–13.

TEUBNER, G. (ed.) (1987), *Juridification of Social Spheres*, Berlin: de Gruyter.

THOMPSON, F. (1993), "Matching Responsibilities with Tactics: Administrative Controls and Modern Government," *Public Administration Review* 53: 303–18.

WALDO, D. (1968), "Scope of the Theory of Public Administration," in J. C. Charlesworth (ed.), *Theory and Practice of Public Administration*, Philadelphia: American Academy of Political and social Science/American Society for Public Administration, ch. 1.

ZIFCAK, S. (1994), *New Managerialism*, Buckingham: Open University Press.

CHAPTER 2

PUBLIC MANAGEMENT

A CONCISE HISTORY OF THE FIELD

LAURENCE E. LYNN, JR.

2.1 INTRODUCTION

A HISTORY of the field of public management arguably might begin with any of the following statements:

- The contemporary study of public management has its origins in the 1970s: in America, in the curriculums and research of the new public policy schools (Perry and Kraemer 1983; Rainey 1990); in Europe, in efficiency-driven managerial reforms originating in Great Britain and New Zealand (Aucoin 1990; Pollitt 1990).
- The field of public management has its roots in the scientific study of the modern administrative state in America beginning in the late nineteenth and early twentieth centuries (Mosher 1975; Waldo 1955, 1980; Minogue, Polidano, and Hulme 1998).
- The origins of the field of public management are to be found in the systematic study and practice of cameralism and *Staatswissenschaften* beginning in

seventeenth- and eighteenth-century Germany and Austria (Barker 1944; Rosenberg 1958).

- The field of public management is rooted in early appearances of bureaucratic government and of administrative doctrines and "best practices" in ancient China and in medieval regimes in the Orient and the Occident (Lepawsky 1949; Creel 1964).

Choosing among these starting points begs two questions of definition: of "field," together with its boundaries, and of "public management" as distinct from both public administration and private or generic management.

"Field" shall mean, following Bourdieu (1990), "an arena for the play of intellectual forces and power relationships" (Lindenfeld 1997: 5), but in a capacious sense. Evidence of such play shall not be limited to academic knowledge but shall include the "common knowledge" of educated and ruling elites concerning how to conduct the affairs of state (Hood and Jackson 1991). Thus, for example, the requirement of formal training for government service in ancient China and German import of experienced French officials for customs and excise administration and of British models of local governance are evidence of a field. Moreover, although intellectual boundaries have from time to time been narrowly-drawn around the common knowledge of ruling elites, the "sciences of state," or administrative law, the field now encompasses, in addition to those elements, social and behavioral disciplines that furnish conceptual and empirical footings for the contemporary study and practice of public management (Frederickson and Smith 2003).

As for "public management," one question concerns whether or not a distinction can be drawn between "management" and "administration." Numerous attempts to do so, from Fayol (1916) to Aucoin (1990), have variously asserted the primacy of one over the other (to the point of drawing invidious distinctions, for example, between "management" as unduly masculine, instrumental, and undemocratic, and the more holistic and polycentric "administration") without producing consensus. In this chapter, public management will be viewed broadly as encompassing the organizational structures, managerial practices, and institutionalized values by which officials enact the will of sovereign authority, whether that authority is prince, parliament, or civil society. Public management, in other words, is regarded as synonymous with public administration (Lynn 2003; Pollitt and Bouckaert 2000). As for whether or not there is a distinctive *public* management, there is widespread professional acknowledgement that constitutions, collective goods production, and electoral institutions create distinctive managerial challenges that justify a separate field (Pollitt 2003; Rainey and Chun this volume).

Thus defined, the field of public management is surely of older vintage than American scholars have been wont to assert and is arguably even older than the popular starting point for administrative histories: the advent of European absolutism in the seventeenth century. To establish an appropriate historical perspective, however, it will be useful to consider the case for each of the four starting points.

2.2 ADUMBRATIONS, AT LEAST

The existence of organized bureaucracies and systematic administration in Egyptian, Chinese, Greek, Roman, and other early civilizations has long been acknowledged. Though Lepawsky found only limited evidence in early civilizations for "the rise and the development of administration as an art, of organization as a science, or of management as a technique," in other words, for the existence of a field (1949: 82), that there is any evidence at all is notable.

The field may have originated in ancient China. Confucius held that the conductor of a government should "hold the mean," meaning "to approach a problem by seeking the widest differences of opinions and by making the most careful study of the facts in the spirit of absolute impartiality and unselfishness, and then to solve it moderately, practicably, and logically, in accordance with the best ethical rules," a precept on which it is hard to improve (Lepawsky 1949: 83, quoted from Hsü 1932). H. G. Creel makes the strongest (albeit controversial) claim for the existence of Chinese doctrines of administration that were influential in later times. By the second century BC, Creel says,

an increasing number of [administrative] officials was selected by civil service examinations. . . . An increasing proportion of officeholders were educated in an imperial university that was expressly founded, in 124 B.C., for the purpose of inculcating in future officials the values and attitudes desired by the government. Many of them were career bureaucrats from an early age. (Creel 1964: 155–6)

Creel finds further support for his claim not in Confucianism, which had little to say about statecraft, but in the career of Shen Pu-hai (d. 337 BC), who was chancellor of a small state in north-central China. A book attributed to his authorship was widely read and influential as late as the reign of Emperor Hsüan (74–48 BC). Not a Confucian, Shen Pu-hai "is concerned, with almost mathematical rigor, to describe the way in which a ruler can maintain his position and cause his state to prosper by means of administrative technique and applied psychology" (Creel 1964: 160).

Chinese influence on the subsequent history of public administration and management is proverbial, and not just because examinations for entry into public service originated there. Creel and other scholars find Chinese influence specifically in the regimes of the Kingdom of Lower Italy and Sicily, where Frederick II's statutes promulgated at Melfi in 1231 have been characterized by Ernst Kantorowicz as "the birth certificate of modern bureaucracy" (quoted by Creel 1974: 58). As late as the seventeenth century, there may have been knowledge of the doctrines of Shen Pu-hai, according to Creel, and Shen's book was extant as late as the early eighteenth century. Whatever their provenance, reforms recognizable to modern students of public administration and management were adopted in several medieval regimes (Rosenberg 1958). Of particular interest is the emergence of a concept of "public trust" in numerous cities, "established as legal associations under a corporate authority and vested with varying rights of self-government" that "adumbrated some of the modern ideas of public need and public service" (Rosenberg 1958: 6, 8).

What we know of the history of organized administration across time and civilizations, therefore, suggests that common forms of self-awareness and codification concerning the structures, practices, and values of public administration and management accompanied the emergence of organized societies (Waldo 1984). Broadly construed, public administration and management has been a concomitant of the earliest quests for order, security, wealth, and civilization. Such a view is controversial, however.

2.3 ABSOLUTISM AND ADMINISTRATIVE SCIENCES

"The modern bureaucratic state is a social invention of Western Europe, China's early civil service notwithstanding," declared Hans Rosenberg (1958: 2). These early "bureaucrats," he argued, were indistinguishable from the household staff of the dynastic ruler and cannot be considered embryonic civil servants. If, with Ernest Barker, we regard management as "the sum of persons and bodies who are engaged, under the direction of government, in discharging the ordinary public services which must be rendered daily if the system of law and duties and rights is to be duly 'served',"(1944, 3), then the emergence of modern public administration and management awaited two historic developments: the rise of absolutism in Europe following the Peace of Westphalia in 1648 and the revolutionary idea of "national sovereignty" institutionalized in France after 1789 (Barker 1944: Merkle 1980). Perhaps the most conspicuous precursor of the contemporary field was a recognized field of study and practice called *cameralism*.

2.3.1 Early Administrative Science

The reign of Louis XIV characterized absolutism in paradigmatic form. The break with the past was in the growth of large bureaus of officials and a new system of financial administration under the powerful Colbert. Revolutionary change occurred at the local level with the institution of the *intendant*, a permanent administrator answerable to the king and his ministers, especially in matters of finance, and the *intendant*s, too, required staffs. Against the background of the scientific spirit created by Bacon, Galileo, and Descartes, scholars such as Vaubon and Jonchère began addressing the needs of absolutist institutions (Deane 1989; Merkle 1980). Such scientific thinking (in contrast to descriptive or philosophical thought) "drove the mysticism from statecraft" (Merkle 1980: 141; Raadschelders and Rutgers 1999).

The main story occurred in the German states, however. Beginning in 1640, a succession of German rulers—Frederick William (The Great Elector), his grandson Frederick William I, and Frederick the Great (who died in 1786)—created an absolutist state that broke with medieval tradition by instituting public management by trained and competent civil servants acting on behalf of a "public interest" rather than (solely) out of narrow dynastic concerns (albeit on behalf of Hohenzollern and Hapsburg political interests as against powerful rivals) (Morstein Marx 1935). The Great Elector established public service as a duty to the people (rather than to the feudal nobility) in the army and the revenue, postal, and education systems; Frederick William I initiated the training of officials and established two university chairs in administrative subjects in the 1720s (by end of eighteenth century there were twenty-three such chairs, Wagner 2003); Frederick the Great instituted examinations and a civil service commission. The consequence was the emergence of a field of study and practice termed "cameralism." (The word refers to the room or place (*kammer*) where the domain is ruled.)

"Cameralism," said Albion Small (1909: 591), "was an administrative technology..., a theory of managing natural resources and human capacities so that they would be most lucrative for the prince in whose interest the management was conducted." According to Johann Justi, one of its most eminent scholars and practitioners, the aim of cameralism, or *Staatswissenschaften*, is to achieve the common happiness of the ruler and his subjects (an early version of the concept of "public will" or "public interest") through rules that amount to applications of benefit-cost economics (Small 1909: Lindenfeld 1997). Cameralism, according to Carl Friedrich (1939: 130–1), "was the academic counterpart of modern bureaucratic administration and, hence, in its essence was administrative science."

As an academic discipline, cameralism amounted to what would today be called a "managerialist ideology" (Pollitt 1990). It advocated meritocracy rather than noble birth, administrative science rather than feudal law, standardized principles rather than local particularity, and formalism and professionalism rather than traditionalism (Hood and Jackson 1991). The best interests of the prince and the people lay in economic development which, in turn required active management by administrators who were trained, examined, evaluated, and held loyal to a strongly led state. Its central tenets are sufficiently modern that Hood and Jackson refer to the late twentieth-century New Public Management as a "new cameralism" (Hood and Jackson 1991: 182).

Cameralists were often successful practitioners. Schumpeter (1954: 143–208) described them as "Consultant Administrators". In contrast to modern deductive science, "[t]he cameralists proceeded much more by the statement and elaboration of practical maxims than through the construction and logical manipulation of analytical models" (Wagner 2003: 7). Administrators participated at a high level in literary discussions of cameralistic topics and produced a "massive German literature" that addressed general problems and issues of public management (Morstein Marx 1935; Tribe 1984: 273).

Beginning in the late eighteenth century, intellectual and political developments began that were to culminate in fundamental structural change—national sovereignty, *Rechtsstaat*, the *Code Napoleon*, the bureaucracies that were to be idealized by Max Weber, and law as the basis for training officials—and to undermine the pre-eminence of *Staatswissenschaften* as the intellectual foundation for public administration and management. Royal servants became state servants (for example, in Prussia's Legal Code of 1794), servants became officials, government by officials became known as bureaucracy, and bureaucracy became both powerful and controversial.

2.3.2 The Imperial Bureaucracy

With state building largely accomplished on the Continent, "the struggle for legalizing or constitutionalizing these great administrative mechanisms" began (Friedrich 1939: 132). Thus was initiated a decisive shift toward the rule of law and reliance on bureaucracy as a primary instrument of institutional change and social mobility (Anderson and Anderson 1967; Dunsire 1973). Consequently the foundations of official training, academic discourse, and political agendas also shifted, albeit at different times in different states. By the end of the nineteenth century, the field of public administration and management had become preoccupied with the *de facto* separation of policy and administration and the resulting tensions between an institution, bureaucracy, which exhibited imperialistic proclivities and the revolutionary idea of popular sovereignty, with its expectation of democratic accountability.

The "age of reason" had proclaimed the supremacy of law, and Holland and England (the latter led by Sir Edward Coke and prominent English lawyers) had embraced the idea of law as right reason as early as the seventeenth century. The motive for abandoning *Staatswisschaften* on the Continent was widespread dissatisfaction with what was coming to be known as "bureaucracy," a pejorative term coined by a Frenchman in the eighteenth century (although the term was correctly used by Mill and others to mean "rule by officials"). The historical irony, now no less than then (Morone 1990), is that reforms to ensure democratic accountability actually tended to strengthen bureaucratic institutions.

The French *bourgeoisie*, for example, finally rebelled against the taxation needed to support their kings' propensities to wage war. "A new conception of the state now appeared in the doctrine of 'national sovereignty'" (Barker 1944: 13). Far from displacing the role of administrators, however, "France retained the administrative machine of the past, but gave it a new motive power" (ibid.). *L'état* was now the collective people, not the person of the king. Napoleon was, as Barker puts it, the successor to both Louis XIV and Colbert, and organized a new administration around a *Conseil d'État* and the system of *Préfets* nominated and controlled by the central government. The result was that "the Revolution left its new theory of democracy curiously united with the old practice of bureaucracy" (Barker 1944: 13–14). State administration under the *Code Napoléon* "was to learn to govern France without ever losing continuity through successive periods of revolution" (Merkle 1980: 144).

Following its defeat by Napoleon at Jena in 1806, the Prussian state, too, was quickly revolutionized. Freiherr vom Stein, head of the Prussian civil service, had already transferred official allegiance from the person of the king to the head of state. But prior to 1806, administrative theory was dominated by the idea of the *collegium*, collective responsibility for advising the ruler. Following Napoleonic logic, after 1806 and the advent of a representative parliament, the *collegium* was replaced by the *Buro-* or *Einheitssystem*, in which, in the interests of efficiency, responsibility was clearly vested in an individual at each level of authority up to a minister. Moreover, the term *Rechtsstaat* entered the discourse: law as the foundation for public administration. Professors of the sciences of the state "generally held liberal views, such as beliefs in the rule of law, a limited degree of popular representation, a free press, and a vital public opinion" (Lindenfeld 1997: 91). Under Rechtsstaat, these academics believed, a strong, positive government could be reconciled with individual and social autonomy.

In practice, however, the emphasis was placed on law, not on *Staatswissenschaften*. "[T]he rising emphasis upon law as the necessary form of all governmental action ... engendered a considerable shift in the concept of what was necessary for the training of governmental officials" (Friedrich 1939, 133): law, not the administrative sciences. Despite an emancipated peasantry and a liberated townsfolk in a new system of municipal administration, Prussian absolutism endured, as did the power of the administrative class, university-trained and office-experienced. Over time, the Prussian bureaucracy was to become iconic. The sciences of the state, though not bureaucracy itself, were also undermined by the growing influence of Adam Smith's *The Wealth of Nations* and the emergence of the field of economic analysis, which shifted the focus of thinking away from the state as the engine of wealth creation toward individuals and entrepreneurs operating in free markets. Thus law—legal reasoning—along with economics eclipsed completely the older administrative sciences in intellectual discourse.

During a century marked by revolutions in the name of popular sovereignty, therefore, the dominant institution of public administration and management became bureaucracy. The dominant idea became the ideological separation of policy and management, the latter governed by *Rechtsstaat*. Issues relating to management of hierarchies (what are now called "techniques of management") came to the fore: the content of the education and training of officials at different levels; the use of entrance examinations and apprenticeships; the use of performance standards and evaluations; discipline; reassignment; promotion; salary structures; retirement benefits; status and rights of workers in state enterprises; and retention of personnel (Anderson and Anderson 1967).

This bureaucratic "paradigm" engendered widespread popular and professional criticism. Balzac's best-selling novel *Les Employés* imprinted contempt for bureaucracy on popular consciousness. Von Mohl's definitive analyses tended to fuse the term bureaucracy with a system of state administration that was inherently unresponsive to public concerns (Albrow 1970). For Frederick Le Play, bureaucracy "meant the dissemination of authority among minor officials, absorbed in details, intent upon complicating business, and suppressing initiative in others" (Albrow 1970: 30). Hintze cited the weaknesses of bureaucracy as "corruption and laziness, excessive ambition, servility toward superiors, brutality toward inferiors, conceitedness, and narrowmindedness" (Anderson and Anderson 1967: 183). Said Austrian scholar Josef Redlich, "[t]he combination of parliament and a traditionally authoritarian bureaucracy evoked the worst qualities of each body" (quoted by Anderson and Anderson 1967: 184). By the end of the nineteenth century, the idea that bureaucracy and democracy are incompatible had become popular with the critics of "imperial bureaucracy" (Friedrich and Cole 1932), an idea that has been given new life in postmodern democratic theory.

Rechtsstaat, too, had come under criticism. Earlier in the century, tension became apparent between the idea of a *Rechtsstaat* and the idea of a eudaemonic welfare state responsible for the well-being of its inhabitants and concerned with protecting civilians against the state (Raadschelders and Rutgers 1999). Later, Stein argued that *Rechtsstaat* "left no room for a proper conceptualization of administration" (Lindenfeld 1997, 201). In Stein's view, according to Lindenfeld (1997: 201), "administration was the wave of the future," a view that found its way to the heart of Goodnow's seminal American treatises. Later, Schmoller attempted a revival of the sciences of the state in the form of social science, and despite the opposition of many law professors, a doctorate in the sciences of the state was established in 1880 (Lindenfeld 1997).

The dominant intellectual "memory" of the era, however, is Max Weber's positive analysis of bureaucracy. The power of Weber's work has obscured the intellectual ferment that preceded it. *Rechtsstaat*, moreover, had become deeply entrenched and has endured to the present.

2.3.3 Anglo-Saxon Exceptions

An island nation, like England, or a former colony isolated in an aboriginal hemisphere, like America, face different state-building tasks than Continental nations such as France and Germany, where protection of territorial integrity and enforcement of unity were paramount (Barker 1944). The differences widen when the influence of democratic institutions and the nature of legal systems are taken into account. Unlike Continental nations, democracy in England and America was built on a system of common law that preceded and governed the development of public bureaucracies. The idea of the "state" as independent of the political régime, and officials as "servants of the state," is, as König observes (1997: 217), "still not understood easily in the Anglo-American administrative culture"; in contrast, the idea of popular sovereignty and public accountability, staples of Anglo-American discourse, are not as easily understood on the Continent (Peters 1997).

Despite their similarities, the field of public administration has evolved in quite distinctive ways in Great Britain and the United States. The reasons lie in the differences between the two nations' constitutions and political institutions. Great Britain is a parliamentary democracy with virtually no separation of powers. The field of public administration and management in the US, and the intellectual and practical challenge of conceptualizing managerial responsibility there, directly reflect constitutional tensions between executive, legislative and judicial branches of government. These differences did not become apparent, however, until the emergence of the American administrative state in the late nineteenth and early twentieth centuries. The field of public administration and management in the Anglophone world originated in England.

2.3.4 Limited Government in England

After the Commonwealth and the violence of parliamentary power, the Glorious Revolution of 1688 established a monarchy with curtailed powers. While France and Prussia "made a science of the service of the State," England "considered [governing] a task for intelligent amateurs" (Barker 1944: 29, quoting Pollard in Acton et al. 1902–12: 10. 353). Government in England, moreover, was parliamentary and local. "[T]he theory of the English State [after 1660 and 1688] is a theory not of the administrative absolutism of a king, but of the legislative omnipotence of a parliament" (Barker 1944: 31) and the power of justices of the peace and municipal councils. Whereas the French, for example, hoped to overcome "the intractable nature of the human material" by imposing order, the British preferred to rely on liberty and free choice to produce rational action (Merkle 1980: 210).

A series of developments in the nineteenth century gradually brought elements of bureaucracy into English public administration and management. Various reforms established common patterns of education for officials modeled on classical instruction; "practical technology and organization were considered beneath the attention of a gentleman" (Merkle 1980: 209). In 1853, open competition for appointment to the civil service in India was adopted (and became the rule in British government in 1870). Two years later, following the Northcote–Trevelyan report ("a classic case of argument from 'common knowledge' in order to draw (apparently) obvious conclusions," Hood and Jackson 1991: 141), Gladstone overrode Parliamentary objections to engineer the Order in Council of 1855, which created a civil service commission and required a minimum of competence among public officers" (White 1935: 1). The result was creation of a civil service which has become a model, and in many respects a caricature (as was the Prussian bureaucracy), of such an institution.

None of these developments belied English acquiescence in bureaucratic government, however. English intellectuals compared the bureaucratized Continent with "free England" (Dunsire 1973). In his *Principles of Political Economy*, John Stuart Mill "set himself against 'concentrating in a dominant bureaucracy all the skill and experience in the management of large interests, and all the power of organized action, existing in the community'" (quoted by Albrow 1970: 22). Herbert Spencer warned that "[a]n employed bureaucracy regularly [becomes] a governing bureaucracy, inflexible, fond of power, but enslaved by routine" (quoted by Albrow 1970: 25). French and German critics of the rigid Prussian system envied English self-government. Nonetheless professionalism in public service has had its effects. Ramsey Muir could argue by 1910 that bureaucracy was becoming a reality in England (Albrow 1970: 26).

The English civil service has enjoyed high prestige for integrity, capacity, and intelligence (White 1935). It has also been viewed as having frozen "gentlemanliness" into "a type of neo-mandarinism which saw government of every type the fit province of the generalist and the classicist" (Merkle 1980: 209). Even though amateurism gave way to professionalism, "not only had England avoided bureaucracy, it had also avoided schools for public servants; and with them, administrative science textbooks" because there was no incentive to produce them (Dunsire 1973: 57). While creating the capacity for self-government and engaging in the study of administrative law, England remained unengaged with the study of administrative science.

2.3.5 American Separation of Powers

Textbooks on public administration would not appear in America until the late nineteenth century, when Goodnow's *Comparative Administrative Law* (1893, 1902) appeared. In the meantime, the central issue for Americans was: "Would public administration find a place in a government without a crown?" (Stillman 1982: 6). Still a primary example of self-awareness, *The Federalist* (which Rohr (2002) sees as taking a managerial view), together with early debates over governance in the new republic and early experience with governing, have been distilled into distinct (if not distinctive) administrative traditions or heuristics (Stillman 1982; Kettl 2002): a Hamiltonian tradition, which echoes cameralism in emphasizing strength in the executive to promote national economic interests; a perhaps uniquely American Madisonian tradition, emphasizing the interplay of group interests; a Jeffersonian tradition reminiscent of the English tradition of local government; and, dominant throughout much of the nineteenth century, the Jacksonian tradition of party control of all aspects of administration.

Emerging as the central feature of American public administration and management, however, was the reverential authority acceded to the constitution and to the principle of separation of powers (Lincoln 1838; Story 1840). Since the institution of judicial review was established early in the nineteenth century, the constitution has served as the kind of stabilizing element in American government that public bureaucracies have served in Europe and Parliament has served in England. But America's separation of powers, and the superordinate role of the courts, also greatly complicated the matter of establishing a legitimate role for "unelected bureaucrats."

As early progressive-era reforms were beginning to give shape to a positive state, Frank Goodnow stated the problem of public administration and management concisely (Goodnow 1900: 97–8):

[D]etailed legislation and judicial control over its execution are not sufficient to produce harmony between the governmental body which expresses the will of the state, and the governmental authority which executes that will.... The executive officers may or may not enforce the law as it was intended by the legislature. Judicial officers, in exercising control over such executive officers, may or may not take the same view of the law as did the legislature. No provision is thus made in the governmental organization for securing harmony between the expression and the execution of the will of the state. The people, the ultimate sovereign in a popular government, must...have a control over the officers who execute their will, as well as over those who express it.

Separation of powers, Goodnow recognized, creates a discontinuity in the constitutional scheme such that the people cannot be fully assured that their wishes will be carried out or enforced. The problem is one of coordination between law and implementation—the central, multibranch relationship in American public management—without creating unaccountable power in executive agencies.

2.4 AN AMERICAN CENTURY

The profession of public administration is an American invention, Frederick Mosher once declared (Mosher 1975). Dwight Waldo's similar claim, echoed by Minogue, Polidano, and Hulme (1998), was more implicit: "[O]ccasionally throughout history there were training programs for administrative personnel.... [T]he eighteenth century Prussian course of preparation for royal service known as Cameralism will surely come to mind.... But my reading of the record is that only around the turn of [the twentieth] century did administration attain self awareness" (1980: 64).

The American field's founders were more Eurocentric than is now remembered, however. Wilson, Goodnow, and others sought to adapt European precedents to the American political culture. In his 1926 American textbook, Leonard White noted, in addition to two French journals, that "the most important periodical" dealing with public administration was *Public Administration*, published on behalf of the English Institute of Public Administration, whose founding preceded the American Society for Public Administration and its *Public Administration Review* by over fifteeen years. The work of Henri Fayol, Harold Laski, Lorenz von Stein, Otto Hintze, Henry Berthélemy, and other Europeans was familiar to American scholars, many of whom had studied in Germany. Early American contributors to the field that was beginning to emerge there—Cleveland, Willoughby, Dickinson, Friedrich, Fairlie, Pfiffner—were familiar with, and often wrote about, European and English institutions in both administrative law and public management, and many advocated at least selective adaptation of such precedents to the specific needs of America's rapidly expanding administrative state.

Americans have nevertheless tended to see their government, with its formal separation of powers, federal distribution of authority, and "Bill of Rights," as an exception to European *étatism* and *Rechtsstaat* and to English parliamentarianism. Americans regard their own view of democratic governance as unique, even paradigmatic, and their methods of study, especially their emphasis on theory-based quantitative analysis, as more rigorously scientific. The emergence of a profession of public administration and management in the United States and of a productive academic enterprise both within and independent of political science has attained intellectual pre-eminence in Europe (Dunsire 1973, Kickert 1997). The American approach gave legitimacy to ideas and methods that the reigning European legalism regarded as irrelevant (Rugge 2004).

In any event, the modern era, owing much to American intellectual leadership, has brought more organized and detailed attention and a high degree of academic prestige to a continuously evolving field (Lepawsky 1949).

2.4.1 Scientific Management

American public management (not unlike that in Europe) arguably began in the cities, with the bureaus of municipal research and with Progressive reforms in city management (Mosher 1975; Kickert 1997). The nineteenth-century spoils system (which, Carpenter notes (2001: 41), "bore curious similarities to the medieval European notion of property-in-office") had deteriorated into "political clientelism, nepotism and corruption" (Kickert 1997: 19). Much of the early literature by Goodnow, Cleveland, Willoughby, White, and others was concerned with municipal problems and reforms.

To suit the American temper, which reveres individualism and free enterprise, the replacement for a politically micromanaged public administration, notes Caiden (1984: 53), "had to appear nonpartisan, scientific, universal, efficient, and purposeful. It was sought first in comparisons with foreign experience, then in possible application of selected foreign practices, and finally in conceptualization of general principles derived from observation or hunch that could be elevated into universal laws governing human organization." The ideas most widely attributed to early American administrative thought, of a dichotomy between politics and administration and of scientific principles as the basis for management, "gave a form and purpose, a self-confidence, to both the practice and the study of administration in the 1920s and early 1930s" at all levels of government (Dunsire 1973: 94).

"Scientific management," both as a method and as a body of principles, was embraced because, owing to its business origins, it promised legitimacy for administration in the face of congenital American skepticism of the kind of bureaucratic power associated with European étatism. Writing in 1914, Hamilton Church (1914: iv) captured the excitement of the idea:

The question of formulating some approach to a true science of management has been in the air for some time. The first and most forceful stirring of the subject is unquestionably due to Mr. Frederick W. Taylor, whose paper on "Shop Management," issued in 1903, opened most persons' eyes to the fact that administration was ceasing to be...a kind of trade secret, known only to a few men...and that it was entering a stage where things could be reasoned about instead of being guessed at.

Dunsire notes that the term *science* meant "something more than the eighteenth- and nineteenth-century writers on 'administrative science' (or indeed 'economic science' or 'political science') had meant by the word—something like 'disciplined study'" (1973: 93).

In 1937, the Report of the President's Committee on Administrative Management (the Brownlow Report), became "a landmark statement of 'managerialism' in public administration and is closely associated with the alliance between Progressivism and the scientific management movement" (Hood and Jackson 1991: 135; Dunsire 1973; Merkle 1980). The Brownlow Report (PCAM 1937) brought scientific management to bear on problems at the federal level of American government. The solution to weak presidential control over the burgeoning bureaucracy "is couched in terms of a more centralized top-down reporting structure based on a private business management analogy, with a large general staff apparatus around the chief executive" (Hood and Jackson 1991: 136). Like the Northcote–Trevelyan report, it ran into immediate political trouble, but it had an "agenda-setting" effect in the longer term and "has acquired unquestionably 'classic' status.... It appeals to the march of history and the laws of administrative science to back up its assertions" (Hood and Jackson 1991: 136–7), although it "no more demonstrates the validity of the measures it advocates than does the Northcote–Trevelyan Report" (Hood and Jackson 1991: 142).

Release of the Brownlow report was accompanied by the publication of the report's background papers, *Papers on the Science of Administration*, edited by Luther Gulick and Lyndall Urwick (1937) (which first brought Henri Fayol's ideas to an American audience). This volume served as a lightning rod for critics of a depoliticized, scientific managerialism. Scientific management in a narrow sense had never been as dominant an idea in democratic America as is often supposed (Dunsire 1973), not even with Gulick. Moreover, human relations scholarship, the debate between Herman Finer (1940) and Carl Friedrich (1940)—Finer argued for detailed control of bureaucracy by legislation, Friedrich for managerial professionalism and self-control—and works such as Herring's *Public Administration and the Public Interest* (1936) and Barnard's *The Functions of the Executive* (1938) established the human and political dimensions of management. Within the next decade or so, a series of intellectual challenges to so-called "orthodoxy"—apolitical, scientific management—was to create an "intellectual crisis" in American public administration (Ostrom 1973) that swept away not only orthodoxy but memory of the spirited thirty-year discourse on democratic governance that had shaped the field (Lynn 2001*b*).

2.4.2 Dissent and Divergence

The end of orthodoxy was savagely quick. Robert A. Dahl (1947) and Herbert A. Simon (1950) argued from different intellectual vantage points that the search for principles was naive and unscientific. Their argument was amplified by Dwight Waldo in his widely influential *The Administrative State* (1948). Any pretense at unity now shattered, decades of heterodoxy ensued, wherein the behaviorism of Simon, the organization theories pioneered by March and Simon, older versions of institutional managerialism, newer versions of scientific managerialism, the normative manifestos originating in Minnowbrook and Blacksburg (Frederickson 1971; Wamsley et al. 1990), and developments in the social sciences such as public choice theory, "the new economics of organization," and the study of institutions in sociology, economics and political science competed for "the soul of public administration." The stakes in this competition rose, moreover, as the agenda of the maturing welfare state presented perplexing new intellectual and practical challenges to public managers.

As Aberbach, Putnam and Rockman have emphasized, communication is a key managerial aspect of American exceptionalism (although there are others, including the tolerance of enormous variation across states and municipalities and the fluidity of the legal framework: Peters 1997). "[T]he American separation of powers means that face-to-face encounters... are actually more frequent in Washington than in European capitals.... Institutions and history have pushed American bureaucrats toward more traditionally political roles as advocates, policy entrepreneurs and even partisans, and have led congressmen to adopt a more technical role" (Aberbach, Putnam, and Rockman 1981: 243). It was this activist aspect of American public management that provided the pretext for a new phase in the history of the field: the "discovery" of public management by the newly formed public policy schools beginning in the 1970s.

2.5 THE SEARCH FOR EXCELLENCE AND EFFICIENCY

However much one might acknowledge the intellectual depth and historical continuity of the field of public administration and management from 1660 to 1970, something "new" did come into the picture in the 1970s in both America and Europe. Economic crises, fiscal scarcity, and weariness with the liberal governance of preceding decades gave impetus to more conservative political agendas wherein public-management-cum-private-management was viewed as a means, if not a panacea, for a more frugal, efficient government.

2.5.1 "Best Practices" in America

When choosing to complement technocratic training in policy analysis with an emphasis on public management as a subject for research and teaching in the early 1970s, public policy scholars at Harvard, Princeton, and the University of California rebuked "traditional public administration" for having too little regard for the public manager as a strategic political actor (Lynn 1996). The new emphasis was on how to "realize the potential of a given political and institutional setting" (Moore 1984: 3), that is, on public management as craft, an emphasis neglected, although far from ignored, in traditional American literature. Craft-oriented pedagogy and scholarship featured experiential learning and the extensive analysis of cases, with the goal of identifying "best practices" and universal principles, rules, and check-lists for effective public management (Bardach 1987). Works that distill managerial principles from case analyses have become one of the most popular genres in the field (cf. Kettl 2002).

Although its largely ahistorical, "institutions-are-given" perspective was contro-versial outside the policy schools, this orientation, as later manifest in Osborne and Gaebler's best-selling *Reinventing Government* (1992) (a spawn of *In Search of Excellence*, by Peters and Waterman 1982), with its universal "steer-don't-row" prescription and canonical principles, was to prove congenial to a new generation of reform-minded activists, including the practitioner-dominated National Acad-emy of Public Administration and officials associated with the Clinton adminis-tration's National Performance Review. As Guy Peters has noted (1997: 255), "[p]erhaps the one defining feature of reinvention is a disregard of some of the conventions associated with traditional public administration and an associated desire to rethink government operations from the ground up." Although often regarded as a brand of New Public Management, the American "reinvention" movement featured managerial deregulation, quality, and entrepreneurship and placed far less emphasis on the kinds of market-mimicking reforms that, in any event, had long been popular in state and local government. NPM in America is better represented by the 1993 Government Performance and Results Act, a Con-gressional initiative, and by President George W. Bush's "Management Agenda", which emphasized performance-driven, outsourced management in federal depart-ments and agencies and use of a "program assessment rating tool" in budgeting.

2.5.2 Administrative Reform in Europe

Something "new" was abroad in Europe as well by the 1980s (Aucoin 1990; Pollitt 1990; Kickert 1997). Unlike America, the awakened European interest in public management was more a political than an academic invention. It was directly inspired by the economic crises of the mid-1970s, although it was also influenced by the complex challenges of the post-war welfare state.

Similar to their American counterparts, some European students of bureaucracy and management sought to repudiate a seemingly entrenched paradigm: the legalistic thinking that had continued to dominate training and practice since the nineteenth century (Kickert 1997). In France especially, owing to the influence of Crozier, Friedberg, and other sociologists, the concept of *management public* became central, and the *Institut de Management Public* was created in the 1960s (Crozier and Friedberg 1980). (An awakening interest in public administration in Germany, and such latent interests as existed in Great Britain, were not to bear fruit until later.)

Although the substantive orientation of this new European interest in public management was not toward best practices (the influence of *in Search of Excellence* is, however, evident in both places), "the appeal of the recent managerialist literature lies in the fact that it has been packaged in ways which have addressed issues from the perspective of managers rather than from the perspective of the theorist" (Aucoin 1990: 118). European approaches reflected more traditional concepts of administrative science and public administration, however (Pollitt and Bouckaert 2000).

Aucoin (1990) sees two sets of such ideas at work. The first is a private-sector-oriented managerialist ideology first conceptualized by Pollitt (1990) and manifest in the Thatcher reforms that became the foundation of the New Public Management, which asserts the primacy of management over bureaucracy. In this respect, it is notable that the academic study of public management migrated from departments of public administration or political science towards schools of management, and selected, younger civil servants began to study in those schools. The second, more political, perspective is inspired by public choice theory or its stablemate principal-agent theory (Lane 1993), which establishes the primacy of representative government over bureaucracy. These two sets of ideas are, in Aucoin's analysis, in sharp tension: managerialism requires a politics/administration dichotomy, public choice theory repudiates it.

The new approaches have been sharply contested. Metcalfe and Richards, for example, argue that public choice "largely fails to contribute usefully to our understanding of real world public management problems" (1993: 115). In König's view, legalistic reasoning may be superior to economic reasoning: "Assessments of effects and successes, analyses of costs and benefits fall short of what legal argumentation is able to perform" (König 1997, 226). The unit of analysis for Metcalfe and Richards and for König is the system as a whole, not the individual or the transaction. Metcalfe and Richards prefer a network perspective, however, whereas König argues for "the primacy of politics and democracy as well as the constitutional system of order" (König 1997: 228).

The fact that practical, theoretical and methodological issues in Europe and the U.S. have been tending to converge is both cause and consequence of the direction the field has taken since the 1990s: toward a globalization of the discourse on public administration and management and, in a real sense and for the first time, an internationalization of the field.

2.5.3 The Globalization of Public Management

"[T]here has been an increasing degree of cross-fertilization throughout advanced political systems," Aucoin noted in 1990, "and some considerable spread of these ideas to less advanced political systems" (119). A year later, Christopher Hood (1991) was to coin a term that became a banner for the globalization of public management: New Public Management (NPM). That term was meant to characterize a neo-Taylorite, neo-cameralist approach to managerial reform, originating with the Thatcher regime in Great Britain and with managerialist reforms in New Zealand and Australia. In a popular interpretation, NPM began propagating itself globally both because of the inherent appeal of the ideas and because of the support of the Organization for Economic Cooperation and Development, the United Nations, the United Nations Development Program, and other international and regional forums. That is, NPM referred to a simulacrum of the allocation of resources by competitive markets that suited neo-conservative times: managerial, customer-oriented, performance-driven (Pollitt 1990, Hood and Jackson 1991, Kickert 1997). A compact view of NPM is König's: "a popularised mixture of management theories, business motivation psychology and neo-liberal economy" (1997: 219).

Impressed by the apparently global nature of public management reform and by the family resemblance of its motivations and strategies, academics began creating new international forums for professional discourse on the subject in the 1990s. As König (1997: 226) noted, "management has become the...lingua franca in an increasingly internationalised administrative world. It signals that public administration implies planning and coordination, staff recruitment and development, personnel management and control, organisation, and so on, and that allowances must be made in all these respects for the scarcity of resources."

Motivations to create and participate in these forums (which, though international, have drawn less interest from the French- and Spanish-speaking worlds, Asia, and the less developed countries), have varied. Some promoted New Public Management as an ideology and sought an audience for positive assessments, however premature. Others were impressed with the apparent convergence of management institutions, practices, and values, even seeing a global consensus that the private sector could out-perform traditional institutions (Minogue, Polidano, and Hulme 1998). König insisted, for example, that the challenge of NPM to Continental Europeans "goes beyond the claim to an internal rationalization of the public administration by means of good management" (1997: 213) and posits a slenderized state with well functioning competitive markets. Others sought to promote a wider understanding of national institutions in responding to the managerial challenges of globalization, seeing divergence and the possibility of new theoretical insights to processes of managerial reform (Pollitt 2002). Academics sought a dialogue among scholars with the more modest ambition of encouraging both theory building and lesson drawing among jurisdictions confronting similar challenges (Lynn 1997, 2001a).

Whatever the specific motivations, the idea that there existed entering the twenty-first century a field of public administration and management that transcended national political boundaries was beginning to take hold among prominent scholars, a milestone in the field's history.

2.6 ON WINE AND BOTTLES, OLD AND NEW

If governments are viewed as bottles, then codified, rationalized managerial structures, practices, and values are the wines that fill them. The configurations of actual wine bottles vary widely, as do their contents. But wine mavens recognize each other the world over, new versions of wines from noble grapes are celebrated, and the discovery of an Etruscan amphora or an ancient Roman bottle is cherished by all. So, too, there is a professional field of public administration and management, of ancient origins, which its mavens across the world do not fail to recognize and whose variations delight, enlighten, and unite its members. As Leonard White said in 1926, "the natural history of administration connects its ancient and modern forms in an unbroken sequence of development" (4).

That there is a coherent and enduring intellectual agenda for the field of public administration and management is becoming more widely recognized, albeit from different perspectives. "All administrative reform, like basically all administrative theory," argues Werner Jann, "deals with the same set of problems: *legality, ... legitimacy, ... efficiency* and *effectiveness*" (1997: 94). Raadschelders and Rutgers argue that without studying three dichotomies—public/private, policy/administration, and state/society—"public administration cannot be understood at all" (1999: 30). "[A]ll governments," argue Aucoin and Neintzman, "must now govern in a context where there are greater demands for accountability for performance on the part of a better educated and less deferential citizenry, more assertive and well organized interest groups and social movements, and more aggressive and intrusive mass media operating in a highly competitive information-seeking and processing environment" (2000: 46). Amongst particulars, in other words, there are universals, although no agreement on what these universals are.

If there is a transcendent issue, it is the relationship between bureaucracy and democracy, between administrators and the people, between managerial responsibility and popular sovereignty and the rule of law. As Riggs has noted (1997a: 350), "[i]t has never been easy in even the most democratic countries for the organs of representative government to sustain effective control over their bureaucracies."

Perhaps no development illustrates this proposition better than finding Great Britain (much more than New Zealand) at the forefront of sustained administrative reform in the era of globalized public management and Germany a distinct laggard. Not only did Margaret Thatcher restructure and refocus British public administration but, of the Blair government, it has been said, perhaps too breathlessly, that "[a]t a stroke, a whole new central architecture for managing he implementation of policy in England has been created" (Lee and Woodward 2002: 54). From the perspective either of *Rechtsstaat* or of a formal separation of powers, the fact that, as König notes, "the British administrative 'revolution' with its market testing, compulsory competitive tendering, and so on, has turned out to be the most uncompromising" (1997: 219) is arresting. From a German or French perspective, a state that malleable could not provide the continuity that settled institutions have provided (König 1997). For Americans, who, lacking integrative institutions (Page 1992), have always had to settle for incrementalism on matters of managerial reform, such malleability can only be envied.

The explanation for such differences lies not in craft or structure but in constitutions, in national institutional arrangements that establish and regulate the balance between managerial capacity and external control. The British "fusion of [executive and legislative] powers in a cabinet permits them to maintain effective control over an intrinsically powerful mandarinate" (Riggs 1997b: 274; Stillman 2000). In Germany, in contrast, the inclusion of "traditional principles of civil service" in the Federal Constitution was, Jann (1997) argues, a kind of constitutional guarantee of Weberian principles of administration, and only the sudden belated popularity of the "New Steering Model" at the local level threatened Weberian continuity by seeking to diminish the difference between public and private sectors. America's separation of powers accounts for its exceptional approach to public administration and management.

The fact that public management reform remains primarily a national (and constitutional) matter (König 1997; Rohr 2002) despite the globalization of resources, technology, and ideas is of less significance to the field, however, than that these issues can be intelligibly studied and debated by academic and practicing professionals of widely different national experiences. While their orientations to disciplines, theories, methods, and national agendas will differ (Stillman 2000), these professionals have in common a grasp of larger issues that transcend the descriptive particulars of national regimes or tenets of disciplinary training. National differences may be inimical to reaching that elusive consensus on the universal principles of public administration and management, but such differences are the lifeblood of scientific inquiry and thus well serve the goal of building the theories and empirical understanding that, as they have from ancient times, sustain a professional field on a global scale.

REFERENCES

ABERBACH, J. D., PUTNAM, R. D., and ROCKMAN, B. A. (1981), *Bureaucrats and Politicians in Western Democracies*, Cambridge, MA: Harvard University Press.

ACTON, J. E. E. D., WARD, A. W., PROTHERO, G. W., LEATHES, S. M., and BENIANS, E. A. (1910–12), *Cambridge Modern History*, New York: Macmillan.

ALBROW, M. (1970), *Bureaucracy*, New York: Praeger Publishers.

ANDERSON, E. N., and ANDERSON, P. R. (1967), *Political Institutions and Social Change in Continental Europe in the Nineteenth Century*, Berkeley: University of California Press.

AUCOIN, P. (1990), "Administrative Reform in Public Management: Paradigms, Principles, Paradoxes and Pendulums," *Governance* 3 (2): 115–37.

—— and NEINTZMAN, R. (2000), "The Dialectics of Accountability for Performance in Public Management Reform," *International Review of Administrative Sciences* 66: 45–55.

BARDACH, E. (1987), "From Practitioner Wisdom to Scholarly Knowledge and Back Again," *Journal of Policy Analysis and Management* 7(1): 188–99.

BARKER, E. (1944), *The Development of Public Services in Western Europe: 1660–1930*, London: Oxford University Press.

BARNARD, C. (1938), *The Functions of the Executive*. Cambridge, MA: Harvard University Press.

BOURDIEU, P. (1990), "The Intellectual Field: A World Apart," in *In Other Words*, tr. M. Adamson. Stanford: Stanford University Press, 140–9.

CAIDEN, G. (1984), "In Search of an Apolitical Science of American Public Administration," in J. Rabin, and J. S. Bowman (eds.), *Politics and Administration: Woodrow Wilson and American Public Administration*, New York: Marcel Dekker, 51–76.

CARPENTER, D. (2001), *The Forging of Bureaucratic Autonomy: Reputations, Networks, and Policy Innovation in Executive Agencies, 1862–1928*, Princeton: Princeton University Press.

CHURCH, A. H.. (1914), *Science and Practice of Management*, New York: The Engineering Magazine Co.

CREEL, H. G. (1964), "The Beginnings of Bureaucracy in China: The Origin of the Hsien," *Journal of Asian Studies* 23: 155–84.

—— (1974), *Shen Pu-Hai: A Chinese Philosopher of the Fourth Century B.C.*, Chicago, IL: University of Chicago Press.

CROZIER, M., and FRIEDBERG, E. (1980), *Actors and Systems: The Politics of Collective Action*, Chicago: University of Chicago Press.

DAHL, R. A. (1947), "The Science of Public Administration: Three Problems," *Public Administration Review* 7(1): 1–11.

DEANE, P. (1989), *The State and the Economic System: An Introduction to the History of Political Economy*, Oxford: Oxford University Press.

DUNSIRE, A. (1973), *Administration: The Word and the Science*, New York: John Wiley & Sons.

FAYOL, H. (1916), "Industrial and General Administration," in *Bulletin de la société de l'industrie minerale*, No. 3.

FINER, H. (1940), Administrative Responsibility in Democratic Government. *Public Administration Review* 1: 4: 335–50.

FREDERICKSON, H. G. (1971), "Toward a New Public Administration," in Frank Marini, (ed.), *Toward a New Public Administration: The Minnowbrook Perspective*. Scranton, PA: Chandler, 309–31.

—— and SMITH, K. B. (2003), *Public Administration Theory Primer*, Boulder, CO: Westview Press.

FRIEDRICH, C. J. (1939), "The Continental Tradition of Training Administrators in Law and Jurisprudence," *The Journal of Modern History* 11: 129–48.

—— (1940), "Public Policy and the Nature of Administrative Responsibility," in *Public Policy: A Yearbook of the Graduate School of Public Administration, Harvard University, 1940*, ed. C. J. Friedrich and E. S. Mason. Cambridge, MA: Harvard University Press, 3–24.

—— and COLE, T. (1932), *Responsible Bureaucracy*. Cambridge, MA: Harvard University Press.

GOODNOW, F. J. (1893 and 1902), *Comparative Administrative Law: An Analysis of the Administrative Systems National and Local, of the United States, England, France and Germany*, New York: G. Putnam's Sons.

—— (1900), *Politics and Administration: A Study in Government*, New York: The Macmillan Company.

GULICK, L., and URWICK, L. F. (eds.) (1937), *Papers on the Science of Administration*, New York: Institute of Public Administration.

HERRING, E. P. (1936), *Public Administration and the Public Interest*, New York: McGraw-Hill.

HOOD, C. (1991), "A Public Management for All Seasons," *Public Administration*, 69: 13–19.

—— and MICHAEL JACKSON. (1991), *Administrative Argument*. Aldershot: Dartmouth.

HSU, SHIH-LIEN. (1932), *The Political Philosophy of Confucianism: An Interpretation of the Social and Political Ideas of Confucius, His Forerunners, and His Early Disciples*. New York: Dutton.

JANN, W. (1997), "Public Management Reform in Germany: A Revolution without a Theory?" in W. J. M., Kickert (ed.), *Public Management and Administrative Reform in Western Europe*. Cheltenham: Edward Elgar, 81–100.

KETTL, D. F. (2002), *The Transformation of Governance: Public Administration for the Twenty-First Century*, Baltimore: Johns Hopkins University Press.

KICKERT, W. J. M.. (1997), "Public Management in the United States and Europe," in W. J. M. Kickert (ed.), *Public Management and Administrative Reform in Western Europe*, Cheltenham, UK: Edward Elgar, 15–38.

KÖNIG, K. (1997), "Entrepreneurial Management or Executive Administration: The Perspective of Classical Public Administration," in W. J. M. Kickert (ed.), *Public Management and Administrative Reform in Western Europe*, Cheltenham: Edward Elgar, 213–32.

LANE, J.-E. (1993), "Economic Organization Theory and Public Management," in K. Eliassen and J. Kooiman (eds.), *Managing Public Organizations. Lessons From Contemporary European Experience*. London: Sage, 73–83.

LEE, S., and WOODWARD, R. (2002), "Implementing the Third Way: the Delivery of Public Services under the Blair Government," *Public Money & Management* (October–December), 49–56.

LEPAWSKY, A. (1949), *Administration: The Art and Science of Organization and Management*, New York: Alfred A. Knopf.

LINCOLN, A. (1838), "An Address Before the Young Men's Lyceum of Springfield, Illinois," at http://www.barefootsworld.net/Lincoln1838.htm (accessed January 2004).

LINDENFELD, D. F. (1997), *The Practical Imagination: The German Sciences of State in the Nineteenth Century*, Chicago: University of Chicago Press.

LYNN, L. E., JR. (1996), *Public Management as Art, Science, and Profession*. Chatham, NJ: Chatham House.

—— (1997), "The New Public Management as an International Phenomenon: A Skeptical View," *International Public Management Journal* 1:1 (1997), reprinted in L. R. Jones and Kuno Schedler, (eds.), *International Perspectives on the New Public Management* (Greenwich, CT: JAI Press, 1997).

—— (2001*a*), "Globalization and Administrative Reform: What is Happening in Theory?" *Public Management Review* 3(1): 191–208.

—— (2001*b*), "The Myth of the Bureaucratic Paradigm: What Traditional Public Administration Really Stood For," *Public Administration Review* 61(2): 144–60.

—— (2003), "Public Management," in B. G. Peters and J. Pierre (eds.), *Handbook of Public Administration*, London: Sage, 14–24.

MERKLE, J. A. (1980), *Management and Ideology: The Legacy of the International Scientific Management Movement*. Berkeley: University of California Press.

METCALFE, L., and RICHARDS, S. (1993), "Evolving Public Management Cultures," in K. Eliassen and J. Kooiman (eds.), *Managing Public Organizations. Lessons from Contemporary European Experience*. London: Sage, 106–24.

MINOGUE, M., POLIDANO, C., and HULME, D. (eds.) (1998), *Beyond the New Public Management: Changing Ideas and Practices in Governance*, Cheltenham: Edward Elgar.

MOORE, M. H. (1984), "A Conception of Public Management," in *Teaching Public Management*, Boston: Boston College, 1–12.

MORONE, J. A. (1990), *The Democratic Wish: Popular Participation and the Limits of American Government*, New Haven: Yale University Press. Rev. edn. 1998.

MORSTEIN MARX, F. (1935), "Civil Service in Germany," in L D. WHITE, C. H. BLAND, W. R. Sharp, and F. Morstein Marx (eds.), *Civil Service Abroad: Great Britain, Canada, France, Germany*, New York: McGraw-Hill, 159–275.

MOSHER, F. C. (1975), "Introduction," in F. C. Mosher (ed.), *American Public Administration: Past, Present, Future*. University, AL: University of Alabama Press.

OSBORNE, D., and GAEBLER, T. (1992), *Reinventing Government: How the Entrepreneurial Spirit is Transforming the Public Sector*, Reading, MA: Addison Wesley.

OSTROM, V. (1973), *The Intellectual Crisis in Public Administration*. University, AL: University of Alabama Press. Rev. edn. 1989.

PAGE, E. C. (1992), *Political Authority and Bureaucratic Power: A Comparative Analysis*. Hemel Hempstead: Harvester Wheatsheaf.

PERRY, J. L., and KRAEMER, K. L. (1983), *Public Management: Public and Private Perspectives*. Palo Alto, CA: Mayfield.

PETERS, B. G. (1997), "A North American Perspective on Administrative Modernisation in Europe," in W. J. M., Kickert (ed.), *Public Management and Administrative Reform in Western Europe*, Cheltenham: Edward Elgar, 251–66.

PETERS, T. J., and WATERMAN, R. H., JUN. (1982), *in Search of Excellence: Lessons from America's Best-Run Companies*, New York: Harper & Row.

POLLITT, C. (1990), *Managerialism and the Public Services: The Anglo-American Experience*, Oxford: Basil Blackwell.

—— (2002), "Clarifying Convergence: Striking Similarities and Durable Differences in Public Management Reform," *Public Management Review* 4(1): 471–92.

—— (2003), *The Essential Public Manager*, Maidenhead: Open University Press.

—— and Bouckaert, G. (2000), *Public Management Reform: A Comparative Analysis*, Oxford: Oxford University Press.

PRESIDENT'S COMMITTEE ON ADMINISTRATIVE MANAGEMENT (PCAM). (1937), *Report of the Committee with Studies of Administrative Management in the Federal Government*. Washington, DC: US Government Printing Office.

RAADSCHELDERS, J. C. N., and RUTGERS, M. R. (1999), "The Waxing and Waning of the State and its Study: Changes and Challenges in the Study of Public Administration," in W. J. M. Kickert and R. J. Stillman II (eds.), *The Modern State and its Study: New Administrative Sciences in a Changing Europe and United States*, Cheltenham: Edward Elgar, 17–35.

RAINEY, H. G. (1990), "Public Management: Recent Developments and Current Prospects," in N. B. Lynn and A. Wildavsky (eds.), *Public Administration: The State of the Discipline*, Chatham, NJ: Chatham House, 157–84.

RIGGS, F. W. (1997a), "Modernity and Bureaucracy," *Public Administration Review* 5(4): 347–53.

—— (1997b), "Presidentialism versus Parliamentarism: Implications for Representativeness and Legitimacy," *International Political Science Review* 18(3): 253–78.

ROHR, J. A. (2002), *Civil Servants and their Constitutions*. Lawrence, KS: University Press of Kansas.

ROSENBERG, H. (1958), *Bureaucracy, Aristocracy and Autocracy: The Prussian Experience, 1660–1815*, Boston: Beacon Press.

RUGGE, F. (2004), Personal communication.

SCHUMPETER, J. (1954), *History of Economic Analysis*, Oxford: Oxford University Press.

SIMON, H. A. (1950), *Public Administration*, New York: Knopf.

SMALL, A. W. (1909), *The Cameralists: The Pioneers of German Social Polity*, Chicago: University of Chicago Press.

STILLMAN, R. J., II. (1982), "The Changing Patterns of Public Administration Theory in America," in J. A. Uveges Jun. (ed.), *Public Administration: History and Theory in Contemporary Perspective*, New York: Marcel Dekker, 5–37.

—— (2000), "American versus European Public Administration: Does Public Administration Make the Modern State, or Does the State make Public Administration?" in W. J. M. Kickert and R. J. Stillman II (eds.), *The Modern State and its Study: New Administrative Sciences in a Changing Europe and United States*, Cheltenham: Edward Elgar, 247–60.

STORY, J. (1840), *A Familiar Exposition of the Constitution of the United States*. Boston: Marsh, Capen, Lyon, and Webb.

TRIBE, K. (1984), "Cameralism and the Science of Government," *Journal of Modern History* 56: 263–84.

WAGNER, R. E. (2003), "The Cameralists: Fertile Sources for a New Science of Public Finance," http://mason.gmu.edu/~rwagner/cameralist.pdf (accessed in March).

WALDO, D. (1948), *The Administrative State: A Study of the Political Theory of American Public Administration*, New York: The Ronald Press.

—— (1955), *The Study of Administration*, New York: Random House.

—— (1980), "Public Management Research: Perspectives of History, Political Science and Public Administration," in *Setting Public Management Research Agendas: Integrating the Sponsor, Producer, and User*. Washington, DC: US Office of Personnel Management (OPM Document 127–53–1), 63–70.

—— (1984), *The Administrative State: Second Edition with New Observations and Reflections*, New York: Holmes & Meier.

WAMSLEY, G. L. et al. (1990), *Refounding Public Administration*, Newbury Park, CA: Sage Publications.

WHITE, L. D. (1926), *Introduction to the Study of Public Administration*, New York: Macmillan.

—— (1935), "The British Civil Service," in L. D. White, C. H. Bland, W. R. Sharp, and F. Morstein Marx (eds.), *Civil Service Abroad: Great Britain, Canada, France, Germany*, New York: McGraw Hill, 1–54.

CHAPTER 3

BUREAUCRACY IN THE TWENTY-FIRST CENTURY

KENNETH J. MEIER
GREGORY C. HILL

ALTHOUGH numerous pundits claim the eminent demise of bureaucracy (Lane 2000; Osborne and Gaebler 1992; Handler 1996; Kanter 1989), in this chapter we argue that bureaucracy will not only survive in the twenty-first century but will flourish. The core of the argument is that the large-scale tasks that government must perform—national defense, a social welfare system, political monitoring of the economy, etc.—will remain key functions of governments in the twenty-first century and that bureaucracies, likely public but possibly private, will continue to be the most effective way to do these tasks. Bureaucracy has weathered other calls for its demise before (Bennis 1966; Marini 1971; Thayer 1973); current efforts are likely to meet similar fates. After a brief discussion of definitions and the meaning of bureaucracy, the major sections of this chapter will deal with six challenges to bureaucracy. Some of these challenges are intellectual; others are part of real-world ongoing reform efforts in a variety of countries.

3.1 DEFINING BUREAUCRACY

Reading much of the current literature on bureaucracy suggests that two highly inconsistent definitions are being used. The advocates of administrative reform tend to define bureaucracy by a series of stereotypes. According to Jreisat (2002: 38), "Conventional wisdom has it that bureaucracy is conformist, seeks standardization and routinization of work, and therefore, causes inflexibility and resistance to change in managing public organizations." Bureaucracy, in this view, is slow, inept, and wasteful. Striking in the prescriptive literature is the degree that this stereotype is simply accepted without any empirical evidence other than an occasional anecdote (see Goodsell 1983 for an early critique and discussion). If one accepts this definition of bureaucracy, then the normative need to rid oneself of bureaucracy is self evident. Advocates of this view, however, are then left with the task of explaining why an institution with such a record of poor performance continues to persist in all modern societies. At best such explanations focus on rent-seeking and budget-maximizing bureaucrats who conspire to exploit the polity for their own ends (Niskanen 1971). Empirical evidence to support such claims and why such behavior would be tolerated by politicians and citizens, however, is lacking (see Blais and Dion 1991; du Gay 2000).

More promising than the stereotypical definition is to treat bureaucracy as an empirical organizational form and to determine if this organizational form has any competitive advantages over other organizational forms. In defining bureaucracy, one should go to the authoritative source, Max Weber (1946) who defined bureaucracy in formal, structural terms. Bureaucracy is characterized by the following.

1. Fixed and official jurisdictional areas ordered by rules, laws, or regulations.
2. The principle of hierarchy whereby structures are established with superior and subordinate relationships.
3. Management of the office relies on written files.
4. Occupation of offices based on expertise and training.
5. Full time employment of personnel who are compensated and who can expect employment to be a career.
6. Administration of the office follows general rules that are stable and can be learned.

With one exception, Weber's nineteenth-century definition will be applied to the twenty-first-century world of reinvented government.[1] That exception is, of course, the requirement of written documents or files to guide the administration of programs. Technology has moved beyond paper so that many documents are written only in electronic form. Computer files and paper files, however, are equivalent in function even though a poor transition from paper to computer files can create serious organizational problems (Pollitt 2000). At the outset, we should also note that Weber's definition of bureaucracy does not apply specifically to the public sector; one of his archetype bureaucracies was the Catholic Church, a nonprofit organization.

As we probe the contemporary challenges to bureaucracy, we need to keep these six characteristics of bureaucracy in mind. Some of the challenges to bureaucracy are intellectual and take place in the rarified world of academia; others are practical and take place in the political debates that shape the direction of governments and governance.

3.2 THE CHALLENGE OF POLITICS

Bureaucracies are forged in the smithy of politics. The decision to create such structures and maintain them, whether conscious or not, is made by political actors involved in the process of governance. We assume here that modern democratic governance requires a supporting bureaucratic apparatus because only an effective and efficient bureaucracy can generate the surplus capacity to absorb the high decision and transaction costs inherent in democracy (Meier 1997; Suleiman 2003). A nation that cannot feed or educate its citizens is unlikely to be able to support a functioning democracy. This functional necessity, however, plays out in practice in a variety of ways.

The relationship of bureaucracy to the electoral (often misnamed the political) institutions of government influences bureaucratic structures, delimits the scope of its activities, and creates pressures to restrict or reduce bureaucracy. Hood (2002) argues that different combinations of political institutions result in different implicit bargains with the bureaucracy, thus defining bureaucracy's responsibilities and scope of action. Political systems vary in their concentration of political power and decision-making processes; some political systems are highly centralized with unitary governments, others are decentralized with semi-autonomous governments exercising power in a fragmented political system. In centralized political systems (e.g., UK, France), power is an accepted fact of life; and the role of bureaucracy in establishing and maintaining state power is generally recognized (Peters and Pierre 1998; Pollitt and Bouckaert 2000). Along with the higher status accorded to bureaucrats in these countries, bureaucracy is seen as a legitimate state actor. In France, as an illustration, the bureaucracy is viewed as the instrument by which republicanism seeks equality and other fundamental values (Suleiman 2003: 173–5). Such states provide a clearer "contract" with the bureaucracy by being more precise in defining political roles and accepting the idea of significant discretion among career bureaucrats (Hood 2002). Calls for the elimination of bureaucracy might be made in such countries, but they are more likely to fall on deaf ears since politicians will recognize that removing bureaucracy will directly limit the actions that they can take and undercut policies that they support. France, for example, has increased the size of its bureaucracy by 25 percent in the last fifteen years (Suleiman 2003: 176).

Fragmented political systems create a different environment for bureaucracy because no political institution can generate sufficient consensus to make an enduring bargain with the civil service.[2] In some cases a formal fragmentation of powers can be overcome by alternative institutions such as strong political parties or corporatist decision processes. In fragmented systems where electoral institutions fail to define a precise role for bureaucracy, the bureaucracy itself becomes a more political institution that seeks to aggregate political power in support of policies and their implementation. The classic case of a fragmented political system failing to provide the political consensus to create a relationship with bureaucracy is the United States (Long 1949). Because the formal institutions of government cannot concentrate power and thus define political ends, the bureaucracy is left with the task of building support for its own mission from the bottom up rather than via a principal—agent contract with political branches. In this situation bureaucracy is seen as a competitor for political power, and politicians perceive that running for election by campaigning against the bureaucracy is a viable political strategy. In such systems calls for the elimination of bureaucracy find receptive ears. The irony of decentralized systems such as the United States is that political principals shirk, that is, they fail to define political goals for the bureaucracy. Such shirking allows political attacks on the bureaucracy, but at the same time it creates the incentive for bureaucracies to generate their own political support. Rather than increasing political control over the bureaucracy, the process lessens it because the bureaucracy supplies its own political legitimacy.

The challenge of politics is more than American exceptionalism (or Anglo exceptionalism if one includes Australia and New Zealand) because of recent efforts to shape the structures of democracy. Via both international political pressures and direct economic pressures via the International Monetary Fund, non-European countries have both downsized their governments and decentralized authority to local governments. Particularly among the nascent democracies in Latin American, the argument is made that democracy is enhanced by creating more authority for governments closer to the people (that is local governments, see Blair 2000; Conaghan 1996). The argument is that via fragmented local governments, with each developing a unique set of services, individual citizens can vote with their feet to select the community that best meets their preferences for taxes and services (Tiebout 1956; Ostrom 1973; but see Lyons, Lowery and DeHoog 1992). The argument, however, has implicit in it that local governments have the capacity to provide effective services or can purchase them from the private sector. Without such capacity, decentralization is as likely to bring corruption and dissatisfaction, thus undercutting support for democracy. Building this capacity in a system that denigrates bureaucracy and generally lacks a competitive market system for providing local government services would appear to be virtually impossible.

The political-bureaucratic working agreement, itself a challenge to bureaucracy in terms of legitimacy, also affects the ability of bureaucracies to deal with each of the five other challenges to bureaucracy in the twenty-first century. It determines how much pressure there is to reduce or eliminate bureaucracy, and it influences how realistic politicians are likely to be in pressing for government reforms. The idea of a twenty-first century free from bureaucracy is a plausible one only within some political systems. Even in those systems, however, the idea flourishes because the implications for governance are not fully considered.

3.3 THE NEW PUBLIC MANAGEMENT

The New Public Management both challenges and reinforces bureaucracy (Kettl 2000). One wing of NPM seeks to eliminate government, and thus government bureaucracy, by moving as many of the functions of government to the private sector (Lane 2000; Savas 1987). Government agencies become contract administrators rather than persons who deliver services; the quest is guided by the idea that private bureaucracies are more efficient than government bureaucracies (an open question despite the wealth of research on the topic, see Hodge 2000). Government employment in this scenario shrinks even as larger numbers of people indirectly work for government via contracts (Light 1999).

Two distinct approaches of this anti-bureaucracy New Public Management exist—the Westminster model and the US model (Pollitt and Bouckaert 2000). The Westminster model, so named after the United Kingdom but practiced in Australia and New Zealand also, starts with a fundamental question, what should be the proper role and scope of government (the starting premise of the field of public finance)? Once the overall size of government and the essential functions are defined, then government can rationally establish priorities for reducing government bureaucracy by paring those that do not fit within the defined function. As an example, the UK determined that operating a telephone system was not a government function thus leading logically to the divestiture of British Telecom (Durant, Legge, and Moussios 1998; Suleiman 2003: 199).

The US model of the New Public Management lacks this integrating coherence but rather simply acts to contract out or divest public functions (but see Hall, Holt and Purchase 2003). For example, nowhere in the periodic debates over US agricultural policy is the question of why we subsidize wheat farmers but not soybean producers raised, let alone the question of whether subsidizing agriculture is a government function. This lack of an overall plan, as a result, means that US governments often cut taxes without concern for which programs should be reduced or demand privatization without determining if sufficient private sector organizations exist to create a competitive market. The end result is both an inconsistent approach to government size and an erratic fiscal policy.

The second wing of the New Public Management seeks to liberate bureaucratic managers by freeing them from the rules and restrictions that government managers face. This second goal of NPM is clearly inconsistent and often contradictory relative to the first goal. The liberation of public managers requires the capacity to act, but the diminution of government reduces this capacity (Terry 2003). O'Toole's (1991) studies of local government waste water treatment contracting finds that cities that contract out these functions lose the capacity to restore them if the private contract arrangement does not work. Similarly Durant (1993) found Reagan administration budget cuts in natural resources agencies prevented that administration from implementing its policy changes. Even if private organizations retain this capacity on behalf of government, the different goals of private sector organizations render the capacity less flexible and less useful than it previously was for pursuing government ends (see O'Toole 1991). The privatization of government functions can also diminish government capacity in another sense; it can lead to increases in corruption and a loss of citizen faith in government efforts. In the United States, those federal government programs that rely heavily on private sector implementation are consistently marked by greater corruption than those implemented by government bureaucracies (Perry and Wise 1990; Meier 2000). An irony of the New Public Management, therefore, is its quest to rid itself of unresponsive government bureaucracies actually replaces them with private sector bureaucracies that are more difficult to hold accountable.

The liberation management version of NPM is often accompanied by benchmarking and performance standards with the idea being that public managers are free to experiment but will be held to a clear bottom line. Hall, Holt, and Purchase's (2003) assessment of benchmarking in the UK Next Steps agencies concludes that this generates a narrow accountability system that produces numbers but not necessarily better performance (see also Martin 2002). Goal displacement, as a result, is a distinct possibility as highly bureaucratic auditing systems create red tape for local administrators. The decline in bureaucracy in service delivery agencies is merely displaced to auditing and control agencies with the overall system becoming no less bureaucratic (Power 1997; Barberis 1998).

The New Public Management challenge to bureaucracy is to replace bureaucracy with liberated contract managers. They would substitute private bureaucracies for public bureaucracies thus creating institutions that are more difficult to control and oversee. In addition, stripping government of its action functions and replacing them with the mundane process of contract management is unlikely to attract the type of creative, risk-taking individuals that NPM envisions. The New Public Management challenge to bureaucracy, in short, is no challenge at all.

3.4 THE POSTMODERN CHALLENGE

Bureaucracy is an instrument of rationality; it seeks to order processes and produce outputs by regular means that are amenable to systematic analysis. Because postmodern scholarship is in large part a reaction to the rationality of positivism, it logically includes the consideration of bureaucracy within its purview (Farmer 1995).[3] Denhardt (1993), for example, begins his assessment of bureaucracy by disputing the positivist distinction between facts and values and moves on to a critique of bureaucracy. Although postmodernists range widely in views, united only in their temporal relationship with "modernism," they frequently advocate the same set of reforms to counter the problems of bureaucracy—decentralization, greater participation, and client-driven organizations.

In Denhardt's view, if the distinction between facts and value does not hold, one needs to look elsewhere for knowledge about organizations and how they operate (see also Blankenship 1971). In his view organizational rationality is replaced by individualized understanding linked to individual actions. All views become subjective and none has primacy. Reasoning in this view works via dialectical thinking in an effort to understand the dynamic patterns of organizational life. "Such an approach," Denhardt (1993: 204) contends, "would reveal certain contradictions inherent in hierarchical organizations."

Postmodern critiques of bureaucracy have some of their roots in the human relations school of organization theory, an approach critical of the formal, structural approach of Weber and his descendants. Harmon (1981), for example, grounds his critique of bureaucracy in organizational development, an applied organization theory that focuses on organizational change by non-structural means. The stress on the informal side of the organization quite naturally leads to a rejection of "bureaucracy" for more participatory, decentralized organizational processes. Postmodern approaches also view organizational boundaries with some skepticism, seeking to incorporate clientele within the organization (see Waldo 1971: 263). Clientele not only have a say in what the organization produces but perhaps even in the actual production of organizational outputs.

Bureaucracy can marshal several counter arguments to the challenge of postmodern views of organization. First, one of the more interesting markers of a postmodern bureaucracy is the effort to make the organization client-centered rather than bureaucrat-centered. The charge is essentially that bureaucracies are self-serving and emphasize making the lives of bureaucrats easier rather than serving the clientele (Marini 1971, but see Frederickson 1997: 130–1 on evidence to the contrary). The emphasis on client-centered organizations, which is similar to the New Public Management's emphasis on customer-oriented bureaucracy, reflects postmodernism's roots in social welfare bureaucracies. Ignored in the argument is any recognition of some of the most classical, non-postmodern bureaucracies that are client-centered such as US Department of Agriculture or the Japanese Ministry of Industry and Trade. Such agencies are both client-centered and elitist, thus using "postmodern" techniques for decidedly non-postmodern ends. Client-driven organizations, in fact, are only possible when the social construction of the client population is positive (Schneider and Ingram 1997); in numerous cases, felons, some businesses, welfare recipients, negative social constructions are reinforced by strong public views that are unlikely to change. Bureaucracies in such areas are to be kept separate from clientele; their mission is to manage and perhaps to subjugate clientele not to serve them. Postmodernism lacks this recognition of political realities; social constructions reflect the political power of powerful interests, not just bureaucratic whims.

Second, one postmodern movement, the feminist critique of bureaucracy, directly challenges the notion of hierarchy, a defining characteristic of bureaucracy (Thomas and Davies 2002).[4] Hierarchy forces women to take on the role of organizational advocate if they wish to succeed in the organization; in the process a women's identity as woman is submerged beneath her identity as a bureaucrat (Ferguson 1984; Stivers 2002). The solution, in feminist theory, is to restructure bureaucracies as flat, decentralized organizations that operate via norms of consensus. The ideal feminist bureaucracy, however, clashes with the practice of women managers who actually lead organizations. Nicholson-Crotty and Meier (2002), examining the behavior of school superintendents, found that their behavior could be characterized as political rather than decentralizing. Women top-level managers actually increased the level of bureaucracy in the organization, according to the authors, so that they could exert control over an organization that might be hostile to women managers. Further evidence in support of the political rather than the feminist view was that women managers added less bureaucracy in organizations where more women held managerial roles (interpreted as allies in this research); and as women managers spent more time at the helm of the organization, they gradually decreased the levels of bureaucracy, a finding consistent with the notion that such strategies were temporary efforts to exert control and that they would be reduced when supporters held key positions of authority.

Third, the postmodern critique of bureaucracy seeks to separate organizational form from organizational function. It advocates the equivalent of the old scientific management "one best way" to design and organize work processes. Much of organization theory (Thompson 1967) counsels the exact opposite, that

organizations need to be structured based on their tasks and the degree of environmental turbulence. Joan Woodward's (1980) classic studies of organizational
structure showed that the most effective structures fit fairly clear patterns depending on the organization's environment and its internal processes. Some of
these structures were highly bureaucratic; others were not. More recent work on
structural aspects such as span of control (directly linked to decentralization) also
found that there were optimal levels of hierarchy in educational organizations,
organizations that are normally considered relatively unbureaucratic (Meier and
Bohte 2003).

Finally, the postmodern view of bureaucracy may contain the seeds of its own
demise as a criticism of bureaucracy. Postmodern approaches are strongly opposed
to empirical research unless that research is based on subjective methods that are
unlikely to transfer from one scholar to the next. As a result, the approach can be
charged with presenting bureaucratic stereotypes, much like the New Public
Management, but unlike it in rejecting any efforts to determine if their views
represent a significant portion of the world. Virtually every scholar of bureaucracy
points to the informal aspects of the organization that facilitates bureaucratic
action. Bureaucracy in practice, therefore, is likely to be far less rigid and unchan-
ging than it is in postmodern rhetoric (how much, we will not know if we rely on
postmodernists for an answer).

3.5 THE PRINCIPAL-AGENT MODEL CHALLENGE

Principal-agent models are the antimatter to postmodern approaches. Where
postmodernism rejects rationality and empirical analysis, principal-agent models
revel in both. The basic idea behind principal-agent models is that all relationships can be reduced to contractual terms (see Mitnick 1980; Evans 1980; Moe
1984). Based on a modest set of assumptions about the individual actors involved,
a series of relatively simple propositions are derived. Principal-agent models were
originally established to describe voluntary relationships between peers as they
enter into market-like exchanges (originally used for physician-patient relationships and used car sales). The principal in essence is buying something from the
agent, but the transaction differs from the normal market place of pure competition in one key way. Like private markets, the model assumes goal conflict (e.g.,
the patient wishes to be made well and the doctor would like to maximize income,
or at least charge a higher price than the patient would select), but unlike such

markets it assumes information asymmetry, that the agent has specialized knowledge that the principal does not have. Such a situation creates an incentive for the principal to "shirk," to sell more services or sell them at a higher price than actually needed. The solutions are to draft a contract that seeks to control such behavior before the fact (McCubbins, Noll, and Weingast 1987) or to invest in monitoring the agent as the contract is implemented.

The principal-agent model has developed an extensive theoretical base as scholars have modeled various aspects of bureaucracy and its relationships to political actors in principal-agent terms (Banks and Weingast 1992; Bendor, Taylor, and Van Gaalen 1985, 1987; Niskanen 1971; Woolley 1993). There is also an extensive empirical literature that references the principal-agent model but in actual practice does not engage the model in any significant way or use it to derive research hypotheses (Wood and Waterman 1994; Moe 1985, but see Krause 1996).

The challenge of principal-agent models is the contention that bureaucracy as an organizational form does not matter; all relationships can be reduced to contractual ones. Although principal-agent models are purely an academic enterprise, they generally support the conclusions of the New Public Management. After all if there is no need for bureaucracy as an intellectual concept, then the NPM effort to contract out functions and move to non-hierarchical, market-like implementation is a good thing.

Despite the influence of these models in academia, the argument here will be that such models are woefully incomplete in that sphere and not particularly useful in practical situations. First, by presenting all relationships in contractual terms, the models miss the informal side of bureaucracy, the relationships among individuals that are based on affect and trust. Agents will frequently provide what the principal wants for normative reasons or because the principal's demands are within the agents' zone of acceptance (Simon 1997). The important questions are what values are resident in the bureaucracy and how those values compare with both those of electoral institutions and those of the general public. Second, the language of principal-agent models often prevents its broader use. Goal conflict and information asymmetry inevitably lead to shirking. The common language meaning of shirking is that the agent will not act. In many cases, the real problem is the agent will act even more than the principal seeks. Third, the principal-agent model misses the element of coercion in bureaucracies. The model was designed to examine voluntary relationships between equals in a market-like setting. In this case it is applied to mandatory relationships between unequals in a nonmarket-like situation. Although bureaucratic relationships contain more than coercion (see Barnard 1938), at the end of the day bureaucracies are an ordering of power. The utility of principal-agent models in these situations is open to question. This position also applies to the use of principal-agent models to describe relationships between bureaucracy and electoral institutions.

3.6 THE RISE OF NETWORKS

An increasing body of scholarship argues, and in some cases demonstrates, that public management often takes place via networks of actors rather than solely within the confines of a single, hierarchical bureaucracy (Agranoff and McGuire 2003; Bogason and Toonen 1998; Bressers, O'Toole and Richardson 1995; Milward and Provan 2000; O'Toole 1997; Scharpf 1993). A network is a pattern of two or more units in which not all major components are encompassed within a single hierarchical array (O'Toole 1997). Program success, in these settings, requires collaboration and coordination with other parties over whom managers exercise little formal control. Actors in networks are often located in bureaucracies that are in turn connected with other organizations outside the lines of formal authority. Many of these complex arrangements are required or strongly encouraged by policy makers; others emerge through mutual agreement among organizations or individuals who find common interests served by working together on a regular basis (Gains 1999).

Networked arrays may include some combination of: agencies (or parts of agencies) of the same government; links among units of different governments; ties between public organizations and for-profit companies; and public-nonprofit connections, as well as more complex arrangements including multiple types of connections in a larger pattern. Networks range in complexity from simple dyads to bewilderingly complex arrays entailing dozens of units (see Provan and Milward 1991). Networks are generally designed to deal with "wicked problems" that will not fit within a single jurisdiction or that for political reasons cannot be placed within a single bureaucracy. The latter occurs when policy makers wish to take action but still be able to distance themselves from the policies that might develop (see Pollitt and Bouckaert 2000, 175).

Networks pose a major practical challenge to bureaucracy. To the extent that policy makers create networks rather than bureaucracies to deliver public services, then the persistence of bureaucracy as an organizational form is called into question (Peters and Pierre 1998). Networks lack one fundamental defining characteristic of hierarchy—the ability to compel performance. Ferlie and Steane (2002) go so far as to contend that networks undercut the hierarchical nature of New Public Management control systems.

Several reasons, however, call into question whether networks will replace bureaucracy as the implementation organization of choice. First, a large number of programs are still provided in what are traditional bureaucracies. National defense is consistently operated via bureaucracy even if individual combat units are created to somewhat avoid the perceived problems of bureaucracy. Delivering pensions, regulating business, enforcing criminal laws, and numerous other functions remain the province of bureaucracies.

Second, pundits may simply have misread the movement to networks. A systematic study of US legislation by Hall and O'Toole (2000) examined the legislative output from two sessions of Congress, one in the 1960s and the other in the 1990s. Rather than an explosion in the number of mandated network relationships, they found that program design was relatively constant in regard to creating networks. These findings suggest that not only are networks not a new phenomenon in program design, but that networks are not used to the exclusion of formal bureaucracies.

Third, bureaucracies and networks are not mutually exclusive categories. Many networks are composed of, at least in part, individual bureaucracies (many public sector but some private or nonprofit); a key network in US reproductive health policy links local health departments, nonprofit service providers such as Planned Parenthood, advocacy groups such as abstinence only organizations, physicians in private practice, and the regional offices of the Public Health Service among others (see McFarlane and Meier 2001). Similarly, all bureaucracies have within them formal or informal networks that facilitate task accomplishment. These network ties might remain in the organization or they might be to other organizations with people who perform similar duties (e.g., a network of school superintendents or local government managers).

Fourth, the distinction between networks and hierarchies in practice might be significantly less than in theory. In their series of studies of mental health networks Milward and Provan (2000) find that those networks that develop long term relationships that mimic the stability of bureaucracy actually perform better than those that remain more fluid. Similarly, O'Toole and Meier (2003) in their studies of educational networks find that stability of personnel and management, both traits more associated with bureaucracy than networks, were strongly and positively correlated with higher performance on a wide variety of organizational outputs and outcomes. In short, networks may be more effective to the degree they take on bureaucratic traits.

Rather than a challenge to the continued existence of bureaucracies, therefore, networks are more likely to provide greater focus on a range of relationships both formal and informal. Neither networks nor bureaucracies are likely to disappear as policy instruments. They each provide useful functions in implementing public policy so policy makers will continue to use them.

3.7 THE ARCHITECTURE OF COMPLEXITY

Recent work by Bryan Jones (2001) contains an argument that bureaucracy is inherently unstable in the long run. Although radically different in method, a similar argument is made by those advocating chaos theories of public management (Kiel 1994; Bergquist 1993). Jones is interested in dealing with several issues raised by Herbert Simon (1997) concerning the construction of complex systems. What complex systems do is break down complex tasks into simple ones, deal with them as simple problems, and then aggregate these solutions back together. Such a process, common to bureaucracy, assumes that aspects of problems can be treated in isolation from each other without endangering the overall solution. One key aspect of the architecture of complexity is that complex systems narrow the range of processes and outcomes. Jones's (2001) concern is that the distribution of outcomes tends to be leptokurtic, that is, have a very narrow dispersion about the mean. The theoretical distribution, however, is not purely leptokurtic but combines a very narrow range with potentially an increase in highly extreme values that do not fit the normal processes. His analogy is from tectonics. The earth has under its surface a set of large continental plates that gradually move over time. The movement of these plates creates pressures that can lead to earthquakes if the pressures are not relieved. What complex systems do in Jones's argument is try to contain pressures rather than release them. In tectonics, this would prevent frequent and relatively minor quakes but result in more rare but significantly more severe quakes in the future because the underlying pressure between plates continues to build.

Jones then applies the tectonic analogy to human-designed systems arguing that systems that resist environmental changes, that are sticky in translation of inputs to outputs in his terms, will result in much less change in short periods of time, but that pressures will build up on the system that may at some point overwhelm it. Jones tests these ideas by looking at political and economic institutions from elections to Congress, to stock markets. His work shows that such systems that are more complex (or sticky) do generate patterns of outputs that resemble his theoretical distributions. The more complex the system, the more likely that it will narrow the range of outputs in the short run and the more likely that pressures will build up that can result in major catastrophic change.

Jones's work is directly relevant to the future of bureaucracy simply because bureaucracies are the archetype of complex systems. The complexity and stickiness that Jones describes in terms of political and other institutions reaches a much higher level in the bureaucracy than it ever does in political systems. Weberian bureaucracy is designed to be stable, to take varying inputs and generate outputs that are relatively uniform. The implications of Jones's work, therefore, is that bureaucracies have an inherent Achilles' heel that will lead to their demise.[5] Even if these characteristics do not lead to system failure, they suggest, as does much of the organizational theory literature, that more flexible, fluid organizations are more likely to flourish in turbulent environments (Thompson 1967; Kiel 1994).

Although Bryan Jones's innovative theory has not been tested on bureaucratic organizations (the tests are in the form of kurtotic distributions which require thousands of cases to demonstrate a pattern), proponents of bureaucracy have some theoretical arguments to suggest why results might differ from predicted. Basically, the argument relies on the difference between physical systems and human systems. Human systems, unlike physical systems, can learn and adapt. Events that deviate too far from normal (e.g., the great depression, hyperinflation in Latin American countries) trigger the study and redesign of complex systems. Their design frequently contains an intelligence gathering and research function. Rather than waiting for the next problem that cannot be solved, organizations can look to their micro failures, the smaller failures on programs and processes (that is, the build up of pressures) and learn from these errors. A significant portion of public policy is designed in such a way. Welfare reform in the US relied on a series of pilot projects, many of which failed or failed to meet policy makers' goals and were abandoned. The New Public Management reforms in the UK seem to be following a similar process at the local level as the Best Value Indicator System is being transformed by the Comparative Performance Assessment process.

While such a trial and error process might not be an every day occurrence in public policy, organizations are managed systems. Management can adjust organizational procedures, fill in the gaps where regularized procedures are lacking, grant additional discretion to street-level workers who must make immediate decisions, or generate slack capacity that can be devoted to learning and numerous other activities. These actions should allow bureaucracies to continue to transform uneven inputs into relatively stable outcomes.

Both the arguments of Jones and the counter arguments presented here are strictly theoretical as applied to bureaucracies. Systematic tests of these arguments have not been done, and such tests are likely to be difficult. The degree of challenge that Jones's theory holds for future bureaucracies is very much an empirical question.

3.8 BACK TO WEBER

Six challenges to bureaucracy have been discussed. We need to return to Weber's definition of bureaucracy to determine how well it has held up in light of these challenges. Are there parts of the various challenges that make some characteristics of bureaucracy less viable? If so, does the organization change so much that it can no longer be considered "bureaucracy"? Weber, of course, was constructing an ideal type, and we should expect bureaucracy to vary from the ideal type simply because the demands of actually operating an organization are likely to generate some unique problems that need to be solved.

Fixed and official jurisdictional areas ordered by rules, laws, or regulations, the first characteristic of bureaucracy, is so ingrained in modern governance that realistic alternatives simply do not present themselves. One of the building blocks of contemporary liberal governments is defining (and limiting) the sphere of government and correspondingly the power of the state as exercised through its organizations. If anything, this principle of bureaucracy has spread further with the growth of democracies in Eastern Europe, Latin America, and elsewhere (and with the Westminster approach to NPM). While Weber may have oversold the need for bureaucracies to have regularized processes and procedures at the time he was writing, since then it has become even more a part of bureaucracy and will likely continue through this century.

The principal of hierarchy is perhaps the aspect of bureaucracy that has been subjected to the most challenge either intellectually via postmodern challenges or empirically by the creation of networks. The persistence of bureaucracy and hierarchy in the light of the numerous critiques clearly demonstrates that hierarchy must perform some vital function. As Jaques (1990: 127) concludes, "Thirty-five years of research have convinced me that managerial hierarchy is the most efficient, the hardiest, and in fact the most natural structure ever devised for large organizations." The reason is simple: accountability. Although it takes many forms, one of the basic building blocks of modern governance is accountability (see Power 1997). Hierarchy is the default option in creating accountability systems—A is accountable to B for performing task C. To the extent that policy makers seek to create governance systems that can be held accountable, we are likely to see hierarchy as a basic principal. That practical notion has not changed since the time of Weber's writings.[6]

Management of the office relying on written files, as noted in the introduction, seems quaint if only because written files have largely been replaced by electronic files. The functional uses of files in terms of organization memory, definition of process and procedures, and planning work processes have not gone away. Permanent records generate efficiency and equity by making sure similar cases are treated in similar manners. To the extent that equity and efficiency are valued, bureaucracy is a predictable way to obtain them.

The occupation of offices based on expertise and training, if anything, has increased dramatically. The days of politicians running for office contending that anyone could fill a government job are long past. Even those US politicians who relish running against the bureaucracy generally propose New Public Management schemes that rely even more heavily on expertise and training. Government functions continue to expand, the systems government operates continue to increase in complexity, and the net result is the education and training levels of bureaucracies continues to rise year after year. The skills gap between developed and developing nations generates a bureaucratic capacity gap that severely limits what governments without effective bureaucratic capacity can do. If anything, Weber underestimated the role of expertise and training in perpetuating bureaucracies.

Full-time employment of compensated personnel who can expect employment to be a career is one aspect of bureaucracy that has been eroded at the margins. Governments in the past twenty years have moved many public bureaucrats to private organizations via contracting. Careers in government are not looking nearly as long or as secure as they once were; a US state government (Georgia), in fact, has reintroduced the concept of employment at will thus removing protections against removal from office (see also the 1997 German reform of their civil service, Suleiman 2003: 148). At the same time, one would still characterize bureaucratic employment as a career rather than an a vocation. That career might be spread out over several different organizations, but the skills needed (knowledge, managerial ability, etc.) fit the pattern of a career.

Administration of the office following general rules that are stable and can be learned also appears to be ingrained in both structure and management. Despite the great calls for managers as change agents and visionary leaders, organization members operate best in a stable system of expectations where they know the types of problems they will have and the tools they have to address those problems (O'Toole and Meier 2003). Consistency and stability have great value in organizations, even in organizations that seek radical change simply because whatever changes are adopted will need to be implemented over a longer period of time.

3.9 CONCLUSION

Bureaucracy as an organizational form is nothing if not persistent. To the degree that it does not meet the governance needs of societies, we would expect that bureaucracy would be replaced with other organizational forms. In this chapter we noted a wide variety of factors that will contribute to the continued need for bureaucracy. The need to organize large scale tasks will not disappear; even under the most optimistic view of the New Public Management, a fairly extensive bureaucracy will need to manage the contracts that actually implement policy. In this scenario, however, private bureaucracies (and they are bureaucracies in every sense of the term) will grow and flourish. With globalization of the economy, smaller organizational forms will need to adapt a broader scope and thus are also likely to grow.

The need to breakdown complex problems into more simple ones and solve them a step at a time will continue. As of yet, no one has developed an alternative to the architecture of complexity—that is, breaking down large complex tasks into smaller ones that are amenable to solution. The conservative nature of the architecture of complexity means that risk-averse policy makers will continue to opt for bureaucracy.

Consistent, stable administration will still be highly prized. If governments continue to seek equity in processes, and continue to seek equity over time, then bureaucracy remains the most effective way to do so. What for many in the management reform movement is the weakness of bureaucracy is also its strength. The dominance of one organizational form or another, as a result, is merely the product of the types of problems that must be handled. As long as current performance is adequate, stable and consistent administration should be highly valued.

Public policy will continue to demand expertise. While the ability to contract for expertise is widely available in many western democracies, the knowledge of what to contract for needs to reside in the permanent government. In addition, not all expertise is technical, some of it is administrative, related to the problems of implementation and how they can be circumvented. Bureaucracies are exceptionally good at storing expertise since they are built around the principle of specialization.

Accountability concerns will also favor the continuation of bureaucracy. The easiest solution to problems of accountability is hierarchy, establishing that A is to be accountable to B for task C. Although long chains of accountability result in some slippage between the top and the bottom, such hierarchical chains remain the best way to fix accountability in a system. While some argue that bureaucracy defuses responsibility and makes accountability harder (Bauman 1989), others taking the same extreme cases (the German bureaucracy and the Holocaust) come to different conclusions (Lozowick 2000). Governance systems are headed by politicians, in many countries amateur politicians with little experience in governing. To such novices, hierarchy is an accountability concept that is easy to grasp. In practice this requires consistent applications of accountability to make such hierarchical processes work.

In short, bureaucracy will continue to flourish in the twenty-first century for many of the same reasons that it has flourished in the last century, it facilitates the governance process in ways that other organizational forms do not. Challenges to bureaucracy will always be challenges at the margin, moving tasks from a public sector bureaucracy to a private sector one, for example. Underneath these cosmetic responses to reforms, however, one will still see Weberian bureaucracies continue to perform a myriad of tasks.

NOTES

1. See du Gay (2000) for a similar Weberian analysis that takes a more normative approach concerning what bureaucracy should be and examines bureaucratic ethics rather than its survivability.

2. Political systems can be fragmented horizontally with different political institutions sharing political power (that is, independent branches of government) or they can be fragmented vertically in a federal system that permits autonomous or semiautonomous local governments.

3. This discussion will be limited to the more moderate of the postmodern scholars since they are more likely to posit reforms of bureaucracy than more radical elements who would reject the imposition of values on others.

4. Not all of those who study gender and organizations are postmodern (e.g., Guy 1992). Feminist theory and the work cited here on feminist critiques of bureaucracy clearly fall within the postmodern camp.

5. This is our implication of the work of Jones not his, however, in conversations with Bryan Jones he has generally agreed that these are the implications of his work.

6. Some propose that consumer accountability or client accountability will replace downward political accountability. The shortcoming of these proposals is that they fail to consider the idea that the general public (as opposed to the agency's clientele) might have some interests in governance and fail to consider the unrepresentative nature of most clientele (Peters and Pierre 1998).

REFERENCES

AGRANOFF, R., and McGUIRE, M. (2003), *Collaborative Public Management: New Strategies for Local Governments*, Washington, DC: Georgetown University Press.

BANKS, J. S., and WEINGAST, B. R. (1992), "The Political Control of Bureaucracies under Asymmetric Information," *American Journal of Political Science* 36: 509–24.

BARBERIS, P. (1998), "The New Public Management and a New Accountability," *Public Administration* 76: 451–70.

BARNARD, C. I. (1938), *The Functions of the Executive*, Cambridge, MA: Belnap Press of Harvard University.

BAUMAN, Z. (1989), *Modernity and the Holocaust*, Cambridge: Polity Press.

BENDOR, J., TAYLOR, S., and VAN GAALEN, R. (1985), "Bureaucratic Expertise versus Legislative Authority: A Model of Deception and Monitoring in Budgeting," *American Political Science Review* 79: 1041–60.

—— —— —— (1987), "Politicians, Bureaucrats, and Asymmetric Information," *American Journal of Political Science* 31: 796–828.

BENNIS, W. (1966), "The Coming Death of Bureaucracy," *Think Magazine* (November/ December), 30–5.

BERGQUIST, W. (1993), *The Postmodern Organization: Mastering the Art of Irreversible Change*, San Francisco: Jossey-Bass.

BLAIR, H. (2000), "Participation and Accountability at the Periphery: Democratic Local Governance in Six Countries," *World Development* 28: 21–39.

BLAIS, A., and DION, S. (1991), *The Budget Maximizing Bureaucrat*, Pittsburgh: University of Pittsburgh Press.

BLANKENSHIP, L. V. (1971), "Public Administration and the Challenge to Reason," in D. Waldo (ed.), *Public Administration in a Time of Turbulence*, Scranton, PA: Chandler, 188–213.

BOGASON, P., and. TOONEN, T. A. J. (eds.) (1998), "Comparing Networks," Symposium in *Public Administration* 76(2): 205–407.

BRESSERS, H., O'TOOLE, L. J., and RICHARDSON, J. (eds.) (1995), *Networks for Water Policy: A Comparative Perspective*, London: Frank Cass.

CONAGHAN, C. (1996), "A Deficit of Democratic Authenticity: Political Linkage and the Public in Andean Polities," *Studies in Comparative International Development* 31(3):32–55.

DENHARDT, R. (1993), *Theories of Public Organization*. Belmont, CA: Wadsworth.

DU GAY, P. (2000), *In Praise of Bureaucracy: Weber, Organization, Ethics*, London: Sage.

DURANT, R. F. (1993), *The Administrative Presidency Revisited*, Albany: State University of New York Press.

—— LEGGE JUN., J. S., and MOUSSIOS, A. (1998), "People, Profits and Service Delivery: Lessons from the Privatization of British Telcom," *American Journal of Political Science* 42: 117–40.

EVANS, R. G. (1980), "Professionals and the Production Function," in Simon Rottenberg (ed.), *Occupational Licensing and Regulation*, Washington: American Enterprise Institute.

FARMER, D. J. (1995), *The Language of Public Administration: Bureaucracy, Modernity, and Postmodernity*, Tuscaloosa: University of Alabama Press.

FERGUSON, K. (1984), *The Feminist Case Against the Bureaucracy*. Philadelphia: Temple University Press.

FERLIE, E., and STEANE, P. (2002), "Changing Developments in NPM," *International Journal of Public Administration* 25: 1459–69.

FREDERICKSON, H. G. (1996), *The Spirit of Public Administration*, San Francisco: Jossey-Bass.

GAINS, F. (1999), "Implementing Privatization Policies in 'Next Steps' Agencies," *Public Administration* 77: 713–30.

GOODSELL, C. (1983), *The Case for Bureaucracy*, Chatham, NJ: Chatham House.

GUY, M. E. (1992), *Women and Men of the States*, Armonk, NY: M.E. Sharpe.

HALL, M., HOLT, R.,and PURCHASE, D. (2003), "Project Sponsors under New Public Management: Lessons from the Frontline," *International Journal of Project Management* 21: 495–502.

HALL, T. E., and O'TOOLE JUN., L. J. (2000), "Structures for Policy Implementation: An Analysis of National Legislation, 1965–66 and 1993–94," *Administration and Society* 31(6): 667–86.

HANDLER, J. F. (1996), *Down From Bureaucracy: The Ambiguity of Privatization and Empowerment*, Princeton: Princeton University Press.

HARMON, M. (1981), *Action Theory for Public Administration*, New York: Longman.

HODGE, G. A. (2000), *Privatization: An International Review of Performance*, Boulder, CO: Westview Press.

HOOD, C. (2002), "Control, Bargains, and Cheating: The Politics of Public Service Reform," *Journal of Public Administration Research and Theory* 12: 309–32.

JAQUES, E. (1990), "In Praise of Hierarchy," *Harvard Business Review* (January/February): 127–33.

JONES, B. D. (2001), *Politics and the Architecture of Choice: Bounded Rationality and Governance*. Chicago: University of Chicago Press.

JREISAT, J. E. (2002), *Comparative Public Administration and Policy*. Boulder CO: Westview Press.

KANTER, R. M. (1989), *When Giants Learn to Dance: Mastering the Challenge of Strategy, Management, and Careers in the 1990s*, New York: Simon and Schuster.

KETTL, D. (2000), *The Global Public Management Revolution*, Washington, DC: Brookings.

KIEL, L. D. (1994), *Managing Chaos and Complexity in Government: A New Paradigm for Managing Change, Innovation, and Organizational Renewal*, San Francisco: Jossey-Bass.

KRAUSE, G. A. (1996), "The Institutional Dynamics of Policy Administration: Bureaucratic Influence Over Securities Regulation," *American Journal of Political Science* 40: 1083–121.

LANE, J.-E. (2000), *New Public Management*, London: Routledge.

LIGHT, P. (1999), *The True Size of Government*. Washington, DC: Brookings.

LOZOWICK, Y. (2000), *Hitler's Bureaucrats*, London: Continuum Press.

LONG, N. E. (1949), "Power and Administration," *Public Administration Review* 9: 257–64.

LYONS, W. E., LOWERY, D., and DeHOOG, R. H. (1992), *The Politics of Dissatisfaction: Citizens, Services and Institutions*, Armonk, NY: M. E. Sharpe.

McCUBBINS, M. D., NOLL, R. G., and WEINGAST, B. R. (1987), "Administrative Procedures as Instruments of Political Control," *Journal of Law, Economics, and Organization* 3: 243–77.

McFARLANE, D. R., and MEIER, K. J. (2001), *The Politics of Fertility Control Policy*, New York: Chatham House.

MARINI, F. (1971), *Toward a New Public Administration*, Scranton, PA: Chandler.

MARTIN, S. (2002), "The Modernization of UK Local Government," *Public Management Review* 4: 291–307.

MEIER, K. J. (1997), "Bureaucracy and Democracy: The Case for More Bureaucracy and Less Democracy," *Public Administration Review* 57: 193–9.

—— (2000), *Politics and the Bureaucracy: Policymaking in the Fourth Branch of Government*, Ft. Worth: Harcourt Brace.

—— and BOHTE, J. (2003), "Span of Control and Public Organizations: Implementing Luther Gulick's Research Design," *Public Administration Review* 63: 22–31.

MILWARD, H. B., and PROVAN, K. G. (2000), "Governing the Hollow State," *Journal of Public Administration Research and Theory* 20(2): 359–79.

MITNICK, B. M. (1980), *The Political Economy of Regulation*, New York: Columbia University Press.

MOE, T. M. (1984), "The New Economics of Organization," *American Journal of Political Science* 28: 739–77.

—— (1985), "Control and Feedback in Economic Regulation: The Case of the NLRB," *American Political Science Review* 79: 1094–116.

NICHOLSON-CROTTY, J., and MEIER, K. J. (2002), "Benevolent Dictator or Queen of Hearts: Women Managers at the Top of the Organization," Paper presented at the annual meeting of the Midwest Political Science Association.

NISKANEN, W. (1971), *Bureaucracy and Representative Government*, Chicago: Aldine.

OSBORNE, D., and GAEBLER, T. (1992), *Reinventing Government*, Reading, PA: Addison-Wesley.

OSTROM, V. (1973), *The Intellectual Crisis in American Public Administration*, Tuscaloosa: University of Alabama Press.

O'TOOLE JUN., L. J. (1991), "Public and Private Management of Wastewater Treatment: A Comparative Study," in John Heilman (ed.), *Evaluation and Privatization*, San Francisco, Calif.: Jossey-Bass, 13–32.

—— (1997), "Treating Networks Seriously: Practical and Research-Based Agendas in Public Administration," *Public Administration Review* 57(1): 45–52.

—— and MEIER, K. J. (2003) *"Plus ça Change*: Public Management, Personnel Stability, and Organizational Performance," *Journal of Public Administration Research and Theory* 13(1): 43–64.

PERRY, J. L., and WISE, L. R. (1990), "The Motivation Bases of Public Service," *Public Administration Review* 50: 367–73.

PETERS, B. G., and PIERRE, J. (1998), "Governance without Governments?" *Journal of Public Administration Research and Theory* 8: 223–44.

POLLITT, C. (2000), "Institutional Amnesia: A Paradox of the 'Information Age,'" *Prometheus* 18(1): 5–16.

—— and BOUCKAERT, G. (2000), *Public Management Reform*, London: Oxford University Press.

POWER, M. (1997), *The Audit Society*, Oxford: Oxford University Press.

PROVAN, K. G., and MILWARD, H. B. (1991), "Institutional-Level Norms and Organizational Involvement in a Service-Implementation Network," *Journal of Public Administration Research and Theory* 1(4): 391–417.

SAVAS, E. S. (1987), *Privatization: The Key to Better Government*, Chatham, NJ: Chatham House.

SCHARPF, F. W. (ed.) (1993), *Games in Hierarchies and Networks: Analytical and Empirical Approaches to the Study of Governmental Institutions.* Boulder, CO: Westview.

SCHNEIDER, A. L., and INGRAM, H. (1997), *Policy Design for Democracy.* Lawrence, KS: University of Kansas Press.

SIMON, H. A. (1997), *Administrative Behavior*, 4th edn., New York: The Free Press.

STIVERS, C. (2002), *Gender Images in Public Administration: Legitimacy and the Administrative State*, 2nd edn., Thousand Oaks, CA: Sage.

SULEIMAN, E. (2003), *Dismantling Democratic States*, Princeton: Princeton University Press.

TERRY, L. D. (2003), *Leadership of Public Bureaucracies: The Administrator as Conservator*, Armonk, NY: M. E. Sharpe.

THAYER, F. 1973), *An End to Hierarchy! An End to Competition!* New York: New Viewpoints.

THOMAS, R., and DAVIES, A. (2002), "Gender and New Public Management," *Gender, Work and Organization* 9: 372–97.

THOMPSON, J. D. (1967), *Organizations in Action*, New York: McGraw Hill.

TIEBOUT, C. (1956), "A Pure Theory of Local Expenditures," *Journal of Political Economy* 44: 415–24.

WALDO, D. (1971), "Some Thoughts on Alternatives, Dilemmas, and Paradoxes in a Time of Turbulence," in D. Waldo (ed.), *Public Administration in a Time of Turbulence*, Scranton, PA: Chandler, 257–86.

WEBER, M. (1946), *From Max Weber: Essays in Sociology*, tr. H. H. Gerth and C. Wright Mills, New York: Oxford University Press.

WOOD, B. D., and WATERMAN, R. (1994), *Bureaucratic Dynamics*, Boulder, CO: Westview Press.

WOODWARD, J. (1980), *Industrial Organization: Theory and Practice*, 2nd edn., New York: Oxford University Press.

WOOLLEY, J. T. (1993), "Conflict Among Regulators and the Hypothesis of Congressional Dominance," *Journal of Politics,* 55: 92–114.

CHAPTER 4

PUBLIC AND PRIVATE MANAGEMENT COMPARED

HAL G. RAINEY
YOUNG HAN CHUN

As the topic of public management has developed over the last several decades, many people have taken an interest in whether and how public management differs from management in other settings, such as business firms.[1] All nations face decisions about how to design their public and private sectors, including how to design their roles—which sector is to do what? The similarities and differences between organizations and management in the sectors have important implications for such decisions. A worldwide trend of privatizing governmental activities and government-owned enterprises, for example, has proceeded on the premise that organizations and activities managed under the auspices of the public sector show important differences from those managed privately. Usually, the premise holds that the publicly managed organizations operate less effectively and efficiently, and that privatizing them will remedy their malaise. The privatization movement has involved decisions about trillions of dollars worth of assets around the world, and the question of whether public and private management differ has played an important role in this trend, which has clearly been among the most significant developments in organizational management around the world in recent decades.

Reform movements, such as the New Public Management movement that has swept through many nations, often propose alternatives that involve applying to governmental management theories and techniques drawn from business management (Ferlie, Pettigrew, Ashburner, and Fitzgerald 1996; Pollitt and Bouckaert 2000). Transporting a technique across sectors raises much-discussed questions about whether one can apply a business technique in a public organization, and whether one must make certain adaptations or adjustments if one does. In addition, comparisons of public versus private management have important implications for administrative theory and analysis in general. Well-designed comparisons can contribute to analysis of a variety of topics in management.

In spite of these claims about the importance of the public–private distinction, the clearly prevailing consensus among scholars and experts on management holds that the distinction is not worth much. Many scholars have argued that the "sectors" involve such vastly diverse sets of management settings that distinctions such as public, private, and non-profit confuse and mislead us. In addition, over the years, major organization theorists have proclaimed that public and private management show more similarities than differences (Simon 1995, 1998). These proclamations reflect a "generic" orientation among many management and organization theorists, who take the position that managers face common challenges in most or all settings, such as leading, motivating, and decision making. Therefore we need to build a general, broadly applicable body of theory, and not one specific to such categories as public, private, or non-profit. Widely used texts on organizations and management commonly make a point of including examples and cases drawn from the business, government, and non-profit sectors (e.g., Daft 2004).

4.1 THE BLURRING OF THE SECTORS

In addition, for years many people have emphasized the blurred, indistinct boundaries between the private, public, and non-profit "sectors" of national economies.[2] Since human societies formed, there have always been complex relations and interplay between purportedly private economic activity and governmental entities.

This mixing of the sectors for many years has taken various forms and patterns (Dahl and Lindblom 1953). Hybrid forms of organization, such as state-owned enterprises, government corporations, and heavily regulated business firms, mix government auspices and control, with features usually conceived as private economic activity, such as sale of goods or services for a price.[3]

Another pattern of blurring involves contracting-out by governments and other forms of relationship in which government buys from private organizations, or carries out programs and policies by and through them. On their part, nongovernmental organizations often work hard to influence governmental actions and decisions through political means such as lobbying in legislative bodies. Further blurring the sectors, very similar types of organizations, professionals, and work activities occur in all of them. The long list of such organizational forms includes public, private, or hybridized schools, hospitals, universities, transportation organizations, electric and other utilities. Engineers, medical doctors, scientists, accountants, attorneys, security personnel, and numerous other professionals and specialists work in all the sectors. Countless authors have been emphasizing for years that the blurring and sharing of responsibility have been increasing as reform movements in various nations press for more contracting-out and competitive tendering by governments, as well as other forms of government activity by and through nongovernmental organizations.

These complications with the definition of the public, private, and nonprofit sectors and the distinctions among them raise devilish conceptual and methodological problems for those who would seek to clarify and confirm distinctions. The complications also provide justification for those management theorists who express explicit or implicit contempt for such distinctions. Organization theorists have in the past justified efforts to develop empirically based typologies and taxonomies by pointing to the oversimplifications and stereotypes involved in popular discourse about the public, private, and nonprofit sectors. In these research initiatives, organization theorists have never developed a well-confirmed, widely accepted typology or taxonomy of organizations. These studies did, however, establish the fairly obvious point that a public–private distinction will not serve adequately as a general typology of organizations although it may figure in one.[4] In addition, the studies typically found that government organizations did not necessarily cluster together in categories distinct from those in which business organizations clustered (Pugh, Hickson, and Hinings 1969). These studies supported the conclusion that a public–private or government-business distinction does not predict organizational characteristics very well. This evidence put such distinctions into bad repute among organization theorists, who relegate them to the category of "folk" or "commonsense" typologies that can "obscure more than they illuminate" (Hall 2002: 37).

At the same time, however, many political scientists and economists have taken a diametrically opposing position on the public–private distinction. Numerous economists, political scientists, and public administrationists have commonly referred to the distinctive characteristics of government organizations and codified them into theories about the public bureaucracy. Some economists, for example, point out that most government agencies do not sell their outputs on economic markets and assert that this characteristic, among others, causes them to be very different from business firms on many important dimensions (e.g., Barton 1980; Dahl and Lindblom 1953; Downs 1967; Niskanen 1972).

This interesting divergence among major groups of scholars appears to have various sources. Many economists attribute great significance to economic markets in their theories, and this appears to predispose some of them toward the conclusion that the presence or absence of economic markets for the outputs of an organization has a strong influence on the management of that organization. Political scientists interested in public bureaucracy concentrate on analysis of its political context and end up attributing much significance to political influences. Public adminstrationists, focused on such topics as civil services systems and accountability systems for governmental administrators, often come to see these systems as quite distinctive. Organizational sociologists and psychologists, on the other hand, studying processes and people in many different types of organizations, tend to seek and observe commonalities across those settings. The research evidence reviewed below shows points of consensus, but also conflicting findings on some topics. Ultimately, we conclude below that these conflicting findings show the importance of avoiding the over-generalizations to which strong disciplinary orientations can sometimes lead. This interesting divergence among major groups of scholars throws us back into the hunt for ways of clarifying the matter.

4.2 WAYS OF DEFINING PUBLIC AND PRIVATE MANAGEMENT

The ambivalence and disagreements arise because people, including scholars, often refer to the public and private categories of organizations in vague and ill-defined ways, and because the two categories include huge, very diverse populations of organizations and members that overlap or resemble each other across the "sectors" in the ways described above. Some scholars have, however, taken useful steps to clarify the distinction.

Half a century ago, Dahl and Lindblom (1953) acknowledged the blurring and overlap among the public and private sectors, but argued that one can differentiate with reasonable clarity between *agencies* and *enterprises*. The former are government organizations and the latter are business firms, which one can locate as the end points on a continuum of government ownership and operation, with government agencies at one extreme and enterprises under private ownership at the other. In between these two extremes, and representing differing mixtures of governmental and nongovernmental control, lie the various hybrid forms described earlier, such as state-owned enterprises, government authorities or corporations, and heavily regulated private firms.

Dahl and Lindblom (1953) emphasized the distinctions between economic markets and governmental authority (which they called "polyarchy") as alternatives for organizing the economic and social activities of a nation. Markets allow producers and buyers more choice about their transactions and relations, while polyarchies tend to rely on more centralized rules or authoritative directions. Each alternative has strengths and weaknesses (Lindblom 1977). While allowing more freedom of choice, markets can fail to produce public goods and can fail to control externalities.[5] Polyarchies can respond to such market failures, but can create problems due to excessive central control and the inflexibility of centrally developed authoritative directives in relation to local preferences and needs. The organizations under the control of these two broad institutional alternatives, Dahl and Lindblom argued, show tendencies related to their institutional location. More than the enterprises do, they said, the agencies show greater tendencies toward "red tape, rules, and caution." The agencies lack the direct link between sales of their outputs and the revenues they receive that the enterprises have, since the agencies get their money from government funding processes, so people in the agencies have less incentive toward cost-cutting and efficient operations. Thus, Dahl and Lindblom argued that the broad institutional alternatives of markets and political hierarchies determine major characteristics of the organizations most subject to those alternatives, and in turn they asserted about government agencies the view—fairly standard among many economists and in public stereotypes—that the agencies operate less efficiently and with more rules and red tape than business enterprises. Most importantly, however, their analysis showed that one can make a reasonably clear distinction between a core category of public agencies and a core category of private firms.

Wamsley and Zald (1973) took another step in clarifying the distinction by classifying organizations according to whether they are owned and operated under public or private auspices, and whether they receive their financial resources from public or private sources. A typical agency of a general purpose government does not sell a significant proportion of its outputs on economic markets. Many business firms make most of their money through sales, and they usually operate with more independence from governmental authorities than do government agencies. As described earlier, however, hybrid organizations with mixtures of public and private funding and control complicate the effort to clearly separate public and private organizations. When Wamsley and Zald classified organizations according to ownership and funding, however, it helped to clarify the distinction. Their approach designates four categories:

• Publicly owned organizations with public funding (they get their operating funds from government budget allocations), such as Departments of Defense,

Departments of State, Governmental Retirement Pension agencies, and police departments.
- Publicly owned organizations with high levels of funding from private sources such as sales or donations, such as state-owned enterprises in many nations.
- Privately owned organizations that get very large proportions of their financial resources from contracts with government or sales to government, or from government subsidies.
- Privately owned organizations that get most or all of their financial resources from private sources such as sales or donations. Business firms in many nations can be placed in this category.

This classification scheme, like others that scholars have attempted, involves over-simplifications. Nevertheless, it further establishes the point that the blurring of the sectors does not preclude us from making a reasonably clear distinction between public and private organizations, which can serve as basis for research to prove or disprove hypotheses about differences between them.

Bozeman (1988) took the analysis still further by trying to array organizations along two continua of "publicness," economic authority and political authority, rather than breaking these two continua into two broad categories as Wamsley and Zald did.[6] He makes the point that in reality management has varying degrees of authority over the financial resources and activities of their organizations, with business firms typically having more than government agencies. Business firms with higher levels of government funding from government contracts, however, will tend to have less independent authority over the way those funds are used. Government agencies tend to have more political authority than business firms, in that they receive mandates carrying such authority from legislative bodies or other government officials, but all types of organizations have varying degrees of such authority.[7]

Everyone should be aware of the complications involved in trying to define and distinguish between public and private management, because such complications reflect the realities of the political economies of contemporary nations around the world. Dahl and Lindblom, Wamsley and Zald, and Bozeman, however, show that we can make reasonably clear distinctions.

4.3 CHALLENGES IN COMPARING PUBLIC WITH PRIVATE MANAGEMENT

Defining a distinction between public and private management does not prove that important differences between them actually exist. We need to consider those supposed differences and the evidence for or against them. First, however, some intriguing challenges in research on public–private comparisons need consideration. Many factors, such as size, task or function, and industry characteristics, can influence an organization and its management more than its publicness or privateness. Research needs to show that these alternative factors do not confuse analysis of differences between public organizations and other types. Ideally, studies would have large, well-designed samples of organizations and their employees, representing many functions and controlling for many variables. Such studies require a lot of resources and, with the exception of one recent example, have been virtually nonexistent.[8]

Some theorize on the basis of assumptions, past literature and research, and their own experiences (Dahl and Lindblom 1953; Downs 1967; Wilson 1989). Other researchers conduct research projects measuring or observing public bureaucracies and draw conclusions about their differences from private organizations. Some concentrate on one agency (Warwick 1975), some on many agencies (Meyer 1979). Although valuable, these studies examine no private organizations directly.

Many executives and managers who have served in both public agencies and private business firms have offered observations about the sharp differences between the two settings (e.g., Blumenthal 1983; Rumsfeld 1983). Other researchers compare sets of public and private organizations or managers. Some compare the managers in small sets of government and business organizations (Buchanan 1974, 1975; Kurland and Egan 1999; Rainey 1979, 1983; Porter and Lawler 1968). Questions remain about how well the small samples represent the full populations. More recent studies with larger and more diverse samples of organizations still leave questions about representing the full populations, but they add more convincing evidence of distinctive aspects of public management (Hickson et al. 1986; Kalleberg et al. 1996; Pandey and Kingsley 2000).

To analyze public versus private delivery of a particular service, many researchers compare public and private organizations within functional categories. They compare public and private hospitals (Dugan 2000; Sloan et al. 2001), utilities (Atkinson and Halversen 1986), schools (Ballou and Podgursky, 1998), airlines (Backkx, Carney, and Gedajlovic 2002), nursing homes (Chou 2002; Luksetich, Edwards and Carroll 2000), job-training centers (Heinrich 2000), bus companies (Pendleton 1999), mental health care facilities (Forder 2000), business schools (Casile and Davis-Blake 2002), and art organizations (Palmer 1998). Somewhat similarly, other studies compare a function, such as management of computers or information technology innovativeness, in government and business organizations (Bretschneider 1990; Corder 2001; Elliot and Tevavichulada, 1999; Moon and Bretschneider 2002). Still others compare state-owned enterprises to private firms (Bordia and Blau 1998; Hickson et al. 1986; Mascarenhas 1989; MacAvoy and McIssac 1989; Rosenblatt and Manheim 1996). They find differences and show that the public–private distinction appears meaningful even when the same general types of organization operate under both auspices. Studies of one functional type, however, may not apply to other functional types.

A few studies compare public and private samples from census data, large-scale social surveys, or national studies (Houston 2000; Kalleberg et al. 1996; Light 2002; Smith and Nock 1980; US Office of Personnel Management 2000). These have great value, but often such aggregated findings prove difficult to relate to the characteristics of specific organizations and the people in them.

The review of different research approaches in the preceding paragraphs reflects an empiricist approach to the comparison of public and private management, as if we can best resolve such comparisons by looking at empirical social scientific studies. This approach actually has some sharp limitations. There is, for example, much literature in public administration that provides analytical discourse (i.e., essays) and normative discourse on such topics as administrative ethics, administrative accountability, and many others. These authors often imply or explicitly argue the distinctive character of public administration, contending for example that public administration involves issues in ethics and accountability very distinct from those in business. They do not subject these arguments to tests using empirical social scientific methods, but such reasoned discourse should be considered part of the body of evidence. It is not covered here due to space constraints.

In addition, there are many points on which public and private management differ in such abundantly obvious ways that to deny the distinctions becomes absurd. In the United States, for example, the compensation levels for executives in nearly all major private firms so thoroughly dwarf those of most public sector executives that the difference is essentially undeniable. Although this difference is greater in the US it exists in many other nations as well. The review below concentrates on the empirical, comparative social scientific research that has been reported, and does not include some of these self-evident distinctions.

4.4 Distinctive Characteristics of Public Management: Common Assertions and Research Findings

In spite of the challenges in designing conclusive research, the stream of assertions and research findings continues. Various reviews have compiled the most frequent arguments and evidence about the distinction between public and private management (Boyne 2002; Perry and Rainey 1988; Rainey 2003; Rainey and Bozeman

2000). The discourse includes a mixture of the types of studies and statements described above. The Appendix summarizes many of the main points in this admixture, combining in the same summary the theoretical positions, the frequent assertions, and the points for which research evidence exists, noting points of consensus and conflict. Many of the sources of the assertions and evidence are cited in the reviews mentioned above. The discussion to follow will cite examples from the many citations in those earlier sources, but concentrate on citing more recent research contributions.

4.4.1 Differences in Operating Environments

Many of the claims about the differences between public and private management refer to distinctions between the operating environments in the two settings. Many parties to the discussion emphasize that, unlike private management, public management typically involves organizations that do not sell their outputs in economic markets.[9] Researchers do not try to prove or disprove this observation because it is self-evident. One needs merely to look at the source of revenues in the financial reports of organizations to confirm this distinction. Researchers studying the goals of business firms have found that executives name "profitability" as the most important goal more frequently than any other goal (Daft 2004: 67), and while no executives from government-owned and government-funded organizations participated in this research, clearly they could not mention profitability as a goal.[10]

The more contentious issues concern the implications of this difference. Some scholars theorize (and many citizens believe) that this distinction weakens or removes the information and incentives provided by economic markets and in turn weakens incentives for cost reduction, operating efficiency, and effective performance (e.g., Dahl and Lindblom 1953; Niskanen 1971; Downs 1967). This position serves as a guiding principle in nations with more capitalistic and free-market economies, and for the privatization and managerialism movements that have swept the world. On the other hand, critics of business firms point to frequent instances of waste and ineffectiveness in those organizations. Also, as described later, many authors record public management successes and efficiencies. Surprisingly little large-sample research directly compares public and private managers on matters concerning the incentives and indicators they face, but numerous forms of indirect or implicit evidence indicate that public managers do often have weaker incentives and information for achieving operational efficiency and certain types of effective performance, as discussed in the sections to follow. As indicated in the Appendix, scholars also assert that their operating environments provide less inducement for public sector managers (compared with their private-sector colleagues), to achieve economic efficiencies through responding to consumer preferences and apportioning supply to demand.[11]

Theorists emphasizing the importance of the presence or absence of economic markets (e.g., Lindblom 1977) argue that in the absence of markets as sources of incentives and controls on public management, other governmental institutions (courts, legislatures, the executive branch, higher levels of government) must use legal and formal constraints to impose external governmental control. This in turn leads to more external controls on the managerial structures and procedures, spheres of operations, and strategic objectives in public management as compared to those in private management, even in heavily regulated firms. Public management depends on politically constituted authorities for authorization of activities and for funding of them, and hence faces a very different operating environment. In addition, many observers emphasize the division of external authority among multiple institutions (as noted above, legislatures, courts, and the chief executive) in democratic republics and other types of government as well, and point to the significance of this division for the goals and operations of public management, as discussed below.

The governmental institutions on which public management depends for authorization and funding respond to political influences. Even in autocratic regimes popular support for a government activity can bolster it and popular opposition can undercut it. Public management often involves cultivation of political support and avoiding opposition not just from the formal authorities but from constituencies such as influential interest groups, and from the media, public opinion, and other less formally authorized political influences.

4.4.2 Distinctive Transactions with the Operating Environment

Scholars and experts have often linked these differences in operating context to distinct forms of transaction with the external environment. Government, they observe, produces goods and services that private markets will not adequately provide, such as public goods and the management of externalities, and these goods cannot be sold on markets at a unit price. Others emphasize that government activity is often more monopolistic, coercive, and unavoidable than private-sector activities, with a greater breadth of impact, and this necessitates more oversight and controls on public management by other government authorities. Observers also frequently claim that government organizations operate under greater public scrutiny and with unique public expectations for fairness, openness, accountability, and honesty.

4.4.3 Distinctive Public Management Goals, Roles, Structures and Processes

Most of the observations about the distinctive environment and environmental transactions for public management link them to further distinctions in goals, managerial roles, structures and processes.

Goals and Performance Criteria. Certainly the most frequently repeated observation about public management contends that such conditions as the absence of the market, the production of goods and services not readily valued at a market price, and value-laden expectations for accountability, fairness, openness, and honesty as well as performance complicate the goals and evaluation criteria of public organizations. Goals and performance criteria are purportedly more diverse, conflict more often (and entail more difficult trade-offs), and are more intangible and harder to measure than is the case for private firms (see Appendix, III.1). Virtually everyone writing about public management makes these observations in some form. Numerous examples illustrate them, including vague and conflicting mandates for many government agencies, conflicting interest group pressures, and the scarcity of clear performance indicators. Executives commenting on their experiences in government compared to their experiences in industry frequently make such observations (Blumenthal 1983; Rumsfeld 1983). On the other hand, executives in industry also face intense goal conflicts and problems with clarity of goals, while the goals of some public management activities—collect taxes, send out benefit checks, issue licenses—do not seem vastly more complex than goals that many business firms pursue. Surprisingly little large-sample research provides evidence for these claims about distinctively vague, multiple, and conflicting goals in public management. Two surveys that asked managers questions about whether their organizations had clear goals found no differences between public and private managers in their answers to such questions (see Rainey 2003: 134). Many public managers must definitely be prepared to deal with vague, multiple, and conflicting goals, but just how distinctive public management is on such dimensions remains an open question in need of further analysis and evidence.

General Managerial Roles. In spite of a broad consensus that public and private management involve many similar functions and activities, numerous studies have found distinctive aspects of the managerial roles in the public sector. Very diverse in methodology, the evidence tends to support the conclusions summarized in III.2 of the Appendix (e.g., Atwater and Wright 1996; Bogg and Cooper 1995; Dargie 1998, 2000; Hooijberg and Choi 2001; Kurke and Aldrich 1983; Lau, Pavett, and Newman 1980; Mintzberg 1972; Palmer 1998; Porter and Van Maanen 1983). Obviously there will be wide variations among the roles of managers in public, private, and nonprofit settings. A manager's involvement in external relations, for example, will depend heavily on organizational level and assignment, with high-level executives more likely then middle managers to interact with leaders from external institutions. In government, many managers will work in isolation from media coverage, direct pressures from interest groups and legislators, and other forms of "political" involvement. The evidence does indicate, however, that many managers in government, such as higher-level politically elected executives and politically appointed agency executives, will play roles that reflect the public and political nature of their setting, involving the sorts of activities indicated in III.2 of the Appendix.

Administrative Authority. Closely related to the assertions and evidence about managerial roles are the observations regarding administrative authority summarized in III.3 of the Appendix. Various experienced observers in several case studies have concluded that the external institutional oversight and control, the constraining administrative systems (such as complex civil service procedures), and the political dynamics of the operating environment, leave public managers with less authority over their organizations than their private sector counterparts (e.g., Lynn 1981, 1987; Warwick 1975). The constraints also make it hard to produce results, according to some observers. In his case study of a set of federal bureau chiefs, Kaufman (1979: 35) concluded that they "make their mark in inches, not in miles," and achieve modest results at best. Subordinates and subunits may have external political alliances and civil service system protections that give them relative autonomy from higher levels. Striving for control because of the political pressures on them but lacking clear performance measures, high-level public managers, according to some observers, become reluctant to delegate authority and inclined to establish even further hierarchical controls and reviews of lower level decisions. Another constraint can arise from frequent turnover of top executives in many political systems, due to elections and appointments of new political appointees in the administrative hierarchy. The frequent turnover allegedly disrupts innovation and change (e.g., Warwick 1975).

In addition to the references cited in the preceding section, numerous studies comparing public and private managers and various forms of evidence—including additional studies cited in sections below—indicate the constrained, shared authority of many public managers, and the need for them to prepare for such roles (e.g., Bogg and Cooper 1995; Atwater and Wright 1996). On the other hand, as described later, in the last two decades a genre of literature has developed that includes numerous books and articles reporting evidence that public managers often thrive in their roles and lead innovative, well-performing organizations and subordinates. In addition, at least one comparison of a large sample of government managers to a large sample of business managers found that the government managers expressed less preference for new and additional rules, a finding that does not support the conclusion that public managers have a stronger propensity than private managers to initiate new rules and hierarchical controls (Bozeman and Rainey 1998).

Organizational structure. For nearly two centuries at least, satirists have ridiculed governmental bureaucracy, and have contributed to the widespread belief that government agencies tend toward particularly complex and constraining structural arrangements and a propensity towards "red tape." Some economists and political scientists have essentially codified this view into their theories of public bureaucracy (Dahl and Lindblom 1953; Downs 1967; Niskanen 1971; Warwick 1975). Numerous studies, however, have produced mixed findings as to whether public managers work with structures very different from those of private firms. A diverse array of studies have found various structural differences, but not necessarily differences indicating more "bureaucracy" in public organizations (see Rainey, 2003: 202–9). A number of surveys have found that public managers report higher levels of "red tape" and procedural delays than do managers in private firms (see Bozeman 2000). A number of studies also find that public managers report higher levels of formalization, centralization, or similar dimensions in their organizations than do private managers, although the public–private differences are usually not very large (e.g., Kalleberg, Knoke, Marsden, and Spaeth 1996: 840; Light 2002; Rainey, Pandey, and Bozeman 1995) and some studies find no difference (Kurland and Egan 1999).

As described below, various surveys find that the largest differences between public and private managers show up when they respond to questions about procedural delays and structural constraints in certain areas, such as personnel management and purchasing/procurement. In most governments, central agencies tend to establish personnel and purchasing rules and policies and to oversee these activities in the other agencies. The pattern of findings supports the interpretation that government organizations tend towards more formalization, rule intensity, and "red tape" than do private firms, but not nearly to as great a degree as many theorists have predicted. In activities where external agencies—such as those concerned with personnel and purchasing—establish and oversee rules and policies for the agencies in a government, however, public managers appear to face significantly higher levels of structural formalization and centralization.

Strategic Decision-Making Processes. The differences in organizational environments and in managerial roles discussed above imply or explicitly relate to observations about differences in decision processes in public and private management of the sort summarized in III.5 of the Appendix. While some studies report mixed support for such conclusions (Nutt 2000), a number of studies support them (Hickson, Butler, Cray, Mallory, and Wilson 1986; Nutt 1999; Richardson 1998; Schwenk 1990; Tan 2002).

Incentives and Incentive Structures. In the many surveys of public and private managers, the sharpest differences between the two groups come in their responses to questions about constraints in incentive structures—about whether it is difficult or relatively easy under the rules governing their organizations to base a person's pay, promotion, or disciplinary actions on their performance. A number of surveys at different points in time, different levels of government, and in different nations find that public managers report much more constraint and difficulty in tying pay, promotion, and discipline (including firing a person) to performance than do private managers (e.g., Atwater and Wright 1996; Kurland and Egan 1999; Porter and Lawler 1968; and additional references in Rainey and Bozeman 2000 or Rainey 2003). Many of these same studies find that public managers and employees, as compared to their private-sector counterparts, report a weaker relationship between their performance and pay, promotion opportunities, and job security. Efforts in many different nations in the last two decades to install "pay for performance" procedures for government employees and to introduce other "flexibilities" into their civil service systems reflect policy makers' responses to such views, often voiced in public managers' complaints about the systems in which they work.

Work-related values and attitudes. For years, an abundance of research has found that samples of public managers and employees differ from their private counterparts in their work-related values and attitudes in the ways summarized in III.7 of the Appendix. The research includes studies that differ widely in method, samples, and the values and attitudes assessed, and includes studies that find no differences on one or more of the values and attitudes mentioned in III.7, such as the value placed on pay (Crewson 1997). While critics frequently allege that civil service protections and the personnel constraints mentioned above attract employees seeking job security to the public sector, the results of public–private comparisons of attitudes about job security tend to be mixed (e.g., Karl and Sutton 1998). Overall, however, numerous studies tend to find that many public-sector managers and employees express a lower valuation of financial incentives as an ultimate goal in work, higher levels of altruistic and public service motives, higher valuation of opportunities for meaningful work and work that affects important public outcomes. Higher level managers express higher levels of these motives and values than rank-and-file employees in the public sector (e.g., Jurkiewicz, Massey, and Brown 1998; Houston 2000; see Rainey 2003: 237–243). In addition, a growing body of research on public service motivation over the last decade suggests special patterns of motivation in public and nonprofit organizations that can produce levels of motivation and effort comparable to those among private sector employees, or higher (e.g., François 2000; Houston 2000; Perry 1996, 2000; Simon 1995, 1998).

Since the 1960s, numerous surveys have also compared the work-related attitudes of public and private sector respondents, on topics such as work satisfaction, and have consistently found that public sector managers and employees tend to respond to general or global questions (e.g., "In general, I like my job.") in ways that express equal, sometimes slightly greater, or sometimes slightly lower general satisfaction than private sector respondents. Studies in various nations, however, have found that the public sector respondents expressed somewhat lower levels of satisfaction with specific facets of their work, such as managers' dissatisfaction with

their autonomy or sense of their impact on their organization, and employees'
dissatisfaction with their supervisors (e.g., Bogg and Cooper 1995; Bordia and Blau
1998; Buchanan 1974, 1975; Kurland and Egan 1999; Paine, Carroll, and Leete 1966;
Porter 1962). The public sector respondents tend to be the ones expressing lower
satisfaction with some aspect of their work, and for some of these differences
managers' responses tend to be consistent with differences discussed in preceding
sections (e.g., the external oversight and interventions appear to explain the public
sector managers' lower level of satisfaction with their autonomy in some studies).
These results tend to support the conclusion that public sector managers and
employees express levels of general work satisfaction as high or sometimes somewhat higher than private sector counterparts, but that some specific frustrations or
demands of work in the public sector frequently show up in work satisfaction
comparisons.

4.4.4 Comparative Performance of Public and Private Management

The comparative performance of public and private management, organizations,
and employees figures as the most significant and controversial issue of all. Many
people feel strongly that they know what to conclude about it, even though it turns
out to be a very difficult issue to resolve. One encounters very strongly held but
diametrically opposing conclusions. For years, public opinion surveys in various
nations have found that the majority of respondents express the opinion that
government operates less efficiently and effectively than business (e.g., Katz,
Gutek, Kahn, and Barton 1975; Lipset and Schneider 1987; Peters 1984: 44–6).
Among scholars and professionals one finds groups and schools virtually founded
on this same premise about superiority of business performance and by implication the premise that business management outperforms public management. The
"public choice" school in economics, and economists such as Milton Friedman
represent such a view (e.g., Downs 1967; Niskanen 1971; Tullock, Seldon, and Brady
2002), as do numerous treatises on the public bureaucracy by political scientists
(e.g., Barton 1980; Warwick 1975). This general view of public management as
inferior to business management and in need of improvement has fueled reform
movements in nations around the world that continue to this day, such as the New
Public Management reforms in various nations. On the other hand, as described
below, a stream of books and articles in the last two decades have claimed that
public management performs very well, and often just as well or even better than
private business in many instances.

As indicated in the Appendix, some of this debate turns on questions about
whether public managers and employees have lower levels of incentive and

motivation, less innovativeness and more cautiousness, and hence lower levels of individual performance, than people in business. As described earlier, a number of surveys have found that public managers and employees report that they perceive weaker linkages between their performance and incentives such as pay, promotion, and job security (including the prospect of being fired), compared with their private sector counterparts. The public sector respondents also report other constraints on incentives, such as elaborate rules protecting public employees from discipline and discharge.

Whether these and other conditions, such as intense political oversight, make public managers and employees cautious and risk averse, has received a lot of attention from researchers, with mixed results. Surveys in several nations (such as the US, the UK, Sweden, and Israel) have found that public managers and employees, compared to private sector respondents, express similar levels of receptivity to innovation, reform, and change (Elliot and Tevavichulada 1999; Rainey 1983; Rosenblatt and Mannheim 1996; Wise 1999), and perceive similar levels of risk-taking in their organizations (e.g., Bozeman and Kingsley 1998). Golembiewski (1985) and Robertson and Seneviratne (1995) report evidence of similar success rates for organizational development and planned change initiatives in samples of public and private organizations. In addition, for years authors have described numerous examples of innovations and "revitalization" in government agencies and programs (e.g., Altshuler and Behn 1997; Donahue 1997). On the other hand, some recent studies have found that public managers express less enthusiasm and optimism about organizational change and reform initiatives than do their private sector counterparts (e.g., Boyne, Jenkins, and Poole 1999; Doyle, Claydon, and Buchanan 2000; Lozeau, Langley, and Denis 2002; Denis, Langley, and Cazale 1996). A key distinction in the various studies about dispositions toward change and innovation appears to be whether the public sector respondents are asked for their views about changes generated within their organizations, as opposed to changes initiated or imposed externally, such as a general reform initiative mandated by a legislative body for all agencies in a government. Public management appears for obvious reasons to be more frequently subject to such externally imposed or mandated changes, and public sector respondents tend to express less enthusiasm and support for these types of change than for changes originating within their organizations.

Many of the assertions about the distinctive aspects of public management imply or aggressively claim that individuals in the public sector will display lower motivation and performance than people in business. One encounters difficulties in trying to resolve these claims, because organizational psychologists have never developed a well-validated questionnaire measure of motivation and one faces obvious problems in seeking to compare the individual performances of people working in different jobs in the public and private sectors. In numerous surveys over the years, people in public management have reported high levels of motivation and effort, levels comparable to respondents from business organizations (among many examples, see US Office of Personnel Management 2003; Kilpatrick, Cummings, and Jennings 1964: 607; Rainey 1983). For example, the US Office of Personnel Management (2003) survey of US federal employees found that 91 percent of them believe the work they do is important, and 81 percent believe that they do work of high quality, a percentage that approximates the 83 percent of respondents in a survey of private sector managers and employees who believe that they do work of high quality. On the other hand, when government employees respond to questions that focus less directly on their own motivation and effort, they often express more negative views about such matters. For example, fewer than half of the respondents to the USOPM survey agreed that awards in their agency depend on how well employees do their jobs. Only 27 percent agreed that steps are taken to deal with poor performers and only 36 percent agreed that their leaders generate high levels of motivation and commitment. Langbein and Lewis (1998) compared survey responses by engineers in the public, private, non-profit, and private defense-related firms and found evidence of lower productivity among the public and private defense-related engineers than among those in non-defense-related private firms; they also found that the public and non-profit sector engineers were significantly underpaid compared to their private sector counterparts. In these survey results and many others, people in public management settings report that they display high levels of motivation and effort, but they also often express concerns that appear to reflect the public sector context, such as concerns that the civil service personnel system may protect poor performers more than it should, and that rewards such as pay are not based on individual performance as much as they should be (also see Light 2002).

Whether or not people in the public sector have levels of motivation and individual performance comparable to those in business, there remains the question of whether private sector organizations simply outperform government organizations on such criteria as operating efficiency and the general quality of their products and services. This, too, is a difficult question to resolve. Some Nobel Laureates in economics, such as Milton Friedman and James Buchanan, take the position that free markets and freedom of choice produce generally superior outcomes to those produced by government, and by implication that public management and government organizations will not function as well as private firms and their management. On the other hand, the late Nobel Laureate Herbert Simon (1998: 11) flatly asserted that it is false to claim that "public and non-profit organizations cannot, and on average do not, operate as efficiently as private businesses." The diametrically opposing views of Nobel Laureates in economics reflect the problems in comparing two diverse populations of organizations with dissimilar products and services, and the absence of such measures as profit and sales indicators for most public organizations.

On some general performance criteria public and private management seem quite similar. For example, the American Customer Satisfaction Index (ACSI) has provided customer satisfaction scores for 170 business firms and 30 US federal agencies (American Society for Quality 2001). In 1999, the average score for the business firms was about 3 points higher, on a 100-point scale, than the average score for the federal agencies. In 2001, however, the average for the federal agencies, at 72.1, exceeded the average of 70.0 for the business firms. Customer satisfaction is but one of many measures of performance, but such comparisons suggest that public management quite frequently performs at least as well as private management on important performance criteria.

Much more often, however, researchers conduct before-and-after studies of privatization (such as an ownership change from a state-owned enterprise to a privately owned enterprise) or contracting-out by the public sector, or cross-sectional studies of public and private organizations engaged in the same type of activity. Proponents of privatization report strong and consistent findings in favor of private business, from all these types of study. Savas (2000: ch. 6) reports consistent findings of cost savings as a result of contracting-out, with comparable or better quality of service. He also reports superior economic performance by private forms of organization or service delivery as compared to state-owned enterprise or government service delivery, and of improved performance of government activities that are taken private. Many such studies involving different nations and types of service continue to appear (Backkx, Carney, and Gedajlovic 2002; Boubakri and Cossett 1998; Heinrich 2000; Ballou and Podgursky 1998).

On the other hand, other researchers report either no evidence of private sector superiority, or mixed evidence. Hodge (2000) reports evidence from a large international meta-analysis of contracting-out situations that contracting-out by governments generally produces cost savings, but only in the two service areas of refuse collection and building maintenance. He finds no clear evidence of improvements in service quality. Other recent studies covering many nations have also reported mixed or limited evidence of financial and service improvements due to privatization or public–private status (Villalonga 2000; Parker 1995; Pendleton 1999; Becker, Dluhy, and Topinka 2001; Chou 2002; Luksetich, Edwards, and Carroll 2000; Morris and Helburn 2000; Durant, Legge, and Moussios 1998). At least in terms of the number of studies reporting superior results for private or privatized forms, the weight of the evidence appears clearly in favor of the conclusion that private forms of organization tend to have lower costs and greater economic efficiencies, without general losses in service quality. The continuing appearance, however, of mixed findings or findings of limited improvements or superiority of private forms reminds us that privatization can have many pitfalls and troublesome contingencies. Private management does not necessarily guarantee universal superiority over public management (Sclar 2000).

In addition, in recent years a genre of literature has developed that includes numerous books and articles about very effective public management, many of which draw on evidence from actual instances (for example, Ban 1995; Behn 1991; Borins 1998; Cohen and Eimicke 1995; Doig and Hargrove 1987; Holzer and Callahan 1998; Popovich 1998; Riccucci 1995). Regardless of whether private sector management might have some general or on-average superiority on certain types of performance criteria, these authors mount a strong claim that examples and evidence of excellence in public management abound.

4.5 CONCLUSIONS

This chapter has reviewed the claims and assertions about differences between public and private management, and sought to assess them with a review of research findings. Ultimately both sides in the continuing controversy over whether public and private management differ get to be right, in a sense. The evidence indicates points on which the two domains of management do not differ significantly, or in the ways certain claims and stereotypes would suggest. These findings support those who object to the distinction and who, with great justification, argue the applicability of general management theory and techniques to public management. The review also shows, however, a number of points of interesting and important differences between the two categories of management, knowledge of which can aid the understanding and practice of public management.

For example, the weight of the evidence indicates that most public managers will face conditions much more strongly influenced by the governmental institutions and processes designed to direct them and hold them accountable, and by the goals of producing public goods and services in the absence of profit indicators and incentives, than will most managers in business firms. At higher levels of management and in certain externally oriented managerial roles at lower levels, public managers will be more engaged with, and constrained by, political and governmental processes such as nurturing support from interest groups and managing relations with legislative bodies and the chief executive. In other managerial roles less directly in contact with such political and governmental processes, public managers will still confront influences from those sources, such as complex governmental systems for purchasing and procurement, and for personnel administration.

In relation to this last point, we have substantial evidence of greater concerns among public managers, compared to their counterparts in business firms, about complex administrative rules and "red tape." The public managers perceive, for example, more problems with personnel administration, such as complexities in the rules about pay and discipline that weaken relations between performance and such incentives. They more often report concerns about the motivation and performance of their co-workers. On the other hand, they reports levels of their own motivation and general work satisfaction that differ very little from those of private sector counterparts, and they tend to express higher levels of altruistic and public service motivation. These seemingly rather contradictory findings actually point to the sensible conclusion that public managers face greater challenges in managing their administrative systems in certain senses, such as in managing pay and discipline systems, but that we should avoid over-generalizing about such distinctions. The challenges may be greater in certain ways, but the research is continuing to indicate alternative incentives that can induce high levels of motivation in public organizations.

Similarly, the seeming contradictions in the body of evidence about the relative performance of public and private organizations actually points to constructive conclusions. Most published studies report higher levels of operating efficiency and lower costs on the part of private sector providers compared with similar public sector activities, yet other studies find no such differences or find that the superiority of the private firms is limited to certain service areas. Such findings support the conclusion that management in many private firms does generally have advantages over public management, in achieving operating efficiencies, but not always. These findings, in turn, are leading to the development of a more contingent approach to privatization of public services through contracting-out, in which researchers seek to identify the conditions under which such contracting-out can produce efficiencies. For example, the literature on the topic and governmental policies about it are increasingly emphasizing competition as a key to making contracting-out effective. In a similar pattern, the contradictory conclusions about the general performance of public and private management—with some economists positing inherent weakness in public management and pointing to evidence of it, with others denying such a difference and still others describing patterns of excellence in public management—support the conclusion that private management has certain operating advantages over public management but that we should avoid overstating and over-generalizing such a conclusion. The continuing challenge is to determine when, where, and how public management performs well, when it does, and this body of research continues to develop in ways that help in that quest.

APPENDIX

DISTINCTIVE CHARACTERISTICS OF PUBLIC MANAGEMENT: COMMON ASSERTIONS AND RESEARCH FINDINGS

I. Distinctive Environmental Factors

I.1. Absence of economic markets for outputs; reliance on governmental appropriations for financial resources.

- Lower incentives for public managers to achieve cost reduction, operating efficiency, and effective performance.
- Less ability for public managers to achieve economic efficiency in allocating resources (weaker reflection of consumer preferences, less proportioning of supply to demand).
- Public managers have less availability of relatively clear market indicators and information (prices, profits, market share) for use in managerial decisions.

I.2. External control by politically constituted authority: Presence of more elaborate and intensive formal, legal constraints on public managers as a result of oversight by legislative branch, executive branch hierarchy and oversight agencies, and courts.

- Public management operates under more constraints on domains of operation and on managerial procedures (public managers have less autonomy in making such choices), and under more formal administrative controls.
- In democratic republics as well as some other types of governments, public managers work under the authority of multiple formal authorities and influences, with greater fragmentation among them, than private sector managers.

I.3. Presence of more intensive external political influences.

- Greater diversity and intensity of external informal political influences on decisions (political bargaining and lobbying; public opinion; interest-group, client, and constituent pressures).
- Greater need for political support from client groups, constituencies, and formal authorities in order to obtain appropriations and authorization for actions.

II. Organization—Environment Transactions

II. 1. Public organizations and managers are often involved in production of public goods, handling of significant externalities, or other activities in which private organizations do not readily engage.

II.2. Government activities are often coercive, monopolistic, or unavoidable. Government has unique sanctioning and coercive power and often acts as sole provider of certain services and functions. Participation in the consumption and financing of governmental activities is often mandatory.

II.3. Government activities often have a broader impact and greater symbolic significance. There is a broader scope of concern, such as for general public interest criteria.

II.4. Public managers often operate under greater public scrutiny than do private sector managers, from news media, interest groups, and oversight authorities.

II.5. Public managers face stronger expectations for fairness, responsiveness, honesty, openness, and public accountability than do private sector managers.

III. Organizational Roles, Structures, and Processes

The following distinctive characteristics of organizational roles, structures, and processes have been frequently asserted to result from the distinctions cited under I and II. More recently, distinctions of this nature have been analyzed in research with varying results.

III.1. Greater goal ambiguity, multiplicity, and conflict.

- Greater vagueness, intangibility, or difficulty in measuring goals and performance criteria; the goals are more debatable and value-laden (for example, defense readiness, public safety, a clean environment, better living standards for the poor and unemployed).
- Greater multiplicity of goals and criteria (efficiency, public accountability and openness, political responsiveness, fairness and due process, social equity and distributional criteria, moral correctness of behavior).
- Greater tendency of the goals to be conflicting, to involve more trade-offs (efficiency versus openness to public scrutiny, efficiency versus due process and social equity, conflicting demands of diverse constituencies and political authorities).

III.2. Distinctive features of general managerial roles.

- Numerous studies have found that public managers' general roles involve many of the same functions and role categories as those of managers in other settings but with some distinctive features: a more political, expository role, involving more meetings with and interventions by external interest groups and political authorities; more crisis management and "fire drills"; greater challenge to balance external political relations with internal management functions.

III.3. Distinctive aspects of administrative authority and leadership practices.

- Public managers have less decision-making autonomy and flexibility because of elaborate institutional constraints and external political influences. They must contend with more external interventions, interruptions, constraints.
- Public managers have weaker authority over subordinates and lower levels as a result of institutional constraints (for example, civil service personnel systems, purchasing and procurement systems) and external political alliances of subunits and subordinates (with interest groups, legislators).
- Higher-level public managers show greater reluctance to delegate authority and a tendency to establish more levels of review and approval and to make greater use of formal regulations to control lower levels.
- More frequent turnover of top leaders due to elections and political appointments causes more difficulty in implementing plans and innovations.
- Recent counterpoint studies describe entrepreneurial behaviors and managerial excellence by public managers.

III.4. Organizational structure.

- Numerous assertions that public organizations are subject to more red tape, more elaborate bureaucratic structures.
- Empirical studies report mixed results, some supporting the assertions about red tape, some not supporting them. Numerous studies find some structural distinctions for public forms of organizations, although not necessarily more bureaucratic structuring.

III.5. Strategic decision-making processes.

- Several studies indicate that strategic decision-making processes in public organizations can be generally similar to those in other settings but are more likely to be subject to interventions, interruptions, and greater involvement of external authorities and interest groups.

III.6. Differences in incentives and incentive structures.

- Numerous studies show that public managers and employees perceive greater administrative constraints on the administration of extrinsic incentives such as pay, promotion, and disciplinary action than do their counterparts in private organizations.
- Numerous surveys indicate that public managers and employees perceive weaker relations between performance and extrinsic rewards such as pay, promotion, and job security than do their private sector counterparts. These studies find no clear relationship between such perceptions and employee performance—they find no strong evidence that such perceptions weaken performance. The studies indicate a compensating effect of other motives and incentives (see III.7 below) such as public service motives, altruistic motives, involvement in important work and other intrinsic incentives for public employees.

III.7. Individual characteristics, work-related attitudes and behaviors.

- Numerous studies have found different work-related values on the part of public managers and employees, such as lower valuation of monetary incentives and higher levels of public service motivation, altruistic motives, sense of involvement in worthwhile work, and sense of influence on important public policy decisions than their private sector counterparts. These differences between the public and private sectors increase at higher managerial and executive levels.
- Numerous highly diverse studies have found lower levels of work satisfaction among public than among private managers and employees. The level of satisfaction among public sector samples is generally high and on general satisfaction questions comparable to that of private sector respondents. Many studies, however, find that public sector respondents show lower levels of satisfaction with certain facets of their work, such as the autonomy they are allowed in their jobs, and with their supervisors.

III.8. Differences in organizational and individual performance.

- Numerous authors and observers assert that public organizations and employees are cautious and not innovative. The research evidence is mixed. Some surveys find that public employees do not differ from private sector employees in self-reported receptivity to change and innovation.
- Government managers and employees self-report high levels of motivation and effort in their work, and report levels as high as the levels reported by private sector managers and

employees. On the other hand, survey respondents in government tend to report greater concerns that poor performers are not effectively corrected or discharged.

- Numerous studies indicate that public forms of various types of organizations tend to be less efficient in providing services than their private counterparts, although results tend to be inconclusive in some studies and for certain types of organizations and activities. Other authors strongly defend the efficiency and general performance of public organizations, citing various forms of evidence.

NOTES

1. In this chapter, "public management" will refer to a broad domain of scholarly thought and activity, as well practical applied thought and activity, pertaining to governmental organizations, programs, and activities at all levels of government. "Public management" will refer to people and their behaviors at all levels in those organizations, including people that we might refer to as executives, leaders, managers, members, subordinates, employees, and to research and theory from organization theory and organizational psychology and behavior. Material on all these topics is pertinent to public and private management and their comparison. For example, one finds in the relevant literature a set of studies comparing the organizational structure of public and private organizations, and one might ask whether studies of organizational structure are studies of management. The use of the public management term here assumes that they do, because structure and other organizational characteristics form the context in which management takes place and often reflects the actions and decisions of managers. One also finds many comparisons of survey responses of public and private employees below the managerial level. The chapter will treat such studies as part of the domain of public management. Many of the distinctions mentioned above, such as differences in organizational level, are often extremely important differences, but are all part of the research, theory, and thought relevant to comparing public and private management.

2. One does encounter ideologues who indicate a variant of this perspective, when they express the remarkable belief that privatization and contracting-out by government are original and assuredly effective alternatives for governments. One hopes for their sake that they are not truly ignorant of the history of such alternatives across the centuries, including a history of fairly frequent problems such as corruption on both sides of the arrangement and poor performance by the contractors. Instead, one hopes for their sake that they are referring to the expansion and proliferation of these alternatives beyond their historic levels, and into new areas of public service and public policy where they had not previously been used. Even so, they display either poor memory or ideological zeal when they tout privatization as a panacea for poor performance by governments.

3. Experts on such hybrid organizations have observed for years that decision-makers in government follow no clear policy, typology, or nomenclature in establishing and designing such organizations (e.g., Seidman, 1998).

4. Blau and Scott (1962), for example, proposed a typology of commonweal, business, service and mutual benefit organizations, in which the commonweal organizations included public agencies and the business categories obviously included business firms.

5. See Lindblom (1977, Chap. 6) for a discussion of public goods and other market defects.

6. See Antonsen and Jorgensen (1997) for another, original operationalization of "publicness."

7. See Perry and Rainey (1988) for another effort to define the differences between public, private, and hybrid organizations.

8. Kalleberg, Knoke, Marsden, and Spaeth (1996) report their research as the first organizational study employing a national probability sample. They found that public, private, and nonprofit categories of organization provided some of the significant findings of differences in structural characteristics that they measured.

9. Obviously, this observation may not apply to hybrid forms of organization such as state-owned enterprises and government corporations or authorities that charge customers for their products and services. In many cases, however, such organizations actually operate under greater oversight or influence from political authorities and actors, as a result of government ownership or government participation in their ownership. Among many examples of this point are those nations where political authorities have employed state-owned enterprises for economic development objectives, such as providing jobs in economically depressed regions. This diminishes the importance of profitability in relation to such objectives, thus making the organizations hybrid not just in organizational form, but in operating objectives.

10. The National Organization Survey (Kalleberg et al. 1996) included questions about sales and other economic market indicators. These applied only to the private firms responding to the survey, and the data set contains no responses to these questions for the public organizations in the sample.

11. Many important developments in political science and economics, such as the influential field of public choice economics, have been virtually founded on observations such as these, and the research and debates on such matters are so elaborate that this chapter cannot adequately cover them.

REFERENCES

ALTSHULER, A., and BEHN, R. D. (eds.) (1997), *Innovation In American Government: Challenges, Opportunities, and Dilemmas*, Washington, DC: Brookings Institution.

American Society for Quality (2001), University of Michigan Business School, and Arthur Andersen, "American Customer Satisfaction Index: Federal Agencies Government-Wide Customer Satisfaction Report for the General Service Administration." Available Online: *http://www.customersurvey.gov.*

ANTONSEN, M., and JORGENSEN, T. B. (1997), "The 'Publicness' of Public Organizations," *Public Administration* 75: 337–57.

ATKINSON, S. E., and HALVERSEN, R. (1986), "The Relative Efficiency of Public and Private Firms in a Regulated Environment: The Case of U.S. Electric Utilities," *Journal of Public Economics* 29: 281–94.

ATWATER, L. E., and WRIGHT, W. J. (1996), "Power and Transformational and Transactional Leadership In Public and Private Organizations," *International Journal of Public Administration* 19: 963–89.

BACKKX, M., CARNEY, M., and GEDAJLOVIC, E. (2002), "Public, Private and Mixed Ownership and the Performance of International Airlines," *Journal of Air Transport Management* 8: 213–20.

BALLOU, D., and PODGURSKY, M. (1998), "Teacher Recruitment and Retention In Public and Private Schools," *Journal of Policy Analysis and Management* 17: 393–417.

BAN, C. (1995), *How Do Public Managers Manage?* San Francisco: Jossey-Bass.

BARTON, A. H. (1980), "A Diagnosis of Bureaucratic Maladies," in C. H. Weiss and A. H. Barton (eds.), *Making Bureaucracies Work*, Thousand Oaks, CA.: Sage.

BECKER, F. W., DLUHY, M. J., and TOPINKA, J. P. (2001), "Choosing the Powers: Are Private Managers of Public Housing More Successful Than Public Managers?" *American Review of Public Administration* 31: 181–200.

BEHN, R. D. (1991), *Leadership Counts*, Cambridge, MA: Harvard University Press.

BLAU, P. M., and SCOTT, W. R. (1962), *Formal Organizations*, Novato, CA: Chandler & Sharp.

BOGG, J., and COOPER, C. (1995), "Job Satisfaction, Mental Health, and Occupational Stress Among Senior Civil Servants," *Human Relations* 48: 327–41.

BORDIA, P., and BLAU, G. (1998), "Pay Referent Comparison and Pay Level Satisfaction in Private versus Public Sector Organizations in India," *International Journal of Human Resource Management* 9: 155–67.

BORINS, S. (1998), *Innovating with Integrity: How Local Heroes are Transforming American Government*, Washington, DC: Georgetown University Press.

BOUBAKRI, N., and COSSET, J. (1998), "The Financial and Operating Performance of Newly Privatized Firms: Evidence from Developing Countries," *Journal of Finance* 53: 1081–110.

BOYNE, G., JENKINS, G., and POOLE, M. (1999), "Human Resource Management in the Public and Private Sectors: An Empirical Comparison," *Public Administration* 77: 407–20.

BOZEMAN, B. (1987), *All Organizations Are Public: Bridging Public and Private Organizational Theories*, San Francisco: Jossey-Bass.

—— and KINGSLEY, G. A. (1998), "Risk Culture In Public and Private Organizations," *Public Administration Review* 58: 109–18.

—— and RAINEY, H. G. (1998), "Organizational Rules and the Bureaucratic Personality," *American Journal of Political Science* 42: 163–89.

BRETSCHNEIDER, S. (1990), "Management Information Systems in Public and Private Organizations: An Empirical Test," *Public Administration Review* 50: 536–45.

BUCHANAN, B. (1974), "Government Managers, Business Executives, and Organizational Commitment," *Public Administration Review* 35: 339–47.

—— (1975), "Red Tape and the Service Ethic: Some Unexpected Differences Between Public and Private Managers," *Administration and Society* 6: 423–38.

CASILE, M., and DAVIS-BLAKE, A. (2002), "When Accreditation Standards Change: Factors Affecting Differential Responsiveness of Public and Private Organizations," *Academy of Management Journal* 45: 180–95.

CHOU, S. (2002), "Asymmetric Information, Ownership and Quality of Care: an Empirical Analysis of Nursing Homes," *Journal of Health Economics* 21: 293–311.

COHEN, S., and EIMICKE, W. (1995). *The New Effective Public Manager*, San Francisco: Jossey-Bass.

CORDER, K. (2001), "Acquiring New Technology: Comparing Nonprofit and Public Sector Agencies," *Administration and Society* 33: 194–219.

CREWSON, P. E. (1997), "Public Service Motivation: Building Empirical Evidence of Incidence and Effect," *Journal of Public Administration Research and Theory* 7: 499–518.

DAFT, R. L. (2004), *Organization Theory and Design*, 8th edn. Cincinnati, Ohio: South-Western College Publishing.

DAHL, R. A., and LINDBLOM, C. E. (1953), *Politics, Economics, and Welfare*, New York: HarperCollins.

DARGIE, C. (1998), "The Role of Public Sector Chief Executives," *Public Administration* 76: 161–77.

—— (2000), "Observing Chief Executives: Analysing Behavior to Explore Cross-Sectoral Differences," *Public Money and Management*: 20: 39–44.

DENIS, J., LANGLEY, A., and CAZALE, L. (1996), "Leadership and Strategic Change under Ambiguity," *Organizational Studies* 17: 673–99.

DONAHUE, J. D. (ed.) (1997), *Making Government Work: Tales of Innovation In the Federal Government*, Washington, DC: Brookings Institution.

DOWNS, A. (1967), *Inside Bureaucracy*, New York: Little, Brown.

DOIG, J. W., and HARGROVE, E. C. (eds.) (1987), *Leadership and Innovation*, Baltimore: Johns Hopkins University Press.

DOYLE, M., CLAYDON, T., and BUCHANAN, D. (2000), "Mixed Results, Lousy Process: the Management Experience of Organizational Change," *British Journal of Management* 11: 59–80.

DUGGAN, M. G. (2000), "Hospital Ownership and Public Medical Spending," *Quarterly Journal of Economics* 115: 1343–73.

DURANT, R. F. (1998), LEGGE, J. S., and MOUSSIOS, A., "People, Profits, and Service Delivery: Lessons from the Privatization of British Telecom," *American Journal of Political Science* 42: 117–40.

ELLIOT, R., and TEVAVICHULADA, S. (1999), "Computer Literacy and Human Resource Management: A Public/Private Sector Comparison," *Public Personnel Management* 28: 259–74.

FERLIE, E., PETTIGREW, A., ASHBURNER, L., and FITZGERALD, L. (1996), *The New Public Management in Action*, Oxford: Oxford University Press.

FORDER, J. (2000), "Mental Health: Market Power and Governance," *Journal of Health Economics* 19: 877–905.

FRANÇOIS, P. (2000), "'Public Service Motivation' as an Argument for Government Provision," *Journal of Public Economics* 78: 275–99.

GOLEMBIEWSKI, R. T. (1985), *Humanizing Public Organizations*, Mount Airy, MD: Lomond.

HALL, R. H. (2002), *Organizations: Structure and Process*, 8th edn. Upper Saddle River, NJ: Prentice Hall.

HEINRICH, C. J. (2000), "Organizational Form and Performance: An Empirical Investigation of Nonprofit and For-Profit Job-Training Service Providers," *Journal of Policy Analysis and Management* 19: 233–61.

HICKSON, D. J., et al. (1986), *Top Decisions: Strategic Decision Making in Organizations*, San Francisco: Jossey Bass.

HODGE, G. A. (2000), *Privatization: An International Review of Performance*, Boulder, CO: Westview.

HOLZER, M., and CALLAHAN, K. (1998), *Government at Work: Best Practices and Model Programs*, Thousand Oaks, CA: Sage.

HOOIJBERG, R., and CHOI, J. (2001), "The Impact of Organizational Characteristics on Leadership Effectiveness Models: An Examination of Leadership in a Private and a Public Sector Organization," *Administration and Society* 33: 403–31.

HOUSTON, D. J. (2000), "Public-Service Motivation: A Multivariate Test," *Journal of Public Administration Research and Theory* 10: 713–27.

JURKIEWICZ, C. L., MASSEY, T. K., and BROWN, R. G. (1998), "Motivation in Public and Private Organizations: A Comparative Study," *Public Productivity and Management Review* 21: 230–50.

KALLEBERG, A. L., KNOKE, D., MARSDEN, P. V., and SPAETH, J. L. (1996), *Organizations in America*, Thousand Oaks, CA: Sage.

KARL, K. A., and SUTTON, C. L. (1998), "Job Values in Today's Workforce: A Comparison of Public and Private Sector Employees," *Public Personnel Management* 27: 515–27.

KATZ, D., GUTEK, B. A., KAHN, R. L., and BARTON, E. (1975), *Bureaucratic Encounters: A Pilot Study in the Evaluation of Government Services*, Ann Arbor: Survey Research Center, Institute for Social Research, University of Michigan.

KAUFMAN, H. (1979), *The Administrative Behavior of Federal Bureau Chiefs*, Washington, DC: Brookings Institution.

KILPATRICK, F. P., CUMMINGS, M. C., and JENNINGS, M. K. (1964), *The Image of the Federal Service*, Washington, DC: Brookings Institution.

KURKE, L. E., and ALDRICH, H. E. (1983), "Mintzberg Was Right! A Replication and Extension of the Nature of Managerial Work," *Management Science* 29: 975–84.

KURLAND, N. B., and EGAN, T. D. (1999), "Public v. Private Perceptions of Formalization, Outcomes, and Justice," *Journal of Public Administration Research and Theory* 9: 437–58.

LANGBEIN, L. I., and LEWIS, G. B. (1998), "Pay, Productivity, and the Public Sector: The Case of Electrical Engineers," *Journal of Public Administration Research and Theory* 8: 391–412.

LAU, A. W., PAVETT, C. M., and NEWMAN, A. R. (1980), "The Nature of Managerial Work: A Comparison of Public and Private Sector Jobs," *Academy of Management Proceedings*: 339–43.

LIGHT, P. C. (2002), *The Troubled State of the Federal Public* Service, Washington DC: Brookings Institution. Available at *www.brook.edu/views/papers/light/20020627.htm*

LINDBLOM, C. E. (1977), *Politics and Markets*, New York: Basic Books.

LIPSET, S. M., and SCHNEIDER, W. (1987), *The Confidence Gap*, Baltimore: Johns Hopkins University Press.

LOZEAU, D., LANGLEY, A., and DENIS, J. (2002), "The Corruption of Managerial Techniques by Organizations," *Human Relations* 55: 537–64.

LUKSETICH, W., EDWARDS, M. E., and CARROLL, T. M. (2000), "Organizational Forms and Nursing Home Behavior," *Nonprofit and Voluntary Sector Quarterly* 29: 255–79.

LYNN, L. E. (1981), *Managing the Public's Business*, New York: Basic Books.

—— (1987), *Managing Public Policy*, New York: Little, Brown.

MACAVOY, P. W., and MCISSAC, G. S. (1989), "The Performance and Management of United States Federal Government Enterprises," in P. W. MACAVOY, W. T. STANBURY, G. YARROW, and R. J. Zeckhauser (eds.), *Privatization and State-Owned Enterprises*, Boston: Kluwer.

MASCARENHAS, B. (1989), "Domains of State-Owned, Privately Held, and Publicly Traded Firms in International Competition," *Administrative Science Quarterly* 34: 582–97.

MEYER, M. W. (1979), *Change in Public Bureaucracies*, Cambridge: Cambridge University Press.

MINTZBERG, H. (1972), *The Nature of Managerial Work*, New York: HarperCollins.

MOON, M. J., and BRETSCHNEIDER, S. (2002), "Does Perception of Red Tape Constrain IT Innovativeness in Organizations? Unexpected Results from a Simultaneous Equation Model and Implications," *Journal of Public Administration Research and Theory* 12: 273–92.

MORRIS, J. R., and HELBURN, S. W. (2000), "Child Care Center Quality Differences: the Role of Profit Status, Client Preferences, and Trust," *Nonprofit and Voluntary Sector Quarterly* 29: 377–99.

NISKANEN, W. A. (1971), *Bureaucracy and Representative Government*, Hawthorne, NY: Aldine de Gruyter.

NUTT, P. C. (1999), "Public–private Differences and the Assessment of Alternatives for Decision Making," *Journal of Public Administration Research and Theory* 9: 305–49.

—— (2000), "Decision-Making Success in Public, Private, and Third Sector Organizations: Finding Sector Dependent Best Practice," *Journal of Management Studies* 37: 77–108.

PAINE, F. T., CARROLL, S. J., and LEETE, B. A. (1966), "Need Satisfactions of Managerial Level Personnel in a Government Agency," *Journal of Applied Psychology* 50: 247–9.

PALMER, I. (1998), "Arts Managers and Managerialism: A Cross-Sector Analysis of CEO's Orientations and Skills," *Public Productivity and Management Review* 21: 433–52.

PANDEY, S. K., and KINGSLEY, G. A. (2000), "Examining Red Tape in Public and Private Organizations: Alternative Explanations from a Social Psychological Model," *Journal of Public Administration Research and Theory* 10: 779–800.

PARKER, D. (1995), "Privatization and Agency Status: Identifying the Critical Factors for Performance Improvement," *British Journal of Management* 6: 29–43.

PENDLETON, A. (1999), "Ownership or Competition? An Evaluation of the Effects of Privatization on Industrial Relations Institutions, Processes, and Outcomes," *Public Administration* 77: 769–91.

PERRY, J. L. (1996), "Measuring Public Service Motivation: An Assessment of Construct Reliability and Validity," *Journal of Public Administration Research and Theory* 6: 5–24.

—— (2000), "Bringing Society In: Toward a Theory of PSM," *Journal of Public Administration Research and Theory* 10: 471–88.

—— and RAINEY, H. G. (1988), "The Public-Private Distinction in Organization Theory: A Critique and Research Strategy," *Academy of Management Review* 13: 182–201.

PETERS, B. G. (1984), *The Politics of Bureaucracy*, New York: Longman.

POLLITT, C., and BOUCKAERT, G. (2000), *Public Management Reform: A Comparative Perspective*, Oxford: Oxford University Press.

POPOVICH, M. G. (ed.) (1998), *Creating High Performance Government Organizations*. San Francisco, CA: Jossey-Bass.

PORTER, L. W. (1962), "Job Attitudes in Management: Perceived Deficiencies in Need Fulfillment as a Function of Job Level," *Journal of Applied Psychology* 46: 375–84.

—— and LAWLER, E. E., III (1968), *Managerial Attitudes and Performance*, Burr Ridge, IL: Irwin.

—— and VAN MAANEN, J. (1983), "Task Accomplishment and the Management of Time," in J. L. PERRY and K. L. KRAEMER (eds.), *Public Management*, Mountain View, CA: Mayfield.

POSNER, B. T., and SCHMIDT, W. H. (1996), "The Values of Business and Federal Government Executives: More Different than Alike," *Public Personnel Management* 25: 277–89.

Pugh, D. S., Hickson, D. J., and Hinings, C. R. (1969), "An Empirical Taxonomy of Work Organizations," *Administrative Science Quarterly* 14: 115–26.

Rainey, H. G. (1979), "Perceptions of Incentives in Business and Government: Implications for Civil Service Reform," *Public Administration Review* 39: 440–8.

—— (1983), "Public Agencies and Private Firms: Incentive Structures, Goals, and Individual Roles," *Administration and Society* 15: 207–42.

—— (2003), *Understanding and Managing Public Organizations*, 3rd edn. San Francisco: Jossey-Bass/Wiley.

—— and Bozeman, B. (2000), "Comparing Public and Private Organizations: Empirical Research and the Power of the A Priori," *Journal of Public Administration Research and Theory* 10: 447–69.

—— Pandey, S. K, and Bozeman, B. (1995), "Research Note: Public and Private Managers" Perceptions of Red Tape," *Public Administration Review* 55: 567–74.

Riccucci, N. M. (1995), Unsung Heroes: Federal Executives Making a Difference, Washington, DC: Georgetown University Press.

Richardson, K. (1998), "The Effect of Public versus Private Decision Environment on the Use of the Net Present Value Investment Criterion," *Journal of Public Budgeting, Accounting, and Financial Management* 10: 21–52.

Robertson, P. J., and Seneviratne, S. J. (1995), "Outcomes of Planned Organizational Change in the Public Sector: A Meta-Analytic Comparison to the Private Sector," *Public Administration Review* 55: 547–58.

Rosenblatt, Z., and Mannheim, B. (1996), "Organizational Response to Decline in the Israeli Electronics Industry," *Organizational Studies* 17: 953–84.

Rumsfeld, D. (1983), "A Politician-Turned-Executive Surveys Both Worlds," in J. L. Perry and K. L. Kraemer (eds.), *Public Management*, Mountain View, CA: Mayfield.

Savas, E. S. (2000), *Privatization and Public-Private Partnerships*, New York: Chatham House.

Schwenk, C. R. (1990), "Conflict in Organizational Decision Making: An Exploratory Study of Its Effects in For-Profit and Not-for-Profit Organizations," *Management Science* 36: 436–48.

Sclar, E. D. 2000. *You Don't Always Get What You Pay For: The Economics of Privatization.* Ithaca, NY: Cornell University Press.

Scott, P., and Falcone, S. (1998), "Comparing Public and Private Organizations: an Explanatory Analysis of Three Frameworks," *American Review of Public Administration* 28: 126–45.

Seidman, H. (1998), *Politics, Position, and Power*, 5th edn., New York: Oxford University Press.

Simon, H. A. (1995), "Organizations and Markets," *Journal of Public Administration Research and Theory* 5: 273–94.

—— (1998), "Why Public Administration?," *Journal of Public Administration Research and Theory* 8: 1–12.

Sloan, F. A., Picone, G. A., Donald H. T, and Chou, S. (2001), "Hospital Ownership and Cost and Quality of Care: Is There a Dime's Worth of Difference?," *Journal of Health Economics* 20: 1–21.

Smith, M. P., and Nock, S. L. (1980), "Social Class and the Quality of Life in Public and Private Organizations," *Journal of Social Issues* 36: 59–75.

TAN, J. (2002), "Impact of Ownership Type on Environment-Strategy Linkage and Performance: Evidence from a Transitional Economy," *Journal of Management Studies* 39: 333–54.

TULLOCK, G., SELDON, A., and BRADY, G. L. (2002), *Government Failure : A Primer in Public Choice*, Washington, DC: Cato Institute.

US Office of Personnel Management (2000), *Survey of Federal Employees*, Washington, DC: US Office of Personnel Management.

—— (2003), *The Federal Human Capital Survey*, Washington, DC: US Office of Personnel Management.

VILLALONGA, B. (2000), "Privatization and Efficiency: Differentiating Ownership Effects from Political, Organizational, and Dynamic Effects," *Journal of Economic Behavior and Organization* 42: 43–74.

WAMSLEY, G. L., and ZALD, M. N. (1973), *The Political Economy of Public Organizations*. Lexington, Mass.: Heath.

WARWICK, D. P. (1975), *A Theory of Public Bureaucracy*, Cambridge, MA: Harvard University Press.

WILLIAMSON, O. E. (1999), "Public and Private Bureaucracies: A Transaction Cost Economics Perspective," *Journal of Law, Economics, and Organization* 15: 306–42.

WILSON, J. Q. (1989), *Bureaucracy*, New York: Basic Books.

WISE, L. R. (1999), "The Use of Innovative Practices in the Public and Private Sectors: The Role of Organizational and Individual Factors," *Public Productivity and Management Review* 23: 150–68.

CHAPTER 5

PUBLIC MANAGEMENT, DEMOCRACY, AND POLITICS

LINDA DELEON

OVER recent decades and in many nations, the level of citizen trust and support for government has been declining (Behn 1995, 1998; Fukuyama 1995; Ruscio 1996). In the United States, the proportion of Americans who reply that they "trust the government in Washington to do the right thing" some or most of the time has fallen steadily from 70 percent in 1966, to 25 percent in 1992 (Putnam 1995), and to only 15 percent in 1995 (Nye, Zelikow, and King 1997). Public confidence in government has also declined in Canada (Zussman 1997), some European countries (OECD 2001; Pollitt and Bouckaert 2000), New Zealand (Barnes and Gill 2000) and other nations.

Over the same period, a wave of ongoing governmental reform has washed over much of the developed world (Kettl 2000; Kickert 1997; Pollitt and Bouckaert 2000). While improving public trust is not the most direct nor the only vector in the force field of pressures for reform (constraints on resources, as well as pure dissatisfaction with government-provided services are surely others), the goal of maintaining or improving support for government is a potential benefit of such initiatives (Olsen and Peters 1996). As Newman points out, "the adoption of new ideas may be undertaken as much to win external legitimacy as to achieve performance gains" (Newman 2001: 27).

In fact, the contemporary reform agenda does offer two different and often competing prescriptions. One set of reforms aims at improving public goods and services—providing them more plentifully and efficiently and delivering them with promptness and courtesy (Behn 2002; Vigoda 2003). Examples of these include managerialism, "reinvented government" (Osborne and Gaebler 1992) and New Public Management (NPM), which propose increased autonomy for managers ("letting managers manage"), accountability for results ("making managers manage"), entrepreneurial management, and a variety of market mechanisms such as privatization, contracting out, and competition. Although the evidence is not clear that satisfaction with services directly and significantly improves trust, these reforms are often justified as doing so. In the words of US Vice President Gore (1997: ix), "How can people trust government to do big things if we can't do little things like answer the telephone promptly and politely?"

Other reforms, directed more at mistrust than dissatisfaction, target a source that their proponents believe is different and perhaps deeper. In this view citizens are alienated from a government that treats them as customers but holds them at arm's length. In order to build support for government, citizens must be brought into closer relationship with it, through participative institutions such as citizen advisory boards, participatory policy analysis, and a variety of forums for direct and deliberative democracy. Reformers who follow this line of reasoning are vociferous critics of NPM, alleging that NPM reforms weaken democratic institutions, in that citizens should be not merely passive customers but actively engaged in governance. They further argue that entrepreneurship is often associated with rule-bending or rule-breaking and that markets can produce equilibria but not the public interest (Bellone and Goerl 1992; L. deLeon and Denhardt 2000; Moe 1994; Ruscio 1996; Terry 1993). And, from another corner of the professional landscape, policy scholars have taken aim at both formulation and implementation processes, arguing that the policy sciences have become elitist, serving the politically powerful and the technocrats in their direct or indirect employment (P. deLeon 1990; Durning 1993; Fischer 1990).

Contemporary public management includes initiatives that pursue each of the avenues described above. Reforms centered on producing more and better public services include those that aim to tighten and streamline the management of public bureaucracies, those that increase competition in order to offer citizens more choices, and those that center on increasing citizen participation in political and administrative processes. Other reforms attempt to empower workers in the hope of making them more creative and productive. Superficially, it may seem paradoxical that each vision of how to improve public management claims that it preserves and enhances democracy and improves governmental effectiveness. The sections that follow—after a few disclaimers concerning the scope of what this chapter will address—first discuss three very different answers to the question of how public management can be both effective and democratic. Next, the research literature on several mechanisms for making public management more democratic is reviewed. And finally, a separate discussion briefly treats the question of how to make the internal workings of public organizations more democratic.

5.1 A Few Preliminaries and Limitations

The subject of the relationship between politics and administration has inspired an enormous, multifaceted corpus of literature, such that this chapter needs to set boundaries. In the discussion that follows, public management is construed rather broadly to encompass both the contemporary extent of the field and also the neighboring and overlapping disciplines of public administration and public policy. The focus remains fairly narrowly on the executive or administrative branch of government, however, rather than including legislatures, courts, or the electoral process.

Insofar as possible, the discussion will address international public management, though the literature in the United States and other Anglophone countries was more accessible to this author than that covering other European countries and the rest of the world. Nevertheless, an attempt was made to explore at least the English-language literature on the latter. And, although the nature of and possibilities for democracy vary by level of government (national versus local), for the most part this chapter treats issues at a fairly general and theoretical level. How these issues would differ for local or small governments remains a question for further research.

Finally, this chapter recognizes that democracies vary not only with respect to their political processes but also with regard to their administrative cultures. Contemporary public management theorists (Derlien 1995; Konig 1997; Mathiasen 1999; Pollitt and Bouckaert 2000) distinguish "public interest" from Rechtsstaat systems. The former include the Anglophone countries, the latter includes at least France and Germany, and there are exceptions or hybrids (the Netherlands, Finland, and Sweden are often mentioned). Rechtsstaat systems separate politics from administration more strictly than do public interest systems, and they take a perspective that is more legalistic managerial (Konig 1997). The implications for the discussion that follows is that some parts of it—notably the discussion of citizen participation—may not be as clearly relevant to Rechtsstaat systems as to public interest ones.

5.2 Democracy and Management

The reason that every reform initiative can be defended as one that "strengthens democracy" lies in the fact that democracy has varied definitions and many forms. Democracy, said Aristotle (who didn't much like it), is "rule of the poor in their own interests" (Aristotle 1987). Held (1996) uses the more literal "rule by the people," noting the many possible meanings of "rule," "rule by," and "people." Public administration theorist Carl Friedrich (1935: 37) called it "action in accordance with popular preferences," a formulation that supports representative government but not necessarily widespread political participation, while Peter deLeon (1997) uses Cohen's definition of democracy as "that system of community government in which . . . the members of a community participate, or may participate, directly or indirectly, in the making of decisions that affect them" (1971: 7). The common thread in these formulations is that the will of "the people" should be the basis for government and that citizens should have some means of influencing the public policies that shape their lives.

But under the broad umbrella of any definition are crowded many competing visions of the way democracy should work. Kakabadse, Kakabadse, and Kouzmin (2003) contrast liberal democracy, where society is simply a collection of individuals who are completely free to pursue their own unfettered self-interest, with constitutional democracy, in which certain kinds of decisions are taken off the table by their inclusion in a founding document that has deliberately been made difficult to change. In addition to the limitations on individual freedom imposed by a constitution, other limitations stem from a choice (in large systems, often viewed as necessity) to create representative structures, in which popular will is aggregated and articulated through institutionalized channels (elected executives, legislatures and courts) and attendant informal ones (political parties and interest groups).

The focus here is on the implications of democratic theory for the relationship between public management and the political system. In part, this can be formulated as the problem of the legitimacy of public management: what right have managers to make decisions and take action? Democracy entails that the basic source of all legitimate power is the citizenry, so a theory of democratic administration must show a connection between managerial activity and public preferences. Public management is, fundamentally, the coordination of activities that implement public policy, and the contemporary governance literature categorizes alternative strategies for coordination as hierarchies, markets, and networks (Newman 2001). Each of these is not only a strategy for coordinating administrative activity, it is also a strategy by which the managerial system can be coordinated with the political system. In other words, while some theorists see a hierarchical relationship between public managers and their political superiors as the best way to preserve and enhance democracy, others advocate market-based management, and still others favor networks—participative and with multiple sources of power—as the best method of achieving true democracy.

5.2.1 "Overhead" Democracy, Administrative Hierarchy

In a nutshell, the traditional answer to making public management both efficient and democratic centered on direct service provision through bureaucratic organizational structures that were directed by and accountable to elected representatives of the people. This relationship between representative democracy in the political system and hierarchical control in the administrative system has been termed "overhead democracy" by Redford (1969) and "competitive elitist democracy" by Held (1996). In this model, sovereign power flows via the vote (in partisan electoral contests) from citizens to their representatives and thence to the appointed heads of administrative departments. Strict supervision and the other accoutrements of Weberian bureaucracy maintain accountability and responsiveness. (Of course, the American administrative theorists upon whose work Redford built, rooted their ideas in observations of European systems: Bovens 1998.) Redford believed that this system was unequivocally democratic. Acknowledging that discretion is necessary because "law is rigid and policy must be made pragmatically" (1958: 43), Redford argued that constraining discretion in order to direct it toward the public interest—as opposed to the narrow concerns of an interest group or bureau—necessitates close supervision. Therefore authoritative control of subordinates is not anti-democratic, but the opposite (Bertelli and L. Lynn 2003).

The managerialist alternatives in modern administrative reform movements are based in the same sort of logic. Focusing on results, delivering "things citizens value" (Barzelay 1992), and remaining highly responsive to direction from elected officials are characteristics of the bureaucratic model of administrative organization. Although bureaucracy and hierarchy have received a battering in contemporary organization theory, they are not without their defenders (Jaques 1990; Du Gay, 2000; Kaufman 2001). Leman (1989) makes the case that direct government—service provision done directly by government agencies—is efficient, effective, responsive, and innovative. Not only are hierarchical organizations very effective for some kinds of tasks, they also not uncommonly call forth a service ideal and place a premium on sacrificial personal discipline that comports with public-interested idealism. Military and law enforcement personnel are obvious examples, but many employees in social welfare organizations express similar service ideals as well (Balfour and Wechsler 1990).

While a bureaucracy accountable to elected representatives may promise both efficient service provision and popular control of policy, it is also subject to a variety of well-remarked pathologies. For example, are bureaucracies really efficient? Some observers (Behn 1995, 2002; Jones 1992; Pollitt 1996) contend that demands for democratic accountability, ironically, create the red tape that obstructs results. And even where highly structured organizations are optimal for service provision, the democratic question remains whether the policies they are implementing are actually "ruling the poor in their own interests" or in the interests of economic, political or managerial elites (P. deLeon 1992; 1995; Dryzek 1996; Phillips 2002). A strong administrative system can be oppressive, unresponsive and self-serving.

5.2.2 Markets as Democracy

Markets represent another theoretical approach to the problem of combining effective and efficient service provision with democracy. Market competition forces producers to be efficient. Markets are democratic because they respond to consumer demand and are no respecters of persons. By offering choices to citizens, market-based public management reforms preserve and enhance democracy.

There are several ways in which choices can be made available: through competition among sectors or public agencies for citizen patronage, through competition in the political arena for votes, or through the development of a "heterogeneous mix of public goods and services in a public service economy" (Ostrom 1973: 74). The NPM movement makes extensive use of competition—inter-sectoral, or even among agencies of government— as a strategy for improving public management (Gruening 2001). During the 1980s and 1990s, for example, the UK saw the introduction of market mechanisms such as privatization, contracting-out, quasi-markets, and quangos (Newman 2001). Market-based public management reforms have been justified primarily on the ground of making government services less costly or of better quality (Gruening 2001; Mathiasen 1999; Mintrom 2003; Zifcak 2000). But Behn (2002), for example, also suggests that market-based reforms have the potential not only to boost government performance, but also to improve, at least marginally, citizen trust in government.

In cases where competition allows citizens to choose whether to obtain fee-based services from one agency or another (an example would be municipal golf courses), or from private-versus public-sector sources, citizens participate in a market where the currency is literally money. Another way that citizens can make choices, however, is through the political process. The pluralistic model of democracy (Held 1996) introduces institutions such as interest groups that mediate between citizens and political elites. Power in such systems is shared, not hierarchical, and is the subject of endless bargaining. In the "competitive market" of electoral politics, the currency is votes.

Numerous strategies have been proposed as ways to increase the effectiveness of political competition as a means of infusing citizen preferences into policy and administration. In this line of thinking, citizens are empowered when they are able to choose their political representatives. For over fifty years, American political scientists have pointed to the Westminster system as one well designed to produce a responsive administration (APSA 1950), lauding the more disciplined and ideological British parties for presenting voters with clearer policy alternatives than do American ones. Recent work indicates that this idea retains perennial appeal (Green and Herrnson 2003) as a way to improve the effectiveness and responsiveness of overhead democracy.

In an influential book published in 1973, Vincent Ostrom proposed that an intellectual crisis in public administration was the result of an attempt to fuse two incompatible theories, which he labeled "bureaucratic administration" and "democratic administration." His foundation is the premise that pluralist systems are polycentric, fragmenting government authority in order that each center counterbalances the others, protecting against domination by any one of them. Political economists, he argues, see the question in a slightly different but analogous way. Recognizing that public agencies generally do not have the discipline of the market where a consumer is free to choose among alternatives, they nevertheless can engage in "a relatively constrained but open rivalry" (Ostrom 1973: 20). By offering a heterogeneous mix of public goods and services, local jurisdictions can offer citizens the possibility to "vote with their feet"—to choose where they live based on the market basket of public goods and services offered there:

A variety of different organizational arrangements can be used to provide different public goods and services. Such organizations can be coordinated through various multi-organizational arrangements including trading and contracting to mutual advantage, competitive rivalry, [and] adjudication ... By contrast, hierarchical ordering of the public service would reduce the capacity of a large administrative system to respond to diverse preferences among citizens for many different public goods and services. (Ostrom 1973: 112)

The fragmentation of a unitary system into a polycentric one, in which the power of each jurisdiction is limited vis-à-vis the others, should therefore not be viewed as "Balkanization" but rather a means of offering choices. As an important additional benefit, competitive rivalry among public agencies "may offer an alternative approach to the realization of efficiency in government" (Ostrom 1973: 122).

Ostrom does not suggest that democratic administration drives out the bureaucratic alternative, but rather that each has its place (each level of government—national, regional or local—takes on the economically appropriate functions). Interestingly, Ostrom's exegesis on the idea of a democratic administration leads him to the conclusion that the public manager in a democratic society, while respectful of the authority of government officials, is not a neutral and obedient servant to the master's command. The public manager's service is to individual citizens as consumers of public goods and services, and while respectful of authority, she or he acknowledges a responsibility to refuse to exploit the common wealth of the state or to impair the rights of persons (Ostrom 1973: 131).

Critics of market-based democracy argue that it has its own downside. Lane (2000) says the subjective well-being of citizens is not a function of income but of companionship and that materialism and choice are insufficient to produce happiness. A major challenge to NPM reforms arises from this perspective. Various critics have attacked market-based, entrepreneurial, or competitive reforms by suggesting that, fundamentally, the clamor of individual self-interests cannot result in good for everyone. In competition, there are winners and losers, and to say that the "majority rules" does not preclude that the majority may tyrannize the minority. According to one highly critical analysis, liberal democracy in the US, in its current state, favors "self-interested groups over wisdom, deviation over tolerance, short-term gain over spirituality, [and] fierce economic competition over collaboration" (Kakabadse, Kakabadse and Kouzmin 2003: 48).

One of the chief challenges to the validity of markets—economic or political—as a means to enhance democracy asserts that they give disproportionate influence to those with greater wealth. Market-based reforms may mean greater competition among service vendors (public, or a combination of public, private, and non-profit), which would exert pressure on vendors to perform efficiently and to provide good service. Putting services on the market, however, also implies that those without the resources to pay for them would be left out. Furthermore, the dynamics of markets include the drive on the part of participants to escape the rigors of competition by colluding, restricting the flow of information, and pressing for special protections; those with greater wealth or power can use such means to gain disproportionate advantage.

Where the market is in votes, not currency, political equality can fall victim to the distortions of wealth. As Held (1996: 308) writes, "One of liberalism's central weaknesses is to see markets as 'powerless' mechanisms of coordination and, thus, to neglect . . . the distorting nature of economic power in relation to democracy." Without sufficient resources, individuals or groups do not have access to political officials, to media outlets, or to any of the other critical levers of political power. Other defects of malfunctioning representative systems can include political corruption, entrenched interest groups, compromised legislators, blocked access to media channels, lack of transparency, or an over-reliance on technical expertise (Box et al. 2001; Vigoda 2003).

5.2.3 Networks: Participative Democracy

Networks have received sustained attention in modern organization theory and in the public management literature as well. Since society is seen as increasingly diverse, complex, and fragmented, many theorists suggest that governance cannot be accomplished by any single institution—not even the state—but necessarily requires the coordination of public, private, and non-profit sectors. What once was the preserve of government is now the function of highly complex networks of organizations. Coordination in networks is not hierarchical but based on equality and participation (Chisholm 1989). Theorists in the Netherlands and Scandinavia see government as only one kind of actor in a field containing many other institutions with some degree of autonomy (Newman 2001; Klign and Koppenjan 2000).

Networks present yet another way of providing public management that is both effective and democratic. Effectiveness is enhanced by the collaboration of partners that each bring resources and perspectives necessary to the task. Democracy is preserved because the multiple nodes of the network assure many points of access to the governance system for both organizations and individual citizens. Variants of the participatory model of democracy include those of the "New Right" and the "New Left" (Held 1996). The former is characterized by very limited government, leaving a larger sphere of non-governmental activity open to participation by private individuals. The latter involves direct citizen participation in some cases but does not rule out restricting individual participation at the national level, in favor of representative institutions. Klijn and Koppenjan (2000) propose yet another model, which they call "interactive decision making." Based on a "substantive" (as opposed to "instrumental") democratic tradition, it posits an active role for citizens, participating from the earliest stages of developing the policy agenda all the way through implementation, and a facilitative role for politicians.

In addition to the attention to increasing participation in the governance process by involving non-governmental organizations, the public management literature also addresses the matter of direct citizen participation in policy and management. Motives for advocating increased citizen participation stem from both the critique of the bureaucracy and the critique of representative politics, which have been described above. Critics of the bureaucracy argue that it is inaccessible to citizens and unresponsive to their needs; critics of representative politics argue that it disenfranchises many citizens, caters to elites, and may be corrupt. Under these conditions, reforms that increase citizen influence and direct participation are seen both as a way to increase confidence in and support for government (both elected and administrative) and as a necessary corrective to systemic malfunctions.

Mansbridge (1997), for example, posited that citizens' trust in government would increase were they to have a role in making the complex trade-offs required by policy choices. Introducing a recent symposium on New Public Management worldwide, Vigoda (2003) contrasts "responsive" and "collaborative" public administration. The former puts citizens-as-clients at the center of NPM, which tries to ascertain their needs (through surveys, public hearings, and so on) but keeps them at a distance from administrative work in order to serve neutrality, expertise, and efficiency. Collaborative public administration "may be defined as reform in progress" aimed at promoting trust in government: a collaborative public management would be "more willing to share ideas, knowledge and power with others, not merely instruct citizens and patronize them" (Vigoda 2003: 885).[1]

By contrast, direct and deliberative democratic institutions can build community out of individuality, shared values out of diversity, consensus out of partisanship. In the process of debating public issues, individuals can forge a sense of community as they talk through their differences. In addition, a sense of community and norms of reciprocity will constrain disorderly and fractious impulses (Bellah et al. 1985; Dryzek 1990; Gutmann and Thompson 1996). The abundant literature on social capital supports and extends this idea (Putnam 2000, 2002).

Participative processes have their own pathologies, however. They are subject to some of the same problems as representative ones, in that inequalities of wealth—independent of, or combined with, inequalities of social status—can distort the version of the public interest that results from their workings. Lynn (2002: 448) lists a variety of other "vexing issues" arising from direct participation:

Among them are the destructive consequences of rent seeking, ambition, ignorance, avarice, ideology, narcissism, and prejudice...Economists will adduce collective action problems, opportunism, conflicts of interest, and information asymmetries...

In addition, participative institutions—both those that involve direct participation by citizens and those that link organizations in networks—present difficult issues of accountability. To the extent that networks are egalitarian and cooperative, not coercive, they are what political theorists call "anarchies," of which the defining characteristics are, first, that there is no specialization of political roles (that is, no one is the leader all the time) and, second, there is no enforcement of collective decisions (participants are free to join or withdraw from the arena as they wish (Taylor 1982)). In such cases, accountability is diffused—the collective as a whole is the responsible party—and, in a sense, accountability by all means accountability by none. Alternatively, the only means of ensuring accountability is constant, consistent participation: absent enforcement of collective decisions, players must stay at the table to protect their own interests (L. deLeon 1994).

5.3 DEMOCRATIZING PUBLIC MANAGEMENT

Both the contemporary literature of public management and its related disciplines of public administration and public policy contain extensive research on a variety of means by which the practice of public management can be democratized. This section provides a brief overview of a few of them.

5.3.1 Representative Bureaucracy

Where the political system does not function effectively to represent the will of the people (a charge against both overhead democracy and pluralist democracy), another means of achieving representativeness may be provided by the bureaucracy itself. A representative bureaucracy is one in which the workforce reflects the composition of the citizenry with respect to such qualities as class, gender, race, and ethnicity.[2] A representative bureaucracy "symbolizes as well as promotes equal opportunity and equality" (Dolan and Rosenbloom 2003: 6); it is often preferred by clients (Thielemann and Stewart 1996). More importantly, it should result in policy that serves the public interest.

As Meier and Nigro (1976) have argued, however, the effectiveness of representative bureaucracy involves a four-variable causal chain: social origin dictates socialization experiences, which shape attitudes, which motivate behaviors. Challenging this theory, they cite evidence that people from different social backgrounds can have similar socializing experiences (Barber 1970), that organizations are powerful socializers (Baldwin 1968; Janowitz 1960; Kaufman 1960), and that attitudes may be slightly or not related to actions (Wicker 1969).

Research on the linkages among variables in the theory of representative bureaucracy finds mixed results, but contingency theories show promise. For example, Thompson (1976) suggests key conditions under which passive representation turns active: when minority officials deal with issues that clearly will affect persons of their race, when minorities work in close proximity to each other, and when minority officials occupy jobs that have discretion. Recently, Meier and Bohte (2001) reinforce this last proposition in a study of minority teachers. As predicted, when bureaucrats have policy discretion over an area directly linked to their values, they are likely to take concrete action on behalf of those values.

Interestingly, though, Selden, Brudney, and Kellough (1998) found that attitudes can be more important than status—even persons not from minority backgrounds may act on behalf of minority interests if they believe it is important to do so. Furthermore, in a discussion of comparative civil service systems, Van der Meer (1996) distinguishes demographic, opinion, and interest representativeness, suggesting that the opinions of under-represented groups may not necessarily reflect their more general or long-term interests. On the other hand, advocates of representative bureaucracy argue passionately that a "trustee" relationship is insufficient. Feminist theorists attack as deceptive the "long held view that men could represent women without the latter being physically present . . . by acting as a trustee for them" (Kelly 1998: 204). They point out that increasing representation of women in political and social life is related to the implementation of policy that promotes and preserves their interests (Guy 1992; Hale and Kelly 1989; Kelly and Guy 1991; Stivers 1993). As is so often true in social science, causality cannot be definitively established for this association. It seems plausible, however, that the presence of politically disadvantaged groups in the administrative apparatus (and, of course, in legislative bodies as well) does function to keep "their" issues on the agenda and, subtly, gives public managers' sense of responsibility a human face, the face of colleagues.

5.3.2 Proactive Administration

Overhead democracy suggests something akin to economists' notion of "trickle-down" effects, in which benefits bestowed on the rich and powerful eventually make their way down to less favored participants. But perhaps a trickle is not enough; critics who contend that public administration is elitist would prefer a "cascade" theory—citizen input should pour in from all directions—from inside and outside, from above and below. In this conceptualization, representative bureaucracy brings input from inside administration, overhead democracy brings it from above, and so-called iron triangles (Ripley and Franklin 1984) and issue networks (Heclo 1978) portray influence coming from the external environment of interest groups.

Another important source of democratizing influence, however, can come from "below," from the clients whom public agencies serve. One of the earliest explicit statements of this idea of proactive administration was put forward in a volume of essays (Marini 1971) arising from the Minnowbrook conference in New York, which kicked off a movement in the United States called the New Public Administration. Reacting against the increasingly professionalized (Mosher 1968; Mosher and Stillman 1977) civil service, with a workforce that over-represented the educated middle class compared to the impoverished and disproportionately minority underclass, these theorists (particularly Michael Harmon 1971) argued that authoritative decisions in a democracy should not be made only by legislators in the policy selection phase; rather they should be made, proactively, by administrators as well. Some twenty years later, the "Blacksburg Manifesto," which formed the basis for *Refounding Public Administration* (Wamsley et al. 1990), pursued the same notion, suggesting that "the popular will does not reside solely in elected officials but in a constitutional order that envisions a remarkable variety of legitimate titles to participation in governance," and that "Public Administration, created by statutes based on this constitutional order, holds one of these titles" (47).

5.3.3 "Street-level" Bureaucracy

As in the field of public administration, during the 1970s and 1980s a debate within policy implementation studies pitted those who preferred a top-down approach (Matland 1995; Sabatier 1986) —on the ground that elected officials are more likely to be representative of the population from which they are drawn than are bureaucrats—against those who took a bottom-up orientation. Scholars like Michael Lipsky (1980) focused on the activities and beliefs of "street-level bureaucrats"—front-line workers who interact directly with the clients of public agencies. Street-level bureaucrats, though not formally accountable to their clients and protected by civil service rules, unions and limited liability, may nevertheless have a better understanding of and dedication to client interests than do legislators. They are often, in fact, engaged with clients in the co-production of public services (education, law enforcement), so both parties have an interest in success (P. deLeon and L. deLeon 2002). And clients are not without resources to impose their demands on public servants:

Street-level bureaucrats...are also dependent upon clients. Clients have a stock of resources and thus can impose a variety of low-level costs. This is because street-level bureaucrats must obtain client compliance with their decisions, particularly when they are evaluated in terms of their clients' behavior or performance (Lipsky 1980: 57).

In some few cases, street-level bureaucrats may go so far as to exceed the limits of their administrative discretion. Maynard-Moody and Leland (2000) note that the research on the ways in which street-level workers deviate from formal policy suggests that they do so in order to make their work lives easier. Their own study of a variety of front-line bureaucrats, however, found that a sample of social-welfare professionals were sometimes more committed to client needs than to their agency or to government in general. Clearly, this stance runs counter the classic view of managerial responsibility or the prescription that administrators can "exercise autonomy from organizational or hierarchical imperatives only under certain circumstances and for certain "civic" reasons" (Pollitt 2003), such as whistle-blowing or resistance to actions that are wasteful of public resources.

5.3.4 Administrative Responsiveness and Responsibility

Less radical than theories of proactive administration, but consonant with the Blacksburg Manifesto's call for a fuller appreciation of the positive role of authority in administration, is the development of theories of administrative responsibility. Responsibility and its cousin, responsiveness, are processes by which citizens' choices, as conveyed via the electoral system, are converted into administrative practice. Responsiveness, as suggested in the preceding section, requires that public managers conform to law and policy. But the intent of law may be ambiguous or incomplete. In this situation, "managerial responsibility" (Bertelli and L. Lynn 2003) requires the manager to follow laws, rules, and policies created by the legislative branch. This obedience must also, however, be moderated by four elements: judgment as to what the public interest and professionalism require; accountability to law and rules, recognizing that these may emanate from divergent sources; balance, an attempt to take into account contending interests expressed through many and various channels; and rationality, or judgment that is both reasonable and realistic. Bertelli and Lynn insist that responsibility is both a requirement and a right: "However much courts, legislatures and interest groups may wish it to be otherwise, fulfilling legislative mandates in conformity with both individual and collective justice requires principled deference to public managers, who bear the primary burden of administration" (265).

In an intriguing analysis of responsibility, Bovens (1998) suggests that the older conception of hierarchical responsibility – in which individuals were expected to be strictly obedient to superiors, has given way to a view that managers should also be loyal to peers, their professions, and citizens. Situations in which loyalty to the organization (or, by extension, its political controllers) are in conflict require choices between loyalty, voice and exit (Hirschman 1980). Each of the alternative conceptions of responsibility has less legitimacy than the older notion, and thus public employees must be skillful in balancing their organizational citizenship with their role as citizens of a political community. Because modern notions of proper loyalty and obedience are so fluid, the quest for responsibility, Bovens suggests, will never end.

5.3.5 Citizen Participation

The literature on citizen participation is extensive in both time spanned and quantity. With roots in political science, it investigates questions such as the relationship between participation and the sense of political efficacy, the socio-economic correlates of participation, and the spillover among political, social, and economic participation (Berry, Portnoy, and Thomson 1993).

There are many ways of involving the public in public management. Pollitt (2003) uses a tripartite classification that ranges from informing them, to consulting them, to allowing them full two-way and iterative participation. He also describes "market" and "forum" models; participation is more intensive (along the scale described above) and also more extensive (from participation by individuals to participation by collectivities) in the latter. Moynihan (2003) offers a very similar typology and then asks why, when participation seems to be such a good idea, is there so little of it? His answer reflects a concern that is very widespread among theorists, elected officials, public managers, and even citizens: participation is time-consuming and frustrating and may not even produce better outcomes than decision making by professionals. Other concerns are that democratic activities absorb resources that could be better spent on needed services or that democratic initiatives sometimes backfire—in an effort to secure the participation of socially excluded groups, they in effect discriminate against access by other, established groups (Lowndes, Pratchett, and Stoker 2001). An interesting approach is the contingency theory proposed by Thomas (1995), suggesting that successful outcomes are more likely when participative mechanisms (public hearings, consultation, etc.) are appropriately matched to a variety of decisional and situational conditions.

One way to reduce the costs of participation is to use technology. A number of case studies, drawn from various nations, describe the use of email, websites, networked laptops, and wireless keyboard pads, among other things, to make citizen input easier to obtain and manage, or to provide information to citizens in support of their involvement in decision making (Chen, Huang, and Nsaio 2003; Kakabadse, Kakabadse, and Kouzmin 2003; La Porte, Demchak, and de Jong 2003; Moynihan 2003). Drawing conclusions from a worldwide survey of government websites, La Porte, Demchak, and deJong note that government websites can be justified either on the ground that they increase product efficiency (service provision) or that they increase civic participation, or both. "Hence, the use of the Web is likely to rise irrespective of the philosophical choices and is likely to be included in commonly accepted definitions of democracy" (2003: 437).

Finally, several observers note that the public management literature places undue emphasis on political participation. Social and economic participation are also important avenues by which citizens can achieve public outcomes that meet their needs. Nonprofit or nongovernmental organizations (NGOs) as well as informal clubs and associations, exemplify the former, while private sector activity exemplifies the latter. Lam (2003) makes this argument in the context of Hong Kong: participation may take the form of demonstrations and social movements that favor or protest government activity. Hong Kong residents have a reputation as politically apathetic, but in fact they are quite expressive, if this broader definition of participation is used.

5.4 DEMOCRACY WITHIN PUBLIC ORGANIZATIONS

The preceding sections have focused on the relationship between public management and the political systems by which policy is made and implemented. Several lines of research and theory address the separate question whether public agencies themselves should be run democratically. In Dwight Waldo's famous question, is "autocracy at work" really the necessary price for "democracy after hours" (Waldo 1984: 75). Denhardt (1993) is unequivocal in asserting that public organizations in a democracy must themselves be exemplars of workplace democracy: "Democratic outcomes require democratic processes" (1993: vii). As in a hologram, the democratic nature of the larger system should be repeated in its subunits.

The justification for a democracy within public organizations, like that for public management's relation to the polity and civil society, takes two forms, one arguing from grounds of efficiency and the other from the premise that it helps to build social capital. The argument from efficiency is very well known; its major conclusions are that the persons or groups involved in making a decision are more likely to support it, that diverse input into decisions results in better ones, and that the workers closest to the front lines know best how work should be done.

The second argument holds that workplace democracy develops skills for citizenship (Pateman 1970), such as collaboration and conflict management. As they interact, citizens and public servants take account of each others' wishes and needs, and they become more open to the influence of others. In this way, they arrive at shared values and mutually agreeable actions. It also develops desirable traits in individual citizens and employees, such as a regard for the general interest, a sense of personal efficacy, and a sense of community. Democracy "does not suffer bureaucracy gladly" (Thompson 1983). Values essential to democracy, such as equality, participation, and individual rights, are incompatible with hierarchy, specialization, and impersonality. Employees within the organization may also have opinions and demands to make of management. These impulses toward employee participation stem from various roots (sometimes from the idea that democracy equals participation, sometimes from the view that workers should be empowered in their struggle with capital) and include a wide variety of forms, such as TQM, quality circles, through self-managing work teams, all the way to genuine, all-out workplace democracy. Denhardt quotes Waldo's "plaintive" call for a "working world in which all participate as both 'leaders' and 'followers' according to 'rules of the game' known to all" (Waldo 1952:103, cited in Denhardt 1993: 78).

Feldman and Khademian (2001) make the argument that "managing for inclusion" (of employees in decision processes in public organizations) is a way to solve the democratic problem of the tension between participation and control. The traditional bureaucratic model, which they call "managing for process," was characterized by centralized authority and close supervision to rules and regulations. A newer model, much-touted in NPM, manages for results. Control over process, in this model, is decentralized, but there is centralized control (accountability) for results. Both models are ineffective, however, because in a complex world, process does not always produce anticipated results, and therefore specifying either process or results may be dysfunctional. Managing for inclusion places its faith in the ability of a fully empowered workforce to use teamwork to go after continuous improvement. Managers therefore must let go of control of process or results, focusing instead on building the capacity of both workers and the public to participate in the policy process. "They exert authority and control through the way they implement participation" (Feldman and Khademian 2001: 155).

Theorists of democracy in the workplace do acknowledge that citizen and worker empowerment present problems for traditional notions of accountability and responsibility. In discussing Harmon (1971), Denhardt (1993) concludes that traditional mechanisms of accountability must be followed in most cases. But he also cites approvingly Harmon's argument that the value of human action is found in the action *per se*, rather than exclusively in the results obtained by the action. Another way of expressing this idea is that policy is the outcome of process—we are what we do. Justice and freedom as substantive outcomes can therefore be produced only when the processes for decision making are themselves just and free.

Furthermore, asking managers to let go of control opens up the possibility of allowing for the untoward outcomes that older models ("managing for process" or "managing for results") are designed to prevent. Feldman and Khademian (2001) argue that abuse and corruption resulted in the older models, too, with the added disadvantage that so much red tape was used to patch the system that action was often stalemated. They conclude that "Employees and management must be held to high standards and must both be able to account for their behavior" (164).

Democratizing the workplace can take various forms, on a continuum of increasing empowerment. Participative decision making (PDM) refers to processes that involve workers in the management of organizations, while workplace democracy, industrial democracy, and the like are terms for organizations in which all employees share management responsibility. In between these poles are phenomena like self-directed work teams, where empowered teams may manage their own work but within the framework of a hierarchical organization (Yeatts and Hyten 1998).

5.4.1 Participative Decision Making

PDM refers to the involvement of employees in decisions that are normally the prerogative of management (Parnell and Bell 1994). It is not organizational democracy. By analogy with Barber (1984), it is "weak democracy" in that it filters input either through managers and supervisors or through worker representatives to management councils. Kearney and Hays (1994: 50) write that "By fostering a new cooperative spirit between public management and public employees, organizational democracy becomes a natural extension of dominant societal values, and represents a promising new chapter in the American democratic experience." Employee participation schemes vary by nation: American versions are highly individual, emphasizing empowerment of individual managers and employees, while European ones tend to represent workers through unions (Sagie and Koslowsky 2000). In both cases, advocates of PDM proclaim its benefits for both productivity and worker satisfaction.

Research on PDM dates back to the 1950s. There have been four reviews of the literature on PDM over the past twenty years (Cotton et al. 1988; Locke and Schweiger 1979; Miller and Monge 1986; Wagner and Gooding 1987). Locke et al. (1979) concluded that few inferences could be made about the effects of participation, because too many other variables (employee motivation, task, group, and leader attributes) could account for those effects. Their major finding was that the literature until that date seemed to show that participative leadership did not increase productivity but did lead to higher worker satisfaction. Miller and Monge (1986) criticized Locke's methods. Their meta-analysis concluded that participation does affect both satisfaction and productivity, and that specific organization factors have important effects. For example, a participative organizational climate has more effect than occasional participation in specific decisions.

Recent studies have begun to explore the effects of various forms of PDM on organizational performance. Such forms include informal versus formal participation, employee ownership, decisions on goals, and representative participation (Cotton et al. 1988). The evidence suggests that PDM has a number of positive outcomes in organizations, most of the time. PDM enhances employee job satisfaction and individual performance and, through reducing absenteeism and turnover and improving the flow of information, improves organizational effectiveness (Kearney and Hays 1994; Kim 2002). However, clear productivity or efficiency gains show up in only about half the cases (Kearney and Hays 1994; Sagie and Koslowsky 2000).

5.4.2 Workplace Democracy

In the 1950s, Yugoslavia broke away from the Stalinistic model of central planning and developed an economy-wide system of worker self-management. Lynn et al., describe the demise of this great experiment in empowerment, which, over time, degenerated into a "state-supported neo-Taylorism with a 'thinking tank' and a 'working tank,'... which represented little real empowerment" (M. Lynn, Mulej, and Jurse 2002: 797). Contemporary discussions include those by Krimerman (1992), Pencavel (2001), and Lichenstein (1993). Whitty (1996) discusses co-management as a natural evolution beyond self-directed work teams to employees' full participation at all levels of the firm. The key element of co-management is shared decision making, which can take the form of employee ownership, employee or union representation on governing boards, or inclusion of employees on all internal management bodies. Although there are virtually no examples of workplace democracy in government agencies, and few in the private sector, nevertheless advocates believe that workplace democracy offers the "only viable and sustainable strategy for transcending the divergence of interests between capital and labor" (Wisman 1997: 1388).

5.5 SUMMARY AND CONCLUSION

This chapter posits that democracy is more than a set of principles or procedures set down in a constitution. It is not lip service to an ideal, but the living of it, that realizes what Morone (1990) called "the democratic wish." In administration, as in politics, democracy requires constant defense, whether against the ossifying forces of bureaucratization, the machinations of special interests or the tyranny of the majority.

In the course of this discussion, several of the "big questions" concerning public management, democracy, and politics have been addressed. One asks "How can citizen demands for efficient and effective government be balanced against the requirements of democracy?" Three basic answers were offered: through an efficient bureaucracy responsive to elected representatives, through markets that enforce efficiency and offer a wide range of choices from which citizens may select freely, or through networks that allow participation by a variety of organizations and access by individual citizens.

A second big question asks, "Is 'autocracy at work' the price of 'democracy after hours,' that is, should public organizations themselves be run as democracies?" The immediately preceding section reviewed some positive responses—participative decision making and workplace democracy—although the comparative rarity of these structures suggests that the answer to this question is still, generally, "No."

A third big question asks, "Is administration generic, or is there a subspecies of 'democratic' administration?" Denhardt (1993) argues the case for a specifically democratic administration and notes a number of early theorists—such as Levitan (1943), Follett (Metcalf and Urwick 1940), and Waldo (1948)—who argued that democracy should infuse administrative organizations as well as their political environment. Some theorists, notably those who take the first position described above (that the primary goal of administration is the efficient and effective production of government services) consider democracy to be an attribute of the political system, while administration is generic to all political regimes. Others argue that a democratic politics requires a characteristically democratic administration. The thrust of this chapter, taken as a whole, is that administration in democratic political systems must give attention to a range of issues that authoritarian ones are not concerned to address.

This overview of the relationship between democracy and public management may suggest a contingency theory. Direct democracy may be easier to achieve in systems small enough to permit ready communication; it may be easier where there is consensus on shared values; or it may be easier where there is a high level of interpersonal trust and trust in government. Another factor may be the sophistication and penetration of information technology (Kakabadse, Kakabadse, and Kouzmin 2003), which makes poll-taking or even many-to-many communication much faster and cheaper than it has been in the past. An opposing point of view is also plausible, however. Large, complex, diverse polities may actually need infusions of direct democracy in order to build the consensus and trust they require in order for representative democracy—admittedly more "efficient"—to function effectively.

In either case, and this is the bottom line of this argument, it remains true that more democracy is better than less, and more participation is better than less. The default option should be to provide opportunities for participation, to the extent desired and unless other considerations render it impractical. This guideline implies risks, namely, the pathologies associated with participation. The greater risk, however, lies in making it easy for governments or powerful elites to justify restrictions on information, on civil rights, or on access to the levers of power. Kariel (1966) suggested that the criterion for deciding how much democracy is the right amount should be "How much can the system bear without disintegrating?" Obviously public management is tasked with implementing public policy and delivering government services as effectively and efficiently as possible. Equally apparent is its opportunity and obligation to contribute to collaboration among citizens, public managers, and elected officials.

What managerialism and NPM bring to the table is valuable, despite their critics' concerns. Yet the criticism has value too and should not be dismissed. As with the great balancing act that weighs political freedom in one scale against social order in the other, public management cannot escape the need to weigh two essential and, to some extent, competing values. A public management worthy of trust must produce outcomes that are both efficient *and* democratic.

NOTES

1. If citizens speak, however, will administrators be willing to listen? Alkadry (2003) found that both bureaucratic structures and individual administrators' lack of confidence in citizens' expertise on policy issues predispose them to discount citizen input.
2. A number of studies find that US bureaucracies are increasingly representative with respect to gender and ethnicity, though some groups are under-represented (G. B. Lewis 1988; W. G. Lewis 1989). Evidence from other nations suggests that bureaucracies typically under-represent ethnic minorities, women, and the economically disadvantaged (Kingsley 1944; Krislov 1974; Krislov and Rosenbloom 1981; Heady 2001; Haque 2003).

References

ALKADRY, M. G. (2003), "Deliberative Discourse between Citizens and Administrators: If Citizens Talk, Will Administrators Listen?" *Administration & Society* 35: 184–209.

American Political Science Association, Committee on Political Parties (1950), "Toward a More Responsible Two-Party System." *American Political Science Review* 44(3).

ARISTOTLE (1987), *Politics*. London: Penguin Classics.

BALDWIN, S. (1968), *Politics and Poverty*. Chapel Hill, NC: University of North Carolina Press.

BALFOUR, D. L., and WECHSLER, B. (1990), "Organizational Commitment: A Reconceptualization and Empirical Test of Public-Private Differences," *Review of Public Personnel Administration* 10: 23–40.

BARBER, B. R. (1984), *Strong Democracy: Participatory Politics for a New Age*. Berkeley: University of California Press.

BARBER, J. A., JR. (1970), *Social Mobility and Voting Behavior*. Chicago: Rand McNally.

BARNES, C., and GILL, D. (2000), "Declining Government Performance? Why Citizens Don't Trust Government" (Internet) *www.ssc.govt.nz/display/document.asp?NavID=82andDocAI=1871* New Zealand State Services Commission.

BARNETT, N. J. (1998), "Community Identity in the 21st Century: A Postmodernist Evaluation of Local Government Structure," *International Journal of Public Sector Management* 11: 425–39.

BARZELAY, M. (1992), *Breaking through Bureaucracy*, Berkeley: University of California Press.

BEHN, R. D. (1995), "The Big Questions of Public Management," *Public Administration Review* 55: 313–24.

—— (1998), "The New Public Management Paradigm and the Search for Democratic Accountability," *International Public Management Journal* 1: 131–64.

—— (2002), "Government Performance and the Conundrum of Public Trust," in J. D. Donahue and J. S. Nye, Jr. (eds.), *Market-Based Governance*, Washington, DC: Brookings Institution, 323–48.

BELLAH, R. N., MADSEN, R., SULLIVAN, W. M., SWIDLER, A., and TIPTON, S. M. (1985), *Habits of the Heart*, New York: Harper and Row.

BELLONE, C. J., and GOERL, G. F. (1992), "Reconciling Public Entrepreneurship and Democracy," *Public Administration Review* 52: 130–4.

BERRY, J. M., PORTNOY, K. E., and THOMSON, K. (1993), *The Rebirth of Urban Democracy*, Washington, DC: Brookings Institution.

BERTELLI, A. M., and LYNN, L. E., JUN. (2003), "Managerial Responsibility," *Public Administration Review* 63: 259–68.

BOHMAN, J. (1996), *Public Deliberation: Pluralism, Complexity, and Democracy*, Cambridge, MA: MIT Press.

BOVENS, M. (1998), *The Quest for Responsibility*, Cambridge: Cambridge University Press.

BOX, R. C., MARSHALL, G. S., REED, B. J., and REED, C. M. (2001), "New Public Management and Substantive Democracy," *Public Administration Review* 61: 608–19.

CHEN, D., HUANG, T., and NSAIO, N. (2003), "The Management of Citizen Participation in Taiwan: A Case Study of Taipei City Government's Citizen Complaints System," *International Journal of Public Administration* 26: 525–47.

CHISHOLM, D. (1989), *Coordination without Hierarchy*, Berkeley: University of California Press.

COHEN, C. (1971), *Democracy*, Athens, GA: University of Georgia Press.

COTTON, J., VOLLRATH, D. A., FROGGATT, K. L., LENGNICK-HALL, M. L., and JENNINGS, K. R. (1988), "Employee Participation: Diverse Forms and Different Outcomes," *Academy of Management Review* 13: 8–22.

DAHL, R. A. (1985), *A Preface to Economic Democracy*, Cambridge, MA: Polity Press.

DAWSON, S., and DARGIE, C. (1999), "New Public Management: An Assessment and Evaluation with Special Reference to UK Health," *Public Management* 1(4): 459–82.

DELEON, L. (1994), "Embracing Anarchy: Network Organizations and Interorganizational Networks," *Administrative Theory and Praxis* 16: 234–53.

—— and DENHARDT, R. P. (2000), "The Political Theory of Reinvention," *Public Administration Review* 59: 89–97.

DELEON, P. (1990), "Participatory Policy Analysis: Prescriptions and Precautions," *Asian Journal of Public Administration* 12: 29–54.

—— (1992), "The Democratization of the Policy Sciences," *Public Administration Review* 52: 125–9.

—— (1995), "Democratic Values and the Policy Sciences," *American Journal of Political Science* 39: 886–905.

—— (1997), *Democracy and the Policy Sciences*, Albany, NY: State University of New York Press.

—— and DELEON, L. (2002), "What Ever Happened to Policy Implementation? An Alternative Approach," *Journal of Public Administration Research and Theory* 12: 467–92.

DENHARDT, R. B. (1993), *Theories of Public Organization*, 2nd edn., Belmont, CA: Wadsworth.

DERLIEN, H.-U. (1995), "Public Administration in Germany: Political and Societal Relations," in J. Pierre (ed.), *Bureaucracy in the Modern State*, Cheltenham: Edward Elgar, 64–91.

DIBIE, R. (2003), "Local Government Public Servants' Performance and Citizens' Participation in Governance in Nigeria," *International Journal of Public Administration*, 26, 1061–84.

DOIG, J. W., and HARGROVE, E. C. (1987), *Leadership and Innovation: A Biographical Perspective on Entrepreneurs in Government*, Baltimore: The Johns Hopkins University Press.

DOLAN, J., and ROSENBLOOM, D. H. (eds.) (2003), *Representative Bureaucracy: Classic Readings and Continuing Controversies*, Armonk, NY: M. E. Sharpe.

DONAHUE, J. D. (2002), "Market-Based Governance and the Architecture of Accountability," in J. D. Donahue and J. S. Nye, Jr. (eds.), *Market-Based Governance*, Washington, DC: Brookings Institution, 1–25.

DRYZEK, J. S. (1990), *Discursive Democracy*, Cambridge: Cambridge University Press.

—— (1996), *Democracy in Capitalist Times*, New York: Oxford University Press.

DU GAY, P. (2000), *In Praise of Bureaucracy*, London: Sage.

DURNING, D. (1993), "Participatory Policy Analysis in a Social Service Agency: A Case Study," *Journal of Policy Analysis and Management* 12: 231–57.

FELDMAN, M. S., and KHADEMIAN, A. M. (2001), "Managing for Inclusion: Balancing Control and Participation," *International Public Management Journal* 3: 149–67.

FISCHER, F. (1990), *Technocracy and the Politics of Expertise*, Newbury Park, CA: Sage.

FREDERICKSON, G. (1997), *The Spirit of Public Administration*, San Francisco: Jossey-Bass.

FRIEDRICH, C. J. (1935), "Responsible Government Service under The American Constitution," in C. J. Friedrich, W. C. Beyer, S. D. Spero, J. F. Miller, and G. A. Graham (eds.), *Problems of the American Public Service*, New York: McGraw-Hill, 3–74.

FUKUYAMA, F. (1995), *Trust: The Social Virtues and the Creation of Prosperity*, New York: Free Press.

GAWTHROP, L. C. (1970), *The Administrative Process and Democratic Theory*, Boston: Houghton Mifflin.

GORE, A. (1997), *Businesslike Government: Lessons Learned From America's Best Companies*, Washington, DC: National Performance Review.

GREEN, J. C., and HERRNSON, P. S. (eds.) (2003), *Responsible Partisanship? The Evolution of American Political Parties Since 1950*, Lawrence, KS: University Press of Kansas.

GRUENING, G. (2001), "Origin and Theoretical Basis of New Public Management," *International Public Management Journal* 4: 1–25.

GUTMANN, A., and THOMPSON, D. (1996), *Democracy and Disagreement*, Cambridge, MA: The Belknap Press of the Harvard University Press.

GUY, M. E. (ed.) (1992), *Women and Men of the States: Public Administrators at the State Level*, Armonk, NY: M. E. Sharpe.

HABERMAS, J. (1983 and 1987), *The Theory of Communicative Action: Reason and the Rationalization of Society*, 2 vols., trans. T. McCarthy, Boston: Beacon.

HALE, M. M., and KELLY, R. M. (eds.) (1989), *Gender, Bureaucracy, and Democracy: Careers and Equal Opportunity in the Public Sector*, New York: Greenwood Press.

HAQUE, M. S. (2003), "Citizen Participation in Governance through Representation: The Issue of Gender in East Asia," *International Journal of Public Administration* 26: 569–90.

HARMON, M. (1971), "Normative Theory and Public Administration : Some Suggestions for a Redefinition of Administrative Responsibility," in F. Marini (ed.), *Toward a New Public Administration*, Scranton, PA: Chandler, 172–84.

HEADY, F. (2001), *Public Administration: A Comparative Perspective*, 6th edn., New York: Marcel Dekker.

HECLO, H. (1978), "Issue Networks and the Executive Establishment," in A. King (ed.), *The New Political System*, Washington, DC: The American Enterprise Institute for Public Policy, 87–124.

HELD, D. (1996), *Models of Democracy*, Stanford, CA: Stanford University Press.

HIRSCHMAN, A. O. (1970), *Exit, Voice and Loyalty*, Cambridge, MA: Harvard University Press.

JANOWITZ, M. (1960), *The Professional Soldier*, New York: Free Press Glencoe.

JAQUES, E. (1990), "In Praise of Hierarchy," *Harvard Business Review* 90: 127–33.

JONES, J. R. (1992), *Beyond Distrust: Building Bridges between Congress and the Executive*, Washington, DC: National Academy of Public Administration.

KAKABADSE, A., KAKABADSE, N. K., and KOUZMIN, A. (2003), "Reinventing the Democratic Governance Project through Information Technology? A Growing Agenda for Debate," *Public Administration Review* 63: 44–60.

KARIEL, H. (1966), *The Promise of Politics*, Englewood Cliffs, NJ: Prentice-Hall.

KAUFMAN, H. (1960), *The Forest Ranger*, Baltimore: Johns Hopkins University Press.

—— (2001), "Major Players: Bureaucracies in American Government," *Public Administration Review* 61: 18–42.

KEARNEY, R. C., and HAYS, S. W. (1994), "Labor Management Relations and Participative Decision Making: Toward a New Paradigm," *Public Administration Review* 54: 44–51.

KELLY, R. M. (1998), "An Inclusive Democratic Policy, Representative Bureaucracies, and the New Public Management," *Public Administration Review* 58: 201–8.

—— and GUY, M. E. (1991), "Public Managers in the States: A Comparison of Career Advancement by Sex," *Public Administration Review* 51: 402–12.

KETTL, D. F. (2000), *The Global Public Management Revolution*, Washington, DC: Brookings Institution.

KICKERT, W. J. M. (1997), "Anglo-Saxon Public Management and European Governance: The Case of Dutch Administrative Reforms," in J.-E. Lane (ed.), *Public Sector Reform*, London: Sage, 168–87.

—— and VAN VUGHT, F. A. (eds.) (1995), *Public Policy and Administration Sciences in the Netherlands*, Englewood Cliffs, NJ: Prentice-Hall.

KIM, S. (2002), "Participative Management and Job Satisfaction: Lessons for Management Leadership," *Public Administration Review* 62: 231–41.

KINGSLEY, J. D. (1944), *Representative Bureaucracy: An Interpretation of the British Civil Service*, Yellow Springs, AR: Antioch Press.

KLIJN, E.-H., and KOPPENJAN, J. F. M. (2000), "Politicians and Interactive Decision Making: Institutional Spoilsports or Playmakers?" *Public Administration* 78: 364–87.

KONIG, K. (1997), "Entrepreneurial Management or Executive Administration: The Perspective of Classical Public Administration," in W. J. M. Kickert (ed.), *Public Management and Administrative Reform in Western Europe*, Cheltenham, Edward Elgar, 213–32.

KRIMERMAN, L., and LINDENFELD, F. (eds.) (1992), *When Workers Decide: Workplace Democracy Takes Root in North America*, Philadelphia: New Society.

KRISLOV, S. (1974), *Representative Bureaucracy*, Englewood Cliffs, NJ: Prentice-Hall.

—— and Rosenbloom, D. H. (1981), *Representative Bureaucracy and the American Political System*, New York: Praeger.

LAM, W.-M. (2003), "An Alternative Understanding of Political Participation: Challenging the Myth of Political Indifference in Hong Kong," *International Journal of Public Administration* 26: 473–96.

LANE, R. E. (2000), *The Loss of Happiness in Market Democracies*, New Haven: Yale University Press.

LA PORTE, T. M., DEMCHAK, C. C., and de JONG, M. (2003), "Democracy and Bureaucracy in the Age of the Web: Empirical Findings and Theoretical Speculations," *Administration & Society* 34: 447–54.

LEMAN, C. (1989), "The Forgotten Fundamental: Successes and Excesses of Direct Government," in L. M. Salamon (ed.), *Beyond Privatization*, Washington, D.C., Urban Institute Press, 48–79.

LEVITAN, D. M. (1943), "Political Ends and Administrative Means," *Public Administration Review* 3: 353–9.

LEWIS, E. (1980), *Public Entrepreneurship*, Bloomington, IN: Indiana University Press.

LEWIS, G. B. (1988), "Progress toward Racial and Sexual Equality in the Federal Civil Service?" *Public Administration Review* 48: 700–7.

LEWIS, W. G. (1989), "Toward Representative Bureaucracy: Blacks in City Police Organizations, 1975–1985," *Public Administration Review* 49: 257–68.

LICHENSTEIN, N., and HARRIS, H. J. (1993), *Industrial Democracy in America*, New York: Cambridge University Press.

LIPSKY, M. (1980), *Street-Level Bureaucracy*, New York: Russell Sage Foundation.

LOCKE, E. A., and SCHWEIGER, D. M. (1979), "Participation in Decision-Making: One More Look," *Research in Organizational Behavior* 1: 265–339.

LOWNDES, V., PRATCHETT, L., and STOKER, G. (2001), "Trends in Public Participation: Part 1 Local Government Perspectives," *Public Administration* 79: 205–22.

LUPIA, A., and McCUBBINS, M. D. (1998), *The Democratic Dilemma: Can Citizens Learn What They Need to Know?* Cambridge: Cambridge University Press.

LYNN, L. E., JR. (1987), *Managing Public Policy*, Boston: Little, Brown.

—— (1996), *Public Management As Art, Science and Profession*, Chatham, NJ: Chatham House.

—— (2002), "Democracy's 'Unforgivable Sin'", *Administration & Society* 34: 447–54.

—— LYNN, M. L., MULEJ, M. J., and JURSE, K. (2002), "Democracy Without Empowerment: The Grand Vision and Demise of Yugoslav Self-Management," *Management Decision*, 40(8): 788–95.

MANSBRIDGE, J. (1997), "Social and Cultural Causes of Dissatisfaction with U.S. Government," in J. S. Nye, Jun., P. D. Zelikow, and D. C. King (eds.), *Why People Don't Trust Government*, Cambridge, MA: Harvard University Press, 133–54.

MARINI, F. (ed.) (1971), *Toward a New Public Administration: The Minnowbrook Perspective*, San Francisco: Chandler.

MATHIASEN, D. G. (1999), "The New Public Management and Its Critics," *International Public Management Journal* 2: 90–111.

MATLAND, R. E. (1995), "Synthesizing the Implementation Literature: The Ambiguity–Conflict Model of Policy Implementation," *Journal of Public Administration Research and Theory* 5: 145–74.

MAYNARD-MOODY, S., and LELAND, S. (2000), "Stories from the Front Lines of Public Management: Street-Level Workers As Responsible Actors," in J. L. Brudney, L. J. O'Toole, Jr., and H. G. Rainey (eds.), *Advancing Public Management: New Developments in Theory, Methods and Practice*, Washington, DC: Georgetown University Press, 109–23.

MEIER, K. J., and BOHTE, J. (2001), "Structure and Discretion: Missing Links in Representative Bureaucracy," *Journal of Public Administration Research and Theory* 11: 455–70.

—— and NIGRO, L. G. (1976), "Representative Bureaucracy and Policy Preferences: A Study in the Attitudes of Federal Executives," *Public Administration Review* 36: 458–69.

METCALF, H. C., and URWICK, L. (eds.) (1940), *Dynamic Administration: Collected Papers of Mary Parker Follett*, New York: Harper and Row.

MILLER, K. L., and MONGE, P. R. (1986), "Participation, Satisfaction, and Productivity: A Meta-Analytic Review," *Academy of Management Journal* 29: 727–53.

MINTROM, M. (2003), "Market Organizations and Deliberative Democracy: Choice and Voice in Public Service Delivery," *Administration & Society* 35: 52–81.

MOE, R. C. (1994), "The 'Reinventing Government' Exercise: Misinterpreting the Problem, Misjudging the Consequences," *Public Administration Review* 54: 111–22.

MORONE, J. A. (1990), *The Democratic Wish*, New York: BasicBooks.

MOSHER, F. C. (1968), *Democracy and the Public Service*, New York: Oxford University Press.

—— and STILLMAN, R., JUN. (1977), "Symposium on the Professions in Government," *Public Administration Review* 37: 631–86.

MOYNIHAN, D. P. (2003), "Normative and Instrumental Perspectives on Public Participation: Citizen Summits in Washington, DC," *American Review of Public Administration* 33: 164–88.

NEWMAN, J. (2001), *Modernising Governance: New Labour, Policy and Society,* London: Sage Publications.

NYE, J. S., JUN., ZELIKOW, P. D., and KING, D. C. (eds.) (1997), *Why People Don't Trust Government,* Cambridge, MA: Harvard University Press.

OECD. (2001), *Citizens as Partners: Information, Consultation and Public Participation in Policy-Making,* Paris: OECD.

OLSEN, J. P., and PETERS, B. G. (1996), *Learning from Experience: Experiential Learning in Administrative Reforms in Eight Democracies,* Oslo: Scandinavian University Press.

OSBORNE, D., and GAEBLER, T. (1992), *Reinventing Government,* Reading, MA: Addison-Wesley.

OSTROM, V. (1973), The *Intellectual Crisis in Public Administration,* University, AL: University of Alabama Press.

PARNELL, J. A., and BELL, E. D. (1994), "The Propensity for Participative Decision-Making Scale: A Measure of Managerial Propensity for Participative Decision-Making," *Administration & Society* 25: 518–30.

PATEMAN, C. (1970), *Participation and Democratic Theory,* Cambridge: Cambridge University Press.

PENCAVEL, J. (2001), *Worker Participation: Lessons from the Worker Co-ops of the Pacific Northwest,* New York: Russell Sage Foundation.

PHILLIPS, K. (2002), *Wealth and Democracy,* New York: Broadway Books.

PLUNKETT, L. C., and FOURNIER, R. (1991), *Participative Management: Implementing Empowerment,* New York: John Wiley and Sons.

POLLITT, C. (1996), "Antistatist Reforms and New Administrative Directions: Public Administration in the United Kingdom," *Public Administration Review* 56: 81–7.

—— (2003), *The Essential Public Manager,* Buckingham: Open University Press/McGraw Hill.

—— and Bouckaert, G. (2000), *Public Management Reform: Comparative Analysis,* Oxford: Oxford University Press.

PUTNAM, R. D. (1995), "Bowling Alone: America's Declining Social Capital," *Journal of Democracy* 6: 65–78.

—— (2000), *Bowling Alone,* New York: Touchstone (Simon and Schuster).

—— (ed.) (2002), *Democracies in Flux,* New York: Oxford University Press.

REDFORD, E. (1958), *Ideal and Practice in Public Administration,* University, AL: University of Alabama Press.

—— (1969), *Democracy in the Administrative State,* New York: Oxford University Press.

RIPLEY, R., and FRANKLIN, G. (1984), *Congress, the Bureaucracy, and Public Policy,* 3rd edn., Homewood, IL: Dorsey.

RUSCIO, K. P. (1996), "Trust, Democracy, and Public Management: A Theoretical Argument," *Journal of Public Administration Research and Theory* 6: 461–78.

SABATIER, P. A. (1986), "Top-Down and Bottom-Up Approaches to Implementation Research : A Critical Analysis and Suggested Synthesis," *Journal of Public Policy* 6: 21–48.

SAGIE, A., and KOSLOWSKY, M. (2000), *Participation and Empowerment in Organizations,* Thousand Oaks, CA: Sage.

SELDEN, S. C., BRUDNEY, J., and KELLOUGH, J. E. (1998), "Bureaucracy As a Representative Institution: Toward a Reconciliation of Bureaucratic Government and Democratic Theory," *American Journal of Political Science* 42: 719–44.

SEMLER, R. (1989), "Managing without Managers," *Harvard Business Review* 67: 76–84.

STAYER, R. (1990), "How I Learned to Let My Workers Lead," *Harvard Business Review* 68: 66–83.

STILLMAN, R. J., JUN. (1991), *Preface to Public Administration*, New York: St. Martin's.

STINEHART, K. (1995), "Revitalizing a Continuing Education Department through Self-Managed Work Teams," *Continuing Higher Education Review* 59: 93–109.

STIVERS, C. (1993), *Gender Images in Public Administration*, Newbury Park, CA: Sage.

TAYLOR, M. (1982), *Community, Anarchy and Liberty*, Cambridge: Cambridge University Press.

TERRY, L. D. (1993), "Why We Should Abandon the Misconceived Quest to Reconcile Public Entrepreneurship with Democracy," *Public Administration Review* 53: 393–5.

THIELEMANN, G., and STEWART, J., JUN. (1996), "A Demand-Side Perspective on the Importance of Representative Bureaucracy: AIDS, Ethnicity, Gender and Sexual Orientation," *Public Administration Review* 56: 168–73.

THOMAS, J. C. (1995), *Public Participation in Public Decisions: New Skills and Strategies for Public Managers*, San Francisco: Jossey-Bass.

THOMPSON, D. (1983), "Bureaucracy and Democracy," in G. Duncan (ed.), *Democratic Theory and Practice*, Cambridge: Cambridge University Press.

THOMPSON, F. J. (1976), "Minority Groups in Public Bureaucracies: Are Passive and Active Representation Linked?" *Administration & Society* 8: 201–26.

TRIST, E. L., and BAMFORTH, K. W. (1951), "Some Social and Psychological Consequences of the Longwall Method of Coal-Getting," *Human Relations* 4: 3–38.

VAN DER MEER, F. M., and ROBORGH, R. L. J. (1996), "Civil Servants and Representativeness," in H. A. G. M. Bekke, J. L. Perry, and T. A. J. Toonen (eds.), *Civil Service Systems in Comparative Perspective*, Bloomington, IN: Indiana University Press, 119–33.

VIGODA, E. (2003), "Performance and Democracy in the Public Sector: Exploring Some Missing Links in the Study of Administration and Society (Part A: Administrative Performance, Trust in Governance, and Social Equality)," *International Journal of Public Administration* 26: 883–90.

WAGNER, J. A., and GOODING, R. (1987), "Shared Influence and Organizational Behavior: A Meta-Analysis of Situational Variables Expected to Moderate Participation-Outcome Relationships," *Academy of Management Journal* 30: 241–62.

WALDO, D. (1948), *The Administrative State*, New York: Ronald Press.

—— (1952), "Development of Theory of Democratic Administration: Replies and Comments," *American Political Science Review* 46: 494–502.

—— (1984; orig. 1948), *The Administrative State*, 2nd edn., New York: Holmes and Meier.

WALL, T. D., KEMP, N. J., JACKSON, P. R., and CLEGG, C. W. (1986), "Outcomes of Autonomous Workgroups: A Long-Term Field Experiment," *Academy of Management Journal* 29: 280–304.

WAMSLEY, G. L., GOODSELL, C. T., ROHR, J. A., STIVERS, C. M., WHITE, O. F. and WOLF, J. F. (1990), "Public Administration and the Governance Process: Shifting the Political Dialogue," in G.L. Wamsley, *Refounding Public Administration*, Newbury Park, CA: Sage Publications, 31–51.

WELLINS, R. S., BYHAM, W. C., and WILSON, J. M. (1991), *Empowered Teams*, San Francisco: Jossey-Bass.

WHITTY, M. (1996), "Co-Management for Workplace Democracy," *Journal of Organizational Change Management* 9: 7–11.

WICKER, A. W. (1969), "Attitudes Versus Actions," *Journal of Social Issues* 15: 41–78.

WISMAN, J. D. (1997), "The Ignored Question of Workplace Democracy in Political Discourse," *International Journal of Social Economics* 24: 1388–403.

YEATTS, D. E., and HYTEN, C. (1998), *High-Performing Self-Managed Work Teams*, Thousand Oaks, CA: Sage.

ZAMBONI, M. (2001), "'Rechtsstaat': Just What is Being Exported by Swedish Development Organisations?" *Law, Social Justice and Global Development* 2: http://elj.warwick.ac.uk/global/issue/2001-2/zamboni.html.

ZIFCAK, S. (2000), "From Managerial Reform to Democratic Reformation: Towards a Deliberative Public Administration," *International Public Management Journal* 2: 236–72.

ZUSSMAN, D. (1997), "Public Sector Management in Canada," 2: www.ppforum.ca/News-Letters/issue_6/english/(accessed 06/05/03).

SECTION II

THEORETICAL AND DISCIPLINARY PERSPECTIVES

CHAPTER 6

....

LAW AND PUBLIC ADMINISTRATION

....

ANTHONY M. BERTELLI

THE focus of this chapter is what might be termed *national administrative law*, in contrast to international administrative law that governs international organizations such as the World Bank or United Nations tribunals.[1] In democratic states, administrative law for present purposes includes mechanisms: (1) to redress harm to individuals inflicted by government in the pursuit of government objectives, and (2) for positive control[2] of government agencies by branches of government with sovereign authority in lawmaking, e.g., the United States Congress.[3] The latter function is more apparent in separation-of-powers systems, though it has parliamentary analogs (Huber 2000; Strøm 2000). It is part constitutional and rights-oriented, and part procedural. Courts, chief executives, and bureaus themselves demarcate administrative powers.

We can think of administrative law as a constraint that operates on the set of actions, or policy choices, that a bureau or individual bureaucrat can take. These constraints, in the abstract, have a profound effect on policy. Nonetheless, much of what is interesting about the interaction of law and administrative policy making happens because (a) administrative law develops over time, and in response to politics, and (b) that the rules of administrative law are rarely wholly determinative of administrative behaviour. When bureaus or bureaucrats make decisions, they condition those decisions on the rules of applicable administrative law. As such, one should not expect to find administrative law compiled in casebooks, but rather in statutes, codes, executive orders, policy memoranda, and the norms of administrative procedure in departments throughout the administrative state.

We begin with a general discussion of the elements of administrative law regimes. From this, it should be apparent that the questions of administrative law, whether in parliamentary, separation-of-powers political systems, or any on the continuum between are questions arising from the politics of delegation, namely the delegation of sovereign power to be executed by administrative agents.

The chapter then turns to a discussion of the archetypal French and British administrative law regimes. The censorate—an administrative body that originated in imperial China now seen most clearly in Taiwan, that records and analyzes government functions, impeaches bureaucrats for legal or moral violations or on the basis of citizen complaint, oversees the bureaucracy generally, and remonstrates the government regarding specific policies—the Communist Procuracy's general supervision function, and the ombudsman, which originated in Sweden and Finland and is now found throughout the world in one form or another, are discussed. Variations in these canonical regimes in Germany and Canada are briefly examined.

We then propose a theory of national administrative law as an institutional response to the legislative politics of credit-claiming in the settings of particular national institutions. It is argued that administrative law gropes toward a rather flexible equilibrium represented by standards set forth in cases such as *Chevron USA v. NRDC* (467 U.S. 837, 1984) in the United States and the "pragmatic and functional" approach of Canadian courts.

The chapter concludes with a brief discussion of the challenges of administrative law under the privatization initiatives of the "New Public Management." The nexus of contracts that emerges from such schemes tends to move a fundamentally reactive administrative law regime from a macro-level, public interest focus, to a micro-level notion of transactional justice. This, some commentators argue, frustrates the purpose of administrative law, but in any event creates the need for doctrinal adjustment.

6.1 THE ROLE AND STRUCTURE OF ADMINISTRATIVE LAW

In civilian systems, an essential distinction in public law between constitutional law (dealing with the making of laws and the powers of government) and administrative law (dealing with the execution of those laws) is well known. Yet for the public administrationist, this distinction is unduly simplistic given the importance of constitutional questions in the expansive administrative states of modern democracies. To be sure, administrative law operates at various levels of govern-ment, and the following typology attempts to categorize its influence across the spectrum of governance.

Constitutional administrative law concerns issues of delegation and the raw authority for agency action. It also deals with concerns of *standing*, or the avail-ability of proceedings in which citizens can seek redress for administrative mal-treatment. The underlying principles for this level of administrative law need not be found in a constitution; rather they may be elements of common law doctrine, statutory law, or unwritten, yet defining, principles of specific national govern-ment. As an example of the latter, unwritten elements of administrative law—*légalité*, due process, hearing rights, equality of treatment, legitimate expectations, proportionality of action—have been central to the development of administrative law for the European Union (Schwartze 1993).

Bureau-centric administrative law surrounds the provision of services, the prac-tice of regulation, and the operations of highly regulated private enterprises. In the final section of the chapter, our discussion of the New Public Management and administrative law focuses at this level, since government service reforms under this mantra devolve services to government contractees, who consequently have a hand in creating administrative law. Here, as we shall see, principles of public and private law reside in an often uneasy fusion of rules and purposes. *Client-centric administrative law* deals with the means through which bureaus serves their clients. Informal grievance procedures would also be found here. This is the most ubiqui-tous form of administrative law, but also the hardest for academicians to study, as it is typically embodied in standard operating procedures and norms collected in the organizational cultures of bureaus.

This mélange of law, regulations, and procedures that emerges as administrative decisions are made and reviewed is somewhat systematically depicted in Figure 6.1. Constitutional administrative law operates in courts through judicial review of agency action or constitutional-level litigation (i.e., actions brought under the United States Constitution or Canadian Charter of Rights and Freedoms).[4] Bur-eau-centric administrative law is found and developed in both courts through judicial review, and agencies through rulemaking and adjudication. It includes the civilian categories *contentieux administratifs*, or suits arising from administrative action when authorized,[5] and *contentieux gracieux*, in which an aggrieved party seeks redress from the same authority that brought it harm. All of these proceed-ings can involve a single or several agencies. *Contentieux administratifs* are what we have categorized as judicial review of administrative action, while *contentieux gracieux* operate between the client and bureau and may be more or less trial-like in character depending on the administrative law regime in place in a particular country. In the United States, these are one class of administrative adjudications (e.g., a hearing between a client and the federal Social Security Administration occasioned by the reduction or termination of that client's entitlement benefits). In

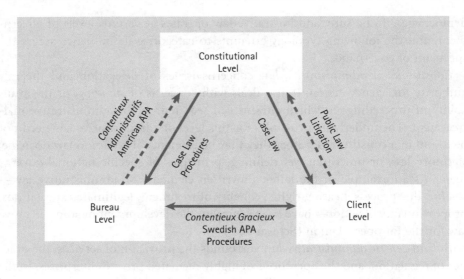

Fig. 6.1 Administrative law and levels of governance

the French system, the *Conseil d'État* lies formally within the executive, and, thus, both types of proceeding take place within the "administration," though as we shall see, the *Conseil* has long held high status as a court.

In Figure 6.1, the actions of agencies give rise to claims and questions at the constitutional level in the form of *contentieux administratifs* represented by the dashed arrows. Administrative agencies interpret their enabling statutes, or "delegated legislation," as such laws are known in Britain, executive orders, or other grants of power and procedural requirements when they act to make policy. Courts in turn interpret agency actions within the rubric of such statutes, executive orders, constitutional provisions, and so forth, making statutory interpretation a central feature of the operation of administrative law regimes.

Judicial review is represented by the solid arrows, and represents the major theoretical thrust of administrative law. Bureaus take actions to implement public policies, and courts review their propriety. The grounds for assessing propriety are central to the debates of scholars of administrative law, as are the standards of review, which range from *de novo*, or the substitution of judicial for administrative judgment, to deference in the presence of *mere rationality* of the administration's action.

One theoretical model of review, *ultra vires*, is "based on the assumption that judicial review was legitimated on the ground that the courts were applying the intent of the legislature" (Craig 1999, 428). Political theory, it has been copiously argued, makes the threshold question of legislative intent both necessary— the courts have no lawmaking pedigree that exceeds that of a democratically elected legislature—and sufficient, or as Craig (1999, 429) puts it, the "doctrines which make up administrative law derived their legitimacy and content from the fact that the legislature intended them to apply in a particular way in a particular statutory context." Thus, in the British model, sovereign authority is *effectuated* by administrative law, which implies a particularly restrictive role for administrative law on public administration.

The effectuation of sovereign intent varies across nations. In France, as will be considered below, a distrust of courts led to an administrative law regime designed to protect prerogative rights of administration. German administrative law, like its modern American counterpart, has focused on the rights of the citizen as against the administration (Schwartze 1998, 192). The Marxist state is the polity itself, and, as we shall see, the investigation of the procuracy seeks to protect individuals from their administrative agents. In each system, sovereign authority creates the intent that administrative law—like other schemes of legal "default rules," such as the law of contracts—makes more predictable, less uncertain in implementation.

Scholars have been critical of the *ultra vires* theory on the ground that legislatures are rarely sufficiently specific in the exposition of their intent when writing statutes as to make its implementation by courts viable.[6] British legal scholars have advocated, in response, a "common law model of illegality," along the following line of argument:

[T]he principles of judicial review are in reality developed by the courts. They are the creation of the common law...When legislation is passed the courts will impose the controls which constitute judicial review which they believe are normatively justified on the grounds of justice, the rule of law, etc....Agency action which infringes these principles will be unlawful. If the omnipotent Parliament does not like these controls then it is open to it to make this unequivocally clear. If it does so, the courts will then adhere to such dictates. (Craig 1999: 429; see also Oliver 1987)

In the American legal academy, the debate has continued to the question of where courts find legislative intent. Proponents of "textualism" (most notably Justices Antonin Scalia and Clarence Thomas of the US Supreme Court) argue that the plain meaning of the statutory language must be distilled without consulting legislative debates on the theory that statutes are bargains among legislator with no implicit intent. Others argue that intent should be found in debates and elsewhere (see generally Scalia 1998). The common strand in all of this is *ultra vires*, administrative authorities take their cues from the sovereign.

The provisions interpreted in public also include general statutes, known as *Administrative Procedure Acts* (APAs) that circumscribe duties and procedures for agency action across every policy domain of administrative governance.[7] In the United States, the APA of 1946 has been particularly useful for defining the character and limits of judicial review of administrative action.[8] Much of the litigation under the Act has been focused on agency *rulemaking*, or, generally, the bureau-level creation of rules or standards that govern action in a class of cases and for a class of clients. The Act also has procedures for judicial review of *adjudication*, or *ad hoc* determinations of cases, for which case law has required some variant of fair procedural, trial-like hearings. The American APA exemplifies an administrative procedure statute that serves the primary function of demarcating judicial review, and as such, is positioned between the constitutional and bureau levels in Figure 6.1.

A second type of APA can be found in Sweden. To be sure, Swedish administrative courts take the APA into account when deciding matters on review, but the primary emphasis of the law is the dispensation of administrative matters. As a consequence, the act is "short and comprehensible and not more complicated than is required for the kind of matter being regulated" (Sterzel 1994: 549). The Swedish APA operates with *contentieux gracieux* between the bureau and client levels as a national codification of administrative standard operating procedures. It is a guide for public administration. When cases reach the Swedish administrative courts for judicial review, a more detailed Administrative Courts Procedure Act applies. As shall be discussed, Sweden also has an ombudsman's office, which provides less formal resolution of *contentieux gracieux*. The former Soviet procuracy, or prosecutor's office, and the Taiwanese *Control Yuan*, with its origins in the Chinese censorate operate at this level as well, and are, in the abstract, similar to the ombudsman.

The most significant challenge to *ultra vires* as a justification for judicial review of administrative action emerged in the United States as "public law litigation" (see Chayes 1976). Complainants in public law cases are typically represented by advocacy (interest) groups, having, of course, policy preferences. Public law cases bring client level disputes directly to the constitutional level, often reconstructing bureau-centric administrative law—as well as circumventing legislated policy choices—in the process (Bertelli 2004; Bertelli and Feldmann 2003). Exercising their equitable jurisdiction, American courts began using their injunctive power to mandate compliance with Constitutional provisions in the early twentieth century, particularly by blocking strikes during the labor movement (McDowell 1982; Yoo 1996). This action ultimately provoked Congress to pass the Norris–La Guardia Act, which made injunctions illegal in labor cases. After the 1954 holding in *Brown v. Board of Education* (347 US 483, 1954) that separate but equal schools are inherently unequal and a constitutional violation, the courts were faced with significant *de facto* and *de jure* remedial concerns coupled with recalcitrant Southern bureaucrats.

Courts developed three basic techniques to implement remedies. First, a "[c]ourt may directly oversee compliance from the bench, either by requiring periodic reports from the agency or through the use of monitors or masters who serve as intelligence agents." Second, the court may approve a consent decree under which "[a]dministrative discretion is much more limited... because the plaintiffs or monitors are a confirming presence and coequal parties in the negotiations" (Wood 1990: 36–7). Third, the court may order receivership, meaning that "the court may take over, its patience exhausted by the evident ineffectiveness of direct oversight or consent decree negotiations in securing compliance" (Wood 1990: 36). This option is typically chosen after the others fail. Finally, since the relief requested in these cases is overwhelmingly injunctive, courts invite litigants to use their expertise to develop mutually agreeable outcomes, embodied in consent decrees (Bertelli 2004; Diver 1979).[9]

This particularly intrusive form of public law litigation—known as institutional reform litigation—is rare outside the United States, though with the passage of the British Human Rights Act 1998 (Palmer 2000) and the Canadian Charter of Rights and Freedoms (Morton and Knopff 2000), the potential for public litigation may theoretically be growing.[10] Sentiment for such litigation, however, is not. Writes Gavin Drewry (1986, 174), "[t]he continental administrator is in general...a lawyer, specialising in that branch of law—namely administrative law—which is most concerned with the functions of government. And, across the Atlantic, we find that constitutional issues permeate American law and life to an extent that foreign observers find incredible. Americans have become a people of constitutionalists who substitute litigation for legislation and see constitutional questions lurking in every case."

Judicial interest representation, then, emerges as the most substantial challenge to *ultra vires* as a defining principle of administrative law. Interests that "lose" in the legislature are given another opportunity to have their voices heard in court against the public policies created by their legislative opponents. Courts must be extremely careful about the counter-majoritarian problem inherent in this administrative law role. Given that caveat, judicial interest representation can assist, as in the case of African-Americans and civil rights, a "discrete and insular minority" against which legislators, expressing the interests of their constituents, are biased. The US Supreme Court opened this avenue in *United States v. Carolene Products, Co.* (304 US 144, 152, n.4, 1938). and the post-war German administrative law system has stressed it as a value (Schwartze 1998).

We shall next discuss administrative law regimes, as defined above, as outgrowths of delegating sovereign powers to administrative agents.

6.2 COMPARATIVE ADMINISTRATIVE LAW REGIMES

The widespread nature of the "French Model" of administrative law is important to understanding comparative regimes, and it is a part of the distinction between private law and public law that often differentiates common law and civilian systems. Civilian public law emerged as a separate discipline in the sixteenth century with the publication in 1572 of Vigelius' *Institutionum Iurus Public*. Subsequently, the field grew "mainly in response to the need of the rulers, states, and free cities for skilled counsel as well as effective public advocacy of their causes" (Schlesinger et al. 1998: 274). In civilian systems, the jurisdiction of ordinary courts extends only to matters of private law, or disputes arising from relationships among individuals. When disputes arise between individuals and the government—especially, for our purposes, from the appropriateness of some administrative action—public law jurisdiction is invoked, and such cases are processed through the administrative tribunals.[11]

That the courts of the *ancien régime* were unpopular among the revolutionaries is a dramatic understatement. One year after the regime fell, "the Constituent Assembly decided that Judges who interfered with the execution of the laws of the Nation by public officials were guilty of a criminal offence, and that is still the law today" (Schlesinger et al. 1998: 540; see generally Schama 1989). This implied *no* judicial review *at all* for bureaucratic action. Consequently, to check against arbitrary administrative action, the *Conseil d'État* was established in the Constitution of 1799. Napoleon charged the *Conseil* with addressing complaints against civil servants, and the executive branch review of administrative actions was born (Schlesinger et al. 1998: 541). Moreover, there is virtually no legislative control through administrative procedure—what has been called "deck stacking" in the positive theory of political institutions (e.g., McCubbins, et al. 1989)—in France, with the overwhelming majority of administrative procedures emerging from the decisional law of the *Conseil* (Schlesinger et al. 1998: 543).

But in Britain, "the common law courts asserted, and through centuries of political and indeed military struggles successfully preserved, their power to curb abusive official action" (Schlesinger et al. 1998: 276). Thus, the common law courts retained jurisdiction over all disputes, public and private. It is in this sense unsurprising that A. V. Dicey (1885) famously rejected the public-private distinction. He wrote:

the notion which lies at the bottom of the "administrative law" known to foreign countries , that affairs or disputes in which the government or its servants are concerned are beyond the sphere of the civil courts and must be dealt with by special and more or less official bodies (*tribunaux administratifs*) is utterly unknown to the law of England, and indeed is fundamentally inconsistent with our traditions and customs (Dicey 1885: 215–16).

Dicey was not sympathetic to the French separation-of-powers system, which he considered to be a product of Montesquieu's erroneous interpretation of the fundamental nature of the English constitution, and a corresponding misconception by the French revolutionaries of what Montesquieu had written (Allison 1996). Moreover, "Dicey condemned the *Conseil d'État* for its origins in the *ancien régime* and for its revival by the despot Napoleon" (Allison 1996: 19). He was not patently wrong. As a non-judicial administrative body, the power of the *Conseil* was particularly abused by Napoleon III, resulting in a purge of its members with the emergence of the Third Republic in 1878. Ever since that time, the *Conseil* has been a court with stature equal to the French high *Cour de Cassation*.

The strength of party control over ministers in the Westminster system has created a situation in which virtually no national level administrative review cases are heard before the courts (e.g., Huber 2000). The bulk of judicial review of administrative action arises from the actions of municipal government, which does not have the constraints of party discipline that operate on cabinet ministers. Thus, the potential for administrative drift and incentives for political control of bureaucracy—as we shall see in the American case—are lower in the Westminster context. Separated powers induce political control problems, and the institutions that enforce political control arrangements are embodied in all levels of administrative law.

The French model is widespread, as are separated powers systems. It underlies the administrative regimes of numerous civilian jurisdictions, from Mexico to the Vatican (Schlesinger et al. 1998: 541). The Diceyan influence limited British and Commonwealth administrative law significantly until the 1980s (Schlesinger et al. 1998: 277).

The British Model was present in the United States well into the twentieth century (as the nondelegation doctrine to which our discussion will return), however, the advent of the modern administrative state coupled with a separation-of-powers system not present in Britain brought the political control problem into the focus of Congress. Controlling public bureaucracy is political. "The problem," Douglas Yates (1982: 151) writes, "is whether a given president, cabinet secretary, congressional committee, interest group, or administrator possesses too much or too little control in the course of advancing or curbing particular interests." In the nineteenth century patronage-driven "state of courts and parties," this problem was quite benign (Skowronek 1982). As the administrative state came to embrace substantive expertise and was charged with the responsibility for implementing complex social and regulatory programs, a politics of bureaucratic control quickly emerged. Leonard White (1935: 418) aptly summarized the pre-bureaucratic epoch in American administrative law:

So long as American administrative systems remained decentralized, disintegrated, and self-governmental and discharged only a minimum of responsibilities, the necessity of highly developed machinery for its control was unknown. Administration was weak and threatened no civil liberties; it was unorganized and possessed no power of resistance; it was elective and quickly responsive to the color and tone of local feeling.

By the early twentieth century, federal courts were determining whether agency adjudication and policy making was not performed simply for private or factional purposes—the judicial interest representation rationale for judicial review. By the

1970s, however, "the main thrust of administrative law," Epstein and O'Halloran (1999: 21) write, "was to make agencies look like pluralistic enterprises, open to the public and reviewable by higher courts." As a consequence, "the focus of the administrative law literature was the role of interest groups and courts as checks on bureaucratic power" (Epstein and O'Halloran 1999: 21).

On this view, Richard Stewart (1975: 1675) noted that the "traditional model of administrative law...conceives of the agency as a mere transmission belt for implementing legislative directives in particular cases [, which] legitimates intrusions into private liberties by agency officials not subject to electoral control by ensuring that such intrusions are commanded by a legitimate source of authority— the legislature" (see e.g., Goodnow 1905; Berle 1913). With regard to the transmission belt, "the court's function is one of containment; review is directed toward keeping the agency within the directives which Congress has issued" (Stewart 1975: 1675). The transformation of agencies into "pluralistic enterprises" was, Stewart (1975: 1723) indicated, "in large degree achieved through an expansion of the class of interests entitled to seek judicial review of agency action" and "the expansion of the concepts of liberty and property that has been a response to large-scale government." Thus, particularly in the regulatory state, interest groups were given the opportunity to influence bureaucratic operations through judicial review. The logical conclusion of this effect is the dramatic oversight role, which we have seen in discussing institutional reform litigation.

Between British parliamentary dominance and French concerns of administrative effectiveness, German administrative authority is subjected to a strong form of *ultra vires* based on constitutional rights guarantees and the *Rechtsstaatsprinzip* (principle of the rule of law in Article 20 of the German Basic Law): "[A]ny state action interfering with the rights of individuals must be authorized by parliamentary statute" (Groß 2000: 587). Moreover, under Article 80, any statutory grant of administrative rulemaking authority must be stated explicitly and with precision. As Groß (2000, 587) characterizes it, "[a]ny independent regulatory power of the administration has been abolished. Only internal affairs of the administration and beneficial actions, like subsidies or the creation of public services, are excepted from that principle." German courts are organized into five divisions—ordinary, administrative, fiscal, labor, and social—to create a pluralistic expertise in scrutinizing Germany's famously detailed code. The administrative courts, which perform the bulk of judicial review of administrative action, are confined to questions of law— not the quality of administrative decisions—and Germans enjoy a right of review in all cases alleging rights interference by the administration (Groß 2000: 589–90).

To preserve sovereign authority, the German judicial check on administrative action is strong, while Canadian (like British) administrative law is strikingly subservient to parliamentary will through a formally weak role. Parliamentary sovereignty over the Canadian judiciary, which extends even to the abolition of the courts themselves, permits it to insert *privative clauses* into statutes that shield administrative activity from judicial review for activities taken under statutes including such language (J. F. Smith 2000: 560). Such clauses do not, however, protect the administration from *ultra vires* review: "an agency's decision beyond its jurisdiction leaves nothing for the privative clause to shield, because no lawful decision has been made" (J. F. Smith 2000: 561).

The rise of the European Union has been the impetus for the creation of some common principles of administrative law across these diverging systems. Schwartze (1998) notes that doctrinal "convergence" has been achieved on several principles. For example, though French law has long regarded that the obligation to give reasons for administrative action as an impediment to the effective execution of laws, this *principe de non-motivation* has begun to see some relaxation (Schwartze 1998: 198). Though British administrative acts traditionally received deference unless a decision was "so unreasonable that no reasonable authority could ever come to it," (*Associated Provincial Picture Houses, Ltd. v. Wednesbury Corp.* [1948] 1 KB 223) the principle of proportionality common in German law—administrative actions must be proportional to their ends—has been gradually effectuated in British courts, though not explicitly referenced (Schwartze 1998: 195). The instrumentality of law in political and economic change is apparent in this transformation.[12]

6.3 THE OMBUDSMAN, THE CENSORATE, AND THE PROCURACY

Centralized oversight of administration may be court-centered, as in the French model, or informal and sovereign-centered, as is typical of ombudsman schemes, the Chinese censorial model and the oversight role of the former Soviet procuracy. The most prevalent example of a bureau-centered administrative review procedure is the *office of the ombudsman*—an official to whom citizens may appeal when they have been wronged by a government agent. The ombudsman originated in Sweden and Finland as a parliamentary construction. In Sweden, the *Justitiekanseler* encompasses the role of an American attorney general as well as a responsibility for supervising all public servants on behalf of the crown (Jacobini 1991: 199). Writes Jacobini (1991: 197): "If [the office of ombudsman] functions usefully, [it] does so well within existing political context, not, it must be emphasized, against it." The ombudsman, then, is an agent of legislative control of the bureaucracy—"police patrols" in the language of McCubbins and Schwartz (1984)—which identically relates to the administrative law regimes we have heretofore discussed.

Ombudsmen save time and resources over trial-type review procedures in complaint processing (especially with regard to client-level matters), and for this reason, they are ubiquitous in complex organizations. At the national level, these offices conserve time and resources in the general and administrative courts, and save individual complainants litigation costs. Moreover, the ombudsman's "chief means of effectiveness is in bringing a supposed injustice to the attention of the allegedly misbehaving office or officer, and the threat of publicity may well be enough to bring about a change" (Jacobini 1991: 198). In addition to Sweden and Finland, strong ombudsmen exist in Denmark, Norway, New Zealand, and similar institutions are present in a host of other nations.

In New Zealand, for example, the ombudsman, who serves a five-year term, has been present since 1962, and investigates agency action both on the basis of complaints and *sua sponte*. With the exception of certain national security matters and other limited areas, where concerns of secrecy are pressing, the ombudsman may investigate any type of administrative action. The ombudsman has no jurisdiction over parliament, cabinet, ministers, or court decisions, though the office can investigate local governments (Jacobini 1991: 203). The office is constrained to avoid usurping judicial review authority when it is available, and is not meant to be an agent of *ex post* remedy. As Gellhorn (1966: 103) puts it, the ombudsman's mission is "not to clean up a mess, but rather simply to provide insurance against future messes." New Zealand's system has been a model for the creation of similar offices in Nigeria, Tanzania, Zambia, and Canada (Jacobini 1991: 204).

Another central overseer with some similarities developed in imperial China. The censorate (*Yu-shih*) "was simply a device designed to help assure the ancient Chinese emperor that his orders were in fact being carried out . . . It had little to do with the modern concern with the citizen's right to be treated properly by the state" (Jacobini 1991: 12–13). In this sense, it differs markedly from the Marxist theory of the procuracy. The censorate is an Asian phenomenon, with variants existing in contemporary Taiwan (the *Control Yuan*) and some other Asian states. Though it has significant similarities to the ombudsman, it was nowhere to be found in Roman law, and consequently was not present in civilian systems (see Hucker 1966).

The theory of the censorate is twofold. First, it was seen as a method of keeping the government true to its legal obligations, a rule of law concern like that embodied in the British *ultra vires* doctrine or German *Rechtsstaatsprinzip*. Second, it advanced two Confucian doctrines relating to disagreement with government action: (1) "If a ruler's policies are bad and yet none of those about him oppose them, such spinelessness is enough to ruin a state," and (2)"for one whose place is near the throne, not to remonstrate is to hold office idly for the sake of gain" (Hucker 1959: 193). The Censorate could record and analyze government functions, impeach bureaucrats for legal or moral violations, survey the bureaucracy generally, impeach officials on sound citizen complaints, remonstrate the Emperor regarding policy, mete out low-level punishments (Hucker 1966: 2–3). A "complaint drum" sat outside the palace for making complaints known to the emperor through the censorate (Hucker 1966: 99–100).

Dr. Sun Yat Sen was a proponent of the censorial system, and since 1931, Taiwan has had a version of the institution called the *Control Yuan*, which has gradually moved away from dominance by the *Kuomintang* party (Ma 1963). The Control Yuan is elected, and has a role in administrative appointments like the United States Senate. It can consent, censure, impeach, and audit, propose corrective action, and act *sua sponte* or on the basis of a complaint (exceptions are national and diplomatic secrecy). Impeachment, a court proceeding for "neglect of duty and for violation of law," is usually directed at high level officials, including the president, but not against elected personnel, like the Control Yuan. Censure, a similar administrative (usually no court involvement) procedure, is directed toward lower officials. "Correction . . . focuses not on individuals, but on the actions of agencies of the government itself" (Jacobini 1991: 184). As such, correction is a micro-level relative of structural reform litigation in the United States. Taiwan also has a formal administrative court in the Judicial Yuan that provides a forum for individual claims for redress of rights infringement due to agency action (Jacobini 1991: 185).

In the former Soviet Union and satellite socialist states, the *procuracy*, or prosecutor's office, had, under the doctrine of "general supervision," the right to oversee the bureaucracy and receive and investigate complaints from citizens. When informed of inappropriate agency action, the Soviet procuracy would confront the agency and demand correction, though it did not have the power to directly order remedial action. Its real power, as with ombudsman-type institutions in general, came predominantly from its ability to create publicity for agency wrongdoing, and in so doing, enforce consistency in administrative behavior throughout the government (G. B. Smith 1978). In that regard, it served as a *parens patriae* for the clients of Soviet administration, and given its centralization, a check on process consistency throughout the administrative state.[13]

Some form of ombudsman institution exists in countries throughout the world. In the United States, lieutenant governors have such a role in Illinois, Missouri, New York, Colorado, and New Mexico (Jacobini 1991: 219). In virtually every nation, there is also informal, fragmented complaint registering machinery that invites citizens to make complaints that will be internally investigated, which serve as micro-level *contentieux gracieux* procedures.

6.4 DELEGATION

Though administrative law operates at various levels, doctrine and procedures, as well as their development revolves around the quintessential problem of *delegation*: When and under what conditions and restrictions may power entrusted by the people to their sovereign governmental authority be delegated to non-majoritarian (or sub-sovereign) institutions? The political control theme in our discussion of American administrative law brings this into sharp relief. In separation-of-powers systems, politics ensues among the political branches over policy choices.

The typical delegation—enabling legislation, delegated legislation—entails a grant of authority to an administrative agency, and as such creates an agency relationship between sovereign authority (e.g., Parliament, the Monarch) as the constitutional level principal and a bureau-level administrative agent. This problem has been copiously studied in the political science literature.[14] Courts through administrative law regimes act as third-party enforcers of the statutory "contract" created between the sovereign and its administrative agent (Huber 2000). Administrative law *regimes*, then, develop as courts or adjudicatory authorities like the *Conseil d'État* answer questions such as these.

- *Does the sovereign have the authority to delegate the function in question to its agent?*
- *Under what conditions was the delegation made?* or *What precise powers were delegated?*

In the common law, this latter question lies at the heart of *ultra vires* inquiry, while the former is implied in the (possibly dormant) American non-delegation doctrine.[15] The non-delegation doctrine, which was the Diceyan rule in American administrative jurisprudence until the 1910s, held that no legislative power could be delegated by Congress since the Constitution establishes it as the sole law-making body in the American government. Such a rule has roots in Locke, and more generally in Anglo-American statism:

The legislative cannot transfer the power of making laws to any other hands; for it being but a delegated power from the people, they who have it cannot pass it over to others . . . The power of the legislative, being derived from the people by a positive voluntary grant and institution, can be no other than what the positive grant conveyed, which being only to make laws, and not to make legislators, the legislative can have no power to transfer their authority of making laws and place it in other hands. (Locke, *Second Treatise on Government*, Section 14)

Both non-delegation and *ultra vires* demonstrate the extent to which the British model restricted the growth of administrative law regimes in the commonwealth and, until the New Deal era, in the United States. Any regime development had to be generated through threshold considerations of the power of administrative agency action under delegation. The French Model also deals with delegated powers, but policing of agency behavior is not performed, in theory, by third party courts, as in the British Model. Nonetheless, the *Conseil d'État* has been a court since 1878, and its decisional law is the backbone of the French administrative law regime. In the censorial, procuracy, and ombudsman regimes, enforcement is truly done through a *non*-judicial third party.

6.5 THE EVOLUTION OF ADMINISTRATIVE LAW REGIMES

The development of administrative law regimes at all levels shapes and defines the institutional environment of public administration. Regardless of the model of administrative law, or even the common law or civilian system, that was initially at work in a country, regimes evolve through changes in decisional law. This development, it is argued, corresponds to a political interaction—one of credit claiming and blame shifting—of the sovereign (e.g., legislature) with the bureau, leaving the courts to determine where the onus of policy making lies in each case.

In the simplest evocative model of government policy choice, legislatures create policy by writing statutes, while administrative agencies make policy through their actions and choices at the bureau and client levels of governance. Taking the initiative to create policy leaves an institution responsible if that policy making is harmful. General delegations allow bureaus to make mistakes and pay for them politically, while specific delegations make legislatures answerable. The messy admixture of delegation techniques found in practice places practitioners of administrative law—on the bench, in the bureau, and at the bar—in the business of statutory construction. Moreover, if legislatures are to blame for harm to citizens, questions are often constitutional, while if agencies are the locus of critical legal authority, principles of tort, contract, and property operate (often through constitutional and statutory filters). Regimes of administrative law develop in response to these political tensions, and the judge may be seen as a "thermostat" that regulates the outcomes of the credit claiming game. Of course, when making delegations, the sovereign *knows* of the courts' thermostatic role, relying on it when making its delegations. Thus, our present theory is a strategic one.

Kaare Strøm (2000: 269) has argued that parliamentary and presidential systems differ on the basis of the directness of the chain of authority between voters and those administrative agencies that craft public policy. In parliamentary systems, the chain of authority flows from the voters through parliament to the prime minister and finally to the department ministers. The system is very direct. Alternatively, separation-of-powers systems diffuse voter control at the beginning of the authority chain. Authority flows from the voters to the separated *political* branches—president and chambers of the legislature—and then to the heads of administrative agencies. Other rules—such as Senate confirmation of administrative appointments in the United States—convolute the chain of authority between the political and executive branches.

In either scheme, the delegation of authority down the chain is insulated against bureaucratic drift by the "default rules" of an administrative law regime. Such a regime creates a (judicially enforceable, and therefore) credible commitment that administrative policy making that falls outside delegated authority will be actively checked, or that the bounds of administrative discretion will be enforced. Such enforcement is not the same as "deck stacking" (e.g., McCubbins et al. 1989). The existence of administrative law regimes allows political "principals" to tighten or relax checks on administrative policy choice in each delegation. Thus, the legal regime is an institutional resource for legislators and agencies playing the credit claiming game, as is contract law for the parties to an agreement. These public officials have control of the temperature dial on the thermostat.

The equilibrium of these political dynamics is a flexible standard under which deference is given to administrative action authorized by the sovereign authority when the authorization is sufficiently specific for at least *ultra vires* review. In cases where it is not easy for courts to interpret sovereign intent, they rely on the common law, decisional law, or general principles of fairness (such as proportionality) to make decisions. This is the standard of *Chevron, USA v. NRDC* in the United States, or the "pragmatic and functional" approach of *Canada v. Public Service Alliance of Canada* [1991] 80 D.L.R. (4th) 520), and it exists in one form or another in many national jurisdictions. Since courts exercise power as the result of a "substitution of law and office for consent" of the parties invoking their jurisdiction, a concern for the *legitimacy* of judicial action is omnipresent (Shapiro 1981). The general form of this standard allows the courts to establish legitimacy from *ultra vires* grounds when sovereign authority makes specific delegations, but from the fundamental notions of fairness, impartiality, and so forth inherent in the courts as institutions when the intent of the sovereign is ambiguous.

6.6 ADMINISTRATIVE LAW AND THE NEW PUBLIC MANAGEMENT

The Westminster reforms of the 1980s, which have evolved into the "new public management" (NPM) require at least an expansion of the reach of administrative law to the contractee-state. H. Wade MacLauchlan (1997, 118) has argued that the values of administrative law and NPM are in "prima facie tension." The conflict comes between the administrative law concerns "with hierarchical order, with due process, with rules and standards, with systemic coherence, and with the manners and sustainability of institutional practice" and NPM's assumption that "the state is too large and too costly, and that centralised or rule-oriented solutions are part of the problem." This view, some commentators argue, becomes problematic as public administration moves farther from the confines of administrative agencies.

One challenge lies with government counsel. MacLauchlan (1997: 123) states that it is the role of the government lawyer "to articulate legal advice and other legal services in terms that leave the ultimate choices with the responsible bureaucratic or political decision-makers." Under the "old public management," he continues, "[t]he main dynamic was one of edifice-building, and the rule of law was styled accordingly. In its negative sense, the rule of law enforced the *ultra vires* principle and prevented arbitrary exercises of power, applying the same law to all, including government. In its positive sense, it encouraged systemic coherence, predictability and due process" (MacLauchlan 1997: 123) But, in Canada and Australia, user-pay programs have been developed for government law practice, whereby an agency needing legal assistance would simply "hire" lawyers within government, implying tighter client control.

Given such systems, MacLauchlan (1997: 130) asks: "Where are the assurances of consistency or independence of judgment? Who will look out for the "central agency" or whole government perspective?" User-pay programs trim government fat, but they may be doing so at significant cost to intergovernmental equilibria. He concludes by opining that "[t]he check against a descent into an "anything goes, eat-what-you-kill" entrepreneurialism has to be professional discipline, accompanied by effective communication with clients about the value of independent judgment and the rule of law" (MacLauchlan 1997: 132).

In an extreme view, Jerry Mashaw (1996) argues that NPM contradicts the core purpose of administrative law. Writing of United States' federal administrative agencies, Mashaw argues that the misdirection begins with the notion of what administrative agencies do. He writes (1996: 412–13), "talk about doing better for less fundamentally misunderstands the purpose of most federal administrative activity... most federal agencies develop general norms and adjudicate cases. They are in the governance business, not the service provision business". The second error comes with understanding the purpose of administrative law: "The long-term commitment of American administrative law has been to assure that administrative discretion is structured, checked, and balanced." He continues, "American administrative law tends to presuppose clear lines of authority, hierarchical control, and responsibility focused on the top level management of agencies" (Mashaw 1996: 414).

"The basic idea," Mashaw (1996: 420) concludes, "[w]hile arguably reinforcing the accountability, reasonableness, and procedural fairness of administrative policy making, these 'regulatory reforms' are designed to stall and derail many rulemaking efforts." Through procedural controls, "Congress is bent on adding 'red tape' at least as fast as the executive purports to eliminate it" (Mashaw 1996: 421). The combination of new procedural requirements created by a legislature seeking bureaucratic control and a pared down administration that is less likely to make rules with the requisite procedural rigidities will lead to an untenable situation. This is not, however, as acute in Westminster systems, where political control is more direct.

More mundane, but equally problematic, is the problem of the legal identity of contractees, to which we alluded earlier. Though, for example, Britain's "Next Steps" agencies enter into performance agreements with cabinet agencies that are genuinely contractual in nature, these relationships "cannot take the form of private law contracts, because the parties have no separate legal identity. Legal identity precedes and cannot be derived from a contractual relationship" (Harden 1992: 46). Nor do these agencies possess "corporate personality deriving from public law; otherwise they would be able to make contracts" (Harden 1992: 46). Such agencies, then, fall outside the reach of both British private and public law. Writes Freedland (1994, 91 emphasis added), "it becomes quite remarkable that public authorities . . . are *assumed* to have an inherent power, freedom to enter into contracts." When the party is a "corporate public authority" lying outside the government, this power apparently is derived from its corporate nature, though in the case of the government, it may be one of the "residuary prerogative powers of the Crown," though British courts have provided little clarity (Freedland 1994: 91). *Churchward v. R.* ([1865] L.R. 1 Q.B. 173) stated that executive contracts are enforceable only where an appropriation from parliament was made as a condition precedent. But, writes Freedland (1994: 93), "[t]o the extent that this reasoning holds good, it means that a government department is free to privatize the performance of almost any of its functions (in the sense of contracting that performance out to the private sector) without statutory authority for so doing."

The contractual nature of NPM reforms places administrative law in something of a disequilibrium, though it is nothing that "pragmatic and functional" jurisprudence cannot handle. The courts, quite simply, will catch up with these reforms should they indeed have a lasting presence in governance.

6.7 CONCLUSION

In this chapter, our aim has been to develop some analytical categories through which we can better understand national administrative law regimes. Administrative law exists at multiple interfaces in governance—between the political branch(es) and the bureau, among the hierarchical levels of the bureau, and between the bureau and client. We have seen that variation in political regimes has important consequences for the type of administrative law regime that can be implemented. The reason that politics is so influential is that administrative law regimes exist to police the delegation of powers from sovereign authority to bureaus. The commitment to uphold administrative law is made credible in most of the world by a third party. In many nations, this third party is the courts. However, parliamentary institutions (such as the ombudsman) or central governmental authorities (such as the censorate or procuracy) have been and are being employed. These bodies generate decisional law that is, of necessity, reactive to political dynamics in the delegation game.

Recent trends in public administration that can be characterized as manifestations of the New Public Management can be problematic for this general operation. Diverse populations of agents—government contractees—are changing the political control problem, even in Britain, where New Public Management initiatives are among the strongest and most lasting in the world. We will find it necessary to revisit these topics again in fifteen years, and will likely find an interesting story of the legal logic of updating this component of administrative law.

Notes

The author would like to thank the students enrolled in his course entitled "Comparative Law and Administration" at Texas A&M University during the summer and fall of 2003 for their invaluable comments and reactions to this material.

1. The basic principles of administrative law apply in the international context as well, but a line must be drawn so as to achieve coherence in the presentation.
2. A positive theory of the control of bureaus through judicial review is presented in Shipan (1997).
3. In contrast, the term "public law" in the lexicon of civilian jurisprudence is more broadly construed to include legal institutions and processes regarding the operation of the state.
4. Morton and Knopff (2000) provide an excellent background in Canadian Charter litigation for the interested reader.
5. As we shall see, it is judicial review of this form that so concerned the British legal icon A.V. Dicey (1885).
6. Notwithstanding the hermeneutic traps identified by postmodern legal scholars (see Kelman 1987), Sunstein (1989) provides an exemplary discussion of the role of statutory interpretation in the American administrative state.
7. Though the United States passed the first such statute, nations having an APA include Australia, Austria, Germany, Netherlands, Switzerland, Sweden, Argentina, Georgia, Korea, Latvia, Poland, Slovenia and Taiwan (see Council of Europe 1996).

8. Rosenbloom (2001) provides a public administrationist's account of the impact of the APA on the American administrative state. McNollgast (1999) provides a view from positive political theory.

9. For a discussion of the impact of this type of litigation on the norms of responsibility and accountability in public administration, see Bertelli (2004) and Bertelli and Lynn (2001; 2003).

10. Though privative clauses and the inferior position of the Canadian Supreme Court, as will be discussed, make this even more difficult.

11. Often legislatures and even the administration itself can choose the default rules for administrative activity. A striking example of this is in the legislative creation of quasi-autonomous, non-governmental organizations, or *quangos* for policy implementation. For example, under Article I, Book II of the Netherlands Civil Code, a quango only has legal personality—a recognition that it, as with a person, can be the subject of a suit—if its enabling statute so provides. Otherwise, depending on its task, the quango is considered part of the administration. For an excellent discussion of quangos in the Netherlands, see Van Thiel (2001). Bertelli (forthcoming 2005; forthcoming 2006) examines the incentives that legislatures face when delegating authority to quangos.

12. Chinese administrative law provides another interesting case study. Deng Xiaoping's economic reforms in the 1970s–1980s provided the impetus for administrative law development. With the promulgation of the Administrative Litigation Law in 1989, citizens (as well as the multinational interests of the new Chinese economy) could bring actions against administration with procedural safeguards (Feng 1996).

13. This check was put to terrible use in the Stalinist era as a threshold screening mechanism for purges (Smith 1978).

14. Bendor, Glazer, and Hammond (2001) provide an excellent review of this literature.

15. For a fuller discussion of the *ultra vires* doctrine in Britain, see Forsyth (1996); the non-delegation doctrine in America is discussed in Barber (1975).

References

ALLISON, J. W. F. (1996), *A Continental Distinction in the Common Law: A Historical and Comparative Perspective on English Public Law*, Oxford: Clarendon Press.

BARBER, S. A. (1975), *The Constitution and the Delegation of Congressional Power*, Chicago: University of Chicago Press.

BENDOR, J., GLAZER, A., and HAMMOND, T. A. (2001), "Theories of Delegation," *Annual Review of Political Science* 4: 235–69.

BERLE, A. (1917), "The Expansion of American Administrative Law," *Harvard Law Review* 30: 430–48.

BERTELLI, A. (2004), "Strategy and Accountability: Structural Reform Litigation and Public Management," *Public Administration Review* 64(1): 19–33.

—— (forthcoming 2005), "Governing the Quango: An Auditing and Cheating Model of Quasi-governmental Public Authorities," *Journal of Public Administration Research and Theory*.

—— (forthcoming 2006), "Delegating to the Quango: Ex Ante and Ex Post Ministerial Constraints," *Governance*.

—— and LYNN, L. E., JUN. (2001), "A Precept of Managerial Responsibility: Securing Collective Justice in Institutional Reform Litigation," *Fordham Urban Law Journal* 29: 317–86.

—— —— (2003), "Managerial Responsibility," *Public Administration Review* 63(3): 259–68.

—— and SVEN E. FELDMANN. (2003), "Structural Reform Litigation: Legislative Mandates Under Remedial Bargaining," Working Paper. Center for Economic and Business Research. Copenhagen, Denmark.

CHAYES, A. (1976), "The Role of the Judge in Public Law Litigation," *Harvard Law Review* 89: 1281–316.

Council of Europe. (1996), *The Administration and You: A Handbook*, Strasbourg: Council of Europe Publishing.

CRAIG, P. (1999), "Competing Models of Judicial Review," *Public Law* 91: 428–47.

DIVER, C. S. (1979), "The Judge as Political Powerbroker: Superintending Structural Change in Public Institutions," *Virginia Law Review* 65: 43–106.

DREWRY, G. (1986), "Public Lawyers and Public Administrators: Prospects for an Alliance?" *Public Administration* 64: 173–88.

EPSTEIN, D., and O'HALLORAN, S. (1999), *Delegating Powers: A Transaction Cost Politics Approach to Policy Making Under Separate Powers*, New York: Cambridge University Press.

FENG, L. (1996), *Administrative Law Procedures and Remedies in China*, Hong Kong: Sweet & Maxwell.

FORSYTH, C. (1996), "Of Fig Leaves and Fairy Tales: The Ultra Vires Doctrine," *Cambridge Law Journal* 55: 122–48.

FREEDLAND, M. (1994), "Government by Contract and Public Law," *Public Law* 86: 86–104.

GELLHORN, W. (1966), *Ombudsmen and Others: Citizen's Protectors in Nine Countries*, Cambridge, MA: Harvard University Press.

GOODNOW, FRANK J. (1905), *The Principles of the Administrative Law of the United States*, New York: Putnam's.

GROß, T. (2000), "Monism(s) or Dualism(s)?: Germany," *European Review of Public Law* 12(2): 585–93.

HARDEN, I. (1992), *The Contracting State*, Buckingham: Open University Press.

HUBER, J. D. (2000), "Delegation to Civil Servants in Parliamentary Democracies," *European Journal of Political Research* 37: 397–413.

HUCKER, C. O. (1959), "Confucianism in the Chinese Censorial System," in D. S. Nivison and A. F. Wright, *Confucianism in Action*, Stanford, CA: Stanford University Press.

—— (1966), *The Censorial System of Ming China*, Stanford, CA: Stanford University Press.

JACOBINI, H. B. (1991), *An Introduction to Comparative Administrative Law*, New York: Oceana.

KELMAN, M. (1987), *A Guide to Critical Legal Studies*, Cambridge, MA: Harvard University Press.

MA, H. H. (1963), "The Chinese Control Yuan: An Independent Supervisory Organ of the State," *Washington University Law Quarterly* 1963(4): 401–26.

McCUBBINS, M., NOLL, R., and WEINGAST, B. R. (1989), "Structure and Process, Politics and Policy: Administrative Arrangements and the Political Control of Agencies," *Virginia Law Review* 75: 431–82.

McDowell, G. L. (1982), *Equity and the Constitution: the Supreme Court, Equitable Relief, and Public Policy*, Chicago: University of Chicago Press.

MacLauchlan, H. W. (1997), "Public Service Law and the New Public Management," pp. (118–133), in Michael Taggart, *The Province of Administrative Law*. Oxford: Hart Publishing.

McNollgast. (1999), "The Political Origins of the Administrative Procedure Act," *Journal of Law Economics and Organization* 15(1): 180–217.

Mashaw, J. L. (1996), "Reinventing Government and Regulatory Reform: Studies in the Neglect and Abuse of Administrative Law," *University of Pittsburgh Law Review*, 57: 405–22.

Morton, F. L. and Knopff, R. (2000), *The Charter Revolution and the Court Party* Peterborough, Ont.: Broadview Press.

Palmer, E. (2000), "Resource Allocation, Welfare Rights: Mapping The Boundaries Of Judicial Control In Public Administrative Law," *Oxford Journal of Legal Studies* 20(1): 63–88.

Rosenbloom, D. H. (2001), *Building a Legislative-Centered Public Administration: Congress and the Administrative State, (1946–1999)*, Tuscaloosa: University of Alabama Press.

Scalia, A. (1998), *A Matter of Interpretation: Federal Courts and the Law*, Princeton: Princeton University Press.

Schama, S. (1989), *Citizens: A Chronicle of the French Revolution*, New York: Knopf.

Schlesinger, R. B., Baade, H. W., Herzog, P. E., and Wise, M. E. (1998), *Comparative Law*, 6th edn., New York: Foundation Press.

Schwartze, J. (1993), "Developing Principles of European Administrative Law," *Public Law* 229–39.

—— (1998), "The Convergence of the Administrative Laws of the EU Member States," *European Public Law*, 4(2): 191–210.

Shapiro, M. (1981), *Courts: A Comparative and Political Analysis*, Chicago: University of Chicago Press.

Shipan, C. R. (1997), *Designing Judicial Review: Interest Groups, Congress, and Communications Policy*, Ann Arbor: University of Michigan Press.

Skowronek, S. (1982), *Building a New American State: The Expansion of Administrative Capacities, (1877–1920)*, New York: Cambridge University Press.

Smith, G. B. (1978), *The Soviet Procuracy and the Supervision of Administration*, Alphen aan den Rijn: Sijthoff and Noordhoff.

Smith, J. F. (2000), "Comparing Federal Judicial Review of Administrative Court Decisions in the United States and Canada," *Temple Law Review* 73(2): 503–96.

Sterzel, F. (1994), "Public Administration," in Bengtsson, et al., *Swedish Law: A Survey*, Stockholm: Juristförlaget.

Stewart, R. B. (1975), "The Reformation of American Administrative Law," *Harvard Law Review* 88: 1669–813.

Strøm, K. (2000), "Delegation and Accountability in Parliamentary Democracies," *European Journal of Political Research* 37: 261–89.

Sunstein, C. (1989), "Interpreting Statutes in the Regulatory State," 103 *Harvard Law Review* 405.

Van Thiel, S. *Quangos: Trends, Causes, and Consequences*, Abingdon: Ashgate.

White, L. D. (1935), *Introduction to the Study of Public Administration*, New York: Macmillan.

Wood, R. (ed.) (1990), *Remedial Law: When Courts Become Administrators*, Amherst, MA: University of Massachusetts Press.

Yates, D. (1982), *Bureaucratic Democracy: The Search for Democracy and Efficiency in American Government*, Cambridge, MA: Harvard University Press.

Yoo, J. C. (1996), "Who Measures the Chancellor's Foot? The Inherent Remedial Authority of the Federal Courts," *California Law Review* 84: 1121–77.

PUBLIC MANAGEMENT AS ETHICS

J. PATRICK DOBEL

7.1 THE ENDURING CHALLENGE

IN 1996 the United Nations overwhelmingly passed an *International Code for Public Officials* as an Annex to a General Assembly resolution *Action against Corruption* (United Nations Resolution 51/59). The code stated "public office" is "a position of trust." Public officials should "ensure that they perform their duties and functions efficiently, effectively and with integrity, in accordance with laws or administrative policies." The code runs less than 1,000 words and stipulates that public officials "shall be attentive, fair, and impartial in the performance of their functions." It prohibits officials from giving "undue preferential treatment" and "improperly discriminate against any group or individual, or others abuse the power and authority vested in them."[1]

The Code represents a remarkable consensus about fundamental administrative values that lie at the heart of public management and administration.[2] Its distillation calls to mind that public management is a value-driven activity with deep moral groundings. Public management ethics covers the principles and values by which public managers may determine right and wrong as well as the character needed to sustain judgment and action. Although the exact structure of the obligations and the weightings of values vary across political regimes and time, all regimes have to solve certain basic problems (Wren 1994; Kettl 2002). First, regimes need institutions and ideas that legitimize their rule. Second, regimes need to find and train individuals who possess the skills and reliability to achieve the regime's aims with competence. Third, regimes and societies struggle to create institutions that will serve the common good and not use power for their own benefit or to tyrannize the population.

Management and administration lie at the center of the governmental enterprise because activities that sustain society and provide public goods require consistency under conditions of uncertainty. These persistent activities involve significant skill and investment. To take a lowly example, if garbage is not picked up on a regular basis, the quality of life as well as public health will deteriorate. Picking up garbage needs elaborate organization of pick up points, delivery points, equipment, and people who perform despite lousy conditions. Oversight ensures the job is done. Disposal points must be monitored to avoid further public health problems. The creation and sustaining of the structures to achieve public ends become the never-ending task of public administration (Kettl 2002).

Public management and administration are justified by moral purpose: they provide the political and institutional conditions that permit human beings to survive, flourish and exercise virtue and excellence. Interestingly, however, almost all historical forms of bureaucracy and government emphasize at the rhetorical level, the ethical responsibilities of public administrators to serve impartially "all" citizens of the state with competence. The successful provision of public goods such as sanitation or defense benefits all citizens. The consensus that emerged in the *United Nations International Code of Officials* was not an accident.

This chapter discusses the ethical values and character that modern public managers and administrators should possess to perform their duties in liberal democracies. The chapter analyzes the strains within liberal democracy that pose unique and persistent tensions between the values of liberal democracy and public management. It focuses upon framing discretion as the moral focal point of public management and looks at the range of values central to morally defensible public management. Finally it discusses the role of ethics policies to imbed values at the core of the public management enterprise and address corruption.

7.2 LIBERAL DEMOCRACY

Liberal democratic regimes establish an array of institutions designed to perform the traditional functions of government by ensuring common and public goods and community solidarity while relying upon the consent of the governed for its legitimacy and guidance. This means the citizenry should have ample opportunities to participate in the process of creating government policy and holding government accountable via elections, self-organization, lobbying, and informal politics. In some variations public participation is encouraged not just to hold government accountable but maximize the power and political development of citizens as a positive good (Fishkin 1991; Gutmann and Thompson 1996; Barber 1984).

The ethical sources of liberal democracy flow from two streams. The democratic promotes popular sovereignty and participation as the means to express human potential for self-rule and civic virtue as well as preventing tyranny. Deliberation among citizens promotes not only better policy and support but more virtuous citizens. On the other hand, the liberal stream insists upon respect for the rights and freedom of the individual as the basic obligation of acknowledging human dignity. Respecting individual rights can run counter to the communal dimensions of democratic participation and accountability but also puts limits upon the ability of communities to dominate or deprive minority groups and individuals of their dignity and chance for flourishing.

Both democratic and liberal sources distrust the administrative state and public management. As Rousseau pointed out in his foundational work on popular sovereignty, government develops its own particular will that differs from the general will of the people. Government institutions pose a profound problem for democratic sovereignty. The theoretical solution resides in keeping the community small, having regular deliberations where all citizens participate and ensuring a constant rotation of any offices by lot or election (Rousseau 1968; Barber 1984). If a country grows in scale, the dangers to sovereignty from government rise and only vigilant efforts to rotate office work; most democracies struggle with permanent government, office, and specialization. Modern variations of democratic distrust offer different ways around the dilemmas. A patronage system seeks democratic control by insisting that political loyalty and responsiveness to the last election, not merit, training, or bloodline should be the major requirement for positions. Each administration brings wholesale changes in administrative personnel. Feminist critics analyze the implied gender roles and exclusions that hierarchical management models carry (Ferguson 1984; Stivers 2002). Postmodern theorists argue that government imposes one narrative that overwhelms other narratives and voices in the political system. Both argue for decentralizing and bringing public organizations and managers closer to the populations, as well as for active attempts to open systems to more voices. The public manager should essentially surrender authority to local democratic deliberation. For New Public Management (NPM) theorists this decentralization should be allied with greater use of market mechanisms. Together they can break the sclerosis and nonresponsiveness that NPM imputes to hierarchical models. Ideally decentralization and markets should make for better service and more effective learning and adaptability (Osborne and Gaebler 1992; Fox and Miller 1995; Hood 1991, 1998; Denhardt and Denhardt 2003). Postmodern theorists and feminists distrust the claims of privileged authority of public management and evince sensitivity to the need for government to attend to the diversity of the citizenry and include marginalized people in the political process (Fox and Miller 1995).

The liberal tradition has its own concerns that overweening government can unjustly dominate individuals or groups. This concern covers not just governmental abuse but also the capacity of sovereign democracies or legislatures to abuse the rights of individuals or groups especially minorities or outcasts. The liberal sources argue for protection of human rights both by limiting the scope of government but more vitally by creating constitutional guarantees, political resources and appeals to protect rights against governmental incursion (Rawls 1971, 1996; Dworkin 1977; Nozick 1974). Oversight and electoral scrutiny provide assurances of governmental respect for rights and deliberation (Finer 1941; Burke 1989). The liberal tradition informs the search for procedural protections with demands for consultation and transparency. Increasingly both domestic and international agreements protect "entrenched human rights" and challenge claims implicit in national democratic or legislative sovereignty (Szablowski 2000). Liberal proposals place the protection of rights as a central value for public managers regardless of their area. For instance at the recent birth of the European Union, Article 41 of the Charter of Fundamental Rights guarantees all citizens the "*right to good administration*" (italics added). It specifies that "every person" has a right to "be heard," have "access to his or her file," and have "affairs handled impartially, fairly, and within a reasonable time" (European Ombudsman 2002).

The size and scope of modern government stresses both sources of legitimacy for the liberal democratic state. In addition, many democratic and liberal values require state action to ensure rights protection or that silenced voices be heard (Dworkin 1977; Rawls 1971). What I will call the "classic" solution to delegated power in liberal democratic regimes emerged in the nineteenth century. It emphasizes that the moral obligation of public managers lies in obedience to the mandates of law and policy mediated by the elected and appointed officials of democratic regimes. No one has articulated this solution more clearly than Max Weber's famous formulation: "The honor of the civil servant is vested in his ability to execute conscientiously the order of his superior authorities, exactly as if the order agreed with his own convictions...Without this moral discipline and self-discipline in the highest sense, the whole apparatus falls apart" (Weber 1946a: 95).

With suitable caveats and adaptations, the classical solution aligns public managers with democratic power by ensuring a line of continuity from people to election, to law and appointment, to institutional authority, to implementation. The oath of the public official mediates the ethical relationship and pledges the official to judge and act in accordance with law, process, and policy. The manager and administrator remain true to their moral obligation to respect the democratic process by voicing their insights prior to decision and deference after decision even

if they disagree with the policy. The liberal tradition built in procedural requirements and in many cases oversight or judicial remedies for individuals that
constrained the exercise of bureaucratic power and enhanced transparency. Transparency makes electoral accountability more real and closes the circle of answerability.

This classic model still holds enormous influence and provides powerful moral
strength to public managers seeking to maintain professional excellence and
provide fair and impartial service to all citizens. The model anchors an abiding
ethical role identity for public administrators that transcends family, ethnic,
gender, racial, and religious affiliation. Public managers provide fair and competent service or advice to all citizens and officials. Officials are asked to promote and
act for the agency on the basis of the good of agency and merit, not primary
affiliations. The modern evolution of the classic model accepts that public management is imbedded in an accountability structure linked to law, constitutional
guarantees, oversight, and hierarchy. It seeks to incorporate long-term, national or
international dimensions of management. It offers continuity and an ethos of
impartial and fair service and has been forced to work aggressively to build
inclusive personnel policies that respond to gender and other diversity critiques.
It seeks to ensure strong consultative systems to supplement the legislative system
(Chapman 1988, 2000b; Vickers 1983; Aberbach et al. 1981; Denhardt 1998; Burke
1986; Cooper 1990; Huber and Shipan 2002). The continuing moral force of the
model comes into sight when *The United Nations International Code of Conduct
for Public Officials* enumerates in its first paragraph that the ultimate loyalty of
public officials "shall be to the public interests of their country as expressed
through *the democratic institutions of government*" (italics added; United Nations
Resolution 51/59).

7.3 THE CHALLENGE OF DISCRETION

Ethical action in public management plays out in discretion. Discretionary
judgment involves a cognitive dimension of framing a situation and identifying
significance. The frame grows from training and experience and enables professionals to adapt to unique challenges in the way consistent with norms and
creative engagement (Schon 1983; Bolman and Deal 1997). Discretion differs from
following rules or direct orders because it grows from latitude within the framework to balance among and give content to the criteria while adapting to unique
circumstances.

Public administrative discretion lives at the nexus point of three lines of moral consideration. First, if discretion exists for public managers, the problem of accountability and the link between administration and liberal democracy becomes much more complicated. Second, discretion isolates and highlights the moral responsibility of public managers. Finally, framing and managing competent, effective, and accountable discretion becomes the focus of ethics policy and institutional design.

The existence of ineluctable discretion for public managers is widely acknowledged (Warwick 1981; Lynn 1987; Rainey 1991; Frederickson 1997; O'Toole 1989). Laws arrive vague, aspirational, and underdetermined. Their mandates reflect the coalitions that pass them and compromise among multiple purposes. Public managers and administrators often draft or consult on legislation. Public managers weight priorities after passage (Bardach 1977; Rohr 1989; Lowi 1979; Lynn 1987; Behn 1998). Laws require implementing rules written by public administrators or contracts written and overseen by public managers, and discretion suffuses this writing and oversight. Making administrative rules follows procedures that involve participation or consultation (Peters 1993; Thompson 1980; Dobel 2001). Public managers influence who participates and what is heard. Often laws may come into conflict with each other or multiple purposes imbedded in a law may require balance or compromise by public managers (Dobel 1990a; Behn 1998). Public managers influence decisions about budget priorities as well as responding to cuts or scale backs (Lynn 1987; Peters 1993). Finally, decisions at the street level where public officials meet citizens they regulate, inspect, and serve involves discretion and negotiation (Lipskey 1980; Bardach and Kagen 1982; DiJulio 1994).

The existence of discretion increases the tension between liberal democracy and public management and administration. The classic solution depends on the ability of people through elected officials to inscribe clear and consistent behavioral requirements. This clarity meant that obedience and honor as Max Weber articulated would ensure that the public servants acted consistent with the mandates of democracy (Weber 1946a). The pervasive and wide range of discretion disrupts the clean lines of accountability in the classical solution (Holzer and Gabrielian 1998; Fry and Nigro 1998; Denhardt 1993, 1998; Hunt and O'Toole 1998a).

The dynamics of organizational life add more pressure to ensure consistent ethical standards and character from public mangers. Public choice theory suggests that public managers will be tempted to become budget maximizers and empire builders more concerned with expanding agency power than achieving goals of law and policy (Niskanen 1971; Ostrom and Ostrom 1971; Moe 1984;). This goal displacement distorts allocation of resources and erects inertia to change reinforced by iron triangles and policy networks (Heclo 1977; Buchanan 1985). Predictable stresses of organizational life pressure ethics, integrity, and autonomy. The incessant press of promotion, linguistic distortion, peer influence, hierarchical demands, and information metamorphosis push individuals to disassociate their standards of judgment and character from official actions. They lose their ability to accept responsibility or to gain moral perspective. Gradually they internalize the hermetic standards and practices of their organization, even if this involves immoral, illegal or questionable activities. When these practices are overlaid by secrecy the subversion of ethical responsibility grows (Milgram 1975; Jackall 1988; Adams and Balfour 1998; Sabini 1982; Dobel 1999).

The pervasive reality of discretion means public servants possess a degree of ineluctable personal responsibility in decisions and outcomes. The actual range of responsibility varies given the chain of commands and multiple principals involved, but it grows as one's stature, influence and expertise expand (Thompson 1980, 1983, 1987). The linking of discretion and responsibility challenges the classical model's emphasis upon the obligation of public administrators to express their position and obey the outcomes. Responsibility reminds public mangers of their unique contribution to their positions that flow from their distinctive skills, style, character and intelligence (Vickers 1983; Applbaum 1999; Dobel 1999, 2003). Responsibility offsets the penchant for excessive reliance upon controls that deflect personal responsibility (Anechiarico and Jacobs 1998; Light 1993). Consequences unfold through discretion-based judgments and enmesh individual administrators in personal responsibility for policy and actions.

Responsible public managers possess a range of ethical options from obedience, to voice, to exit but also to work through time to change the policy or to obstruct or slow down or whistle-blow (Hirshman 1970; Dobel 1999; Chapman 1988; Lundquist 1993). This range of moral options means hierarchical or professional subordination does not exculpate individuals from participating in illegal or morally troubling policies (Thompson 1987; Applbaum 1999).

Recognizing personal responsibility highlights the basic moral compromise public managers and administrators make. They take on strong moral obligations to maintain democratic accountability and defer to the authorized and accountable policies from democratic processes. They commit to institutions and policies that are imperfect and often implement policies with which they disagree. Sometimes officials stay in to implement policy to the best of their ability but also to work to change it over time. Often they may implement troubling policies to balance commitment to other policies or the institution (Thompson 1987; Chapman 1988; Dobel 1999; Rohr 1989). Defenders of the classical model worry that such discretion undermines accountability and honor; they emphasize respect for law and process and deference to the democratic process. This interpretation admits a much narrower range of discretion and initiative (Chapman 1988; Burke 1986, 1989; Cubbon 1993; O'Toole 1998).

The central importance of responsibility and discretion increases with the emphasis upon the mission-driven nature of modern administration (Senge 1990; Block 1993; Moore 1995; Barnard 1938; Collins 2001). Many reform proposals and schools of public administration emphasize the importance of public managers taking initiative in light of their mission. Missions are explicitly value-driven conceptualizations of the legal mandates and public functions of institutions. When they work, they bridge the legal mandates with frames of judgment that permit public managers to judge consistent with legal and accountable intent but also with a spirit of initiative and creating public value and common good. The mission orientation and increase of discretion makes internalized ethics vital to maintaining the integrity of government (Moore 1995). The emphasis upon mission, however, may only inadequately compensate for the loss of centralized bureaucratic control and oversight (Painter 2000; O'Toole 1998).

The institutional design challenges posed by mission, discretion, and managerial ethics depend upon how one conceptualizes the relationships between individual ethics and judgment in public office. Public choice theory influences a wide range of modern public management and posits that the challenge of managerial ethics and democratic accountability reduces to an extended principal–agent problem. The people delegate their power and aspirations through a chain of agents who will make laws, refine them, and implement them. Their elected agents become the principals to oversee public agencies to achieve the common good. This circles back through participation and electoral accountability to ensure alignment over time of principal and agent. The problem is that the extended chains of command, information asymmetries, self-interest, and the desire for autonomy generate constant slippage between principals and agents (Moe 1984; Dunleavy 1992; Lynn 1996). The theory is widely utilized in analysis and design and explains many of the pathologies of bureaucratic life. Some aspects inform the New Public Management school (DiJulio 1994; Pollit 1993, 2003).

Because of the theory's default position to individual self-interest, the implications for designing institutions where public managers achieve high ethical performance are pessimistic. This approach begins with the type of assumptions that informed James Madison's ideas about the dynamics of self-interest, interest, and conflict while trying to achieve some level of public virtue (Hamilton and Madison 1961: 10, 51; Kettl 2002). Accordingly it advocates limiting the scope of organizations to clear functions via design or contracted outcomes while providing discretion to perform. Limited government will be augmented by a preference that powers be devolved when not necessary to be centralized. The approach to ethical actions requires ongoing oversight at multiple levels because of the assumption of constant slippage. It entails significant procedural demands to ensure that voices are heard and that transparency exists in the decision making.

Another public choice tactic writes laws with performance specifications or replaces management with clear and strong contractual language that specifies performance outcomes with government or contractors. Both approaches minimize discretion at one level but increase discretion when bound by clear outcomes and public scrutiny. To the extent that ethics enters into design, ethics focuses on minimizing conflict of interest that would subvert judgment or demanding transparent procedure and disclosure (Stark 2000; Mackenzie 2002). The use of incentives around performance should promote active adherence to goals and utilize self-interest in a positive manner. The design of institutions minimizes concern to inculcate standards and employs limited government, devolution, transparency, multiple forms of oversight, procedures to ensure proper consultation and participation, and use of clear laws, contracts, and outcomes. If done well, these methods should harness self-interest in support of public interest and minimize the predictable tendencies to abuse or the need for integrity oriented leadership.

A different conception of ethical design flows from a different set of assumptions about human beings. While acknowledging the influence of self-interest, this focuses upon the capacity of human beings to act with integrity based upon promises to act according to standards of conduct and judgment. It relies less upon "devices" and more upon creation of culture and ethos that socialize values and practice, what Weber noted as a "vocation" (Payne 1991; Weber 1946a). Theoretically this approach argues that humans can commit and act within institutional roles in ways that transcend narrow personal self-interest. Duty, solidarity, integrity emerge as strong independent aspects of judgment capable of channeling or framing self-interest. Internalized values and character sustain consistent duty-bound behavior in face of obstacles and temptations (March and Olsen 1989, 1995; DiJulio 1994; Mansbridge 1990; Dobel 1999).

This institutional project builds on Chester Barnard's ground-breaking insistence that good organizations possess a "moral" center (Barnard 1938). Empirical work strongly suggests public employees and managers display a sense of mission and character that sustain duty and creating social capital. These attributes enable them to act in accountable and effective ways and manage the tension between personal moral responsibility and democratic responsiveness (Wilson 1989; Rohr 1989; Goodsell 1985; Perry and Wise 1990; Brewer 2003). The autonomous role of commitment and values also inform high performing private and nonprofit organizations (Senge 1990; Collins 2001). A commitment to public office integrates into their sense of identity and enables them to act within the obligations of the office with flexibility. The integrity approach enables humans to surmount prejudices and short-term self-interest on behalf of role obligations. This unfolds as an ethos or tradition of values and character internalized by public servants. The socialized moral attributes take on a self-sustaining aspect that while not sufficient to deter all pressures on high ethical performance provides a strong buttress for judgment and action (Cooper 1987, 1990; Cooper and Wright 1992; Rohr 1986, 2002; Chapman 1988, 1993a, 1993b; O'Toole 1998; Dobel 1999).

This design places culture at the center management (Wilson 1989; Dilman 1998; Denhardt 1998). The organizational design and management strive to achieve what Peter Senge calls "commitment" not "compliance" (Senge 1990). Psychological and social pressures, symbols and rituals as well as solidarity converge to support norms and reinforce performance and judgment. It accentuates the centrality of culture and formal and informal norms in design and management. This begins with clarity about the values but also an awareness of the character needed to maintain high standards. Strong leadership commitment, modeling and mentoring build from the cornerstones. Mission orientation or codes of ethics focus upon principles and character to frame judgment rather than detailed prohibitions. Culture and leadership sustain ethical discretion, practices, and norms. Training and socialization with a special emphasis upon influencing the informal cultures focus daily managerial life. The design requires good pay and benefits to make public integrity compatible with obligations to family. The design depends upon the emergence of trust as a primary attribute of public management but also enables public managers to address the diversity of identities within public organizations in ways that permit solidarity and trust across identity boundaries (Priore 1995). The culture creates organizational boundaries and offers the support, norms and frameworks for mangers to engage the political and external environment.

Neither design strategy sustains ethical performance on its own. Although proponents sometimes seem to suggest the approaches exclude each other, this is more an artifact of theoretical assumptions than reality. The most sophisticated design approaches weave ethics into the organization by aligning it with incentives in hiring, evaluation and promoting where competence and integrity reinforce each other. A unified approach requires that that ethics issues be taken seriously and welcomed in deliberations, culture, and should pervade hiring and firing, performance evaluations and align with incentives (Lewis 1991; OECD 1997; Klitgaard 1988; Klitgaard et al. 2000; Uhr 1999; Gilman 1999).

7.4 WHAT VALUES SHOULD INFORM PUBLIC MANAGEMENT?

The unique and enduring power of government to use coercion, generate revenue, and provide security guarantees that the values its administrators hold will be of great concern. The reality of discretion and the centrality of mission to modern public management reinforce the importance of ethics—character and contextual standards of right and wrong—for public managers. The importance of ethics increases along the jagged borders where career officials meet the elected and appointed agents of accountability (Campbell 1993). The need for re-election and more relaxed standards of elected political leaders complicates this borderland (Stark 2000; Thompson 1995). This becomes a more interesting question because if the world is moving towards one of "governance" then the range of discretion and judgment will become even wider. In a governance world, the reality of resource constraints, trans-jurisdictional problems, and interdependencies increases the range of judgment of public managers. The bleeding out of public responsibilities across organizations adds the compelling need for public managers to lead at the intersection of multiple sectors without clear legal guidance (Bozeman 1987; Kettl 2002). This means that public managers will function at the seams and boundaries building partnerships, interpreting complex cross-cutting regulations and jurisdictions and negotiating ongoing results. The question becomes what ethical standards and characteristics should frame judgment and action by public managers? A number of strong claims exist for the norms and character of public managers. The most obvious discuss what it means to hold a public "trust" or be a "steward" as the United Nations Code postulates. Another set follow from the explicit values built into the traditions of democracy and liberalism. Finally, a number of answers balance personal responsibility and values within legally accountable discretion.

The ideal of holding a public trust or being a public steward brings to mind the reality that public institutions exist in time. They or their responsibilities exist prior to individual public managers exercising responsibility and will exist after one exits the scene. This means that public managers hold their positions as temporary charges to be protected, performed, and handed on.

The steward and trustee dimensions generate unique obligations. First, trusteeship introduces a long-term frame and asks public managers and administrators to attend to the long-term consequences in ways that private organizations have few incentives to. Second, the duty to hand on responsibilities sets special charges to public institutions to keep accurate records and history for accountability and to ensure that those who come after know their historical and technical responsibilities. Government possesses a "store of knowledge and experience" that results from "slow accretion and accumulation." (Chapman 1993a, 2000a). Third, the ability of institutions to perform depends upon maintaining the related obligations of competence and credibility. Public managers have strong responsibility to attend to the institution itself and build competent capacity but also to earn legitimacy for the institution and regime. The integrity of process, capacity and legitimacy abide as key institutional responsibilities (Frederickson 1997; O'Toole 1998; Chapman 1988; Rohr 1989; Wamsley et al. 1990). Fourth, trusteeship and stewardship require a focus upon the common, that which cuts across all cleavages in society. Demanding that the common be addressed means attention to inclusiveness and representation of all viewpoints and all parts of society. It puts special obligations that public organizations attend to and involve marginalized groups. Public managers should work to prevent one group from dominating for its own ends. Even in a governance-based world, public institutions possess unique obligations to introduce long-term views, keep strong records, build capacity and legitimacy of common institutions, include all sectors, and induce deliberation beyond the mere aggregation of private interests (Terry 1995).

Both democratic and liberal streams inform public management values. Both traditions converge on transparency of governmental activity and a demand for strong accountability. Both see accountability requiring maximum participation where possible and inclusive participation where individuals or groups are not denied voice or due process. While both demand inclusiveness, responsiveness and accountability, the liberal tradition places strong obligations to respect rights and process against majority tyranny or a pure outcomes approach.

The insistence upon the personal responsibility of public officials generated a movement to introduce autonomous moral reasoning into discretion. Public administrators were encouraged to use moral theory to work through their conundrums. Texts and training offered multiple moral frameworks to master and provide perspective (Denhardt 1988; Geuras and Garofalo 2002). The approach takes the personal responsibility of managers profoundly seriously, but struggles with ensuring that the introduction of personal judgments remains consistent with the promise to abide by the laws, processes, and legitimate outcomes of the democratic process. It can be very easy for moral persons to introduce their own values to guide government office and usurp the values embodied in law, process and constitution.

The New Public Management school offers different value priorities. It insists that discretion can be expanded to unleash the latent initiative and value possibilities in government. Declining trust and resources make it imperative that efficiency become an overwhelming value driver. Public managers possess obligations to maximize the public value and good that can be wrung from limited resources. The efficiency drive can lead to considerable use of private contractors which concentrates accountability through contracts. Devolving decision power to the local level permits more responsiveness as well as experimentation freed from centralized legalistic requirements. NPM focuses upon outcomes as the mechanism to ensure accountability. The outcomes force public managers to think hard about the real substance of their mission and provide incentives to direct action in desired ways (Hood 1991, 1998; Pollit 2003; Gore 1993). NPM influenced the United Kingdom, Australia, the United States, and most extensively New Zealand. Other countries have been slower to accept its tenets. However its emphasis upon initiative to create public good within a mission-based context, efficiency through contracting as well as devolution have widely influenced public management values. It also inspired critiques that a narrow focus upon efficiency and outcomes diminishes the trustees' longer-term obligations to institutional capacity, records, public memory, and stewardship, of which efficiency is just one aspect (Terry 1995; Frederickson 1997). The outcome-driven focus can displace process-centered goals that respect rights and voice or push production to the exclusion of equity (Frederickson 1997). Others suggest that the entrepreneurial emphasis undermines transparency, respect for law, due process, and institutional solidarity (Borins 1999; O'Toole 1998; Lynn 2001). While the debates continue how different its priorities really are, the prominence of an active quest for the public good and rethinking accountability in a governance-based world continue to ripple through public ethics.

Remembering that law and process remain the moral moorings for public managers is crucial. Without these anchors, discretion becomes arbitrary action in the name of government (Rohr 1989, 2002; Lynn 1996, 2001). The classic model of public administration and accountability places respect and deference to law and democratic process at the core of the values. Action directed and framed by law and process remains the unwavering hallmark of public management ethics (Rainey 1991; Pollit 1993, 2003). The primary importance of law and responsiveness to chains of accountability with elected and appointed officials connects the values and virtues of conscientiousness, competence, honest advice, and duty to law and authority. The classic ethical model, however, can generate passive ethics, unresponsive inertia, irresponsible action, pathological obedience, or paralysis. One potential way to reconcile the classic model with wider discretion builds upon public administration's foundation in law but also in deeper constitutional principles and processes. This bases ethical responsibilities in the official role but permits a range of initiative and responsibility (Cooper 1987, 1990; Chapman 1988). John Rohr's theory of regime values argues that discretion should be informed by primary constitutional values. The theory's many variants provide a way to reunite discretion with a commitment to law, process and institutional accountability (Rohr 1986, 1989, 2002). The increasing use of Constitutional Review both within countries and internationally gives greater weight to this model (Rohr 2002).

The Minnowbrook School and later the Refounding School of public adminis-tration in the United States extended the ethical range of discretion. The Minnow-brook School invested public administration and management with responsibilities to ensure the requirements of fairness and equity infused management and policy making. Real world democratic systems often denied groups voice, participation, or adequate resources for dignity. The Minnowbrook School argued that public administrators had responsibility to give actuality to the moral foundations of liberal democracy. It envisioned introducing more democratic processes into management with greater emphasis upon teams, participation, and responsiveness (Marini 1971; Frederickson 1971). The Refounding School continued many of Minnowbrook's claims but added a strong emphasis upon the agency perspective and requirements of trusteeship obligations to maintain government capacity and agency (Wamsley et al. 1990). Both schools enriched the ethical repertoire of public managers and provided richer frameworks for decision but also added urgency to the question of how to sustain accountability and transparency if public managers self-consciously assumed initiatives in the name of these values (Rosenbloom 1989; Denhardt and Denhardt 2003).

The key to reconcile management discretion and ethics lies in seeing law as an enabler and promise of accountable and effective action, not a constraint or problem as some new public management advocates hint. This compels public managers and administrators to embrace the leadership dimension of responsibilities. Their own values, commitments, character, and attributes buttress their managerial responsibility. Modern public management can link with the foundations of public administration to emphasize that lawful and accountable responsibility can be sustained by the initiative of public managers as leaders.

7.5 THE ETHICS AGENDA AND PUBLIC POLICY

It's a sad joke that many people view political ethics as an oxymoron. Most people do not easily associate ethics and politics or ethics and policy, yet almost by accident, ethics has emerged as a policy domain. Ethics as a rhetorical policy issue usually enters the agenda after a scandal. Bribery, extortion, conflict of interest, regulatory negligence or collusion, or abuses of power cover the normal range of ethical failures. Often ethics failures mirror illegal activities, but while legality defines the minimum of public management ethics, it seldom captures the full spirit and range of public ethics. In these cases public managers betray the legally sanctioned frames of judgment but also use their authority or resources in a way that benefits them or their collaborators. In another form of abuse, they enforce their own personal preferences or prejudices upon others in the name of public power and authority (Stark 2000; *Political Scandals* 1990; Williams 1998; Dobel 1999; Rose-Ackerman 1999; Noonan 1984).

Ethics policies end up ad hoc responses to the latest scandal to quiet public disgust or restore trust (Mackenzie 2002; Anechiarico and Jacobs 1998). Government scandals provide grist for the media, and modern media scrutiny not only uncovers more abuses and scandals but makes them a regular part of its strategy to gain viewers and readers. Media frenzies accompany "ethics scandals" and incite public institutions to lurch from one solution to another without integrating them into a holistic policy.

Ethics policy, however, matters profoundly for government. It lays the foundations for high performance and excellence as the center of public administration. Ethics policy enables public employees and managers to unite personal commitment and public task. High integrity and ethics build legitimacy for the political order. Public ethics harnesses internal managerial practice to public accountability.

Finally ethical public administrators and managers build community and social capital for a regime.

The policy agendas focus in three areas. The first cluster delimits the boundary between public institutions and the environment. Laws try to discourage corruption or abuse of power through disclosure of interests and contacts. Conflict of interest laws require officials to disclose and recuse themselves from decisions where they have conflicts or to divest investments in sensitive areas. Bribery laws penalize incursions of private interest into public office (Noonan 1984).These requirements in theory enable citizens and media to anticipate and discourage interest-distorted decisions. The traditional merit-based civil service insulates civil servants from outside blandishments with reasonable salaries and protection from politically arbitrary removal. Post-employment limitations discourage anticipation of future gain by altering judgments. A few courageous jurisdictions struggle to control campaign contributions or set up public finance of elections to ward off the corrosive influence of money on elected leaders.

The second cluster addresses internal management practice. The most common tactics craft codes of ethics that enumerate the obligations and responsibilities of public managers and employees. To be effective the code should support an internal culture of high ethical and performance standards. The emphasis upon culture combines with education, modeling, and ensuring that incentives and promotion match promulgated values. Often the codes assemble the disclosure, conflict of interest, and often post-employment limitations. United States' codes tend to be long, explicit, and punitive. Ethics offices with investigatory and sometimes quasi judicial power augment the power of the codes. Most codes of ethics written over the last thirty years arose as responses to scandals and narrowed discretion combined with legal and parallel enforcement agencies. More than a few jurisdictions write fine codes only to turn them into dead letters with no strong institutional backing, education, or enforcement. A recent backlash argues, to an extent correctly, that the cumulative impact has been to hurt government flexibility, talent, and responsiveness (Anechiarico and Jacobs 1998; Light 1993). Others see codes as being of no help or clouding the issue that depends upon a deep ethos (Kernaghan 1993). More recent codes under the influence of the OECD and NPM school tend to be terse and principle-based with adaptations to unique institutional cultures. These codes unfold with a precedent-based record that permits adjustment and enforcement. Cynics might see this as the only way to get "vague" language through legislatures, but such codes give rhetorical leverage and distill the essence of the values that liberal democracies have been discussing. The codes often ally with the media to steadily erode the distinction between private and public lives, and senior public managers find their private lives under increasing scrutiny (Thompson 1987; Dobel 1999).

As a recent example, the European Parliament passed "The European Code of Good Administrative Behavior" in 2001 (European Ombudsman 2003*b*).

A European Ombudsman with investigatory, subpoena, and punishment powers supports the Code. In classic manner the Code enumerates all "rights and interests have a basis in law and that their content complies with law." (Article 4) The classic values are "Equality of treatment is respected" and any "difference in treatment" is "justified by objective relevant features." (Article 5) The Code prohibits discrimination for a wide range of genetic, national, and religious reasons. In an important addition, it demands that measures should be "proportional to the aim pursued" and should avoid restricting citizen rights where possible. Addressing the importance of discretion, it posits that public officials "shall respect the fair balance interests of private persons and general public interest." Consistent with the UN it requires that powers be vested in law, articulate public purpose, and avoid abuse. It reiterates the classic position that officials should be "impartial and independent" and abstain from preferential treatment and avoid conflict of interest.

Recognizing the wider values of institutional stewardship and legitimacy, the Code discusses the ethical importance of public precedent, consistency, and public accounting of changes as well as the importance of getting all relevant information to be objective (Articles 9, 10, 11). Addressing recent insights, the Code enshrines respect for citizens at the core of the interaction demanding courtesy, apologies, timely response, public transparency, and notification of appeal rights. The European Code embodies a fascinating amalgamation of the classic emphasis upon public service and the newer concerns for creating value and respect for citizens (European Ombudsman 2002, 2003*b*).

The last policy cluster focuses on oversight or outside scrutiny from parallel agencies like ombudsmen and inspector generals, also from an active civil society. While European and Oceanic countries largely rely upon ombudsmen, the United States, especially at the federal level, relies upon inspector generals (OECD 2000*a*; Light 1993).The emerging strong international consensus to fight corruption has led the United Nations, the OECD, and the United States to conclude that maintaining high ethical standards requires active civil society. While many aspects of administrative ethics should be adapted to particular societies, this policy argues that non-abusive and competent government entails a capacity for self-scrutiny, investigation, exposure, and rectification of government abuse. A free and plural media with investigative journalism provides a foundation for this, so much so that each year journalists are killed. Transparent public finances, plural power centers, and freedom of association help. Autonomous professional associations can create standards that support and help beleaguered government officials.

The most thoughtful approaches to ethics policy conceptualize the role of ethics as central to administrative and managerial life. They integrate ethical values through a mission and with an analysis of the societal preconditions to sustain those values. Managerial and administrative strategies instill the values. The integrated approach connects personal integrity-based cultural approaches with strong oversight and compliance and incentive alignment. This approach builds upon the fundamentals of transparency and accountability. Strong reporting requirements, heavy use of audits, and independent auditing powers enhance the course of action. The integrated policy complements old and new public management and administration and wider or narrower ranges of discretion. The strategy needs strong disclosure requirements for senior officials but not necessarily for all public servants. The disclosure alerts the public and agencies to conflict of interests that undermine judgment and legitimacy. It devotes efforts to exposing the role of incentives in sustaining corruption and the need to align incentives with ethical aspirations (Klitgaard 1991; Klitgaard et al. 2000).The emphasis upon integrating incentives into management identifies how clear and strong disciplinary actions should support the policies. More than a few countries, however, construct ethical Potemkin villages with no serious enforcement.

A wide range of international agreements weave an increasingly dense and sometimes effective web of support for strong public management ethics.[3] The agreements range from outlawing the tax deductibility or expensing of bribes to new international audit standards or financial transparency standards. They continue to be developed often with the support of international professional associations and reflect a deepening consensus across many jurisdictions (Cooper and Yoder 2002). This builds an international civil and legal regime to support ethical standards. They give support and succor to administrators and managers seeking to realize the core values of public management in often hostile and unreceptive environments. They also strengthen the efforts of reformers and committed public servants in more stable liberal democracies.

Even as ethics policy evolves, the modern world of public management poses new challenges especially in how to extend its ethos and values across networks of partners and contractors. It is not clear that contracts will capture the range of ethical subtleties and responsibilities that public servants address in decisions. Neither is it clear whether the ethos of impartiality, fairness, or stewardship can be extended across contractors or partners in private and nonprofit sectors. One of the more intriguing and defining concerns arises in the uniformed services. The military services traditionally rely upon very powerful codes of internalized ethics to maintain discipline and accountability in face of the dangerous and difficult tasks they have to manage (French 2003). At the same time the outsourcing of tasks has led to complex situations where military contractors in war zones not only face deadly fire, but sometimes refuse to perform duties that flow from the ethics of service but not from a contract (Bianco and Forest 2003). This example highlights emergent ethical challenges for public management. The increasing number of contracts and outcome measurements intensify problems with guaranteeing due process and equity in performance while increasing incentives for electoral subversion by potential contractors. The world of networks and partnerships increases the dangers that accurate reporting and accountability across sectors and institutions will be subverted (Hood 1998).

7.6 CONCLUSION

A strong consensus exists on the importance of ethics in public management. While an unadorned listing of the values and attributes may not seem like much help, it aids not so much because it solves the problems, but identifies the checklist that institutional design issues and mangers must attend to. Obviously the values will come into conflict and require compromises (Dobel 1989). The existence of a values checklist, however, provides rhetorical and moral leverage for administrators throughout the world and legitimizes decisions, actions, and managerial strategies that support them against more limited efficiency, self-interested or outcome driven conceptions. The values inhere in a theory of personal responsibility where individuals promise within an institutional context to give serious weight to the values.

These values begin with a commitment to:

- Recognize public institutions as trusts and managers as stewards
- Ensure the long-term and the inclusive commons are addressed in deliberations and decisions
- Demand competence to serve those who rely upon public management
- Frame decisions by law and authorized policy
- Demand good information for decision
- Create accurate durable records
- Build durable and competent institutional capacity
- Impartially serve "all citizens"
- Address efficient use and waste as part of stewardship
- Do not abuse position for personal or group gain

Liberal democracy adds values that supplement and deepen the standards.

- Require maximum transparency
- Require public reasons for actions
- Seek inclusive participation and engage the diversity of society
- Maximize citizen participation
- Engage and respond to citizen deliberations
- Respect citizens and honor rights in treatment and process

Finally, the contemporary discussions of the new public administration, public management, and the new public management reinvigorate an understanding of public managers and administrators as leaders with discretion and values.

- Actively seek better means of service performance
- Respond to citizen concerns with care and timeliness
- Ensure that equity and long term considerations are addressed in public decision

- Work to create organizations that integrate multiple voices in their deliberations
- Be effective and work within the constraints of law and process to achieve measurable and real outcomes
- Gain strong resource and political support for sustainable programs
- Work across sectors to address complex multi-sector problems

Herbert Simon pointed out many years ago, such lists will not provide clarity on decision because they often conflict and under-determine decisions (Simon 1947). But no list of principles, even ones with clear ordinal rankings, can provide clear answers for complex, ever-changing political and organizational situations. They do provide a universe of justifications that public managers should take into account in making and evaluating decisions and provide a legitimate rhetorical opening for managers, citizens, and elected officials to deliberate and critique decisions. A listing of values also delimits what can be ruled out and increases the threshold of justification for policies and actions that run counter to the values. They illuminate how the values interconnect and reinforce providing deeper and stronger grounding. As the values reinforce it, so the clarity and power of the ethics position increases proportionately.

Public management unfolds through choice, and choice involves ethical decision through hundreds of daily actions that impact the welfare of others and give reality to the rights and aspirations of government. Choices define the activity as ethical bounded by obligation and personal responsibility. These ethical commitments provide meaningful and powerful criteria to inform institutional design and managerial discretion. They present design imperatives that can adapt to multiple institutional arrangements and governmental systems. The role of ethics and ethics policy becomes even more central to public management in a time of devolved power, increased discretion and initiative as well as battle with significant and often transnational corruption.

Notes

1. The Code goes on to spell out requirements for disqualification under conditions of conflict of interest and disclosure of assets, limitations on accepting gifts, and respect for confidential information.
2. Although whole books and schools of thought have grown up around the dissection of the difference between public administration and public management, I will assume for all intents and purposes they represent the same enterprise bound by the same values. Although the term "public management" has been used as a descriptor to emphasize a more active and senior management orientation but also one that emphasized initiative, responsibility, and outcome accountability, it is now fairly clear that the administrative tradition of public administration also possessed such points in abundance and the degrees of emphasis disguise the commonalities and continuum of

attributes, values, and skills (Lynn 1987, 2001; Dobel 1999; Uveges and Keller 1998; Pollitt 2003).

3. The United Nations, OECD, and professional associations have been particularly active in these areas. For instance in one area of how efforts overlap and reinforce, see The International Monetary Funds Code of Good Practices on Transparency in Monetary and Financial Practices (2000), or the INTOSAI Code for auditors in the Public Sector (1998), and the irreplaceable Transparency International yearly sourcebook.

REFERENCES

ABERBACH, J. D., PUTNAM, R. D., and ROCKMAN, B. A. (1981), *Bureaucrats and Politicians in Western Democracies*, Cambridge, MA: Harvard University Press.

ADAMS, G. B., and BALFOUR, D. L. (1998), *Unmasking Administrative Evil*, Thousand Oaks: Sage Publications.

ANECHIARICO, F., and JACOBS, J. B. (1998), *The Pursuit of Absolute Integrity: How Corruption Control Makes Government Ineffective*, Chicago: University of Chicago Press.

APPLBAUM, A. I. (1999), *Ethics for Adversaries: The Morality of Roles in Public and Professional Life*, Cambridge, MA: Harvard University Press.

BARBER, B. R. (1984), *Strong Democracy: Participatory Politics for a New Age*, Berkeley: University of California Press.

BARDACH, E. (1977), *The Implementation Game: What Happens after a Bill becomes a Law*, Cambridge, MA: MIT Press.

—— and KAGEN, R. A. (1982), *Going by the Book: The Problem of Regulatory Unreasonableness*, Philadelphia: Temple University Press.

BARNARD, C. I. (1938), *The Functions of the Executive*, Cambridge, MA: Harvard University Press.

BEHN, R. E. (1998), "What Right Do Public Managers Have to Lead?" *Public Administration Review* 58: 204–9).

BIANCO, A., and FOREST, S.A. (2003), "Outsourcing War," *Business Week*, September 15, 69–78.

BLOCK, P. (1993), *Stewardship: Choosing Service over Self-Interest*, San Francisco: Berrett-Koehler.

BOLMAN, L., and DEAL, T. (1997), *Reframing Organizations: Artistry, Choice, and Leadership*, San Francisco: Jossey-Bass.

BORINS, S. (1999), "Innovating with Integrity: Evidence from the Ford Foundation-Kennedy School of Government Awards," *Public Integrity* 1(4): 375–87.

BOZEMAN, B. (1987), *All Organizations are Public: Bridging Public and Private Organizational Theories*, San Francisco: Jossey-Bass.

BREWER, G. A. (2003), "Building Social Capital: Civic Attitudes and Behavior of Public Servants," *Journal of Public Administration Research and Theory*, 13(1): 5–26.

BUCHANAN, J. M. (1985), *Liberty, Market and State*, New York: New York University Press.

BURKE, J. P. (1986), *Bureaucratic Responsibility*, Baltimore: Johns Hopkins University Press.

—— (1989), "Reconciling Public Administration and Democracy: The Role of the Responsible Administrator," *Public Administration Review* 49: 180–5.

CAMPBELL, S. J. (1993) "Public Service and Democratic Accountability," in Chapman 1993c: 111–34.

CHAPMAN, R. A. (1988), *Ethics in the British Public Service*, London: Routledge.

—— (1993a), "Reasons of State and the Public Interest: A British Variation on the Problem of Dirty Hands," in Chapman 1993c, 93–110.

—— (1993b), "Ethics in Public Service," in Chapman 1993c, 155–171.

—— (ed.) (1993c), *Ethics in Public Service*. Ottawa, Canada: Carleton University Press.

—— (ed.) (2000a), *Ethics in Public Service for the New Millennium*. Aldershot: Ashgate.

—— (2000b), "Setting Standards in a New Organization: The Case of British Civil Service Commission, in Chapman 2000a: 93–110.

CHANDLER, R.C. (1989), "A Guide to Ethics for Public Servants," in Perry 1989: 602–818.

COLLINS, J. (2001), *Good to Great: Why Some Companies Make the Leap and Others Don't*, New York: Harper Business.

COOPER, T. L. (1987), "Hierarchy, Virtue and Practice in Public Administration," *Public Administration Review* 47(4): 320–8.

—— (1990), *The Responsible Administrator: An Approach to Ethics for the Administrative Role*, 3rd. edn., San Francisco: Jossey-Bass.

—— and WRIGHT N. D. (1992) *Exemplary Public Administrators: Character and Leadership in Government*, San Francisco: Jossey-Bass.

—— and YODER, D. (2002), "Public Management Ethics Standards in a Transnational World," *Public Integrity* 4(4): 333–51.

CUBBON, B. (1993), "The Duty of the Professional," in Chapman 1993c: 7–15.

DELEON, L., and DENHARDT, R. B. (2000), "The Political Theory of Reinvention," *Public Administration Review* 60(2): 89–97.

DENHARDT, J. V., and DENHARDT, R. B. (2003), *The New Public Service: Serving not Steering*. Armonk, NY: M. Sharpe.

DENHARDT, K. G. (1988), *The Ethics of Public Service: Resolving Moral Dilemmas in Public Organizations*, Westport, CT: Greenwood.

DENHARDT, R. B. (1998) "Five Great Issues in Organization Theory," in Rabin et al., 1998: 117–43.

DiJULIO, J. J. (1994) "Principled Agents: The Cultural Bases of Behavior in a Federal Government Bureaucracy," *Journal of Public Administration Research and Theory* 4: 277–320.

DILMAN, D. L. (1998), "Leadership in the American Civil Service," in Hunt and O'Toole 1998.

DOBEL, J. P. (1978), "The Corruption of the State," *American Political Science Review*.

—— (1990a), *Compromise and Political Action: Political Morality in Liberal and Democratic Life*, Savage, MD: Rowman & Littlefield.

—— (1990b), "Integrity in the Public Service," *Public Administration Review* 50(3): 354–66.

—— (1998), "Political Prudence and the Ethics of Leadership," *Public Administration Review* 58(1): 74–81.

—— (1999), *Public Integrity*, Baltimore: The Johns Hopkins University Press.

—— (2001), "Paradigms, Traditions, and Keeping the Faith ," *Public Administration Review* 61(2): 166–71.

—— (2003), "The Odyssey of Senior Public Service: What Memoirs Can Teach Us," *Public Administration Review* 63(1): 16–29.

DUNLEAVY, P. (1992), *Democracy, Bureaucracy and Public Choice Economic Explanations in Political Science*, New York: Prentice Hall.

DWORKIN, R. (1977), *Taking Rights Seriously*. Cambridge, MA: Harvard University Press.

THE EUROPEAN OMBUDSMAN (2002), *Annual Report 2001* (http://www.euro-ombudsman. eu.int) (July 9, 2002).

—— (2003*a*), *Annual Report 2002* (http://www.euro-ombudsman.eu.int) (September 28, 2002)

—— (2003*b*), *The European Code of Good Administrative Behavior*, Luxemburg: Office for Official Publications of the European Communities.

FERGUSON, K. E. (1984), *The Feminist Case against Bureaucracy*, Philadelphia: Temple University Press.

FINER, H. (1941), "Administrative Responsibility in Democratic Government," *Public Administration Review* 14: 335–50.

FINN, P. (1993) "The Law and Officials," in Chapman 1993*c*: 135–46.

FISHKIN, J. S. (1991), *Democracy and Deliberation*, New Haven: Yale University Press.

FLEISHMAN, J. L. et al. (eds.) (1981), *Public Duties: The Moral Obligations of Government Officials*, Cambridge, MA: Harvard University Press.

FOX, C. J., and MILLER, H. T. (1995), *Postmodern Public Administration: Towards Discourse*, Thousand Oaks, CA: Sage.

FREDERICKSON, H. G. (1971), "Toward a New Public Administration," in Marini 1971.

—— (ed.) (1974), "Symposium on Social Equity and Public Administration," *Public Administration Review* 34(1): 1–51.

—— (1997), *The Spirit of Public Administration*, San Francisco: Jossey-Bass.

FRENCH, S. E. (2003), *The Code of the Warrior: Exploring Warrior Values Past and Present*, Lanham, MD: Rowman & Littlefield.

FRIEDRICH, C. J. (1940) "The Nature of Administrative Responsibility," *Public Policy* 1: 3–24.

FRY, B., and NIGRO, L. G. (1998), "Five Great Issues in the profession of Public Administration," in Rabin et al. 1998: 1163–223.

GEURAS, D., and GAROFALO, C. (2002), *Practical Ethics in Public Administration*, Vienna, VA: Management Concepts.

GILMAN, S. C. (1999), "Public Sector Ethics and Government Reinvention: Realigning Systems to Meet Organizational Change," *Public Integrity* 1(2): 175–92.

GOODSELL, C. T. (1985), *The Case for Bureaucracy: A Public Administration Polemic*, Chatham, N.J.: Chatham House.

GORE, A. (1993), *The Gore Report on Reinventing Government*, New York: Times Books.

GREGORY, R. J. (1999), "Social Capital Theory and Administrative Reform: Maintaining Ethical Probity in Public Service," *Public Administration Review* 59(1): 63–75.

GUTMANN, A., and THOMPSON, D. F. (1996), *Democracy and Disagreement*, Cambridge, MA: Harvard University Press.

HAMILTON, A., MADISON, J., and JAY, J. (1961), *The Federalist Papers*, ed. and introd. Clinton Rossiter, New York: New American Library.

HARMON, M., and MAYER, R. T. (1986), *Organization Theory for Public Administration*, Boston: Little Brown.

HECLO H. (1977), *A Government of Strangers: Executive Politics in Washington*, Washington, DC: Brookings Institution.

HIRSHMAN, A. O. (1970), *Exit, Voice and Loyalty: Responses to Decline in Firms, Organizations and States*, Cambridge, MA: Harvard University Press.

Holzer, M., and Gabrielian, V. (1998), "Five Great Ideas in American Public Administration," in Rabin et al., 1998: 49–102.

Hood, C. (1991), "A Public Management for All Seasons," *Public Administration* 69: 13–19.

—— (1998), *The Art of the State: Culture, Rhetoric, and Public Management*, New York: Oxford University Press.

Hunt, M., and O'Toole, B. J. (1998*a*), "Reform, Ethics and Leadership in Public Service," in Hunt 1998, pp. 175–90.

—— —— (1998*b*), *Reform, Ethics and Leadership: A Festschrift in Honour of Richard A. Chapman*. Aldershot: Ashgate.

International Monetary Fund (2000), Code of Good Practices on Transparency in Monetary and Financial Policies (http://www.imf.org/external/np/mae/mft/index) (May 5, 2003).

INTOSAI (1998), Code of Ethics for Auditors in the Public Sector (http://www.intosai.org/3_ETHICe) (May 9, 2003).

Kettl, D. F. (2002), *The Transformation of Governance: Public Administration for the Twenty-First Century*, Baltimore: Johns Hopkins University Press.

Kernaghan, K. (1993), "Promoting Public Service Ethics: The Codification Option," in Chapman 1993*c*: 15–30.

Klitgaard, R. (1991), *Controlling Corruption*, Berkeley: University of California Press.

Klitgaard, R., MacLean-Abaroa, R., and Parris, H. L. (2000), *Corrupt Cities: A Practical Guide to Cure and Prevention*, Oakland, CA: Institute of Contemporary Studies Press.

Lewis, C. (1991), *The Ethics Challenge in Public Service: A Problem-Solving Guide*, San Francisco: Jossey-Bass.

Light, P. C. (1993), *Monitoring Government: Inspectors General and the Search for Accountabilty*, Washington, DC: Brookings Institution.

—— (1999), *The New Public Service*, Washington, DC: Brookings Institution.

Lipsky, M. (1980), *Street-Level Bureaucracy: Dilemmas of the Individual in Public Services*, New York: Russell Sage Foundation.

Lowi T. J. (1979), *The End of Liberalism: The Second Republic of the United States*, 2nd edn., New York: W. W. Norton.

Lundquist, L. (1993), "Freedom of Information and the Swedish Bureaucrat," in Chapman 1993*c*: 43–58.

Lynn, L E., Jun. (1987), *Managing Public Policy*, Boston: Little, Brown.

—— (1996), *Public Management as Art, Science and Profession*, Chatham, NJ: Chatham House.

—— (2001), "The Myth of the Bureaucratic Paradigm: What Traditional Public Administration Really Stood For," *Public Administration Review* 61(2): 144–60.

Mackenzie, G. C. (2002), *Scandal Proof: Do Ethics Laws Make Government Ethical?* Washington, DC: Brookings Institution.

Mansbridge, J. (1990), *Beyond Democracy*, New York: Basic Books.

March, J. G., and Olson, J. P. (1989), *Rediscovering Institutions: The Organizational Basis of Politics*, New York: Free Press.

—— —— (1995), *Democratic Governance*, New York: Free Press.

Marini, F. (1971), *Toward a New Public Administration: The Minnowbrook Perspective*, Scranton, PA: Chandler.

MILLS, A. (2003), "Strengthening Domestic Institutions against Corruption: A Public Ethics Checklist," in *Integrity Improvement Initiatives in Developing Countries*, Paris: OECD, 141–50.

MOE, T. M. (1984), "The New Economics of Organizations," *American Journal of Political Science* 28(3): 765 ff.

MOORE, M. H. (1995), *Creating Public Value: Strategic Management in Government*, Cambridge, MA: Harvard University Press.

MORRIS, D. (1998), "Moving from Public Administration to Public Management," in Hunt 1998: 55–68.

NISKANEN, W. A. (1971), *Bureaucracy and Representative Government*, Chicago: Aldine Altherton.

NOONAN, J. T. (1984), *Bribes*, New York: Macmillan.

NOZICK, R. (1974), *Anarchy, State and Utopia*, New York: Basic Books.

OECD (1997), *Managing Government Ethics*. PUMA Policy Brief (http://www.oecd.org/puma/gvrnance/ethics/index.htm) (August 10, 2003).

—— (1998), *Principles for Managing Ethics in Public Service*, PUMA Policy Brief No. 4 (www.oecd.org/puma/gvrnance/ethics/) (October 2002).

—— (2000a), *Trust in Government: Ethics Measures in OECD Countries*, Paris: OECD.

—— (2000b), *The Fight against Bribery and Corruption*, OECD Policy Brief. Paris: OECD.

OSBORNE, D., and GAEBLER, T. (1992), *Reinventing Government: How the Entrepreneurial Spirit is Transforming the Public Sector*, Reading, MA: Addison-Wesley.

OSTROM, E., and OSTROM, V. (1971), "Public Choice: A Different Approach to the Study of Public Administration," *Public Administration Review* 31: 203–16.

O'TOOLE, B. J. (1998) "We Walk by Faith, Not by Sight: The Ethic of Public Service," in Hunt and O'Toole 1998, pp. 84–102.

O'TOOLE, L. J. (1989), "The Public Administrator's Role in Setting the Policy Agenda," in Perry 1989: 225–36.

PAINTER, M. (2000), "Contracting, the Enterprise Culture and Public Sector Ethics," in Chapman 2000a: 165–81.

PAYNE, B. (1981), "Devices and Corruption," in Fleishman et al., 1981: 175–203.

PERRY, J. L. (ed.) (1989a), *Handbook of Public Administration*. San Francisco: Jossey-Bass.

—— (1989b), "The Effective Public Administrator," in Perry 1989a: 619–28.

—— and WISE, L. (1990), "The Motivational Basis of Public Service," *Public Administration Review* 50(3): 367–73.

PETERS, B. G. (1993) "Tragic Choices: Administrative Rulemaking and Policy Choice," in Chapman 1993c: 43–58.

Political Scandals and Cause Celebres: An International Reference Compendium (1990) Harlow: Longman.

POLLITT, C. (1993), *Managerialism and Public Services*, 2nd edn., Oxford: Blackwell.

—— (2003), *The Essential Public Manager*. Maidenhead, UK: Open University Press.

PRIORE, M. J. (1995), *Beyond Individualism: How Social Demands of the New Identity Groups Challenge American Political and Economic Life*, Cambridge, MA: Harvard University Press.

RABIN, J., HIDRETH, W. B., and MILLER, G. J. (eds.) (1998), *Handbook of Public Administration*, 2nd edn., New York: Marcel Dekker.

RAINEY, H. A. (1991), *Understanding and Managing Public Organizations*, San Francisco: Jossey-Bass.

RAWLS, J. (1971), *A Theory of Justice*, Cambridge, MA: Harvard University Press.

—— (1996), *Political Liberalism*, Cambridge, MA.: Harvard University Press.

ROHR, J. A. (1986), *To Run a Constitution: The Legitimacy of the Administrative State*, Lawrence, KS; University of Kansas Press.

—— (1989), *Ethics for Bureaucrats: An Essay on Law and Virtue*, New York: Dekker.

—— (1998), "Comparative Constitutionalism as a School for Administrative Statesman," in Hunt 1998: 103–22.

—— (2002), *Civil Servants and Their Constitutions*, Lawrence, KS: University of Kansas Press.

ROSE-ACKERMAN, S. (1999), *Corruption and Government: Causes, Consequences, and Reform*, Cambridge: Cambridge University Press.

ROSENBLOOM, D. H. (1989), *Public Administration*, 2nd edn., New York: Random House.

ROUSSEAU, J. J. (1968), *The Social Contract*, trans. Maurice Cranston. Harmondsworth: Penguin.

SABINI, J., and SILVER, M. (1982) *Moralities of Everyday Life*, New York: Oxford University Press.

SCHON, D. A. (1983), *The Reflective Practitioner: How Professionals Think in Action*, New York: Basic Books.

SENGE P. M. (1990), *The Fifth Discipline: the Art and Practice of the Learning Organization*, New York: Doubleday.

SIMON, H. A. (1946), " The Proverbs of Administration," *Public Administration Review* 6: 53–67.

STARK, A. (2000), *Conflict of Interest in American Public Life*, Cambridge, MA.: Harvard University Press.

STIVERS, C. (2002), *Gender Images in Public Administration: Legitimacy and the Administrative State*, Thousand Oaks, CA: Sage.

SZABLOWSKI, G. J. (2000), "Courts, Parliament, and Public Authorities under the British Human Rights Act 1998," in Chapman 2000a: 51–70.

TERRY, L. D (1995), *Leadership of Public Bureaucracies: The Administrator as Conservator*, Thousand Oaks, CA: Sage.

THOMPSON, D. F. (1980), "Moral Responsibility in Government: The Problem of Many Hands," *American Political Science Review* 74: 905–16.

—— (1983), "Ascribing Responsibility to Advisers in Government," *Ethics* 93: 546–60.

—— (1987), *Political Ethics and Public Office*, Cambridge, MA: Harvard University Press.

—— (1995), *Ethics in Congress: From Individual to Institutional Corruption*, Washington, DC: The Brookings Institution.

TRANSPARENCY INTERNATIONAL (2003), *Introducing the Global Corruption Report 2003*, Peter Eigen. (www.transparency.de/documents)

UHR, J. (1999), "Institutions of Integrity: Balancing Values and Verification in Democratic Government," *Public Integrity* 1(1): 94–106.

UNITED NATIONS RESOLUTION 51/59, 82nd Plenary Meeting, 12 December 1996, Action Against Corruption & Annex International Code of Conduct for Public Officials (http://www. un.org/documents/ga/51/a51r059.htm) (5/5/2003)

UVEGES, J. A., and KELLER, L. F. (1998), "One Hundred Years of Public Administration and Counting: Moving into a Second Century in the Study and Practice of Public Management in American Life," in Rabin et al., 1998: 1–48.

VICKERS, G., Sir (1983), *The Art of Judgment: A Study of Policy Making*, London: Harper and Row.

WAMSLEY, G. et al. (1990), *Refounding Public Administration*, Newbury Park, CA: Sage.

WARWICK, D. P. (1981), "The Ethics of Administrative Discretion," in Fleishman et al., 1981: 93–130.

WEBER, M. (1946a), "Politics as a Vocation," in Weber 1946b: 77–128.

—— (1946b), *From Max Weber: Essays in Sociology*, trans. and ed. H. H. Gerth and C. Wright Mills, Oxford: Oxford University Press.

WILLIAMS, R. (1998), *Political Scandals in the USA*, Edinburgh: Keel University Press.

WILSON, J. Q. (1989), *Bureaucracy: What Government Agencies Do and Why They Do It*, New York: Basic Books.

WREN, D. A. (1994), *The Evolution of Management Thought*, 4th edn. New York: John Wiley & Sons.

CHAPTER 8

PUBLIC ACCOUNTABILITY

MARK BOVENS

8.1 THE CONCEPT OF PUBLIC ACCOUNTABILITY

PUBLIC accountability is the hallmark of modern democratic governance. Democracy remains a paper procedure if those in power cannot be held accountable in public for their acts and omissions, for their decisions, their policies, and their expenditures. Public accountability, as an institution, therefore, is the complement of public management.

As a concept, however, "public accountability" is rather elusive. It is a hurrah-word, like "learning," "responsibility," or "solidarity"—nobody can be against it. It is one of those evocative political words that can be used to patch up a rambling argument, to evoke an image of trustworthiness, fidelity, and justice, or to hold critics at bay.

Historically, the concept of accountability is closely related to accounting. In fact, it literally comes from bookkeeping. According to Dubnick (2002: 7–9), the roots of the contemporary concept can be traced to the reign of William I, in the decades after the 1066 Norman conquest of England. In 1085 William required all the property holders in his realm to render *a count* of what they possessed. These possessions were valuated and listed by royal agents in the so called Domesday

Books. This census was not held just for taxing purposes, it established the foundation of the royal governance. The Domesday Books listed what was in the king's realm; moreover, the king had all the landowners swear oaths of allegiance. In the early twelfth century this evolved into a highly centralized administrative kingship that was ruled through centralized auditing and semi-annual account giving.

Nowadays, accountability has moved far beyond its bookkeeping origins and has become a symbol for good governance, both in the public and in the private sector.[1] Moreover, the accounting relationship has almost completely reversed. "Accountability" does not refer to sovereigns holding their subjects to account, but to the reverse, it is the authorities themselves who are being held accountable by their citizens.

8.1.1 What is "Public" about Public Accountability?

Here we will concentrate on *public* accountability. Most importantly, "public" relates to openness. The account giving is done in public, i.e. it is open or at least accessible to citizens. Therefore, we will only in passing take up the, often more informal, confidential, if not secret, forms of internal accountability. Secondly, for the purpose of this chapter, "public" refers to the public sector. We will concentrate on public managers, on officials spending public money, exercising public authority, or managing a corporate body under public law. We will therefore not discuss the public accountabilities of managers of purely private entities in great detail.

8.2 ACCOUNTABILITY AS AN ICON

In the centuries that passed since the reign of William I of England, accountability has slowly struggled out of its etymological bondage with accounting. In modern political discourse, "accountability" and "accountable" no longer convey a stuffy image of bookkeeping and financial administration, but they hold strong promises of fair and equitable governance. Accountability has become a Good Thing, and, so it seems, we can't have enough of it (Pollit 2003: 89). The concept has become a rhetorical device; it serves as a synonym for many loosely defined political desiderata, such as transparency, equity, democracy, efficiency, and integrity (Mulgan 2000b: 555; Behn 2001: 3–6; Dubnick 2002).

Melvin Dubnick (2002: 2–3) has made a scan of the legislation that has been proposed to the US Congress in the past years. The word "accountability" occurs in the title of between fifty and seventy proposed bills in each two-year term. The focus of these "accountability bills" is extremely broad and ranged in 2001–2 from the Accountability for Accountants Act, the Accountability for Presidential Gifts Act, and the Arafat Accountability Act, till the Polluter Accountability Act, the Syria Accountability Act, or the United Nations Voting Accountability Act. The use of the term "accountability" is usually limited to the title of these acts. In most bills the term rarely is mentioned again, let alone defined. It is merely used as an ideograph, as a rhetorical tool to convey an image of good governance and to rally supporters (McGee 1980). Dubnick calls this the iconical role of the word "accountability." Accountability has become an icon for good governance.

Anyone reflecting on public accountability cannot disregard these strong evocative overtones. It has made the concept less useful for analytical purposes and turned it into a garbage can filled with good intentions, loosely defined concepts, and vague images of good governance. Nevertheless, it is worth saving the concept from its advocates and friends, as Dubnick (2002) summons us. We then have to move from a rhetorical or discourse analysis to a more descriptive, sociological analysis.

8.3 Accountability as an Institutional Arrangement

8.3.1 Accountability as a Social Relation

"Public accountability" is not just another political catchword, it also refers to institutionalized practices of account giving. Accountability refers to a specific set of social relations that can be studied empirically. This raises taxonomical issues: when does a social relation qualify as "public accountability"?

Accountability can be defined as *a social relationship in which an actor feels an obligation to explain and to justify his or her conduct to some significant other* (Day and Klein 1987: 5; Romzek and Dubnick 1998: 6; Lerner and Tetlock 1999: 255; McCandless 2001: 22; Pollit 2003: 89). This relatively simply defined relationship contains a number of variables. The actor, or *accountor*, can be either an individual or an agency. The significant other, which I will call the *accountability forum* or the *accountee*,[2] can be a specific person or agency, but can also be a more virtual entity, such as, in case of devout Christians, God or one's conscience, or, for public managers, the general public.

The relationship between the actor and the forum, the account giving, usually consists of at least three elements or stages. First of all, the actor must feel obliged to inform the forum about his conduct, by providing various sorts of data about the performance of tasks, about outcomes, or about procedures. Often, particularly in the case of failures or incidents, this also involves the provision of justifications. The conduct that is to be explained and justified can vary enormously, from budgetary scrutiny in case of financial accountability, to administrative fairness in case of legal accountability, or even sexual propriety when it comes to the political accountability of Anglo-American public officials.

The obligation that is felt by the accountor can be formal and informal. Public managers often will be under a formal obligation to give accounts on a regular basis to specific forums, such as their superiors, supervisory agencies, or auditors. In the wake of administrative deviance, policy failures, or disasters, public officials can be forced to appear in administrative or penal courts or to testify before parliamentary committees. A tragic example of the latter is the arms experts David Kelly, of the British Ministry of Defence, who was forced to testify before two parliamentary committees in the summer of 2003 about his press contacts regarding the Cabinet's claim that the regime of Saddam Hussein in Iraq could launch weapons of mass destruction—and subsequently committed suicide. But the obligation can also be informal, or even self-imposed, as in the case of press conferences, informal briefings, or public confessions.

Second, the information can prompt the forum to interrogate the actor and to question the adequacy of the information or the legitimacy of the conduct. This is the debating phase. Hence, the close semantic connection between "accountability" and "answerability."

Third, the forum usually passes judgment on the conduct of the actor. It may approve of an annual account, denounce a policy, or publicly condemn the behavior of a manager or an agency. In passing a negative judgment the forum frequently imposes some sort of sanctions on the accountor. These sanctions can be highly formalized, such as fines, disciplinary measures or even penal sanctions, but often the punishment will only be implicit or informal, such as the very fact of having to give an account in front of television cameras, or of having your public image or career severely damaged by the negative publicity that results from the process, as was the case with David Kelly.

To qualify a social relation as a practice of public accountability, an actor should, therefore, at least feel obliged to publicly explain and justify his conduct to a specific forum. More specifically, this qualification contains five elements: (1) public accessibility of the account giving—and not purely internal, discrete informing; (2) explanation and justification of conduct—and not propaganda, or the provision of information or instructions to the general public; (3) the explanation should be directed at a specific forum—and not be given at random; (4) the actor must feel obliged to come forward—instead of being at liberty to provide any account whatsoever; and (5) there must be a possibility for debate and judgment, including an optional imposition of (informal) sanctions, by the forum—and not a monologue without engagement.

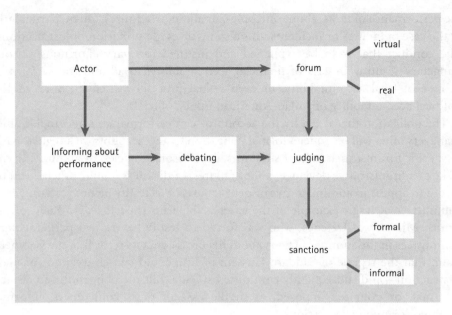

Fig. 8.1 Accountability

8.3.2 The Problem of Many Eyes: Who is the Accountee?

From a sociological perspective, public managers face multiple accountabilities. They may have to account for various elements of their conduct to a variety of forums. In classifying types of accountability it usually helps to distinguish two different questions: *to whom* and *for what*? The latter question is about the substance of accountability and would lead to distinctions such as managerial, financial, programme, or process accountability (Day and Klein 1987: 26; Sinclair 1996; Behn 2001: 6–10). Here I will limit myself to a relational classification of public accountability and I therefore concentrate on the various types of forums— on answers to the *to whom* question.[3]

In the daily life of modern public managers operating in a democratic system, there are at least[4] five different sorts of forums that they may have to face up to, and therefore also at least five major types of potential accountability relationships.[5] To make things even more complicated, each of these forums may require different data, and may have different expectations, based on different sets of norms, about the propriety of the manager's conduct, and may therefore pass different judgments. Public managers, therefore, face a problem of many eyes: who are they to account to and on the basis of which criteria will they be judged?

Organizational accountability: Superiors. The first and most important account-ability relation for public managers is organizational. Their superiors, both administrative and political, will regularly, sometimes on a formal basis, such as with annual performance reviews, but more often in daily informal meetings, ask them to account for their assignments. This usually involves a strong hierarchical relationship and the accounting may be based on strict directives and standard operating procedures, but this is not a constitutive element.[6] Senior policy advisers and project managers, working in a highly professional setting, will often have a considerable amount of autonomy in performing their tasks, and yet may strongly feel the pressures of organizational accountability. Strictly speaking, this is not yet "public" accountability, because these internal account givings are usually not accessible to the public at large. Nevertheless, this organizational accountability is the *sine qua non* for the other, external forms of public accountability.

Political accountability: Elected representatives and political parties. For managers in the public sector, accountability to political forums, such as elected representatives or political parties, can be very important facts of life. In parliamentary systems with ministerial responsibility and a general civil service, such as Britain and The Netherlands, this political accountability usually is exercised indirectly, through the minister. Increasingly, however, public managers too have to appear before parliamentary committees, for example in the case of parliamentary inquiries. In the American presidential system, senior public managers—heads of agencies for example—are often directly accountable to Congress. In administrative systems that work with political cabinets and spoils, as for example in the US, France, or Belgium, public managers will also find they have an informal and discrete, but not to be disregarded, accountability relationship with party bosses. Public managers, especially those with a professional or legal background, often find political accountability difficult to handle, if not threatening, because of the fluid, contingent, and ambiguous character of political agendas and political norms. The criteria for political judgment are often contestable and contested and may depend on media coverage, coalition building, and political opportunity. Sometimes they may even be established after the fact, as was the case with Derek Lewis, the Director General of the British Prison Service, who had achieved almost all the performance tasks set in his contract, but was nevertheless dismissed because of a politically sensitive prison escape by IRA terrorists (Barberis 1998: 457–8; Pollitt 2003: 28, 92).

Legal accountability: Courts. Public managers can also be summoned by courts to account for their own acts, or on behalf of the agency as a whole. These can be the "ordinary" civil courts, as in Britain, or also specialized administrative courts, as in France, Belgium, and the Netherlands (Harlow 2002: 16–18). In some spectacular cases of administrative deviance, such as the *affaire du sang* (the HIV contaminated blood products) in France or the *Tangentopoli* prosecutions in Italy, public officials have also been summoned before penal courts. In most western countries legal accountability is of increasing importance to public managers as a result of the growing formalization of social relations (Friedman 1985; Behn 2001: 56–8) or because of the greater trust which is placed in courts than parliaments (Harlow 2002: 18). For European public managers in particular, the directives of the EU are an additional and increasingly important source of legal accountabilities (Harlow 2002: 156–7). Legal accountability usually will be based on specific responsibilities formally or legally conferred to authorities. Therefore, legal accountability is the most unambiguous type of accountability as the legal scrutiny will be based on detailed legal standards, prescribed by civil, penal, or administrative statutes, or precedent.

Administrative: Auditors, inspectors, and controllers. Next to courts, a whole series of quasi-legal forums, that exercise independent and external administrative and financial oversight and control, has been established in the past decades—some even speak of an "audit explosion" (Power 1994).[7] These new administrative forums vary from European, national, or local ombudsmen and audit offices, to independent supervisory authorities, inspector generals, anti-fraud offices, and chartered accountants.[8] Also, the mandates of several national auditing offices have been broadened to secure not only the probity and legality of public spending, but also its efficiency and effectiveness (Pollitt and Summa 1997). These administrative forums exercise regular financial and administrative control, often on the basis of specific statutes and prescribed norms.[9] This type of accountability can be very important for public managers that work in quangos and other executive public agencies.

Professional accountability: Professional peers. Many public managers are, apart from being general managers, professionals in a more technical sense. They have been trained as engineers, doctors, veterinarians, teachers, or police officers (Abbot 1988; Freidson 2001). This may imply accountability relationships with professional associations and disciplinary tribunals. Professional bodies lay down codes with standards for acceptable practice that are binding for all members. These standards are monitored and enforced by professional bodies of oversight on the basis of peer review. This type of accountability relation will be particularly relevant for public managers who work in professional organizations, such as hospitals, schools, psychiatric clinics, police departments, or fire brigades.

8.4 ACCOUNTABILITY AS A SCHEME FOR BLAMING

8.4.1 Accountability as Liability

Public managers may shrug their shoulders at the sociological variety of public accountabilities and the accompanying obligations and relations. For them, they all have one thing in common: being held accountable means being in trouble. To quote Behn (2001: 3): "They recognize that if someone is holding them accountable, two things can happen: When they do something good, nothing happens. But when they screw up, all hell can break loose. Those whom we want to hold accountable have a clear understanding of what accountability means: Accountability means punishment." Politicians and public managers, therefore, can get involved in extensive "blame games," that involve presentational, policy, or agency strategies to minimize or avoid blame in case of failures and to maximize credits for successes (Hood 2002).

In the world of modern public administration, accountability relations are important venues for delivering blame in case things go wrong. Being accountable means being responsible, which, in turn, means having to bear the blame. This too raises important analytical issues, this time of a more normative and substantive nature: Who qualifies as the accountor, who is to be held liable, and on the basis of what criteria?

8.4.2 The Problem of Many Hands: Who is the Accountor?[10]

Accountability forums often face similar problems as public managers, but then in reverse. They can be confronted with multiple potential accountors. For outsiders, it is often particularly difficult to unravel who has contributed to the conduct of an agency, and in what way, and who can be made to account for its actions, and to what degree. Dennis Thompson has called this the *problem of many hands*: "Because many different officials contribute in many ways to decisions and policies of government, it is difficult even in principle to identify who is morally responsible for political outcomes" (1980: 905). Policies pass through many hands before they are actually put into effect. Decrees and decisions are often made in committees and cross a number of desks before they (often at different stages and at different levels) are implemented. New members of committees, of administrative bodies, and of departments conform to the traditions, rules, and existing practices (or what they think are the traditions, rules, and existing practices) and sometimes contribute ideas and rules of their own. However, they often leave before those ideas and rules can be put into practice, or before it becomes obvious that they did not work very well. Thus, the conduct of an organization is often the result of the interplay between fatherless traditions and orphaned decisions.

Who then, should be singled out for blame and punishment? With large public organizations, there are four accountability strategies for forums to overcome the problem of many hands.

Corporate accountability: The organization as accountor. Many public organizations are corporate bodies with an independent legal status. They can operate as unitary actors and can be held accountable accordingly. Most western countries accept corporate liabilities in civil, administrative, and even criminal law. Public organizations are usually included in these corporate liabilities, with the exception of criminal liability. Most European countries acknowledge penal immunities for all public bodies. Some, such as the UK, France, and The Netherlands, accept criminal liabilities for local public bodies, but not for the organs of the state. Only Norway, Denmark, and Ireland accept criminal liability of both central and local government (Roef 2001).

This corporate accountability strategy is often followed by legal and administrative forums. They can in this way circumnavigate the troublesome issues of identification and verification of individual actors. In the event of organizational deviance, they can turn directly to the organization and hold it to account for the collective outcome, without having to worry too much about which official has met what criteria for accountability. This strategy also assumes that the organization, just as natural persons, will learn from being held accountable and will adjust its policies accordingly. This assumption does not always hold true in practice. External norms do not automatically penetrate through into the organization; and even if they do so, they tend to lose out to other objectives. Sanctions that are directed against the organization may come too late, hit the innocent as well as the guilty, will be paid for by the public treasury, or cannot be made effective because of the actual or threatened liquidation of the public organization (Bovens 1998: 53–73).

Hierarchical accountability: One for all. This is the official venue for public accountability in most public organizations, and with regard to most types of accountability relationships, with the exception of professional accountability. It is particularly dominant in organizational and political accountability relations, for example in the Westminster system of ministerial responsibility. Underlying hierarchical strategies of accountability is a pyramidal image of complex organizations. Processes of calling to account start at the top. The rank and file do not appear before that external forum but hide behind the broad shoulders of the minister, the CEO or the commander in chief, who, at least in dealings with the outside world, assume complete responsibility and take all the blame. The lower echelons can in their turn, however, be addressed by their superiors regarding questions of internal, organizational accountability. In the case of hierarchical schemes, processes of calling to account thus happen along the strict lines of the "chain of command" and the middle managers are in turn accountor and accountee.

Hierarchical schemes are by virtue of their simplicity and clarity highly attract-ive. Whenever one wants to hold someone to account for the conduct of a public organization, one knows immediately whom to turn to: the political or organiza-tional top. It is not necessary to penetrate the organization and to unravel the intricate complex of powers and contributory actions. In practice, this strategy has serious limitations. The lines to the top are long, much vital information comes too late or is incomplete, and many agencies have formal or informal discretionary powers. Political leaders are by definition outsiders in their own organization. In Parliament there has been a tendency to restrict political accountability to that business of which the minister has had personal knowledge and that he was in a position actually to influence. This is documented for the UK (Turpin 1994: 432), Australia (Mulgan 1997: 32), and the Netherlands (Bovens 1998: 88). This means that in political practice, the hierarchical strategy has only limited power of control and preventive effects.

Collective accountability: All for one. Public organizations are collectives of individ-ual officials. Theoretically, a forum could therefore also apply a collective strategy of accountability and pick any member of the organization and hold it personally accountable for the conduct of the organization as a whole, by virtue of the fact that it is a member of the organization. This makes quick work of the practical sides of the problem of many hands. In the case of organizational misconduct, every member of the organization can be held accountable.

The major difficulty with collective accountability lies with its moral appropri-ateness. Collective arrangements of personal accountability are barely reconcilable with legal and moral practices and intuitions current in modern western democ-racies. They are not sophisticated enough to do justice to the many differences that are important in the imputation of guilt, shame, and blame. It makes a substantial difference whether someone, for example in the case of the Eurostat frauds, is the director of Eurostat who ordered secret accounts to be opened, the head of the financial department who condoned the unofficial deposits, or a simple statistician who was just collecting and processing data. A collective accountability strategy will only be appropriate and effective in specific circumstances, for example with small, collegiate public bodies.

Individual accountability: Each for himself. This is the most specific strategy for the attribution of blame. In this strategy an attempt is made to do justice to the circumstances of the case. Each official is held liable in so far as, and according to the extent to which, he has personally contributed to the malperformance of the agency. With this model, junior officials are not spared; the forum does not need to restrict itself to the general managers of the organization, but can hold to account each official of whom it might be supposed that he was involved in the misconduct. Furthermore, the imputation of responsibility will differ from person to person, whether one is at the top or at the bottom of the organizational hierarchy, one is judged on the basis of one's personal conduct. This strategy is typical for professional accountability, which operates on the basis of a strictly individual responsibility.

Such a strategy assumes that individual public managers have sufficient opportunities within their organization to make up their mind and to act accordingly. However, the hierarchical relationships within complex organizations, the powerful social pressure to conform to the aims and practices of the organization, and manifestations of "groupthink" and "peer-group pressure" can form real obstacles for individual officials who intend to act in a morally acceptable way. Hence, internal or external venues for exit and voice, such as whistle-blowing provisions, are an important complement (Bovens 1998: 113–34).

8.5 THE FUNCTIONS AND DYSFUNCTIONS OF PUBLIC ACCOUNTABILITY

8.5.1 Why do we Need Public Accountabilities?

Public accountability is not just the hallmark of democratic governance, it is also a *sine qua non* for democratic governance. Modern representative democracy can be analyzed as a series of principal-agent relations. Citizens, the primary principals in a democracy, transfer their sovereignty to political representatives who, in turn (at least in parliamentary systems) confide their trust in a cabinet. Cabinet ministers delegate or mandate most of their powers to the thousands of civil servants at the ministry, which in its turn, transfers many powers to more or less independent agencies and public bodies. The agencies and civil servants at the end of the line spend billions of taxpayers' money, use their discretionary powers to grant permits and benefits, they execute public policies, impose fines, and lock people up.

The first and foremost function of public accountability, as an institutional arrangement, therefore, is *democratic control*. Each of these principals in the chain of delegation, wants to control the exercise of the transferred powers by holding the agents to account. At the end of the line of accountability relations stand the citizens who judge the performance of the government and can sanction their political representatives by "voting the rascals out." Public account giving, therefore, is a necessary condition for the democratic process, because in the end it provides political representatives and voters with the necessary inputs for judging the fairness, effectiveness, and efficiency of governance (Przeworski, Stokes, and Manin 1999).

Second, public accountability functions to enhance the *integrity* of public governance. The public character of the account giving is a safeguard against corruption, nepotism, abuse of power, and other forms of inappropriate behavior (Rose-Ackerman 1999). The assumption is that public account giving will deter public managers from secretly misusing their delegated powers and will provide overseers, be they journalists, interest groups, members of Parliament, or official controllers, with essential information to trace administrative abuses.

The third function of public accountability is to *improve performance*. Public accountability is meant to foster individual or institutional learning (Aucoin and Heintzman 2000: 52–4). Accountability is not only about control, it is also about prevention. Norms are (re)produced, internalized, and, where necessary, adjusted through accountability. The manager who is held to account is told about the standards he must hold to and about the fact that in the future he may again (and, in that case, more strictly) be called to account. Outsiders are often addressed as well, particularly those outsiders likely to find themselves in a similar position. Parliamentary inquiries into policy fiascos, for example, cast their shadow ahead, way beyond the particular incident—especially when they are broadcast on prime time—and may prompt large numbers of public managers in similar positions to adjust their policies and procedures.

Together, these three functions provide a fourth function of public accountability: to maintain or enhance the *legitimacy* of public governance. Governments in western societies face an increasingly critical public. The exercise of public authority is not taken for granted. Public accountability, in the sense of transparency, responsiveness, and answerability, is meant to assure the public confidence in government and to bridge the gap between citizens and representatives and between governed and government (Aucoin and Heintzman 2000: 49–52).

Finally, in the incidental case of tragedies, fiascos, and failures, processes of public account giving have an important ritual, purifying function; they can help to provide public *catharsis*. Public account giving can help to bring a tragic period to an end and can allow people to get things off their chests, to voice their grievances, but also to give account of themselves and to justify or excuse their conduct. Parliamentary inquiries, official investigations, or public hearings in case of natural disasters, plane crashes, or railroad accidents, often fulfill this function. A recent example is the Hutton Inquiry into the death of David Kelly, which opened within weeks after he had been found dead. Also, the South African "truth commissions," and various war crime tribunals, starting with the Tokyo and Nuremberg trials up to the Yugoslav tribunal are meant to provide this function, at least in part (Dubnick 2002: 15–16). Processes of calling to account create the opportunity for penitence, reparation, and forgiveness and can thus provide social or political closure (Harlow 2002: 9).

8.5.2 Excess of Accountability

Public accountability may be a good thing, but we certainly can have too much of it. Many scholars have pointed to what could be called the *accountability dilemma* (Behn 2001: 11–13) or the *accountability paradox* (Dubnick 2003b: 31). There exists an inherent and permanent tension between accountability and effective performance (Halachmi 2002). Each of these functions of public accountability arrangements can easily turn into dysfunctions if public accountability is too zealously pursued (see Table 8.1).

Too rigorous democratic control will squeeze the entrepreneurship out of public managers and will turn agencies into rule-obsessed bureaucracies. And, as Mark Zegans observed, "rule-obsessed organizations turn the timid into cowards and the bold into outlaws." (quoted in Behn 2001: 30). Too much emphasis on integrity and corruption control will lead to a proceduralism that seriously hampers the efficiency and effectiveness of public organizations (Anechiarico and Jacobs 1996). Too much emphasis on accountability and transparency can lead to suboptimal and inefficient decisions instead of improved performance (Adelberg and Batson 1978; McLaughlin and Riesman 1986; Jackall 1988: 77–82).

In situations in which resources are scarce, a large measure of accountability can lead to an inefficient distribution of those resources. Adelberg and Batson (1978), two social psychologists, constructed a situation in which test subjects had to distribute scholarships to impecunious students, while there was not enough money to guarantee a reasonable grant to all those applicants who satisfied the formal requirements. It turned out that those who knew that they would have to account for their decisions after the event, regardless of whether this accounting

Table 8.1 Functions and dysfunctions of public accountability

Functions	Dysfunctions
Democratic control	Rule-obsession
Integrity	Proceduralism
Improvement	Rigidity
Legitimacy	Politics of scandal
Catharsis	Scapegoating

was to be to the students or to the grant-givers, made much less efficient use of the scarce resources at their disposal than those who did not realise that their actions would be scrutinized. The first group tried to forestall any possible dissatisfaction (and any criticism of their own behavior) by giving each applicant approximately the same amount. However, that procedure led to a situation in which most students received a grant that was so low that they had no real chance of continuing with their studies. The second group, feeling itself under less pressure to honour the principle of equality, made a clear choice. They gave the applicants who were most in need of support a grant that was large enough to enable them to continue with their studies; the rest got nothing. Instead of everybody getting too little, some received enough. A small measure of accountability thus led to a more efficient use of the funds.

The findings of Adeberg and Batson have been replicated and refined in a series of social psychological experiments (Tetlock 1983, 1985; Tetlock, Skitka, and Boettger 1989). Lerner and Tetlock (1999), in an extensive overview of the research literature, come to the conclusion that only special types of accountability relations elicit open-minded and critical thinking: "Self-critical and effortful thinking is most likely to be activated when decision makers learn prior to forming any opinions that they will be accountable to an audience (a) whose views are unknown, (b) who is interested in accuracy, (c) who is interested in processes rather than specific outcomes, (d) who is reasonably well informed, and (e) who has a legitimate reasons for inquiring into the reasons behind participants' judgments" (Lerner and Tetlock 1999: 259). Accountability to an audience exclusively interested in outcomes rather than in decision processes, or to an audience who favors a specific outcome, tends to seriously decrease the complexity and quality of decision making and to amplify cognitive biases (Lerner and Tetlock 1999: 259–66). If accountability is pursued too harshly, public managers may therefore learn the wrong thing, they learn to avoid risk taking, to pass the buck, and to shield themselves against potential mistakes and criticism (Behn 2001: 11).

Similarly, there is no absolute commensurate relationship between transparency and legitimacy. Transparency does not guarantee a favorable press. Each imperfection, each transgression of rules and regulations, however unimportant they may be, each dispute about a decision, can be ruthlessly exposed as a sign of irrationality or deviance. After every affair and fiasco, but even in routine situations, journalists can always find procedures and rules that have not been followed by the book. In contemporary Britain, according to Carol Harlow (2002: 189), "transparency has been taken to extreme lengths, and has become a weapon with which the media presses incursions into private life, howling for punitive action and seeking exaggerated redress for the simplest of errors." Similar concerns have been voiced in Belgium (Elchardus 2002) and the Netherlands ('t Hart, 2001). Increased transparency may thus turn public accountability into a politics of scandal and decrease the legitimacy of governance.

Finally, the institution of tribunals, truth commissions, and parliamentary inquiries may lead to scapegoating instead of forgiving and in lieu of catharsis we may get blaming games in which public managers and policy advisers, such as Derek Lewis or the unfortunate David Kelly, function as lightning rods or sacrificial lambs for politicians (Ellis 1994; Sinclair 1996: 229; Bovens et al. 1999; Hood 2002).

8.6 FROM VERTICAL TO HORIZONTAL ACCOUNTABILITY

In most western democracies, the dominant public accountability relationships traditionally have been vertical in nature. This has been particularly true for countries with a parliamentary system that operates on the basis of the doctrine of ministerial responsibility, such as Belgium, The Netherlands, Germany, and the countries of the former British Commonwealth with their Westminster system, such as the UK, Australia, and New Zealand. Formal public accountability is predominantly exercised through the ministerial responsibility to Parliament. Public managers are not politically accountable; for them organizational accountability prevails, they are accountable only to their direct superiors in the chain of command. Only the apex of the organizational pyramid, the minister, accounts for the organization in Parliament or in the media (Day and Klein 1987: 33–38). Public accountability thus follows the chain of principal-agent relations (see Figure 8.2). Over the past decades, this Weberian, or in Britain Diceyan, monolithic system of hierarchical political and organizational accountability relations has been under serious pressure and is slowly giving way to a more diversified and pluralistic set of accountability relationships.[11]

First of all, the rise of administrative accountability relations, through the establishment of ombudsmen, auditors, and independent inspectors, does not fit within the classic top–down, principal–agent relationships. Although most of these administrative forums report directly or indirectly to Parliament or to the minister, they often do not stand in a hierarchical relationship to the public managers. Some of them, such as ombudsmen, do not even have formal powers to coerce public managers into compliance. Most of these administrative accountability relations are a form of *diagonal* accountability,[12] they are meant to foster parliamentary control, but they are not part of the direct chain of principal-agent relations (Magnette et al. 2003: 836). These controlling agencies are auxiliary forums of accountability that were instituted to help the political principals control the great

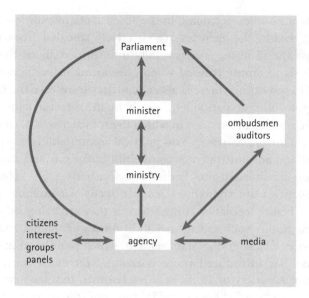

Fig. 8.2 Horizontal accountability

variety of administrative agents, but gradually they have acquired a legitimacy of their own and they can act as independent accountees.

Second, accountability forums increasingly adopt individual strategies of accountability. They are not satisfied with corporate or hierarchical liability, with calling only the agency or its minister to account, but also turn to individual officials. This rupture with the Weberian doctrine started in military and penal law in the Nuremberg and Tokyo Trials after the Second World War. The excuse of superior orders lost much of its legitimacy, first in the military sphere, but gradually also in the civil service (Bovens 1998: 122, 153). Nowadays, in many European countries individual public managers cannot always hide behind their agency or their superiors and can be held accountable by civil courts or sometimes even by penal courts for their personal contributions to organizational misconduct. Parliamentary committees of inquiry are not satisfied with the official view of the department, but do not hesitate to summon individual civil servants to be questioned in their hearings (Barberis 1998: 453, 466).

Third, the rise of quasi autonomous or independent agencies has weakened the legitimacy of the Weberian and Diceyan systems of political control through the minister (Van Thiel 2000; Pollitt et al. 2001). In the case of quangos, the traditional doctrines of ministerial responsibility is counterproductive. Although ministers formally remain answerable to Parliament for the daily performance of these agencies, they have far fewer powers of oversight and control than before. In many cases ministers have only retained a formal responsibility for policy formulation and institutional arrangements, whereas the operational responsibilities have moved to the heads of these agencies. In the absence of any political accountability of these agency heads, the agencies are effectively shielded from parliamentary scrutiny because the minister is structurally uninformed about their daily operations and will stand empty handed when questioned in Parliament about their performance. On top of this, there is also a tendency to reserve the full doctrine of ministerial responsibility to parliament, involving the threat of a loss of confidence and resignation, only to those cases in which the minister was personally involved (Harlow 2002: 22; Bovens 2003: 57). This political accountability gap partly explains the rise of legal and administrative accountability relations and causes a pressure for the creation of shortcuts to Parliament (Barberis 1998). Hence, heads of autonomous agencies are sometimes made directly accountable to Parliament and may appear before legislative committees or they are being subject to administrative scrutiny bodies such as national audit offices (Thatcher 2002: 142).

Fourth, the rise of New Public Management, which went hand in hand with the rise of quangos, has introduced more horizontal forms of accountability into the public sector. A variety of administrative reforms, that have been inspired by the private sector, such as the Financial Management Initiative and the subsequent Next Steps initiatives in the UK, or the Reinventing Government movement in the US, have tried to replace the hierarchical and bureaucratic logic of government operations with a contractual logic (Broadbent et al. 1996; Lane 2000; Pollitt and Bouckaert 2000; Behn 2001: 30–32). Public services are being contracted out to private or semi-public providers and executive agencies have been put "at arms length" from central government, or turned into performance-based organizations (PBO), and are being evaluated on the basis of targets, performance indicators, and benchmarks which have been laid down in (quasi)contracts (Behn 2001: 123).

Semantically, the logic of contracts implies a horizontal relationship, because both parties are free (not) to enter into the contract. In practice, due to a de facto monopoly on the part of the buyer, contract accountability can be another, more subtle form of hierarchical control, because the principal can unilaterally determine the terms of the contract. Some would even argue, that the use of "value for money" audits, with their wide array of performance indicators, allows for "total, 'before and after', supervisory control" (Harlow 2002: 21). Other commentators have warned that the economically informed logic of contracts is inappropriate in the context of professional service delivery, such as in health and education, because these services involve a degree of professional autonomy and tacit knowledge which cannot be spelled out in contracts and performance indicators (Broadbent et al. 1996). Or they worry about the costs, in terms of time-consuming paperwork, an increased overhead, and goal displacement, that are involved in registering and processing all the data that the contracts require for monitoring (Power 1997; Halachmi 2002; Pollitt 2003: 47). Managerialist critics, for example, will argue that public services nowadays have far too many accountability arrangements for efficient performance (Behn 2001: 11–21; Dubnick 2003b: 31–3).

In the fifth place, partly in reaction to a perceived lack of trust in government, there is an urge in many western democracies for more direct and explicit accountability relations between public agencies on the one hand and clients, citizens and civil society, including the media, on the other hand (McCandless 2001). The latter should become forums of political accountability, so the argument goes, and agencies or individual public managers should feel obliged to account for their performance to the public at large or to civil interest groups, charities, and associations of clients. This would be horizontal accountability in the true sense, as the complete hierarchical chain, including Parliament, is surpassed and the agency, the minister, or the public manager is directly accountable to the citizenry.

In the 1990s, many public agencies have established citizen charters, focus groups, and citizen panels to foster public accountability. In the UK, for example, the Blair government in 1998 set up a so called People's Panel, which was made up of approximately 6,000 citizens who were representative for the whole population in terms of age, gender, regional and ethnic background, and a series of other demographic indicators. The panel was used to consult citizens about the quality and content of public services. This national panel came to an end in 2002, but new panels have been established at various government departments. Examples are the British Crime Survey, run by the Home Office annually questioning 40,000 citizens about their opinions on criminal justice, the police, and the courts; Through the Patient's Eyes, a regular survey of in-patients in NHS hospitals, seeking their views on how they were treated; the National Passenger Survey by the Strategic Rail Authority; and a series of surveys run by local government.[13] Likewise, many

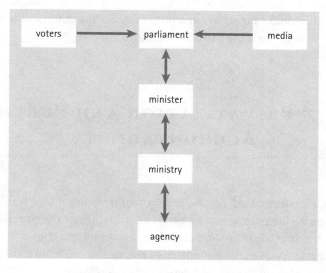

Fig. 8.3 Vertical accountability

agencies have set up smaller consumer panels, or advisory boards with delegations of interest groups, which they can consult about performance or policy changes.

However, most of these panels do not fully qualify as accountability arrangements in the sense of this chapter. To start with, they do not act as accountability forums, there is no formal or informal obligation for these organizations to account for and justify their conduct, let alone a possibility for debate and judgment by these panels. At most these surveys can be used as inputs for other forums, such as parliament, supervisory boards, or the media, who then can hold public organizations to account. The Charter Mark assessments in Britain, in which public organizations volunteer for an extensive assessment of the quality of their public service delivery by independent Charter Mark Assessment Bodies, would probably come closest to horizontal accountability (Bellamy and Taylor 1995; Duggett 1998).[14]

A step further in the direction of genuine horizontal accountability has been the practice of publishing the results of inspections, assessments, and benchmarks on the internet. For example, in The Netherlands, just as in the UK (Pollitt 2003: 41–5), the National Board of School Inspectors, makes its inspection reports on individual schools widely available on the Internet. Parents, journalists, and local councils easily can compare the results of a particular school with similar schools in the region, because quantitative and comparative benchmarks are provided for, but they also have access to the quite extensive qualitative reports. Even though there is little evidence, so far, that many parents exercise their right of exit or chance to voice their concerns on the basis of these qualitative reports, local principals increasingly do feel obliged to publicly account for themselves (Meijer 2004).[15]

Finally, some advocate an even more radical break with hierarchical accountability in favor of "360–degree" accountability in which not only every individual public manager is accountable to everyone with whom he works, but also vice versa: "each individual who is part of a public agency's accountability environment would be accountable to all the others" (Behn 2001: 199–201).

8.7 PRIVATIZATION AND PUBLIC ACCOUNTABILITY

So far we have concentrated on the accountability relations of public managers. However, both the increasing use of private companies in the provision of public services and the privatization of public organizations, raise questions about the public accountability of private managers (Leazes 1997; Gilmore and Jensen 1998; Mulgan 2000a; Minow 2003; Trebilcock and Iacobucci 2003). What does the

NPM-driven shift from public to private service delivery mean for the various forms of public accountability which we have discussed here?

Obviously, the most important consequence is a decrease in intensity and scope of political accountability. Private or privatized organizations are not subject to direct political accountability—that is what privatization usually is about, freeing organizations from the perceived burdens of political control. There is no direct ministerial responsibility to Parliament for the performance of these private bodies and they have far less stringent duties to report to the general public about their performance.

For those companies that have issued shares on the stock market, shareholders stand in a somewhat similar accountability relation to the general managers as citizens with regard to politicians. They usually have the right to certain reports and they may even have the right to pose some questions at general meetings, but the degree of scrutiny and the level of disclosure is far less than required of politicians and public managers; "private sector directors or managers do not open themselves to the same degree of media interrogation as politicians must accept, even on matters of clear public interest" (Mulgan 2000a: 94). Another, major difference is that this "private" form of public accountability is limited to shareholders, there is no general right for citizens to make inquiries into the affairs of private companies, even if these affect their lives. Freedom of information Acts, for example, do not apply to private entities in most countries.

It may be argued that corporations increasingly face public scrutiny, such as Shell did in the case of the Brent Spar or with its operations in Ogonoland in Nigeria. However, this public scrutiny is not yet based on institutionalized forms of public accountability, but only on a rather contingent interplay between interest groups and the media.

In a similar way, corporations and private managers are not subject to the same legal and administrative accountability relations and standards as governmental organizations and public managers are. Private sector companies are not subject to the stringent principles of administrative law, Ombudsmen and national audit offices have no jurisdiction, and there are fewer, or less accessible, mechanisms for external complaints and redress (Gilmore and Jensen 1998: 249; Mulgan 2000a: 90; Minow 2003).

Some argue that, in the long run, given a well-functioning market for public service delivery, free competition among private companies will make most legal and administrative accountability relations superfluous. Market forces will "compel private firms to act as though governed by public accountability rules" (Trebilcock and Iacobucci 2003: 1448). If private schools compete for pupils on the market, there will no longer be a need for public school inspectors who have the right to visit and inspect schools and to publish about their findings on the internet. Private schools, attempting to attract students, will voluntarily disclose information about their performance; and private parties, such as magazines and newspapers, will find it profitable to benchmark and rank them. Market-based accountability will then take the place of administrative accountability.

Others suggest that the trend towards reinventing government will eventually lead to a reinvention of public accountability relations for private bodies delivering public services. Gilmore and Jensen (1998), for example, advocate a protocol for the establishment of appropriate accountability relations in the case of government transfer of authority. And Mulgan (2000a: 94–6) sees some signs of convergence between the public and the private sector, resulting in the extension of public accountability concerns into the private sector. Indeed, in the 1980s and 1990s in western Europe many new independent agencies were created that regulate the operation of markets or promote a variety of public interests (Thatcher 2002: 126). Particularly the privatization of public utilities has given rise to a whole new series of administrative accountability relations in a number of economic sectors.

A somewhat more general convergence can be observed in the case of companies that are quoted on the stock exchange. They operate with public money, albeit not with taxpayers' contributions but with the anonymous deposits of institutional or private investors who buy shares on the public stock exchanges. New accountancy rules, issued in the US in the wake of the Enron bankruptcy and similar financial scandals, also to be introduced in Europe, oblige listed corporations to supply much more financial information to the general public than ever before. Also, the rise of bodies for financial and economic oversight and control, such as the SEC in America, the Competition Commission, the Financial Services Authority and the Securities and Investments Board in Great Britain, or the NMA and the AFM in The Netherlands, is the private sector equivalent of the audit explosion in the public sector.

8.8 THE MANAGEMENT OF PUBLIC ACCOUNTABILITY

Public accountability may be the complement of public management—it certainly is the predicament of public managers. For public managers public accountability has become an important, if not omnipresent, fact of life. Although reporting has always been an important element of the managerial tasks—see the "R" in Gulick and Urwick's PODSCORB acronym (Planning, Organizing, Staffing, Directing, Coordinating, Reporting, Budgeting)—it is not an exaggeration to say that nowadays much of the daily work of public managers consists of managing processes of account giving.

ICT-supported performance indicators and benchmarking systems have only increased the demands of their organizational superiors for frequent management reports and have accelerated the cycle of planning and control. The increasing political role of the media, with their bias for incidents and personal tragedies, has increased the importance, but also the volatility of political accountability. Public managers have to be constantly alert to the media, because the agenda of the media determines in large part the agenda of their political principals. Increasingly too, they may find themselves to be the subject of media attention and political scrutiny (Sinclair 1996: 225–7).

The litigation and audit explosions necessitate them to be alert to legal, financial, and administrative accountabilities. They may be faced with lawsuits and may have to coach staff members who represent their agency in court or consult with lawyers about legal defences and litigation strategies. They have to work their way through rituals of verification, compliance visits, and auditing operations. And the shift to horizontal accountability gives rise to new accountability relations. Panels of citizens and customers are emerging as new forums of accountability, interest groups demand to be treated as relevant stakeholders, and in the background the danger of negative publicity is always looming. Although some of this account-ability management is largely symbolic or ritualistic, most public managers cannot afford to neglect or ignore it.

However, most of these shifts do also offer opportunities for public managers to influence the public agenda to the benefit of their own organization or clientele. They can put these shifts to strategic use by designing their own benchmarks, by setting up their own accountability forums, and by strategically publishing about their successes and positive assessments. The heads of a number of independent agencies in The Netherlands, for example, have voluntarily published a Charter of Public Accountability which established, among others, a board that can visit and inspect their agencies and publicly report on them. This board operates independ-ent from the departments that are the principals of these agencies. In 2002 and 2003 this board inspected four agencies and issued—mostly positive—public reports.[16] These reports were published in the media and sent to parliament and thus became a move in the chess game of politico-administrative relations.

Public managers, therefore, do not need to undergo the rise of public account-ability pressures passively; they can to some extent manage them and become accountability entrepreneurs instead of accountability victims.

Notes

An earlier version of this chapter was presented as a paper at the Annual Conference of the European Group of Public Administration (EGPA), Lisbon Portugal, September 3–6, 2003. I would like to thank the participants in the Study Group on Ethics and Integrity in Governance, my USG colleagues Mirko Noordegraaf and Eugene Loos, and the editors of the handbook for their valuable comments on this earlier version.

1. This emancipation of "accountability" is basically an Anglo-American phenomenon—if only because other languages, such as French, Portuguese, Spanish, or Japanese, have no exact equivalent and do not (yet) distinguish semantically between "responsibility" and "accountability" (Mulgan 2000; Harlow 2002: 14–15; Dubnick 2002). In Germanic languages, such as Dutch, there is a distinction between "verantwoordelijkheid" and "verantwoording," which more or less resembles the distinction between "responsibility" and "accountability." But even here, both obviously are semantically closely related, and connected to "responsibility."

2. The neologisms "accountor" and "accountee" are derived from Pollitt (2003: 89).

3. Others tend to combine the relational and the substantive aspects in making classifications, see Day and Klein (1987: 26) or Sinclair (1996).

4. This is not meant as a limitative enumeration. Sinclair (1996: 230), for example, also mentions personal accountability, in which the public manager is accountable to his or her personal conscience. However, I do not consider this as a form of *public* accountability.

5. These forms are adapted from Romzek and Dubnick (1987) and Romzek (1996). See Sinclair (1996), Behn (2001: 59) and Pollitt (2003: 93) for similar taxonomies.

6. Here I differ slightly from Romzek and Dubnick (1998), Behn (2001), and Pollitt (2003), who would call this hierarchical or bureaucratic accountability. I find these terms somewhat misleading. The defining element in this type of accountability relationship is not hierarchy or bureaucracy as such, but the intra-organizational nature of the forum. Some of the other accountability relationships, such as political or administrative accountability, may involve strong elements of hierarchy too. Also, not all public organizations are by definition bureaucracies; many public managers operate in organizations that do not qualify as bureaucracies in the Weberian or Mintzbergian sense.

7. I have included financial accountability as a subspecies of this larger group of administrative accountabilities. Budgetary experts may of course be inclined to treat it as an independent form of accountability. Compare Laffan (2003: 764).

8. See for the rise of administrative accountability in the EU: Harlow (2002: 108–143), Magnette (2003), Laffan (2003), and Pujas (2003).

9. The rise of these administrative watchdogs raises interesting reflexive issues: how do these accountability forums account for themselves? See Pollitt and Summa (1997).

10. This paragraph is adapted from Bovens (1998).

11. See Day and Klein (1987: 10–29) for the general context and Barberis (1998) for the British context; see Mulgan (1997: 25–26) and Aldons (2001) for an overview of the Australian discussion; see Bovens (2003: 46–67) and Algemene Rekenkamer (2004) for the Dutch discussion. For an overview of the multi-level and composite character of accountability and control in the EU, see Harlow (2002), Costa et al. (2003) and Héritier (2003).

12. I owe this term to Thomas Schillemans.

13. http://www.cabinet-office.gov.uk/servicefirst/2001/panel/newsletter.final.htm

14. http://www.chartermark.gov.uk/.

15. See Halachmi (2002) for the possible dysfunctions of too strict public performance measurement regimes.

16. http://www.publiekverantwoorden.nl

REFERENCES

ABBOTT, A. (1988), *The System of Professions: An Essay on the Division of Expert Labor.* Chicago: University of Chicago Press.

ADELBERG, S., and BATSON, C. D. (1978), "Accountability and Helping: When Needs Exceed Resources," *Journal of Personality and Social Psychology* 36: 343–50.

ALDONS, M. (2001), "Responsible, Representative, and Accountable Government," *Australian Journal of Public Administration* 60(1): 34–42.

ALGEMENE REKENKAMER (2004), *Verbreding van de publieke verantwoording: Ontwikkelingen in maatschappelijke verslaglegging, kwaliteitszorg en governance,* Den Haag. (no publisher)

ANECHIARICO, F., and JACOBS, J. B. (1996), *The Pursuit of Absolute Integrity: How Corruption Control Makes Government Ineffective,* Chicago: University of Chicago Press.

AUCOIN, P., and HEINTZMAN, R. (2000), "The Dialectics of Accountability for Performance in Public Management Reform," *International Review of Administrative Sciences* 66: 45–55.

BARBERIS, P. (1998), "The New Public Management and a New Accountability," *Public Administration* 76: 451–70.

BEHN, R. D. (2001), *Rethinking Democratic Accountability.* Washington, DC: Brookings Institution.

BELLAMY, C., and TAYLOR, J. (1995), "The New Right Conception of Citizenship and the Citizen's Charter," *Government and Opposition* 30: 469–91.

BOVENS, M. (1998), *The Quest for Responsibility: Accountability and Citizenship in Complex Organisations,* Cambridge: Cambridge University Press.

—— (2003), *De digitale republiek: Democratie en rechtsstaat in de informatiemaatschappij,* Amsterdam: Amsterdam University Press.

—— HART, P. 'T, DEKKER, S., and VERHEUL, G. (1999), "The Politics of Blame Avoidance: Defensive Tactics in a Dutch Crime-fighting Fiasco," in: H. K. Anheier (ed.), *When Things go Wrong: Organizational Failures and Breakdowns,* Thousand Oaks, CA: Sage: 123–47.

BROADBENT, J., DIETRICH, M. and LAUGHLIN, R. (1996), "The Development of Principal-Agent, Contracting and Accountability Relationships in the Public Sector: Conceptual and Cultural Problems," *Critical Perspectives on Accounting* 7: 259–84.

COSTA, O., NICOLAS JABKO, LEQUESNE, C., and MAGNETTE, P. (2003), "Diffuse Control Mechanisms in the European Union: Towards a New Democracy?," *Journal of European Public Policy* 10(5): 666–76.

DAY, P., and KLEIN, R. (1987), *Accountabilities: Five Public Services,* London: Tavistock.

DUBNICK, M. J. (2002), "Seeking Salvation for Accountability," paper presented at the 2002 Annual Meeting of the American Political Science Association, Boston.

—— (2003a), "Accountability and Ethics: Reconsidering the Relationships," *International Journal of Organization Theory and Behavior* 6: 405–41.

—— (2003b), "Accountability and the Promise of Performance," paper presented at the 2003 Annual Meeting of the American Political Science Association, Philadelphia.

—— and ROMZEK, B. S. (1993). "Accountability and the Centrality of Expectations in American Public Administration," *Research in Public Administration* 2: 37–78.

DUGGETT, M. (1998), "Citizen's Charter: A People's Charter in the UK," *International Review of Administrative Sciences* 64: 327–30.

ELCHARDUS, M. (2002), *De dramademocratie*, Lannoo: Tielt.

ELLIS, R. J. (1994), *Presidential Lightning Rods*, Lawrence: University of Kansas Press.

FRIEDMAN, L. M. (1985), *Total Justice*, New York: Russell Sage.

FREIDSON, E. (2001), *Professionalism: The Third Logic*, Cambridge: Polity Press.

GULICK, L., and URWICK, L. (eds.) (1937), *Papers on the Science of Administration*, New York, 12–13.

HALACHMI, A. (2002), "Performance measurement: A look at some possible dysfunctions," *Work Study* 51(5): 230–9.

HARLOW, C. (2002), *Accountability in the European Union*, Oxford: Oxford University Press.

HART, P. 'T. (2001), *Verbroken verbindingen: Over de politisering van het verleden en de opkomst van een inquisitiedemocratie*, Amsterdam: De Balie.

HÉRITIER, A. (2003), "Composite Democracy in Europe: The Role of Transparency and Access to Information," *Journal of European Public Policy* 10(5): 814–33.

HOOD, C. (2002), "The Risk Game and the Blame Game," *Government and Opposition* 2002(1): 15–37.

GILMORE, R. S., and JENSEN, L. S. (1998), "Reinventing Government Accountability: Public Functions, Privatization, and the Meaning of 'State Action,'" *Public Administration Review* 58(30): 247–58.

JACKALL, R. (1988), *Moral Mazes: The World of Corporate Managers*, New York and Oxford: Oxford University Press.

LAFFAN, B. (2003), "Auditing and Accountability in the European Union," *Journal of European Public Policy* 10(5): 762–77.

LANE, J.-E. (2000), *New Public Management*, London: Routledge.

LEAZESS, F. J. (1997), "Public Accountability: Is It a Private Responsibility?" *Administration and Society* 29(4): 395–411.

LERNER, J. S., and TETLOCK, P. E. (1999), "Accounting for the Effects of Accountability," *Psychological Bulletin* 125: 255–75.

MCCANDLESS, H. E. (2001), *A Citizen's Guide to Public Accountability: Changing the Relationship Between Citizens and Authorities*, Victoria, BC: Trafford.

MCGEE, MICHAEL C. (1980), "The Ideograph: A link between Rethoric and Ideology," *The Quarterly Journal of Speech* 66: 1–16.

MCLAUGHLIN, J. B., and RIESMAN, D. (1986), "The Shady Side of Sunshine," *Teachers College Record* 87: 471–94

MAGNETTE, P. (2003), "Between Parliamentary Control and the Rule of Law: The Political Role of the Ombudsman in the European Union," *Journal of European Public Policy* 10(5): 677–94.

—— LEQUESNE, C., JABKO, N., and COSTA, O. (2003), "Conclusion: Diffuse Democracy in the European Union: The Pathologies of Delegation," *Journal of European Public Policy* 10(5): 834–40.

MEIJER, A. (2004), *Maatschappelijke controle in de publieke sector via internet*. Forthcoming.

MINOW, M. (2003), "Public and Private partnerships: Accounting for the New Religion," *Harvard Law Review* 116: 1229–1260.

MULGAN, R. (1997), "The Processes of Public Accountability," *Australian Journal of Public Administration* 56(1): 25–36.

—— (2000*a*), "Comparing Accountability in the Public and Private sector," *Australian Journal of Public Administration* 59(1): 87–97.

—— (2000*b*), "'Accountability': An ever expanding Concept?" *Public Administration* 78: 555.

—— (2003), *Holding Power to Account: Accountability in Modern Democracies*, Houndmills: Palgrave/MacMillan.

POLLITT, C. (2003), *The Essential Public Manager*, London: Open University Press/McGraw-Hill.

—— BATHGATE, K., CAULFIELD, J., SMULLEN, A., and TALBOT, C. (2001), "Agency Fever? Analysis of an International Fashion," *Journal of Comparative Policy Analysis: Research and Practice* 3: 271–90.

—— and BOUCKAERT, G. (eds.) (2000), *Public Management Reform: A Comparative Analysis*, Oxford: Oxford University Press.

—— and SUMMA, H. (1997), "Reflexive watchdogs? How supreme audit institutions account for themselves," *Public Administration* 75(2): 313–36.

POWER, M. (1994), *The Audit Explosion*, London: Demos.

—— (1997), *The Audit Society: Rituals of Verification*, Oxford: Oxford University Press.

PRZEWORSKI, A., STOKES, S. C., and MANIN, B. (eds.) (1999), *Democracy, Accountability, and Representation*, Cambridge: Cambridge University Press.

PUJAS, V. (2003), "The European Anti-Fraud Office (OLAF): A European Policy to Fight against Economic and Financial Fraud?" *Journal of European Public Policy* 10(5): 778–97.

RADIN, B. A., and ROMZEK, B. S. (1996), "Accountability Expectations in an Intergovernmental Arena: The National Rural Development Partnership," *Publius: The Journal of Federalism* 26(2): 59–81.

ROEF, D. (2001), *Strafbare overheden: Een rechtsvergelijkende studie naar de strafrechtelijke aansprakelijkheid van overheden voor milieuverstoring*. Antwerp: Intersentia.

ROMZEK, B. S. (1996), "Enhancing Accountability," in James L. Perry (ed.), *Handbook of Public Administration*, 2nd edn., San Francisco: Jossey Bass.

—— (1998), "Where the Buck Stops: Accountability in Reformed Public Organizations," in P. W. Ingraham, J. R. Thompson, and R. P. Sanders (eds.), *Transforming Government: Lessons from the Reinvention Laboratories*, San Francisco: Jossey Bass.

—— and DUBNICK, M. J. (1998), "Accountability," in J. M. Shafritz (ed.), *International Encyclopaedia of Public Policy and Administration*, vol. 1: *A-C*, Boulder, CO: Westview Press.

ROSE-ACKERMAN, S. (1999), *Corruption and Government: Causes, Consequences, and Reform*, New York Cambridge University Press.

SINCLAIR, A. (1996), "The Chameleon of Accountability: Forms and Discourses," *Accounting, Organisations and Society* 20: 219–37.

TETLOCK, P. E. (1983), "Accountability and the Perseverance of First Impressions," *Social Psychology Quarterly* 46: 285–92.

—— (1985), "Accountability: A Social Check on the Fundamental Attribution Error," *Social Psychology Quarterly* 48: 227–36.

—— SKITKA, L., and BOETTGER, R. (1989), "Social and Cognitive Strategies for Coping with Accountability: Conformity, Complexity, and Bolstering," *Journal of Personality and Social Psychology* 57: 632–40.

THATCHER, M. (2002), "Delegation to Independent Regulatory Agencies: Pressures, Functions and Contextual Mediation," *West European Politics* 25: 125–47.

THOMPSON, D. F. (1980), "Moral Responsibility of Public Officials: The Problem of Many Hands," *APSR* 74: 905–16.

—— (1983), "Ascribing Responsibility to Advisers in Government," *Ethics* 93: 546–60.

—— (1987), *Political Ethics and Public Office*, Cambridge, MA: Harvard University Press.

TREBILCOCK, M. J., and IACOBUCCI, E. M. (2003), "Privitization and Accountability," *Harvard Law Review* 116: 1422–53.

TURPIN, C. (1994), *British Government and the Constitution: Text, cases and materials*, 2nd edn., London.

VAN THIEL, S. (2000), *Quangocratization: Trends, Causes and Consequences*, Utrecht: ICS.

CHAPTER 9

ECONOMIC PERSPECTIVES ON PUBLIC ORGANIZATIONS

AIDAN R. VINING

DAVID L. WEIMER

9.1 INTRODUCTION

THE "New Public Management" became prominent in the 1990s (Hood 1991; Osborne and Gaebler 1993; Borins 1994; Aucoin 1995; Lane 2000). New public management (NPM) ideas concerning the functions and boundaries of government agencies and the delivery of public services—often summed up as "reinventing government"—have influenced governments around the world. Initially associated with public sector restructuring in New Zealand (Scott 2001), and then Australia, NPM ideas now influence organizational change in many countries including the restructuring of health care (Propper, Wilson, and Soderlund 1998) and secondary education (Bradley and Taylor 2002) in the United Kingdom and municipal government services in the United States. While there is some disagreement as to exactly what NPM encompasses, there is reasonable consensus that

NPM's core features include privatization, user charges, contracting-out, vouchers, performance measurement and assessment, managerial flexibility, and an emphasis on service receivers as "customers" (Gruening 2001: 2).

Although most of the leading proponents of NPM are political scientists or public management experts, many of its core ideas are drawn from economics. Partly as a result of this "disconnect," NPM critics have argued that it has shallow, even atheoretical, foundations and that it does not offer much practical advice to public management (Lynn 1994; Bryson 2002; Gruening 2001). This criticism is not assuaged by the almost messianic tone of some of the leading proponents of NPM (Abrahamson 1996).

The purpose of this chapter is to relate some of the core ideas of NPM directly to their economic foundations by reviewing relevant theory and empirical evidence. This overview is limited in two ways. First, we focus on the more strategic end of the NPM agenda and have relatively little to say about important tactical issues, such as improving accounting procedures within agencies, more visionary leadership, or the potential of performance auditing. As far as we can tell, economics offers little specific advice to public managers about these issues. (For an overview of performance measurement, see Propper and Wilson 2003.) We focus, therefore, on issues such as contracting-out and privatization that we think are informed by economics.

Second, our focus is primarily normative, though managers' motivations cannot, and should not, be completely ignored. Some positive theory proponents believe that a primarily normative focus is largely a waste of time—that contracting-out decisions, for example, will be driven by bureaucratic self-interest, however complex that self-interest is to model (Dunleavy 1992). A logical consequence of this view is that "reform" will be only incidentally influenced by normative, specifically efficiency, concerns. This critique is certainly well established in the public administration literature (Wildavsky 1966). While we believe that healthy scepticism about the prevalence of disinterested behavior by public actors, whether politicians or civil servants, is always appropriate, we also believe that a totally cynical view ignores two important points. First, normative ideas, including those about the value of efficiency, do appear to influence the design of public organizations and public policy in general (Hall 1989; Kelman 1990). There is a growing literature about the factors that induce the "ebb and flow" of such ideas in actual policy making, which goes beyond the scope of this essay (see, for example, Rodrik 1993 and Walsh 2000). Second, in a competitive institutional environment public managers are likely to see efficiency as at least instrumental to their other goals.

Finally, it worth emphasizing that the focus here is not about the appropriate use of economics and efficiency in analyzing policies and programs; in other words, the role *in policy analysis* of techniques such as cost–benefit analysis. While also of central interest to public managers, it is a different topic that is dealt with in many other places (e.g., GAO 1998; De Alessi 1996). Our focus is on effective public management.

9.2 What Public Management Questions Can Economics Address?

....

Public managers use scarce resources in order to produce social value (Moore 1995). Usually they carry out this task within established institutional arrangements—managing existing organizations and their contractual relations. Sometimes, however, they face decisions that would restructure organizational roles. Of course, as they ponder restructuring, the political process imposes various constraints on public managers and sets various goals for the agencies they manage. Yet the normative proposition is simple. In satisfying these constraints and promoting these goals, public managers should seek to use resources efficiently.

In order to help public managers (and those who study them in order to help them) think about the efficient use of public resources, we proceed as follows. First, what does economics say about how to use resources more efficiently *within existing public agencies?* The answer requires understanding how exchange among organizational members can be inefficient and the difficulty that intra-organizational hierarchies face in efficiently regulating these exchanges. Second, what can economics tell managers about how to decide *what should be produced within public agencies and what should be purchased from external sources?* This question concerns the appropriate boundaries of public organizations. It inevitably deals with the interaction between the public agency and other organizations, such as suppliers, contractors, and other public agencies. A related question is *what services should be left to markets?* Where such services are being provided by markets, this tends not to be a major issue. But in many countries during the twentieth century governments provided almost all goods and services. For these jurisdictions, the question is whether to redraw radically organizational boundaries and privatize, so that government only directly provides goods that meet an economic test of market failure or market power.

9.3 How Can Resources Be Used More Efficiently within *Existing* Public Agencies?

....

Three intellectual sources within economics can throw some light on intra-organizational efficiency: neoclassical economics (the theory of market failure), agency theory (the theory of hierarchy), and the rational choice theory of institutions (the theory of norms).

9.3.1 Intra-Organizational Market Failures

Neoclassical economics is primarily concerned with market allocation. Its normative side, welfare economics, has as its fundamental theorem the Pareto efficiency of the ideal competitive economy: no reallocation could be made that would make some-one better off without making someone else worse off. Under a number of assumptions about the nature of goods, individual preferences, and production technology, the self-interested behavior of consumers and firms will result in a Pareto-efficient allocation of factors (land, labor, and capital) and goods. The efficiency implications of violations of the assumptions of the idealized competitive economy are of particular interest to public policy. These market failures represent situations in which market allocation fails to achieve Pareto efficiency. Market failures thus provide a rationale for considering corrective public policies to increase efficiency. Although the list can be expanded, welfare economics has focused on four market failures: public goods, externalities, natural monopolies, and information asymmetries.

Their relevance here is that public managers may find the concept of market failure useful for framing, and perhaps solving, intra-organizational problems (Vining and Weimer 1999) as well as for their traditional role in assessing the value of government intervention in markets. New Zealand has been at the forefront of recognizing the role of internal organizational markets, for example, with the development of explicit contracts with chief executives of government bureaus (Scott 2001). Three kinds of market failure have direct analogies as organizational, or public bureau, failure: organizational public goods, organizational externalities, and organizational natural monopoly. While all hierarchical organizations, including private firms, are subject to these failures, characteristics of the public organization, especially lack of competition and intangibility of outputs, make them particularly vulnerable to them.

As an illustration, consider organizational public goods. Public organizations, for example, face the problem of getting employees to contribute to the production of organizational reputation and innovation, which have the characteristics of "pure public goods" because everyone in the organization enjoys whatever levels of reputation and innovation are achieved. Yet individual employees often see contributing to reputation or innovation as involving greater costs than benefits. If one employee makes an extra effort, then she bears a cost; if no other employee makes such efforts, then she will have borne personal costs for perhaps no meaningful improvement in organizational output. On the other hand, if all other employees make such contributions, then why bear the personal costs of doing so when it will only have a very small incremental impact? Of course, if all employees make such calculations the pure public good is not produced at all. Everybody ends up "shirking."

Public managers face the challenge of convincing ordinary civil servants to make organizational public goods contributions. Indeed, one of the key focuses of the

NPM has been to strengthen incentives to provide organizational public goods, especially those relating to more subtle organizational public goods such as client service and innovation by offering individual and group, intrinsic and extrinsic rewards. The empirical literature shows the importance of *intelligently and sensitively* aligning employee incentives to the goals of public organizations (Grady 1992; Glor 2002). There are a number of mechanisms for doing so. Public managers may try to link contributions to employee evaluations, perhaps by lowering the costs to clients of communicating to managers about the quality of the service they have received. If employee evaluations translate only weakly into direct rewards like salary and promotion, then managers may use programs such as "employee of the month" in an attempt to provide social status rewards. Appropriate social norms within the organization may help solve the problem, though they may be hard to develop or maintain for large groups or in situations where turnover is high. Organizing small work teams to which reputations can be attributed may facilitate the operation of favorable social norms. Yet moving in this direction is not without risks. If the ordinary public servant perceives that the norms being promoted are not being adhered to by their superiors, then the resulting organizational cynicism can result in highly dysfunctional agencies.

9.3.2 Hierarchies and Agency Loss

The market failure of information asymmetry is fundamentally important to understanding organizational problems. Indeed, it lies at the heart of neo-institutional economics, which maintains the core assumptions of neoclassical economics, specifically utility maximizing behavior and equilibria, but explicitly takes account of the distribution of information and contextual constraints that affect individual behavior (Eggertsson 1990). Two branches of neo-institutional economics have developed: transaction cost theory and agency theory. We draw on transaction cost theory as the conceptual basis for drawing the boundaries of public organizations. Here we consider agency theory as a conceptual basis for assessing the efficiency of hierarchies (Ross 1973; Jensen and Meckling 1976; Sappington 1991; and Banks 1995; see Hesterly, Liebeskind, and Zenger 1990, for a review of empirical research).

Agency theory focuses on two types of information asymmetry between principals and their agents (Hart and Holmstrom 1986). One type is hidden information: the agent enjoys an advantage relative to the principal in terms of some knowledge about the outcome of uncertain events. The other type is hidden action: the agent enjoys an advantage relative to the principal in terms of knowledge about the actions of the agent.

The key insight of agency theory is the recognition that an efficient hierarchy is one that minimizes agency costs, which include the "cost of structuring, monitoring, and bonding a set of contracts among agents with conflicting interests, plus the residual loss incurred because the cost of full enforcement of contracts exceeds the benefits" (Jensen and Meckling 1976: 305). So, for example, public managers may impose rules (contract structuring) that prohibit employees from using work time for personal tasks, but not fully enforce them because the resource costs of monitoring and disciplining violations, as well as the cost of the harm to employee morale and productivity, would be larger than the benefits of the gains in employee work time that would result from full enforcement.

Political scientists have begun to move from using agency theory as a metaphor to constructing and empirically testing formal models of delegation from legislatures to agencies. Prominent examples include Epstein and O'Halloran (1999), who model and test hypotheses about congressional delegation and Huber and Shipan (2002), who model and test hypotheses about both separation-of-powers and parliamentary systems. These models harness agency theory (games of incomplete information) to Niskanen's (1971) conception of information asymmetry favoring bureaus.

In most mature democracies, the contracts under which the managers perform involve considerable constraints on discretion. General civil service rules typically severely limit the discretion of public managers with respect to hiring, firing, rewarding, and disciplining the employees of their bureaus. Numerous historical examples of cronyism and nepotism emphasize the importance of such constraints. These restraints go beyond personnel decisions. Line item budgets often restrict the discretion of managers with respect to the choice of inputs. Further, managers do not have direct access to capital markets that enable them to borrow against future savings to fund potentially cost-saving innovations. The problem faced by the public manager is how to structure intra-organizational "contracts" within these constraints.

In the absence of such constraints, public managers could minimize agency loss by choosing the right balance between *ex ante* rules and *ex post* rewards (Thompson and Jones 1986). In world of no, or minimal, constraints *ex post* rewards will be relatively more attractive than *ex ante* rules. It is easier to assess performance after observing it. In the public sector, however, civil service rules and line item budgets tend to make it more difficult to structure contracts, whether explicit or implicit, with *ex post* rewards.

Nevertheless, agency theory offers some insights for public managers. Hidden information can be modeled as a situation in which the principal knows the distribution from which a random outcome is drawn but only the agent knows the value of the draw. For example, the manager of a training program may know that the difficulty of finding a job in a particular market will range somewhere from "easy" to "very hard," but the trainer who actually has to place clients with employers knows the actual difficulty quite precisely. The problem facing the manager is separating out the effort made by the trainer (hidden action) from the placement difficulty. If difficulty is correlated across agents, say because they work with clients in the same or closely related markets, then the manager may be better able to assess relative performance rather than absolute performance. In an extreme case where managers have substantial discretion over the allocation of rewards, contracts might be structured as tournaments that reward relative performance (Knoeber and Thurman 1994). Emphasizing relative performance, however, can be misleading when the variance of the hidden information is high and the correlation across agents is low (Kane and Staiger 2001).

Some of the implications of agency theory simply reinforce common management wisdom. For example, in circumstances in which some dimensions of employee effort are only imperfectly observable (hidden action) reward structures that focus solely on observable behavior will divert effort toward those behaviors, resulting in the well known problem of "goal displacement." Team production, in which output depends on the hidden actions of its members, will generally suffer from shirking if rewards depend solely on team output (Holmstrom 1982).

Perhaps the most general lesson from agency theory is the importance of incentive compatibility: To what extent do the reward structures facing agents give them incentives to act in ways that promote the goals of the principal? Asking and answering this question goes a long way to helping public managers anticipate the inefficient use of resources.

9.3.3 Leadership and Corporate Culture

As previously argued, line public managers usually have relatively little discretion over the structure of employment contracts. Even if they did, caution would be warranted in translating agency theory into practice, because agency theory tends to focus on one-time interactions while the very nature of the organization is an ongoing employment relationship (Miller 1992). In recent years, considerable effort has been devoted to understanding how norms that require individuals to act against their own short-term interests, such as making contributions to organizational public goods, can be sustained in ongoing groups.

The primary vehicle for this has been the rational choice theory of institutions (Taylor 1976; Schotter 1981; Axelrod 1984; Calvert 1995). The theory begins by modeling a social interaction as a game. It then considers whether behaviors that are not equilibria in the one-time play of the game become equilibria if there is repeated play. The equilibria in repeated games can often be interpreted as organizational norms. To the extent these norms are organizationally beneficial they provide a basis for thinking about how managers can obtain more desirable outcomes within the same formal organizational structure.

Managers may be able to affect the nature of organizational interactions (that is, repeated play) through decisions concerning the size and stability of work groups.

They can also help maintain desirable norms by ensuring that new employees are aware of the norms, so that their inadvertent defections do not undercut it. For example, small unit cohesion in military settings may be enhanced by withdrawing depleted units from the line so that replacements can be trained with veterans (Shils and Janowitz 1948). In situations in which an undesirable norm has taken hold, such as employees cooperating in covering up each other's shirking, the managers may try to break the norm by bringing in new employees who will undermine it.

Note that the so-called Folk Theorem shows that repeated games generally have multiple equilibria (Fudenberg and Maskin 1986). In the example, another equilibrium would be "always defect." Yet another would be "tit-for-tat," in which each defection is punished by defection only once. The likelihood of multiple equilibria provides a theoretical interpretation of leadership: helping groups reach relatively favorable equilibria in repeated games. Leaders may send signals that help players (employees) coordinate on the same strategy. How can this be done in practice? One way might be to create "focal points" that psychologically predispose players to particular strategies (Schelling 1960). This might be done by making clear statements about what is expected of the players, or even simply letting the players know when they are playing the game. It can be supported by encouraging or admonishing employees in person by "walking around" as well as by identifying exemplary cases of behavior in compliance with the norm that will become vivid focal points for coordinating future behavior.

It may be difficult for managers to establish a norm because employees may be concerned that it will change when leadership changes. In other words, leaders will have difficulty making long-term compliance with the norm credible. To get around this problem, leaders may attempt to embed the norm within an agency culture that will persist beyond their tenures (Kreps 1990). The culture sets the expectation that following the particular norm will be rewarded, thus increasing the "shadow of the future" beyond the tenure of the leaders of the day.

9.4 *CHANGING* THE BOUNDARIES OF PUBLIC AGENCIES: CHOOSING AMONG IN-HOUSE PRODUCTION, CONTRACTING-OUT, AND PRIVATIZATION

Public managers sometimes have opportunities to influence their organizational boundaries. Most often, this opportunity arises in the choice of what to produce in-house and what to purchase from other organizations. Sometimes, however, public managers can shape decisions about the more fundamental question of whether the government will relinquish decisions about the provision of goods to either the private or nonprofit sectors (that is, "markets").

9.4.1 Government Production versus Contracting-out

The major purpose of redrawing organizational boundaries of public agencies should be to improve the efficiency with which public services are delivered (Hodge 2000: 25). A rationale for public provision based on market failure or the achievement of other social goals does not necessarily imply a rationale for government production or service delivery (Vining and Weimer 1990). Government can finance provision of services so that they are delivered by either for-profit, private not-for-profit, or other public organizations.

All governments face the choice between internally producing a given good or service or contracting-out its delivery after they have made a decision to provide the good. Public managers have become increasingly aware that this is a *decision*. Contracting-out has grown substantially in the United States, Great Britain, Australia, and many other countries over the last two decades (Domberger and Hall 1996; Dilger, Moffett, and Struyk 1997; Chi and Jasper 1998; Morley 1999; Hodge 2000: 88-92). In order to decide appropriately about what should be contracted-out, and how it should be contracted-out, public managers must consider all costs.

Three types of costs are relevant to the choice between direct production by public agencies and contracting-out: production costs, bargaining costs, and opportunism costs (Globerman and Vining 1996; Vining and Globerman 1998). Production costs are the costs associated with directly producing the good or service. Bargaining and opportunism are costs of governance. We deal with governance costs first. In order to do so, we draw from transaction cost economics, the branch of economics that arose to explain why some economic activities are organized as markets while others are organized as hierarchical entities.

Bargaining costs can be separated into the following categories: (1) the costs arising from negotiating the details of the contract; (2) the costs of negotiating changes to the contract in the post-contract stage to accommodate any unforeseen circumstances; (3) the costs of monitoring performance by other parties to determine if they are adhering to the contract, and (4) the costs of handling disputes that arise if neither party wishes to utilize pre-agreed dispute resolution mechanisms, especially those for breaking the contract. While only the first cost is experienced at the time of contracting (the others are experienced in the post-contractual period), almost all of these costs can be anticipated at the time of contracting. Bargaining costs arise when both parties act with self-interest, but in good faith (Williamson 1985). The incremental bargaining costs of contracting-out are relevant because a potential advantage of not contracting-out is that the distribution of costs within the organization can be resolved at relatively low cost by managers. Nonetheless, bargaining within organizations, for example over internal transfer prices or areas of responsibility, always involves some costs (Jensen and Meckling 1976: 310-11). In highly politicized, large bureaus with many units, these costs can be high.

Opportunism can be thought of as trying to change the rules during the game. It involves behaviors by a party, acting in *bad* faith, to alter the terms of the contract more in that party's favor. There is usually more latitude for opportunism in the context of contracting-out than in agency production, because the issue of who gets rents (payments in excess of costs) is usually less clear in the non-hierarchical relationships between organizations. This inter-organizational battle for rents applies even if the other organizations are other public sector organizations or nonprofits, although the nature of the rent is typically more varied—it can include influence, prestige, bigger budgets, etc. Another factor that dampens rent wars within organizations is that employees have better and more frequent opportunities to punish opportunistic fellow employees (in other words, the interaction has the characteristics of a repeated game). But opportunism can also occur within public organizations (Holstrom 1982; Weimer and Vining 1996). Therefore, it is incremental opportunism costs that are relevant for purposes of organizational design. Opportunism is more often considered to occur *after* contracting has taken place, but some behaviors prior to contracting have opportunism-like characteristics (Klein, Crawford, and Alchian 1978). For example, one party may advance contract provisions that appear neutral but actually facilitate exploitative behavior later.

Opportunism and bargaining costs are often difficult to distinguish in practice. Opportunistic parties have an incentive to claim that their behavior results from an unexpected change in circumstances; often there are informational asymmetries that prevent the other party from determining if the claim is genuine. The difficulty of distinguishing between legitimate bargaining and opportunism raises contracting-out costs (Akerlof 1970).

Production costs are the opportunity costs of the real resources actually used to produce the output. Economic theory suggests that production costs will normally be lower where there is competition, except for well-defined exceptions. Both theory and evidence also suggest that in a competitive environment private, profit-oriented firms have lower costs than public or mixed-ownership organizations (Vining and Boardman 1992). Production costs are likely to be lower with competitive contracting-out for two reasons.

First, in-house production levels may be too low to achieve economies of scale (McFetridge and Smith 1988; Prager 1994). A specialized producer, selling to multiple buyers, can better achieve scale economies. In contemporary public organizations producing complex, intangible services, the most significant economies of scale may be for factors such as administrative systems, knowledge, expertise and the capacity to learn. Scale economies alone, however, are not a sufficient argument for private sector production. Public organizations could engage in co-operative production that utilizes economies of scale. In practice, however, it is often difficult to design government organizations that can span several political jurisdictions to achieve scale economies. In addition, this co-operation also engenders bargaining and opportunism costs. However, large, boundary-spanning not-for-profits may be able to compete on this dimension (Tuckman 1998).

Second, public provision may fail to achieve the lowest production costs that are technically feasible (Leibenstein 1976). The failure to produce at lowest cost results from public agencies being monopolies, rather than from intrinsic attributes of government ownership *per se* (Vining and Weimer 1990), though civil service and other restrictions imposed on public managers may hinder the use of available resources in their most efficient combinations. Government monopoly blunts efficiency incentives because it eliminates comparative performance benchmarks for customers and overseers. Furthermore, when services are funded through lump-sum budget allocations to multi-service agencies rather than through sales to consumers, the marginal costs of services are obscured.

Competition appears to improve technical efficiency, the production of output at the minimum possible cost (Hodge 2000; Greene 2002: 49; Henry 2002). For example, evidence suggests that greater intensity of competition in the hospital sector, regardless of ownership, lowers costs and prices (e.g., Melnick et al. 1992; Dranove, Shanley and White 1993).

More importantly, there is considerable empirical evidence from a range of governmental activities that contracting-out by government to private suppliers generally lowers production costs (e.g., Domberger, Meadowcraft, and Thompson 1987; Pack 1989; Milne and McGee 1992; McDavid and Clemens 1995; Ohlsson 1996; Dilger, Moffett, and Struyk 1997; Domberger, Jensen, and Stonecash 2002). British and Australian studies have found that production cost savings are in the 20 percent range (Morlock 1987; Walsh 1991; Szymanski and Wilkins 1993; Domberger and Hall 1996). A recent survey of the contracting-out experience of the 66 largest cities in the US found that the annual cost savings were between 16 and 20 percent; respondents also estimated that contracting improved service quality by between 24 and 27 percent (Dilger, Moffett and Struyk 1997). Hodge (2000: 103) provides a comprehensive review and meta-analysis of the empirical evidence on costs and finds there are only "around three dozen studies" with "reasonable research integrity." As a result of the meta-analysis, Hodge (2000: 128) concludes:

This analysis has shown that contracting studies have typically reported real cost savings ... These effect sizes were found to be highly significant and were interpreted as being equivalent to an average cost saving of 8 to 14 percent. Overall, the reliability of this average saving was beyond doubt. Cost savings differed between services and a general rule could not be applied to all.

The evidence suggests that much of the cost reduction comes from productivity improvements, which implies that although nominal wages do not change, there are decreases in effective wage rates (Milne and McGee 1992; Szymanski and Wilkins 1993; Domberger, Jensen, and Stonecash 2002). Higher internal costs also result from higher pay rates and civil service restrictions that limit productivity growth (Johnson and Libecap 1989; Kodrzycki 1994).

There are two important caveats to the findings of cost savings from contracting-out. First, studies that have examined the relative production costs of internal provision versus contracting-out have not included bargaining and opportunism costs, which *a priori* might be expected to be higher with contracting-out (Vining and Globerman 1998; Sclar 1997; Hodge 2000). Researchers are just beginning to examine this issue. One recent study finds that governments engage in more monitoring, and bear more monitoring costs, when the risks of opportunism are greater (Brown and Potoski 2003). These conditions are discussed below.

Second, cost comparison studies should control for quality differences. In practice, this is much more important with complex services where quality variance can be high. A few studies have controlled for quality (e.g., Berenyi and Stevens 1988; Holcombe 1991; Domberger, Hall and Li 1995), but the great majority have not. Therefore, there is currently relatively little rigorous empirical evidence on this question (Domberger and Rimmer 1994; Hodge 2000). One important piece of recent evidence is from Williams (1998) who surveyed 723 US local governments that provided residential waste collection. Approximately half provided the service directly and half contracted-out service provision. Eighty-seven percent of the contracting-out jurisdictions reported "satisfactory" service, as against 79 percent of the direct provision municipalities.

A couple of notes of caution are warranted. Not all forms of contracting-out can be expected to lower production costs, particularly if cost-plus contracts are used (McAfee and McMillan 1988). Also, and perhaps obviously, if the contracting-out decision is driven by the pure self-interest of politicians or managers, efficiency gains would be unlikely, or at least purely fortuitous. On positive reasons for contracting-out, see Lopez-de-Silanes, Shleifer, and Vishny (1997).

In summary, public managers should seek the regime that minimizes the sum of production, bargaining, and opportunism costs across government, external suppliers, and third-parties (citizens) for any given level and quality of service. This objective emphasizes that public managers should be as concerned with the costs that they impose on external suppliers or third-parties, as with the budgetary costs that they bear. However, at the organizational level (e.g., a welfare agency or an individual hospital) it is unrealistic to expect managers to act with this degree of altruism without appropriate incentives. Consequently, the highest level of government may have to set appropriate frameworks for contractual conditions (i.e., design meta-contracts). For example, requirements for cost-benefit analysis to support decisions force attention on social costs, including the costs borne by third-parties.

How can bargaining and opportunism costs be assessed in any specific contract-ing-out context? We briefly consider there relevant factors: the task complexity, the degree of contestability, and the degree of asset specificity.

9.4.1.1 Degree of Task Complexity

Task complexity refers to the dimensionality and imperfect transparency of the goods (or services) in the transaction. The greater is the task complexity, the more difficulty the parties face in specifying the terms and conditions of the contract and how they are to be monitored. The empirical literature confirms that high task complexity raises bargaining and opportunism costs (Praeger 1994; Whelan 1999: 52; Brown and Potoski 2003). For example, specifying and measuring the quality of food served by an external supplier is relatively easy; specifying, measuring and enforcing the quality of complex medical services where patients have widely varying risk factors is relatively difficult (Croxon, Propper, and Perkins 2001).

The degree of task complexity largely determines both the uncertainty surround-ing the contract (this effects both contracting parties equally) which raises the probability that "bounded rationality" will come into play (Cyert and March 1963) and the potential for information asymmetry, or hidden information, in which one party to the contract has information that the other party does not have. It also influences the probability that there will be externalities that will affect other organizational activities. Complex tasks involve uncertainty about the nature and costs of the production process itself. Additionally, complex activities are more likely to be affected by various sorts of "shocks," or unforeseen changes in the task environment. Greater uncertainty raises bargaining costs, both during contract negotiations and post-contract. Masten (1984), for example, found that more complex components were considerably more likely to be produced internally in the aerospace industry than to be contracted-out.

High task complexity usually contributes to greater information asymmetry, because it implies specialized knowledge or assets whose characteristics are only initially known to external firms or other external experts (Crawford and Krahn 1998). Information asymmetry usually raises costs, especially if the quality of the contracted services is only revealed considerably after the transaction occurs (Vining and Weimer 1988). Consequently, information asymmetry creates circum-stances conducive to opportunism, which can arise either at the contract negoti-ation stage or, especially, at the post-contract stage.

9.4.1.2 *Degree of Competition or Contestability*

Highly competitive markets for goods and services, whether intermediate or final products, provide opportunities for public agencies to realize lower production costs by contracting-out without great risk for high negotiation and opportunism costs. Public agencies, however, may still be able to reduce production costs by contracting-out activities even if there is little or no direct competition (Vining and Weimer 1990). If the contracted goods involve extensive scale economies (itself an important rationale for contracting-out, as explained above), there may be some degree of local, regional, or even national, natural monopoly (this is also usually related to the extent of asset specificity, to be discussed next). However, if firms are able to switch production to the good without sinking large up-front costs, the market for the good is contestable, in spite of the lack of direct competition. A market is contestable if other firms or nonprofit organizations would quickly become available if the price paid by the governmental organization exceeded the average cost incurred by external suppliers (Baumol, Panzar and Willig 1982). For example, the markets for standard accounting and payroll services are highly contestable as many firms have the capabilities to supply such services, even if they are not currently doing so in a given market.

Higher levels of contestability generally reduce opportunism costs. During contract negotiations, a potential external supplier in a market with no, or very limited, contestability is tempted to offer services at a price above marginal cost (or average cost in circumstances where average cost is declining for the demanded good). This higher price can be thought of as a bargaining cost to the agency, because it must be paid to achieve the contract.

At the post-contract stage low levels of contestability increase the risks of opportunism for two reasons. First, the external supplier cannot be quickly replaced (temporal specificity). Second, there is a heightened risk of "contract breach externalities," which affect third parties (Globerman and Vining 1996). Services that are essential to networks are especially vulnerable to opportunism costs. For example, a firm providing computer services might undermine users both in and outside of the agency by withdrawing services. This could effectively shut down a government. Of course, public agencies do not necessarily eliminate such externality problems by carrying out production themselves. Their own employees can act opportunistically by withholding essential services (passive breach) or by picketing and various forms of sabotage (active breach).

Some of the same problems that contribute to the desire for contracting-out also limit competition and contestability. For example, services for small and geographically dispersed populations that involve economies of scale are unlikely to involve high levels of competition among local private suppliers (Steel and Long 1998); large sunk costs may act as a barrier to *de novo* entry of suppliers, limiting contestability.

In some cases it may also be possible for governments to increase competition by expanding the size of the relevant geographic market through exchange agreements among themselves, such as allowing consumers to acquire services across jurisdictional boundaries with payments made to their suppliers from the agencies serving their home jurisdictions. For example, some US states allow parents to send their children to school districts in which they do not live. Such agreements often face political obstacles because government purchasers are often reluctant to allow funds to flow outside their administrative boundaries, perhaps threatening the financial viability of their own provider organizations.

9.4.1.3 Degree of Asset Specificity

Asset specificity arises when an asset essential to production has much lower value in alternative uses (Klein, Crawford, and Alchian 1978). Specificity can be physical, locational, human (Williamson 1985: 55), and temporal (Masten, Meehan, and Synder 1991: 9; Pirrong 1993). Contracts that require either party to employ assets (usually physical capital assets, but in some circumstances human capital assets) that have little or no value in alternative uses (that is, they are largely "sunk") raise the potential for opportunism. The contracting party that commits assets is vulnerable to hold-up (Shelanski and Klein 1995; Ulset 1996). No matter what prices are agreed to in the contracting stage, the other party may be able to behave opportunistically by reneging and offering lower prices that only cover incremental costs. In effect, the investment in specific assets reduces the contestability of contract renewals. While this question has not been studied systematically in the public sector context, extensive analogous private sector outsourcing evidence suggests that high asset specificity reduces contracting-out (e.g., Hallwood 1990; Lyons 1995; Ang 1998). The public sector evidence does suggest that governments engage in more monitoring when they contract out services that involve higher asset specificity (Brown and Potoski 2003).

If we adopt a social efficiency perspective (as we argued earlier, the correct perspective), then governmental opportunism is as undesirable as external supplier opportunism. Where external suppliers provide and own specific assets (such as, highly specialized buildings), they have to worry about the potential for opportunistic behavior by government agencies. Governments can behave opportunistically once external suppliers have made asset specific investments.

9.4.1.4 Building Capacity to Expand Contracting Options

Managers may be able to increase the range of services for which contracting is feasible by adding to in-house resources. Ironically, adding personnel with expertise relevant to a service may increase the organization's capacity for effectively writing and monitoring contracts for contracting it out. For example, the first step in contracting-out for a sophisticated computer system may be to hire personnel who have experience with candidate systems and vendors. Building organizational capacity to monitor service quality may reduce opportunism in the post-contract phase as well. More generally, the appropriate starting place for effective contracting-out of services may be adding capacity to the administrative core of public agencies.

Managers may also be able to influence their external environments to promote more effective contracting. In situations in which the initial awarding of a contract may confer an advantage to incumbent external suppliers, it may be desirable to multi-source the task among several firms or nonprofit suppliers to enhance the prospects for competition when the contract expires. This strategy involves a conscious decision to bear higher contract administration costs, and perhaps forgo some economy of scale to preserve or foster competition and hence reduce the risk of future opportunism.

9.4.2 Privatization

The presence or absence of market failure is the central issue in evaluating the efficiency consequences of public ownership. During the 20th Century, however, in many countries around the world, the linkage between market failure and the provision of goods via state-owned enterprises (SOEs) was tenuous. In the United States, in contrast, most SOEs, have been, and still are, in sectors for which there is at least some prima facie evidence of market failure or market power (Boardman, Laurin and Vining 2003). Vining and Boardman (1992) provide a summary of the literature that compares the performance of privately-owned firms to SOEs in competitive environments during the era of extensive state ownership (see also Dewenter and Malatesta 2001). Although not universally so, this review tended to show superior private sector technical efficiency.

Extensive privatization, or what might also be called desocialization, has now taken place in a wide range of countries with widely differing institutions and at differing states of economic development, including the United Kingdom, France, Canada, and New Zealand, the former Soviet bloc countries, and countries in Asia and South America. At the urging of the World Bank and International Monetary Fund, many developing countries have also engaged in major privatization programs. Apart from anything else, the large numbers of privatization in a variety of industry, country, and institutional settings permit a sharper (before/after) test of the efficiency consequences of public ownership. The aggregate global evidence on privatization is that there have been major efficiency gains, both in allocative and technical efficiency (e.g., Parker and Martin 1995; D'Souza and Megginson 1999; La Porta and Lopez-de-Silanes 1999; Boardman, Laurin and Vining 2002). Sometimes, these efficiency gains are made in anticipation of privatizations, rather than subsequently to them (Dewenter and Malatesta 2001). For a comprehensive global review of the empirical evidence on the efficiency impacts of privatization, see Megginson and Netter (2001).

In sectors with evidence of natural monopoly or oligopoly, such as electricity, gas, and water distribution, the empirical evidence on privatization suggests improvements in technical efficiency. One recent study concludes that even rail privatization in the UK, probably the most maligned privatization of all, led to significant operating efficiencies, without evidence of lower output quality (Pollitt and Smith 2002). However, realization of efficiency gains in these sectors for consumers and governments (especially longer-run gains) appears to be dependent on effective post-privatization regulatory structures (e.g., Newbery and Pollitt 1997; Saal and Parker 2000; Domah and Pollitt 2001; Wallstein 2001). In practice, this requires regulatory structures that encourage ongoing dynamic efficiency improvements which, in turn requires attempting to achieve a high degree of incentive-compatibility between regulators and regulated firms (Robinson 2001). Although the privatization evidence from the former Soviet bloc countries has been somewhat mixed, considerable evidence is now beginning to emerge concerning the benefits of privatization (e.g., Berkowitz and DeJong 2003; Pivorarsky 2003). The evidence from developing countries is also generally positive in terms of technical efficiency change (Plane 1999; Boubakari and Cossett 1998; Rossi 2001).

9.4.3 Privatization and Regulation

Replacing government with market provision often shifts the functions of public agencies. As the original decision for government provision was likely motivated by perceived market failure or distributional concern, reliance on market provision may call for some sort of public intervention. So, for example, vouchers are often used to subsidize purchases in markets by those who might under-consume some merit good if left to their own resources. Market failure may be inherent in the characteristic of the good or service, or it may result from the path from government to market provision: where a privatized SOE previously enjoyed a legal monopoly, its specific assets may give it the characteristics of a natural monopoly. In such cases, regulation may be required to achieve efficiency.

There is an extensive economic literature on regulation—see Viscusi et al. (1995) for a review. Here we focus on one of the newer forms, price-cap regulation, which has been developed as an alternative to traditional rate-of-return regulation that guaranteed profits to regulated firms. Price-cap regulation was developed largely in the United Kingdom, but it is being adopted more widely. For example, most US states have switched their regulation of local exchange telephone companies from rate-of-return regulation to price-cap regulation. Price-cap regulation involves the regulatory agency setting an allowed price for a specified time period. The allowed price is adjusted annually to take into account inflation but reduced by a percentage to reflect cost reductions that the regulator believes the firm can achieve, based on an assessment of prior inefficiencies or the potential cost savings from new technology. Typically, the regulated firm is allowed to reduce prices if it wishes to do so.

An advantage of such regulation is that it focuses on dynamic efficiency: managers have an incentive to improve productivity over time because they get to keep the surplus if they can reduce costs faster than the capped price declines. However, price-cap regulation requires the regulator to estimate the achievable cost reductions periodically. Hence, it suffers from some of the same problems as rate of return regulation, including the incentive for the regulated firm and interest groups to lobby regulators (van den Berg 1997). There is one important difference, however, between price-cap regulation and rate-of-return regulation: price-cap regulation requires investors in the firm to carry the risk of profit variability (Alexander and Irwin 1996). There is evidence that price-cap regulation has led to significant efficiency improvements for firms with natural monopoly characteristics. For example, one study found efficiency gains at the British Gas Corporation, even though the firm remained a (vertically integrated) monopoly during the period of study (Waddams and Weyman-Jones 1996).

9.5 CONCLUSION

In this essay we present a number of economic frameworks—intra-organizational market failures, agency theory, and transaction cost theory—that may help public managers think about how to run their organizations more efficiently (mostly by focusing on various aspects of incentives) and, when given the opportunity, to design more efficient organizational structures. We do not claim that these frameworks will necessarily help managers much in their day-to-day management tasks. Help in these matters is legitimately the purview of other disciplinary perspectives. These ideas are most useful as a way of thinking, especially about the meaning of social value. Specifically, they should help provide some conceptual underpinning to a number of prescriptions from the NPM. Without clear conceptual foundations, we believe that NPM is in danger of descending into transient faddism. Indeed, the dominant response by mainline public administration scholars has been, at best, skeptical and, at worst, hostile (Thompson and Thompson 2001: 153). Indeed, this should be its fate, unless it can be linked to clear theory and empirical verification.

As should be clear from the numerous references we have cited, there is an active research project underway to determine when contracting-out and privatization actually produce gains in efficiency. As results from this project continue to accumulate, public managers will be better prepared to know how to draw organizational boundaries. They still face the task of aligning their internal organizational structures to fit well with the organizational boundaries. Although some systematic empirical research on the effectiveness of alternative governance structures is beginning to appear (Heinrich and Lynn 2001), it remains relatively rare. For the full gains from inter-organizational choice are to be realized, public administration scholars must reinvigorate their efforts to increase our knowledge relevant to intra-organizational design.

References

ABRAHAMSON, E. (1996), "Management Fashion, Academic Fashion, and Enduring Truths," *Academy of Management Journal* 21(3): 616–19.

AKERLOF, G. (1970), "The Market for Lemons," *Quarterly Journal of Economics* 84 (3): 488–500.

ALEXANDER, I., and IRWIN, T. (1996), "Price Caps, Rate-of-Return Regulation, and the Cost of Capital," *Public Policy for the Private Sector* 87 (Sept.): 25–28.

ANG, S. (1998), "Production and Transaction Economies and IS Outsourcing: A Study of the U.S. Banking Industry," *MIS Quarterly* 22(4): 535–52.

AUCOIN, P. (1995), *The New Public Management: Canada in Comparative Perspective*, Montreal: Institute for Research on Public Policy.

AXELROD, R. (1984), *The Evolution of Cooperation*, New York: Basic Books.

BANKS, J. S. (1995), "The Design of Institutions: An Agency Theory Perspective," in D. Weimer (ed.), *Institutional Design*. Boston: Kluwer Academic Publishing: 17–36.

BAUMOL, W. J., PANZAR, J. C., and WILLIG, R. D. (1982), *Contestable Markets and the Theory of Industry Structure*, New York: Harcourt, Brace, Jovanovich.

BERENYI, E., and STEVENS, B. (1988), "Does Privatization Work? A Study of the Delivery of Eight Local Services," *State & Local Government Review* 20(1): 11–20.

BERKOWITZ, D., and DEJONG, D. N. (2003), "Policy Reform and Growth in Post-Soviet Russia," *European Economic Review* 47(2): 337–52.

BOARDMAN, A.E., LAURIN, C., and VINING, A. R. (2002), "Privatization in Canada: Operating and Stock Price Performance with International Comparisons," *Canadian Journal of Administrative Sciences* 19(2): 137–54.

—— —— —— (2003), "Privatization in North America," in D. Parker and D. Sallal (eds.), *International Handbook on Privatization*, Northampton, MA: Edward Elgar 129–60.

—— and. VINING, A. R (1989), "Ownership and Performance in Competitive Environments: A Comparison of the Performance of Private, Mixed and State-Owned Enterprises," *Journal of Law & Economics* 32(1): 1–33.

BORINS, S. (1995), "The New Public Management is Here to Stay," *Canadian Public Administration* 38(1): 122–32.

BOUBAKARI, N., and COSSETT, J. C. (1998), "The Financial and Operating Performance of Newly Privatized Firms: Evidence from Developing Countries," *Journal of Finance* 53(3): 1081–110.

BRADLEY, S., and TAYLOR, J. (2002), "The Effect of the Quasi-market on the Efficiency–Equity Trade-Off in the Secondary School Sector," *Bulletin of Economic Research* 54(3): 295–314.

BROWN, T., and POTOSKI, M. (2003), "Managing Contract Performance: A Transactions Cost Approach," *Journal of Policy Analysis & Management* 22(2): 275–97.

BRYSON, J. (2002), "Review of 'The Reinventor's Fieldbook: Tools for Transforming Your Government' by D. Osborne and P. Plastrik," *International Public Management Journal* 5(3): 325–8.

CALVERT, R. L. (1995), "The Rational Choice Theory of Institutions: Implications for Design," in D. L. Weimer (ed.), *Institutional Design*, Boston: Kluwer Academic: 63–94.

CHI, K. S., and JASPER, C. (1998), *Private Practices: A Review of Privatization in State Government*, Lexington, KY: Council of State Governments.

CRAWFORD, J., and KRAHN, S. L. (1998), "The Demanding Customer and the Hollow Organization," *Public Productivity & Management Review* 22(1): 107–18.

CROXSON, B., PROPPER, C. and PERKINS, P. (2001), "Do Doctors Respond to Financial Incentives: UK Family Doctors and the GP Fundholder Scheme," *Journal of Public Economics* 79(2): 375–98.

CYERT, R. M. and MARCH, J. G. (1963), *A Behavioral Theory of the Firm*, Englewood Cliffs, NJ: Prentice Hall.

DE ALESSI, L. (1996), "Error and Bias in Benefit-Cost Analysis: HUD's Case for the Wind Rule," *Cato Journal* 16(1): 129–47.

DEWENTER, K., and MALATESTA, P. (2001), "State-owned and Privately-owned Firms: An Empirical Analysis of Profitability, Leverage and Labor Intensity," *American Economic Review* 91(1): 320–35.

DILGER, R. J., MOFFITT, R. R., and STRUYK, L. (1997), "Privatization of Municipal Services in America's Largest Population Cities," *Public Administration Review* 57(1): 21–6.

DOMAH, P., and POLLITT, M. G. (2001), "The Restructuring and Privatisation of Electricity Distribution and Supply Businesses in England and Wales: A Social Cost-Benefit Analysis," *Fiscal Studies* 22(1): 107–46.

DOMBERGER, S., and HALL, C. (1996), "Contracting for Public Services: A Review of the Antipodean Experience," *Public Administration* 74(1): 129–47.

—— —— and LI, A. L. (1995), "The Determinants of Price and Quality in Competitively Determined Contracts," *The Economic Journal* 105(433): 1454–70.

—— JENSEN, P., and STONECASH, R. (2002), "Examining the Magnitude and Source of Cost Savings Associated with Outsourcing," *Public Performance & Management Review* 26(2): 148–69.

DOMBERGER, S., MEADOWCROFT, S. and THOMPSON, D. (1987), "The Impact of Competitive Tendering on the Costs of Hospital Domestic Services," *Fiscal Studies* 8(4): 39–54.

—— and RIMMER, S. (1994), "Competitive Tendering and Contracting in the Public Sector: A Survey," *International Journal of the Economics of Business* 1(3): 439–53.

DRANOVE, D., SHANLEY, M., and WHITE, W. (1993), "Price and Concentration in Hospital Markets: The Switch from Patient-Driven to Payer-Driven Competition," *Journal of Law & Economics* 36(1): 179–200.

D'SOUZA, J., and MEGGINSON, W. (1999), "The Financial and Operating Performance of Privatized Firms During the 1990s," *Journal of Finance* 54(4): 1397–438.

DUNLEAVY, P. (1992), *Democracy, Bureaucracy and Public Choice*, Englewood Cliffs, NJ: Prentice Hall.

ECCLES, R. G. (1985), *The Transfer Pricing Problem: A Theory for Practice*, Lexington, MA: Heath.

EGGERTSSON, T. (1990), *Economic Behavior and Institutions*, New York: Cambridge University Press.

EPSTEIN, D., and O'HALLORAN, S. (1999), *Delegating Powers*, New York, Cambridge University Press.

FUDENBERG, D., and MASKIN, E. (1986), "The Folk Theorem in Repeated Games with Discounting or with Incomplete Information," *Econometrica* 54(3): 533–54.

GAO (General Accounting Office) (1998), *Regulatory Reform: Agencies Could Improve Development, Documentation and Clarity of Regulatory Economic Analyses.* GAO/RCED-98–142 Washington, DC: General Accounting Office (May).

GLOBERMAN, S., and VINING, A. (1996), "A Framework for Evaluating the Government Contracting-out Decision with an Application to Information Technology," *Public Administration Review* 56(6): 577–86.

GLOR, E. D. (2002), "Is Innovation a Question of Will or Opportunity? The Case of Three Governments," *International Public Management Journal* 5(1): 53–74.

GRADY, D. (1992), "Promoting Innovations in the Public Sector," *Public Productivity & Management Review* 16(2): 157–71.

GREENE, J. D. (2002), *Cities and Privatization: Prospects for the New Century*, Upper Saddle River, NJ: Prentice Hall.

GRUENING, G. (2001), "Origin and Theoretical Basis of New Public Management," *International Public Management Journal* 4(1): 1–25.

HALL, P. A. (ed.) (1989), *The Political Power of Economic Ideas*, Princeton: Princeton University Press.

HALLWOOD, P. (1990), *Transaction Costs and Trade between Multinational Corporations*, Boston, MA: Unwin Hyman.

HART, O., and HOLMSTROM, B. (1986), "The Theory of Contracts," in T. Bewley (ed.), *Advances in Economic Theory*, New York: Cambridge University Press: 77–155.

HEINRICH, C. J., and LYNN, L. E., JR. (2001), "Means and Ends: A Comparative Study of Empirical Methods for Investigating Governance and Performance," *Journal of Public Administration Research & Theory* 11(1): 109–38.

HENRY, N. (2002), "Is Privatization Passe? The Case for Competition and the Emergence of Intersectoral Administration," *Public Administration Review* 62(3): 374–8.

HESTERLY, W. S., LIEBESKIND, J., and ZENGER, T. R. (1990), "Organizational Economics: An Impending Revolution in Organization Theory?" *Academy of Management Review* 15(3): 402–20.

HODGE, G. A. (2000), *Privatization: An International Review of Performance.* Boulder, CO: Westview Press.

HOLCOMBE, R. G., (1991), "Privatization of Municipal Wastewater Treatment," *Public Budgeting & Finance* 11(3): 28–42.

HOLMSTROM, B. (1982), "Moral Hazard in Teams," *Bell Journal of Economics* 13(2): 324–40.

HOOD, C. (1991), "A Public Management for All Seasons?" *Public Administration* 69(1): 3–19.

HUBER, J. D., and SHIPAN, C. R. (2002), *Deliberate Discretion?* New York: Cambridge University Press.

JENSEN, M. C., and MECKLING, W. H. (1976), "Theory of the Firm: Managerial Behavior, Agency Costs, and Ownership Structure," *Journal of Financial Economics* 3(4): 323–9.

JOHNSON, R., and LIBECAP, G. (1989), "Bureaucratic Rules, Supervisor Behavior, and the Effect on Salaries in the Federal Government," *Journal of Law, Economics, & Organization* 5(1): 53–82.

KANE, T. J., and STAIGER, D. O. (2002), "The Promise and Pitfalls of Using Imprecise School Accountability Measures", *Journal of Economic Perspectives* 16(4): 91–114.

KELMAN, S. (1990), "Why Public Ideas Matter," in R. B. Reich (ed.), *The Power of Public Ideas*, Cambridge, Mass.: Harvard University Press: 31–53.

KLEIN, B., CRAWFORD, R., and ALCHIAN, A. (1978), "Vertical Integration, Appropriable Rents and the Competitive Contracting Process," *Journal of Law & Economics* 21(2): 297–326.

KNOEBER, C. R., and THURMAN, W. N. (1994), ATesting the Theory of Tournaments: An Empirical Analysis of Broiler Production," *Journal of Labor Economics* 12(2): 155–79.

KODRZYCKI, Y. K. (1994), "A Privatization of Local Public Services: Lessons for New England," *New England Economic Review* May/June: 31–46.

KREPS, D. (1990), "Corporate Culture and Economic Theory," in J. E. Alt and K. A. Shepsle (eds.), *Perspectives on Positive Political Economy*. New York: Cambridge University Press, 90–143.

LANE, J. E. (2000), *New Public Management*, London: Routledge.

LA PORTA, R., and LOPEZ-DE-SILANES, F. (1999), "The Benefits of Privatization: Evidence from Mexico," *Quarterly Journal of Economics* 114(4): 1193–242.

LEIBENSTEIN, H. J. (1976), *Beyond Economic Man*, Cambridge, MA: Harvard University Press.

LOPEZ-DE-SILANES, F., SHLEIFER, F. A., and VISHNEY, R. W. (1997), "Privatization in the United States," *Rand Journal of Economics* 28(3): 447–71.

LYNN, L. (1994), "Public Management Research: The Triumph of Art over Science," *Journal of Policy Analysis & Management* 13(2): 231–59.

LYONS, B. (1995), "Specific Investment, Economies of Scale, and the Make-or-Buy Decision: A Test of Transaction Cost Theory," *Journal of Economic Behavior & Organization* 26(3): 431–43.

MCAFEE, R. P., and MCMILLAN, J. (1988), *Incentives in Government Contracting*, Toronto, Ont: University of Toronto Press.

MCDAVID, J. C., and CLEMENS, E. G. (1995), "Contracting Out Local Government Services: The BC Experience," *Canadian Public Administration* 38(2): 177–93.

MCFETRIDGE, D. G., and D. A. SMITH (1998), *The Economics of Vertical Disintegration*. Vancouver, BC: The Fraser Institute.

MASTEN, S. E., MEEHAM, J. W., JUN., and SNYDER, E. A. (1991) "The Costs of Organization," *Journal of Law, Economics & Organization* 7(1): 1–25.

MEGGINSON, W., and NETTER, J. (2001), "From State to Market: A Survey of Empirical Studies on Privatization," *Journal of Economic Literature* 39(2): 321–89.

MELNIK, G. A., ZWANZIGER, J., BAMEZAI, A., and PATTISON, R. (1992), "The Effect of Market Structure and Bargaining Position on Hospital Prices," *Journal of Health Economics* 11(3): 217–233.

MILLER, G. J. (1992), *Managerial Dilemmas*, New York: Cambridge University Press.

MILNE, R., and McGEE, M. (1992), "Compulsory Competitive Tendering in the NHS: A New Look at Some Old Estimates," *Fiscal Studies* 13(3): 96–111.

MOORE, M. H. (1995), *Creating Public Value: Strategic Management in Government*, Cambridge, MA: Harvard University Press.

MORLEY, E. (1999), "Local Government Use of Alternative Service Delivery Approaches," in *The Municipal Year Book 1999*, Washington, DC: International City/County Management Association, 34–44.

MORLOCK, E. K. (1987), "Privatizing Bus Transit: Cost Savings from Competitive Contracting," *Journal of the Transportation Research Forum* 28: 72–81.

NEWBERY, D., and POLLITT, M. (1997), "The Restructuring and Privatization of Britain's CEGBC Was It Worth It?" *Journal of Industrial Economics* 45(3): 269–303.

NISKANEN, W. A. (1971), *Bureaucracy and Representative Government*, Chicago: Aldine-Atherton.

OSBORNE, D., and GAEBLER, T. (1993), *Reinventing Government: How the Entrepreneurial Spirit is Transforming Government*, New York: Plume.

OHLSSON, H. (1996), "Ownership and Input Prices: A Comparison of Public and Private Enterprises," *Economics Letters* 53(1): 33–8.

PACK, J. R. (1989), "Privatization and Cost Reduction," *Policy Sciences* 22(1): 1–25.

PARKER, D., and MARTIN, S. (1995), "The Impact of UK Privatisation on Labour and Total Factor Productivity," *Scottish Journal of Political Economy* 42(2): 201–20.

PIRRONG, S. C. (1993), "Contracting Practices in Bulk Shipping Markets: A Transactions Cost Explanation," *Journal of Law & Economics* 36(1): 913–37.

PIVORARSKY, A. (2003), "Ownership Concentration and Performance in Ukraine's Privatized Enterprises," *IMF Staff Papers* 50(1): 10–42.

PLANE, P. (1999), "Privatization, Technical Efficiency and Welfare Consequences: The Case of the Cote d'Ivoire Electricity Company (CIE)," *World Development* 27(2): 343–60.

POLLITT, M. G., and SMITH, A. S. J. (2002), "The Restructuring and Privatisation of British Rail: Was It Really That Bad?" *Fiscal Studies* 23(4): 463–502.

PRAGER, J. (1994), "Contracting-out Government Services: Lessons from the Private Sector," *Public Administration Review* 54(2): 176–84.

PROPPER, C., and WILSON, D. (2003), "The Use and Usefulness of Performance Measures in the Public Sector," *Oxford Review of Economic Policy* 19(2): 250–67.

—— —— and SODERLUND, N. (1998), "The Effects of Regulation and Competition in the NHS Internal Market: the Case of General Practice Fundholder Prices," *Journal of Health Economics* 17(6): 645–73.

ROBINSON, C. (ed.) (2001), *Regulating Utilities: New Issues, New Solutions*, Cheltenham, UK and Northampton, MA: Edward Elgar.

RODRIK, D. (1993), "The Positive Economics of Policy Reform," *American Economic Review Papers and Proceedings* 83(2): 356–61.

ROSS, S. A. (1973), "The Economic Theory of Agency: The Principal's Problem," *American Economic Review* 63(2): 134–9.

ROSSI, M. (2001), Technical Change and Efficiency Measures: The Post-Privatization in the Gas Distribution Sector in Argentina," *Energy Economics* 23(3): 295–304.

SAAL, D., and PARKER, D. (2000), "The Impact of Privatization and Regulation on the Water and Sewage Industry in England and Wales: A Translog Cost Function Model," *Managerial & Decision Economics* 21(6): 253–68.

SAPPINGTON, D. E. M. (1991), "Incentives in Principal-Agent Relationships," *Journal of Economic Perspectives* 5(2): 45–66.

SCHELLING, T. C. (1960), *Strategy of Conflict*, Cambridge, MA: Harvard University Press.

SCHOTTER, A. (1981), *The Economic Theory of Social Institutions*, New York: Cambridge University Press.

SCLAR, E. (1997), *The Privatization of Public Services: Lessons from Case Studies*, Washington, DC: Economic Policy Institute.

SCOTT, G. (2001), *Public Sector Management in New Zealand: Lessons and Challenges*, Wellington: Australian National University.

SHELANSKI, H., and KLEIN, P. (1995), "Empirical Research in Transaction Cost Economics: A Review and Assessment," *The Journal of Law, Economics & Organization* 11(2): 335–61.

SHILS, E. A., and JANOWITZ, M. (1948), "Cohesion and Disintegration in the Wehrmacht in World War II," *Public Opinion Quarterly* 12(2): 280–315.

STEEL, B. S., and LONG, C. (1998), "The Use of Agency Forces Versus Contracting-out: Learning the Limits of Privatization," *Public Administration Quarterly* 22(2): 229–51.

SZYMANSKI, S., and WILKINS, S. (1993), "Cheap Rubbish? Competitive Tendering and Contracting-out in the Refuse Collection: 1981–1988," *Fiscal Studies* 14(3): 109–30.

TAYLOR, M. (1976), *Anarchy and Cooperation*, New York: Wiley.

THOMPSON, F., and JONES, L. R. (1986), "Controllership in the Public Sector," *Journal of Policy Analysis & Management* 5(3): 547–71.

THOMPSON, J. R., and THOMPSON, F. (2001), "The Management Reform Agenda 2001–2010: A Report to the PriceWaterhouseCoopers Endowment for the Business of Government," *International Public Management Journal* 4(2): 151–72.

TUCKMAN, H. (1998), "Competition, Commercialization, and the Evolution of Nonprofit Organizational Structures," *Journal of Policy Analysis and Management* 17(2): 175–94.

ULSET, S. (1996), "R & D Outsourcing and Contractual Governance: An Empirical Study of Commercial R & D Projects," *Journal of Economic Behavior & Organization* 30(1): 63–82.

VAN DEN BERG, C. (1997), "Water Privatization and Regulation in England and Wales," *Public Policy for the Private Sector* 11 May: 9–12.

VINING, A. R., and BOARDMAN, A. E. (1992), "Ownership Versus Competition: Efficiency in Public Enterprise," *Public Choice* 32(2): 205–39.

—— and GLOBERMAN, S. (1998), "Contracting-out Health Care Services: A Conceptual Framework," *Health Policy* 46(2): 77–96.

—— and WEIMER, D. L. (1988), "Information Asymmetry Favoring Sellers: A Policy Framework," *Policy Sciences* 21(4): 281–303.

—— —— (1990), "Government Supply and Government Production Failure: A Framework Based on Contestability," *Journal of Public Policy* 10(1): 1–22.

—— —— (1999), "Inefficiency in Public Organizations," *International Public Management Journal* 2(1): 1–24.

—— —— (2001), "Criteria for Infrastructure Investment: Normative, Positive, and Prudential Perspectives," in A. R. Vining and J. Richards (eds.), *Building the Future: Issues in Public Infrastructure in Canada*. Toronto, Ont: C. D. Howe Institute, 131–65.

VISCUSI, W. K., VERNON, J. M., and HARRINGTON, J. E. (1995), *Economics of Regulation and Antitrust*, 2nd edn., Cambridge, MA: MIT Press.

WADDAMS PRICE, C., and WEYMAN-JONES, T. (1996), "Malquist Indices of Productivity Change in the UK Gas Industry before and after Privatization," *Applied Economics* 28(1): 29–39.

WALLSTEIN, S. (2001), "An Econometric Analysis of Telecom Competition, Privatization, and Regulation in Africa and Latin America," *Journal of Industrial Economics* 49(1): 1–19.

WALSH, J. I. (2000), "When Do Ideas Matter? Explaining the Successes and Failures of Thatcherite Ideas," *Comparative Political Studies* 33(4): 483–516.

WALSH, K. (1991), *Competitive Tendering for Local Authority Services: Initial Experiences*, London: HMSO.

WEIMER, D. L., and VINING, A. R. (1996), "Economics," in D. F. Kettl and B. Millward (eds.), *The State of Public Government*. Baltimore: John Hopkins University Press, 92–117.

WHELAN, R. K. (1999), "Public Administration—the State of the Discipline: A View from the Urban and Local Government Literature," *Public Administration Quarterly* 23(1): 46–65.

WILDAVSKY, A. (1966), "The Political Economy of Efficiency: Cost-Benefit Analysis, Systems Analysis, and Program Budgeting," *Public Administration Review* 26(4): 292–310.

WILLIAMS, R. L. (1998), "Economic Theory and Contracting-out for Residential Waste Collection," *Public Productivity & Management Review* 21(3): 259–71.

WILLIAMSON, O. E. (1985), *The Economic Institution of Capitalism*, New York: The Free Press.

CHAPTER 10

POSTMODERN PUBLIC ADMINISTRATION

PETER BOGASON

10.1 INTRODUCTION

THIS chapter discusses[1] what the conditions of postmodernity are about, distinguishing between conditions in society (is there a postmodern epoch?) and in social research (how does one carry out postmodern research?). The subsequent focus is on how research in Public Administration has been influenced by postmodern ideas.

The chapter's approach is inspired by an understanding that the organization of science matters (Bogason 2001; Fischer 1998: 132–3). Only a brief overview of some aspects of postmodern analysis in Public Administration is delivered. White (1999) and Miller (2002b) have given us a state of the art discussion in Public Administration and Policy Analysis, respectively. Broader and fuller accounts of the social sciences and postmodernism may be found in Rosenau (1992) and Hollinger (1994).

It is not easy to define a sharp borderline of the analysis of Public Administration. The field itself is cross-disciplinary, and many policy analyses concern the role of Public Administration. Therefore, some segments of Policy Analysis are included, mirroring the fact that some scholars are involved both in Public Administration research and Policy Analysis. It makes little sense to keep their work in separate boxes.

The problems of delimitation are reinforced by organizational differences between American and European Public Administration at the universities. The organization of European Public Administration is much closer to public policy than at many American universities. Scholars in Public Administration and Public Policy are often organized within the same department (the names vary), and teaching then takes place so that the fields are merged within the same university degree. Consequently, there is no easily identifiable and organized European group of scholars in the field of postmodern Public Administration.

In the USA, there is a distinct group of scholars within Public Administration working on postmodern terms, i.e., they have a discourse which other scholars can identify and relate to (Bogason 2001). Most of them are associated with the Public Administration Theory Network, *PAT-Net*, which was founded in 1978 (Harmon 2003), and has had annual conferences since 1988. Since the mid-1990s, the international membership has increased, particularly with scholars from Australia and Europe joining. Its journal, the *Journal of Administrative Theory and Praxis* (formerly *Dialogue*), is a quarterly which published its 25th volume in 2003.

10.2 Modernity and Postmodern Conditions

The discourse of modernity and postmodern conditions takes place at several academic levels. Two are presented below: One regarding changes within society, the other discussing changes in the scientific communities. Both discussions primarily relate to conditions in the advanced western democracies, there are few, if any, dealing with third world countries in this respect.

10.2.1 The Fragmentation of Society

Social scientists have for more than 150 years been preoccupied with modernity and the characteristics of modern society—the original masters were Marx, Durkheim, and Weber. Recent participants are too numerous to list, but see Beck, Giddens, and Lash (1994) for a taste of the recent menu of the day. Verbatim, *postmodern* indicates that the modern is gone, and that something new, postmodern, has taken over. That is hardly the case. Rather, we have a situation where many facets of life are thoroughly modern, but some trends indicate that things could be different, and if trends are indicative of future conditions, then society will in the longer run take qualitatively new forms. As things are, modern and postmodern conditions coexist and create tensions with one another.

I shall illustrate what is at stake by pairing examples illustrating the two forms (Bogason 2000: 13–28). *Modernity* may be characterized by rationalization, centralization, specialization, bureaucratization, and industrialization. At the core are advanced uses of scientific knowledge to further economic and social development, controlled and monitored by centers of knowledge and power. Coherence and integration dominate the vision, and the industrial corporation and the bureaucratic welfare state are organizational hallmarks of modernity.

Postmodern conditions are characterized by fragmentation: An overarching rationale or vision is replaced by processes of reasoning, and we see trends towards decentralization, individualization and internationalization. Culture loses its national focus, people organize across organizational and even national boundaries, many feel that they are on the brink of chaos. The worldwide matrix organization, outsourcing, and the user-run public organization are characteristic organizational features of postmodern conditions. The differences are illustrated by examples in Table 10.1.

Table 10.1 Modern and postmodern conditions

Modern rationalization	Postmodern reasoning
Global visions	Particular interests
Production	Consumption
Mass Production	Flexible Specialization
Integration	Differentiation
Interest Organizations	Social Movements
Party Politics	Personality Politics
Bureaucracy	Adhocracy
National Culture	MTV images
Planning	Spontaneity
Reason	Imagination
Wholes	Fragments

Source: Adapted from Bogason (2000: 24)

On the left side is order, on the right chaos—if perceived from the left side. If the left side is viewed from the right side, it is a version of Weber's iron cage. Senior readers of this article probably look at postmodern conditions with modernistic glasses (left side), which were given to us by upbringing and education. Junior readers may view things from the right side. It is, perhaps, ironic that Marx's characterization of modernity—"all that is solid melts into air"—in this interpretation rather characterizes postmodern conditions. Modernity is cohesion, postmodern conditions are disintegrative. But of course, modernity viewed from a traditional society was chaotic: people were uprooted from rural and village life, big city life took over. So this sort of evaluation depends on the viewer's perspective.

Seen from a Public Administration research angle, trends towards postmodern conditions are highly interesting and challenging. Since they are more or less the negation of Weber's bureaucracy, modernistic views of how to organize public agencies are disputed, and consequently, if postmodern thoughts are to be influential, textbooks should be rewritten.

Up to time of writing, this has not happened, and comprehensive postmodern discussions of Public Administration are scarce. A few basic books have appeared (Fox and Miller 1995; White 1999; Miller 2002b), but most textbooks have a few paragraphs (or even a chapter) commenting on postmodernism and leave it there (Frederickson and Smith 2003). Since they are close to Public Administration by theme, it is interesting to note that organization theorists (working primarily with private organizations) have for a long time worked with postmodern trends (Clegg 1990; Gephart, Thatchenkery, and Boje 1996; Hatch 1997). Public administration is less receptive; Rod Rhodes' discussion in the last chapter in his *Understanding Governance* (Rhodes 1997) is probably on the kinder side: Postmodernism cannot be ignored, but much of its critique is not really new, and a little too harsh. Rhodes himself, however, has since tried out a sort of narrative analysis in an article (Bevir and Rhodes 1998), a test which he announced in his book.

10.2.2 The Construction of Science

Changes within the scientific field of Public Administration cannot be understood in isolation from changes within the social sciences as a whole. At the core is a postmodern attack on the basic idea of the Enlightenment, namely that improved knowledge is the means to develop the world—for a better world for the human race. The development of modernity undoubtedly is based on overwhelming uses of science and technology for increased industrial production, improved infrastructure and faster transport, paired with comprehensive representative democracy and massive bureaucratic governments. This development is frowned upon by many postmodernists because of its dark sides. Instead of liberation for mankind, they focus on oppression, repression, and depletion. For instance, where modernists praise the freedom created by increased wealth from industrial production, postmodernists see people disciplined by a powerful workplace, and resources such as rain forests jeopardized.

One consequence of this postmodern view of the world is that science is denied any privileged position as foundation of knowledge (Dickens and Fontana 1994: 8). Since the basic tenet of modernistic science is that it creates the truth about the state of the world, postmodernists remove truth from their conceptual baggage. Modernistic positivism, empiricism, and deductive logic are replaced by postmodern hermeneutic analysis, contextuality, and inductive reasoning (King 1998: 163–4). As a corollary, modern attempts at generalization, synthesis, and determination (prediction) are replaced by postmodern exceptions, diversity (*différance*), and indeterminacy. In politics and administration many postmodernists analyze the marginalized, the oppressed, and peripheral where modernists to a larger degree seek the governors, the powerful, and liberated (Farmer 1997: 13). Metaphorically speaking, the modernist professor goes to Washington, DC to advise the President, while the postmodern professor helps out in the local shelter for the homeless.

As scientists, postmodernists do not work with reality; or rather, they see no adequate scientific means for representing *one* reality. Most of them see *social constructivism* as carrying their research. This concerns the physical world—how are we to represent a bicycle beyond being an invention of metal and rubber? That would depend on the perspective of the viewer, and even in laboratories, it is difficult for the scientist to avoid personal elements in the interpretation of data from, e.g., microscopes (Latour 1987). But in the social sciences, the physical world is mostly only an environmental factor. Social scientists are more interested in asking about how we construct a representation of the social world. Are Iron Triangles (Heclo 1972), Policy Communities (Rhodes and Marsh 1992), and Network Societies (Hajer and Wagenaar 2003) real? Social constructivists would answer that the concepts indicate a particular perspective on social phenomena which we can illustrate by statistics, interviews, narratives or other research techniques, but it is difficult to round up the usual suspects for a photo line-up if we want to present a policy community to the rest of the world.

Even the most ardent positivist will not claim that a voter turnout of 85 percent is but one way of illustrating consequences of a democratic procedure—it *is* not democracy. But postmodern scholars go further than such a trivial observation. First, they contextualize all observations, claiming (following Kuhn (1962) to the extreme) that knowledge is only valid among followers of the scientific paradigm that supported the specific way the data were constructed. Second, language is a medium to transfer observations to the rest of the world, but the truth value remains with that language, it is not possible to establish a one-to-one relationship between expressions about phenomena and their existence outside the linguistic convention. Discourse analysts carry this further than any other analysts. This general approach has several followers—with some variations among them, they pursue analysis as a version of structuration theory (Giddens 1984), using the concept of *poststructuralist analysis* (Wamsley and Wolf 1996; Gottweis 2003) to position their language (or discourse) analytical approach which acknowledges structure, but does not reduce the actors to outcomes of structure. Subjects, on the other hand, do not exist outside relations of various kinds, so the analysts prefers to speak of subject positions which are contingent and strategic locations within a specific discursive domain (Gottweis 2003: 253).

Discourse analysis, however, is a broad label (Torfing 1999; McSwite 2000), and Europeans and Americans tend to use it in different ways. Most Americans lean towards a Habermasian version of discourse as a sphere for communication (Miller 2000), while Europeans largely take their departure from a linguistic conceptual basis (Kensen 2000). Nevertheless, there are, of course, exceptions on both sides of the Atlantic; Fischer (2003) gives an overview of the development of discourse and deliberative analysis, based on post-empiricist Policy Analysis.

10.3 POSTMODERNISM AND PUBLIC ADMINISTRATION

A number of books from the mid-1990s illustrate various postmodern critiques of the state apparatus and Public Administration as a scientific activity. We shall use them to illustrate in some detail how the critiques are voiced.

Postmodern writing on Public Administration started out in the USA in the late 1980s, by members of *PAT-Net*—whose members are not all postmodernists, though (VrMeer 1994; Zanetti 1996). The *PAT-Net* group originally consisted mainly of critical theorists, but Gareth Morgan's *Images of Organization* (1986) triggered a new series of discussions regarding the representation of research results in the group. Linda Dennard (1989) reflected on the shift in approaches in an amusing piece, entitled "The Three Bears and Goldilocks meet Burrell and Morgan," where a postmodern perspective (called the *Radical Humanist Paradigm*) was put on the adventurous Goldilocks, who "was wandering in a dark and solemn woods on a journey of self-discovery. Tired and despairing from the vacuous ethos of technicist society, she lay down to rest . . ." (Dennard 1989: 385). This perspective is contrasted with three others from modernity, of which one is the functionalist paradigm, according to which "at 0600 hours, Goldilocks strayed from her Triple A Travel Agenda and got lost in the woods. She set her digital compass for North" (Dennard 1989: 384).

As those quotes illustrate, the discussions in the *Pat-Net* group concerned attempts to downgrade the traditional aspiration for conceptual precision followed by exact (preferably quantitative) measures to demonstrate accurately the extent and variation of the object of the research. Two years later, the tangible result was an anthology, *Images and Identities of Public Administration* (Kass and Catron 1990). The images or metaphors used dealt with the roles available to public administrators in the political system if they wanted to gain more legitimacy. Examples included the "phronemos" (practical reasoner) (Morgan 1990), a member of the "democratic elite" (Fox and Cochran 1990), the "steward" (Kass 1990) and the "responsible actor" (Harmon 1990). Other contributors discussed the challenges to Public Administration (PA) as a field: It should be understood in terms of icons like the "pyramid" (old PA) and the "circle" (new PA) (Hummel 1990), or how to include the wisdom of the public administrators into the processes—a task far beyond technical rationality and requiring interpretive and critical skills (Kass 1990: 15–16). The authors, then, wanted the reader to relate to the subject of discussion, contemplate, and let the imagination wander on the basis of the impulses from the metaphors used in the text.

In various ways, these themes have been found in subsequent publications on postmodern Public Administration. Much of the theoretical inspiration comes from European scholars. Foucault, Derrida, and Laclau have had strong influence on much postmodern writing, regardless of scientific field. Foucault's main significance may lie in his conception of power as something permeating all spheres of life (Foucault 1980), and thus it is not a phenomenon to be on the lookout for and—if possible—to curb, as modernists would do, but an energy which must be recognized and used variously in different situations. Power constitutes strategic possibilities of variance, thus it puts actors in relationships, developing through discourse which put the relations into terms of speech. The focus of the analysis, then, is on networks of negotiation between actors and fields. The essence of power becomes control of communication in networks (Andersen, Born, and Majgaard 1995: 90). Foucault is also important in launching the concept of *governmentality* (Cawley and Chaloupka 1997; Howe 2001) as his version of what later was labeled *governance* by other scientific camps. When we turn to language, Derrida helps us understand signifiers in ambiguous structures always in play, vibrating and under change, so that we cannot participate in a search for a general truth, we must participate in a game of interpretation concerning how knowledge is constituted, oriented towards ambiguity and the unsettled (Pedersen 1996; Farmer 1997). Laclau (1993) follows this line of reasoning, and he is frequently used as an anchor for analysis which is not aimed at listing facts, but at their conditional possibilities. Language is a structure, and the meaning of a word is not its physical referent, but its meaning in our heads; language is form, not substance. As a consequence, relational and meaningful totalities are to be analyzed as discourses, they combine linguistic and extra-linguistic elements into a totality. They are dynamic regarding their identity, depending on the contexts they are linked to through language or social actions (Hansen 1996: 100).

A persistent postmodern theme is a critique of the modern, rationalistic model of the actor and the public organization, in accordance with other postmodern attacks on the Enlightenment. This is found in *The Language of Public Administration* (Farmer 1995), which is a complex deconstruction of Public Administration theory and a modernistic construct. Using four analytical elements, it offers an alternative understanding. *Imaginization* (as we learned from Morgan (1986) above), is for postmodern analysis what rationalization is for modern analysis. It means that one thinks of possibilities within a wide range (where modernity would tend to reduce possibilities to the "doable"); imaginization is placed between perception and the intellect, and is used to transform impressions into thought. Thereby, particulars are becoming important, instead of the generalizing trends by modern subsumption of any activity under a rule. *Deconstruction*, the second element, is a pervasive way of approaching an understanding of phenomena; it is not restricted to being an analytical method or a critique. It is a way of appreciating texts under particular circumstances with the aim of dismantling received views of what that text stands for. The third element, *deterritorialization*, means that modern understandings of representation are negated; postmodernity means the end of the logocentric metaphysics of presence. This is where the social constructivist understanding of research activities becomes important; the realization that not much may be understood by itself, but only as part of a human interaction about understandings of the phenomenon. Finally, *alterity* means a moral stance that counterweighs the standard bureaucratic-efficiency understanding of Public Administration, an anti-administration stance in Farmer's terms (later analyzed in Farmer 1998a), reducing authority and helping service-orientation, and further developed in Farmer (2001). The message, then, is that there is not only one way of understanding, and diversity must be furthered; thus there would be no category of "woman," but a white, Jewish, middle class, a lesbian, a socialist, a mother; all calling for a particularized understanding of their circumstances.

In several later articles (Farmer 1997, 1998), David Farmer has demonstrated how one can deconstruct bureaucratic efficiency: First, it is a social construct, dependent on how people construe it. It follows that efficiency is culture specific, and modernist–secularist, Weberian, linked to the advancement of production. Since it is not a term that is found in all cultures, it is not an objective fact, but something desired under particular circumstances, as in the discussions led by the OECD, the Reinventing Government campaign led by Al Gore, etc. Third, the binarity between efficiency and inefficiency is ambiguous, e.g., it does not guarantee a just outcome. Finally, the concept of efficiency is only privileged in a society that emphasizes control; this means that for postmodernists, it is not important; for modernists, it is. The role of deconstruction, then, is to question what lies under seemingly well-established categories of the bureaucratic phenomenon.

The consequences of rationalist thinking about realizing responsible government is discussed in *Responsibility as a Paradox* (Harmon 1995), criticizing rationalists for seeing responsible action as synonymous with legally correct action. Harmon elaborates three paradoxes which arise out of rationalist responsibility (Harmon 1995: 8–10). Rationalism splits the meaning of obligation and freedom and creates the paradox of *obligation* which attenuates individuals, who are bound to obey superiors within the rules of the contract agreed with them, from being essentially free. The paradox of *agency* comes on the one hand, from an over-assertion (by conservatives) of the role of the individual in terms of guilt, and hence a neglect of the role of collectivities in the relations that must come up when some one is held accountable. On the other hand, to hold collectivities solely responsible for the conduct of individuals (a liberal reaction) creates nothing but victimization. Rationalism finally creates the third paradox of *accountability* by splitting personal responsibility and political authority into two spheres, hence making them incompatible.

Harmon introduces the skeleton of a social constructivist approach to the problems he confronts. To illustrate his points, he uses a character from a well-known British series of novels, Horatio Hornblower (a navy officer, the King's dutiful servant), as the leading character of Public Administration. He thus introduces a scientific discussion based on a simulacrum. He links the resolution of paradoxes to *practical action*, claiming that practical action in the face of paradox is "to reject any strict distinction between the factual and the moral. Factual understandings of social life always presuppose categories of moral appraisal, while moral judgment is inevitably limited, but also enabled, by factual assessment of their meaning and their likely success or failure" (Harmon 1995: 205). Philosophically, this line of reasoning is pragmatic in character, and there are some signs of relativism or at least denunciations of universal, abstract principles. Still, his understanding of a common good and his quest for solidarity and community makes the text "less postmodern" than Farmer's, in spite of its clever uses of a simulacrum.

In *Postmodern Public Administration* (Fox and Miller 1995), the focus is changed from mainly logic within the bureaucratic system to broader, democratic consequences for the citizenry. It is based on Habermasian discourse theory, stressing the need for analysis based on interactive networks. The authors present a model for authentic discourse than leads to their understanding of the active citizen as a worthy agent in public affairs. The basic premise of the analysis is a dissatisfaction with the basic model of Western democracy, the "loop model," in essence an input–output–feedback understanding of democratic decision making, with dividing lines between politics and administration, and the idea of the neutral public employee having the voter as a client. Fox and Miller's alternative is an authentic and sincere discourse.

Fox and Miller find trends towards postmodern conditions in society, where the self-conscious enlightened individual is transformed into a decentered self, so

"When community is reduced to a series of otherwise atomized individuals brought together usually by the coincidence of their consumptive activity, the community does not develop political skills...meetinggoers are not participants" (Fox and Miller 1995, 69). "Meetinggoers" are quiet observers that do not get involved. With Habermas the authors call for inter-associational democracy in the form it seems to be developing in "extrabureaucratic policy networks and other formations" (Fox and Miller 1995: 75). Participation in authentic discourse would require "warrants for discourse," meaning that one has to involve oneself with sincerity (creating trust), and intentionality in the situation (creating orientation towards solving a problem at hand). Furthermore, one must be attentive (creating engagement, but also the ability to listen), and give a substantive contribution (creating a sense that the process is going forward) (Fox and Miller 1995: 120–7). These are normative demands, expressing the authors' hope that there is, even under postmodern conditions, a possibility to sustain a democratic system of governance, requiring increased levels of direct citizen participation in public affairs. In other words, there is a strong criticism of some of the consequences of postmodern conditions, and the use of Habermas gives the analysis a modernistic twist—although the authors *are* critical of Habermas" image of achievable harmony (Fox and Miller 1995: 118).

Legitimacy in Public Administration (McSwite 1997) also calls attention to the postmodern decentering of the subject, in contrast to modern discussions which focus attention on a simplified human nature, e.g., the economic maximizing agent, or an altruistic person in the community. The concern of the book is how administrators may have a legitimate role in democratic affairs, a "facilitative" Public Administration, striving towards involving citizens through efforts towards collaboration. Discourse-oriented relationships, i.e., a mutual surrender to one another, is offered as an alternative understanding to the egoistic (rational choice) model; it is argued that the problem of legitimacy will evaporate once such a reframing of discourse and institutions is accomplished (McSwite 1997: 15). The advice is to let go of the "pointless" discussion of legitimacy because it has institutionalized and maintained a particular understanding and structure of government. Instead, one needs to go back to the true foundation of American Public Administration: Pragmatism. Fact/value, foundationalist/relativist and phenomenology/positivism dichotomies are all bypassed by the continuing testing of hypotheses by the pragmatist, who denies the prerequisites of rational action by picturing social relationships as collaborative, grounded in a joint project and joint action. The results, then, set the operational definition of truth (McSwite 1997: 135). Purpose is created in relationships with other people, in community, not by abstract principles. The relationship is reached by pragmatic collaboration between administrators and citizens, all such processes are contingent on the situation (McSwite 1997: 272).

The most comprehensive European analysis of postmodern conditions and Public Administration is found in *Politics, Governance and Technology: A Postmodern Narrative on the Virtual State* (Frissen 1999). Noticing the general trends towards organizational fragmentation in society, the book applies the concept to Public Administration in the Netherlands in the information age. Thus, the traditional grand narrative of the state as a hierarchically ordered and democratically legitimized system is being undermined—metaphorically speaking from pyramid to archipelago, from hierarchical to circular processes, from central steering to self-governance. ICT has ambiguous consequences, on the one hand it increases the span of control for the center, but on the other hand local organizations gain a stronger power base in terms of information and enhanced communication possibilities with other actors. In Foucauldian terms: Power gets dispersed, multi-faceted and multi-directional. Therefore, one sees many trends at the same time: A stronger hierarchy in information exchange terms, but more autonomy to local organizations. Territory means less in virtual reality, and the subject—including the politician—tends to become de-centered and hence feel somewhat out of control. These trends are put into a wider perspective of postmodern developments in society: politics, economy and culture.

Public Policy and Local Governance (Bogason 2000) offers a framework for analysis of policy-making under postmodern, fragmented conditions. It applies an extension of institutional analysis, stressing that in the search for solutions to policy problems, various roles and institutional settings are combined within policy networks in a search for meaning—and this happens regardless of the formal organizational setting. The role of the formal organization, then, is to be hypothesized, not taken for granted. The analytical approach therefore favors a bottom–up research design, much in line with fourth-generation Policy Analysis (Guba and Lincoln 1989), permitting the analyst to construct an implementation structure (Hjern and Porter 1983) based on interaction among various actors—not neglecting, though, the possibilities for hidden faces of power (Bachrach and Baratz 1962). The rationale behind the analysis is social constructivist, but the author's call for practiceable analysis forces him to compromise between more traditional (modern) and advanced constructivist analytical tools.

The most advanced—and criticized—operational research tool in European postmodern research is narrative and discourse analysis in various versions. *The Politics of Environmental Discourse* (Hajer 1995) is a case in point. Policy analysis in this version is not about whether there is (in this case) an environmental crisis, the policy questions all are about interpretation of its interpretation. On the one hand, Foucault is used as inspiration to analyze specific practices, and on the other hand an argumentative approach is applied (Fischer and Forester 1993), based on "human agency of clever, creative human beings but in a context of social structures that both enable and constrain their agency" (Hajer 1995: 58), creating discourse-coalitions that in their interaction seek support from other actors and thus, over time, create the actual policy-to-come. *Deliberative Policy Analysis* (Hajer and Wagenaar 2003) has become a theme which joins many postmodern analysts across Policy Analysis and Public Administration; the concept satisfies a demand for dynamic analysis, language discourse and the involvement of a broad public in political and administrative processes. When one includes the scholar in the total understanding of this kind of research, all concepts—theory, research, scholar, action, learning, etc.—are mingled, and any change in any one concept will have consequences for the other ones (Kensen 2003). A challenge for the researcher, then, is to keep score of the various roles that are played out over time in a research project.

10.4 POSTMODERN FACETS

Postmodern analyses have many facets, and this section is by no means an attempt to generalize about postmodernism. But *social constructivism* in some version is present in nearly all postmodern writing. For several analysts, constructivism leads to *pragmatism* and activism in a new, American version. Let us take them in that order.

10.4.1 Social Constructivism

The discussions on social constructivism versus foundationalism concern the stances on objective knowledge: Is it possible to go along the classic Durkheimian (1965) line and measure social facts, preferably in a quantitative fashion and as something being there unrelated to the observer, or may we only understand the world around us as an ongoing discussion of our subjective perceptions of social conditions, as Berger and Luckmann (1966) contend?

A debate within *PAT-Net* in 1996–97 is illustrative. An article by Geuras and Garofolo (1996) criticized the "subjectivist" theorists in Public Administration for not being able to state the ethical basis for the values they insist practitioners must apply to be able to make their decisions. The authors bundled Jay White, Michael Harmon, Richard Box, and Fox and Miller with Marcuse, Habermas, Denhardt, Lyotard, and Jameson in a group whose members would all subscribe to a subjective perspective for Public Administration theory. And by doing so, they maintained, it is not possible to establish an ethical basis for judging, say, abortion. So, "we need to wonder why, even in postmodern circumstances, it is not possible . . . to adhere to a set of fundamental moral principles that, we believe, transcend neotribalism, subcultures, and hyperreality" (Geuras and Garofolo 1996: 9).

Those who were criticized did not take it lightly. Excerpts from Michael Harmon's response indicate what was at stake. He stated that being a subjectivist does not mean that one accepts the reduction of judgmental values to some individual, "emotivist" preferences and "it is this misinterpretation . . . that leads . . . to the unwarranted conclusion that all forms of subjectivism must necessarily regard arbitrary individual preferences as the only conceivable alternative to a universalistic ethics" (Harmon 1997: 5). Morality is a question of process rather than any absolute value, it is a relationship, and it consists of the sentiment, feeling, or impulse of being *for* the Other; morality is an act or process of self-constitution. The morality of ends, then, is dependent on the morality of process, i.e. of social relationships that are meant to regenerate and maintain the social bond, which permit moral impulses of being *for* the Other to be expressed (Harmon 1997: 15–16).

Another side of the debate is coined by the expressions of *Big-T-truth* and *small-t-truth* (Wamsley and Wolf 1996; Miller and King 1998). For instance, McSwite (1996) sees postmodernism as a rejection of the possibility of unambiguous representation or identity. Places change—cities lose their meaning as the locus of civilization, and people become disembedded. Personal identity becomes part of an open-ended, unspecified metaphor of personal development, which is relative and thus explorable for each individual (what does gender mean for an androgynous person?). In other words, the Capital-T truths are gone, and truth(s) must be sought for the at this time relevant purpose (Miller 2002a: 338).

Deconstructivists are also skeptical towards a monopoly on truth, as this quotation illustrates:

There should be no objection to a sensitive use of (say) categories in developing important "little t truths," truths within a language or a way of life. But it is part of postmodernism's philosophical skepticism that the categories of a language do not guarantee non contingent (or transcendental) Big T truth, the whole and complete truth about itself. Undeconstructed categories mean that we get "facts" not quite right. . . . Truths which seem to be interpretation-free facts are shown, through deconstruction, to depend on hidden assumptions (oppositions and metaphors) manufactured by the language used. (Farmer 1998c: 42–3)

Social constructivism indicates where postmodern Public Administration belongs in the Academy regarding scholarship (but it should be stressed that constructivists are not necessarily postmodernists). Foundationalists tend to doubt that constructivists belong among scientists, but such a verdict is out of bounds. But how is good postmodern scholarship to be distinguished from bad? Basically in the same way as among foundationalists: By following rules of thumb. But where traditional science speaks of validity, constructivists speak of credibility and transferability; reliability becomes dependability, and objectivity becomes confirmability. And there are procedures to ensure such trustworthiness (Erlandson, Harris, Skipper et al. 1993: 133).

10.4.2 Pragmatism

Pragmatism goes back one hundred years or so in academic Public Administration, and it has always been in a conflict with modernistic, scientific approaches which dominate the field. It started in the progressive era in the late nineteenth century with Peirce, James, and Dewey, but by the late 1930s it was thoroughly out of vogue among leading theorists; a technocratic and rationalistic spirit dominated for many years, probably helped by the war efforts and the development of operation analysis and other tools of social engineering. Kuhn (1962) paved the way for reconsidering how to organize scholarly work, and pragmatists started to link themselves more with the humanities with Rorty (1989) as an icon, claiming that one cannot pursue essentialist or universalist ideas without "blocking the road of inquiry." Instead, one should let "a thousand flowers bloom."

The—somewhat ancient—hero among American Postmodern pragmatic theorists in Public Administration is Mary Parker Follett, whose writings of the 1920s (see Follett 1980) are referenced time and again. Key concepts are experimentation end experience. Some quotes from Mary Parker Follett's work will illustrate: "People must socialize their life by experience, not by study. . . . Ideas unfold *within* human experience, not by their own momentum apart from experience." Likewise: "We need then those who are frankly participant-observers, those who will try experiment after experiment and note results, experiments in making human interplay productive." Follett did not recognize the functional administrator's call for ability to organize for strategy and success, directed by the top; this is the result of processes of relating, not of managing (Snider 1998: 279). Pragmatists, then, deny the principles of rational action by representing social relationships as collaborative, grounded in joint project and joint action.

Miller and King (1998) follow the pragmatic line by challenging the dichotomy of theory and practice, launching a plea for practical theory which is a "critical reflection on practice as well as imaginative reflection on possible modification of that practice" (Miller and King 1998: 58). Theory, then, is an instrument for transforming reality, rather than having the role of mirroring its essential and invariant features. The characteristics of Public Administration as a discipline defy precise measurement, generalizability across cultures, or universal truths—but theories may be used as frames for discussions to reach some contingent agreements on possibilities. In Miller and King's view there are predictable elements in social life, but this is not due to deductive, rationalistic theory; it is due to humans generating patterns in their daily practices. The practices are of a vague, fragile sort of predictability. Giddens' structuration processes (Giddens 1984) form the theoretical basis for stating that "Practical theory, therefore, takes place at the tangled overlap of practitioners' thoughtful reflection on action and scholars' deconstruction and critique of recursive social life" (Miller and King 1998: 57).

McSwite put forward similar ideas in the book published in 1997 (McSwite 1997); the general idea is to assume a personal posture of permanent doubt, place experimentation in a collaborative context, and then make the results the operational definition of truth. This is pragmatic social construction of reality: Our perceptions of the world are socially conditioned, and we need to state our sense of purpose in order to be able to "measure" our world, we do not perceive in limbo. That purpose, however, is not derived solely from the preferences of the individual, it is created in relationships with other people, in Public Administration it may be reached by pragmatic collaboration between administrators and citizens.

Postmodern Public Administration researchers, then, have an interest in Public Administration practice. But they rarely engage in consulting practitioners, and particularly high-level civil servants, as their more traditional colleagues do. Most of them rather get involved in helping out the clients or challenging the received views among the employees of a public service, attempting to make decision-making more democratic (Kensen 2003). But some advise city governments on how to cope with complex decision situations (Zouridis 2003).

10.5 GOING WHERE?

Postmodernism has fueled the discussions on values in our analyses in Public Administration. According to Inglehart, a high degree of economic security has led to a gradual shift from materialist values (primarily interests in economic and physical security) to postmaterialist priorities (focus on self-expression and the quality of life) in western societies (Inglehart 1997: 4). He offers three versions of postmodernism:

1. Rejecting modernity, its rationality, authority, technology and science, based on the Enlightenment.
2. Revalorizing tradition and particularly norms typically linked to the local community, albeit not old marital and sexual mores.
3. Stressing the rise of new values and lifestyle with great diversity and stress on individual choice.

In all cases, postmodern values emphasize human autonomy and diversity instead of the hierarchy and conformity that are central to modernity. In postmodern discussions of Public Administration, all three versions are present, but versions 1 and 2 seem to dominate.

The classic theme of the *public good* is a case in point. McSwite (1996) has discussed the concept on the basis of an understanding of postmodernism as beginning with a rejection of the possibility of representation or identity; thus, cities lose their meaning as loci of civilization and people become disembedded. Under modernism, the concept of the public interest makes administrators adhere to a number of constitutive rules or values that the term reinforces. But ethical codes do not operate unambiguously—"one person's ethical act is another's evil deed"—therefore, the need for arbitration arises; but when acceptance of the arbitration processes wanes, as may be the case under postmodern conditions, problems arise, and the administrator oriented towards modern conditions cannot deliver the promised "heavenly city" (McSwite 1996: 204–6). Other observers conclude that one "must continually seek the concurrent application of postmodern strategies of observation and dialogue (e.g., deconstruction, ethnography, discourse analysis). Thus, public interest as a symbol is re-presented differently in light of the postmodern experience, expressing what is unstated, suppressed, or unattended to in the traditionalist and modernist conceptualizations of the term" (Marshall and Choudhury 1997: 129).

Dialogue, then, leads to more demands for *participation*, and such discussions permeate especially the American postmodern Public Administration scene.

One version is based on quantum theory, or chaos theory, which in the 1990s became quite popular—at least as a metaphor—in management theory in various forms under the heading of *New Science* (e.g., Wheatley 1992). It is contested whether this is postmodern science, but chaos theory stresses elements that seem close: Unpredictability, the key role of creativity, irreversibility (you never step in the same river twice), and variance in key actors in the organization so that leadership is not privileged. Since identity and the self are not fixed under postmodern conditions, but rather progress in a non-linear and adaptive manner, processes can evolve rather than be seen as fragmented (Dennard 1997: 159–60). Such processes should be understood at a micro (quantum) level. Quantum theory is applicable to learning processes (Morcöl 1997: 310), particularly to understanding complex relations between many organizations, evaluating problems of participation, and using in situations of indeterminacy. This means that the understanding of management changes from top–down control to the empowerment of bottom–up processes; that organizational structure is created by webs of relationships, not vice versa; and that strategic planning is impossible, but visualization and strategic co-evolvement with the environment is possible (Evans 1997). The appeal of quantum theory, then, lies in its rejection of linear understanding of organization and management, and its opening up of the possibilities for practices that evoke relationship and meaning for our collective endeavors in governance. A collection of essays related to quantum theory is found in Morcöl and Dennard (2000)—however, Morcöl's introduction denies links to postmodernism.

Participation is also a core theme for another, relatively diverse group of scholars, rooted in critical theory, but attempting to include some postmodern aspects in their research, for example, Richard Box (1998), who discusses new forms of local governance, suited for the challenges of the twenty-first century. Box uses some of Fox and Miller's (1995) ideas about the warrants for discourse, and sees the world as becoming too fragmented and contentious for institutionalized collective action. New localism recreates an interest in communities and the relations residents have with those who share the experience of their local surroundings. We see more "citizen involvement and self-determination...de-mystification of professionalized systems, a desire to avoid the excesses of political intrusion into routine administration...elite groups are an important feature, an impressive technical-professional capacity, and lively debates about the structure and scope of community government" (Box 1996: 91).

In the USA, however, citizen participation is not unproblematic, since some have a worrisome relation to government. The problems of citizens and community in an "anti-government" era are discussed by King and Stivers (1998). The anti-government sentiment of the American people is based on the anti-bureaucrat movement in the media and among presidents as leading politicians; the feeling that administrators overuse their powers; the failure of effective policies; the sense of being powerless vis-à-vis government. What about the politicians? The authors show that lawmakers in representative government use generalized knowledge about citizens, based on statistics and comparable instruments. Citizens, on the other hand, think in personal terms, or "lived knowledge": The US government, then, is not a democracy of lived knowledge; law aimed at citizens excludes us as individuals; administration works with cases, not individuals, representation creates alienation. Using Arendt, the authors claim that democratic knowledge must be constructed not from re-presented but from experienced knowledge, by opening up the public space and thereby easing processes that let human thoughts and ideas be tested by the examination of other citizens. Here it is important to be able to put oneself into another's place, to understand from another viewpoint (to empathize). Citizens create their sense of the common through active conversations with neighbors. That is when "government becomes us" (King and Stivers 1998: 46–8).

Still, there is something left for Public Administration: in particular, public servants may be seen as intermediaries. Already when *Images and Identities* was published in 1990, the theme of "stewardship" was important, and Catron and Hammond (1990) in their epilogue discussed possible images of the public administrator: (1) the *functionary*, who is the traditional subordinate administrator; (2) the *opportunist* or *pragmatist* who is the utility-maximizing employee; (3) the *interest broker* or *market manager* as the disinterested arbiter; (4) the *professional* or expert technician like the competent analyst; (5) the *agent* or *trustee* acting on behalf of the public; (6) the *communitarian facilitator* asking their colleagues to work in the "proximate" environment of the face-to-face group; and finally (7) the *transformational social critic* monitoring political processes on behalf of the citizens, against oppressing trends.

Quite a list, and several modernist analysts would probably deny the soundness of the two last roles. In their book on citizen governance, King and Stivers (1998: 71–5) discussed possibilities and problems in citizen–administrator collaboration as an "us." On the one hand, the scientific, rationalized, professional knowledge of the bureaucracy is an obstacle for the citizens; on the other hand, there could be problems with citizen's accountability, and established societal interests might work against participation just as much as organizational features. King and Stivers propose a more facilitative, less expertise-driven approach and a differentiation between government for, by, and with the people. Civil servants must develop mediation skills; use advocacy to empower citizen and favor active citizenship. In sum, the images of the active administration are: a transformative, facilitative, public-service practitioner who is a task-oriented but inclusive and balanced convener, and a listening bureaucrat (King, Stivers, and collaborators 1998: 202–3).

Thus, Public Administration may function as helpful towards minorities and the disadvantaged. The critique of modernism as an oppressing force rather than being helpful to the marginalized is persistent among many postmodernists. There is a feminist trend among some (Stivers 1993, 2003), but this should be seen in the broader critical perspective rather than as a movement *per se*. Still, many would see postmodern scholars as an extension of the former left wing within scholarship: not totally untrue, but there are other sentiments involved, too.

10.6 CONCLUSION

Postmodern Public Administration has some thematic focal points of criticism. First of all, there is a criticism of the Enlightenment and its modernistic conse-quences, with the bureaucratic organization and its rational procedures as the icons. The critique leads to an interest in public administrators and how they may serve a broader role as energetic developers of a better society for everyone, but particularly the weak. Therefore, postmodernists have little interest in civil servants serving power holders as well as the power holders themselves (the presidency, etc.). Still, postmodernists have something to add to the field of Public Administration in discussions on the rationales of the expanded state, in particular the welfare state—within such themes as democratic governance, links to the public, interaction with clients, and methods of evaluation of the consequences of public policies.

Second, postmodernists criticize generalizing science, and their anti-founda-tionalist stance leads them to a new pragmatism—theories are to serve a purpose of change, or none. As a consequence, many have an interest in democratic theory as a means of creating better and—in a broad sense—more ethical decisions that support the minorities. The criticism, then goes beyond faultfinding, and leads to pragmatic, and hence constructive solutions.

There is not a unifying, postmodern approach. There are several versions of discourse analysis; one more in the line of Habermasian critical theory, another following principles derived from Foucault, and Laclau and Mouffe. In any case, we witness hermeneutical qualitative discussions rather than statistical analysis. The scholarly characteristics of postmodern Public Administration may aptly be caught by negating McCloskey's "Ten Commandments of the Golden Rule of Modernism" (as quoted by Farmer 1995: 72). The transformation would then lead to something like:

By scholarly endeavors, we want to understand specific events, which we cannot expect to observe in any generalized way, but it will help to make people involved narrate about their understanding. Theory is to be used instrumentally for changing unsatisfactory conditions in the world, and subjective understandings of such conditions matter to the scholar in such work. Qualitative, not quantitative measures are important, and it is not possible to elevate any reasoning above other reasonings because of the application of a particular method. Instrumental use of theory must be justified by the conditions of the case, one cannot use generalized theory to classify action. Scholars have the same right as anyone else to be normative.

Judged by the standards of most textbooks on the ontology, epistemology, and methodology of mainstream social science, such a statement leaves many themes for rather heated discussion between modernists and postmodernists.

NOTE

1. Comments on an earlier draft from Hugh Miller, Kåre Thomsen and the editors are gratefully acknowledged.

REFERENCES

ANDERSEN, N. Å., BORN, A., and MAJGAARD, K. (1995), "Grænser og magt," *Grus* 45: 88–102.

BACHRACH, P., and BARATZ, M. S. (1962), "Two Faces of Power," *American Political Science Review* 56: 947–952.

BECK, U., GIDDENS, A., and LASH, S. (1994), *Reflexive Modernization. Politics, Tradition and Aesthetics in the Modern Social Order*, Cambridge: Polity Press.

BERGER, P., and LUCKMANN, T. (1966), *The Social Construction of Reality. A Treatise in the Sociology of Knowledge*, New York: Doubleday Anchor.

BEVIR, M., and RHODES, R. A. W. (1998), "Public Administration Without Foundations: The Case of Britain," *Administrative Theory and Praxis* 20.1: 3–13.

BOGASON, P. (2000), *Public Policy and Local Governance: Institutions in Postmodern Society.* New Horizons in Public Policy, Cheltenham: Edward Elgar.

—— (2001), "Postmodernism and American Public Administration in the 1990s," *Administration and Society* 33.3: 165–93.

BOX, R. C. (1996), "The Institutional Legacy of Community Governance," *Administrative Theory and Praxis* 18.2: 84–100.

—— (1998), *Citizen Governance. Leading American Communities Into the 21st Century,* London: Sage.

CATRON, B. L., and HAMMOND, B. R. (1990), "Epilogue: Reflections on Practical Wisdom— Enacting Images and Developing Identity," *Images and Identities in Public Administration.* Ed. H. D. Kass and B. L Catron, London: Sage, 241–51.

CAWLEY, R. M., and CHALOUPKA, W. (1997), "American Governmentality. Michel Foucault and Public Administration," *American Behavioral Scientist* 41(1): 28–42.

CLEGG, S. (1990), *Modern Organizations. Organization Studies in the Postmodern World.* (London: Sage).

DENNARD, L. F. (1989), "The Three Bears and Goldilocks Meet Burrell and Morgan," *Administration and Society* 21: 3: 384–86.

—— (1997), "The Democratic Potential in the Transition of Postmodernism," *American Behavioral Scientist* 41(1): 148–62.

DICKENS, D. R., and FONTANA, A. (1994), "Postmodernism in the Social Sciences," in D. R. Dickens and A. Fontana (eds.), *Postmodernism and Social Inquiry,* New York: The Guilford Press, 1–22.

DURKHEIM, E. (1965), *The Division of Labor in Society,* New York: Free Press.

ERLANDSON, D. A., HARRIS, E. L., SKIPPER, B. L., and ALLEN, S. D. (1993), *Doing Naturalistic Inquiry: A Guide to Methods,* London: Sage.

EVANS, K. G. (1997), "Imagining Anticipatory Government: A Speculative Essay on Quantum Theory and Visualization," *Administrative Theory and Praxis* 19(3): 355–67.

FARMER, D. J. (1995), *The Language of Public Administration. Bureaucracy, Modernity, and Postmodernity,* Tuscaloosa: The University of Alabama Press.

—— (1997), "Derrida, Deconstruction, and Public Administration," *American Behavioral Scientist* 41(1): 12–27.

—— (ed.) (1998a), *Papers on the Art of Anti-Administration,* Burke, VA: Chatelaine Press.

—— (1998b), "Social Construction of Concepts: The Case of Efficiency," in D. J. Farmer (ed.), *Papers on the Art of Anti-Administration,* Burke, VA: Chatelaine Press, 95–111.

—— (1998c), "Public Administration Discourse as Play with a Purpose," in D. J. Farmer (ed.), *Papers on the Art of Anti-Administration,* Burke, VA: Chatelaine Press, 37–56.

—— (2001), "Mapping Anti-Administration: Introduction to the Symposium," *Administrative Theory and Praxis* 23(4): 475–92.

FISCHER, F. (1998), "Beyond Empiricism: Policy Inquiry in Postpositivist Perspective," *Policy Studies Journal* 26(1): 129–46.

—— (2003), *Reframing Public Policy. Discursive Politics and Deliberative Practices,* Oxford: Oxford University Press.

—— and Forester, J. (eds.) (1993), *The Argumentative Turn in Policy Analysis and Planning,* London: UCL Press.

FOLLETT, M. P. (1980; orig. 1924), *Creative Experience,* New York: Longmans, Green.

FOUCAULT, M. (1980), *Power and Knowledge,* Brighton: Harvester.

Fox, C. D., and Cochran, C. E. (1990), "Discretionary Public Administration: Toward a Platonic Guardian Class?" in Kass and Catron 1990: 87–112.

—— and Miller, H. T. (1995), *Postmodern Public Administration. Towards Discourse*, London: Sage.

Frederickson, H. G., and Smith, K. B. (2003), *The Public Administration Primer. Essentials of Public Policy and Administration*, Boulder, CO: Westview.

Frissen, P. H. A. (1999), *Politics, Governance and Technology: A Postmodern Narrrative on the Virtual State*. New Horizons in Public Policy, Cheltenham: Edward Elgar.

Gephart, R. P., Thatchenkery, T. J., and Boje, D. (1996), "Conclusion. Reconstructing Organizations for Future Survival," in D. Boje, R. P Gephart, and T. J. Thatchenkery (eds.), *Postmodern Management and Organization Theory*, London: Sage, 358–64.

Geuras, D., and Garofolo, C. (1996), "The Normative Paradox in Contemporary Public Administration Theory," *Administrative Theory and Praxis* 18(2): 2–13.

Giddens, A. (1984), *The Constitution of Society: Outline of the Theory of Structuration*, Cambridge: Polity Press.

Gottweis, H. (2003), "Theoretical Strategies of Poststructuralist Policy Analysis: Towards an Analytics of Government," in Hajer and Wagenaar 2003: 247–65.

Guba, E. G., and Lincoln, Y. S. (1989), *Fourth Generation Evaluation*, London: Sage.

Hajer, M. (1995), *The Politics of Environmental Discourse. Ecological Modernization and the Policy Process*, Oxford: Clarendon Press.

—— (2003), "Introduction," Hajer and Wagenaar 2003: 1–30.

—— and Wagenaar, H. (eds.) (2003), *Deliberative Policy Analysis. Understanding Governance in the Network Society*. Theories of Institutional Design, Cambridge: Cambridge University Press.

Hansen, A. D. (1996), "Strukturalisme, poststrukturalisme og subjektets plads," *Grus* 49: 88–106.

Harmon, M. (1990), "The Responsible Actor as 'Tortured Soul': The Case of Horatio Hornblower," in Kass and Catron 1990: 151–80.

—— (1995), *Responsibility as Paradox: A Critique of Rational Discourse on Government*, London: Sage.

—— (1997), "On the Futility of Universalism," *Administrative Theory and Praxis* 19(2): 3–18.

—— (2003), "PAT-Net Turns Twenty-Five: A Short History of the Public Administrative Theory Network," *Administrative Theory and Praxis* 25(2): 157–72.

Hatch, M. J. (1997), *Organization Theory. Modern, Symbolic and Postmodern Perspectives*, Oxford: Oxford University Press.

Heclo, H. (1972), "Review Article: Policy Analysis," *British Journal of Political Science* 2: 83–108.

Hjern, B., and Porter, D. O. (1983), "Implementation Structures: A New Unit of Administrative Analysis," in B. Holzner, K. D. Knorr, and H. Strasser (eds.), *Realizing Social Science Knowledge*, Vienna and Würzberg: Physica-Verlag, 265–77.

Hollinger, R. (1994), *Postmodernism and the Social Sciences. A Thematic Approach*, London: Sage.

Howe, L. (2001), "Civil Service Reform and Political Culture of Governmentality: Massachusetts 1952–1981," *Administrative Theory and Praxis* 23(2): 151–74.

Hummel, R. P. (1990), "Circle Managers and Pyramidal Managers: Icons for the Post-Modern Public Administrator," in Kass and Catron 1990: 202–18.

INGLEHART, R. (1970), *Modernization and Postmodernization. Cultural, Economic and Political Change in 43 Societies*, Princeton: Princeton University Press.

KASS, H. D., "Prologue: Emerging Images and Themes in the Reexamination of American Public Administration," in Kass and Catron 1990: 9–19.

—— (1990), "Stewardship as a Fundamental Element in Images of Public Administration," in Kass and Catron 1990: 113–31.

—— and CATRON, B. L. (eds.) (1990), *Images and Identities in Public Administration*, London: Sage Publishers.

KENSEN, S. (2000), "The Dialogue as a Basis for Democratic Governance," *Administrative Theory and Praxis* 22(1): 117–31.

—— (2003), "Playing with Boundaries as Democratic Scholars," *Administrative Theory and Praxis* 25(3): 327–51.

KING, C. S. (1998), "Reflective Scholarship: Healing the Scholarship/practice Wounds," *Administrative Theory and Praxis* 20(2): 159–71.

KING, C. S., STIVERS, C., and collaborators (1998), *Government is Us. Public Administration in Anti-Government Era*, London: Sage.

KUHN, T. S. (1962), *The Structure of Scientific Revolutions*, Chicago: Chicago University Press.

LACLAU, E. (1993), "Discourse," in R. E. Goodin and P. Petitt (eds.), *Blackwell Companion to Contemporary Political Philosophy*, Oxford: Blackwell.

LATOUR, B. (1987), *Science in Action: How to Follow Scientists and Engineers Through Society*, Cambridge, MA: Harvard University Press.

McSWITE, O. C. (1996), "Postmodernism, Public Administration, and the Public Interest," in Wamsley and Wolf 1996: 198–224.

—— (1997), *Legitimacy in Public Administration. A Discourse Analysis*, London: Sage.

—— (2000), "On the Discourse Movement—a Self Interview," *Administrative Theory and Praxis* 22(1): 49–65.

MARSHALL, G. S., and CHOUDHURY, E. (1997), "Public Administration and the Public Interest. Re-Presenting a Lost Concept," *American Behavioral Scientist* 41(1): 119–31.

MILLER, H. T. (2000), "Rational Discourse, Memetics, and the Autonomous Liberal-Humanist Subject," *Administrative Theory and Praxis* 22(1): 89–105.

—— (2002a), "Doubting Foundationalism," *Administration and Society* 34(3): 335–41.

—— (2002b), *Postmodern Public Policy*, Albany, NY: State U of New York Press.

—— and King, C. S. (1998), "Practical Theory," *American Review of Public Administration* 28(1): 43–60.

MORCÖL, G. (1997), "A Meno Paradox for Public Administration: Have we Acquired a Radically New Knowledge for the 'New Sciences?'," *Administrative Theory and Praxis* 19(3): 305–17.

—— and DENNARD, L. (eds.) (2001), *New Sciences for Public Administration and Policy*, Burke, VA: Chatelaine Press.

MORGAN, D. F. (1990), "Administrative Phronesis: Discretion and the Problem of Administrative Legitimacy in Our Constitutional System," in Kass and Catron 1990: 67–86.

MORGAN, G. (1986), *Images of Organization*, London: Sage.

PEDERSEN, K. (1996), "Postmoderne planlægning—mellem kritik og styring," *Grus* 49: 59–74.

RHODES, R. A. W. (1997), *Understanding Governance. Policy Networks, Governance, Reflexivity and Accountability*, Buckingham: Open University Press.

RHODES, R. A. W. and MARSH, D. (1992), "New Directions in the Study of Policy Networks," *European Journal of Political Research* 21: 181–205.

RORTY, R. (1989), *Contingency, Irony and Solidarity*, Cambridge: Cambridge University Press.

ROSENAU, P. M. (1992), *Post-Modernism and the Social Sciences. Insights, Inroads and Intrusions*, Princeton: Princeton University Press.

SNIDER, K. (1998), "Living Pragmatism: The Case of Mary Parker Follett," *Administrative Theory and Praxis* 20(3): 274–86.

STIVERS, C. (1993), *Gender Images in Public Administration. Legitimacy and the Administrative State*, London: Sage.

—— (2003), "Administration Versus Management. A Reading from Beyond the Boundaries," *Administration and Society* 35(2): 210–30.

TORFING, J. (1999), *New Theories of Discourse. Laclau, Mouffe and Zicek*, Oxford: Blackwell.

VRMEER, R. W. (1994), "Postmodernism: A Polemic Commentary on Continuity and Discontinuity in Centemporary Thought," *Administrative Theory and Praxis* 16(1): 85–91.

WAMSLEY, G. L., and WOLF, J. F. (1996), "Introduction: Can a High-Modern Project Find Happiness in a Postmodern Era?", in G. L. Wamsley and J. F. Wolf (eds.), *Refounding Democratic Public Administration: Modern Paradoxes, Postmodern Challenges*, London: Sage, 1–37.

WHEATLEY, M. J. (1992), *Leadership and the New Science. Learning About Organization from an Oderly Universe*, San Francisco: Berrett-Koehler.

WHITE, J. D. (1999), *Taking Language Seriously: The Narrative Foundations of Public Administration Research*, Washington, DC: Georgetown University Press.

ZANETTI, L. A. (1996), "Advancing Praxis. Connecting Critical Theory with Practice in Public Administration," *American Review of Public Administration* 27(2): 145–67.

ZOURIDIS, S. (2003), "A Quest for Practical Theory: Theory and Interaction Research in a Dutch City," *Administrative Theory and Praxis* 25(3): 351–71.

CHAPTER 11

NETWORKS AND INTER-ORGANIZATIONAL MANAGEMENT

CHALLENGING, STEERING, EVALUATION, AND THE ROLE OF PUBLIC ACTORS IN PUBLIC MANAGEMENT

ERIK-HANS KLIJN

11.1 INTRODUCTION: A NETWORK PERSPECTIVE ON MANAGEMENT

THE concept of network has become quite fashionable in the academic literature on Public Administration and Public Management. The network concept has not only become very popular as an analytic concept to make sense of the world of complex interactions around policy but has also become a catchword for thinking up and devising and proposing alternative ways of managing complex interactions around policy formation, implementation or service delivery.

The growing literature on networks is not restricted to specific scientific fields or geographical locations. One can find literature on networks in public policy and business administration as well as in sociology and economics. There are contributions from all over the world, although their scope and flavor tends to vary somewhat.

In this chapter we provide a brief overview of the literature on networks and look at what it has to tell us about policy processes and public management. In essence the literature on networks and inter-organizational relations challenges some existing aspects of Public Management that are taken for granted. It stresses the interdependency of various organizations in realizing policy initiatives, it challenges the central position of public actors in decision making and implementation processes and it challenges the way policy processes are managed and evaluated.

Section 11.2 tries to explain the growth in popularity of the network concept. In Section 11.3 we provide an overview of the findings that two decades of network research have delivered. We also devote attention to the main concepts that are used in network research. In Section 11.4 we focus on networks as prescriptive theory and discuss the role of public manager in this perspective and the available strategies. Section 11.5 discusses the way outcomes are evaluated and 11.6 deals with the main criticisms that have been aimed at the literature on networks and inter-organizational relations. We end with some conclusions.

11.2 WHY NETWORKS?

The first question to be addressed, of why there has been such a rise in the popularity of the network concept, is not an easy one to answer. One possibility is that earlier theorizing and empirical research on the concept was already available (for instance, the works of the early inter-organization theorists such as Levine and White 1961; Litwak and Hylton 1962; Emerson 1962; or the discussion in political science between elitist and pluralist where the network concept was used, see Dahl 1961; Truman 1964). Thus the network concept was available for use although in the 1960s (and 1970s) it was not a very prominent concept in social science and certainly not in public administration. Most handbooks on organizational theory or Public Administration did not apportion any space to it.

But this simply changes the question to why the concept became popular instead of remaining obscure. It is probable that two developments in Public Administration and in society generally, or at least in the way many observers looked at and interpreted these phenomena, were responsible for the rise of the network concept: the development of a network society and the growing interest in governance as a way to administer policy and service delivery.

11.2.1 Background: Network Management and Network Society

Several authors have argued that we have seen dramatic changes in our society over the last decades. These changes can be summarized as a development towards a network society in which horizontal relations and networks have grown in importance partly as a result of information technologies but also owing to specialization. According to some authors, other societal trends, such as individualization, have reinforced these developments. Individualization is then considered as one of the major societal developments in western society (Sociaal Cultureel Planbureau 2000) and it seems to go hand in hand with a diminishing of the importance of traditional societal relations (see Putnam's conclusions on the vanishing of social capital (Putnam 1995).

Castells, without a doubt the most prominent author on the development of the network society, states that our societies are increasingly formed in the bi-polar tension between the net and the self (Castells 2000). If we look at Castells' analysis, this development towards a network society is a gradual progression which starts somewhere in the 1970s but accelerates during the final decade of the twentieth century. The implicit assumption, if we accept this analysis, is that there is a growing need for inter-organizational structures between organizations (in the private as well as the public sphere) to deal with this growing complexity of interactions in the public and private sphere (and the interfaces between those spheres). Of course this is all very hard to prove. But the growing number of (international) strategic alliances between firms (Faulkner 1995; Nooteboom 1999), the attentions to chain management and networks of firms (Graeber 1993) the growing attention (at least rhetorical) to forms of co-governance and Public Private Partnerships (Osborne 2000; Pollitt 2003b) seem to point to there being some grounds for this assumption.

But there may be a more convincing argument. There can be no doubt that there is a growing, commonly shared perception among many practitioners (professionals and policy makers) and academic experts on Public Administration and Public Management that the network society calls for more horizontal forms of governance. And the golden law is still: "If men define situations as real, they are real in their consequences" (Thomas, cited in Zijderveld 1974).

11.2.2 Networks and New Public Management (NPM): Two Different Views on Management

A second reason for the popularity of the network concept, and the theoretical development that goes with it, may be that it is connected to the literature and practice on governance, horizontal steering partnerships, and so on. In many countries governments have announced that they want to govern with society instead of above society and that they seek partnerships with societal and business actors. The rhetoric of the modernizing governments and joined-up government by the New Labour administration in the UK (see Pollitt 2003b; Newman 2003) may be the most well known but is not the only one and certainly not the first (see McLaverty 2002).

Network theories can be seen as one of the theoretical underpinnings for these trends (whether theorists like it or not) although they are certainly not the only one. As such, both the governance narrative and the literature on networks represent another way of looking at steering and proposing government reforms.

One can even say that in a way the governance "narrative" forms an alternative to the "narrative" of the New Public Management. That "narrative," especially in its early versions, focused strongly on organizational and institutional changes within public sector organizations and on improving efficiency and effectiveness of public organizations mainly by such means as outsourcing and increasing use of market-like mechanisms in public service delivery. As the governance narrative has grown in popularity over the last ten years it is not surprising that network theory, as one of the possible theoretical underpinnings of that narrative, has also grown in popularity.

11.3 A NETWORK VIEW ON (PUBLIC) POLICY: AN OVERVIEW OF THE RESEARCH

The concept of networks first emerged in Public Administration and Public Management in the mid-1970s and early 1980s. This section provides an elaboration on what the network perspective has to offer by giving a brief account of empirical and theoretical findings that have been achieved using this perspective.

11.3.1 Early Research on Networks: The Complexity of Public Policy

The first time the network concept emerges in Public Administration research is in implementation studies and research on intergovernmental relations which were being conducted in the late 1970s and early 1980s. In implementation studies it was used to analyze the network of actors who were involved in implementation. This "bottom–up" approach as it was labeled focused on the views and strategies of local implementing actors regarding the effects of policy outcomes instead of regarding the goals and strategies of central actors (Hjern and Porter 1981). The bottom–up approach showed that central programs offer more opportunities to local implementing actors, which forms one of many considerations in implementation processes. They have been successful in highlighting the importance of other actors in implementation processes but also in highlighting unanticipated effects of implementation. The bottom–up approach, however, also stresses interaction processes between implementing organizations as well as between specific parts of organizations (Hjern and Porter 1981).

The intergovernmental studies focus on the relation and communication networks between different levels of government (local—federal—state) and their strategies, often in the context of policy programs (see Scharpf et al. 1976; Agranoff and McGuire 2003). The studies highlight the fact that governmental actors (especially those outside the center) operate in complex settings where they have to deal with more that one policy program at the same time and where they find themselves in complex networks of actors. This calls for new and different ways of management that focus on managing inter-organizational relations (Lynn 1981; Gage and Mandell 1990).

In one of the first and most famous books on networks in public administration (edited by Hanf and Scharpf in 1978), with the telling title *Inter-organizational Policy Making: Limits to Coordination and Central Control*, which contains several analyses of implementation and intergovernmental policy making, Scharpf writes at the end: "It is unlikely, if not impossible, that public policy of any significance could result from the choice process of any single unified actor. Policy formation and policy implementation are inevitably the result of interactions among a plurality of separate actors with separate interests, goals, and strategies" (Scharpf 1978: 346). According to Scharpf, research should not only be directed towards specific interactions between organizations and the strategic interactions that form policy and implementation, but also to the more structural stable relations between organizations (Scharpf 1978). With this statement he effectively summarized the results of the early empirical and theoretical findings from a network perspective. But it is not until the (late) 1980s and subsequently that networks as a concept receive a more prominent place in Public Administration.

11.3.2 Intensive Interaction, Closed Networks and the Forming and Implementation of Policy

Focusing on interaction patterns between actors in networks, on the nature of closedness and its effects on decision making and policy formation is the main direction taken by network research in the time following the emergence of the concept in the 1970s and 1980s. The research primarily highlights the intensive sector interactions and coordination problems, but also the challenges that forming and implementing complex policy processes and service delivery pose for managers.

11.3.2.1 *Sectoral Networks: Dense Interactions*

If we look at the findings from the literature over the last fifteen years relating to networks which use the idea of networks as an analytical concept, we can see that most studies find strong interactions between actors in specific policy domains. This generalization holds for studies which use quantitative techniques for mapping interactions (see Laumann and Knoke 1987 for one of the best examples) and for studies which use case studies to compare and analyze different networks (see Milward and Wamsley 1985; Rhodes 1988; Hufen and Ringeling 1990; Marin and Mayentz 1991; Marsh and Rhodes 1992; Marsh 1998).

Laumann and Knoke deduce, after an intensive quantitative study of interactions between actors in national policy domains in the US, that these domains consist of a group of core participants made up of public as well as private actors. At the end they conclude:

Despite their lack of formal decision-making authority, many private participants possess sufficient political clout to secure that their interests will be taken into account. This mutual recognition creates and sustains the legitimacy of core actors' involvement in domain issues and events...Within the group of core participants, however, there exists a relatively dense system of knowledge on inter-organizational interaction. (Laumann and Knoke 1987: 375).

Similar findings can be found by Rhodes in his analysis of British Government (1988) and by various researchers in case studies compiled by Marsh and Rhodes (1992), or by an analysis of decision making in the Netherlands (Koppenjan et al. 1987; Hufen and Ringeling 1990). Rhodes describes these integrated policy networks as policy communities. Policy communities are:

networks characterized by stability of relationships, continuity of a highly restrictive membership, vertical interdependence based on shared service delivery, responsibility and insulation from other networks and invariability from the general public (including parliament). They have a high degree of vertical interdependence and limited horizontal articulation. They are highly integrated" (Rhodes 1988: 78).

Intensive interactions in sector networks can be found both at a national level, where actors are strongly focused on policy making processes and at a local level where implementation of sector policy is also at stake (see Lowndes and Skelcher 1998; Clarence and Painter 2000; Klijn 2001). Some of the literature sees a network structure in which sectoral networks consist of vertical and horizontal ties between actors. The vertical ties, which are weaker, are built around streams of money and regulations from the central to the local level (and information and lobbying attempts from local to central levels). The implementation of sector policy is taken care of by these vertical ties but central policy is also refined and changed. Public and private actors at the different horizontal levels (central administrative level and local level) then have strong interaction and dependency relations with each other (see Milward and Wamsley 1985, but also Rhodes 1988; Klijn 2001). The horizontal ties in the network structure secure policy formation and negotiation between various groups of actors. At the central level it is mainly interest groups and the inner circles of implementing organizations that are active while at the local level, in addition to the same implementing public and private organizations, consumer and citizen groups also participate.

Dense interaction patterns are not only found in sector networks but also in empirical work that has been done on local service providing. Most research on service delivery and service contracting also shows a group of actors who interact intensively as a result of their dependency on delivering public integrated services (Milward and Provan 2000; Mandell 2001; Agranoff and McGuire 2003). In the case of contracting, some authors find a tension between the need to tender the service delivery to acquire and maintain incentives for cost efficiency and the need to promote interaction and learning processes between organizations to promote better service delivery. Contracting tends to disrupt the network after which new learning and interaction processes are needed (Milward and Provan 2000).

11.3.2.2 *Closedness of (Sector) Networks*

The intensive interactions between actors in sector networks tend to make these networks rather closed to other actors. Networks can be closed for a variety of reasons that often reinforce each other. The dense interaction patterns of course require a lot of efforts on the part of an actor. Not all actors have the resources or opportunities to make such efforts. In general, although it stresses the involvement of a wide variety of actors, network research does not confirm the old idea of pluralism: that important interests vary with each decision and that the policy arena is relatively open (see Dahl 1961). Network research tends rather to emphasize the involvement of specific actors whose interests are closely tied to the character and nature of the interactions. Networks exist and develop because of mutual dependencies and these are often tied to actors' core interests. It is not by accident, therefore, that local housing networks are characterized by sections of local government administration, housing associations, a few commercial developers and building companies, and occasionally some residents' organizations (Klijn 2001). These are precisely the actors who have something at stake in decisions on local housing policy, the financial transactions which accompany these decisions, and the intended results (restructuring housing areas, new dwellings, improving living conditions in certain areas, etc.). If the reason for the development of networks is mutual dependency, therefore, then it is not surprising that researchers find a varied but nevertheless limited number of actors whose interests are strongly tied to decisions that are being made in those networks.

Thus the policy arenas in networks are dominated by actors who are part of the network and have sufficient resources to organize themselves and promote their (often sectoral) interest in interactions that take place in networks (see Laumann and Knoke 1987; Rhodes 1988; Hufen and Ringeling 1990; Marsh 1998). But even if actors are able to make the investment of resources needed to engage in the variety of interactions in networks, they still have to learn the rules of the network and to become knowledgeable about the dominant perceptions there (Blom-Hansen 1997; Marsh 1998; Klijn 2001). Networks are thus not only closed because it takes transaction costs to engage in necessary interactions, or because actors within the network explicitly try to secure their own positions, but also because network rules which have been formed in earlier interactions resist the entry of other actors or simply create the kind of situation from which actors, issues, or interest are "naturally" excluded.

11.3.2.3 *The Need for Many Linkages to Implement Policy Programs and Policy Initiatives*

Both the research on national policy networks and the research on (local) service delivery networks stress not only the relative closedness of sectors and organizational boundaries but also the coordination problems which result from initiatives that require inter-organizational coordination. Whereas classical studies on subsystems and iron triangles tend to focus on the power of various interest groups to influence or block decision making, the literature from a network perspective tends to focus more on problems with and opportunities for connecting interactions between actors in a network or even between actors in various networks in order to achieve outcomes in policy programs or complex policy projects.

In a recent study on how city officials work with other layers of government and organizations to develop their city economics, Agranoff and McGuire conclude that they need a lot of different vertical and horizontal linkages to achieve that. Or, as they put it: "From the perspective of the city Government, there is not one cluster of linkages to manage but several clusters-some horizontal, some vertical, and some that include both within the context of a single project or program" (Agranoff and McGuire 2003: 123). This complexity of policy processes and the need for many linkages between public actors who start policy initiatives are one of the leading themes in the network research in addition to the themes of intensive interaction and interdependencies and the closedness of networks (see: Kickert, Klijn, and Koppenjan 1997; Lowndes and Skelcher 1998; Milward and Provan 2000; Mandell 2001).

All these empirical findings regarding the network perspective on public policy, whether applied to policy making and implementation at the national level, at the local level, or to locally bound service delivery, affirm the image of the "Hollow State." The Hollow State (see Rhodes 1997; Milward and Provan 2000) refers to the image of a state which does not itself perform the policy making and service delivery tied to the modern functions of government but in some way or another ensures that services and policy outputs are delivered by other organizations. This feature has been strengthened by the recent trends towards outsourcing, privatization, and agentification that have been taking place over the last two decades (Pollitt and Bouckaert 2000).

The emergence of the Hollow State raises a governance problem: How can we organize policy implementation and service delivery with the fragmented set of organizations that are involved? This is the very question that lies at the heart of the more recent literature from a network perspective. The literature thus endeavors not only to formulate an analytical perspective by means of which complex policy processes and interaction patterns between actors can be analyzed but also aims to provide a prescriptive perspective by means of which strategies can be developed to guide these complex processes in order to achieve meaningful outcomes for the actors involved. This prescriptive dimension of network theory is elaborated in the next section. First we try to summarize some conclusions on the network perspective as analytical perspective.

11.3.3 Conclusion: Networks as Analytical Perspective

The network perspective on policy and public management builds on the tradition of public administration and Public Management as far as the main concept used in the analysis is concerned. For the analysis of actors and their interactions, concepts such as strategies, resources, dependencies and perceptions or frames of references are used. In that sense, it builds on and integrates different theories of public administration and organization (Klijn 1997):

- Organizational theories which stress the possession of resources (and their relation to power), the use of strategies to exchange resources (Aldrich 1979; Pfeffer 1981) and the evolving of networks of interaction due to these resource exchanges.
- Public administration theories of complex decision making (Allison 1971; Kingdon 1984) which stress that public policy is the result of the interaction of different strategies by various actors who struggle with the problem definition, possible solutions and choice moments (see also Lindblom and Cohen 1979; Dery 1984).

- Organizational theories of organizational learning and reframing such as the work of Weick (1979), Rein and Schon (1992) and others which point out that actors make sense of their environment by using frames. Analyzing these frames makes it clear how actors understand their world and why they choose certain strategies.

11.3.3.1 *Mutual Dependencies as Core Assumption*

Mutual dependencies are one of the key concepts in most network and inter-organizational theories. Mutual dependencies emerge because actors do not them-selves posses enough resources for survival or for the achievement of interesting goals. They thus have to interact with other organizations in order to exchange resources. Networks develop because these resource exchanges continue over time. With the growing importance of using perceptions or frames of reference to explain stagnations or breakthroughs in interactions in networks, network theor-ists are now building on earlier theories of organizing and learning (Weick 1979; Rein and Schon 1992).

In addition to characteristic concepts that are tied to individual actors in the network (such as resources, strategies, perceptions) network theories try to explain outcomes by using concepts that are tied to the interactions between actors or to the structural characteristics of the network.[1] Explanations that have been explored are, for instance, the nature of the games (for a qualitative attempt, see Crozier and Friedberg 1980; for a more quantitative attempt, Scharpf 1997, who tries to incorp-orate game theory in the analysis). But there are also attempts to explain outcomes based on the characteristics of the network as a whole. This takes the form of trying to develop structural features by means of formal network analysis methods (see Laumann and Knoke 1987) but also by analyzing the rules of networks and their influence on interactions (for an analysis of rules in a formal game theory manner, see Scharpf 1997; for a reconstruction of rules in action in networks and their influence, Klijn 2001).

11.3.3.2 *The Focus of a Network Perspective*

The main focus of a network perspective is the complex policy processes which result from interdependencies of actors by realizing policy initiatives. It tries to develop concepts (networks, games, perceptions, etc.) and methods of analyzing (such as formal network analysis, explicating network rules and frames of reference) in order to clarify the complexity of the interaction processes and their outcomes.

The main differences from earlier theorizing and empirical research are not only a stronger focus on the complexity of the interactions and the nature of depend-encies, but also the attention devoted to coordination and management strategies that are needed to achieve results and the attention devoted to the structural characteristics of networks. Another difference, however, is also a far stronger focus on the limited governing capacities of public actors in forming and implementing public policy and the attention paid to other ways of managing. In this sense the network literature, or at least a substantial part of it, has an explicit prescriptive ambition. This is the focus of the next section.

11.4 NETWORK AS PRESCRIPTIVE THEORY: MANAGEMENT STRATEGIES FOR THE PUBLIC SECTOR

It is clear that, from a network or inter-organizational perspective, policy making and implementation or service delivery is a complex process. Interesting outcomes for the actors involved do not occur automatically but have to be managed and coordinated carefully. In fact, most of the literature on networks and inter-organizational management assumes that without network management it is hardly possible to achieve interesting outcomes. This view challenges conventional public administration which strongly emphasizes political decision making and goal setting as important factors and the way the relationship between political decision makers and implementing bodies is organized (clear goal setting, strong monitoring and steering opportunities, etc.).[2] In the network literature the figure of a network manager is introduced. This is an actor—or more than one actor—who performs and implements the coordination activities required to ensure that the interaction and joint decision making between actors, which is necessary to achieve outcomes in an interdependent world, actually takes place. To be clear: the figure of the network manager is not a superhuman agent in a horizontal world. Most literature considers network management as a function or a set of activities which can also be performed by more than one actor. The question of who manages the interactions of actors in a network setting may even be subject to conflict and struggle. It is necessary, however, to look at the image of the network manager and the strategies elaborated in the literature in order to gain a clear understanding of the concept of the network manager and network management.

11.4.1 The Public Manager as Network Manager

Almost all the literature on networks and inter-organizational management agrees that the role of the public manager differs sharply from that portrayed in the standard textbooks. As early as 1978 Hanf, in one of the first and best known works on networks and inter-organizational policy making, describes network management as inter-organizational coordination. In his opinion that meant "Intervening in the existing structure of interrelationships in order to promote the interactions appropriate for mobilizing a concerted or coordinated effect consistent with the objective interdependencies of the problem situation" (Hanf/Scharpf, 1978: 12). If we look at the literature that followed the influential publication of Hanf and Scharpf (1978) we find more or less the same characteristics applied to the role of the network manager (see Agranoff 1986, 2003; Agranoff and McGuire 2003; Mandell 1990; Kickert, Klijn, and Koppenjan 1997):

- *Power and authority.* Because the network manager is dependent for his initiative on the resources of other actors and mostly does not have any or has only limited authority over other organizations, he operates in a divided power structure and there is no single authority where strategic decisions can be unilaterally made (Bryson and Crosby 1992). The public manager as network manager simply does not have the position and authority to make unilateral decisions. His world is one with a divided authority structure in which he has to achieve coordinated action. This does not mean that there are no power differences or that power does not matter as some critics say. In a network or inter-organizational perspective, the power of an actor depends on his available resources and the way he is dependent on the resources of other actors (see Emerson 1962; Scharpf 1978). The more the various actors are mutually dependent on each other's resources the more equal the power division in the network is. But even powerful actors have limited authority because they have no direct authority regarding the way other actors use their resources.
- *Goal Structure.* Activities are not guided by uniform, clear goals because the various actors involved have different goals. Goals also emerge during the co-operation process (Agranoff 1986; Mandell 1990). This makes a large part of decision and co-operation processes in networks a goal seeking rather than a goal setting process. It also makes the goal structure of inter-organizational co-operations and decision making more like a package deal, where different actors find interesting elements that suit their interests and capacities, rather than a unified common goal (Klijn and Teisman 1997).
- *Management role.* It is clear that the management role differs strongly from that described in the standard textbooks in which the management role is that of system controller (Hunt 1972: 25, see also Robbins 1980). From an inter-organizational network perspective the role of the manager is more that of a mediator, a process manager or a facilitator since network management is in essence an inter-organizational activity (see Friend et al. 1974; Hanf and Scharpf 1978; Lynn 1981; Gage and Mandell 1990; Kickert, Klijn, and Koppenjan 1997).
- *Management Activities.* In the traditional literature on management, the activities of the manager are described as comprising three major tasks: setting the goals

(planning); structuring and designing the organization (organizing); and "getting the job done" (leading) (see Robbins 1980). Managing networks bears little resemblance to these kinds of top—down activities based on clear authority and goal setting. Management activities are more focused on bringing different actors together, adjusting and accommodating goals and perceptions and building organizational arrangements to sustain and strengthen interactions. If we were to name three network management equivalents of planning, organizing, and leading these would probably be: goal finding and perception accommodation; making organizational arrangements; and coordinating.

11.4.2 Strategies of Network Management

The number of network management strategies that has been dealt with in the literature is impressive and this is not the place to describe them all or to even try to describe a number of them (see Gage and Mandell 1990; O'Toole 1988; Agranoff and McGuire 2001). It is clear, however, that if the network manager is to achieve interesting outcomes he has to implement a range of different strategies (see Kickert, Klijn, and Koppenjan 1997; Agranoff and McGuire 2001). He has to activate actors and resources, he has to coordinate goal-achieving mechanisms (which includes influencing the perceptions and goals of other actors), he has to foster or create organizational arrangements to facilitate and enable interactions between actors, and last but not least he has to coordinate the stream of actions and interactions between different actors.

On the other hand, we have seen that networks consist of concrete interactions between actors within a network structure that is created by the actors (partly willingly and consciously, partly as result of interactions and established ways of behaving). This means that network management strategies can be aimed at bringing about changes in the interactions of actors or effecting changes at the network level (Kickert, Klijn, and Koppenjan 1997). Table 11.1 summarizes the main strategies of network management while making no claims to be exhaustive (for an overview of the many different strategies of network management: Hanf and Scharpf 1978; O'Toole 1988; Gage and Mandell 1990; Kickert, Klijn, and Koppenjan 1997; Agranoff and McGuire 2001; Koppenjan and Klijn 2004). Not all the strategies mentioned in any one cell are mutually exclusive. One can, for instance, influence the perceptions of actors by initiating a search process for variety in solutions.

Strategies for the activation of actors or resources are necessary to start the game. The network manager has to identify the actors necessary for an initiative and actually create a situation in which they become interested in investing their resources (see also Lynn 1981). Scharpf calls this selective activation and tells us that the correct identification of necessary participants and the lack of opposition from other actors who possess the resources to block the initiative is crucial for

Table 11.1 Overview of network management strategies

	Activation of actors and resources	Goal achieving strategies	Organizational arrangements	Interaction guiding
Management of interactions	Selective activation, resource mobilizing, stabilization, deactivation of actors and resources, initiating new series of interaction, coalition building	Searching for goal congruency, creating variation in solutions, influencing (and explicating) perceptions, managing and collecting information and research	Creating new ad hoc organizational arrangements (boards, project organizations, etc.)	Mediation, brokerage, appointing of process manager, removing obstacles to co-operation, creating incentives for co-operation
Management of network	network activation, changing composition of networks, changing position of actors	Reframing of perceptions, changing decision rules in networks, changing information flow permanently	Creating permanent organizational constructions	Changing or setting rules for conflict regulation, for information flow, changing pay-off rules or professional codes

inter-organizational policy making (Scharpf 1978). Sometimes the manager has to try to deactivate actors because their involvement is not productive. Once the game has been started it is necessary to clarify the goals and perceptions of actors and to try to invest time and money in developing solutions that create opportunities for actors' participation (Koppenjan and Klijn 2004). But creating temporary organizational arrangements to facilitate interactions is also important. Of course, the transaction costs of these arrangements have to be kept as low as possible. And last but not least, the interactions in the game itself have to be managed. This can be done by appointing a process manager who invests time and energy in connecting the actions and strategies of actors to each other during the interactions.

At the network level, the manager also has opportunities for intervening. These strategies are highly time-consuming, however, and are often more open to conflict and criticism because of the normative questions which are often involved (Koppenjan and Klijn 2004). Nevertheless, one can see many of these strategies in practice where (mostly) central public actors are trying to achieve different outcomes by changing the rules for interactions, changing the positions of actors or using one of the other strategies that are shown in Table 11.1.

11.4.3 Effects of Network Management

What are the effects of these network management strategies on service delivery, outcomes of decision-making processes or the solving of wicked problems? It is very difficult to draw general conclusions regarding the necessity and effectiveness of network management.

The first observation that can be made on this topic is that most of the literature on networks claims that for a lot of societal problems hardly any options exist other than steering by network-like strategies. Especially for wicked problems, problems where a lot of actors are involved and there is much uncertainty about knowledge and disagreement about what the problem is and what the best solutions are, conventional unilateral steering does not usually work very well (Hanf and Scharpf 1978; Rhodes 1997; Agranoff and McGuire 2001). Public actors who want to solve societal problems quite simply need the information and resources of other actors. Furthermore, simple strategies of top—down steering and contracting are based on the assumption that there is a clear goal or product that can be managed by top—down steering and contracting. But frequently this assumption is just not fulfilled so that in many cases public managers are simply bound to all kinds of network-like strategies to achieve outcomes.

Network studies show that there are many obstacles to achieving interesting outcomes in complex decision processes. A lot of research has been conducted into various case studies of complex decision making in networks and the general picture that emerges from the research is that achieving interesting outcomes for the parties involved is not an easy job and much can and does go wrong. In particular, connecting the various actors' strategies to each other and reconciling differences in perceptions and goals requires a lot of energy on the part of the initiator and manager. An active role needs to be played by a network manager (or more than one network manager) in order to achieve interesting results (Gage and Mandell 1990; Alter and Hage 1993; Agranoff and McGuire 2003). But institutional obstacles can also prove a difficult element that hinders successful interaction (Klijn 2001; Koppenjan and Klijn 2004). Many of these studies indicate that the lack of active strategies on the part of network management contribute to failures in interaction (Hanf and Scharpf 1978; Hufen and Ringeling 1990; Mandell 2001; Bueren, Klijn, and Koppenjan 2003).

O'Toole and Meier, who collected data from a large number of Texas school superintendents in different educational districts, have done some interesting research. Superintendents were asked how frequently they interacted with key environmental actors (school boards, local business leaders, other superintendents, and the state education agency). These frequency rankings were used to produce a measurement of network management and were connected to indicators of success and failure in the different educational networks in the districts (Meier and O'Toole 2001). They found that managerial networking was positively correlated with primary goals (they used standardized test scores to measure effectiveness) but also with other indicators of organizational performance. Although Meier and O'Toole did not look at specific managerial strategies (such as those mentioned in Table 11.1) and thus were not able to assess the effect of certain types of strategies, their findings are nevertheless highly interesting and valuable.

The conclusion may be that the empirical research conducted so far points to the fact that network management does matter but that a lot of research still has to be done. The most interesting and necessary areas concern the question of which strategies seem to be most effective and the need for further research on the choice of management strategies by network managers.

11.5 EVALUATING OUTCOMES: A PROBLEMATIC ISSUE

An important question from a network or inter-organizational perspective on public management is how to evaluate outcomes of actors' interaction processes. Most traditional forms of evaluation start with a centrally formulated goal and try to assess the way in which this goal is achieved. This method is problematic from a network perspective, however.

11.5.1 Problems with Conventional Modes of Evaluation

The conventional mode of evaluating has its problems, of course, and these have now been extensively elaborated. It is sometimes difficult to determine the goals of a policy program or policy initiative because these goals are vague, not clearly stated, or change over time. These traditional problems have long been tackled in the evaluation literature, for instance by tracing how goals evolved (see, e.g., Patton 1997).

Yet this is not the essential problem from a network perspective. The main problem is that if one looks at it from this perspective there are a lot of actors involved, each with their own differing perceptions, goals, and strategies. It is not a clear case of which goal the evaluator should take as a starting point for evaluation, especially not if more that one public authority is involved. But even if there is only one public actor involved, the question still remains of whether the goals of this actor have to be the sole evaluation criteria. If one looks at interactions in policy making and management from a multi-actor perspective, it seems logical to look at evaluation from a multi-actor perspective too. It is not very likely, however, that the different actors will have a collectively formulated goal at the beginning of policy interactions that can serve as a keystone for evaluation.

But there are other problems too. From a network or inter-organizational perspective, interactions are complex and knowledge is spread among different actors. This means that a lot of information which could contribute to a satisfactory way of dealing with societal problems (and provide interesting solutions) has to be found and developed during the interaction process. If actors change their perceptions or goals as a result of additional information acquired during the process this can be an indication of learning, and learning is considered a very important aspect of inter-organizational interaction (Gage and Mandell 1990; Kickert, Klijn, and Koppenjan 1997). These learning effects cannot be taken into account if the evaluation is only carried out according to an a priori stated goal.

And last, but certainly not least, there is the problem of exclusion. If policy is being formed and implemented in networks of actors there is a danger of closedness and group-think. It is possible that actors will agree on packages of goals that lay the burden of the costs outside the network on actors who are not represented. Evaluation criteria of outcomes in networks should take this danger into account. Some of these problems are extensively tackled in the literature on evaluation, others are largely neglected, or not dealt with satisfactorily. It is not surprising that network literature has been looking for additional ways to evaluate policy outcomes

11.5.2 Towards a Multi-Actor Evaluation

An adequate yardstick for evaluating outcomes of some of the network literature comes with the solution provided by a multi-actor measurement. This means that evaluation has to be carried out by some method of weighting the various benefits for various actors (a kind of balance sheet) or by assessing their satisfaction afterwards (this is the other side of the coin or something similar to achieving collaborative advantages see: Huxham and Vangen 2000). This then provides an answer to learning processes and the fact that many actors are involved. Thus an outcome of interactions in networks is good if it satisfies a number of actors in the network. This not only takes into account the preferences and goals of the various actors but also measures whether they consider the time and energy spent on achieving those outcomes has been worthwhile (Kickert/Klijn/Koppenjan 1997).

There is of course a danger that actors will suggest rationalizations to hide their potential dissatisfaction with outcomes. A solution might be to take a wider look at the range of potential generated outcomes and to try to relate these outcomes to the interests of various actors. In this way the evaluator could produce a kind of short list or balanced score card of effects and their relations to actors' interests, goals or perceptions. This evaluation step is of course not without its problems because one has to decide which effects have to be taken into account and how they should be weighted. In that sense evaluation can become an ongoing discussion between evaluator and evaluated. This is a trend that fits within the discussion on frame reflection (Fisher and Forrester 1993; Schon and Rein 1994; Roe 1994), utilization-focused evaluation (Patton 1997), and involving stakeholders in evaluation processes. This notion of weighted interests or satisfying actors meets the need to take learning processes and shifting of goals into account as well as the need to evaluate outcomes in a multi-actor setting. It does not, however, provide a solution for the exclusion problem. To address this problem, evaluation also needs to pay attention to the way the process is conducted. In other words it is important that third parties have access to the decision-making process, that processes have legitimacy and that they meet criteria of juridical and procedural scrupulousness. These process norms are thus important additional criteria by which to judge outcomes of interaction processes in network and inter-organizational settings. This may involve strengthening the position of under-represented actors (see also Huxham 2000). If decision making is open to actors who are interested or have an interest in the issue and if the actors involved are satisfied, then this usually creates favorable conditions for ensuring that outcomes are socially good and preferable.

Note that in this sense evaluation criteria from a network perspective devote a lot of attention to the process and development of interesting outcomes at the expense of the previously formulated goals of one actor. This position is certainly not without its critics because, again, it places the goals and positions of (central) public actors in a less central position and it tends to regard a general interest as something which is formulated (and constructed) during the process after confronting problem solutions and information, rather that something which can be formulated in a clear way at the beginning. Learning, creating variety in information and solutions and promoting interaction and joint problem solving should contribute to interesting solutions which are supported by actors who have the indispensable resources to realise solutions for societal problem solving (Agranoff 2003; Koppenjan and Klijn 2004).

11.6 Some Critical Notes on a Network Perspective

Network and inter-organizational perspectives have generated several criticisms. Broadly speaking, the most important criticisms aimed at network theory have been (see Klijn and Koppenjan 2000):

- lack of theoretical foundation and clear concepts (Borzel 1998; Dowding 1995)
- lack of clear evaluation criteria
- neglect of the role of power (Brans 1997; Agranoff and McGuire 2001)
- lack of explanatory power (Dowding 1995; Blom-Hansen 1998; Pollitt 2003b)
- normative objections against networks and the role of public actors in this theory.

11.6.1 Rounding up the Usual Suspects: Some "Traditional Criticism"

The first critique does not appear to be a very valid one. We have shown that network and inter-organizational theory are solidly rooted in the tradition of public administration and certainly contain enough theoretical concepts and elaborations to be taken seriously. The fact that the network concept is used in different ways does not alter this conclusion. Bodies of literature or theoretical schools are not a "unity" but display varieties and differences in scope and flavour. As far as the criticism on evaluation criteria is concerned: in network and inter-organizational theory, attention is certainly devoted to evaluation questions (and this is not markedly less that in other bodies of literature) and as we have seen there are even some thought-provoking ideas on other ways to evaluate outcomes.

The same can be said of the third criticism on power. Almost all the literature on networks and inter-organizational relations builds heavily on the notion of resource dependencies and also includes the notion of a-symmetric power relations. Power then is connected to a-symmetry in resources and their importance. In this sense they build on the earlier work of the inter-organizational theorists (Levine and White 1961; Emerson 1962; further elaborated by Scharpf 1978). The underlying reason for this criticism is perhaps also a question of taste and disciplinary background. Many of the network and inter-organizational theorists are public administration academics or academics in the field of business administration while the critics are often political scientists. Whereas, in political science, power lies at the heart of every explanation this is not the case in Public Administration. Although it does not lie at the heart of every explanation in network theory, attention is certainly devoted to the notion of power. In so far as network literature pays attention to rules (especially informal rules shaped by actors in past interactions) the invisible side of power (the mobilization of bias because of rules that constitute meaning and close networks to outsiders) is also taken into account. Network theory, however, also sees important explanations other than power differences for the stagnation in policy processes such as differences in perceptions, a lack of interaction and organizational arrangements between actors, and institutional obstacles (such as conflicting rules in different networks). Generally speaking, therefore, the first three criticisms are not particularly impressive and appear to provide easy sticks with which to beat a "newcomer" in Public Administration theory.

11.6.2 Further Criticism: Explanatory Power, Attention to the Political Dimension and Normative Questions

The points relating to explanatory power and the normative aspects are more interesting criticisms. In the first place, because they contain a wide variety of critiques and because they concern some sections of the literature more than others: but there are also some points of criticism which seem more important that those previously mentioned.

The criticism relating to the explanatory power of network and inter-organizational theories is a discussion occurring on two levels simultaneously. It is a discussion about whether the literature provides any explanation at all and at the same time a discussion about what type of explanations might be involved. Dowding (1995) has criticized network theory (and especially the British work on policy communities) for the fact that most of the explanations are at the actor level and not at the network level. In this sense, the theories do not greatly differ from other theories (Pollitt 2003b). This criticism certainly holds for a substantial part of the literature. The structural features of networks have had too little attention focused on them in network research so far. These features can, however, be studied in more ways than simply by using network analysis—e.g., quantitative mapping of patterns of interactions—as Dowding propagates. Mapping the interactions does not provide the analyst with any more (though also not less!) than a static picture of the pattern of interactions between actors at any given moment. The research can, for instance, also be directed toward rules actors formed in earlier interactions and the effects of those rules on interactions around issues. But then again, the mapping could also be directed to the perceptions of actors, for instance. So although network theory is certainly far more than a metaphor (see Klijn and Koppenjan 2000), the fact that more attention needs to be devoted to the structural characteristics of networks is a justified point in the criticism.

The same holds for attention to normative issues, especially the problem of accountability in networks and the relation between horizontal forms of govern-ance and existing democratic institutions. Existing democratic institutions have a strong focus on vertical forms of accountability. This sometimes contrasts with the empirical and normative reality of forms of horizontal governance (see Koppenjan and Klijn 2004).

This tension is also visible in recent experiments in many western European countries to involve citizens in complex interaction processes in networks. The new horizontal forms of governance inspired by ideas of more participative democracy often do not mix very well with the traditional political institutions (Edelenbos and Monninkhof 2001; Klijn and Koppenjan 2000b; McLaverty 2002).

A lot of the literature on networks and inter-organizational coordination has a strong managerial flavor. There is nothing wrong with that, although it certainly tends to pay too little attention on the problem of accountability. On those occasions when attention *is* being paid to the issue it is usually in the sense that networks have to be opened up to other actors so that process norms ensure a good weighting of values (see the previous chapter). The problem, however, is that although this solution does improve the transparency of choices that are made, it does not resolve the tension between elected politicians and horizontal forms of governance. This is partly an eternal problem according to the literature on iron triangles and power dating back fifty years. Network literature should therefore probably push the research in the direction of examining how the connections between democracy and horizontal complex forms of decision making can be redesigned using institutional design. This is a controversial path as has been proved by the criticism that has already been aimed at network theories on this point (see Pollitt 2003b). However, the problem of complex horizontal interaction processes which can be empirically observed and that do not match the normative rules and expectations of citizens, politicians and others remains pressing. From a network theory perspective, the theme of accountability can only be addressed logically and in an innovative way to connect it to ideas of promoting openness and value weighting and by looking at and devising attempts to redesign political and other accountability. This is certainly one of the most challenging and necessary research areas for network theory in the coming years.

11.6.3 Some Points for Future Research

We may conclude that the network perspective offers an interesting and promising theoretical perspective. It has generated a lot of empirical material on the complexity of policy making and implementation processes, on the need for extensive horizontal and unorthodox forms of management, and insights into the relative closedness of networks.

Further development is certainly needed, especially in the area of how to analyze structural features of networks and to relate these to interactions around policy initiatives that take place in networks. In addition, the fact that many policy initiatives require the involvement of different networks, whereby institutional features of networks can clash, needs more research. And last, but certainly not least, more attention needs to be devoted to the relationship between horizontal forms of managing and the problem of accountability in networks. The key question to be answered by network theory in the near future is: how can accountability be arranged or, more likely, rearranged so that it ties in with and addresses the problem of the empirical complex world of networks where resources are dispersed, actors have opportunities to block decisions and societal problems can only be solved by the involvement of a large group of actors. And then a final question that is connected to that one: how may citizens be involved in such complex decision-making processes and how may they be tied to the "traditional" institutions of parliamentary democracy?

NOTES

1. Although there are less of these concepts than there are of concepts tied to actor characteristics (see for this criticism Dowding 1995).
2. This statement not only holds for traditional public administration studies and a lot of implementation studies which implicitly take central goals of central (departmental) actors as a starting point for analysis (see for instance the classical work of Pressman and Wildavsky 1983 and 1973), but also more recent theories such as the ideas expressed in New Public Management and many contracting theories.

REFERENCES

AGRANOFF, R. I. (1986), *Intergovernmental Management. Human Services Problem-Solving in Six Metropolitan Areas*, Albany, New York: State University of New York Press.
—— (2003), *Leveraging networks: a guide for public managers working across organizations*, Arlington: IBM Endowment for The Business of Government.
——, and McGUIRE, M. (2001), "Big Questions in Public Network Management Research," *Journal of Public Administration Research and Theory* 11: 295–326.

—— —— (2003), *Collaborative Public Management: New Strategies for Local Governments*, Washington, DC: Georgetown University Press.

AIKEN, M., and HAGE, J. (1968), "Organizational Interdependence and Intra-organizational Structure," *American Sociological Review* 33 (6): 912–30.

ALDRICH, H. A. *Organizations and environments*, Englewood Cliffs: 1979.

ALLISON, G. T. (1971), *Essence of Decision*, Boston: Little Brown.

ALTER, C., and HAGE, J. (1993) *Organizations working together*, Newbury Park: Sage.

BLOM-HANSEN, J. (1997), "A New Institutional Perspective on Policy Networks," *Public Administration* 75: 669–93.

BÖRZEL, T. A. (1998), "Organising Babylon: On the Different Conceptions of Policy Networks," *Public Administration* 76: 253–73.

BRANS, M. (1997), "Challenges to the Practice and Theory of Public Administration in Europe," *Journal of Theoretical Politics* 9(3): 389–415.

BRYSON, J. M., and CROSBY, B. (1992), *Leadership for the Common Good; Tackling Public Problems in a Shared Power World*, San Francisco: Jossey-Bass.

CASTELLS, M. (1997), *The Power and Identity*, Cambridge: Blackwell.

—— (2000, first edn. 1996), The Rise of the Network Society: Economy, Society and Culture, Cambridge: Blackwell.

DAHL, R. A. (1961), *Who governs? Democracy and Power in an American City*, New Haven: Yale University Press.

DERY, D. (1984), *Problem Definition in Policy Analsysis*, Kansas: University Press of Kansas.

DOWDING, K. (1995), "Model or Metaphor? A Critical Review of the Policy network Approach," *Political Studies* 43: 136–58.

EDELENBOS, J. and MONNINKHOF, R. A. H. (eds.) (2001), *Lokale interactieve beleidsvorming*, Utrecht: Lemma.

EMERSON, R. M. (1962), "Power-dependence Relations," *American Sociological Review*, 27: 31–40.

FAULKNER, D. (1995), *International Strategic Alliances*, London: Mc Graw Hill.

FISCHER, F., and FORESTER, J. (eds.) (1993), *The Argumentative Turn in Policy Analysis and Planning*, Duke Durham, NC: University Press.

FRIEND, J. K., POWER, J. M., and YEWLETT, C. J. L. (1974) *Public Planning: The Inter-corporate Dimension*, London: Tavistock.

GAGE, R. W., and MANDELL, M. P. (eds.) (1990), *Strategies for Managing Intergovernmental Policies and Networks*, New York: Praeger.

GRAEBER, G. (1993), *The Embedded Firm: Understanding Networks: Actors, Resources and Processes in Interfirm Cooperation*, London: Routledge.

HANF, K., and SCHARPF, F. W. (1978), *Interorganizational Policy Making: Limits to Coordination and Central Control*.

—— and TOONEN, TH. A. J. (eds.) (1985), *Policy Implementation in Federal and Unitary Systems*, Dordrecht: Nijhoff.

HJERN, B., and PORTER, D. O. (1981), "Implementation Structures: A New Unit for Administrative Analysis," *Organizational Studies* 3: 211–37.

HINDMOOR, A., (1998), "The Importance of Being Trusted: Transaction Costs and Policy Network Theory," *Public Administration* 76: 25–43.

HUFEN, J. A. M., and RINGELING, A. B. (1990), *Beleidsnetwerken; Overheids-semiover heidsen particulire organisaties in wisselwerking*, Vuga: 's-Gravenhage.

HUNT, J. W. (1972), *The Restless Organization*, Sydney: Wiley.

HUXHAM, C. (2000), "The Challenge of Collaborative Government," *Public Management Review* 2: 337–57.

—— and VANGEN, S. (2000), "What Makes Partnerships Work?", in S. Osborne (ed.), *Public-Private Partnerships: Theory and Practice in International Perspective*, London: Routledge.

KAUFMANN, F. X., MAJONE, G., and OSTROM, V. (eds.) (1986), *Guidance, Control and Evaluation in the Public Sector: The Bielefeld Interdisciplinary Project*, Berlin: Walter de Gruyter.

KICKERT, W. J. M., KLIJN, E. H., and KOPPENJAN, J. F. M. (eds.) (1997), *Managing complex networks; strategies for the public sector*, London: Sage.

KINGDON, J. W. (1984), *Agendas, Alternatives and public policies*, Boston and Toronto.

KLIJN, E. H. (2001), "Rules as Institutional Context for Decision Making in Networks: The Approach to Post-war Housing Districts in Two Cities," *Administration and Society* 33(3): 133–64.

—— and KOPPENJAN, J. F. M (2000*a*), "Public Management and Policy Networks; Foundations of a Network Approach to Governance," *Public Management* 2(2): 135–58.

—— —— (2000*b*), "Politicians and Interactive Decision Making: Institutional Spoilsports or Playmakers," *Public Administration* 78(2): 365–87.

KOPPENJAN, J. F. M., and KLIJN, E. H. (2004), *Managing Uncertainties in Networks: A Network Approach to Problem Solving and Decision Making*, London: Routledge.

—— RINGELING, A. B., and te VELDE, R. H. A. (eds.) (1987), *Beleidsvorming in Nederland*, Vuga: 's-Gravenhage.

LAUMANN, E. O., and KNOKE, D. (1987), *The Organizational State: Social Choice in National Policy Domains*, Wisconsin: University of Wisconsin Press.

LEVINE, S., and WHITE, P. E. (1961), "Exchange as a Conceptual Framework for the Study of Interorganizational Relationships," *Administrative Science Quarterly* 5: 583–601.

LINDBLOM, C. E., and COHEN, D. K. (1979), *Usable Knowledge: Social Science and Social Problem Solving*, New Haven: Yale University Press.

LITWAK, E., and HYLTON, L. F. (1962), "Interorganizational Analysis: A Hypothesis on Co-ordinating Agencies," *Administrative Science Quarterly* 6 (4): 395–420.

LOWNDES, V., and SKELCHER, C. (1998), "The Dynamics of Multi-organisational Partnerships: An Analysis of Changing Modes of Governance," *Public Administration* 76(2): 313–34.

LYNN, L. E. (1981) *Managing the Public's Business, The Job of the Government Executive*, New York: Basic Books.

MC LAVERTY, P. (ed.) (2002), *Public participation and innovations in community governance*, Aldershot: Ashgate.

MANDELL, M. P. (ed.) (2001), *Getting Results through Collaboration: Networks and Network Structures for Public Policy and Management*, Westport, CT: Quorum Books.

MARIN, B., and MAYNTZ, R. (eds.) (1991), *Policy Networks: Empirical Evidence and Theoretical Considerations*, Boulder, CO: Westview Press.

MARSH, D. (ed.) (1998), *Comparing Policy Networks in British Government*, Oxford: Clarendon Press.

—— and RHODES, R. A. W. (eds.) (1992), *Policy Networks in British Government*, Oxford: Clarendon Press.

MEIER, K. J., and O'TOOLE, L. J. (2001), "Managerial Strategies and Behaviour in Networks: A Model with Evidence from U.S. Public Education," *Journal of Public Administration and Theory* 11(3): 271–93.

MILWARD, H. B. and WAMSLEY, G. L. (1985), "Policy Subsystems, Networks and the Tools of Public Management," in Hanf and Toonen 1985: 105–130.

—— and PROVAN, K. G. (2000), "Governing the Hollow State," *Journal of Public Administration Research and Theory* 10(2): 359–79.

NEWMAN, J. (2003) "New Labour and the politics of governance", in: A. Salminen et al., *Governance in networks*, Amsterdam: IOS Press.

NOOTEBOOM, B. (1998), *Management van Partnerships*, Schoonhoven: Academic Service.

OSBORNE, S. P. (ed.) (2000), *Public–Private Partnerships: Theory and Practice in International Perspective*, London: Routledge.

OSTROM, E. (1986), "A Method for Institutional Analysis," in Kaufmann, Majone and Ostrom 1986: 459–79.

O'TOOLE, L. J. (1988), "Strategies for Intergovernmental Management: Implementing Programs in Interorganizational Networks," *Journal of Public Administration* 11(4): 417–41.

PATTON, M. (1997), *Utilization Focused Evaluation*, 3rd edn., London: Sage.

PFEFFER, J. (1981), *Power in Organizations*, Boston: Pitman.

POLLITT, C. (2003a), "Joined-up Government: A Survey," *Political Studies Review* 1: 34–49.

—— (2003b), *The Essential Manager*, Maidenhead: Open University Press.

—— and BOUCKAERT, G. (2000), *Public Management Reform: A Comparative Analysis*, Oxford: Oxford University Press.

PUTNAM, R. D. (1995), "Tuning in, Tuning out: The Strange Disappearance of Social Capital in America," *Political Science and Politics* 12: 664–83.

REIN, M., and SCHÖN, D. A. (1992), "Reframing Policy Discourse," in F. Fischer and J. Forester (eds.), *The Argumentative Turn in Policy Analysis and Planning*, Durham NC: Duke University Press.

RHODES, R. A. W. (1988), *Beyond Westminster and Whitehall: The Sub-central Goverments of Britain*, London: Unwin Hyman.

—— (1997), *Understanding Governance*, Buckingham: Open University Press.

ROBBINS, S. P. (1980), *The Administrative Process*, Englewood Cliffs, NJ: Prentice Hall.

ROE, E. M. (1994), *Narrative Policy Analysis: Theory and Practice*, Durham/London: Duke University Press.

SCHARPF, F. W. (1978), "Interorganizational Policy Studies: Issues, Concepts and Perspectives," in Hanf and Scharpf 1978: 345–70.

—— (1997), *Games Real Actors Play: Actor-Centered Institutionalism in Policy Research*, Boulder, CO: Westview Press.

SCHON, D. A. and REIN, M. (1994), *Frame reflection: toward the resolution of intractable policy controversies*, New York: Basis Books.

SOCIAAL CULTUREEL PLANBUREAU (2000), *Sociaal Cultureel Rapport: Nederland in Europa*, Vuga: 's-Gravenhage.

TEISMAN, G. R. (1997), *Sturen via creatieve concurrentie*, Nijmegen: Katholieke Universiteit Nijmegen.

TRUMAN, D. (1964), *The Governmental Process*, New York: Knopf.

WEICK, K. E. (1979), *The Social Psychology of Organizing*, 2nd edn., New York.

ZIJDERVELD, A. C. (1974), *Institutionalisering: een studie over het methodologische dilemma der sociale wetenschappen*, Meppel: Boom.

CHAPTER 12

WHATEVER HAPPENED TO PUBLIC ADMINISTRATION?

GOVERNANCE, GOVERNANCE EVERYWHERE

H. GEORGE FREDERICKSON

12.1 THE CONCEPT OF "GOVERNANCE"

FOR at least the last fifteen years governance has been a prominent subject in public administration.[1] Governance, defined by Lynn, Heinrich, and Hill as the "regimes, laws, rules, judicial decisions, and administrative practices that constrain, prescribe, and enable the provision of publicly supported goals and services," holds strong interest for public administration scholars (2001: 7). This chapter reviews and evaluates the evolution and development of the concept of governance in public administration; then, using regime theory from the study of international relations, the concept of governance as applied in public administration is analyzed, parsed, and framed.

The present scholarly and conceptual use of the concept of governance in the field tends to take one or more of the following forms:

1. It is substantively the same as already established perspectives in public administration, although in a different language.
2. It is essentially the study of the contextual influences that shape the practices of public administration, rather than the study of public administration.
3. It is the study of inter-jurisdictional relations and third-party policy implementation in public administration.
4. It is the study of the influence or power of non-state and non-jurisdictional public collectives.

Of these approaches to public administration as governance, it is the third and fourth—governance as the public administration of inter-jurisdiction relations and third party policy implementation, and the governance of non-state and non-jurisdictional public collectives—that form the basis of a usable theory of governance for public administration.

It was Harlan Cleveland who first used the word "governance" as an alternative to the phrase public administration. In the mid-1970s, one of the themes in Cleveland's particularly thoughtful and provocative speeches, papers, and books went something like this: "What the people want is less government and more governance" (1972). What he meant by governance was the following cluster of concepts.

The organizations that get things done will no longer be hierarchical pyramids with most of the real control at the top. They will be systems—interlaced webs of tension in which control is loose, power diffused, and centers of decision plural. "Decision-making" will become an increasingly intricate process of multilateral brokerage both inside and outside the organization which thinks it has the responsibility for making, or at least announcing, the decision. Because organizations will be horizontal, the way they are governed is likely to be more collegial, consensual, and consultative. The bigger the problems to be tackled, the more real power is diffused and the larger the number of persons who can exercise it—if they work at it. (p. 13)

Like many, Cleveland saw the blurring of the distinctions between public and private organizations, and he associated this blurring with his conception of governance. He reasoned through what it meant as follows: "These new style public-private horizontal systems will be led by a new breed of man and women. I call them Public Executives, people who manage public responsibilities whether in 'public' or 'private' organizations" (p. 14).

Cleveland clearly understood the challenges of individual accountability associated with horizontal multi-organizational systems. Who, exactly, do these modern public executives work for and to whom are they accountable? Consider this remarkably bold argument: "Public ethics are in the hearts and minds of individual Public Executives, and the ultimate court of appeals from their judgments is some surrogate for people-in-general" (p.117). Note, that he does not argue that accountability is ultimately to the people or to the elected officials of one's jurisdiction. Cleveland's idea of public responsibility is much bigger than that. The moral responsibility of public executives includes basic considerations of four fundamental principles: "a sense of welfare; a sense of equity; a sense of achievement; and a sense of participating" (pp. 126–7).

What would be the results of such a grand conception of the moral responsibility of the public administrator?

In a society characterized by bigness and complexity it is those individuals who learn to get things done in organizational systems who will have a rational basis for feeling free. (p. 135)

By the development of their administrative skills, and by coming squarely to terms with the moral requirements of executive leadership, individual men and women can preserve and extend their freedom. Freedom is the power to choose, and the future executive will be making the most choices—whom to bring together in which organizations, to make what happen, in whose interpretation of the public interest. Those who relish that role will have every reason to feel free, not in the interstices but right in the middle of things. (p. 140)

Governance is an especially important word/concept because of the mismatch or disconnect between jurisdictions on one hand and social, technological, political, and economic problems on the other hand. Cleveland understood this, too: "One of the striking ironies of our time is that, just when we have to build bigger, more complicated 'bundles of relations' to deal comprehensively with the human consequences of science and technology, many people are seized with the idea that large-scale organization is itself a Bad Thing. My thesis is the reverse" (pp. 139–40). Big problems, Cleveland believes, require big responses. Those responses will, however, be multi-organizational and will involve both public and private organizations. These responses will, pace Cleveland, be led by not one, but many, leaders.

In the thirty years since Cleveland's initial conception, it would be only a slight exaggeration to say governance has become the subject formerly known as public administration. A leading academic journal, now in its sixteenth year, carries the title *Governance: An International Journal of Policy and Administration*. A careful examination indicates that its contents have mostly to do with what was once called public administration. The most popular and widely read magazine for American state and local governments is *Governing: The Magazine of States and Localities*, now in its fifteenth year. The Brookings Institution recently changed the name of its highly regarded " Governmental Studies" program to " Governance Studies" and launched a series of studies of governance (Benner, Reinicke, and Witte 2003; Birdsall 2003; Graham and Litan 2003; Woods 2003). Scholars at the Kennedy School of Government at Harvard are midway through a large project that has the title, "Visions of Governance in the 21st Century." Schools of governance, teaching graduate curricula not unlike public administration graduate curricula in both Europe and the United States, are now found at several important European universities. In the early 1990s the National Academy of Public Administration essentially dropped the phrase "public administration" in favor of the word "governance," although the work of the Academy continues to be primarily public administration consulting (Fosler 1998). "In much of the modern literature in the field, governance has become a virtual synonym for public management and public administration" (Frederickson and Smith 2003: 225). The problem is that governance has dozens of meanings. Lynn, Heinrich, and Hill say it best:

The term "governance" is widespread in both public and private sectors, in characterizing both global and local arrangements, and in reference to both formal and informal norms and understandings. Because the term has strong intuitive appeal, precise definitions are seldom thought to be necessary by those who use it. As a result, when authors identify "governance" as important to achieving policy or organizational objectives, it may be unclear whether the reference is to organizational structure, administrative processes, managerial judgment, systems of incentives and rules, administrative philosophies, or a combination of these elements.

From Cleveland's tightly defined presentation of what governance was understood to be, and from his carefully set out descriptions of the implications of that understanding, governance is now everywhere and appears to mean anything and everything (Rhodes 2000). Because governance is a power word, a dominant descriptor, and the current preference of academic tastemakers, there has been a rush to affix to it all of the other fashions of the day. Governance is the structure of political institutions. Governance is the shift from the bureaucratic state to the hollow state or to third-party government (Milward and Provan 2000; Salamon 2002; Rhodes 1997). Governance is market-based approaches to government (Kettle 1993; Nye and Donahue 2000). Governance is the development of social capital, civil society, and high levels of citizen participation (Hirst 2000; Kooiman 2001; Sorensen 2004). Governance is the work of empowered, muscular, risk-taking public entrepreneurs (Osborne and Gaebler 1992). In the United Kingdom governance is Tony Blair's "third way," a political packaging of the latest ideas in new public management, expanded forms of political participation, and attempts to renew civil society (Newman 2001). Governance is the new public management or managerialism (Kernaghan, Marson, and Borins 2000). Governance is public-sector performance (Heinrich and Lynn 2000). Governance is interjurisdictional cooperation and network management (Frederickson 1999; O'Toole 2003; Peters and Pierre 1998). Governance is globalization and rationalization (Pierre 2000). Governance is corporate oversight, transparency, and accounting standards (Monks and Minow 2004; Jensen 2000; Blair and MacLaury 1995).

In all, Rhodes (2000: 55–60) found seven applications of governance in the field of public administration: the new public management or managerialism; good governance, as in efficiency, transparency, meritocracy, and equity; international and inter-jurisdictional interdependence; non-government driven forms of socio-cybernetic systems of governance; the new political economy, including shifting from state service provision to the state as regulator; and networks. There are many more applications of governance to the subject once known as public administration, but these few illustrate the capacious range of concepts, ideas, and theories associated with it.

There are as many definitions of the concept of governance as a synonym for public administration as there are applications. Kettl claims an emerging gap between government and governance. "Government refers to the structure and function of public institutions. Governance is the way government gets its job done. Traditionally, government itself managed most service delivery. Toward the end of the twentieth century, however, government relied increasingly on non-governmental partners to do its work, through processes that relied less on authority for control" (2002: xi). To Kettl, governance, as an approach to public administration, has primarily to do with contracting-out and grants to sub-governments.

As was noted at the outset, Lynn, Heinrich, and Hill (2001: 15) use a much bigger approach to governance as an analytic framework. Their model, intended to be a starting point for research, is:

O = f [E, C, T, S, M]
  Where:
O = Outputs/outcomes. The end product of a governance regime.
E = Environmental factors. These can include political structures, levels of authority, economic performance, the presence or absence of competition among suppliers, resource levels and dependencies, legal framework, and the characteristics of a target population.
C = Client characteristics. The attributes, characteristics, and behavior of clients.
T = Treatments. These are the primary work or core processes of the organizations within the governance regime. They include organizational missions and objectives, recruitment and eligibility criteria, methods fro determining eligibility, and program treatments or technologies.
S = Structures. These include organizational type, level of coordination and integration among the organizations in the governance regime, relative degree of centralized control, functional differentiation, administrative rules or incentives, budgetary allocations, contractual arrangements or relationships, and institutional culture and values.
M = Managerial roles and actions. This includes leadership characteristics, staff-management relations, communications, methods of decision making, professional/career concerns, and mechanisms of monitoring, control, and accountability.

The problem is that it is difficult, following Lynn, Heinrich, and Hill, to conceive of anything involving government, politics, or administration that is not governance. That being the case, there appears to be little difference between studying the whole of government and politics and studying public administration. Put another way, public administration is ordinarily thought to have to do with "treatments," "structures," and "management" in the Lynn, et al. governance formula. They tuck the centerpieces of public administration into the broader context of governance. This chapter will later return to these distinctions and to a large-scale synthesis of governance research by Lynn, Heinrich and Hill.

Peters uses an equally big definition of governance as "institutions designed to exercise collective control and influence" (1995: 3). Peters, and Peters with Pierre (2000), settles on the "steering" characteristics of governance as distinct from government.

Public institutions continue to bear the primary responsibility for steering the economy and society. Government may, however, be able to discharge that fundamental responsibility through means other than direct imposition of authority, or use other instruments not requiring directly government involvement in the social processes being influenced. Governance, in the words of Walter Kikert (1997), is "steering at a distance." This style of steering is more palatable politically in an era in which there is significant public resistance to the state and its more intrusive forms of intervention. (Peters 1995: 86)

Doubtless the most comprehensive synthesis of governance as public administration is found in B. Guy Peters' *The Future of Governing* (2001). Like many approaches to governance that use a narrow reading of public administration as a straw man, Peters "sets up" public administration as the old-time religion, riddled with identity crises. Traditional public administration is "five old chestnuts," modeled on an institutionalized and apolitical civil service, organizational hierarchy and rules, a preoccupation with permanence and stability, and reams of internal regulations (Peters 2001: 4–13). These elements of the old-time public administration religion would be recognized by any of the members of that church, all of them having been part of the internal critique of the field long before governance ever appeared (Frederickson and Smith 2003). Traditional public administration, following Peters, floundered because of disappointments in governmental performance, changing demographics, overly large and cumbersome governments, and several other deficits. Governance reform, particularly as seen in Great Britain, New Zealand, Australia, and the United States is modeled on various contributions of four different approaches to public administration—markets and competition, participative administration, greater flexibility, and deregulation. In Table 12.1, Peters provides an excellent summation of the characteristics of these four governance models. Each of these models would be instantly recognized by any senior student of public administration as a part of the literature and theory of the field, entirely independent of applications of the models to governance. Public administration scholars have also long recognized the normative content of each of the models, as does Peters. The question is: Does the application of governance as

Table 12.1 Major features of four models of governance as public administration

	Market Government	Participative Government	Flexible Government	Deregulated Government
Principal diagnosis	Monopoly	Hierarchy	Permanence	Internal regulation
Structure	Decentralization	Flatter organizations	"Virtual organizations"	No particular recommendation
Management	Pay for performance; other private-sector techniques	TQM; teams	Managing temporary personnel	Greater managerial freedom
Policymaking	Internal markets; market incentives	Consultation; negotiation	Experimentation	Entrepreneurial government
Public Interest	Low cost	Involvement; consultation	Low cost; coordination	Creativity; activism

Source: Peters 2001: 21

either as a theory or an analytic framework add value to broader long-standing approaches to public administration? (See particularly Wilson 1989 and Frederickson and Smith 2003.)

Are these so-called governance concepts, with their attendant possible meanings, really useful to students of public administration and public management? Do they add anything of consequence to our understanding of the field? Do they merely repackage public administration in a newer and rather fuzzy language? Could the use of the governance concept have a negative influence on our theory building and research scholarship, obfuscating and confusing rather than clarifying and illuminating, and distorting by concealing bias rather than revealing and removing it? The validity and usefulness of the governance concept can be challenged on at least five rather fundamental grounds. These five points lead, in turn, to two implications or indirect criticisms that question whether further use of the concept of governance as an organizing concept for public administration and management has the potential to contribute substantially to our understanding of the field and ought to be encouraged by leading scholars in the field.

First, the concept of governance is fashionable, the favorite of academic taste-makers, the flavor not only of the month but also of the year and the decade. Does the governance concept bring anything particularly new to the public administration table? Much of the governance literature is "a rehash of old academic debates under a new and jazzier name—a sort of intellectual mutton dressed up as lamb—so that pushy new professors . . . can have the same old arguments as their elders but can flatter themselves that they are breaking new ground by using new jargon" (Strange 1983: 341). Fashions change, and we may already have reached the half-life of the hegemony of governance as an organizing concept for the field. In the same way that miniskirts come and go, so too could governance.

Second, the concept is imprecise, wooly, and, when applied, so broad that virtually any meaning can be attached to it. As described earlier in this chapter, governance, at least at this point, does not have an agreed-upon meaning. Fortunately, some who use the term are serious about the matter of definition and precision; others however are not. Still, there is little doubt that the word governance is useful as a way to describe, as Cleveland does, patterns of inter-jusridictional and inter-organizational relations. The matter of precision in definition is considered again at the close of this chapter.

Third, the concept of governance is freighted with values, values often stated in ways that imply that certain things are understood and agreed-upon when, in fact, they are not. Some approaches to governance as public administration tends to wrap together anti-bureaucratic and anti-governmental sentiments, preferences for markets over governments, and preferences for limited government—all points-of-view masked as given, understood, and agreed-upon (Kernaghan, Marson, and Borins 2000; Osborn and Gaebler 1992). Not the least of the value problems generally associated with some uses of the concept of governance, are its democratic deficits. Standard models of democratic government involve a limited state that is controlled by representative government bound by the rule of law, and also a largely self-organizing civil society independent of the state but protected by the state's laws and administrative procedures. Some models of governance, however, either discount the significance of jurisdictionally based democratic traditions or fail to take them into account, most notably the Osborn and Gaebler reinventing government model (1992; see also Hirst 2000; E. Sorensen 2002). Other models are deeply contextual, based on constitutional, legal, organizational, and political influences and imperatives (Lynn, Heinrich, and Hill 2001). These models are state and jurisdiction-centered understandings of governance in which public administration is contingent on artifacts of constitutions, rules, laws, and politics. This perspective on governance in public administration makes the subject both bigger and grander, a kind of un-public administration.

Fourth, scholars who use the word governance, particularly in Europe, claim that governance is primarily about change, about reform, about getting things right. In addition to the scholars there are policy entrepreneurs using the word governance to lend importance to their policy projects. Such perspectives almost always begin with the notion that things are broken and need to be fixed. Investments in our prevailing institutions, our cities, states, and nations and their established governments are devalued, as are the accomplishments of those institutions. Order, stability, and predictability are likewise undervalued. Governance, it is claimed, is about dynamic change, about reform. It is interesting to remember that the origins of American public administration were closely associated with reform and with the progressive project of the late nineteenth and early twentieth centuries.

In most of the more precise scholarly literature, despite the rhetoric of reform, governance is mostly about order and about how politicians and bureaucrats adapt in orderly ways to changing circumstances and values. There is a surface dynamic to governance as a form of orderly adaptation using the logic of the diffusion of innovation, and so-called best practices borrowed from other organizations or jurisdictions. But the underlying values of governance are not primarily about change, they are about order. Most descriptions of elements of governance—networks, inter-organizational and inter-jurisdictional cooperation, power-sharing federations, public–private partnerships, and contracting-out—are forms of institutional adaptation in the face of increasing interdependence.

Fifth, governance is often centered on non-state institutions—both nonprofit and for-profit contractors, non-governmental organizations, intergovernmental organizations, parastatals, and third parties generally. State- and jurisdiction-centered theory and research is, from some governance perspectives, passé. In the name of the "hollowed-out" thesis, many have criticized that part of the governance perspective that emphasizes privatization, contracting-out, and public–private partnerships (Rhodes 1997; Newman 2001; Milward and Provan 2000).

In their convictions regarding the superiority of the market over the polity, advocates for this governance perspective appear to somehow imagine that there can be governance without government (Peters and Pierre 1998). At a minimum, when this perspective is implemented it seriously diminishes the capacity of the core state executive to steer (Rhodes 2000). Indeed, it can be argued that under hollow-state conditions steering is reversed, the state being steered by its governance partners (Kettl 1993; Frederickson 1999). It is the states and their subjurisdictions that deal with the vexing problems of race, poverty, and justice. In the words of Janet Newman, "It is noticeable that theories of governance fail to deal adequately with the issues of diversity and patterns of inclusion on which it is based" (2001: 171).

From this sketchy critique of governance, two important implications arise. One is that the governance approach to the study of public management and administration emphasizes theory and research, explaining change and reform rather than the functioning of jurisdictions—cities, states, nations, and certain regional or global institutions—which are, after all, the dominant and preferred way to practice governance. Public administration, in practice, is about organization, bureaucracy, and management and the context in which they happen. What people often value about the jurisdictions in which they live and, by implication, the bureaucracies working for those jurisdictions, is the order, predictability, stability, and permanence they provide. National and local identity is important to the people. When will people sing an anthem to a contractor, wear the uniform of a network, or pledge allegiance to non-jurisdictional forms of governance? Probably not soon. Governance scholarship tends to ignore or at least de-emphasize the vast world of non-governance that lies deep in the folds of jurisdiction, organization, and bureaucracy. Are we better off as theorists if we focus on governance and not on government organization, bureaucracy, and management?

Concepts of governance as public administration reflect a long-standing theoretical debate in the field, the matter of distinctions between politics, and policy on one hand and policy implementation or administration on the other. Easy dismissal of the politics-administration dichotomy serves to focus the study of public administration, particularly by some governance theorist, on the constitutional and political context of the organization and management of the territorial state or jurisdiction. From this perspective governance becomes steering and public administration becomes rowing, a lesser phenomenon in the scholarly pecking order, not to mention a lesser subject in governance. Public administration, thus understood, is the work that governments contract-out, leaving governance as the subject of our study. Although the lines between politics, policy, and administration are often fuzzy and changing, and although we know, strictly speaking, there is not a politics–administration dichotomy, it is nevertheless important to understand the empirical distinctions between political and administrative phenomena. Concepts of governance that advance our understanding of public-sector administration and organization are helpful. Concepts of governance that simply change the subject of public administration to politics and policy making are not. In democratic government it is, after all, elected officials who govern. Bureaucrats have roles and responsibilities for governing or governance, but in democratic polities these roles and responsibilities are different than the roles and responsibilities of elected officials. Janet Newman says it well: "Neither 'good governance' nor 'well-managed government' could resolve the contradictions around the popular role of government and the appropriate boundaries of governance" (2001: 170). In the name of stamping out bureaucracy and replacing it with what they describe as good governance, Osborn and Gaebler advocate a range of managerial prerogatives that would significantly intrude on the political and policy-making prerogatives generally assumed to belong to elected officials, and particularly elected legislators, in a democratic polity (1992).

The second implication of the critique is that governance theorists persist in looking for an all-pervasive pattern of organizational and administrative behavior, a "general theory" that will provide an explanation for the past and a means to predict the future. Despite the accumulated evidence based on decades of work on theory and the empirical testing of theory in public administration, no such pattern has been found (Frederickson and Smith 2003). Does the governance concept beguile a generation of scholars to set off in the vain search for a metatheoretical El Dorado (Olsen 2003)?

12.2 CONSTRUCTING A VIABLE CONCEPT OF GOVERNANCE FOR PUBLIC ADMINISTRATION

Although the critique of governance is a serious challenge, does it render the concept useless? The answer is no. There are powerful forces at work in the world, forces that the traditional study of politics, government, and public administration do not explain. The state and its sub-jurisdictions are losing important elements of their sovereignty; borders have less and less meaning. Social and economic problems and challenges are seldom contained within jurisdictional boundaries, and systems of communication pay little attention to them. Business is increasingly regional or global. Business elites have multiple residences and operate extended networks that are highly multi-jurisdictional. States and jurisdictions are hollowing-out their organization and administrative capacities, exporting to contractors much of the work of public administration.

Governance, even with its weakness, is the most useful available concept for describing and explaining these forces. But for governance to become anything more than passing fashion or a dismissive un-public administration, it must respond to the critique of governance. To do this, governance scholars must settle on an agreed-upon definition, a definition broad enough to comprehend the forces it presumes to explain but not so broad as to claim to explain everything. Governance theorists must be ready to explain not only what governance is, but also what it is not. Governance theorist must be up-front about the biases in the concept and the implications of those biases.

The lessons learned in the evolution of regime theory in international relations are relevant here because regime theory predates governance theory and because the two are very nearly the same thing.[2]

To construct a practical and usable concept of governance for public administration, the field would profit by narrowing the subject to its most common usage and returning to Cleveland's original conception. In addition, the field would benefit by using regime theory from international relations to inform the development of governance theory. This would bring some precision to the concept and facilitate theoretical discourse around governance in public administration. In precise terms, then, governance in public administration should be defined as "sets of principles, norms, roles, and decision making procedures around which actors (managers) converge in a given public policy arena (Krasner 1983; March and Olsen 1995; Keohane 2002). It is important to note here that this definition includes many of the elements in the Lynn et al. definition of governance set out on page 286, and does not include others (e.g., outcomes as the dependent variable, environmental characteristics, client characteristics, regimes, judicial decisions, and the phrase "administrative practices that constrain, prescribe, and enable the provision of public services"). Obviously, the definition of governance borrowed from regime theory and applied to public administration significantly narrows the Lynn et al. definition.

The evolution of regime theory in international relations is guiding this insistence that to be useful, governance theory must be both narrowed and precise.

For a longer time than the concept of governance has claimed to be an organizing concept for public administration, the concept of regimes has informed research and theory in international relations (Krasner 1983; Hasenclever, Mayer, and Rittberger 2000). The basic elements of the concept of governance in public administration are similar to the theory of international regimes, and international regime theorists are well ahead of governance theorists. The path that international relations scholars have taken in the development of regime theory serves as a useful guide for the development of governance theory in public administration.

Descriptions of international regimes are very close to the narrower description of governance being presented here.

Regimes are deliberately constructed, partial international orders on either a regional or global scale, which are intended to remove specific issue areas of international politics from the sphere of self-help behavior. By creating shared expectations about appropriate behavior and by upgrading the level of transparency in the issue area, regimes help states (and other actors) to cooperate with a view to reaping joint gains in the form of additional welfare or security. If we classify international issue-areas by the dominant value being at issue, we find that regimes exist in all domains of contemporary world politics: there are *security* regimes such as the nuclear non-proliferation regime; *economic* regimes such as the international trade regime; *environmental* regimes such as the international regime for the protection of the stratospheric ozone layer; and, finally, *human rights* regimes such as the one based on the European Convention on Human Rights. (Hasenclever, Mayer, and Rittberger 2000: 3–4)

One might add to this list: bureaucratic regimes, patterns of cooperation between jurisdictions conducted by appointed officials, almost always in specific policy domains (Haas 1990, 1992).

International relations theory went through a period not unlike the present period in public administration—anything and everything was claimed to be regime theory (Strange 1983; Rosenau 2003). In recent years the subject has returned to its original and narrower definition (Krasner 1983)

Adapting a theory of governance in public administration from international regime theory, suggests a governance theory in three parts: (1) vertical and horizontal inter-jurisdictional and inter-organizational cooperation; (2) extension of the state or jurisdiction by contracts or grants to third parties, including sub-governments; and (3) forms of public non-jurisdictional or nongovernmental policy making and implementation.

The first of these, vertical and horizontal interjurisdictional and inter-organizational cooperation, will be called *inter-jurisdictional governance*. Inter-jurisdictional governance in public administration is:

1. actors in systems of governance either based in jurisdictions representing jurisdictional interests or in nongovernmental profit and nonprofit organizations, representing their interests;
2. participation in such systems of governance as a voluntary form of cooperation;
3. almost always policy-area specific; for example environmental inter-jurisdictional governance, economic development inter-jurisdictional governance, public safety inter-jurisdictional governance, national defense inter-jurisdictional governance.

The second form will be known as *third-party governance*. Third-party governance has the following characteristics:

1. it extends the functioning of the state or the jurisdiction by exporting to third parties (the first party is the elected basis of democratic legislative authority, the second party is executive administration or public administration) jurisdictional tasks and responsibilities for policy implementation;
2. its precise governance roles and responsibilities are based upon formal contractual or grant documents upon which the contractor (the jurisdiction) and the contractee (the profit or non-profit organization or subgovernment) agree;

3. its contracts and grants are time specific;
4. its contract and grants are policy-area specific, as in health research grants or road construction contracts.

The third form will be known as *public nongovernmental governance*. Public nongovernmental governance has the following characteristics:

1. policy making and implementation by nongovernmental institutions or actors that bear on the interests or well being of citizens in the same way and with the same consequences as state or jurisdictional outcomes;
2. jurisdictional or systems of inter-jurisdictional regulation, oversight or accountability have limited affect.

Governance in public administration may take these forms either singularly or in combination.

Inter-jurisdictional, third-party contract and public nongovernmental governance comprehend those aspects of governance most relevant to public administration and the largest and most common forms of governance. While other models of governance are interesting and may be relevant, it is inter-jurisdictional, third-party and nongovernmental governance that come closest to comprehending the traditional practices of public administration, theories of public administration and the modern practices of governance. The critical point here is that instead of governance replacing public administration, governance is a kind of public administration. In simple terms, it could be said that in the day-to-day, internal management of a government agency a person practices public administration. It could also be said that in the management of the extended state or jurisdiction, a person practices the public administration of governance. And it could be said that nongovernmental institutions or organizations making and implementing policies that affect citizens in the same way as the policies or actions of the state are practicing the public administration of governance (Frederickson 1997: 224). Therefore governance, as a distinct form of public administration, has to do with the extension of the state or jurisdiction either beyond its boundaries, through third parties, or by nongovernmental institutions.

Three schools of thought have evolved in international regime theory, schools of thought that are particularly useful as a basis of comparison with the narrower description of governance theory in public administration: the *neoliberal* school; the *realist* school; and the *cognitive* school.

Neoliberals emphasize the role of international regimes in helping states and jurisdictions achieve common interests. In the neoliberal schema, states and jurisdictions are rational egoists that care only for their own interests. Neoliberals draw heavily on economic theories of institutions, focusing on the role of information and transaction costs. Regimes are likened to investments by the territorial state, investments determined by issue density. Game theoretic models such as the

Prisoner's Dilemma are used by neoliberal regime scholars to estimate the probability that, under conditions of mixed motives and in particular situations, a regime might emerge and institutionalize. Thus the " structure of the situation" is central to the logic of the neoliberal school of international regime theory (Hasenclever, Mayer, and Rittberger 2000: 5–9).

The neoliberal school of international regime theory is very nearly the same as the public choice or rational choice school in public administration and policy studies. Consider, for example, studies of the commons (Ostrom 1998); the self-maximizing bureaucrat or bureaucracy (Tullock 1965; Downs 1967; Niskanen 1971); the self-maximizing citizen (Tiebout 1956; Lyons, Lowery, and DeHoog 1992); the conditions of both individual and jurisdictional cooperation (Axelrod 1984); and formal models or organizational or bureaucratic behavior (Moe 1984; Knott 1993) as illustrative of the similarities between international regime theory and the governance perspective in that part of public administration having to do with public choice theory and the empirical work supporting it.

International regime theorists of the *realism* school emphasize political power and its exercise in the territorial state and argue that power is as important to inter-jurisdictional cooperation as it is to conflict. "The overall result for realist students of international institutions is that international regimes are more difficult to create and harder to maintain than neoliberals would have us believe. The likelihood for a regime to be put in place and to be stable is greatest when the expected gains are balanced (at least for the most powerful members) such that relative losses do not accrue" (Hasenclever, Mayer, and Rittberger 2000: 9–10).

The realist school of international regime theory is not unlike a similar school in public administration. In the public administration version the focus is on constitutions, laws, the separation of powers, formal structures and rules, and on the exercise of political and bureaucratic power in the context of such structures (Long 1952). The leaders in the study of the constitutional and legal foundation of public administration (Rohr 1986; Rosenbloom 2003; Cooper 2002; Gilmore and Jensen 1998) tend to focus on elements of third party governance, (see especially, Cooper 2002) as well as inter-jurisdictional governance (see especially the federalism and intergovernmental relations scholars such as Wright 1997; Agranoff 1985; 2003).

Cognitivists (sometimes in regime theory called strong cognitivists) are critical of both neoliberal and realist approaches to international regimes, "for treating actors' preferences and (perceived) options as exogenous 'givens,' i.e., as facts which are assumed or observed, but not theorized about...(and) reject the conception of states as rational actors, who are atomistic in the sense that their identities, power and fundamental interests are prior to international society and its institutions. States are as much shaped by international institutions as they shape them" (Hasenclever, Mayer, and Rittberger 2000: 10–11).

Doubtless the most influential argument in the cognitive school of international regime theory is made by two political scientists primarily associated with public administration, James G. March and Johan P. Olsen (1998: 949). They apply institutional theory to international relations, insisting that "on the one side are those who see action as driven by the logic of anticipated consequences and prior preferences. On the other side are those who see action as driven by the logic of appropriateness and senses of identity. Within the tradition of logic of appropriateness, actions are seen as rule based. Human actors are imagined to follow the rules that associate particular identities to particular situations, approaching individual opportunities for action by assessing similarities between current identities and choice dilemmas and more general concepts of self and situations. Action involves evoking an identity or role and matching the obligation of that identity or role to a specific situation. The pursuit of purpose is associated with identities more than with interests, and with the selection of rules more than with individual rational expectations" (p. 951; see also March and Olsen 1984, 1995; Olsen 2003; Frederickson and Smith 2003).

The cognitive institutional perspective in both international regime theory and in public administration works from the premise that it is not possible to describe international political order, or organizational order or inter-organizational order in terms of the simple notion of rational intention and design. "History is created by complicated ecology of local events and locally adaptive actions. As individuals, groups, organizations, and institutions seek to act intelligently and learn in a changing world involving others similarly trying to adapt, they create connections that subordinate individual intentions to their interactions . . . They coevolve with the actions they produce" (March and Olsen, 1998: 968).

From this review of regime theory and its similarity to concepts of governance it is evident that international relations scholars have about the same "sharp disagreements with regard to both epistemology and ontology" (Hasenclever, Mayer and Rittberger 2000: 33). The neoliberalists and realists (sometimes together called the rationalists) can by synthesized with softer versions of cognitive regime theory in a form of "contextualized theory" that rests positivist tests of truth in the folds of culture, history, demographics, and the general endogeneity of complex regime and governance forces. However, there does not appear to be enough common ground to hold both the strong cognitivists and their logic of appropriateness and the rationalists with their positivist truth tests.

The study of governance and public management is advanced considerably by a recent large-scale synthesis of the literature (70 journals, and 800 articles over a twelve-year period) by Carolyn J. Hill and Laurence E. Lynn, Jr. (2005). They used a state-centric definition of governance adapted from their earlier work, a definition not unlike the standard Krasner definition of international regime theory (1983: 6). They found that the governance research scholarship broke down similarly to the regime theorists: (1) studies that are historical, descriptive, and institutional in the cognitive tradition; (2) studies of examples and "best practices," mostly in the institutional tradition; and (3) studies following the positivist social science canon. Their synthesis focused on studies of the third type. To operationalize the synthesis they used an adaption of their formula presented on page 286 of this chapter, a process hierarchical model from political power at the top to consequences, outputs, outcomes, results, and stakeholder assessments at the bottom.

In the order of their presentation, Hill and Lynn found that: (1) there is notably more research that explains frontline work than research on higher levels of governance; (2) the majority of studies adopt a top–down perspective on governance with little emphasis on outcomes, results, or stakeholders' assessments—studies of street-level bureaucracy and bureaucrat–client interactions are the exception; (3) structures of authority are used to explain, they are not explained; (4) governance matters or, put another way, there is a demonstrable hierarchy of influence from politics clear to the stakeholders, and at each step of the way structure, process, and management matter; (5) in governance studies results are most often described as institutional outputs and not social outcomes; (6) organizational structures and levels of management discretion influence organizational effectiveness; (7) effectiveness and cost-savings associated with third-party governance are influenced by incentives and contract review standards and processes.

Hill and Lynn's most important finding is that hierarchy and, as they put it, hierarchical governance, is alive and well and the primary means by which we govern. It appears that the networked, associational, horizontal, and conjunct forms of governance are less important than governance scholars might think. "[T]he American political scheme remains hierarchical and jurisdictional" and jurisdictional hierarchy is the predicate to networked governance (p. 34). And they identify the likely reasons: "The seemingly 'paradigmatic' shift away from hierarchical government toward horizontal governing (hence increasing the preference for 'governance' as an organizing concept) is less fundamental than it is tactical: the addition of new tools or administrative technologies that facilitate public governance within hierarchical systems" (p. 33). For this reason, it is argued here that the study of governance should focus on inter-jurisdictional, third-party, and nongovernmental governance as a way to narrow the grandness of the governance project.

To return to the three categories of governance set out on pages 294 and 295, in the cases of both inter-jurisdictional and third-party governance it is important to get past the idea that there can somehow be a governance tree floating in space without governmental or bureaucratic roots. Peters and Pierre asked whether there can be, as Cleveland seemed to imply, governance without government (1998). The answer is no, at least following the narrower definition of governance argued here. This suggests a state or jurisdiction-centered approach to governance, an approach ready to accept the importance of hierarchy, order, predictability, stability, and permanence. Despite all the scholarly focus on governance, it appears, even from the synthesized research of governance scholars, that the old-time religion, trad-itional public administration, is the basis of policy implementation in government, and government is an essential precondition of governance.

It follows from this reasoning that one of the best hopes for an empirically robust theory of governance might be to turn somewhat in the direction of the cognitive and institutional research perspective. Lynn and Hill, in their justification for studying primarily the positivist–rationalist literature, acknowledge that their approach "sacrifices verisimilitude and nuance but gains in transparency and replicability" (p. 5). But they found "the fact that relatively few studies examined more complex patterns of causality may reflect the paucity of data, but it may also reflect something more significant: conjunctions by hundreds of specialized inves-tigators that the world of practice remains more hierarchical than many of us want to concede. When it comes to answering multi-level 'why' questions, the evidence suggests that hierarchy 'still' matters" (pp. 33–4).

It may be that causality is more likely to be found in the cognitive and institutional literature. March and Olsen's overarching descriptive synthesis is an insightful understanding of democratic governance from the perspective of insti-tutional theory, with an emphasis on the logic of appropriateness as an explanatory variable (1995; see also Wilson 1989). Keohane's application of the institutional perspective to international governance, particularly the formal intergovernmental organizations such as the United Nations, the World Trade Organization and the European Union illustrates a conceptual approach that could be useful in the search for causality in public administration as governance (2002).

12.3 Summing-Up

From its prominence in the 1980s, regime theory would now be described as one of many important theories of international relations. International relations is, of course, the study of relations between nation-states whereas public administration is the study of the management of the state and its subgovernments. It could be said that regime theory accounts for the role of non-state actors and policy entrepre-neurs in the context of the modern transformation of the nation-state. In public administration it could be said that the modern transformation of states and their subgovernments explains the contemporary salience of theories of governance. Both regime theory and governance theory are scholarly responses to the trans-formation of states.

Government in the postmodern state involves multiple levels of interlocked and overlapping arenas of collective policy implementation. Governments now operate in the context of supranational, international, transgovernmental and transnational relations in elaborate patterns of federated power sharing and interdependence. Therefore, it is now understood that public administration as governance is the best description of the management of the transformed or postmodern state (G. Sorensen 2004) Nationhood and community are transformed as collective loyalties are increasingly projected away from the state. Major portions of economic activity are now embedded in cross-border networks and national and local economies are less self-sustaining that they once were (G. Sorensen 2004: 162).

Harlan Cleveland understood very early how governments, economies and communities were changing and how rapidly they were changing. His initial description of public administration as governance was designed to square the theory and practices of the field with the realities of a changing world. His governance model still serves as a compelling argument for plural, inter-jurisdictional, and inter-organizational mediated decision-making networks of public executives operating in the context of blurred distinctions between public and private organizations. Following Cleveland's treatise, the popularity of the word governance soared and while gaining altitude evidently lost oxygen. In an oxygen deprived state many scholars engaged in excesses and failures in their considerations of governance. Some engaged in fuzzy definitions of governance and others simply didn't bother with definitions. Others freighted-up governance with anti-bureaucratic, anti-governmental and pro-market values, often without acknowledging the added weight. Still others made of public administration straw men and then, with exaggerated claims, demonstrated how easily governance could tip them over. And, as is often the case with concept entrepreneurs, governance was seen as the answer, *the* grand theory to replace public administration.

Lynn, Heinrich and Hill brought governance back down to earth and oxygenated it with their analytic framework. And, more recently, they filled in much of their framework with a synthesis of empirical research literature. Many other leading scholars in public administration use the Lynn et al. framework, together building an impressive body of research.

Taking a page from the evolution of regime theory in international relations, it is here suggested that the longer range prospects for the application of governance to public administration would be improved by narrowing the scope of the subject. It is suggested that there be a fundamental distinction between public administration as the internal day-to-day management of an agency or organization on one hand, and public administration as governance, the management of the extended state, on the other. It is further suggested that the public administration of governance include the management of nongovernmental institutions and organizations insofar as their policies or actions affect citizens in the same way as state agencies. Once established, these distinctions lead to a three part definition of governance in public administration. First, *inter-jurisdictional governance* is policy-area specific formalized or voluntary patterns of interorganizational or interjurisdictional cooperation. Second, *third-party governance* extends the functions of the state by exporting them by contract to policy-area specific nonprofit, for-profit or subgovernmental third parties. Third, *public nongovernmental governance* accounts for those activities of nongovernmental organizations that bear on the interests of citizens in the same way as governmental agencies. These three forms of governance are, after all, what is ordinarily meant when the word/concept governance is used in public administration.

The rapid transformation of the state and its subgovernments has profound implications for the practices of public administration. Governance theory, accounting as it does for most of the effects of state transformation, promises to contribute importantly to the development of public administration scholarship.

NOTES

1. The phrase "public administration" is used here only as a convention. The phrase "public management" could have been used, and would have had the same meaning.
2. There is a second and less useful body of regime theory found in urban studies. Urban regime theorists tends to emphasize the role of business leaders in urban economic development and to de-emphasize the roles of elected and appointed government officials (Elkins 1987; Stone 1989). The work of Royce Hansen is a welcome exception to this generalization, and his work is rather similar to the use of regime theory in international relations and as it is used here (2003; see also Frederickson 1999).

REFERENCES

AGRANOFF, R. (1985), *Intergovernmental Management: Human Services, Problem-Solving in Six Metropolitan Areas*, Albany, NY: State University of New York Press.

—— (2003), "Leveraging Networks: A Guide for Public Managers Working Across Organizations," *New Ways to Manage Series* (March), Arlington, VA: IBM Endowment for the Business of Government.

AXELROD, R. (1984), *The Evolution of Cooperation*, New York: Basic Books.

BENNER, T., REINICKE, W. H., and WITTE, J. M. (2003), "Global Public Policy Networks," *Brookings Review* (11(1): 18–21.

BIRDSALL, N. (2003), "Asymmetric Globalization," *Brookings Review* 11(1): 22–7.

BLAIR, M. M., and MacLAURY, B. L. (1995), *Ownership and Control: Rethinking Corporate Governance for the 21st Century*, Washington, DC: Brookings Institution.

CASTELLS, M. (2000), *The Rise of Networked Society*, 2nd edn., Oxford: Blackwell.

CLEVELAND, H. (1972), *The Future Executive: A Guide for Tomorrow's Managers*, New York: Harper & Row.

COOPER, P. J. (2002), *Governing by Contract: Challenges and Opportunities for Public Manager*, Washington, DC: CQ Press.

DESSLER, D. (1989), "What's at Stake in the Agent-Structure Debate?", *International Organization* 43(3): 441–73.

DOWNS, A. (1967), *Inside Bureaucracy*, Boston: Little, Brown.

ELKIN, S. L. (1987), *City and Regime in the American Republic*, Chicago: University of Chicago Press.

FOSLER, R. S. (1998), "The Global Challenge to Governance: Implications for National and Subnational Government Capacities and Relationships," *National Academy of Public Administration*. Presented to the NIRA-NAPA 1998 Tokyo Conference on The Challenge to Governance in the Twenty-First Century: Achieving Effective Central-Local Relations.

FREDERICKSON, H. G. (1999), "The Repositioning of American Public Administration," *Political Science*, 701–11.

—— and SMITH (2003), *The Public Administration Theory Primer*, Boulder, CO: Westview Press.

GILMOUR, R. S., and JENSEN, L. S. (1998), "Reinventing Government, Accountability, Public Functions, Privatization, and the Meaning of 'State' Action," *Public Administration Review* 58: 247–58.

GRAHAM, C., and LITAN, R. E. (2003), "Governance in an Integrated Global Economy," *Brookings Review* 21(2): 2–30.

HAAS, P. M. (1990), *Saving the Mediterranean: The Politics of International Environmental Cooperation*, New York: Columbia University Press.

—— (1992), "Intoduction: Epistemic Communities and International Policy Coordination," *International Organization* 46: 1–35.

HANSEN, R. (2003), *Civic Culture and Urban Change: Governing Dallas*. Detroit: Wayne State University Press.

HASENCLEVER, A., MAYER, P., and RITTBERGER, V. (1996), "Interests, Power, Knowledge: The Study of International Regimes," *Mershon International Studies Review* 40: 177–228.

—— —— —— (1997), *Theories of International Regimes*, Cambridge: Cambridge University Press.

—— —— —— (2000), "Integrating Theories of International Regimes," *Review of International Studies* 26: 3–33.

HEINRICH, C. J., and LYNN, L. E., JR. (eds.) (2000), *Governance and Performance: New Perspectives*, Washington, DC: Georgetown University Press.

HILL, C. J., and LYNN, L. (2005), "Is Hierarchical Governance in Decline? Evidence from Empirical Research," *Journal of Public Administration Research and Theory* 15: 173–96.

HIRST, P. (2000), "Democracy and Governance," in J. Pierre (ed.), *Debating Governance: Authority, Steering, and Democracy*, Oxford: Oxford University Press, 13–35.

JENSEN, M. (2000), *A Theory of the Firm: Governance, Residual Claims, and Organizational Forms*, Cambridge: Harvard University Press.

KEOHANE, R. (2002), "International Organizations and Garbage Can Theory," *Journal of Public Administration Research and Theory* 12: 155–9.

KERNAGHAN, K., MARSON, B., and BORINS, S. (2000), *The New Public Organization*, Toronto: Institute of Public Administration of Canada.

KETTL, D. (1993), *Sharing Power: Public Governance and Private Markets*, Washington, DC: Brookings Institution.

KIKERT, W. (1997), "Public Governance in the Netherlands: An Alternative to Anglo-American 'Managerialism,'" *Public Administration* 75: 731–52.

KNOTT, J. (1993), "Comparing Public and Private Management: Cooperative Effort and Principal-Agent Relationships," *Journal of Public Administration Research and Theory* 3: 93–119.

KOOIMAN, J. (ed.), *Modern Governance*, London: Sage.

KRASNER, S. D. (ed.) (1983), *International Regimes*, Ithaca, NY: Cornell University Press.

LONG, N. E. (1952), "Bureaucracy or Constitutionalism," *American Political Science Review* 46: 808–18.

LYNN, L. E., JR., HENRICH, C., and HILL, C. J. (2001), *Improving Governance: A New Logic For Empirical Research*, Washington, DC: Georgetown University Press.

LYONS, W., LOWERY, D., and DeHOOG, R. H. (1992), *The Politics of Dissatisfaction: Citizens, Services, and Urban Institutions*, Armonk, NY: Sharpe.

MARCH, J. G., and OLSEN, J. P. (1983), "What Administrative Reorganization Tells Us About Governing," *American Political Science Review* 77: 281–96.

—— —— (1984), "The New Institutionalism: Organizational Factors in Political Life," *American Political Science Review* 78: 734–49.

—— —— (1989), *Rediscovering Institutions*, New York: The Free Press.

—— —— (1995), *Democratic Governance*, New York: The Free Press.

—— —— (1998), "The Institutional Dynamics of International Political Order," *International Organization* 52: 943–69.

MILWARD, H. B., and PROVAN, K. (2000), "Governing the Hollow State," *Journal of Public Administration Research and Theory* 10: 359–79.

MOE, T. (1984), "The New Economics of Organization," *American Journal of Political Science* 28: 739–77.

MONKS, R. A., and MINOW, N. (2004), *Corporate Governance*, 3rd edn., New York: Blackwell.

NEWMAN, J. (2001), *Modernizing Governance*, London: Sage.

NISKANEN, W. (1971), *Bureaucracy and Representative Government*, Hawthorne, NY: Aldine de Gruyter.

NYE, J. S., and DONAHUE, J. D. (eds.) (2000), *Governance in a Globalizing World*, Washington, DC: Brookings Institution.

OLSEN, J. P. (2003), "Citizens, Public Administration and the Search for Theoretical Foundations," *American Political Science Association*, Annual Meeting, John Gaus Lecture. Philadelphia, August 29.

OSBORN, D., and GAEBLER, T. (1992), *Reinventing Government*, Reading, MA: Addison-Wesley.

OSTROM, E. (1998), "A Behavioral Approach to the Rational Choice Theory of Collective Action: Presidential Address, American Political Science Association, 1997," *American Political Science Review* 92: 1–22.

O'TOOLE, L. J., JR. (2003), "Intergovernmental Relations in Implementation," in B. G. Peters and J. Pierre (eds.), *Handbook of Public Administration*, Thousand Oaks, CA: Sage.

PETERS, B. G. (1995), "Bureaucracy in a Divided Regime: The United States," in J. Pierre (ed.), *Bureaucracy in the Modern State: An Introduction to Comparative Administration*, Aldershot: Edward Elgar.

—— (1996), *Governance: Four Emerging Models*, Lawrence: University Press of Kansas.

—— (2001), *The Future of Governing*, Lawrence: University Press of Kansas.

—— and PIERRE, J. (1998), "Governance Without Government? Rethinking Public Administration," *Journal of Public Administration Research and Theory* 8: 227–43.

PIERRE, J. (ed.) (2000), *Debating Governance: Authority, Steering, and Democracy*, Oxford: Oxford University Press.

RHODES, R. A. W. (1997), *Understanding Governance: Policy Networks, Governance, Reflexivity, and Accountability*, Buckingham: Open University Press.

—— (2000), "Governance and Public Administration," in J. Pierre (ed.), *Debating Governance: Authority, Steering, and Democracy*, Oxford: University of Oxford Press, 54–90.

ROHR, J. (1986), *To Run a Constitution: The Legitimacy of the Administrative State*, Lawrence: University Press of Kansas.

ROSENAU, J. N. (2003), *Distant Proximities: Dynamics beyond Globalization*, Princeton: Princeton University Press.

ROSENBLOOM, D. H. (2003), *Administrative Law for Public Managers*, Boulder, CO: Westview Press.

SALAMON, L. M. (ed.) (2002), *The Tools of Government: A Guide to the New Governance*, Oxford: Oxford University Press.

SORENSEN, G. (2004), *The Transformation of the State: Beyond the Myth of Retreat*, London: Palgrave Macmillan.

STONE, C. (1989), *Regime Politics*, Lawrence: University Press of Kansas.

STRANGE, S. (1983), "Cave! Hec Dragones: A Critique of Regime Theory," in S. D. Krasner (ed.), *International Regimes*, Ithaca, NY: Cornell University Press.

TIEBOUT, C. (1956), "A Pure Theory of Local Expenditure," *Journal of Political Economy* 44: 416–24.

TULLOCK, G. (1965), *The Politics of Bureaucracy*, Washington, DC: Public Affairs Press.

WILSON, J. Q. (1989), *Bureaucracy: What Government Agencies Do and Why They Do It*, New York: Basic Books.

WOODS, N. (2003), "Unelected Government," *Brookings Review* 21(2): 9–12

WRIGHT, D. (1997), *Understanding Intergovernmental Relations*, 3rd edn., Washington, DC: International Thompson Publishing.

CHAPTER 13

....

VIRTUAL
ORGANIZATIONS

....

HELEN MARGETTS

THE dictionary definition of "virtual" is "that is such for practical purposes though not in name or according to strict definition" (Pearsall and Trumble 1995: 1614). More recently, the word virtual has become linked with the potential for information technology to create an environment that is "not physically existing as such but made by software to appear to do so." A virtual organization, therefore is an organization that does not exist as such, but is "there for practical purposes," facilitated either by information technology, or by some other means of linking individuals and groups. This chapter investigates the various visions of virtuality which have been applied to public organizations over the past decade, discerning three ways in which we might expect organizations to become more virtual. It then examines the evidence to assess the extent to which organizations have experienced "virtualization." Although the evidence does not appear to justify the wildest claims of some commentators, there is no doubt that two key trends in public management discussed elsewhere in this volume—e-government and new public management—are bringing virtuality in various guises. The final part of the chapter looks into the future, at the potential for these trends (and the relationship between them) to bring further virtualization.

13.1 Visions of Virtuality

The growing popularity of the word virtual, dating from the early 1990s, is most commonly associated with technological change and the idea of "virtual reality," "images or environments generated by computer software with which a user can interact realistically using a helmet containing a screen, gloves fitted with sensors etc." (Pearsall and Trumble 1995) or (more concisely): "the technological management of the body's senses" (Holmes 1997: 1). For example via a computer keyboard it has become increasingly possible to pay a virtual visit to an art gallery or even, using more controlled environments, to undertake more physically oriented activities such as sailing a boat. In fact, such technologies predate the terminology, flight simulation being an obvious example. The image became more popularly accessible with widespread use of the Internet and web-based technologies, which opened up organizations of all kinds to their customers, giving us the virtual bookshop (Amazon) with no physical location, or the virtual auction (e-bay) where there is no central auctioneer. Using this analogy, a virtual public organization would presumably be one which interacted only using its "virtual" face—probably its web site—in the same way as a "virtual" bookshop such as Amazon deals only with customers on-line and maintains no physical presence for customers. Any organization that does exist is there to serve the web site, rather than the other way round.

From the 1990s, the word "virtual" proliferated in book and journal article titles attached to various aspects of social, economic and political life. The most marked was the rise of the "virtual corporation" and "virtual company" to indicate private sector organizations that used a variety of inter-organizational relationships facilitated by technological development to become loose conglomerations of groups and partnerships. A forerunner was the computer company Dell, "touted by itself and others as a quintessential Internet company," using the Internet to "co-ordinate a network of suppliers and business partners who carry out many of the processes involved in building, distributing and supporting personal computers" (Kraemer and Dedrick 2001: 2). The rise of the virtual corporation led other management literature to promote the virtues of "virtual teams" and "virtual organizations."

Political scientists and sociologists also began applying the term to the public arena—for example, virtual politics (Holmes 1997); the virtual university (Robins and Webster 2002); and the virtual state (Frissen 1999; Fountain 2001; Rosecrance 1999). The more postmodern of sociologists became particularly excited about the potential for multiple realities offered by the Internet and began discussing the concept of virtual communities—an electronic meeting place where disembodied communication takes place (cyberspace) (Holmes 1997: 1). The postmodernist Paul Frissen in a book entitled *The Virtual State* (in Dutch) defines virtualization as:

firstly the direct consequences of applying virtual reality to organizations, and secondly the implications of all those ICT effects for which the term "virtual reality" is employed metaphorically (change in time and space, changes in the experience of reality, changes in physical and social relations). (Frissen 1999: 54)

Specifically applied to organizations, Frissen suggests that:

delimitation of organizations to reflect their physical and bureaucratic identity becomes less important. Relationship patterns with other actors are not only given more weight but become substitute organizations. The network becomes an important, perhaps the most important, work context, both technologically and socially... organizations thus become more fluid and more flexible. (Frissen 1999: 55–6)

In Frissen's terms, information technologies lead to virtualization of organizations, both directly in their capacity to reduce time and space and to replicate reality and indirectly in a metaphorical sense, by providing the analogy of virtual reality.

Less technologically determined visions of virtuality in public administration are provided by Fountain (2001) who uses the term "virtual" to refer to:

capacity that appears seamless but that exists through the rapid transfer and sharing of the capacity of several discrete units and agencies as their partners... clients interact with a virtual government agency as if they are interacting with a coherent physical organization when in fact they are interacting with several agencies that may be integrated only through digital networks. (Fountain 2001: 24–5)

She develops a "technology enactment framework" which focuses on the relationship between information technology, organizations and institutions to explain why many different scenarios for the virtual state are likely to emerge (Fountain 2001: 83–103). In her framework, the term "virtual agency" describes at least four different enactments of the Internet and related technologies by government agencies: single agency web sites; groups of agencies linked by common clients (such as students or senior citizens); intranets within agencies; and a group of agencies that integrate some of their activities both on the web and "behind" the website, within and across the structures of the agencies themselves. Thus virtuality will be associated with moves towards e-government: the use of information and communication technologies (ICTs) by government to communicate and transact internally and externally with citizens, businesses and other government organizations. But in Fountain's institutionalist view, traditional characteristics of government organizations will continue to shape developments: government agencies are "embedded in an institutional environment that discourages horizontal cross-agency initiatives and encourages competition among autonomous agencies for resources," "government agencies face strong institutional constraints on network formation" and "virtual agencies succeed only when the agencies involved can develop and maintain social capital" (Fountain 2001: 101).

Not all ideas of virtuality rely on the increasing capability of ICTs to link organizational units and individuals. In the private sector, the term "virtual corporation" is often used to refer to an increasing tendency of successful corporations to maintain or increase output with a steady or declining amount of labour, by "downsizing." The apparent success of this strategy led to a proliferation of management books such as Quinn's *Intelligent Enterprise* (1992) which advocated the practice of radical outsourcing—a corporation should only do that at which it could be "best in world" and all other activities should be outsourced. The public sector equivalent—to some extent an attempt to mimic the success of the virtual corporation—was the widespread trend towards contracting out, outsourcing and privatization, a key theme of the New Public Management (NPM) described elsewhere in this volume. Contracting trends also fuel virtuality, by ensuring that many government activities are carried out by consortia or chains of private sector organizations. Such arrangements are facilitated by contracts—although often, additionally by technology. The relationship between IT and contracting can become more direct; the predominant role played by technology in contemporary organizations and the multiplicity of skills and expertise needed to provide it means that more than any other function, the provision of technology is contracted out or "outsourced" to third party providers, although the percentage of IT operations that are contracted out varies greatly across governments, in line with variations in NPM trends.

For government, various writers predict increasing virtuality through outsourcing trends. The management theorist Henry Mintzberg (1996: 81) defines "virtual" as synonymous with widespread outsourcing and argues that as illustrated by the UK, the US, and New Zealand "virtual government contains an assumption that the best government is no government.... In virtual government's perfect world, the microstructures (the activities of agencies) would no longer exist within government ... the motto of this model might be Privatize, Contract and Negotiate." Less normative arguments are used by proponents of the "hollow state metaphor" (Milward and Provan 2003: 4) to describe the decision by a government to contract with third parties—nonprofits, firms, other governments—to produce public goods and services, what they describe as a "political theory of devolution of the mantle of government authority to non-profit organizations and private firms" (Milward 1996; Milward and Provan 2000, 2003). The "hollow state" in Milward's terms is defined by a marked degree of separation between the source and use of funds; joint production of services by multiple agencies; and the core task of public management as arranging networks, rather than managing hierarchies (see also Agranoff and McGuire 2001 and O'Toole 1997). More radical visions for the "Virtual State" include Rosecrance (1999) who uses the term to denote modern states with little of the traditional apparatus of states (such as military power, agriculture or manufacturing) but highly developed managerial, financial, and creative skills—Hong Kong, Singapore, and Taiwan being prime examples. The virtual state in these terms is facilitated by the development of the virtual corporation, where the focus is on product design, marketing, and financing while production is left to third-party suppliers dispersed around the world.

Finally, other visions of virtualization come from a more traditional and prescriptive stream within public administration which recognizes the pathologies that arise from departmental silos within governments, whereby all the lines of accountability are vertical and horizontal linkages are difficult to establish and maintain, and prescribe methods of fostering collaboration and co-operation. Bardach (1998) for example, in a book entitled *Getting Agencies to Work Together*, argues for a new type of managerial craftsmanship, whereby problem-centered groupings of agencies work together. Some of the "hollow state" school (both practitioners and academics) have used organizational theory to advocate ways of managing networks of service providers, in terms of cooperation, partnerships, alliances, and services integration, arguing that the more integrated and coordinated the network, the more effective it will be (see Milward and Provan 2003: 9). A similar argument is applied to "one-stop-shops," a "new organizational model to deliver services from the point of view of the 'customer' as citizens and businesses can then be called in their particular role in the process of service delivery" (Hagen and Kubicek 2000: 1). Both practitioners and commentators were early in highlighting the capacity of technology to aid such a process; even in the 1980s, the UK Department of Social Security was arguing that "One-stop shops" were the way forward for social security provision, facilitated through a huge (£2.6 billion eventually) program of computerization of social security. With rising use of the Internet, one-stop shops can become more virtual and might be superseded by "zero touch transactions," currently under discussion in the Netherlands, whereby government agencies would use their own and other agencies' databases of citizen information to proactively contact citizens when (for example) they become eligible for a pension or a child reaches school age. Rather than having to apply for benefits or schools, the agency would complete the transaction for the citizen using existing information, so that they would only have to intervene if the information were wrong. Such ideas are similar to private-sector models already in operation: the computer equipment company Cisco, for example, has since the late 1990s employed a "zero-touch" model whereby orders are routed to third-party suppliers and delivered and invoiced direct to the customer without any employee from Cisco actually "touching" the transaction.

Overall, from these various visions of virtuality (many of which originate from business and management literature based on private sector experience), it is possible to discern at least three meanings of the "virtualization" of public organizations. All three indicate a blurring of organizational boundaries, becoming less of an organization in the traditional sense of the word, a central part of most definitions of virtuality.

1. *A virtual face.* First, a government organization becomes virtual in terms of its relationship with clients—businesses, citizens or other governments—who deal only with some kind of virtual image of an organization, rather than organizations themselves. This notion of virtuality is a "representation" of organizations with a web site as a "window," both drawing citizens and businesses into the organization and divulging information. In its more radical sense, the web site becomes more important than the organization itself, possibly presenting information from several organizations as a coherent whole and receiving information and transactions from citizens and posting them off to relevant organizations without citizens themselves being aware of which organizations they are dealing with. As this process develops, private sector companies have used the Internet and web-based technologies to create new types of relationships with customers—the computer company Dell is "now using the Internet and e-commerce to create closer relationships with customers that it has previously considered transactional—individual consumers, the home and the small business market" (Kraemer and Dedrick 2001: 32). The Internet has, as the company's founder Michael Dell put it, "turbocharged our ability to understand our customers."

2. *Internal virtuality.* A second meaning of a virtual organization is in the sense of not really having any central existence; being somehow hollow or empty—and as such, presumably, less distinct from the outside world. If a virtual state is—in Rosecrance's terms—a state which lacks what it has traditionally meant to be a state, then a virtual organization would be one which lacks what it normally takes to be an organization. Such a development would start with the replacement of bureaucracy by information systems but the progression through radical downsizing owes as much to outsourcing and contracting-out as to technological development. Virtual organization in this sense means a small "core" organization that mainly deals with contracts or chains of contracts, rather than actually doing anything—an organization which lacks organizational capacity. Such an organization could take the form of a partnership with a major vendor—or if subcontracting is employed, then complex chains of contracting organizations with some kind of hierarchy expressed through "prime-" and "sub-" contractor arrangements. However, given the strong tendency of governments to contract-out information technology provision noted above, it is generally associated with technological trends as well.

3. *Virtual networks.* A third meaning of virtuality is in terms of interorganizational relationships, whereby organizations exist only as consortia of groups and individuals grouped together for a particular purpose—linkages are more important than organizations and the network of individuals and organizations (in Frissen's terms) is the most important of all. In the business world, such a

development has been termed 'strategic convergence'—"a mean of strengthening competitive advantage by combining resources to outperform the competition" (Cartwright 2002: 59). A notable example is AutoNation, previously a used-car superstore which has reached a number of agreements with car dealerships, car rental companies, manufacturers, and a car-purchasing web site to become the largest automotive dealer in the US: "in short, the company has worked backward from the consumer to converge used, new and rental car markets, different brands and types of vehicles and technology in one place—a web site" (Cartwright 2002: 59). There are numerous other examples of strategic alliances between major corporations (Starbucks, United Airlines, Barnes and Noble, and Marriott; Deutsche Telekom and DaimlerChrysler; Blaupunkt and Microsoft to name but three) based on telematics, the integration of several technologies, products and services. Networks of inter-organizational relationships can exist through links between groups within organizations—the idea of "virtual teams" working across organizational boundaries with information technology (Lipnack and Stamps 2000). These cross-functional "teams without borders" are made possible by the Internet, the Web, and Intranets, allowing companies to use the combined talents of the best people for the job no matter where they are in the world (although such authors are keen to emphasize the "90/10" rule—90 percent people and 10 percent technology).

13.2 WHERE IS THE EVIDENCE?

Certainly information technologies do offer the possibility of virtual organizations in all three of the senses outlined above. A key breakpoint here was the development of web-based technologies and increasingly widespread use of the Internet. Earlier information technologies were largely internally facing and although creating new possibilities for internal organizational restructuring, they made little difference to organizations' ability to communicate with their customers or clients or with other organizations. Such technologies might facilitate an organization whose central existence is really a complex web of information systems, while radically reducing staff numbers—replacing bureaucracy with information systems (internal virtuality)—but offer little in terms of external linkages. The Internet, in contrast, really does offer potential to transform the relationship between organizations and customers. A web site allows the possibility of all kinds of transactions that would originally have been processed within an organization being processed by the web site alone. As one official in the Australian Tax Office put it in 1999, in the future "this organization will become its Web site" (Dunleavy and Margetts 1999).

13.2.1 A Virtual Face

With respect to clients coming inside the organization, there are all sorts of ways in which the interface between citizens and government organizations has changed. In the most basic sense, most government agencies now have a presence on the Web. In a comprehensive analysis of UK government on the web in 2001, Dunleavy and Margetts (2002) found that 84 percent of central government agencies maintained a web site and those that did not were chiefly small government bodies with few external dealings. Four-fifths of the 310 sites surveyed had general e-mail enquiry services, on-line press releases and annual reports, breakdown of the organizations activities and links to other government agencies. By 2001 the modal UK government organization had between 41–50 percent of a range of features, up from 21–30 percent of the same range for a smaller number of web sites in 1999 (Dunleavy and Margetts 2002: 62). Citizens appear to be obtaining more information about government on-line. Thomas and Streib (2003) found from a survey in the State of Georgia that citizen visits to governmental web sites were increasingly common and "appear to have become a major new form of the traditional citizen-initiated contact." The increasing availability of governmental information on the Web can "by itself promote governmental openness and transparency, and in the process no doubt will facilitate the achievement of democratic values" (Thomas and Streib 2003: 98 and LaPorte et al. 2000). The 2003 Hutton Enquiry in the UK, the investigation into the death of the government scientist Dr David Kelly, is a good contemporary example, whereby all evidence, hearings, and rulings were available for citizens—making the details of the inquiry far more accessible than previous such investigations. Although it had few staff, the inquiry became a tangible entity to huge numbers of citizens, with between 10,000 and 30,000 unique visitors on many days of evidence-giving, and (once the material was so readily available) facilitated dissemination throughout international news networks by media organizations quick to take advantage of an easy and long-running story.

There are some more radical examples of web sites opening up organizations to citizens. The Australian Tax Office, for example, has initiated moves towards opening up the legislative databases upon which decisions are based to taxpayers, so that they can follow in detail how a decision on their particular case has been made. Such moves make organizations more transparent by revealing their decision-making process to customers. In the Netherlands, draft tax legislation has been posted on the internet for public comment; indeed so useful were the comments made by both tax practitioners and consultants that the draft law was substantively changed in response.

The growth of central government portals is probably the strongest cross-national example of governments developing a virtual face. Before use of the Web became widespread, it would have been difficult to point a citizen to any particular contact point (e.g., building, telephone number, or mail address) and say "that is the government." In the twenty-first century, the governments of all liberal democracies and most other countries have a virtual "entry point" which welcomes various categories of national and international visitors to "the government." The US federal government's site, firstgov.gov, has been extremely successful since its creation in 1999 in drawing US citizens to its site, particularly after an impressive response to the terrorist attacks of September 11 2001, when the site became a focal point for news as well as information about the government itself. The Canadian government site at www.canada.gc.ca offers a whole range of information about Canada and the Canadian government. Many central government portals provide different types of entry point for different categories of consumer; businesses, citizens and overseas visitors; in Australia, the business entry point has been particularly successful in changing the ways in which businesses deal with the central government. Governments vary in the extent to which they have used the Internet to develop a virtual presence in this way: for example, both attempts at UK government portals, the non-intuitively named www.open.gov (to 1999) and www.ukonline.gov.uk (from 1999) lacked the comprehensiveness of the other sites mentioned above and there is no central business portal at the time of writing.

In most countries, there is a long way to go before governments maximize the potential for this type of virtuality and government agencies have lagged behind most other types of organization. It is impossible to generalize across the private sector, and indeed there are many variations such as between large and small businesses (the latter are far less likely to use the Internet to deal with customers or even to have Internet access) and between different sectoral fields (airlines and travel companies have been particularly innovative, for example, in terms of developing new relationships with customers). Likewise, it is difficult to generalize across governments in countries with wildly differing levels of internet penetration and e-government development. However, a global survey of e-government usage (Taylor Nelson Sofres 2002) found disappointing levels of usage of many on-line services in the majority of countries, particularly the UK where only 13 percent of citizens had used any government online services in the past twelve months (although the equivalent figure in Sweden, Norway, Singapore and Denmark was over 50 percent). It is difficult to think of a governmental equivalent anywhere in the world of Amazon, an organization based entirely around the web site—so that the organization services the web site rather than the web site servicing the organization. Thomas and Streib (2003) found that their US survey respondents who reported using government web sites were mostly seeking information rather than attempting to communicate information to government, or undertake other forms of interaction. Dunleavy et al. (1999, 2002) found that UK government web sites lagged behind the private sector in terms of transactional facilities and that local government (where one might expect to find most evidence of transformation of government-citizen relationships, as it is where citizens have most contact with government) lagged behind central government. Government agencies in many countries (particularly the UK) have been slow to use the new potential offered by web-based technologies to revitalize the relationship with their 'customers' through (for example) the use of web usage statistics to give new understanding of how citizens use—and would like to use—Internet-based applications to deal with government organizations.

13.2.2 Internal Virtuality

The most obvious sense in which organizations have been "hollowed out" through the use of information technology was through the automation of administrative functions: the replacement of bureaucracy with information systems. In more advanced liberal democracies such as the US and the UK, such a process took place across larger government departments in the 1960s–1980s, when most large-scale computerization projects were cost justified through massive staff savings (see Margetts 1999 for a history). Although the savings actually achieved were disappointing in many cases, with few projects eventually covering their costs in this way, there is no doubt that automation of public administration did remove the need for some types of administrative activity and that the spread of information systems brought new organizational structures. Overall, it meant a shift from organizational capacity to organized expertise, with large departments developing large, technically skilled, information systems departments working to develop and maintain "mission-critical" systems. This might be seen as a shift from "machine bureaucracy" to "adhocracy," using the organizational categorization of Mintzberg (1985). Many commentators (such as Frissen, see above) claimed that the spread of IT across government would bring "leaner, flatter hierarchies," but there has been a tendency in government for IT expertise to remain organizationally separate from the rest of the department and to leave conventional hierarchies more or less intact. In fact, a study of program managers in US county-level public agencies found that IT adoption had very little impact on an agency's structure (Heintze and Bretschneider 2000).

In the last twenty years the tendency has been for governments to contract-out their information technology development and maintenance to private sector computer services providers, giving clear evidence of virtualization in this sense of "hollowing out," particularly in countries where contracting trends have been strong. Here the dual trends of technological development and contracting out by government become strongly inter-related, as information technology will often be at the forefront of centrally mandated contracting initiatives (in the UK, US, Australia, New Zealand, for example). In the US, well over half of the information technology budget of the federal government goes to a bewildering array of private sector computer services providers. New Zealand and Australia were at the forefront of a trend towards contracting-out information technology during the 1990s. In Japan, government information systems have never been "insourced," but are provided "free" (companies recoup their profits via long-standing maintenance contracts) with hardware systems purchases from domestic providers such as Hitachi, Toshiba, and Fujitsu. The consequent extremely low levels of expertise in technological issues resident within the Japanese central government can at least in part explain Japan's poor showing in consultancy e-government rankings (Igarashi 2003).

Contracting trends and regulatory regimes vary across countries, meaning that different markets of computer companies providing IT services to government and distinctive "contracting regimes" develop (Dunleavy et al. 2004). These regimes shape the type of "internal virtuality" that emerges across governments. In the UK, an extremely distinctive contracting pattern developed through a succession of centrally driven contracting initiatives, particularly Market Testing in the 1980s and the Private Finance Initiative (PFI) in the 1990s, an arrangement that was intended to transfer the risk inherent in large-scale government IT systems to the private sector. Sustained contracting has resulted in several huge-scale "partnerships" between UK government agencies and global computer services providers, unique in the world in terms of the length of the contract and contract value. The result is that almost every department and agency is involved in at least one major partnership arrangement and that many aspects of organizational activity are completely reliant on the partnership for successful operation. The Passports Agency was paralysed in 2001 when a new system for allocating passports developed by Siemens crashed and the Contributions Agency miscalculated many hundreds of thousands of NI contributions with the second version of the National Insurance Recording System, developed by Arthur Andersen. The Immigration and Naturalization Directorate was left with 12,000 letters unanswered after a new system developed by Siemens was delayed and finally abandoned in 2001 (for a list of fifteen recent IT disasters which paralysed UK government departments see Organ 2003: 32). All these agencies are now virtual in the sense that they cannot operate without the successful functioning of a major partnership.

There are other examples of governments with much lower levels of information technology outsourcing, particularly across Europe. In the Netherlands, for example, contracts with private sector providers are very small and far more expertise is maintained within government departments. Canada outsources so little of its government information technology that major computer services providers in Ottawa see the federal government as their greatest competitor. Such a strategy does not appear to have damaged Canada's attempt to lead the race in developing an electronic government; the country has been top of the Accenture rankings in e-government for the three years between 2000 and 2003 (Accenture 2003, 2002).

Types of contracting arrangement also vary in the extent to which they actually encourage virtuality; after all, the idea of accountability through a contract is a hierarchical notion. In countries with high levels of information technology out-sourcing, what Garvey (1993) called the "shadow bureaucracy" of "beltway ban-dits" (as he termed the huge range of private sector computer services providers around the suburbs of Washington, dependent upon the US federal government for their existence) is certainly a growing and tangible feature of the govern-ment, accompanying the "formal bureaucracy" of traditional government. In the UK, major long-term partnerships make for a blurring of distinctions between public and private officials: if an employee of the company Electronic Data Systems has spent the last ten years working in Inland Revenue offices as part of the £1 billion contract arrangement between the two organizations, is he a private or public official? Such arrangements can bear a remarkable similarity to more traditional organizational forms.

Furthermore, these partnerships can develop extremely strong external bound-aries, with the computer services providers keen to guard commercial confidenti-ality and shore up the relationship against competition from other market providers. Due to the distinctive nature of public sector contracting (generally adversarial relationships where private sector profits are tightly controlled), gov-ernment agencies tend not to use the more relational style of contracting preferred by the private sector and there is less evidence of the loose configurations of organizations that characterize the "virtual corporation." In this sense, virtuality may exist within the relationship, but organizational boundaries around the so-called partnership may actually be reinforced. Countries operating the Anglo-Saxon model of contracting (the US, the UK, Australia, and New Zealand, for example) tend to develop particularly adversarial relationships where the contract is tightly adhered to and acts as a kind of an internal barrier within the organiza-tion. In Japan, as one official of the Ministry of Economy, Trade, and Industry (METI) put it, "there is a computer system room over there (in the METI building), and people there are only from Fujitsu and few officials have access to the room" (Igarashi 2003: 56). In other countries, such as the Netherlands, a more consensual Rhineland model of contracting means that cross-cutting networks have more of a chance to make both internal and external boundaries less distinct, where the same people have "virtual identities" in both public and private spheres (Margetts et al. 2003).

13.2.3 Virtual Inter-Organizational Networks

The "convergence" sense of virtuality is the most difficult of the three to measure quantitatively. But there is qualitative evidence to suggest that it has been slower than the other two to emerge in government, in the terms envisaged by the postmodernist commentators such as Frissen (1999) or (less optimistically) by those writing of the "hollow state" (Milward 1996; Milward and Provan 2000,

2003). It is hard to identify public sector equivalents of the Dell Computer or Automotive examples provided above. Also, virtual networks are more likely to be necessitated by NPM trends rather than by government maximising the benefits of technological development. Agencification in the UK and New Zealand, governments at the forefront of NPM trends, led to fragmentation of government departments without any subsequent virtual reintegration. It is more the case of such fragmentation posing challenges to technological development rather than technology providing integrative solutions. In the US, Kettl (2002: 110) notes an increasing reliance by government on a wide variety of partnerships with non-profit and voluntary organizations but these inter-organizational relationships seem to owe more to contracting trends and the outsourcing of what were previously core government functions than to technological development. The concept of "governance" which has arizen out of an increasing emphasis on networks as an alternative to bureaucracy owes little to any identification of technological trends and indeed Kettl's own analysis of the "*Transformation of Governance*" in the US has only passing reference to the Internet or ICTs. Likewise, Bardach's (1998) enthusiastic treatize on *Getting Agencies to Work Together* makes little mention of the potential of information technology to aid the process. In the UK the election of a "new Labour" government in 1997 brought many euphoric references to "joined-up" government and "holistic government" (Perri 6 et al. 2002), more "muted" (Ling 2002) but still present in the second term. Although some calls for holistic government rested on the potential of web-based technologies to aid collaborative working (e.g., Perri 6 1997), "joined-up government in Britain . . . is best viewed as a group of responses to the perception that services had become fragmented and that this fragmentation was preventing the achievement of important goals of public policy" (Ling 2002: 616). Surveys of joined-up government (Ling 2002; Pollitt 2003) after five years of the Labour government pointed to the difficulties involved in "joining-up," the long time-frame needed to implement joined-up initiatives and the impossibility of imposing "joined-up-ness" from the top down (see Pollitt 2003: 48–9).

Certainly web-based technologies lend themselves to the notion of joined up government, but the technology alone cannot make such linkages. Rather, it is in countries where there is a culture of networking across organizational boundaries that this kind of development is most noticeable. In the Netherlands, for example, extended patterns of relationships between political actors and interest groups originated in the basic societal partition of a Roman Catholic, Protestant, and general secular block (Godfroij 1995: 179). These relationships remained when the socio-political blocks disintegrated at the end of the twentieth century, meaning that Dutch administrative culture is strongly networked. Such networks are strengthened through the use of modern technologies, but pre-date the development.

Likewise the capacity of the Internet to facilitate the existence of loose configurations of organizations seems to be under-used by governmental organizations in comparison to other sectors. Once again, it is difficult to generalize across whole sectors, but in the private sector, management theorists have started to argue for whole new ways of understanding organizational structure and for organigraphs, composed of "hubs" and "webs" rather than organizational charts to reflect the complex organizational forms that are now commonplace (Mintzberg and Van der Heyden 1999: 89). Pressure groups and protest organizations have been quick to capitalize on the capacity of web-based technologies to circumvent the need for organization and to organize protests between groups and individuals on a global basis. The non-profit organization Médecins Sans Frontières is made up of a set of national offices with no world headquarters: CEOs from the national offices meet periodically and when a crisis arises, people from the offices communicate informally with one another and organizations on the ground, forming a loose web (Mintzberg and Van der Heyden 1999: 92). Terrorist networks also have revolutionized their activities through such technologies, presenting a distinctive challenge to non-networked governments. It is again difficult to generalize across whole sectors—but within individual countries it does seem that governments have been slower than other organizations to form new structures of this kind (see Margetts 2000, for a discussion of protest and participation in the UK). The exception here is those governments with a particularly networked culture, such as the Netherlands where officials have actually identified the increasing web awareness of citizens and social groups as a challenge for government (Margetts and Dunleavy 2002).

13.3 THE VIRTUAL STATE OF THE FUTURE

All three types of virtuality identified here—the development of a virtual face, internal virtuality and the development of virtual networks—are existent within different public organizations in different countries. Both "e-government" and New Public Management trends have brought virtuality in various guises, and look set to continue to do so. What will be the drivers and barriers to change—and how might the virtual organization look in the future? It is clear from both the commentaries and evidence presented above that a variety of scenarios could emerge. Both trends will be important but they are inextricably intertwined and the relationship between them will crucially shape the future of "virtual government."

With respect to e-government, there are a number of drivers towards further change, particularly growth of Internet and web usage (now over 50 percent of UK citizens and well above that in the US, Canada, and Scandinavian countries) which means that as citizens and firms increasingly interact with all other organizations on-line, they will increasingly demand such facilities from government. Web-based technologies offer new potential for quality of service and extensions of services (particularly in terms of 24/7 access). E-government offers major possibilities for reductions in the costs of government, to the extent whereby it can be argued that electronic transactions should be made compulsory for some services for some groups of user (see Margetts and Yared 2003). Such an incentive would expose government to the same drivers as private firms experiencing the competitive disadvantage of not introducing electronic innovations, the key reason why airlines now all offer electronic booking facilities. Other drivers are provided centrally, as governments across the world have imposed strong central "pushes" towards e-government, with prime ministers or presidents imposing central targets and deadlines for progress on e-government in many countries.

To what extent can we expect these drivers to bring "virtual government?" The dominant way of assessing e-government change in the IT industry (see for example UNPAN 2001; Accenture 2002, 2003; Taylor Nelson Sofres 2002, 2003) relies on the so-called "stages model" which maps the development of e-government into distinct phases (Dunleavy and Margetts 2002: 11). Here, e-government proceeds in five stages, following on from each other in increasing order of implementation difficulty, desirability for society and the levels of sophistication of systems which emerge. The stages (for a fuller exposition see Dunleavy and Margetts 2002: 11) start with (1) a *basic web site* which holds basic information about the agency, electronic versions of the agency's documentation and serves as an on-line advertising hoarding. (2) *Electronic publishing* occurs when an agency's web site becomes an important element of its overall communications strategy. Citizens or firms can download forms to fill in and post back, but cannot do on-line submissions and the external web site does not link in any significant way with the agency's back-office systems. (3) The third stage comes when agencies move on to *interactive e-publishing*, where users can personalize how the site works for them, with effective search tools (for instance by specifying an address or postcode to obtain relevant local information) and the external web site links extensively to some back office systems. At least some forms can be submitted on-line and there is email contact with officials. (4) A *transactional web-site* exists when users can accomplish more sophisticated dealings with the agency on-line, through authenticating themselves securely to the agency and then make secure payments or request personalized information from the agency's databases. There are two types of transactional services: one-off transactions, in which the system does not use prior information about the user, or "account management" type transactions, where the transaction relies on full account history of previous dealings with the agency, similar to Internet banking. Finally (5), *joined-up e-governance* would be achieved when the web site can facilitate "one-stop" shop services for citizens, and provide access not just to one agency, but across other relevant central government agencies or tiers of government. On such a model, the "virtual face of an organization" develops first, followed by a hollowing out of the organization as links between internal information systems and the web site replace bureaucratic processes with an eventual emphasis on inter-organizational linkages, "joined-up governance" and the organization as a virtual network represented by a web site.

However, this progression through the stages (much loved by international management consultancies for its help in creating indicators to "measure" countries' relative success in attaining e-government) is misleading and sheds little light on the future of the virtual organization. First, some of the model's criteria of progress are particularly questionable when applied to the public sector. Many agencies do not undertake individual transactions with citizens because of their fundamental role; defense agencies or foreign offices for example. The model seems to privilege certain kinds of agency which do transactions, as they will have more incentive to get further through the stages. For those agencies that don't transact with their customers, a stages model approach would lead them to believe that the jump from 1 to 5 above would be completely unachievable. But in fact agencies can make progress towards this end point in all four remaining ways—by building up full-scale electronic publishing, by pushing more interactive publishing strategies, by developing "one-off" on-line transactions, or by "account management" transactions. There is no automatic reason why government strategy should favor any one of these routes over others. Instead, each agency should ask "Given the type of organization that we are, and the kind of functions that we have, our fundamental mission and role, how far can we and should we move towards fully electronic or digital operations?" (Dunleavy and Margetts 2002: 12). As illustrated above by the example of central government portals, even a basic web site can achieve virtuality in all three senses defined here—in presenting a virtual face to citizens, in reducing the need for internal organizational capacity and in creating virtual networks of organizations and individuals.

Second, the stages model of development is inherently modernist, with an inbuilt assumption that a government or an organization will only proceed forward through the stages. Accenture (2003: 6–7) characterize their version in terms of "maturity": "eGovernment matures through a series of plateaus," with "continual growth of all countries." The assumption is that all governments will go forward towards the next stage and there is no going back, which would involve becoming "less mature." But is such a development inevitable? When applied at the level of a whole government, this assumption will lead policy makers to believe in the inevitability of the eventual realization of the utopian end-goal of holistic e-governance. For UNPAN, this would mean "Seamless government" (the "full integration of e-services across administrative boundaries" (UNPAN 2001); for Accenture, "Service Transformation" will include improved customer service delivery as the vision; take-up of services as a key measure of success; eGovernment will become part of wider service transformation; and multichannel integration will result (Accenture 2003).

In contrast to the stages model view, in the real world there exist a range of barriers to progress towards virtuality. There are a range of "demand side" cultural barriers that work against citizens and businesses using government on-line services and "supply-side" cultural barriers, distinctive to governmental organizations, that could work against a holistic approach (see Margetts and Dunleavy 2002 for a full discussion). A major barrier is the difficulty (or at least, the perceived difficulty) in building linkages between legacy systems (existing IT systems which pre-date web-based technologies) and the web site, or between internal legacy systems, which can create "silos" within organizations as difficult to penetrate as the departmental silos long lamented of UK public administration. Private companies tend to be more relaxed about building software (called "middleware") which translates inputs from web sites into the formats required by legacy systems, and private officials will admit (privately!) that their "legacy systems are a mess." But such an approach is uncongenial to the formal and bureaucratic approach of government agencies to systems development, and (particularly in the UK) they are more likely to pursue complete "transformations" of their existing systems which can paralyse e-government development for many years (Dunleavy and Margetts 2002; Margetts and Yared 2003).

Other barriers to virtuality come from the relationship between e-government and new public management trends, particularly contracting. With respect to contracting of IT itself, Dunleavy et al. (2004) have established the relationship between government and the IT industry through a "contact regime" of computer service providers as a vital determinant of e-government success. With regard to contracting more generally, Milward and Provan (2003) point out that while the key to managing networks of service providers is services integration, any moves to do so in countries where new public management reform has been strong run up against a "competing implicit theory" that explains effectiveness in terms of competitive contracting: "this strategy raises the question of what incentive agencies have to collaborate if they are in competition with one another?" (Milward and Provan 2003: 3). "Holistic e-government" may be the utopian endpoint of e-government change, but as noted above, there is nothing inevitable about its development and its progress will run up against barriers to collaboration and cooperation.

So are public organizations becoming "such for practical purposes although not in name or according to strict definition?". As noted above, there are clear problems with measuring virtuality, but there is enough evidence to suggest that—via the development of a virtual face, internal virtualization fueled by outsourcing (particularly IT outsourcing) and via more limited development of virtual networks—the definition of what it means to be an organization is changing. But the evidence presented above demonstrates that there are strong variations across countries and the relationship between e-government and NPM will shape what sort of virtuality emerges in any government and whether it might be viewed as a positive or negative change. Dunleavy, Margetts et al. (2000, 2004) identified four possible outcomes from the interaction between NPM and "digital era governance":

- *Digital NPM Scenario*: e-government is filtered and sifted by bureaucratic and political decision makers still committed to NPM perspectives, with radical outsourcing still a feature of public management and few of the potential holistic effects of e-government being realized
- *Transition to a Digital State*: full implementation of e-government effects and a "writing off" of NPM
- *Policy Mess*: e-government changes are only half-heartedly implemented, cutting across NPM legacies, particularly fragmentation. Web-based activities are added to—rather than replacing—existing work processes and government bureaucracies slowly add web-based capabilities to existing work processes and government
- *State Residualization*: e-government changes are adopted half-heartedly within an NPM framework, with governments and agencies resisting the logic of reintegration and allowing IT corporations with big government contracts to dictate the pace of change.

The transition to a digital state scenario would bring virtualization of public agencies in the most positive sense, characterized by collaboration, process reengineering, cooperation, reintegration of NPM-fueled fragmentation and ultimately a more holistic style of government—virtualization in all three senses. The digital NPM scenario would involve both radical outsourcing change and e-government change directed at public sector downsizing, meaning that "internal virtualization" would be the most prominent, but "virtual networks" would be unlikely to emerge. In this scenario, the "virtual state" consists of strictly demarcated contract relationships between a small governmental core and private sector providers of on-line services, which are likely to be huge global corporations. Accountability runs through the contract and this type of "virtual state" is furthest removed from democratic control. In the "policy mess" scenario, where NPM trends cut across moves towards digital governance, weak forms of "virtual face" will be added onto existing organizational arrangements but there will be no re-engineering of organizational arrangements left over from the NPM era. The confusing nature of these forms of virtuality will work against transparency and democratic accountability. In the "state residualization" scenario, internal virtuality will be present in its most negative sense, with enfeebled government agencies stripped of organizational capacity struggling—but failing—to capitalize upon technological developments.

REFERENCES

ACCENTURE (2002), *eGovernment Leadership—Realizing the Vision*, Government Executive Series, available at www.accenture.com

—— (2003), *eGovernment Leadership —Engaging the Customer*, Government Executive Series, available at www.accenture.com

BARDACH, E. (1998), *Getting Agencies to Work Together: The Practice and Theory of Managerial Craftsmanship*, Washington: Brookings Institution.

BEYERLEIN, M. (2001), *Virtual Teams*, Elsevier Science.

CARTWRIGHT, P. (2002), "Only Converge: Networks and Connectivity in the Information Economy," *Business Strategy Review* 13(2): 59–64.

CLAYTON THOMAS, J., and STREIB, G. (2003), "The New Face of Government: Citizen-Initiated Contacts in the Era of E-Government," *Journal of Public Administration Research and Theory* 13(1): 83–101.

DUNLEAVY, P. (1994), "The Globalization of Public Services Production: Can Government Be 'Best in World'?" *Public Policy and Administration* 9(2): 36–65.

—— and MARGETTS, H. (1999), *Government on the Web*, London: National Audit Office), HC 87.

—— —— (2000), "The Advent of Digital Government: Public Bureaucracies and the State in the Internet Age," paper to the Annual Conference of the American Political Science Association, Omni Shoreham Hotel, Washington, 4 September 2000, developed for publication as DUNLEAVY, P. MARGETTS, H., and BASTOW, S. (2004), "NPM is Dead—Long-live Digital-era Governance," to be submitted to *Journal of Public Administration Research and Theory* available at www.governmentontheweb.org.uk

—— —— (2002), *Government on the Web II*, London: National Audit Office), HC 764.

—— —— BASTOW, S., and TINKLER, J. (2000), "The Digital State and Government-Business Relations in the Information Age," paper to the Annual Conference of the Political Studies Association of the UK, London School of Economics, April 2000 available at www.governmentontheweb.org.uk

—— —— —— —— (2004), "Government IT Performance and the Power of the IT Industry," paper presented at e-Government: the 4th social study of IT workshop at the LSE, 22 March 2004, accepted for and to be presented at APSA 2004 and submitted to *Public Administration Review.*

—— —— —— —— YARED, H. (2001), "Policy Learning and Public Sector Information Technology: Contractual and E-government Changes in the UK, Australia and New Zealand," Paper for the American Political Science Association's Annual Conference 2001, 28 August –1 September, Hilton Hotel, San Francisco.

FOUNTAIN, J. E. (2001), *Building the Virtual State: Information Technology and Institutional Change*, Washington: Brookings Institution.

FRISSEN, P. (1999), *Politics, Governance and Technology: A Postmodern Narrative on the Virtual State*, London: Edward Elgar.

GARVEY, G. (1993), *Facing the Bureaucracy: Living and Dying in a Public Agency*, San Francisco: Jossey Bass.

GODFROIJ, A. (1995), "Public Policy Networks: Analysis and Management," in W. KICKERT and F. VAN VUGHT (eds.), *Public Policy and Administrative Sciences in the Netherlands*, Prentice Hall, 179–98.

HAGEN, M., and KUBICEK, H. (2000), *One-Stop-Government in Europe: Results from 11 National Surveys*, University of Bremen.

HEINTZE, T., and BRETSCHNEIDER, S. (2000), "Information Technology and Restructuring in Public Organizations: Does Adoption of Information Technology Affect Organizational

Structures, Communications and Decision Making?", *Journal of Public Administration Research and Theory* 10(4): 801–30.

HOLMES, D. (eds.) (1997), *Virtual Politics: Identity and Community in Cyberspace*, London: Sage.

IGARASHI, T. (2003), "Why is the Japanese e-government lagging behind? Reforms towards a virtual government," MSc dissertation, UCL School of Public Policy, September 2003.

KETTL, D. (2002), *The Transformation of Governance: Public Administration for Twenty-First Century America*, Washington: John Hopkins Press.

KRAEMER, K., and DEDRICK, J. (2001), *Dell Computer: Using E-commerce to Sort the Virtual Company*, web-based working paper, Center for Research on Information Technology and Organizations, University of California, Irvine.

LING, T. (2002), "Delivering Joined-Up Government in the UK: Dimensions, Issues and Problems," *Public Administration* 80(4): 615–42.

LIPNACK, J., and STAMPS, J. (2000), *Virtual Teams: People Working Across Boundaries with Technology*, John Wiley.

MARGETTS, H. (1999), *Information Technology in Government: Britain and America*, London: Routledge.

—— (2000), "Political Participation and Protest," in P. DUNLEAVY, A. GAMBLE, I. HOLLIDAY, and G. PEELE (eds.), *Developments in British Politics 6*, London: Macmillan, 185–202.

—— (2003), *Electronic Government: Method or Madness?* Inaugural lecture, University College London, 13 February 2003 available at www.ucl.ac.uk/s

—— and DUNLEAVY, P. (2002), *Cultural Barriers to e-government*, London: NAO), available at www.governmentontheweb.org.uk and www.nao.gov.uk

—— and YARED, H. (2003), *Incentivization of e-government*, London: NAO), available at www.governmentontheweb.org.uk and www.nao.gov.uk

—— DUNLEAVY, P. BASTOW, S. and TINKLER, J. (2003), "Leaders and Followers: E-government, Policy Innovation and Policy Transfer in the European Union," paper to the European Union Studies Association, EUSA), conference, Nashville, Tennessee, USA, 27 March, available at www.governmentontheweb.org.uk

MILWARD, H. B. (1994*a*), "Nonprofit Contracting and the Hollow State: A Review Essay", *Public Administration Review* 54: 73–7.

—— (1994*b*), "Contracting for the Hollow State," in P. Ingraham and B. Romzak (eds.), *New Paradigms for Government*, San Francisco: Jossey Bass, 41–62.

—— (1996), "The Changing Character of the Public Sector," in J. L. Perry (ed.), *Handbook of Public Administration*, San Francisco: Jossey Bass, 77–91.

—— PROVAN, K.G., and ELSE, B. (1993), "What Does the Hollow State Look Like?", in B. Bozeman (ed.), *Public Management: The State of the Art*, San Francisco: Jossey Bass, 309–22.

—— —— (2000), "Governing the Hollow State," *Journal of Public Administration Research and Theory* 10: 359–79.

—— —— (2003), "Managing the Hollow State: Collaboration and Contracting," Working Paper, School of Public Administration and Policy, University of Arizona, see http://www.bpa.arizona.edu/~spap/faculty/milward/

MINTZBERG, H. (1985), *Structure in Fives*, London: Macmillan.

—— (1996), "Managing Government, Governing Management," *Harvard Business Review* (May–June), 75–83.

—— and VAN DER HEYDEN (1999), "Organigraphs: Drawing How Companies Really Work," *Harvard Business Review* (September–October), 87–94.

ORGAN, J. (2003), "The Coordination of e-Government in Historical Context," *Public Policy and Administration* 18(2).

PEARSALL, J., and TRUMBLE, B. (eds.) (1995), *The Oxford English Reference Dictionary*, 2nd edn., Oxford: Oxford University Press.

PERRI 6 (1997), *Holistic Government*, London: Demos.

—— LEAT, D. SELTZER, K., and STOKER, G. (2002), *Towards Holistic Governance: the New Reform Agenda*, London: Palgrave.

POLLITT, C. (2003), "Joined-up Government: A Survey," *Political Studies Review* 1(1): 34–49.

QUINN, J. (1992), *Intelligent Enterprise: a New Paradigm for a New Era*, New York: Macmillan.

ROBINS, K., and WEBSTER, F. (eds.) (2002), *The Virtual University? Knowledge, Markets and Management*, Oxford: Oxford University Press.

ROSECRANCE, R. (1999), *The Rise of the Virtual State: Wealth and Power in the Coming Century*, New York: Basic Books.

TAYLOR NELSON SOFRES (2002), *What is the Online Use of Government?*, November.

—— (2003), *Government Online: An International Perspective 2003*, Global Summary, available at www.tnsofres.com/21451_global_27nov03

THOMAS, J. C., and STREIB, G. (2003), "The New Face of Government: Citizen-Initiated Contacts in the Era of E-Government," *Journal of Public Administration Research and Theory* 13: 83–102

UNITED NATIONS Online Network in Public Administration and Finance, UNPAN (2001), "Benchmarking E-government: a Global Perspective, Assessing the UN Member States," http://unpan1.un.org/intradoc/groups/public/documents/un/unpan003984.pdf

CHAPTER 14

THE THEORY OF THE AUDIT EXPLOSION

MICHAEL POWER

14.1 INTRODUCTION

THE theory of the audit explosion refers to the growth of audit and related monitoring practices associated with public management reform processes (Power 1994). This growth was conspicuous in the UK context during the 1980s and early 1990s, but was also evident to varying degrees in other countries where public sector reforms took place. The theory has two main points of focus, respectively *explanatory* and *critical*. First, it seeks to document and explain the emergence of new patterns and intensities of auditing and inspection. Second, it focuses critically on the consequences of auditing for auditees and, in particular, on a range of side effects and unintended consequences for public services.

This chapter revisits the main elements of the theory of the audit explosion, critically addressing the extent to which its claims have relevance beyond the UK context. The argument begins with the traditional model of auditing, against which the transformations implied by the audit explosion theory can be evaluated. This is

The author is grateful for the financial support of the UK Economic and Social Research Council and of the P. D. Leake Trust, managed by Chartered Accountants Trustees Limited. The author is also grateful for discussions with Christopher Hood in the development of the arguments in this chapter.

followed by a broad, and no doubt familiar, account of the public management reforms which have, in some countries and in some domains, been strongly associated with an audit explosion. Third, an explicit comparison between the UK and the USA is made and its implications for the theory are considered.

The second half of the chapter shifts to the critical focus of the theory of the audit explosion. First, the significance of auditable systems of control for the expansion of audit processes is emphasized. Second, a variety of adverse consequences of the audit explosion are addressed. The chapter concludes with a series of reflections on the normative issues at stake in the design of auditing and inspection practices if the worst excesses of the audit explosion are to be avoided.

14.2 THE TRADITIONAL AUDIT MODEL

Traditional financial auditing in the public sector, which still forms the bedrock of much auditing work and is far from being superseded, is primarily focused on the regularity and legality of transactions. This more or less routine checking function is largely unglamorous and public sector auditors have tended to have low status within administrative and management hierarchies as a consequence. Under this traditional model bureaucratic hierarchies and related oversight mechanisms provide the primary focus for administrative control, with auditing, both internal and external, as rather minor adjuncts of this system. Prior to the 1980s, supreme audit institutions (SAIs) in different countries tended to be relatively invisible technocratic organizations within the public administration fabric, dominated by a transactions and systems focus, with at best a minor role in the policy discourses of public management. Perhaps the most traditional audit of all is reflected in the early history of the US General Accounting Office (GAO) which engaged in *ex ante* transaction authorization. This soon became impractical due to the volume of transactions, and gave way to *ex post* testing of legal compliance with authorization being conducted at the departmental level (Mosher 1979). The "court of auditors" model, which characterizes a number of Continental European SAIs, certainly afforded much higher status to its functionaries, but was traditionally concerned primarily with the legal and managerial authority and regularity of transactions. Even today, the European Court of Auditors continues to operate with very traditional transaction sampling methodologies and newspaper headlines about European Union fraud are estimates based on statistical extrapolations.

The low-key conception of public sector auditing as an *ex post* transaction checking function helped to support institutional myths of its neutrality as a technical practice focused primarily on financial control. Despite some notable exceptions (e.g., Normanton, 1966; Mosher 1979), SAIs also aroused little interest among public administration scholars. Under this traditional model of public sector auditing, it is not relevant to wider discussions of organizational perform-ance and effectiveness. Traditional auditing did not disturb established managerial climates of "mutuality" and hierarchical bureaucratic oversight, and the auditor of the 1960s and 1970s was largely unthinkable as a possible agent of public sector reform. Accordingly, the new auditing mandates in the name of efficiency, effec-tiveness, and performance which came to prominence in the 1980s had to be constructed against the background legacy of a traditional mode of operation which was never entirely superseded and which still constitutes a bedrock of auditing work (Scott 2003).

14.3 Public Management Reform and the Audit Explosion

The audit explosion must be set within the broader context of transformations in public management, namely the wave of public sector reforms experienced in a number of different countries, which has been characterized as the "new public management" (NPM hereafter). NPM is a label for a complex and varied set of transformations involving, *inter alia*, a renewed focus on cost control and efficiency, devolved budgeting and decentralization of managerial authority, the creation of market and quasi-market mechanisms involving new contractual forms, a focus on service quality coupled to new mechanisms for public account-ability, the development of a multiplicity of performance indicators for public services, private–public partnerships and privatization initiatives. Thus character-ized, the NPM is neither a unitary program nor a clearly defined policy. It is perhaps best understood as a wave of reactions against the elements and assump-tions of traditional public administration, radicalizing existing concerns and cri-tiques and borrowing from highly idealized elements of private sector management thinking (e.g., Osborne and Gaebler 1992) to acquire a transnational momentum (Sahlin-Andersson 2001).

Although the NPM has taken different forms, timings, and intensities in differ-ent countries, some common drivers for reform can be identified. The first encompassed political demands for greater accountability of public service pro-viders, coupled to neoliberal preferences for exercising economic control at a distance through the "managerialist" instruments of accounting, budgetary con-trol, auditing, and quality assurance. Second, more or less objective conditions of fiscal constraint created a political determination to reduce public borrowing. A third driver was a long-standing concern with the efficiency and quality of public sector services, which could be newly expressed in terms of performance accountability and customer focus.

The theory of the audit explosion attributes the growth of auditing to these three pressures for change, which specifically extend regularity and legality mandates to operationalize new demands for efficiency and value for money. However, these pressures were in themselves insufficient. The audit explosion was also a function of institutional supply side factors, namely the existence and legitimacy of professional advisory groups, able and willing to redefine their work in the name of new political and legal demands. Thus, in broad terms it can be argued that the timing and extent of the NPM changes outlined above was contingent on the existence of a class of implementers of policy and promoters of best management practice (Saint-Martin 2000). In the UK context, the emergence of these professional groups as re-inventers of auditing in the service of NPM corresponded to the demise in relative status and policy power of other groups, namely service providers (teachers, doctors) and other professionals. This repositioning of expertise in the hierarchy of public management, in which auditors, inspectors and evaluators rise at the expense of other professionals is a variable but critical consequence of the audit explosion to be discussed further below.

In the UK, a crucial supply side factor was the existence of private and public sector accounting professionals, and related consultants in accounting systems, quality assurance and business strategy. However, in jurisdictions without a tradition of external advice or a ready supply of monitors and advisers (e.g., Germany, Japan), or where accounting professionals tended to relatively low status (e.g., USA), the audit explosion was muted. In these contexts existing professional elites, civil servants and service providers such as doctors, were able to absorb managerialist pressures for change within their own ranks. In addition legal frameworks and legalistic approaches to public sector control were able to remain pre-eminent points of reference in some countries, suggesting the importance of institutional factors in determining any audit explosion.

In its most extreme form, visible in the UK, Australia ,and New Zealand, NPM pressures for change resulted in the de-legalization and de-traditionalization of auditing mandates and their emergence as tools of economic modernization. Auditing in its various forms became a policy instrument as it never was before, extending its reach beyond the traditional mandate of verification to encompass and operationalise ideals of cost effectiveness, efficiency and, perhaps most problematic of all, effectiveness. These new auditing mandates are most visible in the work of national audit bodies, which in some countries became explicit instruments of public management reform with a key role in monitoring the activities of the state with ever more regulatory and oversight functions.

14.4 THE AUDIT EXPLOSION IN COMPARATIVE PERSPECTIVE: AMERICA AND BRITAIN

In its original form the theory of the audit explosion was mainly UK based and lacked a comparative focus. Accordingly, a useful test of the explanatory merits of the theory lies in developing the comparative focus a little further. Put simply, why did an audit explosion occur in the UK and not in the United States? Indeed, audit and monitoring more generally do not figure at all in Osborne and Gaebler's (1992) highly influential reform "bible" for NPM in the USA, which focuses mainly on reengineering "business" processes and improving customer responsiveness in public services.

A possible explanation for this difference is to be found in American and British exceptionalism. Following Moran (2003), it can be suggested that the audit explosion was more pronounced in the UK (and New Zealand) because NPM reforms were part of a substantive challenge to an existing system of rule, and a response to an institutional crisis. In contrast, in the United States the crisis was, arguably, more technocratic and organizational in form. Auditing exploded in the UK because it became a key instrument of attack on "club government," understood as a form of closed professional self-regulation, which needed to be reconstituted with "new ambitious systems of surveillance." The audit explosion in the UK was therefore part of a broad institutional reform process to reconfigure modes of government steering via new and existing regulatory agencies, such as auditing and inspection bodies. Such bodies, particularly the Audit Commission dealing with local government reform in England and Wales, were instrumental not merely in management change but also in redrawing the boundary between the public and the private sphere.

Far from signaling an executive government withdrawal from public sector management issues in the UK, the use of auditing and related instruments of control in fact widened the scope of potential intervention, changed its quality to action "at a distance" and added greater formality than hitherto. It is this that essentially characterizes the new British regulatory state (Moran 2003). Auditing was given a radical reforming role which is also visible in New Zealand and Canada, but not in the USA. In the UK, not only was there an army of accountants ready and willing to reinvent themselves, but legislative and judicial frameworks were also relatively weak sources of administrative authority and control as compared with the mutualist "club" legacy of a private style of negotiation among insiders. Indeed, Hood et al. (2004) argue that the UK audit explosion was a process of catch-up, compensating for the lack of oversight provided by these other mechanisms in other countries.

In contrast with the UK, the USA has a longer tradition of powerful regulatory agencies and oversight mechanisms dating from the 1930s, which were further developed in the human rights and welfare revolution in the 1960s and by the creation of Inspectors General in the 1970s. Indeed, a simple answer to the puzzle of the American audit explosion is that it had already happened as a broader oversight explosion in the 1960s in the context of an expansion of welfare and regulatory programs. In this setting the GAO developed a capacity for program evaluation which was profoundly different in character and expertise from the traditional audit model (Mosher 1979). In addition, it can be argued that American institutions of monitoring and oversight were more legalistic and procedural in orientation, and operated in an increasingly adversarial regulatory culture (Kagan and Axelrad 2000). As a consequence of this, regulatory and public administrative institutions developed detailed operational rules, and related audit and monitoring practices were defined as compliance based activities in relation to these rules. In short, American public sector auditing operates in the shadow of the law much more than its UK counterpart. Consequently, accountants are lower status agents of change in the US public administration context and audit is a relatively minor adjunct of other oversight programs.

In contrast to the USA, UK auditing and auditors were able to claim additional jurisdictions over new problems of efficiency and value for money. In both the USA and the UK, NPM-style reforms were stimulated by very similar neoliberal concerns about the quality of public management and the capacity of the state to steer and control. However, in the USA these challenges operated within a more stable set of institutional arrangements than in the UK. In the USA the crisis of public administration was conceptualized as technocratic, and auditing could only grow as a compliance and due diligence function within a regulatory oversight explosion that had already occurred in the 1960s. In the UK the crisis was perceived and articulated as more than technocratic; it concerned the very culture of governance itself. Consequently, the audit explosion was more than just a solution to technical steering and control difficulties; it was also an intervention in this system of governance itself, to reconstitute self-regulation from its club character into something more formal and transparent.

This comparative argument is suggestive but needs greater refinement (See Hood et al. 2004). However, if it is broadly correct, then the theory of the audit explosion can be developed to explain a growth of auditing in only those countries and sectors where there was, and will be, a high degree of technocractic *and* institutional crisis *and* the absence or weakness of compensating oversight institutions. It follows that in countries with a high degree of technocratic crisis, which is not translated into demands for reforms in governance, an audit explosion will be more muted, contained within existing club or hierarchical styles of administration.

To summarize: a comparison between the cases of the USA and the UK suggests that the original theory of the audit explosion can be adapted to take account of the varied institutional conditions under which such a growth of monitoring may take place. The form and substance of auditing will be a function of the distinctive features of the state traditions within which NPM reforms take place. In addition, such a broad brush concept as the audit explosion needs to be sensitive to the variety of institutional levels and sub-sectors which shape very specific audit practices (Hood et al. 2004). Nevertheless, it can be plausibly argued that the British regulatory state was radically overhauled as an attack on club government, and that auditing and related practices were key instruments in this transformation. In contrast, the US regulatory state and related systems of governance were not subject to radical challenge at this time, and the role of audit was a much less significant engine for change than in the UK.

14.5 AUDITING, INSPECTION, AND AUDITABLE SYSTEMS

So far in this chapter, the theory of the audit explosion has been discussed in terms of transformations and extensions of the traditional accounting based concept of audit. However, it is in principle much broader in scope than this, referring also to organizations which have audit-type characteristics, and which are involved in monitoring, inspection and evaluation. This leads to understandable definitional concerns about the scope of the concept of "audit." For example, the audit explosion refers not merely to changing mandates in SAIs, such as such as the General Accounting Office in the USA, The National Audit Office in the UK, the *Bundesrechnungshoefe* in Germany, and the Australian National Audit Office. It also encompasses the many inspectorates and evaluative bodies which address the performance of the "auditee," such as inspectorates for prisons, health and safety in the workplace, educational, medical, and research quality. However, it does not include all institutions of oversight (Hood et al. 2004) and should be methodologically restricted to two convergent families of practices, namely accounting and quality assurance.

The *accounting line of development* of the audit explosion has already been described. NPM reforms placed great emphasis on financial control disciplines and the reform of financial management. From this point of view, accountants emerged as high status actors in a climate of fiscal constraint, shifting the locus of oversight power from bureaucratic elites to financially minded managers. In some countries the financial audit adapted its focus on transaction authority to include the oversight of new performance related mandates, such as cost effectiveness.

Radcliffe (1999) and Everett (2003) document the reconstruction of audit in Canada in the name of "efficiency" and "comprehensiveness."

This accounting dimension of the audit explosion represents a reassembly of the financial audit around new definitions of auditee performance, but anchored in financial concepts. Critically, auditee organizations are to be reformed as part of making them "auditable," so the auditor becomes an explicit change agent, rather than a pure verifier. This transformation has had profound implications for constitutional myths of the independence of SAIs and inspectorates from executive government (Funnell 2003).

The accounting line of development is significant but was probably overstated in the original theory of the audit explosion (e.g., Power 1999: ch. 2 where the financial audit "model" is discussed). A second, equally important, basis for the audit explosion follows a *quality assurance* line of development. This overlaps with the financial auditing transformation and involves the expansion and reform of evaluative bodies and inspectorates operating within the orbit of executive government, such as the French *inspections générales* in France, and the inspectors general in the USA. The inspection process has varied domain specific histories (e.g., prisons, education) drawing on diverse forms of expertise to conduct monitoring, and involving multiple non-financial, auditable indicators of service quality. The audit explosion effect in these settings is reflected in the increasing prominence of quality assurance ideas and practices, building on older concerns with fraud, waste and abuse inside government, together with efforts to focus performance evaluation on outcomes rather than inputs and processes (Hood et al. 2004).

The important link between the two lines of auditing development, accounting and quality assurance, is their emerging common focus on management control systems. ISO 9000 and similar blueprints for management self-knowledge have had a fundamental bearing on the form of the audit and inspection explosion. The design and operation of systems of control is a model of organizational self-observation and creates the possibility of a certain style of external oversight. This is at the very heart of the theory of the audit explosion as a qualitative shift in the lens of auditing and inspection from people, practices and products to systems. Notwithstanding the cross national institutional variations described above, the audit explosion also represents a generic rise in a "control of control" style of monitoring, in which first-order questions of quality are subordinate to a logic of management system integrity, and in which audit serves a virtualist form of "meta-regulation" (Parker 2002: ch. 9; Parker 2003).

Such frameworks for internal control are increasingly (but not exclusively) prescribed in terms of organizational governance and the self-management of risk. From this point of view, auditing is reconfigured as a monitoring tool which provides internal and external assurance of risk management systems (e.g.,

COSO 2004); the risk management explosion of the late 1990s is in essence a risk-based mutation of auditing and inspection processes (Power 2004). However, this governance model which depends on self-inspection processes only works where there is in fact an auditable risk management and internal control process. For example, the European Court of Auditors continues to adopt a traditional trans-actions-based audit largely because it is unable to rely upon the control systems within the European Commission. This is a source of continuing conflict and tension between these two bodies.

The potential standardization of audit and inspection processes in terms of focusing on the formal elements of internal systems should not be underestimated, even if much remains to substantiate the claim empirically. The complex oper-ations of hospitals, schools and police forces become easily "auditable" and "inspectable" by virtue of abstracting from their first order performance objectives and by focusing on the management system for defining and monitoring perform-ance. This transformation of auditing and supervision into a cost-effective "control of control" practice also moves it to center stage of regulatory practices as they evolve modes of "enforced self-regulation" (Ayres and Braithwaite 1992; Parker 2002: ch. 2). Audit emerges as the enforcement arm of regulatory and management systems which prescribe frameworks of internal control and self-management for organizations. Crucially, this focus on systems has had a number of side-effects and unintended consequences which are now discussed.

14.6 CONSEQUENCES OF THE AUDIT EXPLOSION

The importance of the theory of the audit explosion does not just lie in explaining the prominence of auditing in public policy; it also lies in critical intuitions about the consequences of auditing for organizational agents who are audited. It is here that the cross-cultural relevance of the theory is most plausible, but it is also here that the theory takes the argument into less easily visible areas where there have been consequential transformations in working practices.

Audit is not, and never has been, a pure form of observation independent of the domain observed, although this ideal is to be found in text books and is reflected in the traditional model discussed above. Auditing always stands in a transformative relation to organizations, specifically with the imperative of making them auditable by the creation of systems. Accordingly, as the previous section discussed, where an audit explosion can be observed, it is bound up in a wider series of changes having to do with making public sector organizations auditable. This is much more than the technical design of suitable indicators and systems of control, and involves the transformation in the mode of governance of organizations and individuals within them. From this point of view the audit explosion can be characterized by transfers of institutional power to audit bodies who decide on a wide range of issues and who, by definition, overstep their purely auditing jurisdiction to become *de facto* policy makers.

Studies show a variety of strategies by state executives to use audit for political programs (see English 2003; Funnell 2003; Pallott 2003). In contexts where performance is not well defined (e.g., teaching quality as compared with class sizes), the auditor is more likely to become an evaluator or judge in the execution of the audit role (e.g., Everett 2003). Thus, functional sub-areas with weak or contested knowledge bases (social work, psychoanalysis) may exhibit greater tendencies to an audit explosion than those with strongly institutionalized knowledge bases and robust alternative oversight mechanisms. And when the auditor role moves beyond that of inspector of transaction authority to evaluator of target organization performance, there is an inevitable blurring of the audit and advisory roles, as the auditor acts on the organization to create "auditable" systems.

The theory of the audit explosion also suggests that, against traditional myths of neutrality, the growth of auditing has profound impacts on behavior beyond those intended by NPM reform processes, not least in terms of intensifying "auditee mentalities." Work on health (Day and Klein 2001); academia (Strathern 2000; Charlton and Andras 2002); psychotherapy (Davenhill and Patrick 1998), social work (Munro 2004), and counselling (House 1996) all confirm the profound and often perverse effects of the audit explosion. Indeed, it is argued that the growth of auditing, and of systems which seek to represent performance in such a way as to make it readily auditable, leads to a decline of organizational trust (O'Neill 2002) as it generates elaborate and wasteful games of compliance which distract professional attention. Auditing also leads to an excessive concern with representations of individual and collective performance by specialist officers (Miller 2003), to defensive strategies and blamism (Hood 2002) which stifle organizational innovation (Hunt 2003), and to lower employee morale. To this must be added the hidden financial costs of audit compliance as organizations engage in elaborate strategies to make themselves auditable.

The critical part of the theory of the audit explosion challenges audit with the hypothesis that it is a fatal regulatory remedy, which interferes with and distracts the audited organization and its service capability in catastrophic ways. Understanding the behavioral impact of auditing on auditees is the important empirical challenge posed by the theory of the audit explosion. Indeed, the social construction of a new subject, the "auditee," deserves to be the main focus of sociological and anthropological studies of the future. There are suggestions of a profound transformation of the professional subject into an auditable self no longer sure of its right and capability to make judgments (Shore and Wright 2000) and whose civic motivation is "crowded out" by excessive monitoring (Frey and Jegen 2001). Evidence of these negative consequences is increasing but is by no means conclusive (see Parker 2002: ch. 6).

To summarize: the critique of the consequences of auditing contrasts with traditional rationales of auditing and inspection, which state that in situations of distrust between principals and agents, both parties can benefit from auditing which restores trust and enables trade. These rationales require auditors to be operationally suspicious and independent. In order to be credible producers of trust in this way; they must themselves be trusted for their trust production to work. In contrast, the theory of the audit explosion suggests a more complex relationship between auditing and trust, namely where the trust production function threatens to become an end in itself, a self-reproducing industry. First, the theory suggests that, at least in some countries, political systems have demanded more of auditing processes than they can deliver, reflecting an institutionalized trust in audit as a policy instrument which may simply be misguided. Second, the role of audit in the production of trust must be tempered by studies which show that the operation of audits can, by replacing local and tacit forms of professional mutual evaluation with standardized templates, create an excessive preoccupation with representations of performance and associated games, with negative impacts on public service quality. How these pathologies might be designed out of the audit process is the normative challenge for theory of the audit explosion.

14.7 Redesigning Auditing

This final section considers some of the design questions at stake in the preceding analysis, recognising that it is possible to build on empirical evidence to construct a more normative framework (Parker 2002: ix). To answer the question "what would good auditing look like?" a number of dimensions across which the design of auditing might vary can be considered, namely: institutional logic and sanctions; knowledge base; formal organization; operational process; reporting and public responsiveness.

14.7.1 Institutional Logic and Sanctions

Perhaps the most basic issue for the design of auditing and inspection processes is the balance between blame and learning in the treatment of auditees. This balance is not always amenable to explicit control and rhetorics of learning and support at the level of stated mission do not necessarily mean that the process will reflect these values and avoid being blamist in its operations. It is also wrong to suggest that blaming is always undesirable; an ideal design for audit will seek to combine triggers for blaming with a learning, supportive environment. Here, Ayres and Braithwaite's (1992) concept of the ladder of enforcement is helpful by showing how mutualist, supportive modes of auditor and auditee interaction may be combined with possibilities for more blamist strategies when necessary ("mutualist oversight" according to Hood et al. 2004). This requires the institutional design of a rich ladder of trigger points for auditor action, with the most serious sanctions at the top of the ladder. A related issue concerns the overall focus of the audit process and the objects of any possible sanctions: are individual agents the object (subject to discipline, sacking, or shaming) or are organizations the principle focus (subject to fines, closure, or adverse reporting)?

From this point of view, many auditing practices can be seen to be inadequate, having only a limited range of response functions. For example, corporate financial auditing is presently characterized by a thin range of public sanctions i.e., a qualified audit report, which is very serious and is exercised rarely, or the giving of an effective clean bill of health, although this is very coded in form. This suggests that financial auditing predominantly concerns the public production of comfort (Pentland 1993), because the possibilities for anything else are limited and extreme.

The question of institutional logics of blame is relevant to auditors themselves, and not just auditees. One of the pathologies of corporate financial auditing in recent years has been a highly blame-centered and litigious environment for auditors, something which in turn makes them more defensive and therefore less willing to be appropriately blamist about auditees. Borrowing from Hunt's (2003) critique of the pervasive risk-aversity of corporations, it may be suggested that a potential problem of auditing is the "timidity" of "watchdogs who never bark," because the incentives to do so are lacking. The problem of the "timid auditor" is that of a defensive mentality in which avoiding blame and litigation become dominant objectives of the entire audit/monitoring process. From this point of view, it can be observed that prisons, schools, and health and safety inspectors have been historically less timid than, say, financial auditors.

In the end, the question of blame and learning as inherent logics of auditing are a function of the institutional environment within which audit operates, the availability of a ladder of enforcement possibilities and the incentive structure for auditors and inspectors themselves.

14.7.2 Knowledge Base

It was suggested above that the audit explosion is characterized by two principle sources of abstract knowledge: financial auditing and quality assurance. To these must be added the professional logics of evaluation, which are specific to the area in question, such as in medicine and social work. The mix of these three elements can vary over time and the theory of the audit explosion suggests that in some settings the first two have come to dominate and colonize the latter. A specific design issue therefore concerns the relative mix of financial and non-financial expertise, its likely impact on the conduct of the audit and, crucially, its effect on the concept of valuable performance by the auditee which is presupposed by the audit process. Even where public sector auditing mandates have focused on "performance auditing" (Pollitt et al. 1999), realizations of this mandate have been very varied, suggesting considerable operational frictions in making the transition from regularity to "value for money" auditing. For example, Pollitt (2003) notes a tendency in some countries to define performance auditing in terms of efficiency or a more general business review.

These frictions have much to do with the legacy knowledge base of auditing. Notions of performance which become defined in terms of cost-effectiveness, economy and financial regularity will reinforce the financialization of the audit and inspection process. Notions of performance based on values of quality, effectiveness, and outcomes beyond manifest outputs may result in an audit process in which the language of professional judgment still has a voice. And, as suggested above, the audit explosion effect will be dampened by the existence of robust justificatory and evaluative frameworks for determining "good" teaching, "good" medicine, "good" social work as alternative knowledge systems.

14.7.3 Formal Organization and Independence

The question of independence is completely fundamental to the design of audit and inspection processes, and is a persistent source of controversy. However, auditor independence has a number of different dimensions. First, related to the previous discussion of the knowledge base, the degree of *epistemic* independence will determine the extent to which the auditor is dependent on the auditee for knowledge and the extent to which the audit process operates with its own knowledge base. Epistemic dependence will be the norm in complex service settings, although the theory of the audit explosion suggests that auditors develop their own systems based forms of knowledge capable of avoiding much of this complexity.

Second, the degree of *relational* or social independence of the auditor will be critical. From a design point of view, the benefits of learning and information exchange from low relational distance and high mutuality between auditor and auditee must be traded off against the risks of auditor capture. Third, it is possible to contrast the extent to which the auditor's *incentives* are independent from those of the auditee. This matters because auditors and inspectors ideally must have an incentive to make reports when the circumstances require. Where auditors are remunerated by the auditee, and are economically dependent, these incentives may be compromised without the existence of further mechanisms, such as liability law.

Fourth, the degree of formal independence of the body from the audited organization is perhaps the most visible but also least relevant dimension of the independence issue. In the public sector, most SAIs are constitutionally independent of the executive and therefore formally independent of the policy making process. However, as noted above, the audit explosion has been characterized by audit bodies becoming *de facto* interpreters of policy.

These four dimensions of independence suggest its complexity and the need to construct auditing as a trade-off between a number of different elements. Formal independence may be critical for public perception and legitimacy, but epistemic and relational dependence may be operationally desirable and inevitable, provided there are suitable checks and balances.

14.7.4 Operational Process and Style

The operational process of auditing can be designed in a number of ways. First, auditing can be a routine and predictable process or it can be one based more on "contrived randomness" involving surprise visits. Routine visits encourage elaborate pre-visit preparation by the inspectee and have a high degree of legitimacy and defendabiliity. They may be appropriate under conditions of service and information ambiguity where dialogue is needed to construct common frames and to obtain information. In contrast, random visits may use floating resources with rights of access and whistle-blowing potential. Surprise visits may be appropriate in settings where critical performances, e.g., class sizes, numbers of prisoners per cell, are well defined and easily verifiable with forms of direct or pure observation, without reference to other systems of control. Audit processes may be designed with a balance of these routine and non-routine possibilities although, as Hood et al. (2004) note, while contrived randomness can often be found in public administration control activities, it is a relatively weakly institutionalised form of control lacking in advocates and "gurus."

Second, closely related to the contrast between routine and random modes of operation, is a contrast between a focus on auditee control systems and on the first order performances of the auditee. A control of control focus on internal control systems may be efficient and cost-effective, as well as enhancing the self-regulating, self governing capacity of organizations (Parker 2002, 2003). However, it may also have many of the side effects described earlier in this chapter. The control focus is closely related to a risk based approach to audit and inspection, which is increasingly prevalent in a number of areas.

In designing risk-based approaches to auditing, possibilities exist for "light touch" and "proportionate" auditing which modulate audit and inspection activities and give incentives to auditees to develop good internal systems. These risk-based approaches, which trust in the internal self-regulating power of organizations, must be traded-off against the benefits of independent external verification.

Finally, a question arises as to whether it is possible for auditing processes to have the capacity for meta-reflection on their own side effects, such as the costs of compliance, and some of the adverse consequences of the audit explosion described above. The theory of the audit explosion suggests that these negative consequences are rendered systematically invisible, denied, or made irrelevant. In addition, the internalization of these auditing externalities is not likely to be easy to design. Nevertheless, this is the design challenge posed by the theory, for which even some limited cost–benefit analysis would be a modest beginning.

14.7.5 Reporting & Public Responsiveness

The final design dimension of auditing concerns its communicative role via forms of reporting. It is possible to contrast highly standardized and coded forms of report with more customized and extensive narratives seen in performance auditing. It has been suggested that highly legalized environments will tend to create the former, where auditors are reluctant to risk making clear, informative public judgments about auditees. This contrasts with more "intelligent" forms of public audit reporting, which are more accessible to general audiences (O'Neill 2004). The contrast between financial audit reports and those of, say, schools inspectors illustrates these differences. Indeed, public sector auditors have a considerable advantage over their private sector counterparts in this respect.

The degree of public responsiveness will also be reflected in the style of reporting and communicating. Audit can potentially be designed in terms of degrees of public permeability (Parker 2002: ch. 8), meaning the extent to which the audit process is essentially monological, i.e., delivers coded information to a presumed expert community of readers, or whether it is dialogical and engages with the wider publics on whose behalf it speaks (Humphrey and Owen 2000; Watchirs 2003; Courville 2003). Auditor direct engagement with the public is undoubtedly more costly than communicating via reports.

To summarize: auditing practice is not a natural or obvious collection of operations, but has been changed and adapted for different purposes in different settings. This means that it is amenable to conscious design and a number of choices and potential trade-offs have been outlined above. Many of these trade-offs are difficult to engineer because they are a function of wider institutional mechanisms, such as liability law and political culture; others are more amenable to explicit construction. The theory of the audit explosion has suggested a number of potential pathologies of auditing, pathologies which any normative design proposals must take into account and seek to overcome.

14.8 CONCLUSIONS

This chapter has reviewed the theory of the audit explosion across its two primary dimensions: explanatory and critical. The explanatory component requires refinement to account for variation in the scope, timing, and intensity of an oversight explosion in different countries (Power 2000a; Hood et al. 2004). This would take into account the distinctive pattern of NPM reforms in different countries as conditions of possibility for an audit explosion. Such refinements would also enable limited predictions about the likely future shape of an audit explosion. Notwithstanding these weaknesses in the original formulation of the theory, it retains some generic merits, provided that the concept of audit is used broadly, but not too broadly, to characterize a family of monitoring practices ranging from financial audit, to inspections and evaluation. This family, with financial auditing and quality assurance legacies, is characterized by an increasing focus on management systems.

The generic concept and practice of the auditable system of control is central to the critical part of the theory of the audit explosion. Since the theory was originally formulated, considerable regulatory and professional attention has been focused on these internal control systems and the codification of principles of best practice for organizations to adopt a self-monitoring capacity. These principles were further refined to align control practices with risk management broadly understood (e.g., ICAEW 1999; COSO 2004). These developments require a further adaptation of the theory, to embrace not simply a growth in external monitoring requirements but, perhaps more significantly, to account for an intensification and formalization of *internal*, self-monitoring practices at the organizational level (Power, 2000b). Indeed, the internal audit and risk management function in public sector organizations is a conspicuous area for development and growth, with implications for the frequency and intensity of more risk-sensitive external monitoring, as part of a rhetoric of reducing the regulatory burden on organizations.

The critical component of the theory of the audit explosion also focuses on the adverse and unintended consequences of external monitoring requirements, and an increasing body of evidence is available to support the original claims. The difficulty is that more monitoring of various kinds is an easy and politically acceptable solution to perceived problems and scandals in the public and private sector; it is part of the politics of being seen to do something. This, and a generic tendency for regulatory systems to overreact to crisis, means that further unintended, and possibly disastrous, consequences for service provision are likely, but remain invisible or only anecdotally diagnosed.

Finally, the chapter tentatively explored some issues in the design of auditing processes, which might overcome the potential pathologies of the audit explosion. In part, these issues are to do with making the operational level of the audit process more "intelligent," but equally they reflect the wider institutional environment in which auditing functions and this is a matter for political rather than technical design. To conclude, for all the imperfections of its original formulation, the theory of the audit explosion, and indeed the label "audit explosion" itself, denotes a fruitful space for intellectual enquiry into the nature, extent and effects of social and political demands for monitoring.

REFERENCES

AYRES, I., and BRAITHWAITE, J. (1992), *Responsive Regulation: Transcending the De-regulation Debate*, Oxford: Oxford University Press.

CHARLTON, B., and ANDRAS, P. (2002), "Auditing as a Tool of Public Policy: The Misuse of Quality Assurance Techniques in the UK University Expansion," *European Political Science*, 2(1): 24–35

COSO (2004), *Enterprise Risk Management—Integrated Framework*, Committee of the Sponsoring Organizations of the Treadway Commission.

COURVILLE, S. (2003), "Social Accountability Audits: Challenging or Defending Democratic Governance," *Law & Policy* 25: 269–97.

DAVENHILL, R., and PATRICK, M. (eds.) (1998), *Rethinking Clinical Audit: The Case of Psychotherapy Services in the NHS*, London: Routledge.

DAY, P., and KLEIN, R. (2001), *Auditing the Auditors: Audit the National Health Service*, London: The Nuffield Trust.

ENGLISH, L. (2003), "Emasculating Public Accountability in the Name of Competition: Transformation of State Audit in Victoria," *Critical Perspectives on Accounting* 14: 51–76.

EVERETT, J. (2003), "The Politics of Comprehensive Auditing in fields of High Outcome and Cause Uncertainty," *Critical Perspectives on Accounting* 14: 77–104.

FREY, B., and JEGEN. R. (2001), "Motivation Crowding Theory," *Journal of Economic Surveys* 15(1): 589–611.

FUNNELL, W. (2003), "Enduring Fundamentals: Constitutional Accountability and Auditors-General in the Reluctant State," *Critical Perspectives on Accounting* 14: 107–32.

HOOD, C. (2002), "The Risk Game and the Blame Game," *Government and Opposition* 37(1): 15–37.

—— JAMES, O., PETERS, G., and SCOTT, C. (eds.) (2004), *Controlling Modern Government: Variety, Commonality and Change*, Cheltenham: Edward Elgar.

HOUSE, R. (1996), " 'Audit-mindedness' in Counselling: Some Underlying Dynamics," *British Journal of Guidance and Counselling* 24: 277–83.

HUNT, B. (2003), *The Timid Corporation*, London: John Wiley.

HUMPHREY, C., and OWEN, D. (2000), "Debating the 'Power' of Audit," *International Journal of Auditing* 4: 29–50

ICAEW (1999), *Internal Control: Guidance for the Directors of Listed Companies Incorporated in the United Kingdom*, London: Institute of Chartered Accountants in England and Wales.

KAGAN, R., and AXELRAD, L. (eds.) (2000), *Regulatory Encounters: Multinational Coorporations and American Adversarial Legalism*, Berkeley: University of California Press.

MILLER, D. (2003), "The Virtual Moment," *Journal of the Royal Anthropological Institute* 9(1): 57–75.

MORAN, M. (2003), *The British Regulatory State: High Modernism and Hyper-Innovation*, Oxford: Oxford University Press.

MOSHER, F. (1979), *The GAO: The Quest for Accountability in American Government*. Boulder, CO: Westview Press.

MUNRO, E. (2004), "The Impact of Audit on Social Work Practice," *British Journal of Social Work* 34: 1077–97.

NORMANTON, E. L. (1966), *The Accountability and Audit of Government*, Manchester: Manchester University Press.

O'NEILL, O. (2002), *A Question of Trust: The BBC Reith Lectures 2002*, Cambridge: Cambridge University Press.

—— (2004), "Intelligent Trust, Intelligent Accountability," Paper presented at the "Soft Risks, Hard Lessons" Workshop, University of Cambridge, February.

OSBORNE, D., and GAEBLER, T. (1992), *Reinventing Government: How the Entrepreneurial Spirit is Transforming the Public Sector*, Reading, MA: Addison-Wesley.

PALLOTT, J. (2003), "A Wider Accountability? The Audit Office and New Zealand's Bureaucratic Revolution," *Critical Perspectives on Accounting* 14: 133–55.

PARKER, C. (2002), *The Open Corporation: Effective Self-Regulation and Democracy*, Cambridge: Cambridge University Press.

—— (2003), "Regulator-Required Corporate Compliance Program Audits," *Law & Policy* 25: 221–44.

PENTLAND, B. T. (1993), "Getting Comfortable with the Numbers: Auditing and the Micro-production of Macro Order," *Accounting, Organizations and Society* 18: 605–20.

POLLITT, C. (2003), "Performance Audit in Western Europe: Trends and Choices," *Critical Perspectives on Accounting*, 14: 157–70.

—— GIRRE, X., LONSDALE, J., MUL, R., SUMMA, H., and WAERNESS, M. (1999), *Performance or Compliance? Performance Audit and Public Management in Five Countries*, Oxford: Oxford University Press.

POWER, M. (1994), *The Audit Explosion*, London: Demos.

—— (1999), *The Audit Society: Rituals of Verification*, Oxford: Oxford University Press.

—— (2000a), "The Audit-Society—Second Thoughts," *International Journal of Auditing* 4: 111–19.

—— (2000b), *The Audit Implosion: Regulating Risk from the Inside*, London: Institute of Chartered Accountants in England and Wales.

—— (2004), *The Risk Management of Everything*, London: Demos.

RADCLIFFE, V. (1999), "Efficiency Audit: An Assembly of Rationalities and Programmes," *Accounting, Organizations and Society* 23(4):377–410.

SAHLIN-ANDERSSON, K. (2001), "National, International and Transnational Constructions of New Public Management," in T. CHRISTENSEN and P. LAEGREID (eds.), *New Public Management: The Transformation of Ideas and Practice*, Aldershot: Ashgate, 43–72.

SAINT-MARTIN, D. (2000), *Building the New Managerialist State: Consultants and the Politics of Public Sector Reform in Comparative Perspective*, Oxford: Oxford University Press.

SCOTT, C. (2003), "Speaking Softly Without Big Sticks: Meta-Regulation and Public Sector Audit," *Law & Policy* 25: 203–19.

SHORE, C., and WRIGHT, S. (2000), "Coercive Accountability: The Rise of Audit Culture in Higher Education," in M. STRATHERN (ed.), *Audit Cultures: Anthropological Studies in Accountability, Ethics and the Academy*, London: Routledge, 57–89.

STRATHERN, M. (ed.) (2000), *Audit Cultures: Anthropological Studies in Accountability, Ethics and the Academy*, London: Routledge.

WATCHIRS, H. (2003), "AIDS Audit—HIV and Human Rights: An Australian Pilot," *Law & Policy* 25:245–268.

SECTION III

EXPLORING
CURRENT
PUBLIC POLICY
AND
MANAGEMENT
THEMES

CHAPTER 15

PUBLIC–PRIVATE PARTNERSHIPS AND HYBRIDITY

CHRIS SKELCHER

15.1 INTRODUCTION

PUBLIC–PRIVATE partnerships (PPPs) combine the resources of government with those of private agents (businesses or not-for-profit bodies) in order to deliver societal goals. The forms taken by public–private partnerships include contracting-out of services, business management of public utilities, and the design of hybrid organizations for risk sharing and co-production between government and private agents. PPPs give rise to a series of ideological and managerial choices. These concern the relationship between private actors and the state, the extent to which businesses and not-for-profits should substitute for government, and the costs and benefits of different public–private solutions (Linder and Rosenau 2000). The way in which these choices are constituted and resolved is a function of the particular-ities of differing political and cultural contexts. In Australia, New Zealand, Scandinavia, and the UK, PPPs introduce a significant disjunction to the tradition of public provision through a social democratic welfare state (Castles et al. 1996; Savitch 1998). This contrasts with the US where historically there has been closer involvement of business in the provision of government (Moulton and Anheier

2000; Salamon 1981). In Asia, the notion of public–private partnership is difficult to translate to societies whose cultural and political traditions do not easily accommodate the western distinctions between private sector and state (Common 2000). PPPs in the Indian sub-continent, Africa, and Latin America are associated as much with meeting basic needs through small-scale initiatives as reforming large state owned enterprises in the light of internationally directed structural adjustment policies (Batley and Larbi 2004).

Conceptual clarity is a prerequisite of any discussion of public–private partnerships. The terms public, private, and partnership are overworked, individually and collectively, and their meanings are contingent on context (Linder 2000; Pollitt 2003). In western Europe, the phrase public–private partnership refers specifically to a mechanism for spreading risk, gaining off-balance-sheet financing, and increasing innovation in the design, construction and operation of infrastructure-based projects (Commission on Public Private Partnerships 2001; Reeves 2003). The US interpretation, however, is broader and covers a variety of instruments through which government involves businesses and not-for-profits in the realization of public policy goals (Beauregard 1998; Milward and Provan 2000; Rosenau 2000). This chapter uses the term public–private partnership in a generic sense to refer to the ways in which government and private actors work together in pursuit of societal goals.

PPPs arise from the make-or-buy decisions that governments face. Governments can choose to realize societal goals directly, through public employees and collectively controlled facilities (the make decision), or indirectly by means of business and not-for-profit organizations (the buy decision) (Osborne and Gaebler 1992; Williamson 1996). The buy decision leads to a choice between the five main forms of public–private partnership discussed in this chapter, namely public leverage, contracting-out, franchising, joint ventures, and strategic partnering.

The development of these relationships between state and private actors gives rise to the phenomenon of hybridity. This refers to an organization that has both public and private orientations (Ferlie et al. 1996; Koppell 2003; Joldersma and Winter 2002). Hybridity is associated with an indistinct boundary between public and private interests as a result of the close engagement of business and not-for-profits in the governmental process. Public–private partnerships, therefore, generate a series of questions that relate to the legal, ethical and financial conditions for public management.

The chapter has four sections. The first step is to explore the political and theoretical rationales for public–private partnerships. This leads into an analysis of the five types of PPP. The third section discusses the impact of PPPs in terms of cost/quality and organizational hybridity. The final section draws out the main conclusions of the analysis and identifies challenges for the future governance and management of PPPs.

15.2 EXPLANATIONS FOR PUBLIC–PRIVATE PARTNERSHIPS

PPPs do not emerge as a matter of whim or fancy. They are institutions rooted in a specific political and temporal *milieu* (Peters 1998). At particular moments they seem to offer the solution to public policy problems. This is illustrated by examining the make or buy decisions of UK and US governments over the past two centuries. During the nineteenth century these governments undertook infrastructure procurement by franchising to private companies the right to design, finance, build, and operate schemes for power, water supply, and other public utilities (Pietroforte and Miller 2002). During the twentieth century UK governments expanded their direct involvement in public provision, leaving private actors to play specific functional roles, for example in the construction of government-designed facilities (Middleton 1996). In the US, however, business contractors continued to be an indispensable part of the workings of Federal government, with Light (1999) estimating that four times as many people were retained through grants and contracts as were direct employees. This third-party government (Salamon 1981) includes the contractual relationships between government and not-for-profits, especially in social welfare provision (Smith and Lipsky 1993).

Governments around the world made greater use of private actors to design, manage, and deliver public policy during the latter part of the twentieth century. This was motivated variously by the prescriptions of New Public Management, reform programs introduced as a result of government ideology or pressure from international agencies, and social, economic and cultural changes (Batley and Larbi 2004; Clarke and Newman 1997; Halligan 1997). The policy instruments employed ranged from competitively tendering public services through to the sale of state-owned enterprises. However the adoption by governments of market approaches did not follow a single logic. Batley (1996) analyzed private sector involvement in the provision of public services in Latin American, Africa and Asia and concluded ideology was not a significant driver. The prime motivation was the pragmatic of gaining investment through compliance with international donor agencies' structural adjustment demands. In Australia, Domberger and Hall (1996: 134) note variation in the adoption and form of competitively tendered contracting and conclude: "historical factors, local circumstances, political ideologies and economic situations have all played a role." The prevailing political economy in Western Europe has not generated a strong impetus to expand contracting or externalization, other than in the UK which tends to be an outlier in its enthusiasm for marketization. The administrative law tradition in Germany meant that marketization was slow to develop (Jann 2003; Wollmann 2001) while in France the traditions of state technocratic control and integration of public and private enterprise had a similar effect (Durant and Legge 2002). However the impetus of economic liberalization in the transitional states of eastern Europe has resulted in extensive use of contacting-out to reform public services and stimulate private activity (Devas and Horváth 1997).

This evidence enables us to locate the adoption of public–private partnerships within a set of responses to public management reform that are differentiated by national context (Pollitt and Bouckaert 2000). The marketization wave in a number of advanced economies during the latter part of the twentieth century was associated with neo-liberal governments who adopted prescriptions arising from the rational choice view of public officials as budget-maximising bureaucrats rather than neutral proponents of the public interest (Horn 1995; Lane 1995). This ideological stance has undergone some change, for example during the Clinton and Blair administrations in the US and UK respectively, but the emphasis on the positive contribution of business and not-for-profits has been sustained. Its intellectual justification is provided by Third Way politics (Giddens 1998, 2000). This offers a perspective that moves beyond the old alternatives of market or state (Table 15.1). It stresses interdependencies and mutuality, a stakeholder society in which a variety of interests are brought into the governmental process (Newman 2001; Falconer and McLoughlin 2000). The language of public–private partnership in this context symbolizes a disjunction from the more ideologically driven discourse of contracting and privatization, as Linder (2000: 25) observes:

[Public–private] [p]artnerships have been viewed as a retreat from the hard-line advocacy of privatization. From this perspective, they serve a strategic purpose, enlisting the support of more moderate elements that are less opposed to state action on principle. Partnerships are accommodationist; they hold back the spectre of wholesale divestiture and, in exchange, promise lucrative collaboration with the state.

Table 15.1 The third way, social democracy and neo-liberalism

Social democracy	Neo-liberalism	Third way
Class politics of the left	Class politics of the right	Modernizing movement of the center
Old mixed economy	Market fundamentalism	New mixed economy
State domination over civil society	Minimal state	New democratic state
Internationalism	Conservative nation	Cosmopolitan nation
Strong welfare state	Welfare safety net	Social investment state

Source: Newman (2001), after Giddens (1998)

15.3 FORMS OF PUBLIC–PRIVATE PARTNERSHIP

Five different forms of public–private partnership can be distinguished. Some are predominantly state-led, while others are based on a presumed mutuality of interest and risk-taking. Their institutional forms can be further distinguished in terms of time scale, financing, and partner relationships (Table 15.2). In this section we explore the key features of each and the main lines of debate about their application to public policy problems.

15.3.1 Public Leverage

Public leverage occurs where governments use their legal and financial resources to create conditions that they believe will be conducive to economic activity and business growth. Schaeffer and Loveridge (2002) use the term "leader-follower" to capture this approach, since government is encouraging and inducing private sector decision makers to align with public policy goals. Public leverage has a particular significance in regeneration strategies for disadvantaged localities (Boyle 1993; Walzer and Jacobs 1998; Jacobs 1999). Governments around the world have packaged together infrastructure improvements, financial incentives, business support services, and other measures to promote economic regeneration in a locality. Place marketing within an overall policy to attract footloose capital often supports this approach. This strategy may make sense from the perspective of a single jurisdiction, but there is a danger of over-supply of government inducements at the regional, national and global level as localities compete between themselves. Public leverage also occurs where government wishes business or not-for-profits to be the means of realising a goal that might otherwise be achieved through public bureaucracies. An example is US Federal government subsidies to private developers of housing schemes for low-income families (Macdonald 2000). This arm's length leverage avoids the need for government itself to develop and manage public services.

15.3.2 Contracting-Out and Competitive Tendering

Contracting-out involves separating the purchaser of a service from the provider. Government concentrates on the former, defining what services are to be available and to what standard, and then contracts out the provision to a business or

Table 15.2 Forms of public–private partnership

Dimensions	Public leverage	Contracting-out	Franchising	Joint ventures	Strategic partnering
Purpose from government's perspective	To create conditions attractive to private sector investment and business development.	To achieve cost reductions, efficiency gains and quality improvements in public services. To reduce the workforce management responsibilities of public managers.	To transfer management of public enterprise to commercial sector.	To deliver projects where government has commonality of interest with business or not-for-profits. To enable government to gain access to private capital off the public balance sheet. To transfer risk to the private sector.	To enable government to gain significant cost and business process gains over the medium to long term. To integrate business and not-for-profit actors into the public policy process.
Mechanism	Government prepares land for industrial development, provides tax breaks, offers subsidies, etc.	Provision of public service under contract by business, not-for-profit or another public agency, often utilizing competitive tendering against the existing public provider.	Business or not-for-profit is granted licence by government to deliver the service, within public interest regulatory framework. In the case of infrastructure provision, the assets may revert to government after a fixed term.	Contract between government and private partners covering capital works and subsequent operating costs.	Long-term and open-ended relationship between public and private actors based on trust and mutuality rather than formal contract, but may include elements of contracting-out, franchising or joint venture.

Funding	Public.	Public.	User fees, possibly with additional public subsidy tied to provision of uneconomic but socially desirable services. User fees provide basis for access to capital funds through the market.	Private, with government refunding costs over the long term.	Public, but may include private.
Timescale	Medium term. Open ended.	Short to medium term. Fixed period contracts.	Medium to long term. Fixed period franchise.	Long term. Fixed term contract.	Long term. Open-ended relational contract.
Partner relationships	Government seeks to attract business partners.	Public purchaser; private or not-for-profit supplier.	Private provision under public regulation.	Government commissions and specifies the project outcomes, and commits to repaying costs. Private partner finances, and/or builds, and/or manages, and/or operates the facility.	
Example	Economic regeneration areas.	Contracted out refuse collection and social care services.	Railways in the UK.	Construction of major infrastructure projects.	Civic partnerships.

not-for-profit organization. Contracting-out is the logical outcome of a competitive tendering or market-testing process in which the public provider is deemed not to offer the best solution. Fiscally prudent politicians and academic advocates of rational choice theory identified possibilities for efficiency gains by competitively tendering municipal services such as refuse collection, street cleaning and road maintenance. Cost reductions were expected to arise from changes in working practices, employment conditions, and management overheads as a result of exposing the de facto monopoly of the public provider to contestability (Domberger and Jensen 1997; Walsh 1995).

A further potential benefit from the use of competitive tendering is improved service quality. The process of competitive tendering requires the public sector client to specify the nature of the service they wish delivered in order to be able to evaluate bidders' offerings and monitor the performance of the successful supplier. This involves a fundamental change in government's perspective from the traditional input orientation concerned with staff, money, and other resources to a focus on the outputs and outcomes to be achieved (Walsh 1995). There are, however, enduring problems in defining the qualitative aspects of a service, especially where service users are ill-defined (as in the case of recipients of a street cleansing service), are not able to offer an opinion (such as those in receipt of medical advice), or are vulnerable and dependent on public provision (for example, people receiving care for mental health problems) (Stewart and Walsh 1994).

The ability of contracting-out to realize its benefits depends on two conditions—market competition and government capacity (Van Slyke 2003). The need for a competitive market may seem an obvious point, but this does not always exist in services where governments wish to offer contracts (Milne 1997). Government capacity relates to the imperative to be a "smart buyer" (Kettl 1993). Procedures, staff skills, and culture must be transformed from the hierarchical mode of supervising direct service provision to that of service design and contract management. This requires a range of skills, including negotiation, contractor management, dispute resolution, and service auditing, that traditionally have been little valued in public organizations. There are also particular issues for government in monitoring and taking timely action in respect of social welfare and health services where contractor failure can be highly significant politically and in terms of the well being of the individual.

From a theoretical perspective, contracting-out places government and supplier in the roles of principal and agent respectively (Lane 1995). This apparently simple relationship contains significant complexity. There are strong incentives on the successful bidder to minimize their costs and maximize their revenue. Possibilities for opportunistic behavior arise due to the information asymmetry between contractor (who knows what work has been done and to what standard) and the client (who is at one remove from the delivery process) (Kavanagh and Parker 2000). The ability of a contractor to control (at least partly) the quality, quantity, and timeliness of the data provided to the client is a powerful resource in the relationship and raises particular problems in social welfare contracting because the service package is more open-ended (Mackintosh 1997). It is also clear that the introduction of contracting can redirect the mission of not-for-profits toward government's service-delivery objectives (Van Slyke 2003; Deakin 2001).

The reality of contracting-out for public services is more complex than the normative theory indicates. Opportunism, information asymmetry, and complex principal–agent chains, combined with pressure to reduce the client-side overhead, compound the problem. The complexity of contracting-out increases as one moves away from basic municipal services into professional, health, and social welfare provision, where short-termism is counterproductive to the public good. The bureau has been the transaction-cost efficient way of delivering such services, even if it is X-inefficient because of the weakness of constituency interests and the problem of natural monopoly (Horn 1995; Lane 1995). The contemporary public management discourse privileges public–private partnerships over bureau solutions. Consequently the weaknesses of the contracting-out model require a search for alternatives routes to the engagement of private actors in public services.

15.3.3 Franchising

Franchising involves government awarding a licence to a business or not-for-profit to deliver a public service in which the provider's income is in the form of user fees. Savas (2000: 80) sees the difference between franchises and contracts in this way:

> With franchises, as with contracts, government is the arranger and a private organization is the producer; however, the two are differentiated by the means of payment to the producer. Government (the arranger) pays the producer for contract service, but the consumer pays the producer for franchise service.

The licence may require the private agent to develop infrastructure, in which case it would normally transfer to public ownership at term (Pietroforte and Miller 2002).

Under franchising, government is reallocating its monopoly rights to a private entity (Ghere 2001a). The process of allocating these rights may be undertaken competitively and require potential providers to bid a cash value to acquire the franchise. This was the position with the provision of train services in Great Britain after denationalization (Pollitt and Smith 2002). Government auctioned franchises to operate bundles of routes for a fixed time period. The successful train operating companies were then responsible for providing rolling stock and delivering a service subject to price and performance regulation. The customer revenue stream flowed to the franchise holder, but there were also public subsidies to maintain services on socially desirable routes.

Franchising has a particular benefit in the case of a monopoly public-interest service whose revenue is sourced from user charges and where government does not want to develop and/or operate the service directly itself. The monopoly features of the service make privatization (i.e., sale of ownership into the market) undesirable.[1] Franchising provides a means of transferring operational responsibility to the business sector, with government taking on the role of an arm's length public-interest regulator. In the case of a new service or facility, franchising also transfers some risk to the private sector.

15.3.4 Joint Ventures and DBFO Partnerships

Joint ventures occur where two or more parties wish to engage on a collaborative project in a way that retains their independence (Schaeffer and Loveridge 2002). They enable the co-ordination of important decisions by independent actors in respect of a project that is close-ended in terms of its scope and the commitment of partners' resources. The joint venture may be managed through a partnership agreement or a separate corporate entity—a special purpose vehicle (SPV). Joint ventures are now used extensively to realize public goals for infrastructure provision and renewal, including schools (Ball et al. 2000), public transport (Klijn and Teisman 2003), hospitals (Froud and Shaoul 2001), roads (Reeves 2003), air traffic service (Goodliffe 2002), economic sectors (Samii et al. 2002), and prisons (Schneider 2000). These are typically referred to as public–private partnerships in the European context[2] and as Private Finance Initiative (PFI) in the UK.[3] The generic nomenclature is DBFO (design–build–finance–operate).

DBFO involves government stating its intentions in output terms and then entering into a long-term contractual relationship with a company or consortium who undertake to design, finance, and build the facility, and manage and deliver some of the services associated with it (typically, maintenance, cleaning, and security). Government pays for the output over the medium to long term through a shadow toll or other revenue formula. The particular solution in any individual case will be a permutation of these DBFO elements and its lesser variants—e.g. DBF (design–build–finance) and DBO (design–build–operate). For example, the private partners might design, finance, and build a facility, which would then be redeemed by the public sector through a long-term debt arrangement (the turnkey method) (Pietroforte and Miller 2002; Wakeford and Valentine 2001).

DBFO joint ventures offer three potential benefits to government. The first is that the separation of the capital financing of a public project from its ongoing funding does not add to public debt. The infrastructure is treated as incidental to the output, with the benefit that it will not be reflected on the public sector balance sheet (but see below). However the Commission on Public–private Partnerships (2001) warns that the provision of capital by the market brings an assumed benefit of greater diligence in project management and avoidance of cost overruns that may not be borne out in practice. The second motivation for government is to encourage innovative solutions since the project is specified in outcome terms. Daniels and Trebilcock (2000) caution that the less crystallized the project, the greater the risk that creative design will increase the costs of the project and bias the selection process. The third purpose of DBFOs is to transfer the risks of the project to the private partners. Risks include those associated with planning and design, construction, availability and performance, and residual value (Kirk and Wall 2002; Reeves 2003). Van Ham and Koppenjan (2002), however, point out that the private partner also bears unique risks including political discontinuity and high transaction costs due to unfamiliarity with public policy processes (Table 15.3).

15.3.5 Strategic Partnering

Strategic partnering between public and private agents involves a situation in which there is boundarylessness in terms of the distinctions between the constituent parties (Ashkenas et al. 2002) and where there are "permeable organizing practices that are intended to yield mutual beneficial outcomes" (Grimshaw et al. 2002:482). Schaeffer and Loveridge (2002) stress the open-ended nature of strategic partnering, the full sharing of risks and rewards, and the evolving substantive content of the action that arises. The assumptions underlying strategic partnering contrast markedly with those informing contracting-out. Trust-based relationships cement a collaborative endeavour between the organizations and

Table 15.3 Risks and barriers in joint ventures

	Public parties	Private parties
Risks	Substantive risks	Construction and exploitation risks
	Financial risks	Risk of high transaction cost
	Risk of private discontinuity	Policy risks
	Democratic risks	Risk of political discontinuity
	Political risks	Administrative risks
		Social risks
Cultural and institutional barriers	Long-term orientation	Short-term orientation
	Not geared to exploitation and cash flow	Fixation on returns and cash flow
	Political primacy handicaps partnership	Lack of understanding of political and public processes

Source: Van Ham and Koppenjan (2002)

replace the primacy of legal instruments and associated client suspicion of contractor guile (Coulson 1998; Lane and Bachmann 1998; Smith 1996).

From a theoretical perspective, strategic partnering provides a means of reducing the transaction costs of service specification, supplier procurement, and regulation that can arise under contracting-out (Lane 2001). Klijn and Teisman (see Table 15.4) summarize the differences between contracting-out and long-term partnering in this way (2000: 85–6):

> Contracting-out is characterized by a principal-agent relationship in which the public actor defines the problem and provides the specification of the solution . . . Partnership, on the other hand, is based on joint decision-making and production in order to achieve effectiveness for both partners. Relational transparency, or in other words trust, is crucial.

However Teisman and Klijn (2002) warn that strategic partnering schemes can flounder and regress to traditional contracting-out approaches because the institutional norms of government are not sufficiently adapted to this way of working. These conclusions, however, are based on a managerial analysis of strategic partnering. An examination of the political science literature reveals substantial evidence for macro-level strategic partnering between government and business, especially through ongoing corporatist relationships between public and private actors at the citywide level (Austin and McCaffrey 2002; Beauregard 1998). These take place through informal networks that at particular moments give rise to formal partnerships (Lowndes and Skelcher 1998; Pierre 1998b). Regime theory provides an

Table 15.4 Comparison between contracting-out and long-term partnership

Contracting-out	Long-term partnership
Government and company in principal–agent relationship	Government and company involved in joint decision making and production
Government defines problem, specifies solution and selects company to deliver	Both parties develop joint products that contribute to their interests
Benefits are efficiency	Benefits are effectiveness
Key to success is unambiguous specification	Key to success is developing processes for interweaving goals, efforts and products
Project managed with strong requirement to monitor contractor	Process managed with strong emphasis on dialogue and joint problem solving
Contractual transparency, including rules covering tendering, selection of company, service delivery and inspection and monitoring	Relational transparency, involving building enduring and trusting relationships which integrate organizational actors', efforts to work towards common goals

Source: adapted from Klijn and Teisman (2000: 86)

underlying explanation of how such stable governing coalitions oriented to public purpose emerge in urban areas. The process is one in which government merges its capacity to act with those of business and other key groups in the locality, giving the coalition direction and co-ordination in pursuit of mutually beneficial goals (Stone 1989; Stoker 1995). Regime theory is based on research in US cities where the structural conditions for governmental action tend to be different than in the Europe case, for example US metropolitan areas are more jurisdictionally fragmented and in some European states (e.g., the UK; the Netherlands) national government plays a greater role in stimulating governing coalitions at the local level. Consequently there is debate about the wider applicability of regime theory (John 2001). Nevertheless strategic alliances have been established between public and private actors in urban areas, providing an infrastructure of cooperation across sectoral boundaries (DiGaetano and Lawless 1997; Harding 2000).

15.4 Evaluating Public–Private Partnerships

This assessment of public–private partnerships concentrates on two issues. The first concerns the proposition that greater involvement by private agents in delivering public goals increases efficiency and service quality. The second issue involves the impact of public–private partnerships on the governance and management of the public service, especially in the context of hybrid organizational forms.

15.4.1 Cost and Quality Impacts of PPPs

There are two broad sets of financial analyses. Savas (2000), a leading proponent of marketization, reports a range of studies of contracting-out across US government services that found 20, 30, and 40 percent cost reductions[4] when compared with previous in-house provision. These changes arise from reductions in staffing, employment conditions, administrative overheads, new management regimes, and other factors. Support comes from Domberger and Jensen's (1997) analysis of competitive tendering in the UK and Australia where mean savings of around 20 percent are reported. Other studies produce more modest cost reductions and highlight the variance within the overall percentage. Walsh and Davis (1993) analyzed eight services in which there was compulsory competitive tendering and found that expenditure had reduced in some and increased in others. They note that some cost increases were due to the service specification process revealing to local politicians that standards were undesirably low. Boyne (1998: 698) argues that the rational choice theories informing marketization "over-emphasize bureaucrats' desire for budget maximization but also under-emphasize the constraints on their ability to achieve this aim," echoing Dunleavy's (1991) earlier critique.

The evidence on PPP as a stimulus to innovation is mixed. Ball et al. (2000) studied a project to build a school and reported that the client already had a fixed view about its design. In contrast, an evaluation of two prison PFI schemes identified innovative solutions in relation to construction and the control and monitoring of prisoner movements (National Audit Office 1997). The evidence on cost is clearer but still contentious. The Commission on Public Private Partnerships (2001) report a study that estimated cost reductions under PFI of between 10 and 20 percent. However Pollock et al. (2002) challenge the value-for-money methodology employed by the UK government for PFI and provide data to illustrate how important notional risk transfer is in validating the case for private financing (c.f. Ball et al. 2001). Joint ventures can produce rigidities in the budget of the public agency responsible for funding the scheme, with Grimshaw et al. (2002) reporting that a hospital board found 20 percent of its annual revenue budget ringfenced to meet the costs of the PPP contract into which it had entered. Finally, changes in accounting rules can increase costs. This applies particularly where a PPP scheme is presented as a means of purchasing public services without the cost impacting on public debt or government's balance sheet (Reeves 2003).

Judgments about the impact of public–private partnerships on service quality are more difficult to reach. The definition of service quality itself is problematic given its multidimensional and sometimes subjective properties (Pollitt and Bouckaert 1995) and little research on the quality impact of PPP has been undertaken. However some conclusions can be offered. The first observation is that problems of information asymmetry, limited government capacity and regulatory capture might be expected to lead to quality shading, the propensity for contractors to sacrifice performance in order to maintain profitability in a competitive market. This hypothesis was tested in a small-scale study of cleaning contracts and found not to apply, although the authors recognize that the findings should be taken as indicative rather than definite (Domberger et al. 1995). The second conclusion is that the use of contracting-out, franchising, and joint ventures reduces the vertical integration of a service. For example, contracting-out in schools place educational matters and janitorial services within different management structures, even though both contribute to the quality of education received by pupils. Similarly separation of responsibility for track and train services has proved a major problem in the performance of the UK's rail network. The irony is that this decoupling of vertical integration comes at the time when governments also recognize the benefits of greater collaboration between organizations in order better to deliver public policy goals (Sullivan and Skelcher 2002).

15.4.2 Hybridity: The Public Governance Impacts of PPPs

Public–private partnerships are part of a wider process through which business models are imported into the public sphere (Ferlie et al. 1996). The new organizational forms that emerge are hybrids—"organizational arrangements that use resources and/or governance structures from more than one existing organization" (Borys and Jemison 1989: 235). PPP hybrids have both public and private characteristics and are commonly referred to as quasi-governmental, although this term also encompasses organizations such as regulatory agencies and arm's length public bodies that are more firmly located within the public realm (Moe 2001; Skelcher 1998). It is frequently easier to define hybrids by exclusion (not government, not private sector) than by inclusion, although an individual body may also claim publicness in one context and privateness in another (Moe 2001). Koppell (2003: 12) defines a quasi-governmental hybrid body as "an entity created by...government...to address a specific public policy purpose. It is owned in whole or in part by private individuals or corporations and/or generates revenue to cover its operating costs." However there is an empirical problem of applying this definition to a highly differentiated class of organizations where "each is unique in terms of history, purpose and organization" (2003: 2; see also Joldersma and Winter 2002).

There is a tension within a hybrid between public accountability and commercial acumen (Thynne 1998a; Wettenhall 1998). This raises three empirical and normative questions. The first question concerns the degree of constitutional oversight of this emergent class of organizations. This is limited for several reasons. Hybrid quasi-governmental bodies emerge through pragmatic and *ad hoc* processes and in a multiplicity of forms (Guttman 2003; Skelcher 1998). They are frequently a function of executive rather than legislative decision and thus comprise a judgment about technically appropriate means rather than public policy ends (Moe 2001). The choice of public–private hybrid is validated by the discourses of public management reform and marketization, especially in the post-New Right era of collaborative public policy realization, and by the "emotional connotation" of the term partnership that "conveys an image of egalitarian and conflict-free decision-making" (Schaeffer and Loveridge 2002: 185). The creation of effective constitutional oversight requires as a first step the clear demarcation of this class of organizations, but this is problematic.

The second question relates to the accountability of hybrids. The procedural regularity and transparency that informs the normative practice of government is tested by the involvement of private actors with their conventions of commercial confidence in pursuit of competitive advantage. Indeed the choice to create a quasi-governmental body offers government the advantage of reduced public accountability (Moe 2001; Thynne 1998b). Such private actors may well be public spirited and interested in advancing societal goals, but the accountability structures within which they operate are fundamentally different to those applying in the government service. Democratic government operates through public deliberation and the regular testing of authority through elections. Hybrids are largely immune from these processes and this leads to problems in securing accountability (Broadbent and Laughlin 2003; Whorley 2001). Boards are appointed and frequently conduct their business in closed session (Skelcher 1998). Regulatory control is variable in its effectiveness (Koppell 2003). This critique leads to the question of whether a different form of accountability should be applied to hybrids. Ghere (2001b) argues that public managers involved with PPPs have a personal responsibility to assure that the entity is connected to community values, but recognizes that this is likely to be in the context of the private commodification of services that were formerly perceived as in the public realm. This suggests that stronger institutional means for accountability are necessary in order to assert the publicness of a hybrid.

The third question concerns the extent to which involvement by government in a hybrid compromises its impartiality, especially in undertaking its regulatory role (Schaeffer and Loveridge 2002). There is a danger of subordinating public responsibilities to private goals, especially where government carries the final political and fiscal risk (Seidman 1988). Because government is the guarantor, market incentives on the PPP are reduced and there is a corresponding need for effective regulatory oversight to assure the public's policy and fiscal interests are served (Moe and Stanton 1989; Rubin and Stankiewicz 2001). Problems of governmental capacity are even more pronounced in developing and transitional states, leading to problems of fraud, corruption, and non-compliance by providers and thus undermining the economic benefits of competition (Batley 1996; Mills and Broomberg 1998). However there is also evidence from France that there can be strong PPPs in the context of overall governmental control of policy (Nelson 2001).

15.5 CONCLUSION

Buying through a PPP predominates over making through a bureau as the preferred model of public service delivery in the early twenty-first century. The roots of PPPs go back to nineteenth-century relationships between government and private actors that in some nations were dislocated by the growth of welfare state bureaucracies during the twentieth century. In recent years the forms of PPPs have extended from the early models of contracting-out municipal services to encompass longer-term possibilities based on relational contracting. Evidence about the impact of PPPs is emerging, although it is important to separate out the transitional effects of this changing mode of governance from the medium term consequences arising from the new institutional settlement.

The central justification for PPPs rests on the benefits that arise from the combination of public and private resources in pursuit of public policy goals. Notions of complementarity, synergy, and positive-sum outcomes are key elements of the discourse. Trust is presented as a medium that cements the exchange between government and private actors, resolving the conflicting motivations of purchaser and supplier within the old model of contracting-out and the consequent transaction problems of opportunism with guile and information asymmetry. This powerful image appeals to the conceptions of social order and benefit that are intrinsic to the value base of public managers. Better to work together with business and not-for-profits over the longer-term, the argument goes, than to face the problem of regulating short-term contracts where suppliers engage in rent-seeking behaviour.

There are, however, four questions that public managers need to address in the decision to engage in joint ventures, strategic partnering, and trust-based relationships. First, does the rhetoric of common interest between the parties occlude important differences of value and motivation? For the public sector, relational contracting offers the benefit of identifying a preferred partner with whom to work towards societal goals over the long term. This contrasts with the position for the private sector where partnership is a significant business strategy based on an assessment of market conditions and driven by considerations of competitive advantage (Faulkner and de Rond 2000). The ability to gain first mover advantage by establishing an early foothold in a new or expanding market for public services provides companies with an opportunity to create a more secure business environment and to exclude competitors from a close and long-term relationship with government. Second, with what do the partners trust each other? The notion of trust is integral to the normative value set of the public sector and is reinforced through institutional arrangements that provide transparency about the decisions governments make and the processes employed. The same cannot be assumed of the business sector. Confidentiality is as much a part of the core value set of business as transparency is to that of government. From a business context, the building of trust is a process that leads to the cementing of a deal. It is not an intrinsic value. Brereton and Temple (1999) argue that collaborations between government and private actors lead to a shared public service ethos that emphasizes outputs rather than procedural regularity. Ghere (2001b), however, takes a less sanguine view and points to the erosion of governance integrity in local communities as the key issue arising from the use of PPPs.

The third question concerns the extent to which governments have capacity to engage in PPPs. The institutional arrangements in a specific locality—the level of governmental capacity, style of political leadership, quality of managers, and so on—is a key variable in determining the success or otherwise of a public–private partnership (Batley 1996). These are sometimes difficult to resource under conditions of contracting-out; they become even more important within longer-term and relational PPPs in order for the public partner to be an effective player in the enterprise. In their absence, the danger is that the public interest is sidelined. The fourth and final question is: how do PPPs articulate with democratic institutions and processes? Creating public–private partnerships is a highly political venture, but those that have been established are generally opaque to public view and outside the realm of democratic discourse. They occupy a managerial world in which *ex post facto* scrutiny is the primary means of accountability. The paradox is that this is occurring precisely at a time when popular democratic engagement is high on the agenda for many governments. Values of active citizenship stand in contradistinction to the relocation of services from democratically controlled bureaus into the nether world of quasi-governmental hybrids.

The challenge for politicians and public managers when they set out along the road to longer-term PPPs is to retain forms of democratic leverage over hybrid organizations. The effective combination of resources to meet societal goals requires the active participation of government and private actors but also the wider civil society. There is little evidence that democratic considerations have made a significant impact on the governance arrangements for PPPs. Retaining the publicness of a PPP is essential in order to provide democratic steering and societal accountability for its delivery of public policy goals. This relates to the wider debate about the design of democratic institutions in a public policy environment that is characterized by complexity and polycentrism (Koppenjan and Klijn 2004; Skelcher 2005). The failure to engage with these issues will undermine the public dimension of PPPs. The business case for a PPP, therefore, needs to be matched by institutional arrangements for its continued public governance.

Notes

This chapter was researched and written while the author was Public Service Fellow in Governance and Performance at the ESRC/EPSRC Advanced Institute of Management Research. The author would like to acknowledge the support provided through Fellowship Award RES-331-30-000129.

1. Privatization is used here in the European sense of sale of public assets, rather than the US sense of contracting-out.
2. Readers will note that the term public–private partnership as used in this chapter assumes a much broader meaning.
3. Private Finance Initiative refers to a specific policy instrument used by government to encourage private capital financing of public investments and associated provision of services. Somewhat confusingly, it has recently been relaunched as Public–Private Partnerships (Commission on Public–Private Partnerships 2001).
4. The literature on contracting-out can be quite partial. Consequently the term cost reduction is used here since this is what studies are, in the main, measuring. The terms

savings or efficiencies need to be treated with care since they may include changes in service levels or quality standards (Walsh 1995). Readers are also cautioned against the inference that competition is the only means through which efficiencies can be gained (Busch and Gustafsson 2002).

REFERENCES

ASHKENAS, R., ULRICH, D., JICK, T., and KERR, S. (2002), *The Boundaryless Organization: Breaking the Chains of Organizational Structure*, rev. edn., San Francisco: Jossey-Bass.

AUSTIN, J., and MCCAFFREY, A. (2002), "Business Leadership Coalitions and Public–Private Partnerships in American Cities: A Business Perspective on Regime Theory," *Journal of Urban Affairs* 24(1): 35–54.

BALL, R., HEAFEY, M., and KING, D. (2000), "Managing and Concluding the PFI Process for a New High School: Room for Improvement?" *Public Management Review* 2(2): 159–80.

—— —— —— (2001), "Private Finance Initiative—A Good Deal for the Public Purse or a Drain on Future Generations?" *Policy and Politics* 29(1): 95–108.

BATLEY, R. (1996), "Public–Private Relationships and Performance in Service Provision," *Urban Studies* 33(4–5): 723–51.

—— and LARBI, G. (2004), *The Changing Role of Government: The Reform of Public Services in Developing Countries*, Basingstoke: Palgrave Macmillan.

BEAUREGARD, R. (1998), "Public–Private Partnerships as Historical Chameleons: The Case of the United States," in Pierre 1998a: 184–97.

BORYS, B., and JEMISON, D. (1989), "Hybrid Arrangements as Strategic Alliances: Theoretical Issues in Organizational Combinations," *Academy of Management Review* 14(2): 234–49.

BOYLE, R. (1993), "Changing Partners: The Experience of Urban Economic Policy in West Central Scotland, 1980–90," *Urban Studies* 30(2): 309–24.

BOYNE, G. (1998), "Competitive Tendering in Local Government: A Review of Theory and Evidence," *Public Administration* 76(4): 695–712.

BRERETON, M., and TEMPLE, M. (1999), "The New Public Service Ethos: An Ethical Environment for Governance," *Public Administration.* 77(3): 455–74.

BROADBENT, J., and LAUGHLIN, R. (2003), "Control and Legitimation in Government Accountability Processes: The Private Finance Initiative in the UK," *Critical Perspectives on Accounting* 14(1–2): 23–48.

BUSCH, T., and GUSTAFSSON, O. (2002), "Slack in the Public Sector: A Comparative Analysis of a Private and a Public Enterprise for Refuse Collection," *Public Management Review* 4(2): 167–86.

CASTLES, F., GERRITSEN, R., and VOWLES, J. (eds.) (1996), *The Great Experiment: Labour Parties and Public Policy Transformation in Australia and New Zealand*, Auckland: Auckland University Press.

CLARKE, J., and NEWMAN, J. (1997), *The Managerial State: Power, Politics and Ideology in the Remaking of Social Welfare*, London: Sage.

Commission on Public Private Partnerships (2001), *Building Better Partnerships: The Final Report of the Commission on Public Private Partnerships*, London: Institute for Public Policy Research.

COMMON, R. (2000), "The East Asia Region: Do Public–Private Partnerships make sense?", in OSBORNE, S. (2000).

COULSON, A. (1998), "Trust and Contract in Public Sector Management," in A. Coulson (ed.), *Trust and Contracts: Relationships in Local Government, Health and Public Services*, Bristol: Policy Press.

DANIELS, R., and TREBILCOCK, M. (2000), "An Organisational Analysis of the Public–Private Partnership in the Provision of Public Infrastructure," in Rosenau 2000: 93–110.

DEAKIN, N. (2001), "Putting Narrow-Mindedness out of Countenance: The UK Voluntary Sector in the New Millennium," in H. Anheier and J. Kendall (eds.), *Third Sector Policy at the Crossroads*, London: Routledge, 36–50.

DEVAS, N., and HORVÁTH, T. (1997), "Client–Contractor Splits: Applying a Model of Public Management Reform to Local Community Services in Hungary," *Local Government Studies*. 23(4): 100–9.

DIGAETANO, A., and LAWLESS, P. (1999), "Urban Governance and Industrial Decline: Governing Structures and Policy Agendas in Birmingham and Sheffield, England, and Detroit, Michigan, 1980–1997," *Urban Affairs Review* 3(4): 546–77.

DOMBERGER, S. and HALL, C. (1996), "Contracting for Public Services: A Review of Antipodean Experience," *Public Administration* 74: 129–47.

—— —— and Li, E. (1995), "The Determinants of Price and Quality in Competitively Tendered Contracts," *Economic Journal* 105: 1545–63.

—— and Jensen, P. (1997), "Contracting out by the Public Sector: Theory, Evidence, Prospects," *Oxford Review of Economic Policy* 13(4): 67–78.

DUNLEAVY, P. (1991), *Democracy, Bureaucracy and Public Choice*, London: Harvester Wheatsheaf.

DURANT, R., and LEGGE, J. (2002), "Politics, Public Opinion, and Privatisation in France: Assessing the Calculus of Consent for Market Reforms," *Public Administration Review* 62(3): 307–23.

ELSTER, J. (ed.) (1998), *Deliberative Democracy*, Cambridge: Cambridge University Press.

FALCONER, P. and McLOUGHLIN, K. (2000), "Public–Private Partnerships and the "New Labour" Government in Britain," in Osborne: 2000: 120–33.

FAULKNER, D. and M. DE ROND. (eds.) (2000), *Co-operative Strategy: Economic, Business and Organisational Issues*, Oxford: Oxford University Press.

FERLIE, E., ASHBURNER, L., FITZGERALD, L., and PETTIGREW, A. (1996), *The New Public Management in Action*, Oxford: Oxford University Press.

FISHKIN, J. (1991), *Democracy and Deliberation: New Directions for Democratic Reform*, London: Yale University Press.

FROUD, J., and SHAOUL, J. (2001), "Appraising and Evaluating PFI for NHS Hospitals," *Financial Accountability and Management*. 17(3): 247–70.

GHERE, R. (2001a), "Probing the Strategic Intricacies of Public–Private Partnership: The Patent as a Comparative Reference," *Public Administration Review* 61(4): 441–51.

—— (2001b), "Ethical Futures and Public–Private Partnerships: Peering far down the Track," *Public Organization Revie*. 1(3): 303–19.

GIDDENS, A. (1998), *The Third Way: The Renewal of Social Democrac*. Cambridge: Polity Press.

—— (2000), *The Third Way and its Critics*, Cambridge: Polity Press.

GOODLIFFE, M. (2002), "The New UK Model for Air Traffic Services: A Public–Private Partnership under Economic Regulation," *Journal of Air Transport Management* 8(1): 13–18.

GRIMSHAW, D., VINCENT, S. and WILLMOTT, H. (2002), "Going Privately: Partnership and Outsourcing in UK Public Services," *Public Administration* 80(3): 453–74.

GUTTMAN, D. (2003), "Contracting United States Government Work: Organisational and Constitutional Models," *Public Organization Review* 3(3): 301–16.

HALLIGAN, J. (1997), "New Public Sector Models: Reform in Australia and New Zealand," in J.-E. Lane(ed.), *Public Sector Reform: Rationale, Trends, and Problems*, London: Sage.

HARDING, A. (2000), "Regime Formation in Manchester and Edinburgh," in G. Stoker (ed.), *The New Politics of British Local Governance*, Basingstoke: Macmillan.

HORN, M. (1995), *The Political Economy of Public Administration: Institutional Choice in the Public Sector*, Cambridge: Cambridge University Press.

JACOBS, B. (1999), *Strategy and Partnership in Cities and Regions: Economic Development and Urban Regeneration in Pittsburgh, Birmingham and Rotterdam*, Basingstoke: Palgrave Macmillan.

JANN, W. (2003), "State, Administration and Governance in Germany: Competing Traditions and Dominant Narratives," *Public Administration* 81(1): 95–118.

JOHN, P. (2001), *Local Governance in Western Europe*, London: Sage.

JOLDERSMA, C., and WINTER, V. (2002), "Strategic Management in Hybrid Organisations," *Public Management Review* 4(1): 83–100.

KAVANAGH, I., and PARKER, D. (2000), "Managing the Contract: A Transaction Cost Analysis of Externalisation," *Local Government Studies* 26(4): 1–22.

KETTL, D. (1993), *Sharing Power: Public Governance and Private Markets*, Washington, DC: Brookings.

KIRK, R., and WALL, A. (2002), "The Private Finance Initiative: Has the Accounting Standards Board Reduced the Scheme's Value for Money?", *Public Management Review* 4(4): 529–48.

KLIJN, E.-H., and TEISMAN, G. (2000), "Governing Public–Private Partnerships: Analysing and Managing the Process and Institutional Characteristics of Public–Private Partnerships," in Osborne 2000: 84–102.

—— —— (2003), "Institutional and Strategic Barriers to Public–Private Partnership: An Analysis of Dutch Cases," *Public Money and Management* 23(3): 137–46.

KOPPELL, J. (2003), *The Politics of Quasi-Government: Hybrid Organisations and the Dynamics of Bureaucratic Control*, Cambridge: Cambridge University Press.

KOPPENJAN, J., and KLIJN, E.-H. (2004), *Managing Uncertainty in Networks: Public Private Controversies*, London: Routledge.

LANE, C., and BACHMANN, R. (eds.) (1998), *Trust Within and Between Organisations*, Oxford: Oxford University Press.

LANE, J.-E. (1995), *The Public Sector: Concepts, Models and Approaches*, 2nd edn., London: Sage.

—— (2001), "From Long-Term to Short-Term Contracting," *Public Administration* 79(1): 29–47.

LINDER, S. H. (2000), "Coming to Terms with the Public–Private Partnership: A Grammar of Multiple Meanings," in Rosenau 2000: 19–36.

—— and Rosenau, P. (2000), "Mapping the Terrain of the Public–Private Policy Partnership," in Rosenau 2000: 1–18.

LIGHT, P. (1999), *The True Size of Government*, Washington, DC: Brookings.

LOWNDES, V., and SKELCHER, C. (1998), "The Dynamics of Multi-Organisational Partnerships: An Analysis of Changing Modes of Governance," *Public Administration* 76(2): 313–34.

MACDONALD, H. (2000), "Renegotiating the Public–Private Partnership: Efforts to Reform Section 8 Assisted Housing," *Journal of Urban Affairs* 22(3): 279–99.

MACKINTOSH, M. (1997), "Economic Culture and Quasi-Markets in Local Government: The Case of Contracting for Social Care," *Local Government Studies* 23(2): 80–102.

MIDDLETON, R. (1996), *Government versus the Market: the Growth of the Public Sector, Economic Management and British Economic Performance, c. 1890–1979*, Cheltenham: Edward Elgar.

MILLS, A., and BROOMBERG, J. (1998), *Experiences of Contracting: an Overview of the Literature*. Macroeconomics, Health and Development Technical Paper 33, Geneva: World Health Organisation.

MILNE, R. (1997), "Market-Type Mechanisms, Market Testing and Market Making: A Longitudinal Study of Contractor Interest in Tendering," *Urban Studies* 34(4): 543–59.

MILWARD, H. B., and PROVAN, K. (2000), "Governing the Hollow State," *Journal of Public Administration Theory and Practice* 10(2): 359–79.

MOE, R. (2001), "The Emerging Federal Quasi-Government: Issues of Management and Accountability," *Public Administration Review* 61(3): 290–312.

—— and STANTON, T. (1989), "Government-Sponsored Enterprises as Federal Instrumentalities: Reconciling Private Management with Public Accountability," *Public Administration Review* 49(4): 321–9.

MOULTON, L., and ANHEIER, H. (2000), "Public–Private Partnerships in the United States: Historical Patterns and Current Trends," in Osborne, S. (2000),

National Audit Office (1997), *The PFI Contracts for Bridgend and Fazakerly Prisons*, HC 253 Session 1997/8, London: HMSO.

NELSON, S. (2001), "The Nature of Partnership in Urban Renewal in Paris and London," *European Planning Studies* 9(4): 483–502.

NEWMAN, J. (2001), *Modernising Governance: New Labour, Policy and Society*. London: Sage.

OSBORNE, D., and GAEBLER, T. (1992), *Reinventing Government: How the Entrepreneurial Spirit is Transforming the Public Sector*, Reading, MA: Addison-Wesley.

OSBORNE, S. (2000), *Public–Private Partnerships: Theory and Practice in International Perspective*, London: Routledge.

PETERS, B. (1998), "'With a little help from our friends': Public–Private Partnerships as Institutions and Instruments," in Pierre 1998*a*: 11–33.

PIERRE, J. (ed.) (1998*a*), *Partnerships in Urban Governance*. Basingstoke: Palgrave Macmillan.

—— (1998*b*), "Local Industrial Partnerships: Exploring the Logics of Public–Private Partnerships," in Pierre 1998*a*: 112–39.

PIETROFORTE, R. and MILLER, J. (2002), "Procurement Methods for US Infrastructure: Historical Perspectives and Recent Trends," *Building Research and Information*. 30(6), 425–34.

POLLITT, C. (2003), *The Essential Public Manager*, Buckingham: Open University Press.

—— and BOUCKAERT, G. (1995), "Defining Quality," in C. Pollitt and G. Bouckaert. (eds.), *Quality Improvement in European Public Services: Concepts, Cases and Commentary*, London: Sage.

—— —— (2000), *Public Management Reform: A Comparative Analysis*, Oxford: Oxford University Press.

POLLITT, M., and SMITH, A. (2002), "The Restructuring and Privatisation of British Rail: Was it Really that Bad?" *Fiscal Studies* 23(4): 463–503.

POLLOCK, A., SHAOUL, J., and VICKERS, N. (2002), "Private Finance and "Value for Money", in NHS Hospitals: A Policy in Search of a Rationale?" *British Medical Journal* 32(4): 1205–9.

REEVES, E. (2003), "Public–Private Partnerships in Ireland: Policy and Practice," *Public Money and Management* 23(3): 163–70.

ROSENAU, P. (ed.) (2000), *Public–Private Policy Partnerships*, Cambridge, MA: MIT Press.

—— and STANKIEWICZ, G. (2001), "The Los Angeles Community Development Bank: The Possible Pitfalls of Public–Private Partnerships," *Journal of Urban Affairs* 23(2): 133–53.

SALAMON, L. (1981), "Rethinking Public Management: Third Party Government and the Changing Form of Government Action," *Public Policy* 29(3): 255–75.

SAMII, R., VAN WASSENHOVE, L., and BHATTACHARYA, S. (2002), "An Innovative Public–Private Partnership: New Approach to Development," *World Development* 30(6): 991–1008.

SAVAS, E. S. (2000), *Privatization and Public–Private Partnerships*, London: Chatham House.

—— (2002), "Competition and Choice in New York Social Services," *Public Administration Review* 62(1): 82–91.

SAVITCH, H. (1998), "Public–Private Partnerships in Europe from an American Perspective," in Pierre 1998a: 79–93.

SCHAEFFER, P., and LOVERIDGE, S. (2002), "Towards an Understanding of Types of Public–Private Cooperation," *Public Performance and Management Review* 26(2): 169–89.

SCHNEIDER, A. (2000), "Public–Private Partnerships in the US Prison System," in Rosenau 2000: 199–216.

SEIDMAN, H. (1988), "The Quasi-World of the Federal Government," *The Brookings Review* 2(2): 23–7.

SKELCHER, C. (1998), *The Appointed State: Quasi-Governmental Organisations and Democracy* Buckingham: Open University Press.

—— (2005), "Jurisdictional Integrity, Polycentrism, and the Design of Democratic Governance,"*Governance* 18(1): 89–110.

SMITH, S. (1996), "Transforming Public Services: Contracting for Social and Health Services in the US," *Public Administration* 74(1): 113–27.

—— and LIPSKY, M. (1993), *Nonprofits for Hire: the Welfare State in the Age of Contracting*, Cambridge, MA: Harvard University Press.

STEWART, J., and WALSH, K. (1994), "Performance Measurement when Performance Can Never be Finally Defined," *Public Money and Management* 14(2): 45–9.

STOKER, G. (1995), "Regime Theory and Urban Politics," in D. Judge, G. Stoker, and H. Wolman. (eds.), *Theories of Urban Politics*, London: Sage.

STONE, C. (1989), *Regime Politics: Governing Atlanta, 1946–1988*, Lawrence, KS: University Press of Kansas.

SULLIVAN, H., and SKELCHER, C. (2002), *Working Across Boundaries: Collaboration in Public Services*, Basingstoke: Palgrave Macmillan.

TEISMAN, G., and KLIJN, E.-H. (2002), "Partnership Arrangements: Governmental Rhetoric or Governance Scheme?" *Public Administration Review* 62(2): 197–205.

THYNNE, I. (1998a), "Government Companies: Ongoing Issues and Future Research," *Public Administration and Development* 18(3): 301–5.

—— (1998b), "Government Companies as Instruments of State Action," *Public Administration and Development* 18(3): 217–28.

VAN HAM, H., and KOPPENJAN, J. (2002), "Building Public–Private Partnerships: Assessing and Managing Risk in Port Development," *Public Management Review* 3(4): 593–616.

VAN SLYKE, D. (2003), "The Mythology of Privatization for Social Services," *Public Administration Review* 63(3): 296–315.

WAKEFORD, J., and VALENTINE, J. (2001), "Learning through Partnership: Private Finance and Management in the Delivery of Services for London," *Public Money and Management* 21(4): 19–25.

WALSH, K. (1995), *Public Services and Market Mechanisms: Competition, Contracting and the New Public Management*, Basingstoke: Macmillan.

—— and DAVIS, H. (1993), *Competition and Services: The Impact of the Local Government Act 1988*. Department of the Environment, London: HMSO.

WALZER, N., and JACOBS, B. (1998), *Public–Private Partnerships for Local Economic Development*, London: Praeger.

WETTENHALL, R. (1998), "The Rising Popularity of the Government-Owned Company in Australia: Problems and Issues," *Public Administration and Development* 18(3): 243–55.

WHORLEY, D. (2001), "The Andersen-Comsoc Affair: Partnerships and the Public Interest," *Canadian Public Administration* 44(3): 320–45.

WILLIAMSON, O. (1996), *The Mechanisms of Governance*, Oxford: Oxford University Press.

WOLLMANN, H. (2001), "Germany's Trajectory of Public Sector Modernisation: Continuities and Discontinuities," *Policy and Politics* 29(2): 151–70.

DECENTRALIZATION

A CENTRAL CONCEPT IN CONTEMPORARY PUBLIC MANAGEMENT

CHRISTOPHER POLLITT

16.1 INTRODUCTION

FOR the last quarter century or so, decentralization has been virtually unassailable. Almost everyone has been in favor of it, from the centralized French (Guyomarch 1999; Cole 2003) to the already decentralized Germans (Wollmann 2001); from the majoritarian British (Pollitt, Birchall, and Putman 1998) to the consensual Danes and Dutch (Kickert 2000: 30; Christensen 2000); from the West (USA, see Osborne and Gaebler 1992: ch. 9) to the East (Japan, see Yamamoto 2004), and from the North (Horvath 2000) to the (European) South (Italy, see Carbone 2000) and, indeed, the global south (New Zealand, Boston et al. 1996: 81–2). Since the 1992 Maastricht Treaty the European Union has enshrined the doctrine of "subsidiarity"—which in most of its many interpretations has something to do with decentralization—in its arrangements and since the 2001 white paper on European Governance the EU Commission has been officially in favor of decentralizing regulatory functions to autonomous agencies (on subsidiarity see Middlemas 1995; on agencies, Vos 2003). Decentralization plays a central role (pun intended) in the dominant public management ideology of our time, the New Public Management (NPM, see Hood 1991; Pollitt 2003: ch. 2).

When a concept is so universally popular, any self-respecting academic becomes suspicious. Are all these different governments really talking about the same thing? Are they practicing what they are preaching? Are there hidden agendas? Costs as well as benefits?

The aim of this chapter is to probe and problematize the concept of "decentralization." More specifically, it will:

- Take note of the long history of decentralization.
- Explore the concept, and identify its various meanings.
- Identify the key arguments—why the idea has gained such popularity.
- Consider the (often unspoken) alternative—"centralization."
- Review (necessarily superficially) some of the evidence concerning the practice of decentralization.

16.2 DECENTRALIZATION: A HARDY PERENNIAL

Arguments concerning decentralization and centralization are as old as the study of public administration—or considerably older. In British history, for example, the Magna Carta of 1215 can be interpreted as a baronial demand for more decentralized forms of administration, i.e. more power to them and less to the unfortunate King John. Jump forward six centuries or so and figures such as Adam Smith and John Stuart Mill can be lined up as champions of decentralization, while Jeremy Bentham, Napoleon, and Lenin are frequently cast as advocates of centralization. Some political leaders, such as Mao Zedong seem to have swung violently between opposite poles, according to circumstance.

If we lower our gaze from the stratosphere of kings, political leaders, and great philosophers to the humble terrain of public administration, the history of the concept seems almost as long and equally vigorously contested. At the dawn of the modern study of public administration Prussian cameralists were advocating the formalization and standardization of administrative tasks—a highly centralizing approach. In nineteenth-century England a vigorous battle of pamphlets took place between those favoring more or less centralized arrangements for government. Consider this decentralist, from 1851:

CENTRALIZATION is that system of government under which the smallest number of minds, and those knowing the least, and having the fewest opportunities of knowing it...and having the smallest interest in the well working, have the management of it, or the control over it. (Toulmin Smith 1851, quoted in Dunsire 1973: 69–70)

In the United States there is a long, unfinished debate concerning the respective rights and roles of the federal government, the state governments, and local authorities. This argument goes back to the makers of the American constitution (for example, the contests between Hamiltonians and Jeffersonians). Likewise both France and Germany have sustained extended debates about the balance between centralized and decentralized authorities (for some flavor of this, see the Chapter 29).

One could go on—indeed large sections of Lynn's chapter summarizing the history of the field of public management (see above) can be read as a series of debates between centralists and decentralists. However, this chapter is not primarily intended to be a history of the concept. Rather it is an analysis of its contemporary meaning and relevance.

16.3 MAPPING THE CONCEPT

16.3.1 Decentralization: Definitions and Meanings

A word of preliminary warning: this definitional section is substantial. This is because the English term "decentralization" has been used in a variety of ways, and its apparent equivalents in other languages, such as *décentralisation* (French), *decentramento* (Italian) or *decentralisatie* (Dutch), also have somewhat shifting meanings, and may sometimes prove to be "false friends". In the words of a now-largely-forgotten classic, written half a century ago:

It is impossible to standardize the usage of the word decentralization by seeking to give it meanings that would be acceptable universally. The English language took the word from Latin; it shares it with the Romance languages...it is a word that is not confined to public affairs and to formal organization in government or business. It is used in every walk of life. It must be accepted as a word of innumerable applications. Throughout all of them, however, runs a common idea, which is inherent in the word's Latin roots, meaning "away from the centre." (Macmahon 1961: 15)

We cannot remove this diversity but we can seek clarification, identify the major applications within public management, and perhaps locate the centre of gravity of this family of usages. Even a little clarification would be an achievement, considering that, as Henry Mintzberg put it: "this remains probably the most confused topic in organization theory" (Mintzberg 1979: 181).

At the heart of most English usages in public management is the notion of *authority being spread out from a smaller to a larger number of actors—from a* central authority, in Macmahon's terms, to others. So where, say, the authority to buy computers was formerly exclusive to the finance directorate, and now—within certain limits—this authority has been *decentralized* to line managers in operating directorates, we have an example of a mainstream usage. Or when central government relinquishes its control of major hospitals and transfers this responsibility to regional or local authorities, we speak of this, too, as *decentralization.*

It should immediately be noted that there are many different ways of thus spreading authority. Five major distinctions can be made.

1. *Political decentralization and/or administrative decentralization?* Is the authority to be spread out from the central political level to other elected politicians (as when Mr Blair's Labour Government transfers certain powers to the newly created Scottish and Welsh assemblies)? Or are the recipients of the spreading out of authority to be managers and administrators (as when Mrs Thatcher's Conservative government created Urban Development Corporations or National Health Service Trust hospitals, cf. Pollitt, Birchall, and Putman 1998)? Within the category of political decentralization one may make a further distinction: that between "normal" political adjustments and fundamental constitutional change. This chapter will concentrate mainly on administrative decentralization, and will have less to say about political decentralization, and least of all about constitutional change. Nevertheless, the political forms cannot be altogether ignored. The political sets the frame for the administrative, and if one gets well out of line with the other (strong political centralization, say, coupled with administrative decentralization) problems are likely. The two forms are by no means mutually exclusive—one can decentralize politically and administratively at the same time—but they are different from one another, not least in their implications for public accountability, and for the overall coherence of national policy making.

2. *Territorial decentralization, or what?* In a number of works decentralization is treated as primarily a territorial phenomenon: authority is parceled out by larger territorial units to smaller ones (e.g. Smith and Stanyer 1976; Smith 1985). There is, for example, a huge literature on federalism and another on local government, both of which extensively treat with territorial, political decentralization. Unfortunately for advocates of this usage, a large number of the reforms which we have witnessed under the label of decentralization actually do not use territory as the basis for the transfer of authority. There are other ways of categorizing the recipients of decentralized authority than by territory—what Macmahon calls the "nature of the basis of division" (1961: 17). Many instances are primarily *functional* rather than territorial. When countries like the UK or Japan or the Netherlands decentralize powers from ministries to agencies, most of these agencies are territorially just as national in scope as were their parent ministries—this is functional rather than territorial decentralization (Pollitt and Talbot 2004). Other categories are also possible, if not, in practice, so frequent. More than seventy years ago, Luther Gulick categorized the

possible bases of organization into specialization by *purpose (function), process, persons or things to be served or place (territory)* (Gulick 1937). Each of these could thus form the basis for acts of decentralization.

Political and popular attitudes to the different bases for decentralization vary considerably. Typically political decentralization to elected local authorities is construed as "democratic" and "participatory," whereas functional decentralization to a national agency is regarded as neutral or even antipathetic to "democracy." Decentralization to a particular client group (the over 65s; the disabled; Roma people) may be regarded as highly desirable by the members of that group but divisive and inequitable by other groups.

3. *Competitive decentralization or non-competitive decentralization?* If authority is to be parceled out, *how* should this be done? On the basis of an *allocation* (X is henceforth responsible for activity A, Y for activity B), or on the basis of a *competition* (here are the terms for the performance of activities A and B, who would like to bid to do these things?). Competitive markets are, famously, decentralized ways of coordinating decision making, and over the last twenty or thirty years many commentators have favored increased use of market mechanisms in the performance of public tasks (e.g., Lane 2000; Osborne and Gaebler 1992).

4. *Internal decentralization and/or external decentralization?* Authority can be parceled out within an existing organization, or transferred to other (possibly new) organizations. When the House of Commons remits a task to the discretion of a Parliamentary select committee, or the Directorate General of the Budget in the European Commission delegates additional financial discretion to the finance unit of the Directorate General of Agriculture, we are dealing with *internal* decentralization—in-house operations. When the UK government create a new National Assembly for Scotland then *external* decentralization is taking place. *Devolution* is a term sometimes given to external decentralization. For example, the OECD distinguishes between:

Delegation of power to entities that remain legally indistinguishable from the state but which are given some autonomy and/or independence and/or have a quasi-contractual (target-setting) relationship with the reporting ministry.

Devolution of power to entities that are legally separate from the state (they have their own "legal Personality") and are often in contractual relationship with the reporting ministry. (OECD 2001: 7)

However, usage of the term "devolution" varies considerably, and in some cases it is reserved for external decentralization which is *political* rather than administrative (see above). If this latter, narrower meaning is chosen, then the National Assembly for Scotland (which finally arrived a quarter of a century later, in 1998) *is* devolution, but the creation of a Finnish state enterprise for forestry is not.

5. *Vertical decentralization or horizontal decentralization?* It is often assumed that decentralization is primarily a vertical phenomenon—the "center" is "higher," on some vertical scale than the actors to whom the packets of decentralized authority are distributed. Mintzberg, however, is one significant author who has argued that, alongside vertical decentralization, we also need to consider horizontal decentralization. "Horizontal decentralization will refer to the extent to which nonmanagers control decision processes" (Mintzberg 1979: 186). Thus, we can imagine an organization where all groups of staff are tightly controlled by the line managers as being *horizontally highly centralized* and another, where analysts, professional experts or machine operators have considerable discretion as *horizontally decentralized*. Going outside single organizations and into the field of inter-organizational relations, horizontal decentralization is a significant theme in the burgeoning literature on *networks*, network management and partnerships (see, e.g., Kickert, Klijn, and Koppenjan 1997: Rosenau 2000). Here the idea is that relations between organizations (say between central government, local authorities and voluntary associations which are collectively responsible for delivering social care) should be conducted on the basis of specialization and cooperation rather than hierarchical diktat. In reality, we know that such mutually supportive horizontality can be extremely elusive, but the rhetoric of horizontal egalitarianism has a power of its own (Bache 2001; Lowndes and Skelcher 1998).

16.3.2 Decentralization in Other Languages.

This is not the place to mount a full analysis of the different meanings given to decentralization-related terms in other languages. It may nevertheless be useful, however, to refer to one or two of the most common terms and their usages partly as a warning against over-easy translations.

In French *décentralisation* is normally reserved for what we have above termed external, political decentralization, i.e. the giving of new powers and political responsibility to another authority, such as a local government. This is distinguished from *déconcentration* which is the delegation of executive tasks from a ministry to field services. (In English deconcentration is often used to denote the physical decentralization of an operation—such as moving offices from central London to provincial towns—with no necessary connotation of a decentralization of authority.) However, just to keep things complicated, the French *décentralisation* can also sometimes be used to refer to the functional decentralization which occurs when a ministry delegates the performance of some national service not to its own (territorially based) field services, but rather to an autonomous agency or quango. In Italian, apparently, *decremento* is used in ways roughly similar to the English decentralization.

By this stage the reader may be beginning to feel buried beneath the snowstorm of "d-words." Figure 16.1 attempts to sum up what has been said so far, and to show the way in which the terms will be used in this chapter. While no single usage can be established as universally authoritative Figure 16.1 is at least not wildly idiosyncratic. Thus decentralization is used as the generic term, and other words (devolution, delegation, deconcentration) are identified with particular aspects or species of the central concept.

16.4 THE ARGUMENTS FOR AND AGAINST

16.4.1 Why is Decentralization so Popular?

One reason why decentralization is so popular is its multi-valency—its ability to link up with many other arguments, so that, rhetorically speaking, it can be persuasively useful for several agendas at the same time. It appears to bring both administrative and political benefits, and we will quickly review both, though concentrating on the former.

In *Administrative Argument* Hood and Jackson list ninety-nine major administrative doctrines that have circulated and alternated since administration began to emerge as a distinct body of knowledge, or craft (Hood and Jackson 1991: 34–5).

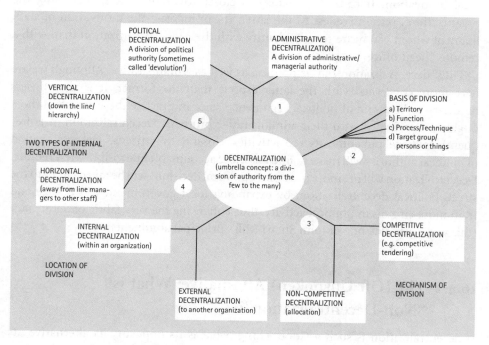

Fig. 16.1 Decentralization: A proposed use of terms

Many can be related to decentralization. For example, there is the doctrine of preferring small-scale organizations over large ones ("small is beautiful"—one of the key features of the NPM—see Boyne et al. 2003). Decentralization does not necessarily mean smaller organizations, but it often does. Or there are the doctrines of preferring short hierarchies over long ones, and narrow spans of control over broad ones—both of which can also readily be associated with decentralization. Both are held to speed decision making and therefore increase efficiency. Or, again, there is the doctrine that pluriform structures are better than uniform structures, because contingencies and contexts vary. Pluriformity goes hand-in-hand with decentralization (once more, not as a necessary feature of decentralization but as a frequent one). Finally, there is the doctrine that an *independent* public bureaucracy (i.e., one at arm's length from a ministry) will be superior in the performance of certain functions such as the regulation of business, the inspection of other parts of the bureaucracy or the investigation of corruption. Hence the independence of audit offices and regulatory bodies for telecommunications, water supply, public transport, and so on. It is a version of this doctrine that the European Commission is using when it argues that:

[t]he creation of further autonomous EU regulatory agencies in clearly defined areas will improve the way rules are applied and enforced across the Union. (European Commission 2001: 24)

Decentralization is said to bring other administrative advantages. It can encourage local innovation. It can bring managers closer to service users, increasing the organization's responsiveness to the latter. It can increase the motivation of staff, many of whom can more readily identify with their local organization than with a remote "head office."

Thus, decentralization can be political as well as administrative. Although we are here more concerned with the latter aspects than the former, it is nevertheless necessary to be aware of political arguments, since in practice these are often thoroughly intermingled with their administrative brothers. Decentralization, it is frequently said, will put authority and activities "closer to the citizens." Decentralization of political authority will make politicians more accountable and visible—less remote. Decentralization will promote trust, since political decisions will be taken closer to the street. Political decentralization, by expanding local government, will engage and train more citizens in political activity, thus enhancing the very fabric of democracy (this was, *inter alia*, one of John Stuart Mill's principal arguments).

16.4.2 The (Oft Unspoken) Alternative: What is "Non-Decentralization"?

If decentralization is such a Good Thing, what is its opposite, its alternative, its antagonist? The obvious answer is "centralization"—but what is that? Given our original definition, centralization must be the *concentration* of authority—political and/or administrative—*in one place* (or, at least, in a smaller number of locations than previously). It is a tribute to the strength of the current fashion for decentralization that that these words—"concentration of authority"—sound so immediately threatening. Surely that is so dangerous, so potentially dictatorial that no right-minded person would wish it? Whole constitutions (notably the American one) have been built around the desire to avoid the possibility of centralized power.

Yet in practice centralization has often been popular. It is easy to produce a list of historical enthusiasms for centralization just as long and as diverse as the catalogue of decentralization initiatives with which this paper opened. For example, in 1970 the new UK Conservative government under Edward Heath produced a white paper entitled *The reorganization of central government* which featured the aggregation of a number of small ministries into giant "super-ministries" and the creation of a "central capability" (the famous Central Policy Review staff—see Pollitt 1984: 89–106). More broadly, executive centralization has often been associated with periods of interventionist political reform, as with Roosevelt's New Deal or Nixon's failed attempt at an "administrative Presidency" in the US. The administrative logic of centralizing reforms such as these is commonly that a single organization will make both *strategy formulation* and *coordination of implementation* less difficult. There may also be *economy of scale arguments*—a larger organization can more easily support expert central units for planning, policy analysis, and program evaluation.

Furthermore, on the political level, it is sometimes argued that centralization will *improve the equity and or equality with which citizens are treated by eradicating the local variability that can come with a decentralized function*. Devolution of political power to the American states was what helped to sustain racialist practices in the American south, until the centralizing federal legislation of the 1960s helped to enshrine the civil and political rights of the black and other ethnic minority citizens. Cole succinctly describes the political case for centralization in his recent review of decentralization in France:

For many French citizens, decentralisation is synonymous with social regression, unequal provision, even a return to the pre-Republican order. Upstanding republicans equate territorial uniformity with ideas of progress, equal opportunity and citizenship. (Cole 2003: 2)

The more one reflects on the historical record, the more it seems clear that the argument between centralization and decentralization is not at all a simple progression from the "bad old days" (when centralization was king) to "modern times" (when we all recognize that decentralization is superior). On the contrary, it looks more like a perpetual struggle—which may well suggest some kind of trade-off between attainable, but mutually incompatible goals (Hood 1998). In a very detailed survey of changes in the structure of Norwegian administrative system over the period 1947–2003, Lægreid et al. comment that: "There appears to be a cyclical process, whereby development in one direction results in a counter-process and sometimes the re-emergence of new values and controls in another" (Lægreid et al. 2003: 8). In a study of American federalism, Kettl remarks that "Decentralization is the usual prescription for troubled centralized systems, centralization for decentralized ones" (Kettl 1983: 169).

What is more, the two trajectories—centralization and decentralization—may often appear simultaneously, either by centralization taking place in one part of the government while decentralization is proceeding elsewhere, or even by centralization and decentralization being thoroughly intertwined within a single reform. One example must suffice. During the late 1980s British schools were the beneficiaries of several important measures of decentralization. One was the Grant-Maintained Schools (GM) initiative, which allowed individual schools to opt out of local authority control. Another was the introduction of Local Management of Schools (LMS) which placed a much larger than hitherto proportion of school budgets under the direct control of the schools themselves (rather than local education authorities). Yet, during precisely the same period that these two decentralizing measures were being promoted, the same central government was taking an unprecedented degree of control of what went on in the classroom. The 1988 Education Act ushered in the first National Curriculum, which prescribed, in considerable detail, what subjects were to be taught and for how long. At the same time batteries of national tests and performance indicators were introduced (Pollitt, Birchall, and Putman 1998).

16.4.3 The Arguments for and against Decentralization: A Summary

Table 16.1 summarizes the arguments for and against decentralization—both those we have already identified and some additional ones. Reading through the list in the table, it is clear that, while every entry has some face plausibility, equally every entry provokes some immediate qualification, such as "only if X and Y," or "yes, but perhaps at the cost of Z." This interconnectedness of decentralization with other features of organizational structures and processes will become even more apparent when we consider a selection of the research literature on the topic.

16.5 CONTEXTS

Before coming to specific studies of decentralization there is a need for a few brief remarks concerning contexts. Decentralization, as we have already seen, can mean something different in France than in Sweden (or in community mental health

Table 16.1 Some common arguments for and against decentralization

A. Arguments in favor of administrative decentralization

1. Decentralization (both vertical and horizontal) speeds decision making by reducing the overload of information which otherwise clogs the upper reaches of a centralized hierarchy. Faster decision making is more efficient.

2. Decentralization means that decisions are taken closer to the users/consumers of an organizations products and services, and this, in turn means that decisions are likely to be more responsive to those users.

3. Decentralization improves the ability of an organization to take account of differences between one local context and another. Services can be better "tuned" to local conditions.

4. Decentralization may be used as one way to reduce political intervention in matters that are best managed without political interference in details (e.g. case work with individual citizens; regulatory functions, etc.).

5. Decentralization encourages innovation (because new ideas no longer have to find their way all the way up the hierarchy to the centre to be approved and authorized).

6. Decentralization improves staff motivation and identification. They feel they can "belong" to a smaller, more comprehensible organization, rather than just being a cog in a gigantic bureaucratic machine.

B. Arguments in favor of political decentralization

1. Devolution of political power puts it closer to the citizen.

2. Devolution of political power makes politicians less remote, more visible and more accountable.

3. Devolution of power encourages more citizens to play some active part in the democratic process—by voting, attending meetings or even standing for office.

4. Devolution of political power allows for greater expression of legitimate local and regional differences.

C. Arguments in favor of centralization (political and administrative)

1. Centralization enables organizations to benefit from economies of scale.

2. Centralization enables organizations to retain a critical mass of experts (in central think tanks and the "technostructure"). Small organizations do not have the resources to do this.

3. Centralization, in the form of standardization, leads to greater equity. All citizens in similar circumstances receive the same service. Autonomous local services are more prone to inequities—both intentional and unintentional.

4. Centralization makes the coordination of policies and programs (especially those which cross sectoral or organizational boundaries) easier to accomplish. "Joined-up" government can be substituted for "hollowed-out" government.

5. Centralization makes the line of accountability clearer and more easily understood by citizens. In highly decentralized systems patterns of accountability are complex, and there are too many opportunities for blame-shifting.

than in the army). Its significance and appeal depends to a considerable extent on what has gone before—on where a jurisdiction is starting from—on the historical and constitutional legacy. For example, the decentralizing components within the NPM carry a very different resonance in the highly centralized UK than in highly decentralized Germany (Wollmann 2001). These path dependencies (Pierson 2000) go further than simply the difference between unitary and federal states. In the federal USA a pro-business, anti-public sector ideology has meant that decentralization has recently been translated into a massive contracting-out of public services, whereas in federal Germany a very different ideology has seen decentralization strengthen the portfolio of activities carried out by multi-purpose local authorities. Clearly, if authority is highly concentrated, as it is in states such as the France, New Zealand and the UK, then decentralization has "further to go," and may come as a greater shock to the system, than in already extensively decentralized states such as Denmark, Germany or Switzerland.

Thus, we need to locate studies of specific acts (or rhetorics) of decentralization within the particular institutional patterns and trajectories of the countries concerned (Pollitt and Bouckaert 2004). In many cases we find that debates about decentralization are virtually permanent features of the states concerned. Thus the American discussion of "states' rights" (i.e., the autonomy of state governments versus the federal government in Washington, DC) began before the framing of the American constitution in 1787, and has continued ever since. In France the tensions between "Paris and the rest" have flared up regularly ever since Napoleon Bonaparte's great centralizing reforms at the end of the eighteenth century and the beginning of the nineteenth. Sometimes the accent is on decentralization and sometimes the flow is the other way. But, whichever way the current fashion is pointing, the issue is always there, and is always framed by the past, especially—given the nature of politics—the recent past.

Institutional differences can also lead to paradoxes. For example, it is arguably easier for highly centralized regimes to achieve radical decentralization than for already highly decentralized regimes. In decentralized regimes such as those of Germany or the USA authority is already parceled out into many different institutional locations, and many of these are protected from sudden change by entrenched constitutional law. In the UK, however, Prime Minister Blair can decide to set up elected assemblies in two country-regions (Scotland and Wales) and force this through with a massive, one-party Parliamentary majority and a simple piece of ordinary legislation. In France, too, Mitterand was able, in the 1980s, to create new regional bodies, and to transfer powers to local authorities, in a way that would have been difficult or impossible for any American President.

16.6 Selected Studies

16.6.1 Decentralization: Theories and Evidence

Despite the very wide use of arguments concerning the causes and consequences of decentralization, the amount of empirical research which has focused specifically on decentralization has been rather limited. With the exception of mainstream organization theory, there does not seem to have been a major set of cumulative studies of decentralization within the field of academic public administration. There are quite a few "one-off," isolated investigations, but no real research program. (A partial exception might be made here for the considerable US principal–agent literature that deals with delegation, but much of that is theory-heavy and empirically light.) Many studies refer to centralization or decentralization in general terms, but do not advance an operationally precise definition. It is as though decentralization is like a popular character actor—he gets lots of walk-on parts, and is immediately recognizable, but is seldom given a starring role. In our review of this scattered *corpus* of work we will divide the material by field and subfield.

16.6.2 Contingency Theory

Donaldson (2001) provides an authoritative synthesis which traces the important role which decentralization has played in the development of contingency theory. Burns and Stalker, Hage, Pugh, Child, and Donaldson himself (and others) have all attempted to operationalize "decentralization" and use it in quantified comparisons of organizational structures—in both public and private sectors. In his summary of the current state of play Donaldson suggests that growth in the size of an organization tends to lead to an increase in the number of hierarchical levels, and that this, in turn, reduces the effectiveness of centralized decision-making. Organizational leaders are then obliged either to suffer a loss of performance (a decreasing "fit" between structure and organizational and environmental contingencies) or to decentralize. The decentralization may be "lagged" (delayed) until organizational leaders recognize the falling performance and correctly analyze its cause, or these same leaders may sometimes act in anticipation of problems, by decentralizing before the vertical information channels become too long and clogged up (Donaldson 2001: esp. chs. 5 and 7).

The efforts of contingency theorists are not to everyone's epistemological taste, but one of the strong points of their work is their insistence on building clear models of relationships between variables (and then the testing of the strength of those relationships across a population of organizations). In most contingency schemes decentralization seems to function as an intermediate variable, in the sense that it is caused by something else (e.g., increasing organizational size, according to bureaucratic theory, or increasing task uncertainty, according to organic /mechanistic theories), but then has effects of its own—principally better "fit" and therefore improved performance.

16.6.3 Other Organization Theorists

Over the past thirty years Mintzberg has been a particularly influential voice, and one that has had a great deal to say about decentralization. He insists that it should be regarded as but one among several organizational "design parameters." Further: "The relationships among the design parameters are clearly reciprocal, not sequential" (Mintzberg 1979: 181). Like the contingency theorists, Mintzberg sees functional efficiency as the main engine of decentralization. However, his classification of organizational forms is considerably more sophisticated and elaborated. After much intricate argumentation, Mintzberg arrives at a centralized type of organizational structure plus four different types of decentralization (Mintzberg 1979: 208–13). These represent different combinations of vertical and horizontal decentralization. His broad conclusion is:

The formalization of behavior takes formal power away from the workers and the managers who supervise them and concentrates it near the top of the line hierarchy and in the technostructure [technostructure = the analytical staff of the organization who generate the definitions, categories and procedures by which work is standardized and controlled] thus centralizing the organization in both dimensions... Training and indoctrination produces exactly the opposite effect: it develops expertise below the middle line, thereby decentralizing the structure in both dimensions... Putting these two conclusions together, we can see that specialization of the unskilled type centralizes the structure in both dimensions, whereas specialization of the skilled or professional type decentralizes it in both dimensions. (Mintzberg 1979: 211)

The implication is that up-skilling and professionalization leads to decentralized structures, because such staff can neither work effectively nor sustain their motivation if constantly and tightly circumscribed by rules and instructions from those at the top of the organization.

Mintzberg's five organizational types have proved widely influential, both in business studies and in public administration. It should be noted, however, that subsequent empirical work seems to indicate that the existence of the "types" is suspect—most organizations occupy intermediate and mixed positions rather than one of the pure positions set out by Mintzberg (Doty, Glick, and Huber 1993, see also Donaldson 2001: 141–52).

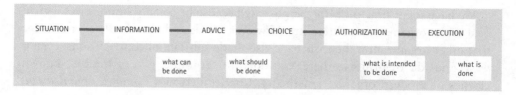

Fig. 16.2 A continuum of control over the decision process

Source: Mintzberg (1979: 188)

In another part of his analysis, Mintzberg offers different types of typology: a "continuum of control over the decision process" (1979: 188) and a continuum of co-ordinating mechanisms' (p. 198). Both are potentially very useful for the analysis of decentralization, and both are reproduced here (Figures 16.2 and 16.3).

These continua suggest that researchers should not content themselves with a generalized enquiry into "decentralization," but should disaggregate that notion so as to identify which steps in the decision process are centralized and which decentralized, and what overall effects this pattern seems to have on the final actions/outputs. Strong echoes of similar thinking can be found in NPM doctrine. Targets should be centralized, but authority over choice of means should be decentralized.

Similarly, in terms of Figure 16.3, NPM doctrine is in favor of a lessening of centralized controls over direct supervision and standardization of work processes, but specifies a strong central voice in the setting of output targets. More recently, much of the partnership literature argues for increased reliance on mutual adjustment as a principal means of co-ordination (see, e.g., Kickert, Klijn, and Koppenjan 1997). One means of achieving this, in decentralized structures, is the adoption of common standards, which is supposed to be a voluntary process (Brunsson and Jacobsson 2002).

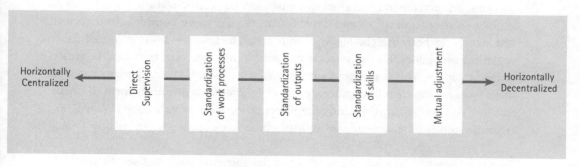

Fig. 16.3 A continuum of coordinating mechanisms

Source: Mintzberg (1979: 198)

We have spent time on Mintzberg partly because he so ably summarizes a great deal of the organizational literature. However, we should also briefly acknowledge that other organization theorists have also made substantial contributions, even if we cannot do them justice here. Consider, for example, two of the best-known classics of modern organization theory, Charles Perrow's *Complex organizations* and W. R. Scott's *Organizations: Rational, Natural and Open Systems* (Perrow 1986; Scott 1987). Perrow devotes very little space—and not even a single subheading—to the centralization/decentralization issue. Despite this he announces early in his book that one of his major insights is that "bureaucracy has become a means, both in capitalist and non-capitalist countries, of centralizing power in society and legitimizing or disguising that centralization"(1986: 5). Unfortunately, this arresting claim is subsequently not followed up in any detail. Scott, by contrast, has quite a lot to say about decentralization. He notes that one of the key features of hierarchical forms of organization is their centralized communications systems, which may be relatively efficient at dealing with middling amounts of routine information, but rather poor at handling high complexity and/or ambiguity (1987: 151–3). Thus, he links the advantages and disadvantages of different degrees of centralization to the nature of the task.

16.6.4 Decentralization in the Public Administration and Public Management Literatures

Transferring contingency theory logic to the contemporary public sector, we might say that changing contingencies mean that increased decentralization is necessary if government performance is to be maintained or improved. The contingencies could be (according to organic theories) changes in tasks, so that, for example, government is nowadays involved in more complex high-tech projects, or in attempts to solve ill-defined but "wicked" social problems such as drug abuse, inner city decay or an ageing population. Or the new contingencies could be (according to bureaucratic theories) an increase in functional specialization and formalization in government, leading to decentralization as a typical feature of a more complex, bureaucratic system. (Note here the challenging—but often forgotten—assumption of much organization theory to the effect that greater bureaucratization equals greater *decentralization*. This is the exact opposite of the position taken by many management writers who treat "bureaucracy" as an inherently *centralizing* form of organization.) At first hearing this kind of argumentation sounds reasonable. We will now examine some of the scholarly groupings which work among these assumptions.

Network theorists draw on the work of social theorists such as Castells (1997) to support a vision of a new world in which governments are "hollowed out" and obliged, by new pressures, to relinquish their central role:

[T]he hollow state is not only characterized by the fact that the implementation of politics is increasingly being done by autonomous actors. The hollow state is also characterized by the complexity of its decision making. Because policy cannot be controlled from the centre, decision making involves more actors and becomes more complex. (Klijn 2002: 151; see also Milward and Provan 1993 for one of the original statements of the "hollow state" concept)

Much of the research that supports this vision is very different from the work of the contingency theorists cited earlier. Some is pitched at a very high level of generalization/abstraction (e.g., Kickert, Klijn, and Koppenjan 1997; Kooiman 1993). Most of it, however, consists of qualitative case studies: some of them rich, subtle and suggestive, but not the kind of material that can easily be cumulated into broad generalizations about the effects of decentralization under a standardized set of circumstances (e.g., Christensen 2001; Lowndes and Skelcher 1998). Some, though not all, this literature is normatively-tinged: its authors not merely believe that decentralized networks are becoming more important, but they also think that this is a desirable, pro-democratic trend.

Milward and Provan (1993; 2003) examined the management of community mental health networks in four US cities. Contrary to the views of the some of the more romantic network enthusiasts, they concluded that networks would work most effectively when integration is centralized through a powerful core agency. What is more, network effectiveness was found to be highest when mechanisms of state fiscal control were direct and not fragmented or indirect. Network stability over time also enhanced effectiveness. In another American study—this time of job training networks—Heinrich and Lynn used quantitative analysis to establish that a degree of central authority seemed conducive to positive program outcomes (2000).

Traditional mainstream public administration. As one might expect, British writers have been frequent occupants of this particular niche. To illustrate the *genre*—and its findings—we may consider a number of works which have examined the very extensive administrative decentralization practiced by NPM-minded British governments between 1980 and 2003.

Pollitt, Birchall, and Putman examined the theory and practice of decentralized management in a sample of sixteen schools, hospitals and social housing departments/associations (1998). All had experienced the decentralizing, "opting out" policies of the Conservative administrations of 1987–97. The research found that substantial decentralization *had* occurred, although often less than had originally been envisaged by the policy makers. Also, it had been accompanied by significant measures of centralization, and especially by a shift from local government control to central government control. As far as performance was concerned, the pace of activity had intensified in all three sectors, and in some cases efficiency measures indicated growing productivity. Certainly, there was greater awareness and transparency with regard to various performance measures, but this was paradoxically, chiefly the result of relentless central government pressure. Evidence with regard to equity was patchy, but suggestive of the likelihood of some equity losses. None of the sixteen organizations could produce convincing time series that would permit comparisons of efficiency or effectiveness before and after the decentralizations.

Boyne et al. (2003) is later work covering much the same territory (reforms in UK health, housing and education) as Pollitt, Birchall, and Putman. The authors survey a great deal of empirical literature in an attempt to test three key propositions from public choice theory. These are that:

- More competition will lead to better performance.
- Making more performance information publicly available will also improve performance.
- And so will a shift from larger to smaller organizations, because larger size equals declining marginal efficiency and reduced responsiveness to customers.

These propositions are closely related (at least *de facto*) to the centralization/ decentralization issue because competition usually means breaking up public sector monopolies (spreading out authority and resources to a larger number of organizations), and so does the shift to smaller organizations. The greater availability of performance information should, in principle, allow us to see whether the hoped-for improvements actually come about.

Boyne et al.'s conclusions are mixed. In health and housing there is some evidence of raised efficiency (in education the picture is obscure). In housing and education there is evidence of greater responsiveness to service users (in health the evidence is insufficient to be sure). However, in all three sectors there appears to have been some loss of equity (Boyne et al. 2003: 156). Thus the public choice propositions are partly confirmed, but the performance improvements in efficiency and user responsiveness have been paid for by a fall in performance against the criterion of equitable treatment. It must be added, however, that Boyne et al. found endless methodological problems—missing evidence and highly imperfect evidence—and their findings are thus heavily qualified.

Talbot (2004) looks at fifteen years of experience with the Next Steps program of creating executive agencies, an administrative decentralization which saw nearly 80 percent of civil servants decanted into well over 100 agencies in just ten years. Structural disaggregation, combined with financial and personnel freedoms and a regime of performance targets, was supposed to be the recipe for greater efficiency and user responsiveness. Talbot's analysis of the evidence leads him to a now familiar-sounding set of conclusions: that there is some evidence for efficiency gains, but that the attribution is problematic (the cause could well be a variety of other developments, not just agency status) and that the frequent absence of comparable data prior to reform makes "before and after" comparison virtually impossible. What is more, even the detailed performance data has rather serious problems, because indicator definitions and sets change rather rapidly. In the first few years of a new agency this "churn rate," year-on-year, may be as high as

60 percent and even with older agencies it can still be 20 percent. In another Next Steps study, James (2003) came to similar conclusions about technical efficiency, but also found evidence of substantial problems with externalities, as agencies focused tightly on their own targets and neglected wider effects within the system of government as a whole.

What we see from these British studies, therefore, is a strong presumption of some efficiency gains (although not of a spectacular order) plus a shift towards greater customer responsiveness. The data, however, are frequently hard to interpret, and time series from before decentralization are usually absent. What is more, decentralization has often been accompanied by measures of centralization, especially the tightening of reporting regimes and categories, and at the same time there have probably been some negative "externalities."

A major empirical study, using an unusually detailed databank built up over many years, has been carried out in Norway. Lægreid et al. (2003) found that, although the coupling of reform visions, reform decisions and actual changes was often loose, nevertheless some broad patterns could be found in the half-century record:

The main reform strategy in Norway has been to avoid privatization by concentrating on structural devolution within the public sector. (p. 27)

Within this broad thrust:

there is an increasingly parallel process of vertical specialization and horizontal despecialization [at least in the period since 1983]...Units are changing their form of affiliation through structural devolution or autonomization at the same time as units within the same form of affiliation are going through amalgamation and merging processes and are being terminated into existing units to an increasing degree. (p. 28)

The Norwegian team did not look for evidence of the effectiveness or efficiency of these reforms. However, their research suggested to them that administrative changes were not the product of some simple drive for efficiency, nor yet the inevitable effects of global forces. On the contrary, they saw what had happened as "a complex interplay between international trends, particular national structures, historical–institutional contexts and specific institutional traditions" (p. 31).

In an overview of developments in American government, one prominent scholar identified devolution as one of the two main dimensions of recent transformations (Kettl 2000). More and more of the work of the federal government is carried out through partnerships—with states, local governments, voluntary associations, and for-profit private companies (see also Peterson 2000). The picture is a complex one in which the new "horizontal" links have been layered on top of the older vertical hierarchies, rather than replacing them. This causes problems for the traditional system of vertical accountability:

The spread of horizontal relationships muddies that accountability. They replace hierarchical authority with networks—sometimes formally constructed through contracts and other legal agreements, sometimes informally drawn through pragmatic working relationships. (Kettl 2000: 494)

Informatics. We now turn to another approach. In recent years the study of information systems has begun to grow as an important new sub-field of public management. Research concerning the impact of changing Information and Communication Technologies (ICTs) has significant implications for the centralization/ decentralization issue. Reading this literature, it soon becomes apparent that diametrically opposite interpretations of the significance of ICTs are in play. Some see them as tools for decentralization, democracy and participation—for a new style of "soft" governance. Others see them as increasing the probability of a "Big Brother" state. Perhaps, as Frissen puts it:

In order for the government to become a Soft Sister it needs access to all the data gathered by Big Brother. Big Brother and Soft Sister are Siamese twins. (Frissen 1998: 35)

Much depends on the technical details themselves—how are the systems designed, what categories and decision rules do they incorporate, who can access the data? Bovens and Zouridis (2002) point out that in many cases "street-level bureaucrats"—those who Lipsky (1980) made famous for their discretionary ability to reformulate policies at the coal face—have now lost much of their freedom to their operating software:

Public servants can no longer take freely to the streets, but are always connected to the organization via the computer. Client data must be filled in, and with the help of fixed templates, in electronic forms. Knowledge management systems and digital decision trees have strongly reduced the scope for administrative discretion. (Bovens and Zouridis 2002: 177)

In short, modern ICTs enable a kind of decentralized centralization. The conclusion which the authors draw from this analysis is that systems designers themselves need to be held to account. Citizens and their elected representatives should be given the opportunity to examine and criticize these systems before they pass the point of no return.

New institutional theorists. Our account would be seriously incomplete if we did not refer to a very different school of thought. This group is much less convinced than Mintzberg or the contingency theorists that efficiency and "fit" are what usually drive organization restructuring. Instead they see a world in which "the logic of appropriateness" (March and Olsen 1989) is often dominant, and in which organizational reforms are adopted as part of a cycle of fashion, to imitate the apparent success of other organizations or to comply with pressures for conformity applied from above (Powell and DiMaggio 1991). Thus reform may be seen as mainly a matter of preserving or enhancing legitimacy (and the careers of the reformers) rather than something principally for improving efficiency or responsiveness. The means and meanings of a particular reform are socially constructed by opinion-leaders and dominant groups—the "real" effectiveness of the change may never be known. Often, it is not necessary for the reforms to be fully implemented for them to have these beneficial (but temporary) effects—the disjuncture between what the leaders of the organization say is happening and the actual effects on the ground (often minimal) may even be helpful in allowing the organization to continue to pursue multiple and mutually incompatible goals (Brunsson 1989; Brunsson and Olsen 1993). Political organizations have a particularly strong need to maintain and exploit these gaps between words and deeds, because they are wrestling with so many competing demands and priorities. What is more, they are subject to the exacting norms of public accountability—indeed, much of their output is talk and text rather than action.

From this perspective decentralization becomes a kind of totem, a rallying cry, a badge of progress and political correctness, a preferred vocabulary for insiders—and perhaps, a way of promoting one's own career. The waxing and waning of calls for decentralization may bear little relation to what happens "on the ground." The multiplicity of slippery meanings which can be ascribed to decentralization permit actors to recruit all sorts of unlikely reforms under its banner. Paradoxes are commonplace—thus NPM reforms ostensibly designed to "free the manager to manage" are accompanied by the stealthy growth of army of straight-jacket of inspectors, auditors, evaluators and monitoring systems, all designed to maintain the control of those at the centre (Hood et al. 1999). Or again, to take a US example:

There has been through the history of the republic, and especially through Nixon's and Reagan's grant reforms, a powerful rhetoric advocating state and local autonomy. At the same time, there has been a growing tide toward a stronger federal role, even in decisions that were once the predominant province of state and local governments. (Kettl 1983: 171)

Federalist studies have a long and honorable history of their own, especially in the USA, but also in countries such as Belgium, Germany, and Australia (e.g., Halligan and Power 1992; Howitt 1984; Peterson, Rabe, and Wong 1986; Riker 1987). It is impossible to do them justice here, but a highly selective glance may yield some insights that are useful to our theme.

Federalist studies frequently show what an intimate and complex relationship there is between political and administrative decentralization. The two may move together, or they may not. They also show some of the alternation between periods of activist, interventionist central government and contrasting periods of decentralization, as alluded to earlier (Beer 1973; Kettl 1983). These alternations occur within a given constitutional framework (path dependency) so that, for example, the US federal government almost certainly has greater leverage over the American states than does the Swiss central government over the Cantons, with the German federal government probably somewhere in between. Occasionally federal systems exhibit the paradox whereby the existence of decentralized autonomy permits a subnational jurisdiction to develop a unique solution to its policy problems, only to see its model borrowed by central government and generalized across other jurisdictions (see, e.g., Halligan and Power 1992).

Federal studies sometimes confirm the existence of substantial gaps between rhetoric and reality. Take, for example, the following assessment of President Reagan's policies of the early 1980s:

Attempts at a more comprehensive decentralization were scuttled by several interrelated factors. The basic ideas undergirding decentralization were never translated into coherent, workable policy proposals by the Reagan administration. Efforts to decentralize . . . suffered from rhetorical excesses and tactical blunders, and decentralization was never elevated to the top of the President's agenda. (Peterson, Rabe, and Wong 1986: 218)

Why, one may ask, was there resistance to decentralization, or, to put it another way, who was trying to preserve central control? Peterson et al. have the answer:

given the formidable political impediments to decentralization, including such well-entrenched institutions as congressional committees, federal agencies and bureaus, and the myriad pressure groups that coalesced around them, it is remarkable that even incremental steps towards decentralization were taken. (p. 219; see also Kettl 1983: 172–3)

In a number of these studies there is an interesting suggestion that certain types of program may be better suited to decentralized solutions than others. Peterson et al. argue that programs with developmental objectives are particularly suited to localized planning and delivery, whereas redistributive programs are more appropriately handled centrally. "It is only the federal government that has the national constituencies and independence from economic competition with neighbouring jurisdictions necessary to facilitate significant redistribution" (Peterson, Rabe, and Wong 1986: 232).

16.7 Conclusions

The first conclusion must be that we are dealing with one of the most protean concepts in the field. Decentralization, in its many guises (and together with its inseparable partner, centralization) has been a hardy perennial since the emergence of public administration as a self-conscious field of study, and it continues to occupy a pivotal place in more recent public management discourses.

A second conclusion might be that there is now considerable accumulated evidence, gathered by a variety of methodologies and seen through a range of theoretical perspectives, to indicate that decentralization *can* lead to increased efficiency and to greater responsiveness to users. *Can* is the crucial word, because the connection is anything but automatic. It is contingent upon a range of other factors. Elements of both agency and structure play a part. Clearly, the managerial and political skill with which a particular decentralization measure is conceived and implemented affects the outcomes. Even a sensible measure can be undermined by incompetent implementation. Clearly also, certain structural factors, such as the size of the organization, and the technical complexity of its main task will influence both the need for decentralization and the type of decentralization which is most likely to prove effective. Finally, there is a strong suggestion that different types of program may be more or less amenable to decentralization. For example, developmental programs may be at the "more" end and redistributional programs at the "less." And it may be easier to exert central control in standardized "production" organizations (where outputs and outcomes can be clearly measured) than in "coping" organizations (where they cannot) (Wilson 1989; Pollitt et al. 2004).

Third, the main thrust of the new institutionalist theorists is hard to ignore. Many pronouncements about decentralization may have more to do with legitimacy and getting a good sound bite than with measurable efficiency or customer responsiveness. It is not unusual for the gap between decentralizing rhetoric and actual experience "on the ground" to be large. How far such gaps are the product of operational complexity baffling good intentions, or how far they result from a cynical use of rhetoric, it is often hard to say. The new institutionalism does not drive out the more traditional analysis of dependent and independent variables, but it does offer a very different kind of perspective, which seeks to pose different questions that are shaped by a different epistemology.

Fourth, existing research gives support to the idea that decentralization often involves trade-offs. This may not *always* be the case, but in practice it seems often to be so. Thus decentralization in the delivery of human services frequently leads to some loss of equity. When decentralization takes the form of partnerships or networking there may also be some loss of transparency. The lines of accountability become complex, if not blurred. It gets harder for the onlooker to understand who is responsible and accountable for what. The more stringent and numerous accountable relationships which characterize many public services make it harder to achieve radical decentralization. The existence of such trade-offs is one important reason why we frequently see alternations over time between more and less centralized arrangements for a particular policy or program. In an important sense, therefore, the "right" balance between centralization and decentralization is usually only a temporary one.

REFERENCES

BACHE, I. (2001), "Different Seeds from the Same Plot ? Competing Models of Capitalism and the Incomplete Contracts of Partnership Design," *Public Administration* 79(2): 337–59.

BEER, S. H. (1973), "The Modernization of American Federalism," *Publius* 3(2): 53–95.

BOSTON, J., MARTIN, J., PALLOT, J., and WALSH, P. (1996), *Public Management: The New Zealand Model*, Auckland: Oxford University Press.

BOVENS, M., and ZOURIDIS, S. (2002), "From Street-Level to System-Level Bureaucracies: How Information and Communication Technologies are Transforming Administrative Discretion and Constitutional Control," *Public Administration Review* 62(2): 174–84.

BOYNE, G., FARRELL, C., LAW, J., POWELL, M., and WALKER, R. (2003), *Evaluating Public Management Reforms*, Buckingham: Open University Press.

BRUNSSON, N. (1989), *The Organization of Hypocrisy: Talk, Decisions and Actions in Organizations*, Chichester: Wiley.

—— and JACOBSSON, B. (2002), *A World of Standards*, Oxford: Oxford University Press.

—— and OLSEN, J. (1993), *The Reforming Organization*, London and New York: Routledge.

CARBONE, L. et al. (2000), *La riforma dell'Amministrazione dello Stato—Presidenza del Consiglio, ministeri, controlli, enti pubblici*, Salerno and Napoli: Edizioni Giuridiche Simone.

CASTELLS, M. (1997), *The Power of Identity: The Information Age: Economy, Society, and Culture*, vol. 2, Oxford: Blackwell.

CHRISTENSEN, J. (2000), "The Dynamics of Centralization and Recentralization," *Public Administration* 78(2): 389–408.

COLE, A. (2003), *Decentralisation in France: Back to Grass Roots or Steering at a Distance?* Paper presented to the UK Political Studies Association Conference, University of Leicester, 15–17 April.

DONALDSON, L. (2001), *The Contingency Theory of Organizations*, Thousand Oaks, CA: Sage.

DOTY, D. GLICK, W., and HUBER, G. (1993), "Fit, Equi-finality and Organizational Effectiveness: A Test of Two Configurational Theories," *Academy of Management Journal* 36: 1196–250.

DUNSIRE, A. (1973), *Administration: The Word and the Science*, London: Martin Robertson.

EUROPEAN COMMISSION (2001), *White Paper on European Governance*, COM (2001), 428 final.

FRISSEN, P. (1998), "Public Administration in Cyberspace: A Postmodern Perspective," in I. Snellen and W. van de Donk (eds.), *Public administration in an information age: A Handbook*, Amsterdam: IOS Press.

GULICK, L. (1937), "Notes on the Theory of Organization," in L. Gulick and L. Urwick (eds.), *Papers on the Science of Administration*, New York: Institute of Public Administration.

GUYOMARCH, A. (1999), " 'Public Service,' 'Public Management' and the Modernization of French Public Administration," *Public Administration* 77(1): 171–93.

HALLIGAN, J., and POWER, J. (1992), *Political Management in the 1990s*, Melbourne: Oxford University Press.

HEINRICH, C., and LYNN, L., JR. (2000), "Governance and Performance: The Influence of Program Structure and Management on Job Training Partnership Act (JTPA) Program Outcomes," in C. Henrich and L. Lynn (eds.), *Governance and Performance: New Perspectives*, Washington, DC: Georgetown University Press, 68–108.

HOOD, C. (1991), "A Public Management for All Seasons," *Public Administration* 69(1): 3–19.

—— (1998), *The Art of the State: Culture, Rhetoric and Public Management*, Oxford: Oxford University Press.

—— and JACKSON, M. (1991), *Administrative Argument*, Aldershot: Dartmouth.

—— SCOTT, C., JAMES, O., JONES, G., and TRAVERS, A. (1999), *Regulation inside Government: Waste Watchers, Quality Police, and Sleaze-Busters*, Oxford: Oxford University Press.

HORVATH, T. (ed.) (2000), *Decentralization: Experiments and Reforms: Local Governments in Central and Eastern Europe*, Budapest: Open Society Institute.

HOWITT, A. (1984), *Managing Federalism: Studies in Intergovernmental Relations*, Washington, DC: CQ Press.

JAMES, O. (2003), *The Executive Agency Revolution in Whitehall: Public Interest versus Bureau-Shaping Perspectives*, Basingstoke: Palgrave/Macmillan.

KETTL, D. (1983), *The Regulation of American Federalism*, Baton Rouge and London: Louisiana State University Press.

—— (2000), "The Transformation of Governance: Globalization, Devolution and the Role of Government," *Public Administration Review* 60(6): 488–97.

KICKERT, W. (2000), *Public Management Reform in the Netherlands: Social Reconstruction of Reform Ideas and Underlying Frames of Reference*, Delft: Eburon.

—— KLIJN, E.-H., and KOPPENJAN, J. (eds.) (1997), *Managing Complex Networks: Strategies for the Public Sector*, London: Sage.

KLIJN, J.-E. (2002), "Governing Networks in the Hollow State: Contracting out, Process Management or a Combination of the Two?", *Public Management Review* 4(2): 149–65.

KOOIMAN, J. (1993), *Modern Governance: New Government–Society Interactions*, London: Sage.

LÆGRIED, P., ROLLAND, V. RONESS, P., and ÅGOTNES, J-E. (2003), *The Structural Autonomy of the Norwegian State, 1947–2003*. Paper presented at the Seminar on the Study of Public Sector Organizations, Public Management Institute, Katholieke Universiteit Leuven, May 2–3.

LANE, J.-E. (2000), *New Public Management*, London: Routledge.

LIPSKY, M. (1980), *Street-Level Bureaucracy*, New York: Russell Sage Foundation.

LOWNDES, V., and SKELCHER, C. (1998), "The Dynamics of Multi-Organizational Partnership: An Analysis of Changing Modes of Governance," *Public Administration* 76(2): 313–34.

MACMAHON, A. (1961), *Delegation and Autonomy*, London: Asia Publishing House.

MARCH, J., and OLSEN, J. (1989), *Rediscovering Institutions: The Organizational Basis of Politics*, New York: Free Press.

MIDDLEMAS, K. (1995), *Orchestrating Europe: The Informal Politics of the European Union, 1973–1995*, London: Fontana.

MILWARD, H., and PROVAN, K. (1993), "The Hollow State: Private Provision of Public Services," in H. Ingram and S. Smith (eds.), *Public Policy for Democracy*, Washington, DC: Brookings Institute, 222–37.

Milward, H., and Provan, K. (2003), "Managing the Hollow State: Collaboration and Contracting," *Public Management Review*,5(1): 1–18.

Mintzberg, H. (1979), *The Structuring of Organizations: A Synthesis of the Research*, London: Prentice-Hall.

OECD (2001), *Distributed Public Governance: Agencies, Authorities and Other Autonomous Bodies* (preliminary draft), Paris, OECD.

Osborne, D., and Gaebler, T. (1992), *Reinventing Government: How the Entrepreneurial Spirit is Transforming the Public Sector*, Reading, MA: Adison Wesley.

Perrow, C. (1986), *Complex Organizations: A Critical Essay*, 3rd edn., New York: Random House.

Peterson, M. (2000), "The Fate of 'Big Government' in the United States: Not Over, but Undermined?", *Governance* 13(2): 251–64.

Peterson, P., Rabe, B., and Wong, K. (1986), *When Federalism Works*, Washington, DC: The Brookings Institution.

Pierson, P. (2000), "Increasing Returns, Path Dependence and the Study of Politics," *American Political Science Review* 94(2): 251–67.

Pollitt, C. (1984), *Manipulating the Machine: Changing the Pattern of Ministerial Departments 1960–83*, London: Allen and Unwin.

—— (2002), "Clarifying Convergence: Striking Similarities and Durable Differences in Public Management Reform," *Public Management Review* 4(1): 471–92.

—— (2003), *The Essential Public Manager*, Buckingham: Open University Press

—— Birchall, J., and Putman, K. (1998), *Decentralizing Public Service Management: The British Experience*, Basingstoke: Macmillan.

—— and Bouckaert, G. (2004), *Public Management Reform: A Comparative Analysis*, 2nd edn., Oxford: Oxford University Press.

—— Caulfield, J., Smullen, A., and Talbot, C. (2004), *Agencies: How Governments Get Things Done through Semi-Autonomous Organizations*, Basingstoke: Palgrave/Macmillan.

—— and Talbot, C. (eds.) (2004), *Unbundled Government*, London: Taylor and Francis.

Powell, W., and DiMaggio, P. (eds.) (1991), *The New Institutionalism in Organizational Analysis*, Chicago: University of Chicago Press.

Riker, W. (1987), *The Development of American Federalism*, Boston and Dordrecht: Kluwer.

Rosenau, P. (ed.) (2000), *Public–Private Policy Partnerships*, Westwood, MA: Massachusetts Institute of Technology.

Scott, W. R. (1987), *Organizations: Rational, Natural and Open Systems*, 2nd edn., Englewood Cliffs, NJ: Prentice-Hall.

Smith, B. (1985), *Decentralisation: The Territorial Dimension of the State*, London: Allen and Unwin.

—— and Stanyer, J. (1976), *Administering Britain*, London: Martin Robertson.

Smith, J. T. (1851), *Local Self-Government and Centralization: The Characteristics of Each and its Practical Tendencies*, London (pamphlet).

Talbot, C. (2004), "Executive Agencies: Have they Improved Management in Government?", *Public Money and Management* (forthcoming).

Vos, E. (2003), "Agencies and the European Union," in L. Verhey and T. Zwart (eds.), *Agencies in European and Comparative Law*, Intersentia Publishing, 113–47.

WILSON, J. Q. (1989), *Bureaucracy: What Government Agencies Do and why they Do It*, New York, Basic Books.

WOLLMANN, H. (2001), "Germany's Trajectory of Public Sector Modernization: Continuities and Discontinuities," *Policy and Politics* 29(2): 151–69.

YAMAMOTO, K. (2004), "Agencification in Japan: Renaming, or Revolution?", in C. Pollitt and C. Talbot (eds.), *Unbundled Government*, London: Taylor and Francis, ch. 11.

CHAPTER 17

E-GOVERNMENT

A CHALLENGE FOR PUBLIC MANAGEMENT

IGNACE SNELLEN

17.1 INTRODUCTION

EVERY activity of a public administration has an informational and a communicative aspect. Therefore, it may be expected that the institutionalization of electronic information and communication technologies (ICTs) in public administration would have a fundamental impact on the way in which public administration functions (Mowshowitz 1992). Although this basic assumption is generally adhered to, it is not uncontested (Kraemer and King 1987; King and Kraemer 1998).

Early empirical studies in the USA on institutionalization of computing in public administration indicate the relative importance of internal and external factors for this institutionalization. Perry et al. (1992) concluded on the basis of their research "that institutionalization of computing innovations is a function of both environmental and internal factors." To their surprise it was not clear whether

The author is grateful to Dr Vincent Homburg for his sparring role in the final phase of the formulation of this chapter.

top management support was essential or conducive to institutionalization. It seemed to play a more mixed role in this respect.

Originally, "Informatization"[1] was the container concept in which the combination of processes, started by computerization or the deployment of ICTS, was lumped together (Nora and Minc 1980). More recently, "e-Government" has become the label and guiding vision for "the intensive use of ICT applications in the fulfillment of functions of politics and public administration" (Lenk and Traunmuller 2000; Peristeras et al. 2002). In the private sector "e-Business" was the catchword that preceded "e-Government." E-government contains processes both inside and between political bodies and public bureaucracies, with businesses, citizens and civic society, at different layers of government: local, regional, national as well as international. Forms of e-Government are spreading mainly within the executive branches of governments, and to a lesser extent, also within the legislatures and the judiciaries. Within the executive branches use is made of:

- *database technologies*, e.g., as data repositories or for file sharing;
- *tracing and tracking technologies*, e.g., for workflow management and monitoring purposes;
- *desk-top technologies*, such as text processors, digital personal assistants (DPAs), e-mail, and other Internet facilities;
- *decision support technologies*, e.g., spread-sheets, all kinds of task directed computer programs and expert systems;
- *network technologies*, such as websites, homepages, call-centres and e-mail.

Through the use of ICTs public organizations enhance their knowledge management (KM) capacities: to algorithmize and to control decisions and activities; to standardize, formalize, and routinize those decisions and activities; to monitor and benchmark the outputs and outcomes of the organization; and to intensify the patterns of communication with all kinds of stakeholders (Bekkers 1993).

So, many ICT developments are at the core of modern transformations of public administration. ICT developments in public administration lead to different kinds of *boundary and jurisdiction spanning networks*. An e-Government strategy, to become effective, has to take those transformations into consideration. It is a major challenge for public management to keep these transformations in balance: technically, organizationally and institutionally. The last sections of this chapter will go into these problems.

When we look at the deployment of ICTs in public administration, we see that originally ICT applications predominantly played a role in the *enhancement of the internal effectiveness, efficiency, and economy* of the executive functions of public administration especially in the sphere of policy implementation. Only later on the improvement of the *quality of public services* to the citizens, as customers, clients, citizens, and subjects; to businesses and social organizations; and to other branches of the public service itself came into focus (Dutton 1999). Many governments plan to do an increasingly large amount of their business within a few years via the Internet (see, e.g., *Die Bundesregierung* 2002; Margetts 2004).

More modest, however, are the applications of websites and homepages which aim to support the involvement of citizens in *democratic policy making*. These include tools such as instant polling, interactive policy making, co-production of policies, and so forth. The importance of ICTs for democratic purposes is still hardly realized (Nieuwenhuizen and Snellen 2001; Zouridis and Thaens 2003; Chadwick and May 2003).

These contentions, and their implications, as a challenge for management, will be elaborated below. The perspective of this chapter is managerial: the art or science of directing, conducting, and administering the work of others to achieve defined objectives (Johannson and Robertson 1968); the allocation of human and material resources; the determination of structures and processes; and the boundary spanning of the relations with the environment. Academic discussions, whether the penetration of ICTs in all nerves and veins of public administration has to be characterized as modernist, hyper-modernist, or postmodernist (Margetts 2003), are left aside. Ratings, which seek to show which countries are more advanced than others, and which countries are lagging behind (Accenture 2002; Margetts 2004), are interesting, but not relevant for this chapter. Stories about ICT projects that failed abound (Pollitt 2003; Heeks 2003[2]). In this chapter, failed projects are considered important warning signals for management. Apart from that, they may be seen as "normal accidents" (Perrow 1984) during a learning process.

In the following sections, first the shifts in management attention during the early phases of ICT use within public administration will be presented. Second, some theoretical approaches to informatization will be discussed. Third, the dominant focus of public managers on effectiveness, efficiency, and economy as the main purpose of the use of ICTs in the implementation of policies will be highlighted. Fourth, the growing emphasis on service delivery with ICTs will be commented upon. Fifth, the democratic possibilities of ICT applications will be discussed. Finally, the main strategic challenges of e-Government for public management, in terms of the technical, organizational and institutional barriers that will have to be surmounted, will be demonstrated.

The structure of this chapter will do justice to the historical dominance of financial considerations during the development of ICTs in public administration. "The dominant analytical perspectives in the information systems field have traditionally been tied to the supply-push world of technical development, coupled with a rational-economic interpretation of managerial behavior" (Kraemer and King 1994). Improvement of the service orientation and the democratic orientation by e-Government emerged only recently (Nieuwenhuizen and Snellen 2001; Zouridis and Thaens 2003; Chadwick and May 2003). The barriers that are to be surmounted, discussed in the final part of the chapter, may make clear, why so many ICT projects failed.

17.2 PRELIMINARY STAGES OF e-GOVERNMENT

In the pioneering phase after the Second World War, computers started to be used in public administration, national scientific research institutes, and large international businesses (Maes 1990; Brinckmann and Kuhlmann 1990; Snellen 1998). In this phase they were mainly used for bulk applications in the financial sphere, such as calculation of salaries, and for complex research calculations. The computers in use at that time at the central level of government were expensive, failure prone, and required a large amount of space. Expectations were that even the larger countries would have use for only a few computers. In the early 1950s IBM estimated that only a few dozens of computers were needed in the whole world. In this pioneering phase, the main concern of management was the *technical control* of the technology and the costs of its application. In public administration computers were mainly used for what we would now call "back-office" registration of transactions (Bellamy and Taylor 1998). Transactions were registered in separate databases. Many mistakes were made during manual data-entry. However, when the data was stored, it was easy to retrieve and to process in routine operations. "Calculation Centres" were created for central government and cooperating regional and local governments.

In the following phase, starting around 1960, the managerial policy focus shifted to large computers, the so-called "main frames," the technical problems they brought with them, and the *cost of their applications*. Later on, this expanded to mini-computers. Electronic engineers and administrative accountants dominated the scene. The next decade can be characterized as a period in which the number and scope of computer applications increased rapidly. Computer programmers and system developers played a major role. Computer terminals were spreading all over public administration. The attention of management was mainly focused on the costs of computer hardware and software, and on the *scarcity of programmers*. The salaries of the programmers had to be adjusted to accommodate market circumstances. During the 1980s, the price of computers decreased dramatically, and the first generations of micro (or personal) computers were introduced. The mere "automation" of routine activities was gradually replaced by "informatization," as described in the introduction to this chapter: a combination of information management, (re)organization management, and policy making. Standard software entered the market. "Islands" of computerization were created, based on claims of autonomy. This "individualism" made cooperation and streamlining of activities for the benefit of effectiveness, efficiency, and economy of integrated services almost impossible. Even within departments, computer applications were often incompatible. As a consequence of this, the management focus shifted toward an *integrated approach* of the existing computerization. This integration was reinforced by the growing interdependencies and chain relationships between different sector policies, (e.g., in social security) and between sequential policy interactions (e.g., in the sphere of criminal justice).

This situation became even more pressing during the 1990s, in which *networks and network applications* became ever more prominent. Secured, dedicated Intranets were created within departments, and separated sectors of public administration. The creation of Extranets, which are (partly) accessible for authorized outsiders, led to a blurring of boundaries and to an interpenetration of public and (semi)private organizations with a shared public task. During this period, websites and homepages began to be used for information, communication, and transactions with the general public. The introduction of e-mail made public administration accessible in new informal ways. One of the last network developments is the introduction of so-called "web services,"[3] through which electronic cooperation between different organizations, different computer applications, and different technical systems is facilitated.

The challenges of technical, organizational, and institutional network developments for management were, and still are, formidable. Databases began to be coupled, responsibilities diffused. Boundaries between organizations became blurred and redefined, organizational jurisdictions were changed. New demarcations in the division of powers, with regard to the principles of "checks and balances," had to be found and established (Bekkers 1998). Examples of this will be discussed in the final parts of this chapter.

17.3 Some Theories on Informatization

Public administrative theorizing about informatization concentrates mainly on three themes:

1. pro or contra technological determinism;
2. organizational implications of the use of ICTs;
3. policy implications of ICTs.

As far as the discussion about *technological determinism* is concerned, three positions can be distinguished: deterministic; voluntaristic; and mixed deterministic–voluntaristic. According to the deterministic position the properties of ICTs are the result of autonomous technological developments. These developments are characterized by an inner logic that articulates what one can aspire, ought to aspire, and will aspire (Ozbekhan 1968; Winner 1977). According to the voluntaristic position "little causal power can be attributed to computers themselves" (Kling 1982). The way in which informatization is given shape may serve predominantly the power position of the person(s) who decide about its deployment (Danziger et al. 1982). According to the mixed deterministic–voluntaristic position the consequences of informatization are the outcome of more or less contingent interactions between actors and their intentions on one side and technological and social circumstances on the other side (Frissen 1996).

As far as the *organizational possibilities and implications* of ICTs are concerned the managerial viewpoints of Hammer and Champy (1993), Davenport (1993), Malone et al. (2003), and Hirst and Norton (1998) stand out. In a "manifesto for business revolution" Hammer and Champy advocated a complete "reengineering" of business organizations, with the help of the new information and communication technologies. The promise of this reengineering is expected to be the simultaneous delivery of huge cost-savings and a huge improvement of the quality of the provided services.

Malone et al. attempt to "invent" the organizations of the twenty-first century. They speculate about a scenario of radical decentralization in an "e-lance economy" (e-lance meaning: "electronically connected freelancers"). These organizational developments in the private enterprise sector are imitated by public administration (Homburg 1999).

The structure of *central government* is being affected as well (Fountain 2001). An analysis of the Parliamentary Office of Science and Technology in the UK (Hirst and Norton 1998) gives some interesting indications about structural changes at the central level of government, which can also be recognized in other countries. According to this analysis, when e-Government is fully installed, not only the executive branches of public administration but also the political and administrative top-structure of cabinet and departments will be reshaped.

As far as the *policy implications* of ICTs are concerned, the main implications are related to the workflow level and its operational management (Lenk 1998). Functions of ICTs in the workflow are: technical coordination and synchronization of processes, storage and retrieval of information used in these processes, automated support of case handling, and generation of secondary (e.g., managerial) or aggregate (e.g., statistical) information (Lenk 1998; Zuboff 1988).

17.4 THREE ROLES OF ICTS IN e-GOVERNMENT

....

17.4.1 Supporting Economy of Implementation

As indicated above, public administration benefits predominantly from ICTs in the executive functions of administration and rule application: the domain of the street-level bureaucrats. Initially, routine calculations of salaries, alimonies, subsidies, and other complicated financial entitlements were executed by computers. Later on advisory information systems and expert (support) systems were added to the toolbox of street-level bureaucrats. Whilst advisory information systems cover only a limited part of the decision space (mostly of complicated calculations), expert (support) systems advise experts on a whole decision trajectory and also dispose of an explanation facility. The next logical step in the development of decision support systems was the building of case-processing systems. Case-processing systems take over the whole discretionary space of street-level bureaucrats. When data entry also takes place electronically, inputted by citizens or businesses, or by automatic document imaging and document retrieval, the street-level bureaucrat is completely "decentered" (Snellen 1998; Johnson 2001). However, without fully automated case-processing systems modern welfare states would not be able to provide the masses of citizens with the support and allowances to which they are entitled. Automatic administrative decision taking is growing steadily within public administration (e.g., in the penal sphere automatic ticketing systems exist, that are based on camera detection of speeding. These systems then look up the addresses of offenders in a population register, and collect the fines by automatic pre-printed giro credit slips) (Zouridis 2000).

Apart from the increase in efficiency (a direct result of the replacement of street level bureaucrats by electronic information devices), management is further enabled to more strictly control administrative activities of the workforce through the use of ICT applications. These applications include: workflow management systems; front end verification tools; and the prescription of text building blocks.

Workflow management systems coordinate, synchronize, and guard the process requirements of administrative tasks. They support the coordinated distribution of information, the documentation, and the division of labour. In workflow management an "engine" drives activities along prescribed administrative channels. It guards the correct input of data (as the case may be retrieved through data repositories outside the organization), ensures that the right sequence of activities are followed, safeguards the deadlines that have to be respected, and constructs the "critical path" of the cooperation between departments. In this way, operational management is relieved from many of its burdens, its span of control may be expanded and, in sum total, economies are achieved.

Front end verification tools enable the street-level bureaucrat to check the information given by clients and thus fight fraud. This verification is facilitated by network connections between different kinds of registers and databases, located in various authorities, both inside and outside the sector to which the office of the contact official belongs. Examples of this are to be found in several countries such as Australia, Belgium, the Netherlands, and the UK.

Text building blocks. The justification of the administrative decisions by the street-level bureaucrat is made easier (and controlled) through the introduction of so-called "text building blocks." Text building blocks are pre-fabricated motivations to justify administrative decisions before citizens. They are also used by the judiciary in complaint or appeal procedures. By pre-fabricating the motivations, and by obliging street-level bureaucrats to use only these "template" communications, management and the "technostructure" (Mintzberg 1983) of public administration dominate the decision space of the officials involved in these organizations. In this way, text building blocks are a powerful tool of management to speed the work processes and to standardize decision making by the street-level bureaucrats. Moreover, this kind of "knowledge management" reduces the need to employ highly professional personnel. Savings are attained by downgrading the function of the officials, without affecting the professional content of their decisions.

Combinations of workflow management systems, information infrastructure networks, and text building blocks, may be more developed in some parts of public administration (such as procurement) than in others. The development of these systems is dependent upon the volume of activities concerned and the potential to algorithmize them. They represent, however, a dominant trend in e-Government at the operational level of public administration.

17.4.2 Supporting Public Service Provision

As indicated above, financial and economic considerations were paramount in the early development stages of e-Government. However, the private sector (e.g., banks and insurance companies) set an example by also applying ICTs to integrate and improve their service delivery. Through these "e-Business" examples, the expectations of people with respect to the service level of public administration also rose. They played a major role in the design of service delivery of e-Government. When the private sector can deliver services 24 hours, 7 days a week, 365 days of a year, why should the public sector lag behind? The introduction of Internet and portals (websites, containing links to commonly used services) particularly boosted electronic service delivery by public administrations (Margetts 2003).

Although, in practice, service delivery and Internet applications are most of the time associated, that as far as service provision is concerned, e-Government is more than websites and portals alone. Service aspects are also involved in the improvement of effectiveness, efficiency and economy of e-Government, such as more speed and transparency, fewer mistakes and more equality. In this section the focus will be on Internet applications for service delivery.

In the first instance, the web sites of public authorities were mainly used to give *information to citizens*. The initiative was often taken by officials who made Internet applications their hobby. The kind of information given was generally a replication of the paper brochures, which citizens and businesses could find also in public kiosks. Apart from the ease with which the information could be attained, the added value of the use of Internet was small. Many government bodies are still in this development stage (Pardo 2000). It is often underestimated how labor-intensive keeping the website up to date actually is. If the official policy is that "on-line may not be privileged above off-line," extra effort has to be given to improve off-line (e.g., mass media) information provision. Gradually, public authorities gain web experience, and become experienced in the organizational arrangements that are required for the public function of the websites. However, many political and administrative bodies are still more focused on providing a mere presence on the Internet, rather than on the value of the content of the information they provide. Furthermore, this content is generally based on an "inside-out" approach to the needs of citizens, as opposed to an awareness of the needs and interests felt by the citizens themselves (DeConti 1998). Also, superficial information may be offered that is actually better provided by commercial parties. Other actors can often more reliably care for the continuity, actuality, and integrity of such information.

A further development is the use of websites to give citizens an opportunity to *ventilate their opinions* on activities, plans, or proposals of public authorities, and also on their life situation. The higher the degree of penetration of Internet access amongst the population, the more efficient kinds of "instant polling" are. However, a danger of this is that it may deepen the "digital" divide (the gap between those who can effectively use new information and communication tools, such as the Internet, and those who cannot: Norris 2001), because the voice of the "digital illiterates" will become unheard. Another caveat is that the consistency of policies may be totally lost, when people are asked to express their preference for *A* (more collective provisions) on one day, and for *B* (the opposite of *A*—tax reduction) the following day.

Only a minority of public authorities make *transactions* via Internet possible. In this respect, e-Government lags behind e-Business. This is understandable because, in many transactions with public authorities, sensitive personal data is involved.

The authentication of the identity of the citizens via the net requires an expensive authentication infrastructure, a so-called "Public Key Infrastructure." Nevertheless, in many countries (e.g., UK, Germany, France, Finland, Singapore) plans are made to handle a large part of the transactions between citizens, businesses, and government in the coming years via the Internet. (In some countries the declaration of personal income, and the settlement of income tax, already takes place automatically.)

One of the fundamental issues at stake where transactions via websites are concerned, is the legal equality of digital "haves" and "have-nots." The "haves" are served quickly and expediently, while the "have-nots" are subjected to traditional bureaucratic procedures. Another danger is that, due to a pronounced bureaucratic rationality, the burden of administrative pre-selection is passed on to the clients of the administration (Snellen 2001b). Moreover, while the procedures at the website front-office may be speeded up, the back-offices, with their administrative routines, may remain as slow as ever.

To improve service quality, websites are increasingly organized along the lines of "*demand patterning*." Interdependent questions and the needs of clients are grouped together and answered coherently. In this way the functional division of labor in the administration is not taken as point of departure of the service delivery. Rather it is formed around the life-world situation of the citizen or client. The "products" of the administration are grouped together on the basis of "life events" or "life episodes," such as moving house, a death, or renovating a house. These life events entail a whole range of connected questions and require different contacts with the administration with regard to compulsory notifications and permits.

To meet the needs and wishes of citizens and clients even further, administrations may use portals on which private suppliers and services are also mentioned. Such an *extended demand patterning* requires much inter-organizational networking and fine-tuning. The effort necessary to keep such websites and portals updated is often underestimated. It is even questionable whether it is a task of government to create portals in cooperation with private parties. Involvement of government may entail an obligation to guarantee a level playing field for competing private parties. Does it mean that the list of flower shops at the portal related to death has to be exhaustive, and that the government accepts any responsibility for the quality and reliability of the private parties on the website?

An even more elaborate form of service delivery via websites is the so-called "one-stop-shop" or *singular window* approach. Through the creation of a virtual single counter on the web, citizens are thus able to handle all their business with the government via one screen. Ideas about one-stop-shops were already brought forward some decades ago (Lenk and Traunmuller 2000). Initiatives in that direction were boosted by the development of Internet technologies, especially during the last decade. Prevention of the time-honored bureaucratic vice of citizens being sent "from the pillar to the post," and—let us not forget—the interests of suppliers of ICTs dominated the scene. The approach here is very ambitious. In principle, via one access point (a virtual front-office) a whole variety of back-offices are put into operation. In addition to this, the variety of back-offices has to be formed into integrated and carefully tuned service delivery to citizens and businesses.

Less ambitious one-stop-shop projects are limited to the business of citizens and enterprises with the administration within only one sector, e.g., social security.

The organizational and institutional problems created by the introduction of one-stop-shops were grossly underestimated (Adler and Sainsbury 1993). The technical interconnection of computer hardware, and the interoperability of software between the single front-offices and the many disparate back-offices, with divergent information systems and communication protocols, appeared to be more difficult and costly than expected. Furthermore, rivalries between different back-offices, their fear of loosing their autonomy and control on "their" information, as well as an inevitable lack of balance between the benefits and costs of alignment with other back-offices are some of the forces against the necessary systems' integration.

Meanwhile, the single window approach with one front-office via the Internet is being replaced by projects, which connect a whole *set of front-offices and public access points*. These include the traditional office, the website, a kiosk, the telephone, and mobile phones. To streamline the connections between such a variety of front-offices and back-offices, so-called "*mid-offices*" are created, acting as e-brokers or gateways. The mid-office routes requests for information, and transactions, from the virtual front-offices to the back-offices. The mid-office may be structured in such a way that it not only routes information between front-offices and back-offices, but may also add information, as it keeps in its own records and registers. An example of the mid-office approach is the Irish Reach Broker project, sketched in Figure 17.1.

It is clear that a one-stop-shop is not simply an add-on facility. It requires an "Integrated (Service) Access Management" that not only deals with one-stop access, but also with several other functions in the interaction process which accompanies any service delivery, such as:

- citizen pre-information at various stages and to various depths
- help in filling in forms, etc., if necessary
- "translating" the demand for a service (a license, etc.) from the citizen's life-world to the required legal–administrative jargon
- matching the demand with the jurisdictional structure (competencies in the legal sense), routing the citizen demand to the relevant back-office (which may also be a completely automated process)
- keeping track of the process, handling "Freedom of Information" requests and other "due process" requirements (Lenk and Traunmuller 2000)

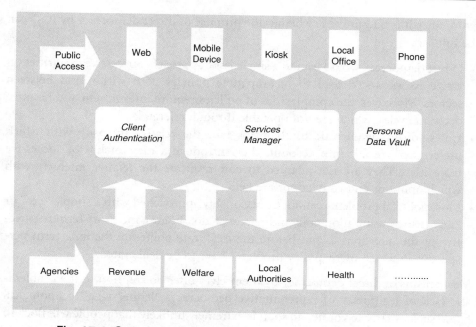

Fig. 17.1 Overview of the Reach Broker as originally conceived

Source: Bannister and Walsh (2002)

Some of the technical–organizational problems, related to this, will be discussed later on in this chapter.

17.4.3 Supporting Democracy

As indicated above, the emphasis of e-Government is more on financial and economic aspects of public administration, and on service delivery for citizens and enterprises, than on the democratic possibilities of ICTs (Clift 2000; Hoff, Logren, and Torpe 2003).

As far as these potentialities are concerned, much is expected from forms of direct democracy, especially referenda, made possible by ICTs. Expectations are that direct democracy might replace representative democracy. For many, representative democracy is, as it was once called by an American thinker on democracy, "a sorry substitute for the real thing" (Dahl 1989).

Representative democracy is deemed antiquated, an arrangement of the past, necessitated by the impossibility to realize direct democracy by giving all citizens an equal opportunity to participate in the collective decision making processes. ICTs, however, promise direct democracy in the form of continuous opinion polling, instant referenda, tele-conferencing, digital cities, and discussion groups. It is expected that the erosion of the legitimacy of representative democracy will stop, since it is questionable whether the promise of direct democracy by ICTs can be fulfilled.

- Direct democracy would lead to a single issue approach. Successive majorities on single issues would lead to incompatible policies both within and between sectors. Moreover, the complexities of policies require intermittent and iterative decision cycles, which are not operable through referenda.
- Unless direct democratic mechanisms take the relative intensity with which preferences are felt into account, they introduce a dictatorship of successive majorities. They are not adapted to communicate the relative intensity with which opinions and convictions are held.
- Most political problems cannot be reasonably approached with a simple "yes" or "no" answer, as opinion polls and referenda do. Besides, the short-term perspective of the questions as put before the electorate obliterate the long-term perspective in which many policy problems have to be deliberated.

Mechanisms of direct democracy by themselves offer no solution to the problematic lack of legitimacy of representative democracy. Neither will "technological fixes," such as remote voting, do so. It is extremely unlikely that people will flock to the polling booth, just because they are offered the opportunity to cast their vote close to the shopping mall, their office, or wherever they happen to be. In this respect, even less can be expected of the electronic voting machine, although it is a device which can prevent unpleasant, and hardly democratic, surprises such as the vote-counting fiasco in Florida during the presidential elections of 2000. ICTs may even be dysfunctional, in so far as they de-emphasize arrangements for deliberation as the core of a democratic polity.

More promising, from a democratic point of view, are arrangements for interactive policy making and co-production of policies. Interactive policy making can be defined as involving citizens, social organizations, enterprises, and (other) public authorities, in the early policy making stage, in order to form a dialogue and solution of commonly articulated problems. More and more governments start to publish draft legislative and policy proposals in an early stage, so as to involve interested parties (Clift 2000). As such, interactive policy making is a reaction of governments to the network dependencies within which they have to develop their policies. The contributions of participants to interactive policy making may relate to agenda-setting, defining priorities, informing political bodies about any kind of preference, and also indicating the desired implementation of policies (Mattila 2003). The Internet-related ICT facilities which are used in this respect are e-mail, usenets and newsgroups, Internet relay chat, and the World Wide Web. These facilities may also be used to organize resistance against policy proposals, and to build up countervailing power against authorities.

In more and more countries, policy proposals are published at an early stage on the Internet, to enable people to air their opinions about them. A positive effect of this is the growing transparency of policy deliberations. By analyzing relevant websites, interested citizens and organizations can easily get an overview of the positions which the different stakeholders take with respect to the policy proposals. The organization of communities and interest groups on the net is also facilitated. One of the drawbacks, however, of the use of ICT facilities in the modes of interactive policy making is that political representatives are marginalized (Raab and Bellamy 2000). In the (interactive) preparation of policies, public servants make use of a whole plethora of information and communication technologies. As a result, their level of knowledge about the needs and wishes of the electorate is higher than that of the politicians. Whilst non-elected officials are actively engaged in negotiations with interested parties, the politicians—elected officials who have the last say—abstain from negotiations. Meanwhile, their room for maneuver is narrowed by the agreements which non-elected officials have reached with the population. In complex issues, the margin to influence the result is becoming extremely small (Snellen 2002).

From a democratic point of view, co-production of policies is more promising than interactive policy making. Co-production of policies is, also, a reaction to existing network relationships, in which governments have had to operate in the last few decades. This co-production may be seen as the common preparation (together with the directly concerned parties) of the operational implementation or the "filling-in" of a chosen policy framework. When the authority has decided to create a provision, an infrastructure or a physical amenity, then the local population, which is affected most by the decision, may be invited to participate in the exact design. The opportunity to participate in such a way may ease the community's acceptance of the political decision, and further the necessary cooperation of the local population. ICTs can be helpful at this stage too, using the same devices (e.g., tele-conferencing) that are used for interactive policy making. They can enable the population to visualize what the outcomes of their choice processes would look like. At the local level of public administration, co-production of policies is becoming more and more a normal practice, letting people decide on the design of street furniture or upon the lay-out and destination of neighborhood facilities. Interactive websites, computer simulations, and virtual designs are very useful for these sorts of purposes.

Combinations of interactive policy making and co-production of policies are also practiced in situations where municipalities make so-called "neighborhood budgets" available to the different neighborhoods. The inhabitants may then use this money to purchase provisions according to their own liking (Mattila 2003).

These kinds of participative policy making are a challenge for public management in a democracy. As indicated above, marginalization of politicians may endanger the democratic quality of the policy outcomes. Bishop (2000) notes with respect to this: "While the current public sector management environment tends to emphasize the relationship between the bureaucracy, agencies and the community, they have underplayed the political connections between the delivery of public goods and representatives." As far as Denmark is concerned, Hoff (2000) remarks: "consumer democracy aims not so much to challenge as to bypass the tired institutions of representative democracy. It seeks, in effect, to re-centre democracy from the political nexus, a nexus formed around parliamentary and electoral processes, onto the consumer nexus, a nexus formed largely around the consumption of public services." There is a danger that ICT applications will follow those tendencies slavishly.

That does not, however, alter the fact that political parties and parliamentarians increasingly make use of ICT applications on the Internet. The dominant trend in political parties is, still, to use the Internet to spread the ideological message to the local party organizations, and to keep the ranks closed. This "top–down" approach is more and more countered by "down–up" reactions (Smith 1998). Parliamentarians, especially the younger generations, are quickly making up these arrears. They appear to have, however, an ambivalent attitude toward the information available to them via ICT applications. They continuously move in a field of tension in which information and knowledge at this moment are a means of power, and at the next moment, are inconvenient possessions for which they can be blamed. In addition to this, when in opposition they want parliament to know more; when in the reigning coalition or majority party, they want the individual members to know more (Nieuwenhuizen and Snellen 2001). So, in the practical absence of politicians and elected public officials, non-public officials effectively have a free playing field (Snellen 2002).

17.5 e-Government: Barriers and Challenges

As a contribution to a Handbook for Public Management, the final part of this chapter will focus on some of the key barriers management will be confronted with, while shaping, through e-Government, an effective, efficient and economic, service-oriented, and democratic public administration. These barriers are mainly *technical*, *organizational*, and *institutional* and have to do with the growing interdependencies of network organizations in e-Government. The former sections may have made it clear that the establishment of e-Government involves more than just introducing ICT applications into public administration.

17.5.1 Technical Barriers

Everybody who has experience with the introduction of sizable ICT innovations into public administration knows that it progresses with great difficulty and runs high risks. To fully realize e-Government through technical and (inter)organizational networks, as described in this chapter, measures have to be implemented at three levels: (1) intra-organizational and intra-sectoral with respect to sharing of information; (2) intra-sectoral with respect to service delivery and client registration; (3) inter-sectoral with respect to overall information architectures.

17.5.1.1 *Intra-Organizational and Intra-Sectoral*

The *first* level is about electronic sharing of data related to clients and societal situations. Negotiations concerning the following aspects are then at stake:

1. The definition of the shared data (which are often further defined in local regulations).
2. The definition of messages required for the execution of tasks (operational work processes, about which administrative departments wish to maintain a certain autonomy).
3. The technical standards and protocols (to which administrations are accustomed and wish to stick).
4. The quality of data in terms of actuality (which may differ quite substantially between the parties).
5. Safeguarding the security of shared data by technical and organizational measures and authorizations (the importance of security for the continuity of business, or for privacy, may differ between parties).
6. The establishment of a control authority on the observance of the set of agreements with respect to data and messages.
7. The bearing of costs of the common facilities (often the unbalance of benefits and costs for some of the parties leads to protracted discussions and much delay).
8. Object identification and numbering (of major importance for statistical research and prevention of fraud).

Commitment to the same objectives, a common sense of direction, for a longer period of time, is often lacking in e-Government initiatives. Too many different functionaries, each with their own specialty and "trained incapacity," are participating in larger e-Government projects. Without a strong management, too many partial decisions are taken, which are at cross purposes with the common design. The staffing is often discontinuous, the dependency on outside specialists intensive, and the documentation of the projects failing.

17.5.1.2 *Intra-Sectoral with Respect to Service Delivery and Client Registration*

The *second* level concerns the transformation of service delivery and the registration of clients and citizens. If a functional bureaucratic orientation has to be replaced by a client orientation, different agreements have to be reached.

1. Public services, which move in the direction of becoming parts of one-stop-shops, will have to agree on the portal-functions they will develop in common. Where will the common boundaries of the network of connections with other organizations be drawn?
2. The management of the content of the website has to be organized with regard to information about rights and obligations, procedures, contacts with sister organizations and independent experts, "what-if" questions, and calculations of the entitlements with respect to provisions.
3. Content management systems have to be developed, e.g., with respect to standardization and possible changes by one of the partners in the network.
4. the required levels of identification and authentication for the different transactions via the net have to be determined. Questions about electronic signature, encryption, and Public Key Infrastructure present themselves.
5. Differences between the participants at a one-stop-shop arrangement, with regard to freedom of information, active disclosure of policy initiatives, and existing databases have to be balanced.

17.5.1.3 *Inter-Sectoral with Respect to Overall Information Architectures*

The *third* level concerns the exchange of information between different sectors of public administration. If different sectors "feed" databases which are managed and used by other sectors, a need arises for an overarching information architecture for the whole public administration, as well as separate architectures for each of the sectors. In this overarching architecture a number of factors have to be established: where registrations will be kept, what kind of infrastructure will be built and maintained for the routing of the data, and how this infrastructure will be positioned. Every time regulations in one of the relevant sectors are changed, the effect on the architecture will have to be checked. On the basis of the architecture, the most practical solutions as to introduction, costs and administrative burdens can be chosen.

17.5.2 Organizational Barriers

In former sections, many forms of reorganization prompted by the introduction of ICTs are discussed. Jane Fountain (2001: 27) emphasizes the role of standardization in bringing about organizational changes.

First, standardization renders redundancies across agencies transparent. Second, standardization weakens the rationale for having different agencies collect and store highly similar or identical data elements. Third, data standardization suggests new forms of analysis that may lead to a change in the structure and organization of agencies. Fourth, structural changes in the federal bureaucracy are inevitable as redundant data collection, storage, and analysis by different agencies is eliminated.

So, a "virtual state" is being built "consisting of virtual agencies overlaid on a formal bureaucratic structure" (2002: 99).

The barriers which are involved in those reorganizations will be treated only shortly. Many of them are of a general nature and well known from the literature on organizations (Homburg 1999). Loss of autonomy, a feeling of "ownership" with respect to data, information and knowledge within repositories of the own organization, a one-sided view on societal problems specific for the "trained incapacity" of experts, and general inertia, are some of the barriers to e-Government encountered.

In the following example, extracted from a German study (Reinermann and von Lucke 2002), some of the more specifically ICT-oriented organizational barriers can be distinguished.

The size and complexity of the existing governmental structures limit their adaptability to new situations, such as emerging e-Government. Cooperative behaviour is hindered by the separation of powers, the tier structure of public administration and the right of self-determination at the different levels of government. The necessity to come to an agreement leads to compromises at the level of the lowest common denominator. The flexibility which is required by e-Government is opposed to the immobility of existing public authorities. The legal necessity to maintain off-line facilities makes on-line e-Government facilities extra-expensive. Many organizational changes, inspired by e-Government, relate to horizontal cross-boundary processes, while public administrations, in general, are mainly interested in vertical-jointed jurisdictions. And finally, e-Government measures are too much directed at cost savings in the existing departments, instead of at interconnected chains of activities.

17.5.3 Institutional Barriers

Persistent institutional barriers with respect to e-Government have mental, legal and cultural backgrounds. From a mental point of view, public servants, especially those at street level, are incited to resist the downgrading of their jobs through information infrastructures, and through a knowledge management approach, which does not leave them any form of discretion. In former sections of this chapter, the influence of the convergence of workflow management, a prescribed use of outside databases, and text building blocks on the job quality of officials at the operational level of public administration, was indicated. A source of legal resistance comes from the fact that ICTs lead to blurring of boundaries between organizations. The moment information is shared between parts of public administration, responsibilities for the authenticity, accuracy, and integrity of the information also become blurred. What is even "worse," the boundaries of the jurisdictions of public organizations as the constituent parts of public administration also become blurred. Jurisdictions can be defined as "the exclusive authority of an actor as a unified entity to determine rights and obligations of citizens in a task domain with (a certain degree of) discretion for which this actor is legally and politically accountable" (Bekkers 1998). In some countries information may not be shared between ministerial departments that belong to different sectors of society (Reinermann and von Lucke 2002). For reasons of privacy, such boundaries for the sharing of information are also advocated by ethicists (Van den Hoven 1998). As far as information sharing is concerned, e-Government might thus have a negative effect on the perception of reliability of public administration. Other elements of e-Government may also have the same kind of effect. Uncertainty may still exist about the validity of administrative acts via the Internet, of electronic signatories, or of electronic transactions. Apart from that, many laws have to be adjusted to the introduction of e-Government.

Cultural resistance to e-Government may come from lack of confidence in the new technologies. The traditional carefulness, seen as a bureaucratic virtue, may turn to risk-avoidance, and a lack of innovation.

17.6 STRATEGIC MANAGEMENT OPTIONS FOR E-GOVERNMENT

It would be an easy, superficial, and probably very costly strategic option to follow indiscriminately the ambitions and aspirations of the ICT branch of industry. This would not necessarily imply that the values, norms and interests of democracy, public administration, and civil society are met. A more considerate managerial strategy would be to take the real interests of the citizenry as the point of departure for electronic service delivery and democratic facilities. Many high-flying ICT applications (in the sphere of one-stop-shops and e-voting) would not pass the test of straightforward citizen orientation (Pardo 2000). Creating technologically highly advanced services and democratic facilities is not a goal in itself, but has to be related to the legitimacy of governmental institutions. The following strategic options for e-Government deserve to be discussed.

- In the field of service delivery, the strategic options to be considered are: a shift from a supply oriented to a demand-oriented public service delivery; from a ready-to-wear to a tailor made service; and from a fragmented to an integrated service offer. An "outside-in" approach would also imply a shift from a functional bureaucratic to a holistic design of service delivery, from a one-service counter to a "multichanneling" entry to the service, and from a reactive to a proactive orientation. Recognition of modern citizenship would result in a shift from "passive" citizen participation to "active" citizen participation in service delivery (Van Duivenboden and Lips 2001).
- In the field of democratic potentialities a strategic option is to let ICTs enhance the possibilities of citizens to freely access statistical and administrative data deposited with the government and public administration. Geographic Information Systems (GIS) could play a major role in giving insight into the geographical spread of societal problems, and the activities of governments in that respect. Performance indicators, and benchmarking, are interesting strategic options, not only to improve the top–down oversight of levels of government and parliaments, but also to make it possible for citizens and their interest organizations to execute horizontal oversight over organizations of the civil society, such as schools, hospitals, housing corporations, and the like (Barrados et al. 2000).

Interactive policy making and co-production of policies are modalities of policy agenda formation and policy implementation, which are increasingly important. It is becoming impossible to imagine democratic practice today without some ICT applications. In the field of modernization of the overall structure of government and public administration e-Government can be used as a driving force. Knowledge management, which is facilitated by ICTs, may enhance the effectiveness of policy making and policy execution in policy-chains, such as the judicial chain from police arrest to prison, or the food chain from farm to family home. In more and more fields of governmental activity, integral and institutional boundaries crossing policies are developed, such as safety policy, youth policy, and the like. New structures will have to be designed to make cooperation across those institutional boundaries possible. Many of the barriers and obstacles, indicated above, will occur for this strategic transformation of public administration. It remains to be seen whether and in what time span managers in public administration will succeed in overcoming the barriers and obstacles on the road to the information polity.

Notes

1. As far as public administration is concerned, the elements of informatization are (Snellen and van de Donk 1998): the introduction of various applications of ICT in order to (re)shape important parts of information processing and communication

facilities; the introduction of specialized expertise (officers, departments and organizations with explicit tasks and responsibilities) in the area of information processing; the (re)establishment of internal and external information flows and information relations; the development of information policies within and between organizations; the redesign of internal and external organization structures and work-processes that are related to the introduction of ICTs (Lenk 1997).

2. According to Heeks (2003) 35 percent of e-Government projects in developing/transitional countries are total failures, 50 percent are partial failures, and 15 percent are successes.

3. Programmatic interfaces for application to application communication.

REFERENCES

ACCENTURE (2002), e-Government Report. May 2002.

ADLER, M., and SAINSBURY, R. (1993), "The 'One Stop Shop': Haven't We Been Here Before?", *Benefits* 6: 35–37.

BANNISTER, F., and WALSH, N. (2002), "The Virtual Public Servant: An Overview of Ireland's e-Government Initiatives and its Public Services Broker." Paper EGPA, September, Vaasa: Finland.

BARRADOS M. et al. (2000), "Involving Others in Governing: Safeguarding the Public Interest." Paper IIAS Conference Bologna, 19–22 June.

BEKKERS, V. J. J. M. (1993), *Nieuwe vormen van sturing en informatisering* (New forms of steering and informatization). Delft: Eburon.

—— (1998), "Wiring Public Organisations and Changing Organizational Jurisdictions," in Snellen and Van de Donk 1998: 57–77.

BELLAMY, C., and TAYLOR, J. A. (1998), *Governing in the Information Age*, Buckingham: Open University Press.

BISHOP, P. (2000), "Representative Democracy, Participation and Globalisation." Paper IIAS Conference Bologna, 19–22 June.

BRINCKMANN, H., and KUHLMANN, S. (1990), *Computerburokratie. Ergebnisse von 30 Jahren Offenllicher Verwaltung mit Informationstechnik*, Opladen: Westdeutscher Verlag.

CHADWICK, A., and MAY, C. (2003), "Interaction between States and Citizens in the Age of the Internet: 'e-Government' in the United States, Britain, and the European Union" *Governance: International Journal of Policy, Administration and Institutions*, 16(2), 271–300.

CLIFT, S. (2000), *The E-Democracy E-Book: Democracy is Online*, http://www.publicus.net

DAHL, R. A. (1989), *Democracy and its Critics*, Princeton: Yale University Press.

DANZIGER, J. N., DUTTON, W. H., KLING, R., and KRAEMER, K. L. (1982), *Computers and Politics: High Technology in American Local Governments*. New York: Columbia University Press.

DAVENPORT, T. H. (1993), *Process Innovation: Reengineering Work through Information Technology*, Boston: Harvard Business Press.

DECONTI, L. (1998), "Planning and Creating a Web Site: Learning from the Experience of US States." Working Paper Institute for Development Policy and Management, The University of Manchester.

Die Bundesregierung (2002), "Modern State–Modern Administration: Progress Report." Berlin.

DUTTON, W. H. (1999), *Society on the Line: Information Politics in the Digital Age*, Oxford: Oxford University Press.

FERLANDO, G., and QUIRCHMAYR, G. (eds.), "Advances in Electronic Government." Pre-Proceedings of the Working Conference of the International Federation of Information Processing WG 8.5 Zaragoza, 10–11 February.

FOUNTAIN, J. E. (2001), *Building the Virtual State: Information Technology and Institutional Change*, Washington, DC: Brookings Institution.

FRISSEN, P. H. A. (1996), *De Virtuele Staat. Politiek, bestuur, technologie: een postmodern verhaal*, Schoonhoven: Academic Service.

HAMMER, M., and CHAMPY, J. (1993). *Reengineering the Corporation: A Manifesto for Business Revolution*, New York: HarperCollins.

HEEKS, R. (2003), "Most e-Government-for-Development Projects Fail: How Can Risks be Reduced?" IDPM e-Government Working Paper no. 14, University of Manchester, UK.

HIRST, P., and NORTON, M. (1998), "Electronic Government: Information Technologies and the Citizen." Report for the Parliamentary Office of Science and Technology of the UK Parliament.

HOFF, J., LOFGREN, K., and TORPE, L. (2003), "The State we are in: E-democracy in Denmark," *Information Polity* 8(1, 2): 49–67.

HOMBURG, V. M. F. (1999), *The Political Economy of Information Management*, (Diss.), Capelle a/d Ijssel: Labyrint Publication.

JOHANNSEN, H., and. ROBERTSON, A. B. (1968), *Management Glossary*, London: Longmans.

JOHNSON, P. W. (2001), *An Analysis of Three Strategic Criteria to Guide Policy Development in E-Government: A Bibliographic Essay*, http://filebox.* vt.edu/arh/psk2/papa6664

KING, J. L., and KRAEMER, K. L. (1998), "Information Technology in the Establishment and Maintenance of Civil Society," in SNELLEN and Van de Donk 1998: 509–22.

KLING. R. (1982), "Social Analyses of Computing: Theoretical Perspectives in Recent Empirical Research," *ACM Computing Surveys* 12(1): 61–110.

KRAEMER, K. L., and KING, J. L. (1987), "Computers and the Constitution: A Helpful, Harmful or Harmless Relationship?" *Public Administration Review* 47(1): 93–105.

—— —— (1994), "Social Analysis of Information Systems: The Irvine School, 1970–1994," *Informatization and the Public Sector* 3(2): 163–82.

LENK, K. (1997), Business Process Reengineering in the Public Sector: Opportunities and Risks. In: J.A.Taylor et al. Beyond BPR in Public Administration: Institutional Transformation in an Information Age. Amsterdam: IOS Press 1997: 151–63.

—— (1998), "Policy Execution in an Age of Telecooperation," in Snellen and Van de Donk 1998: 473–83.

—— and TRAUNMULLER, R. (2000), "Perspectives of Electronic Government," Presented at the IFIP WG 8.5 Conference on "Advances in Electronic Government", Zaragoza 10–11/2/2000.

—— (2002), "Electronic Service Delivery: A Driver of Public Sector Modernization," *Information Polity* 7 (2,3): 87–96.

MAES, R. (1990), "Informatie-infrastructuur: een sleutelbegrip voor het plannen, ontwikkelen an gebruiken van infomatiesystemen," in J. Truyens, *Informatie-infrastructuur*, Kluwer Bedrijfswetenschappen, 1990: 18–32.

MALONE, T. W., LAUBACHER, R., and SCOTT MORTON M. S. (eds.) (2003), *Inventing the Organizations of the 21st Century*, Cambridge, MA: MIT Press.

MARGETTS, H. (2003), "Electronic Government: A Revolution in Public Administration?", in G. Peters et al. (eds.), *Handbook of Public Administration*. London: Sage, 366–76.

—— (2004), "E-Government in Seven Liberal Democracies: Obstacles and Achievements.", Paper for Symposium on Internet and Governance, Oxford Internet Institute, 8–10 January 2004, Oxford University.

MATTILA, J. (2003), "Participatory E-governance—a New Solution to an Old Problem?" in A. Salminen (ed.), *Governing Networks. EGPA Yearbook*, Amsterdam: IOS Press, 161–69.

MINTZBERG, H. (1983), *Structures in Fives: Designing Effective Organizations*, Englewood Cliffs: Prentice Hall.

MOWSHOWITZ, A. (1992), "Virtual Feudalism: A Vision of Political Organization in the Information Age," *Informatization and the Public Sector* 2(3): 213–31.

NIEUWENHUIZEN, B., and SNELLEN, I. (2001), "Informatisation Policies in the Dutch Parliament: Do ICTs Support the Dutch Parliament as a Learning Organisation?", in P. Falconer et al. (eds.), *Managing Parliaments in the 21st Century*, Amsterdam: IOS Press, 67–75.

NORA, S., and MINC, A. (1980), *The Computerization of Society: A Report to the President of France*. Cambridge, MA: MIT Press.

NORRIS, P. (2001), *Digital Divide: Civic Engagement, Information Poverty, and the Internet Worldwide*, New York: Cambridge University Press.

OZBEKHAN, H. (1968), "The Triumph of Technology: 'Can' implies 'Ought,'" in S. Anderson (ed.), *Planning for Diversity and Choice*, Cambridge: MIT Press 204–34.

PARDO T. (2000), "Realizing the Promise of Digital Government: It's more than Building a Web Site." Paper, Center for Technology in Government, Albany, NY: SUNY.

PERISTERAS, V., TSEKOS, TH., and TARABANIS, K. (2002), "Realising e-Government: Architected/Centralised versus Interoperable/Decentralised ICTs and Organizational Development." Proceedings of European Group for Public Administration Annual Conference (EGPA Conference 2002), 4–7 September, Potsdam, Germany.

PERROW, C. B. (1984), *Normal Accidents: Living with High-Risk Technologies*, New York: Basic Books.

PERRY, J. L., KRAEMER, K. L., KING, J. L., and DUNKLE, D. (1992), "The Institutionalisation of Computing in Complex Organizations," *Informatization and the Public Sector* 2(1): 47–73.

POLLITT, C. (2003), *The Essential Public Manager*, Maidenhead and Philadelphia: Open University Press.

RAAB, C., and BELLAMY, C. (2000), "Hollowed, But not Yet Out: Postmodernising Parliamentary Democracy." Paper, EGPA Conference Glasgow, 30 Aug.–2 Sept.

REINERMANN, H., and VON LUCKE, J. (eds.) (2002), *Electronic Government in Deutschland: Ziele, Stand, Barrieren, Beispiele, Umsetzung*. Spyerer Forschungsberichte 226.

SMITH, C. (1998), "Political Parties in the Information Age: From 'Mass Party' to Leadership Organization?" in Snellen and Van de Donk 1998: 175–89.

SNELLEN, I. TH. M. (1998), "Street Level Bureaucracy in an Information Age," in Snellen and Van de Donk 1998: 497–505.

—— (2001a), "Administratieve lastenverlichting: Wie is er voor het algemeen belang?", in Van Duivenboden and Lips 2001: 335–46.

—— (2001b), ICTs, "Bureaucracies, and the Future of Democracy," *Communications of the ACM* 44(1): 45–48.

—— (2002), "Electronic Governance: Implications for Citizens, Politicians and Public Servants," *International Review of Administrative Sciences* 68: 183–98.

—— and VAN DE DONK, W. B. H. J. (eds.) (1998), *Public Administration in an Information Age: A Handbook*, Amsterdam: IOS Press.

VAN DEN HOVEN M. J. (1998), "Privacy and the Varieties of Informatonal Wrongdoing," *Austr. Journal of Professional and Applied Ethics* 1(1): 30–43.

VAN DUIVENBODEN, H., and LIPS, M. (eds.) (2001), *Klantgericht Werken in de Publieke Sector: Inrichting van de Electronische Overheid*, Utrecht: Lemma BV.

WINNER, L. (1977), *Autonomous Technology: Technics-out-of-Control as a Theme in Political Thought*, Cambridge MA: MIT Press.

ZOURIDIS, S. (2000), *Digitale Disciplinering. Over ICT, organisatie, wetgeving en het automatiseren van beschikkingen* (Diss.), Tilburg University.

—— and THAENS, M. (2003), "E-Government: Towards a Public Administration Approach," *The Asian Journal of Public Administration* 25(2): 159–83.

ZUBOFF, S. (1988), *In the Age of the Smart Machine: The Future of Work and Power*, Oxford: Heinemann Professional.

CHAPTER 18

PROFESSIONALS IN PUBLIC SERVICES ORGANIZATIONS

IMPLICATIONS FOR PUBLIC SECTOR "REFORMING"

EWAN FERLIE

KEITH J. GERAGHTY

18.1 INTRODUCTION

PROFESSIONALS play a major role in the organizing and provision of public services. A distinctive feature of the contemporary public sector is the presence of many different professions such as doctors, lawyers, nurses, and teachers. The

Thanks are due to Professors Stephen Harrison and Mike Reed for their generous sharing of ideas and working papers.

privatization of nationalized industries, contracting-out and reinvention and reengineering initiatives in the 1980s and 1990s led to a downsizing of manual workforces across many public sectors, as well as a delayering of middle management. However, core areas of the Welfare State—where human service professionals are concentrated—proved more difficult to privatize. Professionals also remain strongly represented as expert advisers in central government, for example, economists, and some "new professions" or rather knowledge workers may be emerging (e.g., Information Technologists). Given these trends, the role of professionals within public service organizations assumes great significance.

There are many ways of analyzing the public service professions: the terrain is vast and complex. One lens is to classify and analyze professions by different location and role, for example, the difference between professions in local and central government or elite professions and para-professions. A second focus could be to analyze changing relations between the public service professions and more demanding service users. A third would be tracking the evolution of professionalization projects, for example, the central civil service (at least in the UK) appears to be moving from a long tradition of "gentleman amateurs" to a new notion of the civil servant as a professional.

All these perspectives are interesting to scholars and important to public policy. However, our particular focus here is the relationship between public service professionals and current public management "reform." This focus limits a vast field yet is of strategic importance in helping us to understand challenges facing public sector reformers. New Public Management reforms challenge professionalism as a governing principle (Sehested 2002), but also depend on professionals for their implementation. The alignment or divergence between policy and professional interests and agendas may determine the outcome of current reform efforts. We need to connect the traditionally separate public sector reform and professional literatures and draw out possible implications.

The chapter reviews the evolving literature on professionals in public service organizations. It then presents two contemporary, but alternative, narratives of public service reform, that of "New Public Management" and that of the "Governance Model," considering implications for public service professionals. Examples are presented particularly from health care and higher education in different countries. These settings are selected because of their central role in many current reform strategies. We outline possible scenarios for the future and consider implications. More theoretical and empirical work is needed, but emergent evidence points to more varied responses by professionals to public sector reform than often assumed.

18.2 A MULTI DISCIPLINARY LITERATURE IN EVOLUTION: PROFESSIONAL DOMINANCE, MANAGERIALIZATION OR WHAT?

There is a well-developed scholarly literature on the professions, some of which considers implications for public sector organizations but which in general does not connect with a traditionally separate literature on public policy reforming. Key theoretical perspectives on professional work have been reviewed in Leicht and Fennell (2001), including career theory (how professional careers unfold), theories which analyze professions as institutions, power theory, and organizational change theory (the particular interest of this chapter). Within the study of the emblematic case of medicine, power theories (Harrison 2003) distinguish between continuing professional dominance, a more pluralist model of "countervailing powers" (e.g., growth of user influence, the emergence of new expert occupations), and finally deprofessionalization or even the alleged proletarianization of medical professionals. Reed's (1996, 2003) conceptual framework for classifying different approaches to the study of professional work differentiates between a "continuity thesis" (where professions have successfully institutionalized occupational closure and control), a "transformation thesis" (which supposes a radical loss of professional control), and a "fragmentation thesis" (where traditional professional work co exists with expanding forms of novel expertise such as the information and communications technologies) (Reed 1996, 2003). Broadly speaking, recent literature is moving away from the old "continuity" or dominance theses but it is unclear whether the alternative is transformation or fragmentation.

Writers' perspectives vary by academic discipline. In the USA, "professional careerists" have long been seen as an important subsystem by political scientists within the public bureaucratic system, growing in importance from the 1930s onwards as the use of the merit system matured. The use of professional expertise (lawyers; scientists) was here seen as a way of combating corruption as well as inefficiency in American government (Stillman 2000). Public bureaucrats may also recruit professionals as a way of changing or "modernizing" the profile of a public agency: Wilson (1989) gives the example of the US Forest Service employing new environmental professionals. Political scientists have also considered whether the influence of professionals on public policy should be seen as part of a closed "iron triangle" or a looser "issue network" model (Heclo 1978), essentially reflecting a broader debate between elitist and pluralist models of State power. They are also interested in the ways in which State and health care systems are bound together (Moran 1999) at a macro level.

Other political scientists (Lipsky 1980) have analyzed at a more micro level the ways in which low-level officials or "street-level bureaucrats" use conditions of high discretion in "people processing" agencies and erode the power of senior policy makers to set meaningful direction. Lipsky (1980) notes the existence of groups of client orientated "New Professionals" (e.g., community lawyers), coming into public service agencies from social movements. Sociologists also alert us to "professionalization projects," the process by which an occupation seeks to become a profession (Abbott 1988). Organizational change theorists study the dynamics of change in distinctive professionalized organizations (Mintzberg 1979), with weak managerial capacity and typically resistant to macro or top down change. The chapter will use an organizational sociological perspective to analyze current change processes.

Economists often take a skeptical view of the behavior of professionals, including those in public agencies. They note that professionals typically seek to establish monopolies based on the possession of credentials which exclude possible alternative suppliers (Friedman 1962). The result is lack of competition and consumer choice, excessive supply and inflated prices, particularly where the professions control entry into and exit from the labor market. These market-led approaches have been (Freidson 2001) of rising influence since the 1970s in such areas as US health policy, where medicine has come under increasing challenge to control costs. Agency theory suggests the use of more explicit contracts between managers and professionals, aligned to stronger forms of incentives (Leicht and Fennell 2001), to bring professionals into concordance with policy objectives.

Classic literature on the professions argues for a model of "professional dominance," based on the case of American medicine (Freidson 1970, 2001) in the 1950s, when clinicians obtained near total control over the labor market. Clinicians dominated managers as well as users, reflecting inequality in the basic distribution of power between social groups (Alford 1975). The transition from free-standing professional work to large-scale public bureaucracies in the 1950s and 1960s did not end professional control. Mintzberg (1979) proposes an archetype of the "*professional bureaucracy*," where senior professionals represent the real core. The organizational form is one of "bureau-professionalism" (Clarke and Newman 1997) with *both* many bureaucratic rules *and* strong professional control over working practices. The style of administration is facilitative rather than directive. Professionals form "bubbles" in these bureaucracies which protect them from standard managerial processes (Ackroyd 1996). For example, the UK National Health Service (NHS) has been strongly influenced by senior clinicians, even given public ownership and strong bureaucratization. (Rhodes 1997) suggests that professional groups capture the policy domain: senior clinicians dominate closed policy networks, such as advisory machinery at the Department of Health. These "iron triangles" are more restricted than the American pattern presented by (Heclo 1978).

The old assumption that post-industrial societies would lead to the "professionalization of everyone" has not been realised. Literature more recently paints a picture of rising managerialization (Clarke and Newman 1997; Broadbent and Laughlin 2001) in public service organizations. Why might this be the case? Public service "reforms" in a number of countries have sought to increase managerial power and dilute the traditional power of professionals. Their motivation comes from the political desire to reduce the escalating costs of social programs (Freidson 2001) funded by the taxpayer and to empower consumers. This raises the prospect of significant change rather than continuity: even institutionalised professions such as medicine are finding the reproduction of professional dominance difficult and are coming under increasing external pressure to be more accountable to patients and their political and institutional representatives.

18.2.1 Professionalization Projects Stalled

While policy makers and public managers seek to reduce professional autonomy; the professions seek increase it in profession building. Recent professionalization projects have not however been successful. Nursing has long sought to win similar status and autonomy as medicine, putting in place institutions of self-regulation, accreditation systems, and graduate-only posts. However, these claims have yet to be fully accepted by the State. One possible reason is the gender divisions that demarcate the high ranking professions of medicine and law (male dominated) from the lower status female dominated professions of teaching, social work, and nursing. Another view is that the historic conditions which allowed the emergence of elite professions have ended, so that further professionalization projects will not achieve success. Some authors now speak more broadly of "knowledge workers" or "experts" rather than professionals (Scarborough 1995; Reed 1996), such as new groups of Information Technologists or management consultants (although the growth of the "Expert State" has long been evident in the USA, as already mentioned). One implication is that public sector managers may seek to transform themselves into a new profession but are unlikely to succeed. One can usefully distinguish between the old "professionalised State" and a new "Expert State" (where knowledge workers remain influential, but have not developed the elaborate self regulatory institutions of the old elite professions).

18.2.2 Inter-Professional Relations: Workload Shifts and Turf Disputes

(Abbott 1988) refers to the competition for turf and "jurisdictions" between overlapping professions. The relationship between professional groups is as important as that between professionals and managers. The public sector contains an extensive range of professional groupings. Dominant professions typically seek to marginalize the jurisdictions of subordinate professions. (Freund and McGuire

1999) suggest that the dominance of the medical profession entailed the "subordination, co-option, or elimination of all competing health care professions." However, this established pattern may not be evidence in certain conditions. Recent staffing shortages and capacity short falls have led UK doctors to relinquish routine work to senior nurses, where new roles have been created. Workload shifts become less contentious given high work bombardment. Routine work also appears to be moving from teachers to classroom assistants and from lawyers to para legals.

Concurrent professionalization projects across the public sector can create an immobile pattern of multi-professionalization, slowing down public services reforms to the pace of the slowest profession (Ferlie, FitzGerald, Wood, and Hawkins 2004). So how might public policy reformers respond to multi-professionalization? One response is to "divide and rule" over the different professions. Typically, public policy reforms empower subordinate public service professions vis-à-vis dominant ones (e.g., moving work away from medicine to nursing). However, multi-professionalization threatens public services reform as rapid and significant change to the traditional division of labor becomes problematic, outside the specific conditions of excessive work bombardment mentioned earlier. Yet ensuring cooperation between different professional groups is critical to achieving high quality and "seamless" services. So another policy response is to introduce initiatives to "free up" the inter-professional division of labor, for example, in recent attempts to deregulate legal services in the UK, relaxing constraints on the arcane division of labor between solicitors and barristers.

18.2.3 Knowledge Based Professions?

The possession of scarce, valued, abstract, and accredited knowledge has often been seen as a core trait of a profession. Reed (2003) points out that such professionalized knowledge is increasingly being supplemented and contested by expertise produced by new knowledge workers. This arena becomes ever more important with the rise of knowledge-based firms (Alvesson 2004) or more broadly knowledge-based organizations that primarily produce knowledge rather than goods or services. There may also be more explicit attempts to control that knowledge through knowledge management strategies. There appear to be contradictory pressures at work within current public sector settings in relation to professional knowledge. On the one hand, we see attempts at bureaucratization, codification, and control. For example, there is the rise of scientific bureaucratic forms of knowledge in the profession of medicine internationally as part of the Evidence Based Medicine movement, with the erosion of tacit clinical judgment and the creation of new governmental agencies producing an ever increasing number of guidelines and protocols which formalize and codify knowledge (Harrison

2002). In the UK, teachers have lost control over curriculum development to national agencies. On the other hand, Moran (1999) draws attention to the continuing ability of the clinical research elite in American medicine to win huge research budgets in the National Institutes of Health and the relationship between such basic research and the development of new drugs and technologies. Research-based knowledge is here a major and largely autonomous motor of product and indeed economic development. Research intensive Universities are differentiating themselves from the bulk of the University population. Finally, there is some evidence of knowledge fragmentation and contestation as new knowledge workers (e.g., health economists' work on the cost effectiveness of medical interventions) produce alternative knowledge which supplements and indeed challenges old professional knowledge. Knowledge does not flow readily between the different public services professions, rather it "sticks" at the boundaries, as each profession generates a distinct social and cognitive "community of practice" (Ferlie et al. 2004).

18.2.4 Managerialization of the Public Service Professions?

In the 1980s and 1990s, "the fiscal crisis of the Welfare State" resulted in policy interventions designed to lower costs and improve the quality of services provided by public services professionals in the face of taxpayers' revolts. This led to the introduction of managerial roles and external systems of regulation to weaken professional control. Some see this managerialization process as radical and sustained in nature (Clarke and Newman 1997; Broadbent and Laughlin 2001).

An example is Higher Education where traditional academic freedom may be in retreat. Prichard (2000) suggests that UK higher education academics are increasingly in conflict with a rising cadre of new managers (often themselves originally academics). This has led to the decomposition of traditional academic work and a shift to work intensification driven by managerial target setting. Reed and Deem's (2002) study of rank and file academics found that many of them perceived far greater managerial control over their work, augmented by new control technologies which enabled the collection of performance data (what might be termed "rule by spreadsheet"). From a gender perspective, some detect a shift from feminine to masculine styles of the management of academics within UK universities, with emphasis on appraisal, performance measurement and performance management (Thomas and Davies 2001). Internationally, a trend to managerialization within universities is also reported in the USA. El-Khawas (2002) argues that there has been a strengthening of the strategic core in many American universities, as predicted in Clark's (1998) new model of the "entrepreneurial" and more business orientated university. In France, Musselin and Mignot-Gerard (2002) detect a strengthening of corporate university leadership capacity, although in this case reform has not been imposed from above but rather associated with regionalization.

But might the managerialization process be less forceful than some of these accounts suggest? Prominent professions in the private sector (Brock, Powell, and Hinings 1999) are also experiencing the development of increased managerial and corporate systems at the expense of professional autonomy. However, the basic drivers (market forces, globalization, over capacity, and sharp customer pressure) remain weaker in the public sector, so the old pattern of professional dominance may have more staying power there (Elston 1991). Reform strategies in European nations with strong traditions of State welfare provision—and weak market forces—may find managerialization especially difficult (Dent 2000). In the US, where insurance rather than taxpayer-based forms of payment are stronger, purchaser organizations, such as Health Maintenance Organizations in health care, have more muscle to lever change in professional practice through control over payment (Moran 1999).

18.2.5 Alternative Scenarios?

The professionalization (vs) managerialization debate reviewed above may be crude and overstated. Are there other, more subtle, scenarios? A first alternative is the emergence of professional–managerial hybrids: many of the new managers are themselves professionals by training. Here professionals take on additional managerial roles later on in their careers, seeking to link the professional and managerial worlds. The policy system may need to develop this cadre by investment in personal and organizational development as they move into their new roles. This is a strategy of incorporation (Harrison and Pollitt 1994), at least of an elite subgroup. In health care, medical managers (Clinical Directors in the UK) have emerged as an important leadership grouping, often more influential than the general (lay) managers introduced in the 1980s. Some senior academics have also moved on from a pure academic career to undertake strategic managerial positions (e.g., Heads of Department). In the USA, broader perspectives have been encouraged by the provision of joint degrees, for example between medicine or law and public policy/management or between social work and business administration.

Second, some "entrepreneurial professionals" welcome increased market freedoms associated with reforms which enable them to escape from a rigid "professionalized bureaucracy." Not all professionals are opposed to a "freeing up" of the public services, especially where they have a right to private practice and have experienced the private sector. Whittington, McNulty, and Whipp (1994) found, contrary to prevailing literature, that some NHS clinicians relished the opportunity to market their services within NPM style reforms. Clark's (1998) emergent ideal type of the "entrepreneurial" university exhibits a strengthened strategic core but also a greater openness to markets. So is some of the literature critiquing professionals' response to managerialization in the public services normatively driven rather than empirically founded?

Third, professionaliszed public service organizations are characterized by collective rather than individualized forms of leadership, particularly in strategic change (Pettigrew, Ferlie, and McKee 1992; Denis, Langley, and Cazale 1996). Team-based forms of leadership mix managers and professionals, as neither group can succeed in managing major change without support from the other. Conflict gives way to bargaining and perhaps even cooperation. The division of labor benefits both sides in managing major change: managers concentrate on securing support from the political and policy systems, while senior level professionals negotiate with the professional rank and file.

In summary, there is an extensive scholarly literature on the sociology of the professions within public service organizations. Present developments may be characterized by a period of organizational change as reform strategies attempt to control public services professionals and reconstitute traditional professional work. The literature is generally moving from a presumption of professional dominance to that of managerialization, although there is debate about how deep or broad this shift is. Alternative and nuanced outcomes are possible so we need more contemporary thinking and empirical study.

18.3 Two Narratives of Public Sector Reform and Implications for Public Service Professionals

18.3.1 New Public Management and the Public Service Professions

We move on to consider specifically the relationship between governmental public sector reform strategies and the public sector professions. We distinguish two meta-level reform narratives. Over the past two decades, ideas of New Public Management have been (Pollitt and Bouckaert 2000; McLaughlin, Osborne, and Ferlie 2001) influential in countries such as the UK, New Zealand, Canada, and Australia (Hood 1991, 1995; Ferlie et al. 1996). The NPM critiques powerful professions for dominating public sector agencies and blocking politically driven or user-orientated reform (Dent 2000; Sehested 2002). Public service organizations are seen as hijacked by professionals who run services for the benefit of producers rather than consumers (Broadbent and Laughlin 2001). Traditional high levels of trust in professionals are then replaced by mistrust and rigorous control and audit devices (Power 1997).

NPM reforms typically introduce higher levels of accountability for public service professionals. Poor performance is uncovered through individual appraisal, short-term job contracts or performance-related pay. Contrary to the assumption that policy networks are captured by professional groups (Rhodes 1997), NPM-style governments have withdrawn from professionalized public policy networks: the UK Department of Education distanced itself from teaching trade unions, seeing them as no more than producer-based interest groups. This disengagement led to antagonistic relations, yet the UK Department of Education argues that its imposition of targets on professionals safeguards the interests of users (e.g., achieving rising literacy and numeracy levels) and challenges poor professional performance.

While NPM represents the infusion of private sector managerial ideas and techniques into the public services, there are different NPM subtypes (Ferlie et al. 1996) reflecting distinct managerial schools of thought. We distinguish between "hard NPM" and "soft NPM," each with different implications for public service professionals.

18.3.2 "Hard NPM" and Public Service Professionals

Broadbent and Laughlin (2001) argue that NPM regimes seek to control public service professions through the introduction of an "accounting logic" which places greater emphasis on the explicit measurement of outputs and outcomes, makes linkages between them and connects them with financial flows so as to reward performance. Within hard NPM there is a rise of audit, performance measurement, performance management, and performance-related finance. This new paradigm assumes (1) performance identification through measurement and (2) a reward-or-punish strategy, using hard numbers and performance indicators as the basis of judgment. These hard NPM ideas have more recently been adopted within UK Higher Education (Reed and Deem 2002) through performance management systems, institutional assessment of research and teaching performance, and linking to grant flows. This finding is counter intuitive as higher education has been historically seen as a sector with a strong self-steering capacity, a condition which predicts low NPM impact.

18.3.3 "Soft NPM" and the Public Service Professions

While hard NPM has been evident since the 1980s, there has more recently been a growth of soft NPM. Soft NPM is associated with the human relations school of private sector management, rather than accounting logic. The emphasis here is on user orientation, quality improvement, organizational and individual development and learning. While this is a different management style to the more aggressive

NPM model, it still moves the locus of control and decision making away from professionals to a new internalized management function. The aim is to absorb professionals into more inclusive and responsive management systems. The "culture of excellence" approach (Peters and Waterman 1982) in the 1980s and "high commitment" human resource models (Tichy, Fombrun, and Devanna 1982; Sparrow and Hiltrop 1994) contribute to this style of management. Newer corporate quality systems such as Total Quality Management, Business Process Reengineering, and process redesign have emerged in public management reform strategies, not just in the UK, but internationally as part of reinvention initiatives (Joss and Kogan 1995; Morgan and Murgatroyd 1997; Kaboolian 2000; McNulty and Ferlie 2001). The model of "the Learning Organization" has been imported into some public service organizations (Senge 1990). There is increased recourse to the appraisal of professionals, linked to a consideration of their development needs as well as the pursuit of organizational objectives. These "change programs" often suffer from weak professional support or even at times resistance (Morgan and Murgatroyd 1997; Kaboolian 2000; McNulty and Ferlie 2001). Nevertheless, the increasing stress placed upon organizational development (OD) and learning has raised the profile of "soft HRM" ideas. These are viewed as a more attractive and engaging option than hard NPM, not only for public managers seeking to implement change but for some professionals who themselves are self motivated to engage in service improvement initiatives and find these managerial technologies to be helpful tools. Some professionals may actively embrace a learning organization model, seeing it as an organizational reenforcer of their preexisting individual desire to learn throughout their careers: Lipsky (1980) refers to "new professionals" aligned to social movements. A key issue here is how to "keep new professionals new" by protecting and expanding this core and preventing burn-out and routinization. Reflective practice and ensuring rich supervision is one response to this problem.

18.3.4 The Governance Narrative and the Public Service Professions

Some commentators are skeptical about the impact of NPM ideas (Lynn 1997), seeing them as faddish. Other critics suggest that NPM reforms exhibit dysfunctional consequences: an over concentration on strong vertical reporting lines, a neglect of lateral working, and a lack of social or democratic legitimacy. In response, an alternative post-NPM "governance" narrative has emerged in the UK, associated with the election of New Labour in 1997, and lately exported to some other Anglophone countries.

So called "Third Way" theory (Giddens 1997) examines the dangers of the over directing State and the need to rebalance its relationship with civil society.

The so-called "governance" model emphasises social inclusion and partnership working across various stakeholders and boundaries, including public service professionals. Governance implies creating coalitions, hybrids, and "win-win" situations in which public sector professional groups are included. Newman (2001) specifically identifies greater consultation with staff and their inclusion in the development of policy as an important development in the shift from NPM to governance-based modes of working. UK public policy reform documents (Cmnd. 4310 1999; 4818 2000) outline measures for staff as well as users to create "buy-in" (e.g., family friendly working; better education and development) to public service reform. The rhetoric around the distinctive value of public services has been strengthened. This discourse indicates a more inclusive stance towards the public service professions than NPM rhetoric. Governance working abandons the hard NPM strategy, accepting the existence of networks which possess substantial autonomy. Networks and partnerships are new steering mechanisms which complement the traditional hierarchies fragmented by NPM reforms. These networks include the public service professions along with new actors drawn from outside the public sector through public–private partnerships (PPPs). Rhodes (1997) states that "governance blurs the distinction between State and civil society. The State becomes a collection of inter-organizational networks made up of governmental and societal actors with no sovereign actor able to steer and regulate. A key challenge for government is to enable these networks and seek out new channels of cooperation."

Newman (2001) suggests that the governance model implies a move away from hierarchies and markets to networks and partnerships as steering mechanisms; the recognition and incorporation of policy networks into the process of governing; and use of influence, persuasion, and leadership by Government, rather than direct command and control. This supposedly results in a more legitimate and consensual basis for State–society interaction, involving professionals as well as users in collaborative and high trust partnerships. It is more likely that professionals will "own" the change agenda, rather than feel that it has been imposed on them from above. The search for greater legitimacy may also lead to a greater acceptance of the ethical benefits of strong, self regulating professions. The governance discourse might be expected to chime with public service professionals' values more than the NPM paradigm, and public sector workers were an important electoral constituency for New Labour in 1997. Newman (2001: 122–4) presents a relatively optimistic picture of at least some UK public sector professionals engaging with the partnership agenda, seeing it as a release from traditional constraints and opening up of new career paths. She also notes that the governance paradigm has run alongside the old NPM paradigm rather than displacing it. These "Third Way" governance ideas may diffuse out of their UK heartland, at least to other Anglo-Saxon political cultures. Similar trends are observable in Australia and New Zealand, where ideas and practices of networking and cooperation have taken on greater significance (New Zealand Ministry of Health 2001) within the public services.

The New Public Management (NPM) and Governance models suggest two distinct narratives of public sector reform and more specifically different patterns of professional-managerial relations. The discussion of future scenarios below considers their distinctive consequences and under which circumstances each scenario might be expected to flourish.

18.4 Four Scenarios for the Public Services Professions

We now take a more forward-looking perspective and outline four scenarios which may govern the future of public service professionals. The relations between the State and the public service professions will vary strongly by political economic context: the Anglo-American model(s) present a different and more hostile context for the professions than either the *Rechtstaat* model in Germany and France or a Nordic model based on decentralization, corporatism, and consensus (Premfors 1998). A recent empirical study of the Danish hospital field suggested a relatively "soft" pattern of NPM impact on the professions there, mixed also with preexisting reform ideas (Jespersen, Nielsen, and Sognstrup 2002). Four different scenarios are presented:

1. Hard NPM and Radical Managerialization
2. Soft NPM and Indirect Managerialization
3. Professional Managerial Hybridization
4. Governance, Expert Networks, and Partial Re-professionalization.

These scenarios lie along a continuum, beginning with hard NPM and ending with governance.

18.4.1 Hard NPM and Radical Managerialization

This is the most hostile scenario (Broadbent and Laughlin 2001) for the public service professions. Where the conditions that helped trigger the NPM wave during the 1980s and 1990s (political resistance to rising public spending and taxation; rising concern about non-responsive services and poor quality) are still prominent, hard NPM strategies may endure as governments respond to continuing political unease. This direction will be strengthened in jurisdictions where political institutions are centralized and under strong executive control (Pollitt and Bouckaert 2000). The degree of influence of managerialist ideas—and more broadly capacity—in the public sector varies strongly from one jurisdiction to another (Saint-Martin 2000). Management has emerged as a much more powerful directing function in Anglo Saxon cultures than in *Rechtstaat* cultures where lawyers are more prominent. The rise of management as a new elite grouping has been marked in a number of Anglo Saxon jurisdictions in the 1980s and 1990s and does not appear to have gone into reverse. In more managerialized regimes and societies, an abandonment of the "tacit contract" between the State and professions is likely, whereby professional control is curtailed or even eradicated (Davies 2000) by well-developed managerial cadres.

Checking the power of the public sector professions and increasing their productivity will here remain a strategic imperative within public policy reforming which cannot easily be abandoned. Political energy and NPM interventions will be concentrated in electorally high-profile sectors (e.g., education; health). In this scenario, the "value for money" NPM agenda will continue, with progressive managerialization, marketization, and the growth of performance measurement systems. Professional services will be explicitly contracted for and performance measured against stated service levels developed within the "accountancy control" logic. Trust levels will continue to erode. The growth of general managerial roles will be apparent, with a tightening up of professionals' job contracts to remove traditional bases of autonomy. There will be a decline of self-regulation and the emergence of externally driven and more transparent regulatory offices. More data on the performance of individual professionals will be made available to consumers to enable them to make informed choices, for example surgeons' death rates, or school teachers' exam results, or the recent "star rating scheme" for hospitals in UK health.

The continuance of hard NPM is likely in some historically high-impact NPM jurisdictions, such as the UK and New Zealand (Hood 1995) while its emergence remains unlikely in more consensual western European regimes, at least in the absence of a full fiscal crisis. Will any further countries now join the group of "high-impact" NPM countries or have the historical conditions which gave rise to hard NPM come to an end? Will existing hard NPM countries be able to move away from an NPM archetype—even if the political rhetoric changes—or are they now stuck on a long-term track (Ferlie and FitzGerald 2001)? The desire to move onto a post-NPM agenda may depend on whether it is widely perceived that NPM-led reforms have become "unimplementable" or have generated perverse effects, due to their lack of legitimacy amongst non-State actors.

18.4.2 Soft NPM and Indirect Managerialization

In this scenario soft NPM leads to a more subtle and indirect form of managerialization. Professionals are drawn into newly developed managerial processes
based on principles of joint learning, high commitment and culture change, rather
than measurement, audit and external regulation. However, they lose their old
separate identities and become more incorporated within the organization. The
stated intention is to create a new corporate culture of collaboration and continuous improvement within public services. Soft NPM initiatives may be used with
senior professionals who have resisted more direct managerial control. As public
service organizations become "learning organizations," professionals become more
engaged with reform and are self-motivated to reflect, change, and improve (Senge
1990). A number of other implications follow. Systems of self-regulation and
accreditation will be developed further, as well as internally developed systems
(e.g., quality circles) designed to reinforce quality. The HRM function takes on a
more strategic role (Tichy, Fombrun, and Devanna 1982) within public policy
reform, as the knowledge base and skills of the public sector workforce become
critical in delivering better quality services. There is a drive to ensure consultation
and involvement of professional staff so as to secure their "buy-in" to reform,
especially with professional opinion leaders who are important change agents
(Rogers 1995). The desire to achieve "cultural change" as well as structural change
reinforces the use of organizational development strategies which are likely to focus
on "the management of change" and "transformational leadership" programs,
again using managerial ideas and techniques originating in the private sector.
Government will seek to increase its control over entry into and exit from public
sector professions. It may expand the numbers of entrants into key public service
professions (e.g., using manpower planning for medical schools to expand entry)
to dilute the professional power created by scarcity.

The above scenario may be too optimistic. Even the more subtle approach of
"soft NPM" may not be able to bridge the underlying tensions between professional interests and managers who are seeking higher commitment and performance levels as defined against political and managerial criteria. There is skepticism
about importing private management models to rectify public sector problems, in
soft as well as hard NPM. For example, a recent study of an attempt (McDonnell
et al. 2003) to create "learning organizations" in UK primary care, reported
considerable implementation difficulties as underlying conditions were not receptive to these new organizational forms. Managers found it difficult to grasp these
somewhat nebulous concepts; were unable to protect the long-term OD agenda
from the pressure of short term fire-fighting; and many rank and file professionals
remained disengaged.

Where might soft NPM approaches to the management of public service professionals be expected to flourish? As with hard NPM, these ideas will be more

influential in States and societies where there is a strong managerial capacity and ideology so that politicians trust in the efficacy of private sector based management ideas to reform the public sector. Given that these OD interventions require top level political support and financial investment across the public services if they are to have a system wide impact, the presence of centralized political institutions may also be helpful. These are similar conditions to hard NPM. But in the case of soft NPM, the previously dominant accountancy logic has given way to alternative HRM logic. Soft NPM requires the HRM function to have secured a truly strategic role and for accounting logic to become subordinate. This becomes more likely under conditions of full employment, fiscal balance and in advanced economies where knowledge based organizations (as opposed to manufacturing) are pervasive. Within the public services, soft NPM is a more likely response in knowledge based services (health; education) than in high volume, routine, services (social security).

The reform agenda of governments which favor soft NPM approaches will be distinctive from the old value for money agenda. Key policy objectives are instead centred on quality and capacity development, rather than productivity, cost control or increasing activity levels. These approaches require long time scales to be effectively implemented and interventions (for example) in the cultural sphere are not easily controlled or managed. The implication is that governments adopting soft NPM approaches need time and political stability: they may be attractive in countries with relatively stable governments based on one historically dominant party or a coalition. They are less politically viable in majoritarian and volatile political systems with short electoral cycles and where parties quickly alternate in government.

18.4.3 Professionals Colonise Management: Hybrids and Self Reform

Within this scenario, the presumption that managers will colonize the world of public service professionals goes into reverse: rather, public service professionals colonize the world of management. Specifically a subgroup emerges of senior professionals who seek to "manage" their erstwhile professional colleagues. In contrast to the first two scenarios, professional managerial hybrids replace non-professional general or HRM managers as the principal managerial element. Such hybridization is an important trend in public services management (e.g., in health care or higher education), reflecting a more organic strategy as opposed to bringing in general management from outside to direct groups of public service professionals. In order to be effective, however, these "hybrids" have to link very different professional and managerial worlds and remain credible in both. At one level, these hybrids work to a managerial agenda which they take to the professional rank and file, for example the challenging of poor performance within management systems constructed by government. However, they can also act to protect the professional rank and file from managerial excess, such as the over-bureaucratization of audit systems, and help ensure that core professional values (clinical and academic excellence) are not subverted by reform programs. They are likely to prefer quality-led soft NPM approaches than productivity-led hard NPM.

Important questions arise about the extent and impact of hybridization: are these hybrids able to balance the interests of the professional rank and file and the managerial constituency effectively, or is there in the end a contradiction between the two? Is there a separation out of the new hybrid elite from the professional rank and file (Montgomery 1990) which leads to increasing conflict between the two groups originally located within the same profession? What are their training and development needs as they move into these very different roles and how are these being met? What interventions are being undertaken by the policy system to invest in this key linking group? Public service professionals are not just the passive recipients of top–down public service reform (FitzGerald and Ferlie 2000), but shape its enactment at local level (Hoff and McCaffrey 1996).

Many professionals learn and adapt quickly to new roles and seek to shape them to protect their own preexisting core agendas. Some public service reforms have more ambiguous implications for managerial and professional leadership roles than assumed in the managerialization thesis. New forms of professional practice may evolve that contradict the assumption of inward-looking behavior assumed in much of the NPM style literature on public service professionals here and which undercut the case for managerialization. The public service professions here manage to reform themselves (albeit under the threat of imposed managerialization) and to introduce more effective systems of self-regulation which obviate the need for external regulation. For example, Argyris (1999) writes of so-called Mode 2 professionals who are, in terms of their own values much more user-centered in their practice than earlier generations of professionals, for example, progressive primary care doctors who explore options with their patients within co-decision making. The reformed education and training programs of the 1990s may in the end help produce a new generation of more user-centered public service professionals.

This strategy may be thought to be more likely in societies where managerial roles, ideas, and prestige are strong: management is a desirable field for elite professionals to seek to move into. However, government plays a more limited role in reforming than in the two previous scenarios. Its role is limited to building up managerial and reformist capacity within the professions themselves. The behavior of the professional bodies and individual professionals becomes more important: Do they want to colonize the world of management and if so, are they able to learn and adapt to their new roles quickly?

Governments which adopt this strategy may be motivated by three possible considerations: (i) they decide that modest rather than radical strategies of public service reform are more likely to produce a political pay off; (ii) they have respect for alternative and legitimate power centres such as the liberal professions; (iii) earlier strategies of hard or soft NPM reforming have been tried and have foundered on the rocks of professional resistance.

18.4.4 Legitimacy Deficits, Partial Reprofessionalization and the Expert State

The hard NPM model of confrontation with public service professionals can generate two perverse effects. First, it can lead to implementation deficits as front line professionals fail to "buy into" top–down change initiatives and indeed block or reshape them (McNulty and Ferlie 2001). Do managerially led and top–down strategies of macro public policy reform promise much; but in the end deliver little? Second, NPM-based approaches erode their own legitimacy as professional groups highly trusted by the public, such as doctors or teachers, are removed from policy making and may even become public critics of reform. Where such managerially led reform strategies have failed either substantively or politically, there may be a partial move back either to reprofessionalization or alternatively a new form of an Expert State.

For example, the significance and utility of governmentally imposed targets in UK public services are currently being publicly questioned by leading clinicians or teachers. Do the recently introduced hospital star ratings mean anything substantive at all? Primary health care is an interesting example, as family doctors are an extreme case of trusted public service professionals. In response to growing legitimacy deficits, there has been a (still ambiguous) move back to including representatives of the primary health care professions on the boards of local health care organizations. Policy networks here undergo some reprofessionalization in line with governance-based approaches in order to reduce legitimacy deficits. This scenario depends on the professions retaining high levels of societal legitimacy: user or customer based movements are apparent in some societies where notions of customer focused organizations are strong (e.g., USA), challenging the traditional prestige of public service professionals.

A second counter trend (at least at the meso and macro levels of the policy system) is the increasing premium placed on highly esoteric and technical knowledge within public policy making. This development is broader than simple reprofessionalization, and fits with the fragmentation thesis (Reed 2003). We may be seeing the rise of the "Expert State" in which high-level technical experts are increasingly influential. These individual experts may be acting as individuals rather than representative of traditional professional bodies but nevertheless are important "knowledge workers" whose valued knowledge remains resistant to managerialization, marketization or performance management. An important example to consider is the interface between science and public policy. We see the incorporation of high level technical advisers, such as leading scientists, within policy networks. UK examples would be the recent use of elite scientists to advise on the formulation of policy on GM Foods, or the use of scientific experts to advise on Weapons of Mass Destruction. These policy networks are outside the conventional control of line management but shape overall policy at national level. The fundamental driving process is the continuing need for expert knowledge, increasing sub-specialization and differentiation in its production, in turn leading to a move back to forms of self-regulation such as peer review through the publication process rather than external regulation by non experts.

Beck's (1992) analysis of contemporary "risk society" suggests fundamental trends in the assessment and management of the hazards of large-scale risk, such as nuclear energy or genetic modification, that cause a migration of the potential for structuring society from the conventional political subsystem to the alternative subsystem of scientific, technological, and economic modernization. As Beck states (1992: 186): "the political becomes non-political; and the non-political becomes political." The proliferation of expert advisory machinery set up to manage technically founded and systemic sources of risk increases the power of senior experts over policy makers and managers who lack the technical knowledge to assess or challenge their recommendations. In response to "mad cow disease" (Spongiform Encephalopathies), for example, the UK Government set up the Spongiform Encephalopathy Advisory Committee (SEAC) whose membership is almost entirely comprised of clinical academics, veterinary academics, and public health physicians with little consumer or managerial representation.

A second example where new expertise may be becoming increasingly important within the public services is in program evaluation. We see the increasing role of applied social science within the Evidence Based Policy movement (Davies, Nutley, and Smith 2000) which proved increasingly influential in the late 1990s in the UK, USA, and Canada. Here public policy reforms are increasingly subjected to technical evaluations to ascertain "if they worked." There is a significant growth of the evaluation industry within public policy reforming, albeit from a low level of capacity in some countries. While political considerations will not be removed from reforming, the increasing access of social scientists to decision making is important. Analysis and debate within the evaluation community is highly technical (e.g. the strengths and weaknesses of different forms of quasi experimental design), from which lay audiences are excluded. Evaluators can be seen as an emergent new group of "experts," but they still lack the traditional structure or trappings of a profession, such as a common paradigm or a College which can insist on standards of entry, accreditation and discipline.

18.5 Concluding Discussion

We have argued that professionals play a major role in the delivery of public services so that any analysis of public services reform should explicitly consider the behaviour and power of public service professional groups. Conditions of high professionalization are increasingly characteristic of contemporary public sectors, as they shrink into a knowledge intensive core.

18.5.1 The Theoretical Domain

Within the theoretical domain, there is already an extensive scholarly literature on the professionalization vs. managerialization debate as applied to public services organizations, often drawing on the basic ideas of Freidson. The general trend suggested is towards managerialization, but there is controversy about how radical or internationally based this shift is. New ideas and perspectives can supplement and refresh this by now well-established debate. We should explore whether some unexpected responses and hybrid roles are emerging (FitzGerald and Ferlie 2000). In addition, Evetts (2002) draws attention to the international level of analysis at which professional labor markets are increasingly structured; Johnson (1995) uses the Foucaultian notion of "governmentality" to challenge the supposed dichotomy between the professions and the State (rather the State grew up incorporating professional expertise as a mode of discipline and governing, for example, the construction of mental asylums). Lipsky's (1980) argument about "keeping new professionals new" draws attention to the need to explore the value base of some professionals and how this connects to social movements. This may link to the concept of professional "identity" stressed by Alvesson (2004) which needs further exploration. Reed's (2003) important fragmentation thesis alerts us to the possibility of the coexistence of traditional forms of professional knowledge with new forms of knowledge produced by emergent occupational groups or sub-elites who capture the Expert State (Beck 1992). There are then a number of ways in which thinking about public services professionals could now be refreshed.

18.5.2 The Empirical Domain

Empirically, we need more up-to-date material in particular in relation to key cases such as the UK (high impact NPM State), France and Germany (ideal typical *Rechtstaat* States), and the USA (knowledge intensive economy involving important professional groups but combined with strong market forces and relatively weak government). Is the empirical material conventionally used in the literature now badly dated? Well-structured comparative analysis across key cases is particularly helpful. We have some already: Harrison and Schultz (1989) compared and contrasted dimensions of clinical autonomy in the USA and UK. Pollitt (1993) compared the introduction of medical audit in the USA and UK. Moran (1999) compares the governance of the "health care State" in America, the UK, and Germany. Some recent work suggests a softer impact of NPM on public service professional groups in a Nordic political economy such as Denmark than Anglo-Saxon countries (Jespersen, Nielsen, and Sognstrup 2002; Sehested 2002). It would be interesting to explore more comparative material from *Rechtstaat* polities such as France and Germany or other regional groupings (e.g., Southern Europe; South East Asia) as well as variation within the Anglo-Saxon bloc.

Finally, we should remember the limitations of the chapter. Many of our examples have been taken from medicine, an extreme example of a historically successful profession. Weaker professions (such as social work or nursing) present a different pattern. The phenomenon of developed public service professions may apply only to some countries where there are certain assumptions and legal frameworks governing relations between government and liberal professions. Such assumptions need not necessarily apply in the old Second World countries, nor in some developing countries.

References

Abbott, A. (1988), *The System of Professions: An Essay on the Division of Expert Labour*, London: University of Chicago Press.

Ackroyd, S. (1996), "Organisation Contra Organisations: Professions and Organisational Change in the UK," *Organisational Studies* 17(4): 599–621.

Alford, R. (1975), *Health Care Politics*, London: University of Chicago Press.

Alvesson, M. (2004), *Knowledge Work and Knowledge Intensive Firms*, Oxford: Oxford University Press.

Argyris, C. (1999), *On Organisational Learning*, Oxford: Basil Blackwell.

Beck, U. (1992), *Risk Society*, London: Sage.

Broadbent, J., and Laughlin, R. (2001), "Public Service Professionals and the New Public Management: Control of the Professions in the Public Services," in K. McLaughlin, S. Osborne, and E. Ferlie (eds.), *New Public Management: Current Trends and Future Prospects*, London: Routledge, 95–108.

Brock, D., Powell, M., and Hinings, C. R. (eds.) (1999), *Restructuring The Professional Organisation*, London: Routledge.

Clark, B. R. (1998), *Creating Entrepreneurial Universities*, Oxford: Elsevier Science Ltd.

Clarke, J., and Newman, J. (1997), *The Managerial State*, London: Sage.

Cmnd. 4310, (1999), "Modernising Governance," London: HMSO.

Cmnd. 4818, (2000), "The NHS Plan," London: HMSO.

DAVIES, C. (2000), "The Demise of Professional Self Regulation: a moment to mourn?", in G. Lewis, S. Gewitz, and J. Clarke (eds.), *Rethinking Social Policy*, London: Sage.

DAVIES, H. T. O., NUTLEY, S., and SMITH, P. C. (2000), *What Works? Evidence Based Policy and Practice in Public Services*, Bristol: The Policy Press.

DENIS, J., LANGLEY, A., and CAZALE, L. (1996), "Leadership and Strategic Change Under Conditions of Ambiguity," *Organisational Studies* 17(4): 673–99.

DENT, M. (2000), *Professions, New Public Management and the European Welfare State*, Stoke on Trent: Staffordshire University Press.

EL-KHAWAS, E. (2002), "Governance in US Universities: Aligning Internal Dynamics with Today's Needs," in A. Amaral, G. A. Jones, and B. Karseth (eds.), *Governing Higher Education: National Perspectives on Institutional Governance*, Dordrecht: Kluwer Academic Publishers, 261–78.

ELSTON, M. A. (1991), "The Politics of Professional Power," in J. Gabe, M. Calnan, and M. Bury (eds.), *The Sociology of the Health Service*. London: Routledge.

EVETTS, J. (2003), "The Construction of Professionalism in New and Existing Occupational Contexts: Promoting and Facilitating Occupational Change," in *Health Professions, Gender, and Society*, Special Issue of *International Journal of Sociology and Social Policy* 23(4/5): 22–35.

FERLIE, E., ASHBURNER, L., FITZGERALD, L., and PETTIGREW, A. (1996), *The New Public Management in Action*, Oxford: Oxford University Press.

—— and FITZGERALD, L. (2001), "The Sustainability of the New Public Management in the UK," in K. McLaughlin, S. Osborne, and E. Ferlie (eds.), *New Public Management: Current Trends and Future Prospects*, London: Routledge, 341–53.

—— —— WOOD, M., and HAWKINS, C. (2004), "The (Non Spread) of Innovations: The Mediating Role of Professional Groups." *Academy of Management Journal* 48(1): 117–34.

FITZGERALD, L., and FERLIE, E. (2000), "Professionals—Back to the Future?", *Human Relations* 53(5): 713–39.

FREIDSON, E. (1970), *Professional Dominance: The Social Structure of Medical Care*, New York: Atherton Press.

—— (2001), *Professionalism: The Third Logic*, Cambridge: Polity.

FREUND, P., and McGUIRE, B. (1999), *Health, Illness and The Social Body*, Englewood Cliffs, NJ: Prentice Hall.

FRIEDMAN, M. (1962), *Capitalism and Freedom*, Chicago: University of Chicago Press.

GIDDENS, A. (1997), *The Third Way*, Cambridge: Polity Press.

HARRISON, S. (2002), "New Labour, Modernisation and the Medical Labour Process," *Journal of Social Policy* 31(1): 465–86.

—— (2003), "Health Policy," in M. Hawksworth and M. Kogan (eds.), *Routledge Encyclopaedia of Government and Politics*, London: Routledge.

—— and POLLITT, C. (1994), *Controlling Health Professionals*, Buckingham, Open University Press.

—— and SCHULTZ, R. (1989), "Clinical Autonomy in the UK and the USA - Contrasts and Convergence," in G. Freddi and J. W. Bjorkman (eds.), *Controlling Medical Professionals: The Comparative Politics of Health Governance*, London: Sage, 198–209.

HECLO, H. (1978), "Issue Networks and the Executive Establishment," in A. King (ed.), *The New American Political System*, Washington, DC: American Enterprise Institute of Public Policy Research, 87–124.

Hoff, T., and McCaffrey, D. P. (1996), "Adapting, Resisting and Negotiating—How Physicians Cope With Organisational and Economic Change," *Work and Occupations* 23(2): 165–89.

Hood, C. (1991), "A Public Management for All Seasons?", *Public Administration* 69: 3–19.

—— (1995), "The New Public Management in the 1980s: Variations on a Theme," *Accounting, Organisation and Society* 20(2/3): 93–110.

Jespersen, P. K., Nielsen, L. M., and Sognstrup, H. (2002), "'Professions, Institutional Dynamics and the New Public Management Field,'" *International Journal of Public Administration* 25(12): 1555–1574.

Johnson, T. (1995), "Governmentality and the Institutionalisation of Expertise," in T. Johnson, G. Larkin, and M. Saks (eds.), *Health Professions and the State in Europe*, London: Routledge.

Joss, R. and Kogan, M. (1995), *Advancing Quality: TQM in the NHS*, Buckingham, Open University Press.

Kaboolian, L. (2000), "Quality Comes to the Public Sector," in R. Cole and W. R. Scott (eds.), *The Quality Movement and Organisation Theory*, London: Sage.

Leicht, K. T., and Fennell, M. L. (2001), *Professional Work: A Sociological Approach*, Oxford: Basil Blackwell.

Lipsky, M. (1980), *Street Level Bureaucracy*, New York: Russell Sage.

Lynn, L. E. (1997), "The NPM as an International Phenomenon: A Skeptical Vire," *Advances in International Comparative Management*, JAI Press. Supplement 3: 105–12.

McDonnell, J., Ferlie, E., Thomas, P., McCulloch, J., and While, A. (2003), "Organisational Development Strategies Adopted By Primary Care Organisations to Facilitiate Quality Improvement: Some Empirical Evidence," London: Centre for Public Services Organisations, The Business School, Imperial College London.

McLaughlin, K., Osborne, S., and Ferlie, E. (eds.) (2001), *New Public Management: Current Trends and Future Prospects*, London: Routledge.

McNulty, T., and Ferlie, E. (2001), *Reengineering Health Care: The Complexities of Organisational Transfomation*, Oxford: Oxford University Press.

Mintzberg, H. (1979), *The Structuring of Organisations: A Synthesis of The Research*, Englewood Cliffs, NJ: Prentice Hall.

Montgomery, K. (1990), "A Prospective Look at the Specialty of Medical Management," *Work and Occupations* 17(2): 178–98.

Moran, M. (1999), *Governing the Health Care State: A Comparative Analysis of the United Kingdom, the United States and Germany*, Manchester, Manchester University Press.

Morgan, G., and Murgatroyd, S. (1997), *TQM in the Public Sector*, Buckingham, Open University Press.

Musselin, C., and Mignot-Gerard, S. (2002), "The Recent Evolution of French Universities," in A. Amaral, G. A. Jones, and B. Karseth (eds.), *Governing Higher Education: National Perspectives on Institutional Governance*, Dordrecht, Kluwer Academic Publishers, 63–86.

Newman, J. (2001), *Modernising Governance*, London: Sage.

New Zealand Ministry of Health (2001), "The Primary Health Care Strategy," Wellington: New Zealand, Ministry of Health.

Peters, T., and Waterman, R. H. (1982), *In Search of Excellence*, London: Harper and Row.

Pettigrew, A., Ferlie, E., and McKee, L. (1992), *Shaping Strategic Change*, London: Sage.

POLLITT, C. (1993), "The Politics of Medical Quality: Auditing Doctors in the UK and USA," *Health Services Management Research* 6(1): 24–34.

—— and BOUCKAERT, G. (2000), *Public Management Reform: A Comparative Analysis*, Oxford: Oxford University Press.

POWER, M. (1997), *The Audit Society*, Oxford: Oxford University Press.

PREMFORS, R. (1998), "Reshaping The Democratic State: Swedish Experiences in Comparative Perspective," *Public Administration* 76(1): 141–58.

PRICHARD, C. (2000), *Making Managers in Universities and Colleges*, Buckingham, Society for Research into Higher Education and Open University Press.

REED, M. (1996), "Expert Power and Control in Late Modernity," *Organisational Studies* 17(4): 573–98.

—— (2003), "Alternative Professional Futures: Professional Change in Advanced Capitalist Societies," Cardiff: Cardiff Business School.

—— and DEEM, R. (2002), "New Managerialism: The Manager Academic and Technologies of Management in Universities: Looking Forward to Virtuality," in K. Robins and F. Webster (eds.), *The Virtual University*, Oxford: Oxford University Press, 126–47.

RHODES, R. A. W. (1997), *Understanding Governance*, Buckingham, Open University Press.

ROGERS, E. (1995), *The Diffusion of Innovations*, New York: Free Press.

SAINT-MARTIN, D. (2000), *Building The Managerialist State: Consultants and the Politics of Public Sector Reform in Comparative Perspective*, Oxford: Oxford University Press.

SCARBOROUGH, H. (ed.) (1995), *The Management of Expertise*, London: Macmillan.

SEHESTED, K. (2002), "How New Public Management Reforms Challenge The Roles of Professionals," *International Journal of Public Administration* 25(12): 1513–37.

SENGE, P. (1990), *The Fifth Discipline*, London: Doubleday.

SPARROW, P., and HILTROP, J. M. (1994), *European Human Resource Management in Transition*, London: Prentice Hall.

STILLMAN, R. J. (2000), "Inside Public Bureaucracy," in id., *Public Administration: Concepts and Cases*, Boston, Houghton Muffin, 183–206.

THOMAS, R., and DAVIES, A. (2001), "The Costs to Academic Service: Managerialism, Accountability and Women Academics," *Critical Perspectives on Accounting* 12(6).

TICHY, N. M., FOMBRUN, C. J., and DEVANNA, M. A. (1982), "Strategic human resource management," *Sloan Management Review* 23(2): 47–61.

WHITTINGTON, R., McNULTY, T., and WHIPP, R. (1994), "Market Driven Change in Professional Services - Problems and Processes," *Journal of Management Studies* 31(6): 831–45.

WILSON, J. Q. (1989), *Bureaucracy*, New York: Basic Books.

CHAPTER 19

RETHINKING LEADERSHIP IN PUBLIC ORGANIZATIONS

JEAN-LOUIS DENIS

ANN LANGLEY

LINDA ROULEAU

By leadership, most people mean the capacity of someone to direct and energize the willingness of people in social units to take actions to achieve goals...Leadership in one sense can draw mainly on blunt power, but usually the term implies legitimate authority.

Rainey 1991: 157

The failure of revolutionary leaders to achieve their proclaimed claims—liberty, equality, prosperity—is also taken as evidence of the minor impact of leadership. Yet it is not that simple; after a revolution, its supporters often divide and fall out among themselves...and once they attain absolute power, many leaders are blinded by it and indulge in megalomaniac fantasies. Thus it is no surprise that revolutions often fail to achieve their pre-revolutionary aims. However, this does not mean leadership is insignificant, only that its impact is complex.

Goldstone 2001: 157

THE notion of leadership has a long history in the administrative sciences and in popular management writings. Leadership is at the heart of what seems to make things happen in groups, organizations, or societies. In this chapter we will first provide an overview of some of the dominant conceptions of leadership in the scholarly literature on organizational behavior and management. We will then examine previous treatments of this topic in the public administration literature before offering three alternative conceptions that we suggest merit further development. These conceptions are grounded in a series of novel developments in sociology and organization theory that we shall argue can enrich thinking about leadership in public organizations because they recognize the pluralistic nature of the organizational context within which the leaders of public sector organizations operate as well as the dynamic and collective nature of leadership processes in these settings.

19.1 CONCEPTIONS OF LEADERSHIP IN ORGANIZATION STUDIES

We will first briefly review the conceptions of leadership that represent landmarks in scholarly works on management and organizations, taking a historical approach. In the 1940s and 1950s, researchers focused mainly on the identification of traits that ensure exceptional leadership capabilities (Leatt and Porter 2003; Rainey 1991; Bryman 1996; Stogdill 1948). According to this approach, leadership is intrinsic to a given individual—it is not the result of socialization or learning. Although these studies identified a vast array of traits exhibited by exceptional leaders (House and Aditya 1997), it is difficult to establish a consistent set of findings across leaders from this body of work (Stodgill 1948; Bryman 1996; Rainey 1991). The "traits" approach reappeared in new guise in the 1980s in the form of "upper echelons" theory (Hambrick and Mason 1984), leading to a series of studies that attempted, with varying degrees of success, to relate the demographic characteristics of top management team members to variables such as consensus and performance. One of the interesting aspects of this revival to which we shall return is that its unit of analysis is the top management team (i.e., leadership group) rather than the individual leader. Another feature of interest is the emphasis on leadership as the capacity to relate an organization to its environment (so-called "strategic leadership") rather than the more internally oriented focus associated with earlier work (Boal and Hooijberg 2001).

The second stream in leadership studies emphasizes not the attributes of individuals but their behaviors in collective settings. These studies try to relate generic behaviors or leadership styles to levels of work-group performance or satisfaction (Leatt and Porter 2003; Bryman 1996; House and Aditya 1997). These studies dating mainly from the 1950s and 1960s used questionnaires to inquire about the perceptions that followers have of the behaviors of their leader. They suggested that leaders with "high levels of both consideration and initiating structure had the best leadership style" (Bryman 1996: 278). However, critics have questioned the rigor of the methods, the theoretical basis behind the research in this stream, and the lack of consideration for different contexts for the exercise of leadership (House and Aditya 1997). In order to better understand and explain variations in the impact of different leadership behaviors, some researchers there-fore tried to take into account the influence of various situational or contextual factors using a contingency approach (Fiedler 1967; Bryman 1996). For example, Fiedler (1967) empirically identified two leadership types: a relationship-oriented type and a task-oriented type. These two types were found to be potentially effective if they are adapted to some situational or contextual variables. The contingency approach led over time to the development of an increasingly complex set of leadership effectiveness models, such as path–goal theory, vertical–dyad linkage theory, cognitive resource theory, leader–member exchange theory (House and Aditya 1997). The burgeoning numbers of variables and contingent relationships incorporated into these models suggests that this approach to leadership research may have reached its limits.

According to Bryman (1996: 280) a new approach to leadership study emerged during the 1980s: "a conception of the leader as someone who defines organiza-tional reality through the articulation of a vision which is a reflection of how he or she defines an organization's mission and the values which will support it. Thus, the New Leadership approach is underpinned by a depiction of leaders as managers of meaning rather than in terms of an influence process." Such a conception of leadership recalls Weber's work on charisma. This conception is also reflected in the seminal work of Selznick (1957), *Leadership in Administration*, where leadership is described as a process of institutionalization of meaning "to infuse with value beyond the technical requirements of the task at hand" (1957: 17). This approach is well illustrated by the work of Burns (1978), Bass (1985), and Bennis and Nanus (1985) on transformational leadership. According to Bass (1996), transformational leadership is based on four main attributes: idealized influence or charisma, inspirational motivation, intellectual stimulation, and individualized consider-ation. In more concrete terms, a transformational leader is a model for others in the organization, provides a plausible and attractive vision of the organization's future, fosters a more reflexive approach to practices and current ways of organ-izing, and is able to pay attention to individuals' specificities. This type of leader-ship is opposed to transactional leadership based on contingent reward and management processes that pay attention to exceptions with a view to improving or adjusting the behaviors of subordinates. Again, according to Bass (1996), transformational leadership amplifies transactional leadership but does not replace it.

The work on transformational leadership devotes more attention to leadership and change than previous conceptions. However, the emphasis on "great leaders" typical of this approach has its own limits (Bryman, Gillingwater, and McGuiness 1996: 851). The transformational leadership perspective does not take into account the informal and complex dynamics that are at the basis of achieving influence and sustaining legitimacy. In his review of leadership theories, Bryman (1996) refers to emerging alternative conceptions of leadership. Amongst other ideas, he refers to the term "dispersed leadership" which may foster a more "processual" approach to leadership research (see also Pettigrew 1992). Such a perspective pays more attention to how leadership emerges in concrete social or organizational settings and to interactions between organizational context and leaders' capabilities. Leadership is considered less as an attribute of single individuals but more as a collective process, where individuals negotiate their position with respect to others in more unpredictable ways than a rational view of organizations would suggest. This more collective and processual perspective on leadership has driven some of our own research (e.g., Denis, Lamothe, and Langley 2001) and will form the basis for discussion later in this paper.

19.2 Conceptions of Leadership in Public Administration

The notion of leadership is generally associated with the image of a highly autonomous, powerful and influential manager who determines the destiny of his or her organization. This description is obviously too simplistic even for private sector organizations. It falls particularly wide of the mark in the public sector. As many authors have noted, public sector organizations are different (Rainey 1991; Nutt and Backoff 1992). Leaders in public organizations rarely have undisputed sway over people or unlimited autonomy to determine strategic orientations. In fact, these organizations can often be described as inherently "pluralistic" in nature (Denis, Langley, and Cazale 2001) as they are characterized by multiple objectives and diffuse power structures, often extending beyond organizational boundaries. Indeed, because of technological and environmental changes (Alter and Hage 1991) and the evolving nature of social problems (Bryson and Crosby 1992), public organizations are becoming more and more involved in complex networks. This situation of increased pluralism represents new problems for would-be leaders. As

Cohen and March (1986: 195) indicated in their discussion of the dilemmas underlying the university president's role: "When purpose is ambiguous, ordinary theories of decision making and intelligence become problematic. When power is ambiguous, ordinary theories of social order and control become problematic." In addition, public organizations in today's world operate through a complex and often contradictory web of rules, procedures, and safeguards. This proliferation of rules and routines, often applied in a context of scarce resources, both constrains and enables (Feldman 2000) the people who are charged with applying, developing, using, and maneuvering among them—and in particular the leaders of public organizations.

Given this complex organizational context of diffuse power, divergent objectives, and burgeoning rules, the central dilemma of leadership in public organizations can be summarized by the following question: Can leaders intervene proactively or not in public organizations? Two contrasting views of leadership can be identified from current works on public sector organizations: an "entrepreneurial" view (Borins 2002; Boyett 1997; Lewis 1980; Osborne and Gaebler 1992; Osborne and Plastrik 1997; Rainey 1991; Schmid 1992) and a "stewardship" view (Redford 1969; Davis, Schoorman and Donaldson 1997; Saltman and Ferroussier-Davis 2000; Terry 1995; Cooper and Lewis 1992; Fairholm 1991; Riccucci 1995 in Van Wart 2003; Ackroyd, Hughes, and Soothill 1989). These two views hold different assumptions about the legitimacy of administrative discretion in public administration (Van Wart 2003).

The "entrepreneurial view" focuses on the innovative behaviors of leaders in public sector organizations (Borins 2002). It emphasizes the increased attention by leaders/executives to the demands of the environment and to the preferences of various stakeholder groups (Boyett 1997). According to the "entrepreneurial model", the achievement of more effective public services depends on the creativity and dynamism of strong leaders who do not feel constrained by the weight of tradition or formal rules (Osborne and Plastrik 1997; Ferlie et al. 1996; Pollitt 1998; Friedberg 1993; Brunsson and Sahlin-Andersson 2000). To limit the risks of op-portunistic behavior among autonomous leaders, a very explicit and strong incen-tive scheme is proposed (Osborne and Plastrik 1997) analogous to that found in the private sector.

The "entrepreneurial view" of public leaders is close to the model of "trans-formational leadership" described by Bass (1996) and Burns (1978) and to the "decentralized–external" pattern of executive management described by Schmid (1992) in discussing current developments in the management of human services organizations. The feasibility of this model of public leadership is highly contingent on the nature of the relationship between political leadership and people in charge of public bureaucracies or agencies. In order to acquire sufficient trust from political authority, public leaders have to value and strive for increased account-ability regarding the performance of their own organizations (Borins 2002). The mechanisms by which such accountability can be secured are a major issue in the evolution of public management practice. Some analyses of the "New Public Management" in the UK suggest that new managerial dynamics may fosters a certain democratic deficit in the governance of public services (Ferlie et al. 1996). Managerial discretion may be achieved at the expense of the preservation of public service values (Terry 1995, 1998).

The contrasting "stewardship view" takes a much more conservative stance on the role of public leaders. Public leaders are seen as the guardians of public goods and values (Redford 1969; Saltman, and Ferroussier-Davis 2000; Terry 1995; Cooper and Lewis 1992). The legitimacy of public leaders comes from their conformity to the wishes of democratically elected politicians. The elected parliament or legislature decides on policies and the overarching goals of public systems and services. Public leaders execute policies and orientations decided at a superior level. Conservatism is seen as a positive value that guarantees the continuity of public institutions and services. Conformity to bureaucratic rules is not an impediment to the delivery of effective public services, but the means by which public leaders ensure democratic accountability for their decisions and actions. In this view, innovation is appreciated only as long as it contributes to the maintenance of traditional values of service that legitimate public sector production.

In theory then, the stewardship model focuses less on innovation and adaptation than the entrepreneurial model. However, with its focus on public service values, it does encourage a balance between accountability to political authority and sensitivity to citizen expectations (Mintzberg 1996). Public leaders are necessarily involved in bargaining and transactions with various stakeholders groups (Schmid 1992; Gortner, Mahler, and Nicholson 1986; Van Wart 2003). However, undoubtedly, pressures to renew public services represent a challenge for the stewardship perspective.

The issue of effective leadership in public organizations thus easily gives rise to a philosophical debate. On the one hand, proponents of the entrepreneurial model insist that public leaders not only can but *should* be encouraged to intervene dynamically to transform their organizations using conceptions of strategic leadership derived from the private sector (a transformational model). On the other hand, proponents of the stewardship model remain preoccupied with issues of democratic accountability (remaining closer to a transactional model). A realistic picture of leadership in public organizations probably falls somewhere between these two poles. In public organizations, values and normative pressures play a critical role in the assessment of the legitimacy of decisions and actions, and intense political pressures and autonomous professional groups place leaders in a situation of constant negotiations. The alignment of these different sets of pressures and obligations with needs to improve the delivery of public services implies that the practice of leadership will be particularly complex. The "entrepreneurial" and "stewardship" models of public leadership do not tell us much about the processes that may contribute to achieving integrity and service effectiveness in such contexts.

19.3 A Multifaceted Perspective on Leadership in Public Organizations

We argued above that traditional approaches to leadership have remained largely static. Although they incorporate a wide array of variables associated with leadership behaviors, contexts, and outcomes, they rarely situate these phenomena dynamically or focus on the specific actions of leaders. In addition, the emphasis has usually been on isolated individuals in formal leadership positions. Because of the complexity and ambiguity of power in the public organization context, we argue that research on leadership in public administration needs to focus on processes and skills that may or may not always reside in formally designated leaders. Greater emphasis needs to be placed on the complex emergent activity which is dispersed throughout the whole political and administrative context and its effects over time. To this end, a perspective founded upon three new theoretical frameworks from the social sciences will be proposed. The three foundational frameworks have been chosen because they appear particularly relevant to contexts characterized by diffuse power, divergent values and complex systems of rules and routines: they are Actor Network Theory (Callon 1986; Latour 1987), Conventionalist Theory (Boltanski and Thévenot 1991), and Social Practice Theories (Giddens 1984; de Certeau 1984). Together, these frameworks invite researchers and practitioners to pay greater attention to how strategic leadership is sustained through networks, how it is negotiated among people with competing values and how it is constituted through daily practices.

19.3.1 A Network Perspective

In the vast literature on leadership, networking is becoming more and more recognized as a key characteristic of leaders (Marion and Bacon 1999; Regine and Lewin 2000). Until now, it has been largely defined as a notable organizing skill (Hosking 1991). Network leadership refers to the individual ability to establish direct and indirect interpersonal communication patterns of influence (Brass and Krackhardt 1999; Osborn, Hunt, and Jauch 2002). However, networking is not exclusively an ability to constitute interpersonal links and make contacts with people. It is also a set of activities having structural power effects (Marion and Uhl-Bien 2001) which are critical to understanding the distinctiveness of leadership in public administration. In organizations where power is diffuse, success or failure of the strategic process depends, among other things, on the capacity of leaders to constitute and maintain strong and durable networks. The particular importance of networks in the public sector has been underlined in the classic work of Laumann and Knoke (1987) and other researchers (e.g., Kickert, Klijn, and Koppenjan 1997).

Actor Network Theory (ANT) can provide the theoretical anchoring needed to understand how a leader can become more successful in building networks. ANT was originally developed by the French sociologists of science Michel Callon (1986) and Bruno Latour (1987) as an approach to understanding the emergence and dominance of technological and scientific ideas. It is a combined methodological and conceptual tool which considers technologies and the networks of human and non-human actors (or "actants") linked to them as mutually constitutive. The technology and the actor-network are built up gradually and simultaneously as central actors (called "translators" in ANT's specialized language) succeed in mobilizing other participants and non-human entities as supporters of their definition of the technology while simultaneously redefining it in terms that can maintain this support. Technological artefacts become taken for granted ("irreversible") as the actor-networks surrounding them are solidified. Actors are attached to the network as the artefact in question is defined in such as way as to "translate" their needs and their identities, with different actors being quite likely to interpret the emerging "object" and their own role with respect to it in different ways.

The theory as developed by its originators involves an extensive and sometimes rather hermetic set of terms to describe its various elements. For example, theorists speak of "obligatory passage points" as the creation of nodes through which all actors must pass in order to obtain what they need. Theorists also talk of four sub-processes or "moments" of translation: "problematization" in which translators attempt to define an issue and offer an "obligatory passage point" drawing an initial set of actors together to solve it; "intéressement" in which translators determine and fix the interests of key actors so that they are willing to stay with an emerging project; "enrollment" in which representatives of main groups of actors are assigned "roles" and drawn together to build an alliance; "mobilization" in which the actor-network is extended beyond an initial group.

This set of conceptual and methodological tools can be relevant to examining leadership in public sector in three ways. First, the theory describes and explains how despite fragmentation of power and goals, it is possible to build networks of support around common definitions of an object so that they become taken for granted. Second, in this framework, a change, a "strategy" or any other managerial project can be taken as equivalent to a technological artefact or scientific discovery and thus the basis for the construction of a network. Third, ANT also offers a series of ideas about how such projects might be created, implemented and supported. Leadership, within this definition, becomes a "translation" process with all the potential elements of problematization, intéressement, enrollment, and mobilization leading potentially (but not deterministically) to the irreversibility of a well-defined project or initiative.

From the ANT perspective, the leader is a translator who will be recognized by his or her ability to pull together a powerful alliance with diverse internal and external actors. As a translator, an effective leader needs to "enroll" a network of actors so that an object such as a strategy or project may come to exist. An effective leader will recognize the need to think simultaneously in terms of both the project and the networks of support that they can engage (Demers and Charbonneau 2001). He or she will be drawn to consider the diverse meanings that various project definitions may have for others and how those meanings might be reconstructed either discursively or practically to render them more or less attractive. He or she will also be more sensitive to the dynamic and shifting nature of consensus as well as the importance of irreversible investments in solidifying both networks and strategic projects.

19.3.1.1 *An Example of Public Leadership in the Network Mode: Strategic Change in Health Care*

Our own research in the health care field reveals the relevance of an actor-network lens to the understanding of public sector leadership. An example comes from a study of strategic change in a large suburban hospital (Denis, Lamothe, and Langley 1996; Denis, Langley, and Cazale 2001). Interestingly, the focal leader or "translator" in this case was not the chief executive but a community health physician who moved through various administrative positions. Nevertheless, this individual was instrumental in co-constructing over time with several other key actors a network of support around a strategic change project that was to fundamentally transform the organization's mission: the acquisition of a university affiliation.

The story of this strategic leadership episode is a fascinating one because of the cyclical and recursive dynamics associated with the co-evolving nature of the change project, the actor-network supporting it, and the position of the focal leader over time. Initially, the leader was able to mobilize internal support for university affiliation because it was expressed (or "translated") in developmental terms. It was particularly popular with a group of younger medical specialists and was seen by almost everyone as an opportunity to enhance the organization's prestige. The positive image was leveraged into an enhanced role for the initiator of the project and the creation of a strong alliance among the hospital's administrative and medical leaders. This group pursued the university affiliation, extending the network of support beyond the organization's boundaries. The proposed teaching hospital mission happened to fit with the needs of a smaller university's Faculty of Medicine to broaden its base in order to ensure survival—thus, the Dean of the Faculty of Medicine joined the network. The support of the government (and a particular government minister) was obtained in exchange for an organizational commitment to budget reductions. However, through the process of attaching external actors to the network, the project itself was modified: it had to fit the needs of the Faculty of Medicine (implying new modes of physician remuneration) and it had to meet the Government's financial conditions. The project was implemented by the leadership coalition, but its consequences were such that internal enthusiasm was considerably reduced. In other words, the network of internal support became fragmented. This eventually led to the departure of the focal leader and other members who had supported the initiative. Yet the hospital has maintained its university affiliation. In the long term, this initiative has undoubtedly strengthened the position of this hospital and enhanced its value to the community. The focal leader moved on to become the Associate Dean of the (same) Faculty of Medicine and eventually Director of a Regional Health Board.

This vignette illustrates the relevance of actor-network theory to an understanding leadership in the public sector. ANT takes us beyond a static conception of leadership. Leadership initiatives that build and extend networks of support around strategic projects inevitably change the projects themselves. That is the nature of translation. The "intéressement" of new actors may result in the "désintéressement" of others. Conversely, the evolution of strategic projects and their associated networks can also lead to changes in the political positions of focal leaders, as clearly happened in this case. This dynamic and processual perspective surely provide a much richer understanding of leadership processes than more traditional variance models in which leadership behaviors are posited to lead to fixed outcomes frozen in time.

19.3.2 A Value Perspective

Leaders in public sector organizations must not only deal with dispersed power. They also face the challenge of generating sustainable decisions and strategies in a context of multiple or conflicting objectives. They often work with actors belonging to different institutional spheres and supporting divergent viewpoints, interests and values (Townley 2002; Ferlie et al. 1996). A successful leader will therefore have to incorporate a variety of logics or rationalities into organizational strategies which will be legitimate as long as the ordering of multiple logics is acceptable for the various stakeholders inside and outside the organization. Put another way, interacting with people supporting different logics of action necessitates finding a way to articulate appropriate and viable collaborative arrangements that reconcile competing values.

Over the last fifteen years, some researchers have given attention to the paradoxical nature of leadership. Amongst others, Quinn (1988) proposed the competing values framework in order to explain how leaders deal with divergent requirements coming from the competing demands of stakeholders. Quinn defines eight leadership roles on which strategic leaders can draw, depending on who they are interacting with. Here, leadership resides in the ability to exhibit contradictory and opposing behaviors. Following Quinn, other researchers have demonstrated that leaders who perform multiple leadership roles and are more likely to use them are more effective (Denison, Hooijberg, and Quinn 1995; Hooijberg 1996). Although this so-called "behavioral complexity perspective" may be useful for understanding leadership in the public sector, it does not explain the processes by which a leader juxtaposes or reconciles divergent frames.

A recent body of work by French sociologists (Boltanski and Thévenot 1991, 2000; Boltanski and Chiapello 1999), the conventionalist school, may be helpful in redirecting the behavioral complexity perspective to leadership as it pays attention to the processes by which a compromise among competing rationalities may become possible. In conventionalist terms, the world is structured around a limited set of fundamental logics or rationalities. More specifically, following an in-depth analysis of classic work in political philosophy, Boltanski and Thévenot (1991, 2000) identified six "worlds," "cities," or constitutive value frameworks that structure social arrangements: the "inspirational," "domestic," "opinion," "civic," "market," and "industrial" worlds (see also Amblard et al. 1996; Durand and Weil 1997).

The "inspirational" world refers to the legitimacy of the spontaneous vision, imagination and creativity of the artist. The "domestic" world is a world of tradition ruled by the principles of loyalty and the respect of authority based on assigned roles, status and duties among individuals. The world of "opinion" or reputation values the achievement of public recognition and prestige. The "civic" world values civic duties and the suppression of particular interests in the pursuit of the common good. The "market" world is driven by the interests of competing actors who take part in a commercial game in order to achieve their personal goals. Finally, the "industrial" world is driven by the search for efficiency and standardization.

Despite a limited set of recurrent value frameworks, collective settings or situations will rely on a mix of the different worlds according to conventionalist theory. To gain respect in a given world, individuals have to show the attributes that fit best and incarnate their superior principle. Because individuals in an organization will not always identify with similar worlds and because a single individual may identify with multiple worlds, the invention and negotiation of conventions becomes critical to ensure coordination and cooperation. A convention is an artefact or an object that crystallizes the compromise between various logics in a specific context. For example, a convention might be a quality improvement policy in a public service organization where the rules of the market and the industrial worlds act in synergy.

A leader, in conventionalist terms, is someone who will work in order to stimulate a set of processes that generate accommodation or compromise between values that compete for legitimacy. From a conventionalist perspective, an organizational strategy could be defined as a convention and by extension, the processes used to formulate strategies may be an occasion to affirm or reaffirm certain core values. Thus, an effective leader will demonstrate his or her virtuosity in competencies or behaviors that are viewed as appropriate with respect to different worlds. A successful leader must be able to make an appropriate reading of the institutional order because the analysis of prevalent values is critical to reduce the potential for open conflict. Specific organizational devices (committees, internal contracts, incentive schemes, performance indicators) may help him or her to achieve compromise because they represent institutional mechanisms for mediating between the different values while legitimizing his or her own status.

From this perspective, a successful leader will be someone who is able to navigate with credibility between different worlds and also someone who is able to represent the incarnation of the worlds with which organizational members identify. When the competing values of different worlds are intense, one approach to leadership may involve co-leaders (e.g., the administrative and artistic directors of a museum; or the administrative and clinical leaders of a health care organization) who individually represent different worlds but can bridge their differences at the personal level within the "domestic" world (Chiapello 1998).

The strategic leader, for the conventionalist, can also be conceived of as a "critic." The role of the "critic" is central to the argument of Boltanski and Chiapello (1999) in their analysis of contemporary capitalism. In fact, it is only by explicitly contesting dominant or emergent logics that organization members can secure an influential role in the strategy formation process. In conventionalist term, the leader is someone who through his or her personal association with highly valued worlds is able to open up and renegotiate established conventions leading to enhanced organizational and personal legitimacy. Without active critics, organizational change will take shape according to previous arrangements among the different worlds. Critical thinking questions the normative assumptions behind current strategies or developments (which worlds are favoured or rejected) and may help in fostering change.

19.3.2.1 An Example of Public Leadership in the Conventionalist Mode: The National Film Board

This example draws on work by Mintzberg and McHugh (1985) on strategy formation at the National Film Board of Canada (NFB), as well as other public sources. The NFB is a cultural agency that produces and distributes films reflecting the Canadian identity and reality. It is financed by the Federal Government of Canada. In this type of organization, a continuous tension exists between the need to preserve the autonomy of filmmakers (the "inspirational" world) and the need to set up an efficient organization ("the industrial world") to respond to external demands (government bureaucracy, etc.). John Grierson, the founding leader of the NFB incarnated various logics: the inspirational world based on strong identification with and expertise in the British tradition of documentary film, as well as the civic world exemplified by a strong sense of duty and patriotism. By holding these two logics (inspirational, civic) in constructive synthesis, the founding leader was able to secure the growth and legitimacy of the NFB during the Second World War while maintaining the commitment of its film-makers.

However, the end of the war saw a decline of civic values, or at least of patriotism, as a basis for the legitimacy of the NFB. The role of the NFB was contested by private film companies (market logic). The autonomy of the film-makers (the inspirational world) was also criticized for its relationship with certain subversive political forces. The founding leader left and was replaced by an internal member of the NFB and then in 1949 by Arthur Irwin, an external person without film or government experience. In order to restore a balance between the auton-omy of the inspirational world, the demand to rationalize administratively and to maintain the role of NFB in the promotion of civic values, Irwin negotiated an agreement with government officials: a "new film act" (in fact, a "convention") that ensured growth. Design and conventions were used to operationalize a viable compromise between the inspirational and the industrial worlds.

The following periods were marked by continuous evolution stimulated by the leadership of film-makers in the service of creativity and as well as by the need of the NFB to respond to pressures for rationalization while at the same time paying attention to its role as a promoter of civic values. Throughout its history, leaders at the NFB have played various roles in securing or reaffirming a viable compromise between potentially conflicting logics. In a striking example, one leader of the mid-1980s produced a document entitled "Efficacité créatrice" ("Creative Efficiency") that became the basis for yet another evolving compromise between inspirational and industrial logics at a time that the NFB's survival was again threatened. Such leaders acted as "critics," periodically shaking up the organization in order to protect the work of film-makers or to stimulate it. The capacity to align internal production with external expectations is an important component of leading at the confluence of conflicting values.

Tensions such as those encountered at the NFB between the inspirational world and the pursuit of rationalization (industrial world) permeate public organizations in the field of arts, education and research. Others sets of tensions are also common in the public sector. For example, the current appeal of market ideology and mechanisms for renewing public management clashes with pre-existing in-spirational and civic orders. Such situations raise dilemmas for the practice of leadership. This is explicitly recognized in some training programs for public leaders. For example, the so-called "duality program" of the Leadership Center in the UK National Health Service (NHS) is structured around "couples" or pairs of administrative and clinical leaders from different organizations in order to find ways to bridge conflicting worlds.

19.3.3 A Practice Perspective

Public organizations are not only permeated by diffuse power and divergent objectives. They also have to deal with a complex system of rules and procedures which require from people who work within them—managers and professionals—a considerable amount of both technical and informal knowledge. Change in these organizations often takes place through the way in which people exert their discretionary power as they are apply rules and routines on a daily basis (Feldman 2000). Moreover, public administration, particularly in the large public service sectors of education, health care and social services, the quality of services provided is largely dependent on people and their explicit and tacit knowledge. It is not unusual to observe a mismatch in these organizations between decisions made among top managers and the realities of operating professionals or of the "street-level bureaucracy" (Coble-Vinzant and Crothers 1998). A successful leader in this type of organization will need to bridge this gap. In order to do so, would-be leaders need to know how to navigate the contradictions between complex rule systems, how to manoeuvre among multiple foci of decision making, and how to ensure that available expertise is brought to bear on decisions within structures that are respectful of public and professional accountability norms and procedures. Knowledge, and *a fortiori* tacit knowledge gained through experience is crucial. Leaders need to be skilled "practitioners" within the complex web of public sector decision making.

Recently, leadership theory and research have begun to promote ideas about constant experimentation, learning, plausible judgment, active listening, etc. (Boal and Hooijberg 2001). More specifically, two approaches to strategic leadership have been developing some insights into the question of knowledge. These are the so-called cognitive complexity (Jaques 1989) and social intelligence approaches (Zaccaro et al. 1991). Cognitive complexity refers to the mental processes of retrieving and analyzing information. Authors claim that cognitively complex individuals search for more information and interpret it in a more complex way (for reviews, see Stish 1997; Streufert 1997). In addition to cognitive style, some authors suggest that leadership requires interpersonal skills such as empathy, motivation, and communication. According to Boal and Hooijberg (2001), social skills refer to the ability to notice and make distinctions among individuals, to monitor one's own and others' feelings, to discriminate, and to use appropriate information about the social environment gained through experience. Sternberg et al. (1995) found that effective leaders are able to rapidly assimilate tacit (non-articulated) information and use emotion. While offering a new perspective this work, like the leadership literature discussed earlier, remains limited because it tends to retain a persistent variance model perspective. The work is once more centered on the measurability of individual capacities instead of trying to qualitatively capture how strategic leaders put their experience into action in everyday settings.

A social practice perspective can be useful to highlight the question of knowledge in leadership and overcome these difficulties. In a break with positivist American sociology, some social scientists such as Bourdieu, Foucault, Giddens, de Certeau, Vygotski, etc., have in the last few decades manifested a strong interest in the practical accomplishments of skilled social actors in the production of social life. They adopted a position that recognizes the competencies of the individual and the centrality of knowledge to the production and reproduction of the social world. Albeit to different degrees, these authors claim that there is a practical rationality rooted in the concrete detail of daily life. As Gherardi (2001) argued, practice connects knowing with doing. This perspective therefore promotes a focus on the nature of everyday life and the central role it plays in the social world (de Certeau 1984). The everyday is where we enter into a transformative praxis with the outside world, acquire and develop communicative competence, and actualize our normative conceptions.

Drawing on the social practice perspective impacts the way in which leadership is defined. Leadership in practice means looking at how leadership is constituted, how it is accomplished and how it occurs over time in organizations (Whittington 2003). From a social practice perspective, leadership is not something one does by oneself. Leadership's effects and impacts emerge over time from actions and interactions. A practice perspective on strategic leadership implies that leadership is socially constructed through action and daily conversations (Hosking 1991). Such a perspective emphasizes the routinized character of organizational life and tries to understand how strategic leadership emerges from routines and discourses. For example, in one of the first applications of this perspective, Knights and Willmott (1992) proposed conceptualizing leadership processes by looking at the practices of senior managers. They studied a series of verbal exchanges among senior managers in a financial company in Britain in order to show how the dominant definition of the situation is discursively negotiated.

Effective leaders of the social practice perspective are skilled individuals exercising their leadership by mobilizing knowledge in action and by being competent social performers. Mobilizing knowledge successfully implies being able to catch the larger picture emanating from local events. Having a broader vision of how things are working, effective leaders in public organizations try to pattern the attention of their colleagues, subordinates and even their superiors through subtle dialogues and meaningful micro-acts concerning the changes in the environment, the definition of success, the interpretations of political changes and so on (Johnson 2000). They also have the ability to routinely use appropriate tools and words aiming to co-construct meaningful explanations of change and crisis. The practice literature suggests that as competent social performers, effective leaders are people who possess a great understanding of the social characteristics of internal and external actors with whom they are interacting. They deploy professional expertise, political abilities, historical knowledge, emotions, and so forth in an appropriate way and at the right time to influence strategy (Samra-Fredericks 2003). More specifically, they are able to adapt the way they present and convey their objectives depending on their interlocutors and to perform appropriate emotions in order to attract the attention of a recalcitrant employee or an intransigent stakeholder.

In sum, leadership, from a social practice perspective, is produced and reproduced in daily routines and micro-conservations (Westley 1990). Leadership is, in some ways a mundane activity requiring experience, timing, social awareness and relational capability. By suggesting the need to track the activities, knowledge, and skills that are more or less explicit to leadership, such a perspective may produce knowledge that is more adapted to the needs of leaders in public organizations.

19.3.3.1 *Examples of Leadership in the Practice Mode: Universities, Research Agencies, and Museums*

To illustrate how leadership is fabricated through situated and local practices, we will draw on the insights from three papers that present case studies of public organizations (Leitch and Davenport 2002; Jarzabkowski 2003; Oakes, Townley, and Cooper 1998). These papers demonstrate the importance of looking at the multiple micro-processes by which leaders use their tacit knowledge and act routinely.

Leitch and Davenport (2002) studied stakeholder relationship management during a significant change in a major public sector research funding agency in New Zealand. The agency had to move from a role of resource allocation to a support role for research development and integration. During the change, the top management team deployed strategic ambiguity through metaphors to manage the competing demands of various internal and external stakeholders. For example, the agency's leader used the metaphor of "investment in innovation" in order to enter into a dialogue with stakeholders and to stimulate creative engagement from them. But he omitted to consider the contradictory effects of this metaphor. Some stakeholders who had little interest in the new orientation interpreted this metaphor as a symbol of the agency's desire to remain economically oriented and associated the process's ambiguity with managerial incompetence on the part of the research agency's leader. This example illustrates how in a highly political environment such as the public sector, the successful use of strategic ambiguity depends on the leaders' capacity to tacitly decode or reflexively map out the multiple interpretations carried by metaphors whether used officially or not.

In a very different way, Jarzabkowski (2003) studied the role of the top management team (TMT) in three UK universities undergoing strategic change for coping with decreased public funding. Her longitudinal study pays attention to the systemic links between leaders, strategy activities and the collective structures of the universities throughout strategic change. As surprising as it could first appear, one of the findings was that leadership was not the main influence on strategic change in the university. Even though all three cases acquired a new leader during the change, none of them was the catalyst for the changes. Change arose out of evolving interpretations and systemic needs. Rather, the TMT became mediators of the contradictions between internal actors and collectives structures. Through their daily strategic practices (e.g., planning, income generation, etc.) the TMT distributed shared interpretations predisposing continuity or stimulating change. In all cases, leaders drew on past interpretations (e.g., the academic strength of the university is based on research excellence) and activities in order to promote the change (generate more funds). This paper provides an illustration of how leaders support change through existing routines. Part of the leadership process depends on the leaders' ability to adjust, transform and modify existing organizational activities in order to encourage stakeholders to endorse their views.

Given the complexity of rules and procedures in the public sector, leadership in practice also depends on the capacity of leaders to design, diffuse and use appropriate managerial tools for supporting their actions. Oakes, Townley, and Cooper's (1998) work constitutes a fascinating example of how management tools subjectively operate to support a governmental reengineering effort in provincial museum and heritage sites in Alberta (Canada). Although local managers were reluctant to foster the "new public management" ideology, business plans acted as a pedagogical practice by enhancing subtle changes in managerial identity. As managerial tools, business plans induce a form of "learning by doing" and their daily use by the agency's directors pervasively transform who they are as managers in favour of the new orientation. The capacity to promote managerial tools and use their micro-effects to subjectively control the direction of change is intrinsic to the day-to-day practice of leadership.

19.4 IMPLICATIONS FOR PRACTITIONERS AND RESEARCHERS

The three perspectives presented above have drawn attention to the consequences for leadership of some key features of the public sector organizational context that we identified at the beginning of the previous section: diffuse power (associated with the network perspective), divergent objectives (associated with the value perspective) and complex systems of rules (associated with the practice perspective). This multifaceted framework focuses the attention of both practitioners and researchers on the essential features of leadership in public organizations.

For practitioners, the framework suggests a need to look beyond leaders as individuals to examine the processes associated with acquiring and using power, legitimacy and knowledge. For example, drawing on the network perspective, a public leader must see him or herself as embedded in an ongoing process shared with others (an active node in a multifaceted constantly shifting network), not as an external authority able to impose his or her will. Attention must therefore be given to understanding what actors inside and outside the organization want and can support, and designing and redesigning managerial projects that can slide through windows of opportunity where interests converge long enough to ensure irreversibility (see Kingdon 1984).

Drawing on the value perspective, leaders need to consider what fundamental societal value systems are in play, how they are reconciled, and how to modify both the organization and themselves as individuals to best represent values at the heart of the organization's identity. To deal with competing logics, the leader must also attempt to bridge alternate identities and value systems that are nevertheless inherent to the organization's existence and survival.

Finally, the social practice perspective brings the leadership process down to earth by showing how patterns of decision making are embedded in positioned practices and routines. Some leaders are more skillful than others in using routines, interactions and other the tools available to them to move events in directions they seek to promote. These skills can be acquired both individually and organizationally through active participation in the routines of strategic decision making. Achieving genuine impact in complex public sector contexts requires skillful effort over a long time: this is a call for patience, persistence and subtlety. The most successful leaders will be those who are willing to commit both to their organizations and to desired managerial and strategic developments over the longer term.

For researchers, taking into account these three perspectives will direct leadership studies towards a more dynamic, processual, and contextual vision of leadership that adds richness and depth to the static variable based conceptions that have dominated in the past. However, this will require recourse to more qualitative, longitudinal research methods that follow leaders and leadership teams over time to reveal cycles of leadership actions and their consequences.

Even so, this is not a methodology that promotes easy prediction. There are no simple recipes for leadership effectiveness through having appropriate traits, fitting one's style to the context, or "being charismatic" although all these undoubtedly play a role. Moreover, these perspectives do not plump down on one side or other of the entrepreneurship–stewardship debate but could be compatible with both of them depending on whether leaders decide to destabilize old networks, build new ones and act as critics or creators of new routines (the entrepreneurial perspective) or whether they promote the stability of existing networks, defend established conventions that reconcile competing values and develop their leadership skills through the rehearsal and usage of existing routines (the stewardship perspective). Whichever path they take, they will need to build on and deal with the three underlying forces that we have suggested embody leadership in public organizations: power acquired by collectively operating within networks, legitimacy acquired by incarnating and bridging the values that lie at the heart of organizational identity, and knowledge that is embedded in and acquired through participation in organizational routines and practices.

REFERENCES

ACKROYD, S., HUGUES, J. A., and SOOTHILL, K. (1989), "Public Sector Services and Their Management," *The Journal of Management Studies* 26(6): 603–20.

ALTER, C., and HAGE, J. (1991), *Organizations Working Together*, Newbury Park: Sage.

AMBLARD, H., BERNOUX, P., HERREROS, G., and LIVIAN, Y.-F. (1996), *Les nouvelles approches sociologiques des organisations*, Paris: Seuil.

BASS, B. M. (1985), *Leadership and Performance beyond Expectations*, New York: Free Press.

—— (1996), "Is There Universality in the Full Range Model of Leadership?" *International Journal of Public Administration* 19(6): 731–61.

BENNIS, W., and NANUS, B. (1985), *Leaders: Strategies for Taking Charge*, New York: Harper & Row.

BOAL, K. B., and HOOIJBERG, R. (2001), "Strategic Leadership: Moving On," *Leadership Quarterly* 11: 515–49.

BOLTANSKI, L., and CHIAPELLO, E. (1999), *Le nouvel esprit du capitalisme*, Paris: Éditions Gallimard.

—— and THÉVENOT, L. (1991), *De la justification: Les économies de la grandeur*, Paris : Éditions Gallimard.

—— —— (2000), "The Reality of Moral Expectations: A Sociology of Situated Judgement," *Philosophical Explorations* 3(3): 208–31.

BORINS, S. (2002), "Leadership and Innovation in the Public Sector," *Leadership and Organization Development Journal* 23(8): 467–76.

BOYETT, I. (1997), "The Public Sector Entrepreneur: A Definition," *International Journal of Entrepreneurial Behaviour & Research* 3(2): 77–92.

BRASS, D. J., and KRACKHARDT, D. (1999), "The Social Capital of 21st Century Leaders," In Hunt, Dodge, and Wong (eds.), *Out-of-the-box Leadership*, Greenwich, CT: Jai Press, 179–94.

BRYMAN, A. (1996), "Leadership in Organizations," in S. R. Clegg, C. Hardy, and W. R. Nord (eds.), *Handbook of Organization Studies*, Thousand Oaks, CA: Sage: 276–292.

—— GILLINGWATER, D., and McGUINNESS, I. (1996), "Leadership and Organizational Transformation," *International Journal of Public Administration* 19(6): 849–72.

BRYSON, J. M., and CROSBY, B. C. (1992), *Leadership for the Common Goods*, San Francisco: Jossey-Bass.

BRUNSSON, N., and SAHLIN-ANDERSSON, K. (2000), "Constructing Organizations: The Example of Public Sector Reform," *Organization Studies* 21(4): 721–46.

BURNS, J. M., (1978), *Leadership*, New York: Harper & Row.

CALLON, M. (1986), "Some Elements of a Sociology of Translation: Domestication of the Scallops and Fisherman in St Brieuc Bay," in J. Law (ed.), *Power, Action and Belief: A New Sociology of Knowledge*, London: Routledge.

CHIAPELLO. E. (1998), *Artistes versus managers: le management culturel face à la critique artiste*, Paris : Métaillé.

COBLE-VINZANT, J., and CROTHERS, L. (1998), *Street-level Leadership: Discretion and Legitimacy in Front-Line Public Service*, Washington, DC: Georgetown University Press.

COHEN, M. D., and MARCH, J. G. (1986), *Leadership and Ambiguity*, Boston: Harvard University School Press.

COOPER, T., and LEWIS, J. M. (1992), *Exemplary Public Administrators: Character and Leadership, in Government*, San Francisco: Jossey-Bass.

DAVIS, J. H., SCHOORMAN, F. D., and DONALDSON, L. (1997), "Toward a Stewardship Theory of Management," *Academy of Management Review* 22(1): 20–47.

DE CERTEAU, M. (1984), *The Practice of Every Day Life*, Berkeley: The University of California Press.

DEMERS, C., and CHARBONNEAU, M. (2001), "La stratégie discursive d'Hydro-Québec dans la controverse écologique de Grande-Baleine," *Actes électroniques de la 10ième conférence de l'Association internationale de management stratégique*, Québec, 25 pp.

DENIS, J.-L., LAMOTHE, L., and LANGLEY, A. (2001), "The Dynamics of Collective Leadership and Strategic Change in Pluralistic Organizations," *Academy of Management Journal* 44(4): 809–37.

—— —— and CAZALE, L. (1996), "Leadership and Strategic Change under Ambiguity," *Organization Studies* 17(4): 673–99.

DENISON, D. R., HOOIJBERG, R., and QUINN, R. E. (1995), "Paradox and Performance: A Theory of Behavioural Complexity in Leadership," *Organization Science* 6(5): 524–41.

DURAND, J.-P., and WEIL, R. (1997), *Sociologie contemporaine*, Paris: Vigot.

FAIRHOLM, G. (1991), *Values Leadership: Toward a New Philosophy of Leadership*. New York: Praeger.

FELDMAN, M. S. (2000), "Organizational Routines as a Source of Continuous Change", *Organization Science*, 11: 611–629.

FERLIE, E., ASHBURNER, L., FITZGERALD, L., PETTIGREW, A. (1996), *The New Public Management in Action*. Oxford: Oxford University Press.

FIEDLER, F. E. (1967), *A Theory of Leadership Effectiveness*. New York: McGraw-Hill.

FRIEDBERG, E. (1993), *Le pouvoir et la règle*. Paris : Éditions Le Seuil.

GHERARDI, S. (2001), «From Organizational Learning to Practice-Based Knowing». *Human Relations*, 54(1): 131–9.

GIDDENS, A. (1984), *The Constitution of Society*, London: Macmillan.

GOLDSTONE, J. A. (2001), "Toward a Fourth Generation of Revolutionary Theory," *Annual Review of Political Science* 4: 139–87.

GORTNER, H. F., MAHLER, J., and NICHOLSON, J. B. (1986), *Organization Theory: A Public Perspective*, New York: Brooks/Cole.

HAMBRICK, D. C., and MASON, P. A. (1984), "Upper Echelons: The Organization as a Reflection of its Top Managers," *Academy of Management Review* 9: 193–206.

HOOIJBERG, R. (1996), "A Multidirectional Approach Toward Leadership: An Extension of the Concept of Behavioural Complexity," *Human Relations*, 49(7): 917–46.

HOSKING, D. M. (1991), "Chief Executives, Organizing Processes and Skills," *European Journal of Applied Psychology* 41: 95–103.

HOUSE, R. J., and ADITYA, R. (1997), "The Social Scientific Study of Leadership: Quo Vadis?", *Journal of Management* 23: 409–74.

JAQUES, E. (1989), *Requisite Organization*, Arlington, VA: Cason Hall.

JARZABKOWSKI, P. (2003), "Strategic Practices: An Activity Theory Perspective on Continuity and Change," *Journal of Management Studies* 40(1): 23–56.

JOHNSON, G. (2000), "Strategy through a Cultural Lens : Learning Form Manager's Experience," *Management Learning* 31(4): 403–26.

KICKERT, W. J. M., KLIJN, E.-H., and KOPPENJAN, J. F. M. (1997), *Managing Complex Networks*, Thousand Oaks, CA: Sage.

KINGDON, J. (1984), *Agendas, Alternatives and Public Policies*, Boston: Little-Brown.

KNIGHTS, D., and WILLMOTT, H. (1992), "Conceptualizing Leadership Processes: A Study of Senior Managers in a Financial Services Company," *Journal of Management Studies* 29: 761–82.

LATOUR, B. (1987), *Science in Action*, Milton Keynes: Open University Press.

LAUMANN, E. O., and KNOKE, D. (1987), *The Organizational State: Social Choice in National Policy Domains*, Madison: University of Wisconsin Press.

LEATT, P., and PORTER, J. (2003), "Where Are the Health Care Leaders? The Need for Investment in Leadership Development," *Health Papers* 4(1): 14–31.

LEITCH, S., and DAVENPORT, S. (2002), "Strategic Ambiguity in Communicating Sector Public Change," *Journal of Communication Management* 7(2): 129–40.

LEWIS, E. B. (1980), *Public Entrepreneurship*, Bloomington: Indiana University Press.

MARION, R., and BACON, J. (1999), "Organizational Extinction and Complex Systems," *Emergence* 1(4): 71–96.

—— and UHL-BIEN, M. (2001), "Leadership in Complex Organizations," *Leadership Quarterly* 12: 389–418.

MINTZBERG, H. (1996), "Managing Government, Governing Management," *Harvard Business Review*, May–June 1996.

—— and McHUGH, A. (1985), "Strategy Formation in an Adhocracy," *Administrative Science Quarterly* 24(4): 580–9.

NUTT, P. C., and BACKOFF, R. W. (1992), *Strategic Management of Public and Third Sector Organizations*, San Francisco: Jossey-Bass.

OAKES, L. S., TOWNLEY, B., and COOPER, D. J. (1998), "Business Planning as Pedagogy: Language and Control in a changing institutional field," *Administrative Science Quarterly* 43(2): 257–92.

OSBORN, R. N., HUNT, J. G., and JAUCH, L. R. (2002), "Toward a Contextual Theory of Leadership," *Leadership Quarterly* 13: 797–837.

OSBORNE, D., and GAEBLER, T. (1992), *Reinventing Government*, Reading, MA: Addison-Wesley.

—— and PLASTRIK, P. (1997), *Banishing Bureaucracy*, Reading, MA: Addison-Wesley.

PETTIGREW, A. M. (1992), "On Studying Managerial Elites," *Strategic Management Journal* 1: 163–82.

POLLITT, C. (1998), "Managerialism Revisited," in B. G. Peters and D. J. Savoie (eds.), *Taking Stock: Assessing Public Sector Reforms*, Montreal and Kingston: McGill-Queen's University Press, 45–77.

QUINN, R. E. (1988), *Beyond Rational Management: Mastering the Paradoxes and Competing Demands of High Performance*, San Francisco: Jossey-Bass.

RAINEY, H. G. (1991), *Understanding and Managing Public Organizations*, San Francisco: Jossey-Bass.

REDFORD, E. (1969), *Democracy in the Administrative State*, New York: Oxford University Press.

REGINE, B., and LEWIN, R. (2000), "Leading at the Edge: How Leaders Influence Complex Systems," *Emergence* 2(2): 5–23.

RICCUCCI, N. M. (1995), *Unsung Heroes : Federal Execucrats Making a Difference*, Washington, DC: Georgetown University Press.

SALTMAN, R. B., and FERROUSSIER-DAVIS, O. (2000), "The Concept of Stewardship in Health Policy," *Bulletin of the World Health Organization* 78(6): 732–9.

SAMRA-FREDERICKS, D. (2003), "Strategizing as Lived Experience and Strategists'Everyday Efforts to Shape Strategic Direction," *Journal of Management Studies* 40(1): 141–74.

SCHMID, H. (1992), "Executive Leadership in Human Services Organizations," in Y. Hasenfeld (ed.), *Human Services as Complex Organizations*, Newbury Park: Sage, 98–117.

SELZNICK, P. (1957), *Leadership in Administration*, Berkeley: University of California Press.

STERNBERG, R. J., WAGNER, R. K., WILLIAMS, W., and HORVATH, J. (1995), "Testing Common Sense," *American Psychologist* 50(11): 912–27.

STISH, U. (1997), "Behavioral Complexity: A Review," *Journal of Applied Social Psychology* 27(3): 2047–67.

STOGDILL, R. M. (1948), "Personal Factors Associated with Leadership: A Survey of the Literature," *Journal of Psychology* 25: 35–71.

STREUFERT, S. (1997), "Complexity: An Integration of Theories," *Journal of Applied Social Psychology* 27(3): 2068–95.

TERRY, L. D. (1995), *Leadership of Public Bureaucracies: The Administrator as Conservator*, Thousand Oaks, CA: Sage.

—— (1998), "Administrative Leadership, Neo-managerialism and the Public Management Movement," *Public Administration Review* 58(3): 194–200.

TOWNLEY, B. (2002), "The Role of Competing Rationalities in Institutional Change," *Academy of Management Journal* 45(1): 163–79.

VAN WART, M., (2003), "Public-Sector Leadership Theory: An Assessment," *Public Administration Review* 63(2): 214–28.

WESTLEY, F. (1990), "Middle Managers and Strategy: Micro-dynamics of Inclusion," *Strategic Management Journal* 11: 337–51.

WHITTINGTON, R. (2003), "The Work of Strategizing and Organizing: for a Practice Perspective," *Strategic Organization* 1(1):119–27.

ZACCARO, S. J., GILBERT, J. A., THOR, K. K., and MUMFORD, M. D. (1991), "Leadership and social intelligence: linking social perceptiveness to behavioural flexibility," *Leadership Quarterly* 2: 317–47.

CHAPTER 20

ORGANIZATIONAL CULTURES IN THE PUBLIC SERVICES

ROBERT DINGWALL
TIM STRANGLEMAN

HIGH-POWERED TREASURY THINKER: "The public service ethic" we hear so much about, actually it doesn't exist. Never did. I always compare it to a middle-aged man who believes he's attractive to younger women. It's a delusion.

David Hare, *The Permanent Way*

OUR epigraph, from a docu-drama about the condition of the UK rail industry a decade after its privatization, sums up the conventional wisdom of contemporary neo-liberal policy elites. Just as Margaret Thatcher famously proclaimed that there was no such thing as society, so there is no distinction between the cultures of the public and private sectors. This chapter examines that belief and considers how an important social scientific concept became a management fad. We begin with the idea of culture and its history in organizational studies. We then look at contemporary debates about the way that an understanding of culture may contribute to successful management and conclude by considering whether there are differences between public and private sectors that are relevant to this task.

We are grateful for the advice and comments of Graeme Currie.

20.1 Cultural Analysis

As Raymond Williams (1976: 87) noted, "Culture is one of the two or three most complicated words in the English language," because of its use to describe "important concepts in several distinct intellectual disciplines and in several distinct and incompatible systems of thought." From the perspective of organizational analysts, the most significant are the usages within anthropology and literary scholarship.

Anthropologists have traditionally seen the study of culture as a defining feature of their discipline: "Social anthropologists, in studying the institutionalised social relationships that are their primary concern, have found it essential to take account of the ideas and values which are associated with them, that is, of their cultural content. No account of a social relationship in human terms can be complete unless it includes reference to what it means to the people who have it" (Beattie 1966: 13). Culture does not have a material existence, although physical objects may be treated as cultural artefacts, by virtue of the meanings that people assign to them.

[Culture] does not consist of things, people, behaviour or emotions. It is the forms of things that people have in mind, their models for perceiving, relating, and otherwise interpreting them. As such, the things people say and do, their social arrangements and events, are products or by-products of their culture as they apply it to the task of perceiving and dealing with their circumstances. To one who knows their culture, these things or events are also signs signifying the cultural forms or models of which they are material representations. (Goodenough 1957: 167)

For anthropologists, and many sociologists, an organization is the outward expression of its culture, its members' sense of "what goes with what," that certain events, objects and relationships can be brought under a common rubric, which provides for them to mean something distinctive, identifying them as organization-relevant rather than irrelevant. At the same time, the ability to make a contextually appropriate connection between "events, objects and relationships" and the "common rubric" of culture provides a basis for organization members and outsiders to evaluate both claims to membership and to competence as a member (Bittner 1965; Strong and Dingwall 1985).

More recently, there has been a fashion for using literary modes of thinking about culture (Geertz 1973; Clifford and Marcus 1986). Just as texts are no longer assumed to have an authoritative, inherent meaning that awaits discovery by readers, so culture is not given to observers. Readers find meaning in texts according to their values and starting positions: anthropologists find cultures by their acts of observation and recording. "Culture" is the product of anthropological writing, which represents, organizes, and "makes sense" of observed behavior rather than uncovering the state of mind of the people being studied. Where "realist" writers in the tradition outlined above aim to describe behavior and infer culture from specific acts and apparent connections, "constructivist" writers are more concerned to evoke the events they have witnessed or experienced, often adopting literary genres like drama, poetry or autobiography (Ellis and Bochner 1996; Denzin and Lincoln 2000). These developments have inspired considerable contention, particularly as they tend to reject any idea of being disciplined by reference to the experiences they seek to evoke, arguing that these experiences exist only for the observer and that it is a realist error to consider that they have an independent substance that can falsify interpretations (Spencer 2001). Realist ethnographers have rejected this hyperbolic relativism, arguing that there is a genuine difference between literary and scientific work: if the world is not allowed to constrain our observations, we have only the products of our prior knowledge and values, which may stimulate imagination but tell us very little that has practical use (Murphy and Dingwall 2003).

In either sense, organizational culture is not a new phenomenon. Organizations have always had cultures and scholars have always documented them: it is simply that we have only recently labeled them as such.

20.2 ORGANIZATIONAL CULTURE: A HISTORY

Classic studies of organizations repeatedly observed the way in which workers subverted rational economic models of their behavior. In essence, the goal of Frederick Taylor's "scientific management" was to prevent this subversion by removing ambiguity from work design and control (Kanigel 1997). Taylor's contemporary, Henry Ford, also recognized the "problem" of worker norms and values. He famously created a "Sociological Department" of the Ford Motor Company in 1913 to shape the nascent industry's immigrant workforce into mature, sober characters (Beynon 1973). The Hawthorne studies, at the Western Electric plant in Chicago during the 1930s, systematically varied reward systems, workflow organization and environmental conditions without discovering any robust or consistent effects on workgroup output, as Taylorist approaches predicted (Mayo 1975; Rose 1988; Gillespie 1991). Although the authors do not refer to "culture," they have clearly identified the phenomenon:

every item and event in the industrial environment becomes an object of a system of sentiments. According to this way of looking at things, material goods, physical events, wages, hours of work, etc., cannot be treated as things in themselves. Instead they have to be interpreted as carriers of social value...From this point of view the behavior of no one person in an industrial organization, from the very top to the very bottom, can be regarded as motivated by strictly economic or logical considerations. Routine patterns of interaction involve strong sentiments. Each group in the organization manifests its own powerful sentiments...This point of view is far from being the one which is frequently expressed, namely, that man is essentially an economic being carrying around with him a few noneconomic appendages. Rather the point of view that has been expressed here is that noneconomic motives, interests and processes, as well as economic, are fundamental in behavior in business, from the board of directors to the very last man in the organization. (Roethlisberger and Dickson 1939: 557)

Similar observations could be found in many classic studies of industrial or organizational sociology like Roy's (1952, 1953, 1954, 1959) studies of work in a US machine tool factory or the writings of Strauss et al. (1963, 1964) on the negotiated order of US hospitals. Elliott Jaques' (1951) *The Changing Culture of a Factory* seems to have been the earliest published use of the word "culture" within organizational studies and what we would now call "culture management" became integral to the Tavistock tradition of research and consultancy (see Brown 1992).

However, it would be wrong to imply that these were mainstream approaches at the time. Overwhelmingly, organizations were treated as rational, rule-governed systems, where the objective of research was to find associations between goals, structures, incentives, and output that would allow designers to maximize efficiency. To the extent that cultural issues entered in, they were sources of noise or deviance in systems, associated with the persistence of an informal organization that obstructed the formal structures and processes (Benson 1977). Better design or tighter work-discipline would eliminate these obstacles to efficiency. Unfortunately, the desire to produce a rational structural analysis of organizations was simply unable to deliver the promised results. Starbuck (1982: 3), for example, observed that:

Organization theorists have carried out numerous studies of so-called objective phenomena and their aggregate finding is that almost nothing correlates strongly and consistently with anything else. This null finding fits the hypothesis that organizational structures and technologies are primarily arbitrary, temporary and superficial characteristics.

A new direction was signalled by four papers published in the USA between 1977 and 1983 (Meyer and Rowan 1977; DiMaggio and Powell 1983; Zucker 1977; Scott and Meyer 1983), which laid the foundations for what became known as the "new institutionalism" (see Powell and DiMaggio 1991).

The new institutionalists aimed to transcend the division of organizations into formal and informal dimensions, the former governed by rationality and the latter by culture. They insisted, instead, on the cultural basis of all organizational structures and actions. This led them to regard organizational boundaries as open and fluid so that the cultural foundation of action was not contained within the organization but reflected the organization's interactions with its environment.

The prevalence of bureaucratization and formality was an indicator of the strength of these forms in the culture of the wider society, which had the effect of compelling organizations to adopt them in order to be treated as legitimate. Without legitimacy, organizations could not gain access to a range of material resources and sustain themselves. Access to material resources was, however, derived from the "correct" manipulation of symbolic resources, particularly through a range of ceremonial actions that had little relevance to the productive efforts of the enterprise. The search for legitimacy tended to reduce the diversity of organizational forms, a process known as "isomorphism." This may result either from processes of competition, where organizations serving the same market copy the leader, regardless of whether or not this is appropriate to the niche that they occupy, or from processes of institutionalization. The latter is particularly relevant to public sector organizations, which may not operate in a competitive market but are still obliged to be concerned for their legitimacy. Isomorphism is driven by three mechanisms: *coercive*, through law, regulation, and the threat of sanction; *mimetic*, where uncertainty about the correct course of action is resolved by copying apparently successful models from elsewhere; and *normative*, where specialized labor, such as professionals, shares a common cognitive and normative base.

"Culture" in this model has been seen increasingly as fragmented and decoupled. A large part of what organizations do is purely ceremonial and directed to the expectations of their environments rather than to their practical activities. There is no requirement that these ceremonial acts "join up" in any coherent way. Managers are evaluated mainly by their ability to produce stories that make such connections as and when required (Martin 1982, 2001; Martin and Siehl 1983). Within the managerial literature, however, organizational culture has retained many rationalist features. In a sense, no practicing manager can acknowledge that most of his or her actions are purely ceremonial: part of management's legitimation myth is that it makes a difference to practical activity. Academics may point out that accreditation, quality assurance programs, equal opportunities statements, corporate governance policies, and the like are largely ways to display compliance with the expectations of the organization's environment: managers are obliged to treat such productions as real or jeopardize the legitimacy that the organization hopes to derive from them.

20.3 MANAGERS AND ORGANIZATIONAL CULTURE

These new intellectual directions found a market in a corporate world facing challenges that did not seem responsive to rationalist solutions. Since the late 1960s, the core metropolitan economies of the USA and Europe had been rapidly deindustrializing (Bluestone and Harrison 1982), while sucking in industrial imports from Japan and the "tiger economies" of South East Asia (Bello and Rosenfeld 1992). Rather than being seen as the result of complex geopolitical processes, these changes were attributed to the failure of large western corporations to adapt their classic bureaucratic structures of rigid hierarchy, ordered chains of command and impersonal office holding, which had created a disengaged workforce, documented by William H. Whyte's (1956) exploration of the alienation of US white collar workers in *The Organization Man*. This formed part of a wider backlash against the corporatism of the post-war settlement (V. Wright 1994), reflected in the electoral success of neo-liberal politicians in Europe and the USA in the late 1970s. The success of the Asian economies was attributed to their readier cultural accommodation to the requirements of modern capitalism (Bello and Rosenfeld 1992; Elger and Smith 1994; Wilkinson and Wilmott 1995). Western corporations were urged to respond by changing their cultures and adopting new styles of management based on leadership and inspiration rather than bureaucracy.

In the early 1980s, the idea of organizational culture was popularized among managers by books like Peters and Waterman's (1982) *In Search of Excellence*, and Deal and Kennedy's (1982) *Corporate Cultures: The Rites and Rituals of Corporate Life* (see also Ouchi 1981; Ouchi and Wilkins 1985). This literature claimed that really successful companies either possessed or created the right culture. Byrne's story of this conversion experience, by senior management of a US firm on hearing a culture guru's presentation, may be apocryphal but is only a slight exaggeration.

"This corporate culture stuff is great," the chairman raved at dinner following the talk. Then turning to his president, he demanded, "I want a culture by Monday." (Byrne 1990: 10–11, cited in Parker 2000: 16)

"Culture" now acquired a substantive and evaluative sense that it had not previously possessed. Managers were encouraged to develop a new set of skills based on the creation and manipulation of culture. As Tom Peters put it, in a later book with Nancy Austin:

Every coach, at every level, is above all a value-shaper. The value-shaper not only brings company philosophy to life by paying extraordinary attention to communicating and symbolising it, he or she also helps newcomers understand how shared company values affect individual performance. (Peters and Austin 1986: 30)

Deal and Kennedy (1982: 15) equally put new stress on individual managers:

We think that people are a company's greatest resource, and the way to manage them is not directly by computer reports, but by the subtle cues of a culture. A strong culture is a powerful lever for guiding behavior; it helps employees do their jobs a little better.

A small industry grew up to market the idea that culture was a variable that should be managed and to train managers how to do this (Frost et al. 1985; Hickman and

Silva 1985; Louis 1985; Lessem 1990; Wilson 1992; Anthony 1994; Bate 1995; *Harvard Business Review* 2002).

Susan Wright, an organizational anthropologist, noted the way that this approach turned culture:

from being something an organization *is* into something an organization *has*, and from being a process embedded in context to an objectified tool of management control. The use of the term culture itself becomes ideological. (S. Wright 1994: 4)

Such a usage of "culture" was alien and profoundly disturbing to many social scientists (S. Wright 1994; Grint 1995; Lynn-Meek 1988; Alvesson 2002). They objected to the crude way in which the complexity of the concept was ignored so that it could be used in management writing. This literature, and associated practice, assumed that organizational culture *could* and *should* be manipulated by managers to achieve corporate success. As Wright explained:

For an anthropologist reading this literature there are moments of recognition closely followed by the discovery of familiar ideas being used in disconcertingly unrecognisable ways. (S. Wright 1994: 2)

Much of the managerial writing maintains the search for a Holy Grail of rational management. Now, however, rational managers must understand and manipulate the workforce's culture, while their own goals and values remain as unexamined as those of the traditional corporate bureaucrat. Softer, interpersonal skills are given more prominence in the manager's toolkit but these do not extend to acknowledging the degree to which corporate governance rests on the consent of the governed rather than the sanctions of labor discipline. The 1950s vocabularies of legitimation were displaced by the fashions of the 1980s but this did not signify much more than a change of language. The managers who survived corporate downsizing invoked different symbols but were no less managers than before.

Managerial writers also borrowed liberally from structural functional theory, although, by this time, it had been intensively criticized by social scientists. Management writers were, however, attracted by its straightforward dichotomies between good/bad; functional/dysfunctional; healthy/unhealthy. They could declare themselves the arbiters of what was and was not good/functional/healthy. As Lynn-Meek puts it:

Any theory that assumes that culture is the internalization of dominant norms and values, must also assume that all members must hold the dominant value system or else be "outside culture." (Lynn-Meek 1988: 458)

This illustrates the gulf between social scientific and managerial writers. For the former, the "is" in the context of culture is the belief that culture is an emergent property of actions that simultaneously orient to and reproduce an organization.

Culture expresses the interaction of groups among themselves and with their environment. This view of organizations is predicated on an understanding that social life is fundamentally reflexive and therefore subject to change and open to unintended consequences of action. Culture is not simply a variable that can be altered to achieve a specified outcome. However, while this is a powerful critique, it tends to lead into an argument that culture change is impossible. This seems a somewhat exaggerated conclusion although change is certainly not a simple or straightforward process.

20.4 CULTURE AND COGNITION

The differences between managerialist and social scientific perspectives can be seen in studies of the Challenger and Columbia space shuttle crashes in 1986 and 2003. The Presidential Commission that investigated the Challenger crash treated it as a technical failure, booster rocket seals failing under low temperature conditions before launch. However, in a widely acclaimed book, Diane Vaughan (1996), an organizational sociologist, pointed to the Commission's failure to ask why NASA managers, who had been warned of this risk, still decided to proceed. This was, she argued, the result of changes in NASA's organizational culture during the 1970s. Her work's importance is evidenced by an invitation to join the Columbia investigation team and, ultimately, to write chapter 8 of its final report (Columbia Accident Investigation Board 2003). Although the Board found that the crash's technical cause was damage to the shuttle's structure resulting from the impact of a chunk of insulating foam detaching from the booster fuel tank at launch, the report gives as much prominence to failures in NASA's organizational culture, and the extent to which changes made after the Challenger crash had been inadequate or had not been sustained.

In her Challenger study, Vaughan explored the tension between the engineering culture that dominated NASA until the 1970s and the bureaucratic culture introduced during that decade to tighten cost and production control. While the former placed great stress on the uncertainties of technology, the contestability of judgments, and the need for constant learning from experience, the latter emphasized a more formal, rule-governed approach to secure adequate performance at a politically acceptable cost rather than perfection requiring open-ended funding. Vaughan stresses that this is not a simple portrait of amoral managers and heroic professionals, although it has sometimes been read in that way. Her point is more subtle: production concerns had so permeated the culture that potentially ambiguous information was interpreted in ways favorable to maintaining launch schedules and containing costs, even at some risk to safety. The possibility of seal failure had been acknowledged: however, it had not actually occurred and was not high on the list of priorities for corrective investment. In earlier work (1983), Vaughan had shown how commercial organizations, in this case a pharmacy company, managed information about their activities in ways that normalized deviance, defrauding the Ohio State government by false billing. While the State expected the company to behave like a public bureaucracy, complying with reimbursement rules and exactly justifying the disbursement of public funds, the company experienced compliance as disproportionately costly and denials of reimbursement as arbitrary and unfair. It was impractical for senior managers to monitor every transaction with the State: however the consequent process of "internal censorship," reducing the available information to the volume they could handle, created an environment where junior managers engaged in deviant responses to financial pressures caused by denial of reimbursements to which they felt morally, if not legally, entitled. Internal censorship at NASA filtered out engineering concerns that might obstruct the output and resource use goals set for the agency by successive administrations. This was partly a question of language and partly of values: Vaughan (2004) has noted how words like "waiver," "acceptable risk," and "catastrophe" acquired a distinctive meaning within NASA. Although the apparent desensitization was criticized by the Presidential Commission, it did not necessarily amount to more than organizational argot, whose meaning was clear to any competent member. However, internal censorship does mean that decision makers can become unaware of the concerns of those junior to them or to the side of the reporting line: the CAIB report (2003: 191) reproduces a Powerpoint slide that digests safety-critical information while entirely obscuring its significance. This is not evidence of malice or incompetence but the cultural solution to the problem of overload on the information recipients, partly as a consequence of complexity and partly as a result of lack of human and other resources following a decade of ambitious targets and limited funding.

However, there are tensions within the CAIB report. Chapter 7, which also deals with organizational issues, focuses on "high reliability theory" (LaPorte and Consolini 1991). Rational management can design organizations to avoid catastrophic accidents. As the report notes, "high reliability" advocates are optimists whereas "normal accident" theorists, like Vaughan, are pessimists who consider that high reliability simply means that the catastrophic accident has not yet occurred. Vaughan has certainly questioned whether the response to the CAIB report gives "any indication that they understand the systemic nature of the problem that goes beyond individual accountability" (*Orlando Sentinel*, 28 August 2003). Key decisions, like Shuttle launches, require a degree of "behavioral commitment" (Salancik and Pfeiffer 1978), an act that resolves uncertainty by established a fixed point of reference from which everything else makes sense. This commitment provides for the interpretation of the actions of members as relevant or irrelevant (Strong and Dingwall 1985). The result is what Weick and Sutcliffe (2003: 79) call a "culture of entrapment."

This basic social process for constructing reality is common to organizations of all kinds, both those experiencing adversity and those experiencing success. Even though this social process is fundamental, it gets ignored because people tend to blame adversity on operators at the sharp end of the accident chain and fail to look at earlier moments when commitments are hardening. The analytic error is compounded when people are then removed from their organizational contexts [and] judged one at a time, in isolation.

By emphasizing rational design and high reliability, the CAIB report may actually have the unintended consequence of reinforcing behavioral commitment. Intensified cultural discipline is likely to make professional action more rather than less binding—and the pressure to produce and sustain accounts for failure or error is increased. Through repeated cycles of this process, "people enact a sensible world that matches their beliefs . . . increasingly shrill insistence that change is mandatory changes nothing, since neither the rationales nor the binding to action change" (Weick and Sutcliffe 2003: 81).

Culture here is the source of the accounts that organization members use to explain performance—good or bad. It is the way in which they make sense of the world to each other and to outsiders. It also influences the intensity of behavioral commitment. This is partly structural—the visibility of an act to others—but also frames the extent to which accounts are demanded from members as a condition of continued membership. Weick and Sutcliffe suggest, for example, that the key to performance improvement may lie in recognizing commitment as a collective rather than an individual act. As a result, there are incentives to encourage constructive internal feedback, to identify potential hazards and to simulate alternative strategies. Commitment also highlights the link between organizational culture and social cognition.

The relationship between culture and cognition has long been discussed at an individual level. More recently, social scientists have examined cognition as a group phenomenon, particularly in the performance of complex tasks (DiMaggio 1997). Work like that of Hutchins (1990; Hutchins and Klausen 1996) and Goodwin (1994) has identified the way in which many activities, like docking a ship, flying an aircraft, interpreting archaeological remains, or deciding guilt in a trial, are accomplished through the integration of technology and people. Cognition is distributed so that the outcome depends upon the coordinated assembly of relevant information and activities without any participant necessarily being able to specify how this is done. Coordination is achieved by the participants' local culture, their sense of "what goes with what when," whose results are seen but whose existence and process often goes unnoticed. The challenge to the analyst, and the manager, is to make the unnoticed visible in order to consider its adequacy for the task in hand.

The understanding among NASA managers and engineers that they were performing a challenging task under conditions of great complexity was the necessary
condition of performing the task at all. How else could they be motivated to accept
the risk of committing astronauts' lives to a launch decision? Similarly, the marginalization of those who questioned this understanding was produced by their
failure in this distribution of cognition. They did not interpret and connect events
in the way required of competent members as the basis of joint action. However,
they were able to see the flaws in the local culture precisely because they were
structurally marginal.

Although these problems are not exclusive to the public sector, they are common
within it. Child protection work is a classic example where different information is
held on different systems by different agencies employing different professionals.
The participants in this collaborative activity bring to it their experiences of
different organizations of cognition, which they need to transcend in order to
establish a new inter-agency mode of cognition, which may, of course, compromise
their recognition as competent participants in the culture of their own agency
(Dingwall, Eekelaar, and Murray 1983). Courts are another example: much of the
organizational interaction occurs with the virtual participation of the judge, an
imagined audience for the participants who nevertheless provides for the "going-
together" of their various activities (Lynch 1997).

20.5 ORGANIZATIONAL CULTURE AND CULTURE CHANGE IN THE PUBLIC SECTOR

If the main driver for private sector interest in culture management was international competition, the main driver for public sector interest has been the arrival
of neo-liberal governments in the UK and the USA, since 1979 and 1980 respectively, and their colonization of international organizations (see Gamble 1988; Hay
1999; Pollitt 1993). David Marquand (2004: 2) has recently argued "the single most
important element of the New Right project of the 1980s and 1990s was a relentless
kulturkampf designed to root out the culture of service and citizenship which had
become part of the social fabric." The European public sector has been relatively
untouched by these concerns and has tended to follow its own developmental path
(Schedler and Proeller 2002). Although differences between cultures in the UK and
US public and private sectors were acknowledged, these were all framed in terms of
the latter's institutionalization of waste, sloth, and producer control. Public sector
managers lacked the talents and motivation of their private sector counterparts to

challenge this culture. In his autobiography, Peter Parker, former chair of the nationalized UK rail industry, reflected on Margaret Thatcher's attitude, even before her election victory in 1979. While leader of the opposition, she had come to lunch with his board, where:

> She had talked to us about nationalization with a hearty, dismaying adamancy: to be nationalized, she explained, was an industry's admission of failure. She did not spell out the implication, that—well chaps, it must follow surely—only failures would work in the public sector. However, these general views of hers were well enough known, and were not specifically directed against railways. (Parker 1991: 304)

The public sector was thought to be inherently inefficient simply because it was not in the private sector. It lacked the discipline of the market, which allowed both workers, through their trade unions, and managers to make unrealistic demands and decisions because they could always look to the government as paymasters of last resort. As Marquand (2004: 3) notes "For the marketizers, the professional, public service ethic is a con. Professionals are self-interested rent-seekers, trying to force the price of their labour above its market value. The service ethic is a rhetorical device to legitimize a web of monopolistic cartels whose real purpose is to rip off the consumer." In a 1993 Parliamentary debate on the privatization of UK railways, for example, John MacGregor, then Minister of Transport, asserted that British Rail exemplified:

> the classic shortcomings of the traditional nationalised industry. It is an entrenched monopoly. That means too little responsiveness to customer needs...Inevitably also it has the culture of a nationalised industry; a heavily bureaucratised structure...an instinct-ive tendency to ask for more taxpayers' subsidy. (quoted in Bagwell, 1996: 139)

Neo-liberal governments thought the answer to the perceived problems of State bureaucracy was cultural change. This might either be coerced by privatization, imposing, where possible, the disciplines of the market and bankruptcy, or, failing this, by isomorphic pressure on public sector organizations. By establishing the "sovereignty of the customer," public sector organizations would be made more like their private sector cousins, who were assumed to be more responsive to demand (du Gay 1996; du Gay and Salaman 1992). Public sector workers were expected to adopt the beliefs, values, and ideals of the private sector, either through the direct pressures of the market or through a process of reeducation. The legitimacy of the public sector would rest on a new symbolic code of enterprise, innovation, flexibility, and fleet-footedness. As our epigraph suggests, the reform-ers assumed that there was no meaningful difference between private and public sector organizations: the contrary claim merely reflected the sectional interests of producers. Whether privatized or remaining within the public sector, structural changes were imposed on public sector organizations, often through the adoption of customer/supplier models derived from Total Quality Management. Kirkpatrick and Martinez Lucio's (1995) collection charts the simultaneous adoption of the language of quality assurance and the reshaping of the employment relationship in the UK public sector—the Post Office, the NHS, education, and social services.

Initially, the mere movement of a corporation from the public to the private sector was thought to be sufficient to effect cultural change (Rees 1994; V. Wright 1994; Williams et al 1996). State industries sold off in the UK after 1979 included Associated British Ports, British Aerospace, British Airways, British Gas, British Petroleum, British Telecom, Britoil, Cable and Wireless, the electricity, water, coal and finally the rail industry (Ferner 1989; Rees 1994; V. Wright 1994). Different parts of these organizations were often set up as independent cost or budget centres operating in an internal market or quasi-market (Fairbrother 1996). Where industries were not thought appropriate for privatization, like the UK rail industry in the 1980s, isomorphic pressures led to the introduction of an internal market, to promote a shift from a "production-led" to a "business-led" culture. The results were often "culture wars," as Bate describes for the rail industry:

culture and counter-culture fought it out as the old guard in "Production" clashed head-on with the young turks in the "Sectors," each parading before the other ideologies and styles of thought which they knew to be provocative and unacceptable. The one side valued service ("value for money"/the social railway), the other side profit ("money for value"/the commercial railway). These were life issues, issues on which no inch of ground could be conceded. (Bate 1995: 150)

Cultural rhetoric was highly visible during these transitions to the private sector. However, it depended on a basis of coercion, rather than the mimetic or normative processes envisaged by much of the management literature. Ferner (1989: 4) has estimated that major UK public sector corporations employed 445,000 fewer people in 1988 than in 1979. The changes in organizational culture rested on major changes in the structure and conduct of industrial relations, with previous management/union partnerships giving way to the unilateral imposition of new practices including team working, multiskilling, and monthly or annualized hours, although the UK did not match Ronald Reagan's dismissal of the entire workforce of US air traffic controllers. John Welsby, the last chair of the nationalized rail industry, acknowledged that:

One of the objectives of privatization—rarely openly declared but nonetheless real—was to loosen up some of the rigidities of the industry's working practices. "Breaking the power of the unions" is certainly how some people would put it. I would say it was the opportunity to bring working arrangements more into line with the norms applying at the end of the twentieth century. (*Rail*, 1998, 324: 38)

O'Connell Davidson (1993) has described similar processes in the UK water industry. Roberts' (1993) account of British Shipbuilders notes how the collapse of the sector was used to lever change. Increased global competition for ship construction and a saturated market allowed management and politicians to force through major changes to the division of labor. The "old culture" of the craft workers was blamed for the industry's failure to compete.

In those public services that could not be privatized, culture change was introduced by other means. First, non-core services were sold off—as with British Rail's profitable hotel and shipping subsidiaries in the 1980s (Gourvish 2002). Second, ancillary services, such as cleaning, were subjected to competitive tendering between the existing workforce and external contractors. Finally, the system of public sector internal markets was extended to mimic the discipline of external markets. Tim May (1994) analyzes the enactment of a culture change programme within the probation service. Structural changes enacted by senior management effectively enrolled personnel into this new culture. May identifies three techniques used to change established cultural patterns: introducing new layers of management into the organization in order to restore management's prerogative; recruiting business people into the governing structures to show public servants "how it is done"; and importing independent consultants, who are likewise not "of" the public sector. These techniques combined to devalue the cultural capital of existing staff and managers while simultaneously privileging that of those brought in to the service.

These processes have not fundamentally altered since the 1980s and can still be identified in, for example, much of the Blairite agenda for public sector reform in the UK. The residual public sector continues to be depicted by politicians as slow and unresponsive, whether to themselves or to users. It is still said to consist of large, unwieldy bureaucratic and impersonal institutions inhabited by managers and workers who lack dynamism and are rule-bound rather than creative and enterprising. However, the privatized public services are not necessarily perceived to have been any more successful. Ian Braybrook, managing director of the company that took over most of the former rail freight sector, observed:

As for staff–management relations, it is a fresh culture we need to acquire. The lack of the "them and us" mentality, getting people to believe in the company, to want to work for the company... There is an old business school dictum which says: "To turn a company that is performing badly financially takes three years; to turn round a company which has inadequate systems and IT takes six years; to change a culture takes 20." Well we haven't got 20 years. We aim to change the culture in three or four. (*The Railway Magazine*, August 1997: 49–50)

Strangleman (2004) cites numerous other examples. The new owners' and managers' desire to proclaim culture change was matched only by their desire to distance themselves from the former State-owned railway so that any negative aspect of the industry could be blamed on the legacy of nationalization. However, a series of major railway accidents—Southall 1997, Ladbroke Grove 1999, Hatfield 2000, Potters Bar 2002—have questioned the consequences of this process. Several of the official reports into these accidents have employed cultural explanations, most notably the Southall crash report (Uff 2000: 202), which concluded that:

The lesson to be learned seems to be that compliance with Rules cannot be assumed in the absence of some positive system of monitoring which is likely to detect failures. Such a conclusion would, however, be a sad reflection on a fine industry which has been created through the enthusiasm and support of countless individuals who were proud to be thought of as part of "the railway." *Perhaps the true lesson is that a different culture needs to be developed, or recreated, through which individuals will perform to the best of their ability and not resort to delivering the minimum service that can be got away with* [our emphasis].

Since the late 1970s, then, UK governments have certainly assumed that public sector organizational cultures are different from those in the private sector. However, that difference has consistently been associated with inferiority. It has been treated as axiomatic that the public sector must be made to adopt the culture of the private sector. The levers for securing this change are not, though, the measures of persuasion and inspiration envisaged by popular management texts but the traditional labor disciplines of redundancy and dismissal. The pressures for isomorphism are coercive rather than normative or mimetic. The crisis identified by the Southall crash report, among others, is that the results of such coerced change do not lead to worker ownership of the culture. In this case, safety was equated with strict compliance with rules, rather than proactive recognition of emerging problems, that were not covered by rules, and creative improvization, to deal with these problems before they became hazards. Something important was thought to have been lost in the course of privatization and the abandonment of the traditional vision of the "social railway," which was not driven by profit maximization as its overriding goal. The corporate claims to quality were not matched by delivery. The destruction of producer control also destroyed producer "buy-in" and promoted producer cynicism. More broadly, there is an increasingly acknowledged gap between the rhetoric recycled by public sector managers to their political masters and the experience of delivery from those organizations. Schools may hit their test performance targets but still fail to graduate children who can spell, punctuate, or do simple arithmetic. Hospitals meet targets for reducing the waiting lists for surgery by introducing pre-waiting lists and only admitting patients to the waiting list proper when a date can be set for their operation. Such experiences have both contributed to the mistrust of government and begun to reopen the question of whether there is anything distinctive about the culture of public sector organizations and its embedded values.

20.6 ORGANIZATIONAL CULTURE AND THE PUBLIC SECTOR

Paul du Gay (1996, 2000; du Gay and Salaman 1992) has been particularly prominent in arguing against the "entrepreneurial governance" of the new models of public sector management in the US and the UK. Osborne and Gaebler (1992: 19–20) formulated this term to summarize the ten "essential principles" of "reinvented" public sector organizations:

Entrepreneurial governments promote *competition* between service providers. They *empower* citizens by pushing control out of the bureaucracy, into the community. They measure the performance of their agencies, focusing not on inputs but on *outcomes*. They are driven by their goals—their *missions*—not by their rules and regulations. They redefine their clients as *customers* and offer them choices . . . They *prevent* problems before they emerge, rather than simply offering services afterward. They put their energies into *earning* money, not simply spending it. They *decentralize* authority, embracing participatory management. They prefer *market* mechanisms to bureaucratic mechanisms. And they focus not simply on providing public services but on *catalyzing* all sectors—public, private and voluntary—into action to solve their community's problems.

These principles link structure and culture, the former following from the redefinition of goals and the reconstruction of client identities. Du Gay (2000: 6) comments:

If . . . "entrepreneurial governance" has one overarching target—that which it most explicitly defines itself in opposition to—then it is the impersonal, procedural, hierarchical and technical organization of the Weberian bureau. Put simply, bureaucratic government is represented as the "paradigm that failed."

Following Weber, du Gay argues that it is important to understand why public organizations generally developed bureaucratic forms. What is the basis of public sector isomorphism? Weber pointed to the association between bureaucracy and modern capitalism. Bureaucracy triumphed over the private franchising of public services in eighteenth-century states by establishing a stable, orderly, and rule-governed environment in which citizens were dealt with equally and impartially because the administrator had no personal stake in the transaction's outcome. A culture of affective neutrality and the impersonal administration of entitlements replaced discretionary and personalized administration. This change supplied a background of substantively legitimate public order against which private goals and enterprises could be pursued. Bureaucracy was never an enemy of capitalism but its essential partner, working with an eye to permanence rather than the transience of markets (Gurvitch 1964). Celebrating what he calls the "old institutionalism" of

Coase, Commons, Schumpeter, and Selznick, Stinchcombe has recently revisited this classic sociological argument, that capitalism can only work effectively within a normative framework that it cannot itself generate. Stinchcombe (1997) rehearses this through four case studies. The first examines how law and public institutions supply legitimacy and order through substantive rather than formal actions: democracy and the rule of law are values rather than scripts so that politicians and judges are expected to act in ways that reflect these values rather than simply reading their lines. Bureaucratic formality is a means of insisting on substantive rationality rather than a virtue, or a myth, in itself (see Atkinson 1982). The second looks at the extent to which contracts depend upon moral commitments as much as the letter of their drafting. The credibility of an organization's standing as a contractual partner is a precondition of the contract, and can only be salvaged to a limited extent by mechanisms within the contract, such as performance insurance. The third looks at the notion of "creative destruction" and the extent to which this depends on a background of public order to occur peacefully. The fourth looks at the transition to capitalism in eastern Europe and at the "amoral familism" of southern Italy to consider the implications of failing to establish a public realm where the moral preconditions for successful contracts could be nurtured. These societies cannot supply integrity in the delivery of public goods.

Weber believed that there was an essential distinction within civil society. Public officials must conduct themselves quite differently from their commercial counterparts. Their interests, expressed culturally in their duties and their conceptions of duty, were very different and the separation ensured stability and order in civil society. The cultural values of the public sector do not merely keep the private sector honest: they make the private sector possible at all. These values are threatened by the return to charismatic leadership envisaged under entrepreneurial governance (Gouldner 1952; Weber 1952). Bureaucracy is the solution to the problems of charismatic leadership—autocracy, irresponsibility, instability, cronyism, and transience. These are the dark sides of the personalized public service advocated by UK reformers like Leadbeater (2004). Interestingly, Leadbeater writes of "scripts" rather than values: his vision of public services is one where the State offers citizens what they think they want as individuals rather than what they might dispassionately be thought to need as a community. The articulate, well organized, or well connected will be able to enforce their preferences, however collectively perverse, while others receive a residual service or are oppressively subjected to moral reconstitution to fit the identities prescribed for them. User engagement in health care, for example, has favored rich and well-established disease lobbies at the expense of basic services and considerations of cost-effectiveness. A value-driven approach acknowledges that public services cannot be shaped purely by the aggregation of individual preferences, weighted by lobbying power.

The disinterestedness of the public sector may create the pathology of an apparent lack of interest in the problems of consumers, clients, users, or patients.

However, it may also be crucial to the protection of other stakeholders. A user-driven model of healthcare, for example, risks massive over-consumption of antibiotics for minor illnesses, encouraging the emergence of resistant bacteria and compromising the interests of those who contract serious infections in the future. Denial of service may frustrate individuals but benefit the community. The same model may also lead to demands for public funding of alternative and complementary medicines for which no clear evidence of effectiveness is available. The ineffective use of public funds breaches the moral distinction between taxation and extortion, levying citizens to provide services more efficiently and effectively than could be achieved by the market and levying them to achieve some sectional goal of the rulers or those with privileged access to the political process (Brennan and Buchanan 2000). Denial of service to some may be an essential protection of the property rights of others. These tensions are not entirely unique to the public sector: private sector managers may have to balance customer and shareholder interests, and short-term gains, against the long-term benefits of being perceived as a morally legitimate corporate member of the community. However, they are inescapable in the life of any public sector manager and constrain the possibilities for simply cloning cultures from the private sector. Once upon a time economists knew this: High-powered Treasury Thinkers seem to have forgotten.

A new research direction would show much greater appreciation of the evolutionary logic of public sector cultures and respect for what is in place before seeking to promote change. It would also look more carefully at the impact of wider legal and political cultures that surround public organizations. Most of Europe has had very little engagement with the agenda outlined here, with the exception of a few local experiments (Schedler and Proeller 2002). It is not self-evident that these states have public sectors uniformly inferior to those of the US or the UK. The extent of producer control seen in some public organizations has undeniably been pathological. On the other hand, the costs of reducing producer commitment and the degree to which the producers' goodwill and cultural flexibility contribute to the sustainability of services are now becoming apparent. These need to be better understood.

References

ALVESSON, M. (2002), *Understanding Organizational Culture*, London: Sage.
ANTHONY, P. (1994), *Managing Culture*, Buckingham: Open University Press.
ATKINSON, J. M. (1982), "Understanding Formality," *British Journal of Sociology* 33: 86–117.
BAGWELL, P. S. (1996), *The Transport Crisis in Britain*, Nottingham: Spokesman.
BATE, P. (1995), *Strategies for Culture Change*, Oxford: Butterworth-Heinemann.
BEATTIE, J. (1966), *Other Cultures: Aims, Methods and Achievements in Social Anthropology*, London: Routledge and Kegan Paul.

BELLO, W., and ROSENFELD, S. (1992), *Dragons in Distress: Asia's Miracle Economies in Crisis*, London: Penguin.

BENSON, J. K. (1977), "Organizations: A Dialectic View," *Administrative Science Quarterly* 22: 1–21.

BEYNON, H. (1973), *Working for Ford*, London: Penguin.

BITTNER, E. (1965), "The concept of organization," *Social Research*, 32: 239–55.

BLUESTONE, B., and HARRISON, B. (1982), *The Deindustrialization of America: Plant Closings, Community Abandonment and the Dismantling of Basic Industry*, New York: Basic Books.

BONAVIA, M. R. (1971), *The Organisation of British Railways*, London: Ian Allan.

BRENNAN, G., and BUCHANAN, J. M. (2000), *The Power to Tax: Analytical Foundations of a Fiscal Constitution*, Indianapolis: Liberty Fund.

BROWN, R. K. (1992), *Understanding Industrial Organisations: Theoretical Perspectives in Industrial Sociology*, London: Routledge.

BRUBAKER, R. (1984), *The Limits to Rationality: An Essay on the Social and Moral Thought of Max Weber*, London: Routledge.

BYRNE, J. (1990), "Business Fads: What's In—and What's Out," in P. Frost, V. Mitchell, and W. Nord (eds.), *Managerial Reality*. Glenview: Scott, Foresman, 10–18.

CLIFFORD, J., and MARCUS, G. E. (eds.) (1986), *Writing Culture: The Politics and Poetics of Ethnography*, Berkeley: University of California Press.

COLUMBIA ACCIDENT INVESTIGATION BOARD (2003), *Report*, vol. 1, Washington, DC: Columbia Accident Investigation Board.

DEAL, T., and KENNEDY, A. (1982), *Corporate Cultures: The Rites and Rituals of Corporate Life*, London: Penguin.

DENZIN, N. K., and LINCOLN, Y. S. (2000), "Introduction: The Discipline and Practice of Qualitative Research," in N. K. Denzin and Y. S. Lincoln (eds.), *Handbook of Qualitative Research*, 2nd edn., Thousand Oaks, CA: Sage, 1–29.

DiMAGGIO, P. J. (1997) "Culture and Cognition," *Annual Review of Sociology* 23: 263–87.

—— and POWELL, W. W. (1983), "The Iron Cage Revisited: Institutional Isomorphism and Collective Rationality in Organizational Fields," *American Sociological Review* 48: 147–60.

DINGWALL, R., EEKELAAR, J. M., and MURRAY, T. (1983), *The Protection of Children: State Intervention and Family Life*, Oxford: Blackwell.

DU GAY, P. (1996), *Consumption and Identity at Work*, London: Sage.

—— (2000), *In Praise of Bureaucracy: Weber, Organization, Ethics*, London: Sage.

—— and Salaman, G. (1992), "The cult(ure) of the customer," *Journal of Management Studies*, 29: 616–633.

ELGER, T., and SMITH, C. (eds.) (1994), *Global Japanization?: The Transnational Transformation of the Labour Process*, London: Routledge.

ELLIS, C., and BOCHNER, A. (1996), *Composing Ethnography: Alternative Forms of Qualitative Writing*, Walnut Creek, CA: Altamira.

FAIRBROTHER, P. (1996), "Workplace Trade Unionism in the State Sector," in P. Ackers, C. Smith, and P. Smith (eds.), *The New Workplace and Trade Unionism: Critical Perspectives on Work and Organization*, London: Routledge 110–48.

FERNER, A. (1989), "Ten Years of Thatcherism: Changing Industrial Relations in British Public Enterprises," *Warwick Papers in Industrial Relations* 27.

FROST, P., MOORE, L., LOUIS, M., LUNDBERG, C., and MARTIN, J. (eds.) (1985), *Organizational Culture*, Beverly Hills, CA: Sage.

GAMBLE, A. (1988), *The Free Economy and the Strong State: The Politics of Thatcherism*, Basingstoke: Macmillan.

GEERTZ, C. (1973), *The Interpretation of Cultures: Selected Essays, New York*, NY: Basic Books.

GILLESPIE, R. (1991), *Manufacturing Knowledge: A History of the Hawthorne Experiments*, Cambridge: Cambridge University Press.

GOODENOUGH, W. H. (1957), "Cultural anthropology and linguistics," in P. L. Garvin (ed.), *Report of the Seventh Annual Round Table Meeting on Linguistics and Language Study* (Monograph Series on Language and Linguistics No. 9), Washington, DC: Georgetown University, 167–73.

GOODWIN, C. (1994), "Professional vision," *American Anthropologist* 96: 606–33.

GOULDNER, A. W. (1952), "The Problem of Succession in Bureaucracy," in R. K. Merton, A. P. Gray, B. Hockey ,and H. C. Selvin (eds.), *Reader in Bureaucracy*, New York: Free Press, 339–51.

GOURVISH, T. R. (2002), *British Rail 1974–97: From Integration to Privatisation*, Oxford: Oxford University Press.

GRINT, K. (1995), *Management: A Sociological Introduction*, Cambridge: Polity.

GURVITCH, G. (1964), *The Spectrum of Social Time*, Dordrecht: D. Reidel.

HARE, D. (2003), *The Permanent Way*, London: Faber.

HARVARD BUSINESS REVIEW (2002), *Harvard Business Review on Culture and Change*, Boston: Harvard Business School.

HAY, C. (1999), *The Political Economy of New Labour: Labouring under False Pretences?* Manchester: Manchester University Press.

HUTCHINS, E. (1990), "The Technology of Team Navigation," in J. Galegher, R. Kraut, and C. Egido (eds.), *Intellectual Teamwork: Social and Technological Foundations of Cooperative Work*, Hillsdale, NJ, Lawrence Erlbaum Associates, 191–20.

—— and KLAUSEN, T. (1996), "Distributed Cognition in an Airline Cockpit," in Y. Engestrom and D. Middleton (eds.), *Cognition and Communication at Work*, Cambridge: Cambridge University Press, 15–34.

HICKMAN, C. R., and SILVA, M. A. (1985), *Creating Excellence*, London: Unwin.

JAQUES, E. (1951), *The Changing Culture of a Factory*, London: Tavistock/Routledge & Kegan Paul.

KANIGEL, R. (1997), *The One Best Way: Fredrick Winslow Taylor and the Enigma of Efficiency*, London: Abacus.

KIRKPATRICK, I., and MARTINEZ LUCIO, M. (eds.) (1995), *The Politics of Quality in the Public Sector*, London: Routledge.

LAPORTE, T. R., and CONSOLINI, P. M. (1991), "Working in Practice but not in Theory," *Journal of Public Administration Research and Theory* 1: 19–47.

LEADBEATER, C. (2004), *Personalization through Participation: A New Script for Public Services*, London: Demos.

LESSEM, R. (1990), *Managing Corporate Culture*, Aldershot: Gower.

LOUIS, M. (1985), "Sourcing Workplace Cultures," in R. H. Kilmann, M. Saxton, R. Sherpa, and Associates (eds.), *Gaining Control of Corporate* Culture, San Francisco: Jossey-Bass, 126–36.

LYNCH, M. (1997), "Preliminary Notes on Judges' Work: The Judge as a Constituent of Courtroom 'Hearings,'" in M. Travers and J. F. Manzo (eds.), *Law in Action: Ethnomethodological and Conversation Analytic Approaches to Law*, Aldershot: Ashgate, 99–132.

Lynn-Meek, V. (1988), "Organizational Culture: Origins and Weaknesses," *Organization Studies* 9: 453–73.

Martin, J. (1982), "Stories and Scripts in Organizational Settings," in A. H. Hastorf and A. M. Isen (eds.), *Cognitive Social Psychology*, New York: Elsevier, 255–305.

—— (2001), *Organizational Culture: Mapping the Terrain*, London: Sage.

—— and Siehl, C. (1983), "Organizational Culture and Counterculture: An Uneasy Symbiosis," *Organizational Dynamics*, 12: 52–64.

Marquand, D. (2004) *Decline of the Public: The Hollowing-out of Citizenship*, Cambridge: Polity.

May, T. (1994), "Transformative Power: A Study in a Human Service Organisation," *Sociological Review* 42: 618–38.

Mayo, E. (1975), *The Social Problems of An Industrial Civilization*, London: Routledge and Kegan Paul (first published 1949).

Merton, R. K., Gray, A. P., Hockey, B., and Selvin, H. C. (eds.) (1952), *Reader in Bureaucracy*, New York: Free Press.

Meyer, J. W., and Rowan, B. (1977), "Institutionalized Organizations: Formal Structure as Myth and Ceremony," *American Journal of Sociology* 83: 340–63.

Murphy, E., and Dingwall, R. (2003), *Qualitative Methods and Health Policy Research*, New York: Aldine de Gruyter.

O'Connell Davidson, J. (1993), *Privatization and Employment Relations: The Case of the Water Industry*, London: Mansell.

Osborne, D., and Gaebler, T. (1992), *Reinventing Government: How the Entrepreneurial Spirit is Transforming the Public Sector*, New York: Basic Books.

Ouchi, W. G. (1981), *Theory*, Reading, MA: Addison-Wesley.

—— and Wilkins, A. L. (1985), "Organisational culture," *Annual Review of Sociology* 11: 457–83.

Parker, M. (2000), *Organizational Culture and Identity: Unity and Division at Work*, London: Sage.

Parker, P. (1991), *For Starters: The Business of Life*, London: Pan.

Peters, T., and Waterman, R. H. (1982), *In Search of Excellence: Lessons from America's Best-Run Companies*, London: Harper and Row.

—— and Austin, N. (1986), *A Passion for Excellence: The Leadership Difference*, London: Fontana.

Pollitt, C. (1993), *Managerialism and the Public Services: Cuts or Culture Change in the 1990s?* 2nd edn., Oxford: Blackwell.

Powell, W. W., and DiMaggio, P. J. (eds.) (1991), *The New Institutionalism in Organizational Analysis*, Chicago: University of Chicago Press.

Rees, R. (1994), "Economic Aspects of Privatization in Britain," in V. Wright (ed.), *Privatization in Western Europe: Pressures, problems and paradoxes*, London: Pinter, 44–56.

Roberts, I. (1993), *Craft, Class and Control: The Sociology of a Shipbuilding Community*, Edinburgh: Edinburgh University Press.

Roethlisberger, F. J., and Dickson W. J., with Wright, H. A. (1939), *Management and the Worker: An Account of a Research Program Conducted by the Western Electric Company, Hawthorne Works, Chicago*, Cambridge, MA: Harvard University Press.

Rose, M. (1988), *Industrial Behaviour: Research and Control*, 2nd edn., London: Penguin.

Roy, D. F. (1952), "Quota Restriction and Goldbricking in a Machine Shop," *American Journal of Sociology* 57: 427–42.

—— (1953), "Work Satisfaction and Social Reward in Quota Achievement: An Analysis of Piecework Incentive," *American Sociological Review* 18: 507–14.

—— (1954), "Efficiency and 'The Fix': Informal Intergroup Relations in a Piecework Machine Shop," *American Journal of Sociology* 60: 255–66.

—— (1959), "Banana Time: Job Satisfaction and Informal Interaction," *Human Organization* 18: 158–68.

SALANCIK, G. R., and PFEFFER, J. (1978), "A Social Information Processing Approach to Job Attitude and Task Design," *Administrative Science Quarterly* 23: 224–53.

SCHEDLER, K., and PROELLER, I. (2002), "A Perspective from Mainland Europe," in K. McLaughlin, S. P. Osborne, and E. Ferlie (eds.), *New Public Management: Current Trends and Future Prospects*, London: Routledge, 163–80.

SCOTT, W. R., and MEYER, J. W. (1983), "The Organization of Societal Sectors," in J. W. Meyer and W. R. Scott (eds.), *Organizational Environments: Ritual and Rationality.* Beverly Hills, CA: Sage, 129–53.

SPENCER, J. (2001) "Ethnography after postmodernism," in P. Atkinson, A. Coffey, S. Delamont, J. Lofland, and L. Lofland (eds.), *Handbook of Ethnography*, London: Sage, 443–52.

STARBUCK, W. (1982), "Congealing Oil: Inventing Ideologies to Justify Acting Ideologies Out," *Journal of Management Studies* 19: 3–27.

STINCHCOMBE, A. L. (1997), "On the Virtues of the Old Institutionalism," *Annual Review of Sociology* 23: 1–18.

STRANGLEMAN, T. (2004), *Work Identity at the End of the Line? Privatisation and Culture Change in the UK Rail Industry*, Basingstoke: Palgrave.

STRAUSS, A. L., SCHATZMAN, L., BUCHER, R., EHRLICH, D., and SABSHIN, M. (1963), "The hospital and its negotiated order," in E. Freidson (ed.), *The Hospital in Modern Society*, New York: Free Press, 147–69.

—— —— —— —— (1964), *Psychiatric Ideologies and Institutions*, New York: Free Press.

STRONG, P. M., and DINGWALL, R. (1985), "The Interactional Study of Organizations: a Critique and Reformulation," *Urban Life* 14: 205–31.

UFF, J. (2000), *The Southall Rail Accident Inquiry Report*, Norwich: HSE Books.

VAUGHAN, D. (1983), *Controlling Unlawful Organizational Behavior: Social Structure and Corporate Misconduct*, Chicago: University of Chicago Press.

—— (1996), *The Challenger Launch Decision: Risky Technology, Culture and Deviance at NASA.* Chicago: University of Chicago Press.

—— (2004), "Theorizing Disaster: Analogy, Historical Ethnography, and the *Challenger* Accident," http://www2.bc.edu/~vaughand/pdf/theorizing%20disaster.pdf Accessed 5 May 2004.

WEBER, M. (1952), "The Routinization of Charisma," in R. K. Merton, A. P. Gray, B. Hockey, and H. C. Selvin (eds.), *Reader in Bureaucracy*, New York: Free Press, 92–100.

WEICK, K. E., and SUTCLIFFE, K. M. (2003), "Hospitals as Cultures of Entrapment: A Re-Analysis of the Bristol Royal Infirmary," *California Management Review* 45: 73–84.

WHYTE, W. H. (1956), *The Organization Man*, New York: Doubleday.

WILKINSON, A., and WILLMOTT, H. (eds.) (1995), *Making Quality Critical: NewPerspectives on Organizational Change*, London, Routledge.

WILLIAMS, K., HASLAM, C., JOHAL, S., FROUD, J., SHAOUL, J., and WILLIAMS, J. (1996), "The Right Argument: Refocusing the Debate on Privatization and Marketization," *Manchester International Centre for Labour Studies Working Paper* 11.

WILLIAMS, R. (1976), *Keywords: A Vocabulary of Culture and Society*, London: Fontana.

WILSON, D. C. (1992), *A Strategy for Change: Concepts and Controversies in the Management of Change*, London: Routledge.

WRIGHT, S. (ed.) (1994), *Anthropology of Organisations*, London: Routledge.

WRIGHT, V. (ed) (1994), *Privatization in Western Europe: Pressures, problems and paradoxes*, London: Pinter.

ZUCKER, L. C. (1977), "The Role of Institutionalisation in Cultural Persistence," *American Sociological Review* 42: 726–43.

CHAPTER 21

PERFORMANCE MANAGEMENT

COLIN TALBOT

21.1 INTRODUCTION

DISCUSSIONS of the performance of government have existed as long as government itself. Rulers—even autocratic ones—have usually sought to justify their rule by showing how it is beneficial to the ruled. In many modern democracies this has developed into a political theatre of performance where competing parties promise voters that their policies will deliver their version of "the good life" (Talbot 2000). Elections are fought over both future promises and past performance.

Politicians promise to deliver a host of desirable benefits: better health care, safer streets, national security, economic prosperity, and lower taxes and ask to be judged on their record of delivering on their promises. However, a perennial problem is the lack of specificity or measurement of delivery against these promises. This is compounded by what we call "attribution problems": what has caused positive or negative changes in society? If the economy booms, is this due to the policies of our governors, or because consumers in foreign lands have suddenly started demanding our products?

Given this essential link between policies (what is promised) and delivery (what actually happens) it is perhaps hardly surprising that there have been recurrent attempts to formalize systems for measuring, monitoring, and managing the performance of public systems. As the welfare state grew in developed countries

Schuknecht 2000), it was hardly surprising that a frequent question became—what do we get for all this money?

Political discourse has still tended to focus on "getting and spending"—tax and budgets—(Pliatzky 1982) rather than "achieving." But the latter has surfaced again and again as a subsidiary theme. In the USA, especially, some forms of performance measurement have become widely accepted as a relatively uncontroversial technology. In the immediate post-Second World War period there were intense debates about who was best achieving reconstruction results. In the 1960s and 1970s a more technocratic discussion about the best ways of planning and programming public activities and resources emerged with a mainly policy focus (for a substantial US effort in this direction see Moss 1973). Since the early 1970s the Washington based Urban Institute has played a consistently leading role (see Hatry 1999; Morley, Bryant, et al. 2001). In the 1980s, a new wave of discussions about how best to manage the performance of public organizations emerged, mainly focused on issues of efficiency and service delivery (outputs). Under President Clinton in 1993 Congress passed the Government Performance and Review Act (GPRA) which introduced extensive requirements for performance reporting by federal agencies and departments (Mihm 1995; Radin 1998; Forsythe 2000; Long and Franklin 2004). By the late 1990s an "outcome-based government and budgeting" debate materialized. Under President Bush a new "Management Agenda" was launched in 2002 which included a focus on integrating budget and performance (Office of Management and Budget 2002) with agencies being asked to focus on "high quality outcome measures." Along with four other initiatives under the "Management Agenda," this has been subject to a simple, web-published, traffic-light based scorecard system for every federal agency (http://results.gov/agenda/scorecard.html).

These various "tides of reform," with differing emphases on different aspects of performance, may have waxed and waned along with wider public sector reforms (Light 1997) but "performance" in some guise has remained a permanent feature. Nor is this just a US trend—many other countries have had similar waves of change although the details of timing and focus vary enormously.

Each such wave has had specific themes and foci and has been associated with particular tools and techniques—e.g., Management by Objectives (MBO), Quality, Balanced Scorecards, etc. Each has had widespread, but highly uneven, impacts. Each has risen, reached an apogee, and then fallen back—usually leaving a detritus of systems, policies, and procedures behind. Underlying all of them have been on-going debates about perennial issues in democratic government such as policy versus administration; rational decision making versus incremental "muddling through"; and decisive leadership versus consultation and involvement.

That there has been a surge of "performance" related activity in many states over the last couple of decades is indisputable, but it's spread has been far from global or even. The "performance" tide has been closely allied to the "New Public Management" (NPM) trends of the last part of the twentieth century. Broadly speaking, those polities who have been most active in adopting NPM style reforms are the "Anglo" and northern European countries (OECD-PUMA 1997; Pollitt 2000; Pollitt and Bouckaert 2000; Talbot, Daunton et al. 2001). Bouckaert's introductory chapter to a survey of ten countries suggested a strong correlation within the group of "adopters" of performance approaches between top–down and comprehensive approaches on the one hand (Australia, UK and New Zealand) and bottom–up and incremental approaches on the other (Finland and Denmark) (OECD-PUMA 1997). The outlier in this analysis was France, where a very top–down approach was coupled with very ad hoc and incremental (indeed weak) adoption. In seeking to explain variations in the scope of performance auditing Barzelay suggests that several factors, including influence of NPM, government structures, institutional design, and environmental factors can be discerned (Barzelay in OECD-PUMA 1996). A similar, if more sophisticated, analysis of NPM adoption trends (given in Pollitt and Bouckaert 2004) seems as though it could apply equally to performance.

This chapter will start by asking: Where does performance take place—with programs, organizations, or people? It then outlines some of the justifications and doctrines that have been developed in support of performance measurement and reporting and examines some of the counter-arguments which are typically advanced. The chapter then turns to examining some commonly employed models of performance and discusses performance audit. Finally, it examines what new challenges are on the horizon.

This is not an empirical survey of performance measurement practices but rather a conceptual analysis. There have been empirical surveys in the 1990s (e.g., OECD-PUMA 1994, 1997) and, although these had weaknesses, they at least provided some useful raw material. They have unfortunately not been repeated (for a small exception see Talbot, Daunton et al. 2001). Most academic work has consisted of comparative case studies rather than full surveys (e.g., Cave, Kogan, et al. 1990; Carter, Klein, et al. 1992; Halachmi and Bouckaert 1996; Mayne and Zapico-Goni 1997; Abramson and Kamensky 2002). Interestingly, there have been few attempts at developing taxonomies of different performance approaches—for an exception see Bouckaert's work (in OECD-PUMA 1997), and perhaps De Bruijn's normative analysis (De Bruijn 2001).

There certainly exist differentiated trends in "performance." Some countries such as Australia, New Zealand, Sweden, UK, and the USA have adopted a largely top–down approach whilst others, such as Denmark, have adopted a more bottom–up approach, and others, such Canada, Finland, France and the Netherlands, a more balanced one (see Introduction to OECD-PUMA 1997). In some cases governments—e.g., New Zealand and UK—have focused initially on outputs and service delivery issues) whilst in others the initial focus was on outcomes and evaluation—e.g., Australia (Talbot, Daunton, et al. 2001). There are many other differences, not least the overall level of "take-up" of performance ideas—some countries have largely opted-out or only reluctantly subscribed to them whilst others have been positively evangelical (Pollitt and Bouckaert 2004). There is clearly a need for more systematic gathering of evidence and analysis—especially since this seems to have "dried up" since the late 1990s.

21.2 FOCI: PERFORMANCE OF WHAT?

It is worth starting by asking the obvious question of what we mean when we speak about performance in government. There are three very distinct foci in terms of what is supposed to be for "performing" in current theory and practice. These are: organizational performance; performance of policies or programs (which often span more than one organizational boundary or tier of government); and performance by public servants. These distinctions often go unacknowledged in discussions about performance—confusingly, for example, the term "performance management" is used in two different sets of literature to refer to either organizational or individual performance.

21.2.1 Organizational Performance

The primary focus of much of the performance literature, in both the public and private sectors, has been organizational. This is obviously important in the public sector because most accountability and financing systems tend to be built around organizational structures rather than (or sometimes as well as) programs or policies.

Public sector administrative units often have responsibility for multiple policies and programs, some of which may be shared with other public organizations either horizontally (partner organizations) or vertically (at different levels of government) or both. They also have overhead costs which are not associated directly with any one specific program, policy, or activity.

The public sector focus of performance systems on organizations clearly has advantages: it allows performance to be related to resourcing and accountability regimes and it allows for application of performance models and techniques from the private sector (where the emphasis is almost entirely on organizations). It can therefore be a powerful tool for controlling organizations.

On the other hand the lack of a one-to-one relationship with policies, programs, and activities means that the measurement of organizational "performance" cannot adequately address these issues, unless some form of disaggregation of activities within the organization (e.g., activity based budgeting and activity measures) are available. The tricky issue of overhead cost allocation to specific programs can make analysis of individual activities very problematic. This makes performance focused on organizations a weak tool for controlling programs, policies and specific activities but strong in addressing management accountability.

21.2.2 Activity, Programme, and Policy Performance

The alternative to an organizational focus is an activity, program, or policy focus. This is the traditional terrain of evaluation studies, an extremely well-developed and long-standing field (Caro 1977; Carley 1980; Rossi, Freeman, et al. 2004) with a whole battery of methods such as "cost–benefit analysis." Such activity was closely tied to ideas of rational planning in public policy, popular in the late 1960s and early 1970s.

The advantage of a policy focus is fairly obvious: most policy initiatives are not confined to single organizations or tiers of government. It may even be transnational in scope, for example in economic and environment policies.

The disadvantages are largely the obverse of an organizational focus: account-abilities are diffuse and difficult to pin down; accounting, in a financial sense, is difficult as streams of funding for individual policies flow through multiple channels and often overlap; and attribution problems are compounded by multiple actors.

The evaluation tradition in social and public policy has also remained remarkably separate from mainstream public policy and management scholarship (Blalock 1999), with its own journals, associations and traditions (and, it must be added, intense internal doctrinal disputes (Guba and Lincoln 1989; Pawson and Tilley 1997)). This is problematic since a feature of the current emphasis on "outcomes" in performance is a growing need for integration between perform-ance and evaluation (Blalock 1999).

Concentrating on "policy performance" can have the advantage of being focused on the objectives of policy (in improving health or education) but diffuse in accountability.

21.2.3 Individual Performance

A third distinct meaning of "performance" relates to the performance of individuals and forms part of the human resources management (HRM) literature. This is often located within a framework of what and how individual (or team) perform-ance contributes to organizational performance and strategies but the focus is firmly on the individual/team.

This focus is not covered here in detail as it forms a distinctive literature which mainly relates only tangentially to the organizational performance literature (see also Chapter 22). This is not to suggest that this is a desirable state of affairs. Both normatively and empirically it is possible to show that the disjunction between organizational level and individual level performance policies, analyses, and practice is unfortunate. One OECD study of performance-related pay in the public sector, for example, established that in few cases were the individual criteria for "good performance" related in any discernable way to the organizational criteria for good performance (OECD-PUMA 1993).

21.3 EMERGING ARGUMENTS FOR "PERFORMANCE"

There have been several themes in international discussions about performance in the past twenty years or so which constitute a set of emerging "administrative arguments." Such arguments are made up of doctrines of public administration—that is maxims about administrative who's, how's, and what's—linked to justifications (Hood and Jackson 1991). It is noticeable that in Hood and Jackson's analysis of extant administrative arguments, performance hardly figures, except as means of control by input, processes, output or outcome (ibid. 90–4).

The arguments presented here are not comprehensive and nor is it meant to suggest that all of them appeared everywhere, simultaneously and equally. On the contrary, they have been sporadic, uneven, and far from universal in their appearance with some countries adopting them all and some hardly any of them at all.

21.3.1 Performance as Accountability

The first argument is performance as accountability and transparency. This argument suggests that for democratic systems to work citizens need to be given information not just about what is spent on public activities but also what results are achieved. Democratic states have mixed policies on how much spending information they divulge, and in what detail, but most have always published some annual budget information. On the other hand very few states or public institutions regularly published information about their achievements.

This deepens long-running arguments about improving the public accountability of government (Day and Klein 1987; Behn 2001; Flinders 2001) through mechanisms such as audit (Normanton 1966), inspection (Light 1993), and the rise of what has been called the "audit society" (Power 1997). Nor has this trend been limited purely to the public sector, with debates about accountability (and governance) also surfacing in the private sector (Case 1995; Zadek, Pruzan et al. 1997; Bovens 1998).

The argument for publishing "performance" information has been made within many governance traditions, including North America, other "Anglo" countries and large parts of Europe, and is simply axiomatic: the publication of performance information is a good thing in and of itself. Indeed some see it as a democratic right.

An interesting example is the publishing of schools inspections results in the UK. In a recent exchange about the effectiveness of such inspections, the former Chief Inspector of Schools claimed that "despite the mission statement I was saddled with by politicians, I always believed that inspections were about giving information to parents. They are about transparency and accountability" (Chris Woodhead, quoted in the *Guardian*, July 8 2003).

21.3.2 Performance as User Choice

A further development of this argument is the justification that such information also serves a purpose. The example above leads us into "performance as user choice." Where there is not simply a single, monopoly state provider but citizens and users may be able to make choices as to which public institution to utilize then it is argued that there is a need to publish comparative performance information. This is justified by the need of citizens to have sufficient information about public organizations' relative performance in order to make choices (Institute of Economic Affairs 1979; Self 1993).

In this doctrine performance information is treated as analogous to the price and quality information provided in the private sector and can similarly allow informed "consumer" choice (Waldegrave 1993).

In its most developed form the policy of user choice has been linked to resource distribution. Thus in UK Universities, resources, to some degree, follow students— the more students you attract, the more resources come with them. There have also been various attempts to develop "voucher" schemes where users carry a sort of substitute for money which they can "spend" at the public organization of their choice (Flynn 2002).

Furthermore, it is argued, even where public bodies are monopoly providers in their locality, if "league tables" of performance are published then users of these services in low performing cases may bring pressure to improve services. Both the public accountability and public choice arguments expressed above are geared towards user choice, but the former is based on collective decisions and the latter individual. Whilst the latter is a purer form of choice, such systems are seen to work only for the better informed and wealthier middle classes thus it can clash with notions of accountability.

21.3.3 Performance as Customer Service

Another argument applied to monopoly public services is that of performance as customer service. This has emerged from the general "quality" movement (Peters and Waterman 1982; Aguayo 1991; Oakland 1991; Logothetis 1992; George and Weimerskirch 1998) and its public sector branch (Dickens 1994; Morgan and Murgatroyd 1994; Gaster 1995; Joss 1995; Kirkpatrick and Martinez Lucio 1995; Pollitt and Bouckaert 1995).

This argument says that public organizations should make clear statements about the levels of service they intend to supply, in terms of timeliness, accessibility and quality, and then report on their success against these aims (Hadley and Young 1991; Pirie 1991; Prime Minister and Chancellor of the Duchy of Lancaster 1991; Ayeni 2001).

The justifications for this doctrine are various. First, it is suggested that receivers of monopoly service have an entitlement to know what standards of service they can expect and demand since they have no choice. This is essentially a "rights" based justification.

Second, it is suggested that modern consumers of public services are more demanding about quality and flexibility in service delivery as a consequence of improved standards in the private sector. This is essentially an expediency based justification, if public services do not provide the private sector equivalent standards of flexibility and quality, confidence in and support for public services will diminish.

Third, it is argued that as our societies have become more complex, more diverse in ethnic and cultural identities, better at recognizing forms of discrimination and work patterns have become more flexible then public services need to respond to these changes. "One size fits all" delivery is no longer a sensible way of trying to provide services.

A supplementary reform associated with customer focused performance standards and reporting is the idea of "seamless service delivery" (Linden 1994). This is linked to notions about better customer services by overcoming the poor experience of public service users of fragmented service delivery—for example the large number of agencies a small business has to deal with in government. This has led to attempts to set up "one-stop-shops" that minimize the number of transaction points between the state and the citizen in achieving any particular goal.

The focus of this doctrine can be on either "excellence" or on minimum standards or both. Thus, for example, the UK's Citizens' Charter initiative had two components. One related to standards: each government service delivery unit was required to produce a "Charter Statement" setting out the minimum standards in service delivery. The organization was expected to set up reporting mechanisms on its performance against these standards and to provide mechanisms for complaints and in some cases redress to individuals for failures.

The second component was recognition of "excellence" in service delivery standards through the "Charter Mark Awards" which were originally an annual competition which had a fixed number of "winners" who received a Charter Mark.

These two components were eventually fused in a reformed Charter Mark scheme when this became a standards-based, rather than competitive, scheme where agencies received an award for meeting minimum standards of performance. Charter Marks could also be lost as happened in the case of the UK Passport Agency after a particular crisis.

21.3.4 Performance as Efficiency

Perhaps the longest running argument for the production of performance information (but not necessarily its publication) is a managerial one (e.g., Downs and Larkey 1986; Tomkins 1987; Rosen 1993; Popovich 1998). Here, as public organizations have no "bottom-line" which demonstrates their success (or otherwise), a substitute has to be found. Indeed, such managerial levers are also employed in the private sector where markets cannot operate effectively. This is close to the administrative control mechanisms identified by Hood and Jackson (1991). The purpose of such levers is to improve the efficiency of public organizations which are otherwise free from incentives.

Efficiency in this context is x-efficiency, i.e., the internal efficiency of turning inputs into outputs. Allocative or y-efficiency is dealt with in the section on "performance as resource allocation."

The specific form that this argument has taken recently, influenced by principal–agent theories, is that performance contracts should be drawn up which specify the resources to be supplied; the outputs and services to be delivered; the monitoring mechanisms to be used; and finally, reward or sanction mechanisms (Boston, Martin et al. 1996; Chancellor of the Exchequer 1998). The "principals" in this case can either be politicians (as in the USA's GPRA, New Zealand's reforms, and the UK's minister–agency arrangements) or other public administration bodies or officials (as in Swedish ministry–agency relations or UK Treasury–Departmental relations under Public Service Agreements).

It should be stressed that in this argument performance is principally about outputs. Indeed in the UK case of executive agencies and in New Zealand's minister–department contracts, performance targets were specifically limited to outputs and not outcomes.

Many previous performance related initiatives, such as Planning, Program, and Budgeting systems, Policy Analysis and Review, and Management by Objectives, have relied heavily on this type of doctrine and justification (e.g., Schultze 1968; Lyden and Miller 1971).

21.3.5 Performance as Results, Effectiveness, and "What Works"

This argument suggests that government organizations have become too focused on the inputs and processes of administering public policies and have lost sight of the outcomes they intend to achieve. For example, a benefits agency becomes focused on the task of dispensing social security benefits efficiently and equitably, rather than seeing this as a contributory activity to reducing poverty and considering how benefits fit into wider policies or how they may be better delivered to achieve the desired outcomes.

There are two distinct ways in which this argument has surfaced—one focused on the whole system of government and organizations and the other focused more on programs and policies.

The first focus is on what has been variously called "outcome based governance" or "outcome based budgeting" (Molen, Rooyen et al. 2001). In some respects this has emerged as a reaction to the "performance as efficiency" argument. The latter, it is alleged, may produce increases in efficiency and better delivery of specific services but at the cost of losing sight of the overall aims of policy—the eventual outcomes or results to be achieved. This can lead to poor coordination between government agencies that are focused inwards on achieving optimum efficiency and outputs and not on wider goals. In the worst cases it can lead to perverse outcomes where one agency's efficiency increasing measures undermine the work of another agency or of the whole system.

The second focus is on the so-called "what works" agenda. This first seems to have surfaced in the criminal justice field, especially in the USA and UK, around the issue of "what works" in reducing crime and recidivism (McGuire 1995). It has now mushroomed into a whole research agenda and (supposed) practice of basing policy choices on evidence—what has become known as "evidence based policy and practice" (Davies, Nutley et al. 2000).

21.3.6 Performance as Resource Allocation

Closely related to the "what works" argument is that performance information is essential for decision making about resource allocation. This is part of the long-running argument for rational planning in resource allocation (Schultze 1968).

Information about performance, especially about effectiveness and outcomes, it is argued, is necessary to understanding the utility of resources allocated to any specific policy area.

This has been highly developed, at least rhetorically, in systems such as the UK's new Public Service Agreements (Chancellor of the Exchequer 1998), the USA's Government Performance and Results Act (Mihm 1995; General Accounting Office (USA) 1997a and b; Forsythe 2000), and the New Zealand reforms (Boston, Martin et al. 1996).

21.3.7 Performance as Creating Public Value

The final, and most recent, argument for performance measurement, management, and reporting is about "creating public value" (Moore 1995). This argument states that public services are not merely about addressing "market failure" but have a more positive role in creating value which could not be made in the private sector. Public services are viewed not merely as "products" and from a financial or economic standpoint, as much argumentation about performance has done. Rather, public services are seen as adding value through issues like equity, equality, probity, and building social capital—which the private sector not only does not but cannot provide.

This more positive attitude to public services and their achievements has a long history in the UK and was developed in the early 1980s as the so-called "public service orientation" (Clarke 1987; Stewart 1988; Ferlie, Pettigrew et al. 1996). More recently the ideas of Harvard scholar Mark Moore have been picked up and refashioned by the UK's Cabinet Office (Kelly and Muers 2002).

21.4 COUNTER-ARGUMENTS

The arguments recorded are not exhaustive but they do represent the types of doctrine and the types of justifications offered for developing various forms of performance measurement in recent years.

It should be noted that these doctrines and justifications often overlap in terms of the type of performance reporting they focus on—for example, process, efficiency, outputs or outcomes—and in terms of the types of audience that are the alleged beneficiaries, for example, citizens, politicians, or managers.

As with many administrative arguments, for every doctrine and its justification there are often counter-arguments and it is important to record these. Perhaps surprisingly the academic critique of the "performance" movement has been relatively muted. There have been critiques, but these have tended to be tangential to other arguments such as a general opposition to "managerialism" (Cutler and Waine 1997) or defence of the "public space" (Marquand 2004). There have also been extensive criticisms by practitioners (see evidence submitted to Public Administration Select Committee 2003), but interestingly these have been mainly about how performance measurement (and in the UK case, specifically target setting) has been used in a semi-Soviet planning style. Many criticisms have surfaced in the media, from legislators, practitioners, interest groups, and some academics, but as we have said these tend to be partial and fragmentary. Nevertheless we will try to summarize the arguments most commonly deployed.

Interestingly, performance techniques seem to have been relatively uncontroversial at two extremes—in the USA where they have been accepted widely and simply regarded as a specific technology, and in the southern European states and others where they have been largely ignored (Pollitt and Bouckaert 2004). Where debates have mainly surfaced is in the "Commonwealth" countries, such as the UK, Canada, Australia, Jamaica, and Tanzania, and in the northern European states of the Netherlands, Belgium, Germany, Sweden, and Finland, where their use has proved most controversial (for Finland, Netherlands, Sweden and UK, see Pollitt, Talbot et al. 2005).

Given the "popular" nature of these criticisms I have not provided systematic referencing for these arguments which are regularly deployed against performance in general and specific aspects of performance. They are as follows.

21.4.1   Incompleteness

Performance information, it can be argued, is always only able to give an incomplete picture of public activities which are diverse and complex. There is therefore bound to be a degree of distortion and exclusion, and what is not measured is usually of importance to one stakeholder or another. Thus performance measurement can obscure as much as it reveals.

Another version of this argument is that much performance reporting is deliberately kept simple for communications purposes. League table reporting is inevitably crude and distorting and can cause great demoralization amongst those unfairly categorized as "poor" performers, even exacerbating poor results.

21.4.2   Over-complexity

A corollary of the above argument is that there is a tendency for performance measurement systems, in a search for the elusive goal of completeness, to become ever more complex. This results finally in informational overload which renders the system unworkable and creates incommensurate costs.

21.4.3 Transaction Costs

The costs of producing performance information, especially in complex areas, can easily become prohibitive. Costs include staff time in completing detailed reporting schedules; information processing costs and managerial time spent assessing performance information. The costs of inspection and audit regimes put in place to externally monitor or assess performance can also be great (Hood, James et al. 1999). Overall if "performance" criteria, such as cost–benefit analysis, were to be applied to performance systems themselves it is suggested that they would be a net debit to public services rather than a value adding component. Moreover the performance movement is hypocritical insofar as it rarely applies such criteria to itself.

21.4.4 Attribution

Attribution problems are usually discussed in relation to outcomes. Have the outputs of public services resulted in the desired outcomes and, if so, can these be attributed to the outputs?

However it should also be noted attribution problems can also apply to other parts of the production process. For example, is an increase in efficiency due to managerial actions or a general rise in staff morale caused by their country winning the Soccer World Cup? Or, conversely, is a fall in efficiency due to everyone taking unauthorized leave to watch the World Cup? Crude performance measures about efficiency, outputs, or outcomes often tell us little, it is argued, about the real reasons why a change has taken place. Correlation is thus mistaken for causation. Equally difficult is the counterfactual question as we simply don't know what would have happened without many public interventions.

21.4.5 Quantity versus Quality

Performance measurement is inevitably about trying to put quantitative values onto many aspects of public services which are difficult to quantify. Examples such as the inspirational qualities of a teacher are often used. This is often encapsulated in an aphorism like "we make important what can be measured, because we cannot measure what is important." This, it is suggested, has distorting and demoralizing effects, especially in human services where many aspects of "good" performance are not easily measured.

21.4.6 Manipulation and Deception

Where performance measures are imposed and can lead to rewards or sanctions it is argued that they inevitably lead to attempts to manipulate results to present the best possible picture. This argument is usually supported with cases of specific manipulation which have come to light. Aside from the uncertainty this produces about reported performance, it is argued that it encourages a culture of cynicism and amoral behavior which can seriously damage public service ethics and ethos.

21.4.7 Distorted Behaviors and Unintended Consequences

A consequence of the rewards and sanctions, coupled with problems associated with measuring complex areas of professional practice, may result in changes in behavior in which performance is not optimized. A key example is the prioritization of non-medically urgent operations for patients in order to meet waiting time targets in hospitals at the cost of those more urgent. This biasing of clinical judgment is seen as undesirable.

Even where performance is accurately reported and organizations are genuinely improving their own performance it is argued that the complexity of modern public services and the societies they are interacting with can produce perverse results. These can lead to a focus on narrow outcomes or outputs to for one agency, to the detriment of other wider policy and program objectives and to unintended and unwanted outcomes and outputs or to contradictory efforts by different agencies.

21.4.8 Cyclical Incompatibility

Performance measurement to be really effective has to be sustained and consistent over long periods of time. In the case of outcome measurement this may be over decades. It is argued that the political processes of most democracies are such that there is no way that such sustainability and consistency can be achieved. The vagaries of short-term political cycles and the determination of politicians to gain short-term political advantages will always undermine such aspirations.

21.4.9 Measurement Degradation

A recent argument has emerged about performance targets which suggests that there is empirical evidence to support the notion that the effectiveness of perform-ance measurement deteriorates over time, undermining the very possibility of long-term stability in performance measurement which is important for public accountability and for analytic reasons. Called by some the "paradox of performance" this problematic finding suggests insurmountable difficulties in long-term performance measurement.

21.4.10 Politics versus Rationality

The final argument against performance measurement is a much wider argument against all attempts at rational planning, analysis, and evaluation in public services. This argument, first espoused by Charles Lindblom, is that public systems are dominated by politics which inevitably leads to instability, incrementalism, muddling through, messy compromises and value judgments which fatally undermine all attempts at rational decision making. In the case of performance this emerges as partisan interpretation of figures, distortion by ruling parties and their opponents, instability in measurement regimes and priorities in target setting and booming costs of inspection, audit, and verification.

21.5 Models, Techniques and Tools

Having examined the arguments for and against performance measurement, reporting, and management, the focus turns to the specific models, techniques, and tools used. This is a rapidly evolving field and is constantly influenced by wider performance measurement developments (mainly from the private sector) so what is offered here can only be a brief summary and critical comment upon major developments to date.

The clearest trend in the performance literature generally has been towards developing various models, frameworks, or "balanced scorecards" of performance. The sources of such developments have been multiple.

Negative drivers for the development of more comprehensive ways of analyzing organizational performance in the private sector have been widespread discontent with corporate reporting standards and a pure focus on financial measures. Long before the Enron scandal, many analysts had noted that financial reporting by companies rarely gave an adequate picture of a company's true competitive position. Annual reports often only gave anecdotal and of course glowing accounts of achievements and even seasoned analysts found it difficult to estimate the real direction of a company's performance (Elliot and Schroth 2002). In the most extreme cases apparently healthy companies suddenly collapsed causing real anxiety amongst investors.

More positive drivers for comprehensive analysis came from a series of organ-izational improvement initiatives, such as: customer focus; quality initiatives, e.g., TQM; business process reengineering; just-in-time production; human resource management; and benchmarking. Most of these initiatives, it was widely recog-nized, only addressed a specific aspect of company performance and what was needed was some way of taking a comprehensive view.

21.5.1 Performance Models: Generic

Out of these negative and positive forces emerged several attempts at a holistic approach.

The Baldrige Awards (George 1992) were perhaps the first to emerge. These had their origins firmly in the "quality" movement but established a framework for assessing the whole organization rather than just one or two systems. They were also strongly influenced by the benchmarking movement, developing a model which allowed each individual organization to measure its activities against a wide set of standardized criteria through which to compare. As the name implies, this approach also included an annual competitive award process. These awards have given rise to a whole plethora of similar schemes in other countries: in Canada; in Europe (EFQM Awards); and in many individual European countries.

The European Foundation for Quality Management (EFQM) produced a model based on a similar approach to Baldrige. This model is also known as the Business Excellence Model and latterly the Organizational Excellence Model. The EFQM Model has nine high-level performance clusters, such as Leadership and People and Results, underpinned with around 100 specific, standardized criteria. It is also divided into two even higher-level categories: performance enabling (forward-looking and predictive) clusters and performance results (backward-looking and evaluative) clusters.

Both Baldrige and EFQM models are annual snapshots of performance based on either examination by external assessors or self-assessment. They are meant to form the basis of subsequent improvement programs. One interesting difference be-tween the two is the inclusion criteria for "corporate social responsibility" in EFQM in the form of an "impact on society" cluster. It is tempting to suggest this may be due to the differences between the more free-market, liberal demo-cratic, traditions of the USA and more social democratic traditions in Europe.

A rather different approach was developed in the Balanced Scorecard (Kaplan and Norton 1992, 1996a, 1996b). The Balanced Scorecard is simpler than the Baldrige or EFQM Models with only four high-level "perspectives" (Financial; Customer; Innovation; and Internal Process). It differs in that whilst these per-spectives are generic, what is developed beneath each of the top-level groupings is meant to be idiosyncratic to each organization, thus there are no standardized criteria, benchmarking, or awards. Neither is the scorecard purely a performance assessment tool but is also meant to form the basis of strategic and business planning, with plans taking the form of "strategy maps" which show how each organizational strategic priority should be developed and measured in each of the four scorecard categories.

All three models have had some impact in the public sector. Many public sector organizations in the USA (Baldrige), the UK and Denmark (EFQM), and Canada (using their own award scheme) have participated in the annual competitions or used the frameworks for self-assessment (see for the UK experience Samuels 1997, 1998). The Balanced Scorecard perspectives have often been adapted to meet the needs of specific public organizations. Sometimes these models have not explicitly been called balanced scorecards but "performance frameworks" or similar, even where they are clearly analogous in their basic approach.

21.5.2 Performance Models: Public Sector

Over the past twenty years a simple model of public sector performance which might be called "the production model" has been used. The model comprises four components: "inputs–process–* outputs–outcomes" (IPOO). This commonly agreed framework has been adopted in the UK by five central institutions to clarify definitions (HM Treasury 2001).

In a sense IPOO can be used as a "balanced scorecard." It has been argued that old-style public administration concentrated on one end of this linear model: inputs (budgets) and processes (rules) to the exclusion of outputs and outcomes. The recent emphasis given to "outcome-based governance" concentrates on the other end of the production process to the exclusion of inputs and processes. In between, initiatives aimed at "customer service" can be seen as addressing processes and outputs but down-playing inputs and outcomes (for a practical application see Talbot 1999a).

The IPOO model has serious limitations and public sector approaches have been influenced by other developments and a whole series of much more detailed and comprehensive models have emerged. Most similar to the Baldrige and EFQM approach, but pre-dating the latter, are the Speyer Institute Awards for public administration which have been running in the German-speaking countries for around twenty years as a biannual award program. A more specific attempt to create a public sector specific version of this approach was the Public Service Excellence Model (Talbot 1998, 1999a). A much more sophisticated version of the basic IPOO approach was produced in the USA as the "comprehensive public sector productivity improvement model" (Holzer and Callahan 1998). In Canada a new "management assessment framework" developed by the Treasury Board offers yet another model. The weakness of nearly all these models is clearly that they are purely hypothetico-deductive in nature and have little empirical validation.

21.5.3 Performance Audit

Alongside the growing use of performance models or frameworks there have been a number of other developments. Most prominent amongst these has been the use of performance audit as a tool of government and/or legislatures to evaluate performance (OECD-PUMA 1996; National Audit Office 1999; Pollitt, Girre et al. 1999; Swedish National Audit Office (RRV) 1999).

21.6 THEORY

It is noticeable that many of the arguments considered in the previous sections in support of, or against, performance measurement and management are "practitioner" theories or "theories-in-use" (Argyris and Schon 1978). What is striking about most of the policy and practitioner, and even the academic, literature is the absence of theoretical justification for particular models of performance proposed. Most of these are advanced in purely axiomatic, doctrinal, forms which are supposed to appear as self-justificatory. Theory can relate to performance in two ways: theories of performance, which many of the models implicitly embrace, and theories and performance—that is to say the relationship of performance measurement to wider public organization and management theories.

21.6.1 Theories *of* Performance

There are numerous models of performance—as we discuss above but few come with any clear theoretical explanation or empirical validation. The public sector is in strong contrast here to the private sector where alongside the same normative, celebratory and self-justificatory literature there is also a strong theoretical and empirical tradition (see, e.g., Neely and Waggoner 1998). This lacunae in the public sector is being addressed but the literature is currently underdeveloped (for exceptions see Heinrich and Lynn 2000; Ingraham, Joyce et al. 2003). Normative model building has been extensive but few of these have been based on testable models (but see O'Toole and Meier 2000). Others have taken some of the more interesting empirically based critiques from the private sector—for example, Gupta and Meyer's interesting work on the "paradoxes of performance" which suggest weak correlations between performance indicators and performance itself (Meyer and Gupta 1994) and applied these to the public sector (van Thiel and Leeuw 2002). On the question of how do we really know if public organization are performing well Pollitt has offered an extended review of the issues and problems (Pollitt 2000) but not, unfortunately, a clear solution.

Adopting different approaches, others have sought to inductively derive performance models from empirical evidence—for example, the mammoth survey of state and local government in the USA by the Maxwell School (Government Performance Project 2003) or the international comparative study of public agencies (Ingstrup and Crookall 1998). Others have taken the opposite tack and tried to identify the features of permanently failing organizations (Meyer 1989) or the causes of disasters in organizations (Toft and Reynolds 1994)—both cases using predominantly public organizations as exemplars.

21.6.2 Theories *and* Performance

Several theoretical traditions within and around public organization and management theory potentially have something to say about performance: public choice and institutional economics; the new institutionalism; political-economy; postmodern social constructionism; and complexity theories. Unfortunately there have been few explorations of such linkages.

Public choice and institutional economics theories are probably the strongest candidates for addressing performance. Public choice analyses of public sector activities identify problems of monopoly, producer capture and lack of user choice as key issues. Prescriptions include breaking up monopolies, increased use of contracts, more competition, and greater user choice—all of which require information about the performance of organizational units (Boyne, Farrell et al. 2003: 6–11). In one of the few studies to explicitly try to link analyses of performance systems and public choice theory, Boyne et al. offer a normative template of what "good" performance measurement would look like under public choice and empirical data on actual performance measurement systems. Whilst their analysis of performance measurement is useful, they are forced to conclude that assessing whether these public choice related policies have actually worked in terms of increasing performance is "impossible for technical and theoretical reasons" (ibid. 156).

The so-called "new institutionalism" (March and Olsen 1989; Peters 1999) ought to have something to say about performance. The idea that institutional environments and histories would shape policies on performance measurement seems reasonable but there has been hardly any analysis which draws upon this perspective specifically in relation performance (as opposed to wider public sector reforms). One could expect—for example—that taking an institutional perspective those countries with strong executive–majoritarian traditions might adopt performance systems in ways different to nations with strong party-coalition customs (Lijphart 1999). From a more cultural–institutional perspective countries at different points on Hofstede's (2003) cultural dimensions would adopt or adapt performance in very different ways. Unfortunately, with the partial exception of Pollitt and Talbot et al. who use Hofstede and Barzelay's introduction to the OECD survey of performance audit (OECD-PUMA 1996, Pollitt, Talbot et al. 2005) few such attempts at linking institutionalism and performance have been made.

Political-economy based critiques of public sector "managerialsm," with performance seen as merely one component of the latter, have been made (Cutler and Waine 1997). In this view, changes in public sector management reflect wider changes in management and organization consequential upon changing production norms (e.g., from "Fordist" to "Post-Fordist"). Unfortunately this is not a particularly convincing argument because, as Pollitt has long pointed out (Pollitt 1990), performance measurement is more in the Fordist and Taylorian traditions of management than the new wave "cultural" management of the "excellence" approach (Peters and Waterman 1982) which specifically rejects "managing by numbers."

Those approaching public management from a postmodern or social constructionist theoretical stance would see performance measurement as inherently socially constructed and subjective. This could lead to the conclusion that such approaches should be rejected out of hand or, more constructively, that this should lead to an approach to performance based upon dialogue. This would then be somewhat similar to the dialog-based approaches to public policy which have emerged in recent years (Fischer and Forester 1993). Such an analysis has yet to be made of performance developments.

Finally, we turn to the theoretical "new kid on the block"—complexity theory—which can, and is, being applied to public policy areas (Byrne 1998; Rihani 2002) and has potentially important ramifications for performance (Axelrod and Cohen 1999).

If social systems do behave, as complexity theory suggests, as non-linear systems then much of the linear production-process thinking underpinning performance models discussed earlier is faulty. Put simply, the so-called "butterfly effect" can mean that only small inputs might produce massive outputs, and the contrary may also be true (the "butterfly effect" works in both directions). But in both cases only slight differences of context and initial conditions may mean that one act of "performance" may have completely different results from a seemingly quite similar one. Axelrod and Cohen argue, for example, that in these circumstances it is easy to attribute success (or failure) to a part when an ensemble is to blame; to one ensemble when another is the culprit; or a strategy when it was the circumstances which produced the result (Axelrod and Cohen 1999: 139). Their conclusions that (*a*) it is important that performance measures are shaped within the system and (*b*) that defining "success" may mean, paradoxically, using measures that do not include ultimate success (Axelrod and Cohen 1999: 121–2) pose substantial challenges to public services. In the first instance, defining performance purely "within the system" may mean producer or professional capture and lack of democratic accountability. In the second, their findings seem to undermine the move to "outcome-based" performance, suggesting that it is only through experimentation and short-term and piecemeal measurement that desired outcomes can be reached.

21.7 Conclusions and Future Challenges

As has been mentioned before, public services have been subjected to tides of reform (Light 1997) and performance is no exception. However, there is something qualitatively different about the current wave of performance reforms. The actuality of widespread public reporting of performance is now so well entrenched in many countries (especially the Anglo-American ones, but others too) that it is difficult to see it ever completely ebbing. The form that performance policy may take will undoubtedly change, but just as the move towards audit of financial aspects of government and to inspection and complaints procedures has proved permanent, it is likely, so will performance.

The real issue therefore is not will performance, as a policy trend, continue but how will it continue? We conclude with a brief discussion of some of the challenges and changes which may be confronted in the next few years.

21.7.1 Performance and Functions

Much of the discussion of performance has been of a generic nature—analyses which implicitly assume that the same approaches, models, or techniques of performance measurement, management, and reporting are equally applicable across all parts of the public services.

The argument has been strongly made that, on the contrary, a differentiated approach to performance is necessary according to the type of public function being assessed (Wilson 1989). Whilst some initial work has been done of this topic (e.g., on human services see Martin and Kettner 1996; Yates 1996), there is little substantial, insightful and empirically grounded research on what the alternatives and varieties of different performance approaches for different functions might be.

21.7.2 Performance of Partnerships and Networks

As has been well documented there is a perceived increase in partnership and networked forms within public service. These pose specific problems for performance, much of the debate about which has been framed around single-organization, linear, production-like processes. In both the USA's GPRA and the UK's PSA systems, for example, specific measures have been attempted to promote better understanding of performance across organizational boundaries (General Accounting Office (USA) 1997*a* and *b*; Comptroller and Auditor General 2001). There is as yet insufficient research on how well these types of problems are being tackled, or indeed can be tackled. However if the literature about increasing networked forms of governance is correct, this poses a fairly fundamental challenge to much of the existing approaches to performance.

21.7.3 Performance and Democratic Discourse

The final challenge to identify is how "performance" can be integrated into democratic processes? A recent UK Parliamentary Report identifies this as a substantial problem, with both Government and the Legislature failing to give performance information proper regard in debates about policy (Public Administration Select Committee 2003). Similar criticisms have emerged in the United States with performance reporting under GPRA often being used only as a political weapon—for example a partisan "scorecard" based on GPRA reports published by the Congressional Republican leadership as an attack on the Presidency (Armey, Craig et al. 1997). In the field of policy analysis there has been a similar debate simmering for some years (Fischer and Forester 1993; Hajer and Wagenaar 2003).

This is in some ways the biggest challenge to the performance movement. Many of the arguments for performance reporting rest on the assumption that it will be good not just for managerial reasons but for policy and democratic ones too. On that the jury is still firmly out.

REFERENCES

ABRAMSON, M., and KAMENSKY, J. (eds.) (2002), *Managing for Results 2002*, Lanham, MD: Rowman & Littlefield.

AGUAYO, R. (1991), *Dr Deming: The American Who Taught the Japanese About Quality*, New York: Fireside (Simon & Schuster).

ARGYRIS, C., and SCHON, D. (1978), *Organisational Learning*, Reading, MA: Addison Wesley.

ARMEY, D., CRAIG, L. et al. (1997), Results Act: It Matters Now—an interim report. Washington, DC, Published by Republican leadership in the House and Senate.

AXELROD, R. and M. D. COHEN (1999), *Harnessing Complexity—Organizatinal Implications of a Scientific Frontier*, New York: The Free Press.

AYENI, V. (2001), *Empowering the Customer*, London: Commonwealth Secretariat.

BEHN, R. (2001), *Rethinking Democratic Accountability*, Washington, DC: Brookings Institution.

BLALOCK, A. B. (1999), "Evaluation Research and the Performance Management Movement: From Estrangement to Useful Integration," *Evaluation* 5(2): 117–149.

BOSTON, J., MARTIN, J. et al. (1996), *Public Management: The New Zealand Model*, Auckland: Oxford University Press.

BOVENS, M. (1998), *The Quest for Responsibility*, Cambridge: Cambridge University Press.

BOYNE, G. A., FARRELL, C. et al. (2003), *Evaluating Public Management Reforms*, Milton Keynes, Open University Press.

BYRNE, D. (1998), *Complexity Theory and the Social Sciences: An Introduction*, London and New York: Routledge.

CARLEY, M. (1980), *Rational Techniques in Policy Analysis*, London: Heinemann/PSI.

CARO, F. G. (ed.) (1977), *Readings in Evaluation Research*, New York: Russell Sage Foundation.

CARTER, N., KLEIN, R. et al. (1992), *How Organisations Measure Success: The Use of Performance Indicators in Government*, London: Routledge.

CASE, J. (1995), *Open-Book Management*, New York: HarperCollins.

CAVE, M., KOGAN, M. et al. (eds.) (1990), *Output and Performance Measurement in Government: The State of the Art*, London: Jessica Kingsley.

CHANCELLOR OF THE EXCHEQUER (1998), *Modern Public Services for Britain: Modernisation, Reform, Accountability: Public Service Agreements 1999–2002*, London: The Stationery Office.

CLARKE, M. S. (1987), *The Public Service Orientation: Some Key Ideas and Issues*, Inlogov/LGTB.

COMPTROLLER AND AUDITOR GENERAL (2001), *Measuring the Performance of Government Departments*, London: National Audit Office.

CUTLER, T., and WAINE, B. (1997), *Managing the Welfare State*, Oxford: Berg.

DAVIES, H., NUTLEY, S. et al. (eds.) (2000), *What Works—Evidence-Based Policy and Practice in Public Services*. Bristol: The Policy Press.

DAY, P., and KLEIN, R. (1987), *Accountabilities: Five Public Services*, London: Tavistock.

DE BRUIJN, H. (2001), *Managing Performance in the Public Sector*, London: Routledge.

DICKENS, P. (1994), *Quality and Excellence in Human Services*, London: Wiley.

DOWNS, G., and LARKEY, P. (1986), *The Search for Government Efficiency: From Hubris to Helplessness*, New York: Random House.

ELLIOT, A. L., and SCHROTH, R. J. (2002), *How Companies Lie*, London: Nicholas Brealey.

FERLIE, E., PETTIGREW, A. et al. (1996), *The New Public Management in Action*, Oxford: Oxford University Press.

FISCHER, F., and FORESTER, J. (eds.) (1993), *The Argumentative Turn in Policy Analysis and Planning*, Durham, NC: Duke University Press.

FLINDERS, M. (2001), *The Politics of Accountability in the Modern State*, Aldershot: Ashgate.

FLYNN, N. (2002), *Public Sector Management (4/e)*, London: Financial Times /Prentice Hall.

FORSYTHE, D. (2000), *Performance Management Comes to Washington: A Status Report on the GPRA*, New York: Rockefeller Institute of Government.

GASTER, L. (1995), *Quality in Public Services*, Milton Keynes: Open University Press.

GENERAL ACCOUNTING OFFICE (USA) (1997a), *Agencies' Strategic Plans Under GPRA: Key Questions to Facilitate Congressional Review*, Washington, DC: GAO.

—— (1997b), *Performance Budgeting: Past Initiatives Offer Insights for GPRA Implementation*, Washington, DC: GAO.

GEORGE, S. (1992), *The Baldrige Quality System*, New York: Wiley.

—— and WEIMERSKIRCH, A. (1998), *Total Quality Management*, New York: Wiley.

GOVERNMENT PERFORMANCE PROJECT (2003), *Paths to Performance in State and Local Government*, Campbell Public Affairs Institute, The Maxwell School of Syracuse University.

GUBA, E. G., and LINCOLN, Y. (1989), *Fourth Generation Evaluation*, New York: Sage.

HADLEY, R., and YOUNG, K. (1991), *Creating A Responsive Public Service*, London: Harvester-Wheatsheaf.

HAJER, M., and WAGENAAR, H. (eds.) (2003), *Deliberative Policy Analysis*, Cambridge: Cambridge University Press.

HALACHMI, A., and BOUCKAERT, G. (eds.) (1996), *Organizational Performance and Measurement in the Public Sector*, Westport, CT: Quorum Books.

HATRY, H. H. (1999), *Performance Measurement: Getting Results*, Washington, DC: The Urban Institute.

HEINRICH, C. J., and LYNN, L. E. (eds.) (2000), *Governance and Performance: New Perspectives*, Washington, DC: Georgetown University Press.

HM Treasury (2001), *Choosing the Right FABRIC: A Framework for Performance Information*, London: HM Treasury.

HOFSTEDE, G. (2003), *Culture's Consequence's: Comparing Values, Behaviours, Institutions and Organizations Across Nations (2/e)*, New York: Sage.

HOLZER, M., and CALLAHAN, K. (1998), *Government at Work: Best Practices and Model Programmes*, Thousand Oaks, CA: Sage.

HOOD, C., and JACKSON, M. (1991), *Administrative Argument*, Dartmouth: Aldershot.

—— JAMES, O. et al. (1999), *Regulation Inside Government*, Oxford: Oxford University Press.

INGRAHAM, P. W., JOYCE, P. G. et al. (2003), *Government Performance: Why Management Matters*, Baltimore: The John Hopkins University Press.

INGSTRUP, O., and CROOKALL, P. (1998), *The Three Pillars of Public Managemen:t Secrets of Sustained Success*, London: McGill Queen's University Press.

INSTITUTE OF ECONOMIC AFFAIRS (1979), *The Taming of Government*, London: IEA.

JOSS, R. K. (1995), *Advancing Quality: TQM in the NHS*, Milton Keynes: Open University Press.

KAPLAN, R. S., and NORTON, D. P. (1992), "The Balanced Scorecard: Measures that Drive Performance," *Harvard Business Review* (Jan.–Feb.).

—— —— (1996a), *The Balanced Scorecard*, Cambridge, MA: Harvard Business School Press.

—— —— (1996b), "Using the Balanced Scorecard as a Strategic Managment System," *Harvard Business Review* (Jan.–Feb.).

KELLY, G., and MUERS, S. (2002), *Creating Public Value—An analytical framework for public service reform*, London: Cabinet Office Strategy Unit (*www.strategy.gov.uk*)

KIRKPATRICK, I., and MATINEZ LUCIO, M. (eds.) (1995), *The Politics of Quality in the Public Sector*, London: Routledge.

LIGHT, P. C. (1993), *Monitoring Government: Inspectors General and the Search for Accountability*, Washington, DC: Brookings.

—— (1997), *The Tides of Reform: Making Government Work 1945–1995*, New Haven: Yale University Press.

LIJPHART, A. (1999), *Patterns of Democracy*, London: Yale University Press.

LINDEN, R. (1994), *Seamless Government: A Practical Guide to Re-Engineering in the Public Sector*, San Fransisco: Jossey Bass.

LOGOTHETIS, N. (1992), *Managing for Total Quality*, London: Prentice Hall International.

LONG, E., and FRANKLIN, A. L. (2004), "The Paradox of Implementing the Government Performance and Results Act: Top-Down Direction for Bottom-Up Implementation," *Public Administration Review* 64(3): 309–19.

LYDEN, F., and MILLER, E. (eds.) (1971), *Planning Programming Budgeting: a systems approach*, Chicago: Markham.

McGUIRE, J. (ed.) (1995), *What Works: Reducing Reoffending*, London: Wiley.

MARCH, J. G., and OLSEN, J. P. (1989), *Rediscovering Institutions and The Organizational basis of Politics*, Oxford: Maxwell Macmillan International.

MARQUAND, D. (2004), *The Decline of the Public*, Cambridge: Polity Press.

MARTIN, L. L., and KETTNER, P. M. (1996), *Measuring the Performance of Human Service Programs*, Thousand Oaks, CA: Sage.

MAYNE, J., and ZAPICO-GONI, E. (eds.) (1997), *Monitoring Performance in the Public Sector*, New Brunswick, Transaction Publishers.

MEYER, M. W., and GUPTA, V. (1994), "The Performance Paradox," *Research in Organizational Behaviour* 16: 309–69.

MEYER, M. Z. (1989), *Permanently Failing Organizations*, London: Sage.

MIHM, C. (1995), "GPRA and the New Dialogue," *The Public Manager* (Winter-Spring) pp 15–18.

MOLEN, K. V. D., ROOYEN, A. V. et al. (eds.) (2001), *Outcome-based Governance: Assessing the Results*, Cape Town: Heinemann.

MOORE, M. (1995), *Creating Public Value*, Cambridge, MA: Harvard University Press.

MORGAN, C., and MURGATROYD, S. (1994), *Total Quality Management in the Public Sector*, Buckingham: Open University Press.

MORLEY, E., BRYANT, S. P. et al. (2001), *Comparative Performance Measurement*, Washington, DC: The Urban Institute.

MOSS, M. (ed.) (1973), *The Measurement of Economic and Social Performance*, New York: National Bureau of Economic Research and Columbia university Press.

National Audit Office (1999), *What are Taxpayers Getting for Their Money? A value for money guide to examining outputs and outcomes*, London: NAO.

NEELY, A., and WAGGONER, D. (eds.) (1998), *Performance Measurement: Theory and Practice*, 2 vols., Cambridge: Centre for Business Performance, Judge Institute, Cambridge University.

NORMANTON, E. L. (1966), *The Accountability and Audit of Governments*, Manchester: Manchester University Press.

OAKLAND, J. S. (1991), *Total Quality Management*, London: DTI.

OECD-PUMA (1993), *Private Pay for Public Work: Performance Related Pay for Public Sector Managers*, Paris: OECD.

—— (1994), *Performance Management in Government: Performance Measurement and Results Oriented Management*, Paris: OECD.

—— (1996), *Performance Auditing and the Modernisation of Government*, Paris: OECD.

—— (1997), *In Search of Results: Performance Management Practices*, Paris: OECD.

OFFICE OF MANAGEMENT AND BUDGET (2002), *The President's Management Agenda (Fiscal Year 2002)*, Washington DC: Executive of of the President, Office of Management and Budget.

O'TOOLE, L., and MEIER, K. J. (2000), "Networks, Hierarchies, and Public Management: Modeling the Nonlinearities," in C. J. Heinrich and L. E. Lynn (eds.), *Governance and Performance: New Perspectives*, Washington DC, Georgetown University Press.

PAWSON, R., and TILLEY, N. (1997), *Realistic Evaluation*, London: Sage.

PETERS, G. B. (1999), *Institutional Theory In Political Science*, London and New York: Pinter.

PETERS, T., and WATERMAN, R. (1982), *In Search of Excellence: Lessons From Americas Best Run Companies*, New York: Harper and Row.

PIRIE, M. (1991), *The Citizens' Charter*, London: Adam Smith Institute.

PLIATZKY, L. (1982), *Getting and Spending*, London: Blackwell.

POLLITT, C. (1990), *Managerialism and the Public Services (1/e)*, Oxford: Blackwell.

—— (2000), "How Do We Know How Good Public Services Are?", in D. J. Savoie (ed.), *Governance in the 21st Century*, Monteal and Kingston, McGill-Queen's University Press.

—— and BOUCKAERT, G. (eds.) (1995), *Quality Improvement in European Public Services*, London: Sage.

—— —— (2000), *Public Management Reform: A Comparative Analysis*, Oxford: Oxford University Press.

—— —— (2004), *Public Management Reform: A Comparative Analysis*, 2nd edn., Oxford: Oxford University Press.

—— GIRRE, X. et al. (1999), *Performance or Conformance*, Oxford: Oxford University Press.

—— TALBOT, C. et al. (2005), *Agencies: How Governments Do Things Through Semi-Autonomous Organisations*, Basingstoke: Palgrave (forthcoming).

POPOVICH, M. G. (ed.) (1998), *Creating High Performance Government Organizations*, San Francisco: Jossey Bass.

POWER, M. (1997), *The Audit Society: Rituals of Verification*, Oxford: Oxford University Press.

PRIME MINISTER AND CHANCELLOR OF THE DUCHY OF LANCASTER (1991), *The Citizen's Charter*, Cmd 1599, London: HMSO.

PUBLIC ADMINISTRATION SELECT COMMITTEE (2003), *On Target? Government by Measurement*, London: House of Commons.

RADIN, B. (1998), "The Government Performance and Results Act (GPRA): Hydra-Headed Monster or Flexible Management Tool?" *Public Administration Review* 58(4): 307–16.

RIHANI, S. (2002), *Complex Systems Theory and Development Practice—understanding nonlinear realities*, London: Zed.

ROSEN, E. (1993), *Improving Public Sector Productivity: Concepts and Practice*, Newbury Park, CA: Sage.

ROSSI, P., FREEMAN, H. et al. (2004), *Evaluation: A Systematic Approach*, 7th edn., London: Sage.

SAMUELS, M. (1997), *Benchmarking "Next Steps" Executive Agencies—An Evaluation of the Agency Benchmarking Pilot Exercise*, London: Cabinet Office (OPS) Next Steps Team.

—— (1998), *Towards Best Practice—An Evaluation of the first two years of the Public Sector Benchmarking Project 1996–98*, London: Cabinet Office (OPS) Next Steps Team.

SCHULTZE, C. L. (1968), *The Politics and Economics of Public Spending*, Washington, DC: Brookings.

SELF, P. (1993), *Government by the Market? The Politics of Public Choice*, Basingstoke: Macmillan.

STEWART, J. R., (1988), *Management in the Public Domain*, Place: Publisher.

SWEDISH NATIONAL AUDIT OFFICE (RRV) (1999), *Handbook in Performance Auditing: Theory and Practice*, 2nd edn., Stockholm: Riksrevisionsverket (RRV).

TALBOT, C. (1998), *Public Performance—Towards a Public Service Excellence Model*, Llantilio Crossenny: Public Futures.

—— (1999a), "Public Performance: Towards a New Model?" *Public Policy and Administration* 14(3): pp 15–34.

—— (1999b), *Realising Probation Service Objectives: A Workbook*, London: Home Office.

—— (2000), "Performing 'Performance'—A Comedy in Three Acts," *Public Money & Management* 20(4): pp 63–68.

—— DAUNTON, L. et al. (2001), *Measuring Performance of Government Departments— International Developments*, Llantilio Crossenny: Public Futures (for the National Audit Office).

TANZI, V., and SCHUKNECHT, L. (2000), *Public Spending in the 20th Century: A Global Perspective*, Cambridge: Cambridge University Press.

TOFT, B., and REYNOLDS, S. (1994), *Learning from Disasters*, Oxford: Butterworth— Heinemann.

TOMKINS, C. R. (1987), *Achieving Economy, Efficiency and Effectiveness in the Public Sector*, London: Kogan Page.

VAN THIEL, S., and LEEUW, F. L. (2002), "The Performance Paradox in the Public Sector," *Public Performance & Management Review* 25(3): 267–81.

WALDEGRAVE, W. (1993), *The Reality of Reform and Accountability in Today's Public Service*, BDO Consulting.

WILSON, J. Q. (1989), *Bureaucracy: What Government Agencies Do and Why They Do It*, New York: Basic Books.

YATES, B. T. (1996), *Analyzing Costs, Procedures, Processes, and Outcomes in Human Services*, Thousand Oaks, CA: Sage.

ZADEK, S., PRUZAN, P. et al. (eds.) (1997), *Building Corporate Accountability*, London: Earthscan.

SECTION IV

FUNCTIONAL AREAS

....

STRIVING FOR BALANCE

REFORMS IN HUMAN RESOURCE MANAGEMENT

....

PATRICIA W. INGRAHAM

REFORM of human resource management systems has been a prominent part of broader governmental reform and change in many nations for the past twenty years. Most often, however, it has not been the central focus. Budgetary change, downsizing, decentralization, and privatization have been more successful in capturing public and electoral attention. Of course, all of these are concerned with, or have an impact on, public employees' livelihood, compensation, motivation, and commitment to public service, that is to say, on human resource management. Most recently, distress in many western nations over the "War for Talent" or the mismanagement of vital "human capital" has given human resource management (HRM) issues a bit more urgency (McKinsey 1999; Walker 2000). Even the United States, long a champion of modest, incremental change in civil service and HR reform, is confronted by the reality of massive alterations in the way people are managed in two of the largest federal agencies: the Department of Homeland Security and the Department of Defense. Referring to the now inevitable changes in the century-old civil service system, one architect of the new systems observed, "When a house of cards tumbles, it falls fast" (Interview, 2003).

What are the HRM changes that are becoming so common across the world? Are there clear patterns and useful efforts at evaluation? Are there lessons to be gleaned from the experiences of the past two decades, or are each nation's public service and the ways it is managed and reformed culture bound and unique to one national setting (Clark and Pugh 1999/2000)? Certainly the wildfire-like diffusion of New Public Management (NPM) reforms suggests that someone saw commonalities and the potential for policy transfer (Pollitt and Bouckaert 2000). Pay for Performance, lacking a clear record of success in any national setting—or perhaps any other—remains one of the most popular HR reforms in the world (Ingraham 1993). This is apparently due in large part to symbolic appeal. Of course when national cultures, politics, people, and jobs are involved, tidy outcomes and clear lessons are hard to come by. There are nonetheless several broad themes in HR reforms, in their history, and in their implementation experiences in diverse settings that are useful and offer potential lessons in both crafting and implementing HR policies.

22.1 HRM Reforms: What are They?

Reforms to human resource management systems have occurred in a historical/political context that explains much of the look and shape of contemporary systems. In many nations, for example, the mention of HRM brings a smile and a "Oh yes, you mean civil service" response. Classic—which is to say Weberian—civil service structures and management policies are a core part of governmental structure in most nations of the world, whatever their level of economic and social development. These structures and the neutral values and emphasis on technical expertise they embody have had a standardizing impact on the ways in which most governments think about organizing and managing their employees (Bekke, Toonen and Perry 1997). Two systems, standardized classification systems and compensation systems, have contributed heavily to creating the hierarchical structure and authority pattern recognizable since the days of ancient China. Academic analysis of HRM (a relatively recent term; "personnel" is both older and more common) progressed through clear stages in the last century. Initially based on an industrial model, studies such as time-management analyses assumed that both work and the human effort necessary to pursue it could be standardized and made precise. This model fit well with emergent civil service systems, which also attempted to narrowly define work, knowledge, and skills necessary to achieve work objectives, as well as the appropriate compensation for each level of skill. More modern views of the workforce, largely based on the psychology of workplace relations, concluded that managing people was a far more complex task. These two very disparate views of work and workers were summarized by MacGregor's well known "Theory X and Theory Y" approach to management. Theory X represented the rigid, standardized, fundamentally punitive approach; Theory Y was more descriptive of the human relations school of management and motivation thought (Ingraham 1995; Guest 2001). This distinction is also sometimes described as "hard" versus "soft" management, with the fundamental difference being work conditions that are favorable to the employer versus those that are favorable to the employee (Cornelius and Gagnon 2001). Clearly, this definition has implications for those workplaces that are unionized (as are many public organizations) and subject to collective bargaining.

Another notable characteristic of civil service systems is their effort to separate administration *per se* from politics. There is great variation in this regard, primarily through the presence, action, and legitimacy of the higher civil service, which is discussed in more detail elsewhere in this volume. Suffice to say for purposes here, the higher civil service serves as the formal link between the body of the civil service and the external political environment. There are different models for achieving this linkage, with the top levels of American public bureaucracies being only political appointees (or virtually so) and top levels of the French national administrative corps being very elite civil servants who move freely and frequently between the political and administrative worlds (Aberbach and Rockman 2001; Halligan 2003). For HRM, the primary implications of the various arrangements lie in the ways in which organizational managers learn—or do not learn—management skills.

HR reforms have been primarily of three kinds in the past two decades. The first can generally be called increased flexibility or discretion. It implies a movement away from standardized, centralized, often statutorily based civil service systems. Discretion, or greater freedom from overhead controls, is accorded primarily to managers in these reforms and implies giving them greater ability to target the resources and expertise of the people they manage to specific goals and objectives. The New Zealand contract model of awarding flexibility is certainly a leading example of the general trend toward greater managerial and executive discretion (Boston et. al 1996).

The second broad set of reforms is related to pay, and include pay for performance, broad banding (or flexible pay bands), and performance contracts. Because civil service systems were associated with the ideas of automatic promotion and pay increases, pay for performance reforms were intended to refocus the nature of reward systems in public bureaucracies and to clarify performance objectives and expectations for both people and programs within public organizations (Katula and Perry 2003).

The third set of reforms fall into the general categories of decentralization and devolution. Again intended to move away from rigid centralized structures, these reforms were targeted toward allowing for disentangling and bounding of specific missions, as well as for improved direction of financial and people resources toward clear objectives. Experience in many national and subnational governments has been that, following rather extensive decentralization or devolution early in the reform process, there is a movement back toward some central framework or statement of values, but not toward recentralization in the traditional sense (Kernaghan 2001; Selden 2003).

It is important to note that the experience of the emergent nations of eastern Europe and the nations of Central and South America has been quite different in this regard. In the first of these cases, the old central structures were disassembled, but the effort is to create relatively strong new structures in their place so that some stability and predictability can be installed. Very traditional views of management prevail in these settings; the industrial model is tenacious. In the cases of Central and South America, on the other hand, new central structures and frameworks must be created, because none have existed before. As Peters (2002) suggests, this implies the need to decentralize from a stable center. Flexibility, in other words, cannot be created from an unstable base and without a coherent framework. In these settings, creation of a very traditional civil service system is considered a necessary first step in reform.

22.2 HUMAN RESOURCE MANAGEMENT'S PLACE IN THE SEQUENCE OF REFORM

Kernaghan, assessing human resource management reforms in major Westminster democracies, wrote, "It is notable that HRM reforms [in each of the three nations studied] have tended either to follow structural and financial reforms or to be insufficiently aligned with them" (2001: 1). That is certainly the broader pattern as well. The pattern of reforms is due in some part to the influence of large international organizations, such as the OECD and the World Bank, whose focus is primarily economic and budgetary, but whose policy solutions often include civil service reforms as well (Holmes 2001; Brewer, 2002). This focus has been reinforced by the business-like, efficiency oriented emphasis of New Public Management.

Kernaghan's conclusions were reinforced by an analysis of the American federal and state governments, which found that budgetary and financial management reforms and capacity building were the most frequent "leader" in administrative reform (Ingraham, Joyce and Donahue 2003). This was attributed to the clarity and general acceptance of standards of good practice and effective budgetary procedures. Budgets are also the most frequent communicating device between elected officials and citizens. Knowing where the government will get its money and how it will spend it is clearly a foundation step in thinking about governance and management. Thinking about how to recruit and manage the people who will achieve these objectives lags the first level of reform by several years.

Many contemporary "budget reforms," however, focused on budget cutting and downsizing. A frequent target of the cuts is the permanent bureaucracy. Public employees are often the largest cost for a government organization. Their total numbers, pay, and benefits are perceived to be unnecessary drags on national economies and productivity. In addition, technology is often perceived as reducing total employment and the changing nature of public jobs has further decreased the need for routinized jobs and occupations (Pollitt and Bouckaert 2000).

Broad and non-strategic cutting, however, led to a new appreciation of careful management of human resources. In Britain, for example, a 1999 report on civil service reform noted that it was important to create stronger leadership, improved performance management systems, and a better potential to bring in talented staff at all levels of the organization (UK Cabinet Office 1999). In the United States, the Bush Administration's "Management Agenda" and human capital initiatives, followed by the personnel flexibilities built into the Department of Homeland Security legislation and Department of Defense civilian reforms have emphasized the links among performance, results, and a solid and well-managed workforce (Ingraham and Moynihan 2003; US Office of Management and Budget 2002). Sweden notes that its decentralized HR management strategy allows leaders and managers to tailor HR policy to agency mission and needs, but adds, "What makes a manager a true leader is [the] ability to mobilize other people's efforts and lay the foundations of their high motivation and enjoyment of the work" (OECD 2001:69). The need to manage people well, in other words, is now a recurring theme in administrative reforms in many countries. Despite being invited late to the ball, HRM has now established itself as central to public management reform in many nations. There is increased recognition that decentralization or budget cutting—or both—are not adequate solutions by themselves. It is necessary to manage and develop the public employees that remain. Of central importance, therefore, is the recognition that improved HR management capacity is a necessary component of improved public performance and accountability.

How, specifically do the HR reforms and changes look in most nations? Which patterns or combinations of reform components are most in evidence? Again, there is no simple answer but some interesting themes.

22.3 The Components of Human Resource Management Reforms

22.3.1 Decentralization and/or Deconcentration

The first component has been alluded to several times. The rigidity, size, and cost of centralized civil service structures in many countries were a source of frustration to elected officials, public managers, and citizens trying to understand the operations of the governments that served them. Further, the structures and the systems embodied by the civil service removed the very idea of management from personnel; their focus was much more on process and procedure.

The effort to move away from such edifices involved not just the dismantling of civil service activities, but moving away from large, multi-mission, multi-purpose ministries and agencies. The British Next Steps agencies are one example of such reforms. Intended to both downsize central ministries and to introduce business and performance practices into government, Next Steps agencies now include nearly 80 percent of the British public service. Although the UK was not as centralized as other major western nations—Germany, France, and the United States, for instance—the HRM implications and outcomes of the initiative were enormous. The agency executives, of course, gained new visibility and new authority for managing employees. Never a mainstay of the British higher service, the new HRM responsibilities were somewhat unanticipated and difficult to assume. In one case, that of the UK Patent Office, the new agency moved from London to Wales. This was a cost saving device to be sure, but in the end it involved learning to manage a quite different organization, in a different location, with a substantially changed workforce (Annual Report, UK Patent Office 1993).

The tasks and nature of managing are different as well and are, in many ways, more difficult. There are initiatives similar to this in many countries, with similar HRM impacts. It is notable that there are also nations—the United States is one— in which decentralization or similar reforms have *not* been accompanied by HRM flexibilities. In the US, the change of the Patent and Trademark Office to a performance based organization omitted any release from the provisions of USC Title V, the central personnel regulations (Jacobson 2003; Roberts 1997). At least partially as a result of this exclusion, the PTO continues to operate very much as it did when it was a unit of a large central department.

The role of unionization here and in other cases is notable. Again there is substantial variation across nations in terms of proportion of unionized workforce. France has high numbers of unionized employees; New Zealand made elimination of public unions a centerpiece of its management reforms in the late 1980s. Australia created an agency to oversee labor management relationships and collective bargaining agreements. The UK created special labor councils to partici-pate in the reform transitions; the United States is searching for formula for doing that. It is clear, however, that union impact on the nature of reform is significant. In the United States, it was union opposition that eliminated personnel flexibility from the Office of Patent and Trademark's PBO legislation, for example. The earlier definitions of "hard" versus "soft" management patterns makes clear that, while unions generally favor improved workplace conditions for employees, they are hesitant to agree to such reform provisions if greater management prerogatives are also part of the package. Adding some substance to that position, a 2002 Australian study found that Australian Workplace Agreements in Queensland have as their main aim "maximizing hours and minimizing costs, with many employers also using them to undermine unionism"(www.workplaceinfo.com.au). In that study, 38 percent of the agreements increased weekly hours and 42.5 percent removed overtime.

22.3.2 Increased Flexibility and Managerial Discretion Reforms

Although many broader administrative reforms focused on the idea of "letting managers manage," i.e., free them from unnecessary procedural constraints, much of the discretion focused on three areas: hiring, performance, and pay. Hiring reforms were primarily an effort to move from standardized testing for all but the most routine public jobs to more tailored, often "unassembled" examinations that permitted better consideration of individual talents and abilities.

Traditionally, many systems of the world have hired from results of standardized tests, most often with additional limitations placed on numbers of persons from the test result who could be considered for hiring. Most often, that number was from three to five persons (Ingraham 1995). In many settings, veterans—or other groups considered eligible for preferential treatment—had points added to their test totals, so they were often disproportionately represented at the top of the lists. Further, the lag between testing, reporting, and actual hiring was often substantial. Not only were public organizations and their managers very limited in their ability to hire critical personnel, but those people at the tops of hiring lists were some-times—maybe frequently—no longer available when the hiring process got around to them. The ability to compete effectively for scarce talent was a significant problem for many western nations (OECD 2002; Selden 2003). Conversely, the need in many emergent and transitional nations was precisely the opposite: too much discretion in hiring with a resulting emphasis on patronage, corruption, and serious lack of competencies in public organizations. Thus, in relation to hiring, two distinct "models" of reform were evident in the 1990s and beyond. The first was a clear movement away from standardization and toward increased discretion in testing and hiring. The second was a movement away from dysfunctional discretion toward increased standardization and transparency. Mexico is one example of a nation moving in this direction.

A similar pattern is evident in simplification and transparency reforms related to human resource management. Because public personnel systems are often built upon both legal and bureaucratic rules and processes, they are rather Byzantine structures and systems, involving many pages of rules and regulations, multiple processes for consultation and appeal (for employees), and substantial separation from political and other external authority. The plethora of rules and regulations created a significant boundary for central personnel authorities and structures. Furthermore, these intricate complexities removed much of the authority for personnel matters from the hands of the managers and executives for whom the employees worked. Decentralizing agency structures and the concomitant personnel arrangements addressed these problems to some extent, by making the personnel systems both more accessible and more transparent.

Other simplification strategies were put in place in several nations as well, however, to enhance management capabilities and clarify personnel rules after decentralization had occurred. One of the most important of these is classification reform, which collapsed extremely narrow classification categories into much broader "bands" or areas of expertise and knowledge. Broad banding, as it is generally termed, serves to place employees within a broader range of employment opportunities and demands, and also allows managers greater discretion in setting entry pay and pace of promotion. Needless to say, effective broad banding necessitates earlier reform of testing and admission procedures and rests firmly upon an organization's abilities to manage employee performance well. Further, while these reforms enhance transparency by eliminating a good bit of complexity, they create an accountability trade-off in terms of the discretion awarded individual managers and programs. This particular dilemma is at the heart of most HRM reforms. It is notable, however, in relation another popular HRM reform, pay for performance.

Pay for performance (PFP) reforms are generally linked to problems within public bureaucracies that are different from the simplification and transparency reforms just described. The most notable target problem for PFP is the reality of consistent pay increases based on tenure and seniority, rather than on performance or effort (Ingraham 1993; Katula and Perry 2003). Pay for performance reforms vary substantially in their design and application, and actually have very limited concrete evidence of success, despite their presence in nearly every reform effort in the world (Pollitt and Bouckaert 2000). The higher civil service was—and is—a common target of these efforts. The New Zealand contract system for its CEOs is one example (Boston et al. 1996). Australia created the system for its Senior

Executive Service, but discontinued it several years later. The United States has had formal PFP systems for large parts of its national bureaucracy—including the Senior Executive Service—since 1978, and is now considering an expanded pay for performance system a critical part of the reforms for the Department of Homeland Security and the Department of Defense.

The effectiveness of PFP systems rests in large part on two conditions: adequate resources and careful performance evaluation. The first condition is largely a political choice; the latter depends squarely on the ability of managers to clarify and communicate performance objectives, as well as to communicate effectively with employees about their success or failure in meeting objectives. Both conditions have been met infrequently in public settings—and in many private settings as well (Ingraham 1993; Katula and Perry 2003). In the presence of tight public budgets or of public pay caps, PFP programs can quickly become a substitute for annual increases. Similarly, in the absence of a well-developed and trusted performance evaluation system—or in the hands of managers who don't use such systems effectively—PFP can be viewed as an exercise in favoritism. While more formal contracts with executives can eliminate some of these difficulties, in a public setting with lack of consensus about public objectives there is still ample room for debate about appropriate rewards (Schick 2001).

Taken together, the reforms just described redefine the role of management in public organizations. As many advocates of New Public Management accurately noted, "old" bureaucracies created a management cadre not noted for management skills (Kettl 2002). Indeed, civil service systems did not intend to emphasize "good" management as a desirable quality. Rather, narrow expertise, commitment to procedure, and predictable behavior were valued and rewarded. In some nations, Britain and Canada, for example, policy expertise was valued above all else and policy advising was—is—viewed as a more exalted undertaking than management *per se.* The notion of a proactive, discretionary, risk taking public manager is a fairly recent addition to the public management lexicon; the descriptors, at least, fit better with the structures and systems created by reform. As in many other things in life, however, the devil is in the details of HRM reform. The qualities required of the "new" managers were not necessarily cultivated prior to implementation of reform. Nor did many of the managers and leaders with responsibility for implementing the new ways of dealing with the motivation and reward of employees particularly care to do so. The organizational transformations necessary for successful achievement of reform objectives were complicated, long-term and very, very hard. Thompson and Rainey's (2003) account of the transformation of the Internal Revenue Service in the United States documents these difficulties well. A set of newer and less heralded reforms is intended to address the capacity gaps that earlier reform implementation identified.

22.3.3 Capacity Building and Human Capital Reforms

Downsizing of public bureaucracies most often proceeded without strategic analysis of what the organization had to keep, or what it would really need to do its job effectively in the future. This deficiency, in combination with changing demographics of the workforce pool and an apparently decreased interest in public service in younger citizens, caused many countries to step back to take stock of their public workforce (OECD 2002).

An inevitable conclusion for many was that the existing workforce, and particularly its leadership, fell far short of representing the diversity of the nation. One of the most obvious gaps is age. A recent study in the United States indicated that over seventy percent of all federal managers were age 45 or older; for the entire national workforce, the comparable number is 50 percent. (NAPA 2002b: 12). The Le Releve initiative in Canada focused on the need to "refresh" the upper levels of the public service; Japan is struggling with an aging senior service whose insularity from change and renewal has compounded the problem.

More generally, the failure of the public service to reflect population demographics has caused many nations to create diversity initiatives. Britain noted in its 1999 Civil Service Report that there is a demonstrated need to create "a more open, diverse and professional Civil Service," and pledged a "dramatic" improvement in diversity (OECD 2001: 34–5). Sweden, the Netherlands, and many other nations have created initiatives directly intended to increase the numbers of women in the upper ranks of their civil services. To some extent, the simplification and increased discretion reforms discussed earlier may contribute to greater diversity in public service ranks. There is no doubt that rigidly structured classification and promotion systems served to direct women and persons of color away from leadership ranks of civil service systems. Paradoxically, to return to using women as a diversity example, the public service at its lower ranks has historically been an attractive option for women because of the relative lack of discrimination in hiring. Entering and succeeding in the top levels of the organization has been the problem.

Improved diversity is only one prong of strategic workforce planning reform initiatives (NAPA 2002b: OECD 2001). Public organizations in every nation in the world exist in a turbulent environment and must confront changing demands, changing resources, and changing ways of delivering public services, all in the context of heightened performance and accountability expectations. Many civil service entrance procedures were designed to fundamentally screen out prospective employees rather than to gather them in, and a basic operating assumption was that whatever talent was necessary would be readily available (Ingraham 1995). In this context, the need for strategic planning about future needs and acquisition of necessary talent seemed minimal. Standardized routines could address and solve any significant problems. For many nations, that is no longer true. Extensive privatization and contracting activities, dramatic scientific and technological change, and, indeed, greater flexibility and discretion in public organizations has created the need for different talents, skills, and capacities. Many of these skills and talents are in short supply. Government agencies must compete—with one another, with the nongovernmental sector, and with the private sector—for scarce expertise. Further, they must carefully plan for the acquisition of that talent (OECD 2002; Selden 2003). Finally, they must plan for ways to retain critical talent that they cannot afford to lose. Succession planning, therefore, becomes an important part of the enterprise. The Human Capital Initiatives in the United States, the Bringing In and Bringing On Talent initiatives in the UK, and emerging efforts elsewhere emphasize the new importance of coherent approaches to the acquisition and development of core talent and competency in the public service (Lodge and Hood forthcoming).

All of this ties closely to leadership and to its development. Devolution has increased the awareness of the need for leadership at all levels of the organization, not just the top (OECD 2002). The creation and subsequent reform of senior executive corps in many nations has, unfortunately, clarified the general lack of understanding of the components of public sector leadership. Indeed, the appropriate means of acquiring and/or developing such leadership talent and capacity is a topic of hot debate. Should it, on the British model, be "grown"; that is, developed from within the ranks? Should it, rather, on the broader NPM model be "bought"; that is, hired in from the private sector or elsewhere? Is a blend of the two a better option?

Worldwide, there is spirited debate about the desired qualities of leadership, in light of ongoing reform and other challenges facing the public service, however, there is clear consensus about the need. The British *Modernising Government* White Paper stated bluntly that, "The [British] Civil Service needs better leaders at all levels, but it particularly needs them at the top. If change does not happen at the top, it will not happen at all" (Reported in OECD 2001: 35). New Zealand's restructured efforts recognize the central role that leadership plays, not only in leading effective structural change, but also in building the "human resource capability" critical to longer-term success (NZ State Services Commission 2000).

The reform process in most western nations is now adequately advanced to understand that the people management skills deemed necessary to success are rarely nurtured in traditional bureaucratic hierarchies. The cultural changes necessary to develop support for reform and other change efforts in the leadership cadre are part of a very long-term process (Pollitt and Bouckaert 2000).

In that sense, "buying" new leaders presents a strategic option. New skill sets and capabilities come into the organization quickly; new systems and decision points can be established more rapidly. Certainly the contract model adopted in New Zealand, for example, fully embraces the underlying concept of bringing in, rather than bringing up, talent (Boston et al. 1996). The Senior Executive Service in the United States contains specific provisions to allow 10 percent of the membership to be from "outside" (Ingraham 1995). The Canadians herald private sector leadership of public sector rejuvenation. In nations such as Japan and France, close relationships between public sector leaders and private counterparts is believed to alleviate the need for "fresh" talent, but the value of the interchange of views and policy advising is clearly recognized.

Not only for leadership, but throughout the public service, the need for a strong ethical compass and core values also becomes clearer in a less rule driven environment. In developed nations, civil service laws, rules, and procedures cover virtually every variant of potential human misbehavior. If those rules are eliminated or weakened, what replaces them to govern appropriate use of the flexibilities created by reform? Competency frameworks are widely utilized, but the qualitative differences between, for example, being "results driven" and "leading in the public interest" are quite clear (Lodge and Hood forthcoming). In hiring new employees, for example, civil service regulations prescribed a narrow set of choices, and prohibited hiring for political affiliation, family ties, or other "non-qualification" based criteria. There is a clear sense in many nations that the public trust is jeopardized when public service flexibilities in hiring, promotion, and firing are increased. The Department of Homeland Security debate in the United States included charges by one of the leading employee unions that the proposed management flexibilities amounted to a return to the spoils system.

Again, the role of leadership in successfully implementing reforms and in overcoming resistance to their implementation cannot be over estimated. The same charges that can be levied against hiring discretion apply equally to award of bonuses, to decisions to retain "critical" personnel in downsizing, to award of "plum" assignments, and to many other HRM activities. HRM is an enterprise in which decisions—hopefully objective and well reasoned—are made about workplace conditions, rewards, benefits, successes, and failures. The dilemma inherent in performance appraisal and evaluation comes head on: no one likes to be "average" or disadvantaged compared to colleagues and co-workers. Introducing flexibility and discretionary reforms into public human resource management demands that such decisions be made. In the best of all possible worlds, these decisions will be fair and equitable. Even so, not everyone will be happy.

22.4 CONCLUSION: CAN BALANCING BE A LEARNED ART?

This discussion outlines only the bare bones of the many human resource management reforms either being considered or already in place around the world. Although these reforms have rarely been the leading edge of the reform agenda, they are now viewed as key levers for effective change. HRM reforms have followed blunter, and often more visible, efforts: downsizing, privatization, changes in budgetary and financial management processes. Kernaghan's point, cited earlier, is apt: HRM reforms are frequently not strategically aligned with other public management reforms; they are adopted after other public management reports are in place and are, as a result, often in a chronic catching up mode. Further, as noted above, these reforms often have an individualized impact and visibility and are very threatening in that particular sense. HRM reforms generally threaten unions, because they transfer the decision about what is fair and equitable treatment of employees to management. Managers themselves are often skeptical, because the reforms demand a set of skills and capacities that long-term, more traditional managers may not possess. Elected officials, even those who advanced and advocated reforms, do not give up finger pointing rights when something goes wrong or when the new discretionary authority is used in an unpopular way.

Recognition of the need to effectively manage human resources as a resource, and not as a cost, however, continues to gain speed. The recent emphasis on "human capital" is one contributor to the increased awareness. Several early reformer nations have created strategies or mechanisms for tracking human capital management efforts in their own agencies and in other nations. In the United States, the Congress has formally directed the central personnel agency, the Office of Personnel Management, to provide support for such efforts (Thompson and Rainey 2003). This follows the recognized difficulty some nations are having in recruiting and retaining critical personnel. It also confirms that some earlier solutions to performance management—decentralization, for example—came with their own problems, as well as some potential lessons for future change.

Aside from the fundamental need to consider human resources and human capital in early stages of reform, other consistent lessons do emerge. Early decentralization and simplification efforts often occurred without a strategic framework for guidance, and most frequently with few mechanisms for gathering information about changes that were occurring and what difference they might make. This void not only limited efforts to improve, but also fundamentally abandoned managers and leaders trying to address common problems. The learning curve was initially very low. A strategic rebalancing is now evident in many settings, with careful attention paid to "guiding principles," common values, frameworks, and overarching objectives.

Simplification of existing systems is also a common theme in HRM reform and some of the most important lessons are related to it. Many, many national civil service systems had accreted layers of rules and regulations that had little coherence or positive impact. Recognizing that basic purposes could be served with many less overhead and legal controls was an early lesson in HR reforms. Particularly with the current emphasis on performance, multiple levels of complexity directed the activities of both employees and managers away from organizational objectives to more process oriented pursuits. Simplification reforms addressed that problem, but, again, required the presence of clear frameworks and guiding principles to be most effective.

It is important to note, however, that this is primarily the western model. In emergent nations across the world, the emphasis is not on flexibility within a strategic framework, but on creating a coherent and often standardized base. The need for a structured system that can be institutionalized serves a more fundamental need in these nations. In some cases, such as eastern Europe, old, very structured systems needed to be broken down, so others could be erected in their place. The stage and level of the reform process here is obviously very different; lessons from western industrial nations are avidly sought nonetheless.

In the final analysis, the issue of how a government manages its employees is one of accountability, not only to the employees, but also to the broader public. The extent to which overhead controls can be loosened, and flexibilities valued, is a political question. Simplification and flexibility implies risk. Human resource management involves people with different perceptions of fair treatment for them and others. Flexibility and accountability in HRM systems—and reforms to them—can only occur together when there is agreement about the expectations and objectives of the reforms. No matter in which nation the two are juxtaposed, the margin for error is determined in the political environment of public organizations. Absent consensus there, no reform can succeed. Perhaps the most fundamental lesson of all, therefore, is that public organizations are public organizations. Their employees are public employees and voters. Performance objectives, criteria for discretion and flexibility in achieving them, and methods of assessing success or failure are captive to these realities. They need to be carefully shepherded, and their expectations carefully shaped, in HRM—or any other—reform design and in subsequent implementation. That, of course, is the most artful balance of all.

REFERENCES

ABERBACH, J., and ROCKMAN, B. (2001), *In the Web of Politics*, Washington, DC: Brookings Institution.

BEKKE, H., TOONEN, T., and PERRY, J. (1997), *Civil Service Systems in Comparative Perspective* (Bloomington, IN: Indiana University Press.

BOSTON, J. (2001), "Organizing for Service Delivery: Criteria and Opportunities", in B. G. Peters and D. J. Savoie, *Governance in the Twenty-First Century*, Montreal: McGill University Press, 281–381.

—— MARTIN, J., PAILLOT, J., and WALSH, P. (1996), *Public Management: The New Zealand Model*, London: Oxford University Press.

BREWER, G. A. (2002), "Does Administrative Reform Improve Bureaucratic Performance? A Cross-Country Empirical Analysis." Paper Delivered at the Research Workshop on the

Empirical Study of Governance, Management and Performance, College Station, TX, February.

CLARK, T., and PUGH, D. (1999/2000), "Similarities and Differences in European Conceptions of Human Resource Management," *International Studies of Management and Organization* 29(4): 84–100.

CORNELIUS, N., and GAGNON, S. (2001), "Introduction and Overview," in J. Storey (ed.), *Human Resource Management*, 2nd edn., London: Thomson Learning.

GUEST, D. (2001), "Industrial Relations and Human Resource Management", in J. Storey (ed.), *Human Resource Management*, 2nd edn., London: Thomson Learning.

HALLIGAN, J. (2003), "Leadership and the Senior Service from a Comparative Perspective," in B. G. Peters and J. Pierre (eds.), *Comparative Handbook of Public Administration*, Los Angeles: Sage 98–108.

HOLMES, M. (2001), "Does Budgeting Have a Future?" Paris: OECD-PUMA, May.

INGRAHAM, P. W. (1995), *The Foundation of Merit: Public Service in American Democracy*, Baltimore: The Johns Hopkins University Press.

—— (1993), "Of Pigs in Pokes and Policy Diffusion: The Case of Pay for Performance," *Public Administration Review* 53(4): 348–56.

—— and MOYNIHAN, D. P. (2003), "Look for the Silver Lining: When Managing for Results Works," *Journal of Public Administration Research and Theory* 13(4): 469–81.

—— JOYCE, P., and DONAHUE, A. K. (2003), *Government Performance: Why Management Matters*, Baltimore: The Johns Hopkins University Press.

JACOBSON, W. (2003), "A Study of Organizational Change in Two Federal Agencies," Unpublished Ph.D. Dissertation, The Maxwell School of Citizenship and Public Affairs, Syracuse University, Syracuse, NY, June.

KATULA, M., and PERRY, J. (2003), "A Comparative Examination of Pay for Performance Systems," in B. G. Peters and J. Pierre (eds.), *Comparative Handbook of Public Administration*, Los Angeles: Sage, 53–61.

KERNAGHAN, K. (2001), *International Comparison in Human Resource Management Reform*, Ottawa: Canadian Center for Management Development.

KETTL, D. F. (2002), *The Transformation of Governance in the Twenty-First Century*, Baltimore: The Johns Hopkins University Press.

LODGE, M., and HOOD, C. (forthcoming), "Competency and Ineptitude: What's New About Civil Service Competencies and Who Cares?", *Public Administration Review*.

McKINSEY ASSOCIATES (1998), "The War For Talent: Competing for the Best." San Francisco: McKinsey.

NATIONAL ACADEMY OF PUBLIC ADMINISTRATION (2002a), "The Historical Development of the Senior Executive Service," Washington, DC: NAPA.

—— (2002b), "The Twenty-First Century Manager: A Study of Changing Roles and Competencies," Washington, DC: NAPA.

NEW ZEALAND STATE SERVICES COMMISSION (2000), *Annual Report of the State Service Commissioner for Year Ended June 30 2000*, Wellington: State Service Commission.

ORGANIZATION FOR ECONOMIC COOPERATION AND DEVELOPMENT (2001), *Public Sector Leadership for the Twenty-First Century*, Paris: OECD-PUMA.

—— (2002), "Public Sector Employment: Recruiting and Retention," DRAFT (Paris: OECD-PUMA, January.

POLLITT, C., and BOUCKAERT, G. (2000), *Public Management Reform: A Comparative Analysis*, Oxford: Oxford University Press.

ROBERTS, A. (1997), "Performance-Based Organizations: Assessing the Gore Plan," *Public Administration Review* 57(6): 465–78.

SCHICK, A. (2001), "Does Budgeting Have a Future?" Paris: OECD-PUMA.

SELDEN, S.C. (2003), "Comparative Trends in Human Management Resource Reform", in B. G. Peters and J. Pierre (eds.), *Handbook of Comparative Public Administration*, Los Angeles: Sage, 62–71.

THOMPSON, J. R., and RAINEY, H. G. (2003), *Modernizing Human Resource Management in the Federal Government: The IRS Model*, Arlington, VA: IBM Endowment for the Business of Government.

UK CABINET OFFICE (1999), "Progress Report against the Executive Summary of the Modernizing Government," White Paper, London: Cabinet Office.

UK PATENT OFFICE (1993), *Annual Report*, London: HMSO.

US OFFICE OF MANAGEMENT AND BUDGET (2001), *The President's Management* Agenda, Washington, DC: Government Printing Office.

WALKER, D. (2000), "Managing the Human Resources of Government: The Human Capital Crisis," Arlington, VA: Price-Waterhouse-Coopers.

CHAPTER 23

PUBLIC SERVICE QUALITY IMPROVEMENT

JOHN ØVRETVEIT

23.1 INTRODUCTION

AT FIRST sight quality in public services is simple—it is ensuring that users of these services get what they want and need. But any deeper examination of how to do this quickly raises fundamental issues about the purpose of public services, equity and choice, and conflicts and compatibilities between users, potential users, and taxpayers. It raises issues about the role of politicians as consumer representatives, and about economic trade-offs and compromises which are political and not technical in nature. Public service managers contracting for private services face additional challenges: they are held accountable for the quality of these services, yet do not have effective methods to influence the quality of contracted services, especially professional services (Robinson and Le Grand 1995).

Quality often conflicts with managers' primary aims of keeping within budget, increasing efficiency, and meeting the demands of politicians and employees. It is often a confusing subject for all concerned, in part, due to the different languages of the "quality tribes" and "religious wars" fought between different "quality movements." To add to this, safety has also been incorporated or linked to quality in recent years (Editorial, *Quality and Safety in Health Care*, 2002). The academic study of quality in public services has been a needed critical counterbalance to the outputs of the "quality industry." Amongst its contributions has been an understanding of the politics of quality and of the genuine complexity of the issues in applying quality concepts and methods in public services. The academic study of quality in public services since the 1990s has taught us much about the nature of public services, not least about how changes do or do not take place in them.

23.1.1 Questions

The subject of quality methods in the public sector raises a number of issues and questions. Is quality a modern "Taylorism"? Taylor was a time and motion engineer who redesigned work tasks by reducing them to their smallest components and organizing the tasks for the greatest efficiency (Burns 1978). He proposed a clear separation between management, who were to be responsible for conceptualization and design, and workers, who were only to follow the procedures. In a modern world, with democratic ideologies of equality and educated workers seeking personal fulfillment from their work, the quality movement provides a meaning to work and enlists workers' creativity to redesign processes for greater efficiency. Is quality a means of more effectively exploiting and securing the commitment of modern workers, and an ideology suited to a consumerist competitive society? How would such a movement fare in public services?

Some approaches to quality fundamentally challenge the traditional hierarchy of public services, namely those which require managers to work closely with workers as equals in quality project teams and those which demand that managers devolve control to workers' groups to reorganize the work processes. Or do these changes give the impression of empowerment, but really maintain and deepen management control?

In many respects quality originated as a collection of poorly theorized methods which were developed through practice in the workplace. The "quality movement" was built by adherents who tried to provide a theoretical basis and ideology from mostly atheoretical practical tools (Juran 1995). In transferring these methods to the public sector, a similar industry has evolved, developing an ideology and packages of tools for the less competitive and culturally different environment of this sector.

In the definition of what we mean by quality and the different meanings given to the key terms by different theorists we see the fundamental ambiguity and elusive nature of quality. We see a movement attempting to build a science of quality by defining terms, but which is unable to escape the political and contested nature of quality.

The purpose of this chapter is to give a balanced and critical overview of the different ideas and methods of quality assurance and improvement as applied in the public sector. It describes approaches which have been used in multi-professional services, such as health care; in single quasi-professional services, such as education, police, fire, library, and social services; and other government services such as clerical services and industrial-type services which include a physical goods products such as refuse collection and road maintenance.

The chapter starts with a historical background which also considers the question: Why now? Why is quality becoming so important in public services and how does the subject relate to other initiatives such as private service contracting? It then notes definitions of quality and discusses issues of measurement and evaluation. For those considering how to improve the quality of their services, these are important subjects, both in terms of how these issues are decided and in terms of the operational definitions which are decided.

The chapter outlines different approaches which have been taken in terms of their focus and methods, giving illustrative examples from different public services. It then considers the evidence of the results of quality strategies and methods, and also research issues and subjects within the field. The chapter closes by discussing the challenges of improving quality in public services and future directions.

Box 23.1 Definitions

Public service quality: meeting the needs of those most in need of the service, within higher level requirements, available resources and at the lowest cost.

Service user: a person receiving benefit from the service, in private services called a "customer." The person may make use of a direct service (e.g., library, social welfare), or be an indirect user (e.g., public health education).

Quality program: a set of planned systematic activities intended to ensure and improve the quality of one or more organizations services and products, usually organization-wide. Often includes planning and providing training, expertise in quality methods, setting up project teams and quality systems, defining responsibilities for quality, and measuring quality.

Quality project: a time-limited task to solve a quality problem or improve quality, undertaken by a specially created team using quality methods in a structured way.

Quality system: a coordinated set of procedures, division of responsibilities, and processes for setting quality standards and procedures, identifying quality problems and resolving these problems. (BSI 5750 and ISO 9000 are standards for a quality system).

Quality accreditation: a certification through an external assessment of whether a practitioner, equipment, or a service meet standards which are thought to contribute to quality processes and outcomes.

Total quality management: a comprehensive strategy of organizational and attitude change for enabling staff to learn and use quality methods in order to reduce costs and meet the requirements of patients and other "customers."

23.2 HISTORY

23.2.1 The Individual Worker and Professional Quality

The "craft-based" theory of quality is that the "goodness" of the artisan's product—its fitness for purpose and artistry—is largely dependent on their skill, which in turn comes from many years experience and an apprenticeship with a master. By emphasizing the quality of their services to the public, some workers were able to win customers and cast doubts about the proficiency of those who were not members of their exclusive organization. In more recent history, the professions built on this craft approach to quality. The traditional professional approach to quality is individual and through education and regulation, both largely run by the professions.

23.2.2 State Regulation

The involvement of the state and government in service quality also has a long history. The state has acted to regulate certain work or workers, often on the rationale of protecting the public. Neither the professions' nor the state's espoused concern for the welfare of the public, however, were the only factors in their actions. For professions, quality issues coincided with winning and protecting markets. For the state, regulation could provide income and government leaders could trade favors with the rising professional elites. Attention to quality has always combined altruistic and self-serving motives, no less so for the recent managerial focus on quality which provides one way of increasing control or reducing management–employee conflicts in the large professional and unionized workforce of public services.

23.2.3 Large-Scale Manufacturing

Attention to quality in commercial organizations is relatively recent. Up until the 1960s, manufacturing in the West was focused on efficient large-scale production to supply post-Second World War captive markets, and volume production and costs were the main concern. This "era" was supported by the work-organization theories of Taylorism and hierarchical organization. The inspection methods used by craft-based workers were developed into quality control, using statistical methods to sample and assess products (Juran and Gryna 1980).

Changes in society and economy created consumers with more choices, and a more educated workforce which challenged traditional authority. Quality thinking in engineering found an audience in management and managerial philosophies were developed, based around quality (Deming 1986). These ideas emphasized meeting customer needs as well as efficiency, and also the involvement of workers in making quality improvement. They demanded a deeper inner commitment of workers to their work, an organizational "culture" which created and maintained this commitment, and a new role for management in creating and maintaining this atmosphere. Increasing organizational complexity also shifted the focus from individual workers as the source of quality problems to how work was organised and to prevention and improvement rather than inspection and control. With the rise of the service sector, quality ideas and approaches were adapted for commercial services (Norman 1984; Gummeson 1987; Zeithaml et al. 1990).

There are lessons for the public sector from the development of quality methods in industry. One of these is that improvements have been made quickly by giving workers in small teams the methods and power to identify problems and implement their own solutions (Anderson et al. 1991). However, it became clear that larger quality problems originated in relationships between departments. Involving workers from different departments in the teams was less successful because the changes required managers' agreement and involved larger financial and organizational considerations (Godfrey et al. 1992).

This led to a recognition that management needed to be fully involved and that only organization-wide quality programs could address the more significant and costly problems: hence the addition to process-engineering methods of ideas for "total quality management," with managers playing a key role and the whole organization working together (Deming 1986). A further lesson was that this approach was more successful in Japan where both workers and management identified with the company, and a corporate united approach was a natural background to the methods (Athos and Pascale 1981; Schonberger 1982).

Commentators have noted that the traditional worker–management conflicts, weaker management, and professional loyalties in public service made this unified approach problematic (Pollitt 1990). This might explain in part the greater success of small quality team projects within departments, rather than larger organization wide programs or cross-departmental or cross-service team projects (Joss and Kogan 1995).

23.3 PUBLIC SECTOR QUALITY

Concern about public sector quality and using quality methods in this sector emerged in the late 1980s (Ferlie et al. 1996). Consumerism, increasing competition, and the use of quality methods in the commercial sector have led to more choice and higher quality. The contrast between the choice and services people receive from the commercial and public sector has grown (Osborne and Gaebler 1992). There has been an increasing audience for politicians proposing full privatization, and a reversal of the expansion of government service provision. Some left-wing politicians have recognized that the political and social value of public services could only be maintained it these services also responded to the new consumerism (Gaster and Squires 2003). Even left-wing politicians began seriously to consider the option of more contracting of private services: that this could be a way of retaining some of the social and political purposes of the welfare state but also of providing choice and quality, regardless of the lack of conclusive evidence that private services necessarily provide the latter.

Quality improvement has been one of a number of ideas which have been introduced into public services over the last twenty years, many of which were developed and used in the private sector (Pollitt 1990; Ferlie et al. 1996). Quality initiatives have complemented or overlapped with strategies such as more choice for service users, explicit standards and performance management, focus on outputs and efficiency, concern for safety, greater use of competition and contracting, and increase accountability for performance—the latter including inspection, audit, and accreditation (Hughes 1993). These and other strategies have been promoted by national or local government, by professions, or independently by local managers as a way to respond to the pressures on their services.

The experience has been that improving quality in public services is even more difficult than in private services, especially for multiprofessional services such as health care. The chapter later considers some of the theories about why this should be so, as well as the main approaches used: customer service strategies, profession based strategies, standard setting and inspection and, more recently, continuous quality improvement.

23.4 DEFINITION, MEASUREMENT, AND EVALUATION

What do we mean by "quality"? How can we get an agreed understanding of what is good quality? How can we measure and evaluate quality? For those starting quality improvement these are important questions. They also illustrate different views: that a social processes is needed to agree amongst stakeholders how quality shall be defined, or that managers professionals or other experts can and should define quality.

23.4.1 Defining Quality

The answer to "what is quality" for the private sector is simpler than they are for the public sector: It is satisfying or consistently exceeding customer expectations, because survival in a competitive market depends primarily on income from customer-purchasers. However, there are products or services of which the customer, at least initially, is not able to judge quality. A professional is required to assess customer needs or to judge the quality of the product or service. In order to maintain the focus on the customer, definitions have combined the idea of meeting customer wants and their professionally assessed needs by defining quality as "fitness for purpose" (Juran and Gryna 1980), or "conformance to requirements" (Crosby 1979), or "The totality of features and characteristics of a product or service that bear on its ability to satisfy stated or implied needs" (BSI 1990).

However, these definitions do not recognize the economics of quality or the legal and regulatory context, both of which are important in public services. A quality public service is not one which just produces happy customers, but is one which has to meet other higher level regulations and do so economically. One definition which has been used in public services is "meeting the wants and needs of those who need the services most, without waste and within regulations, available resources and the control of the service" (Øvretveit 1992a). This definition includes client quality (meeting users' wants), professional quality (meeting their needs), and management quality (at the lowest cost, without waste and within directives set by higher authorities). There are multiple-component definitions which begin to specify the dimensions of quality which are important to customers. These definitions may or may not have been developed by consulting customers. One example from health care is quality defined as: accessibility, relevance to need, equity, social acceptability, efficiency, and effectiveness (Maxwell 1984).

The idea of basing definitions and models on the concept of "customer" in public services has been challenged. This is not just because public service beneficiaries usually do not pay for public services at the time of use, but also because of the assumptions carried with the term. In public services, better services may be used more, but if no extra income results, then quality is likely to decline (Pfeffer and Coote 1991). There are different views about who the service user is, or whether a pluralistic "stakeholder" definition should be used (Pollitt et al. 1992; Gaster and Squires 2003). Additionally, what should be the process for defining quality? The manager or higher levels deciding a definition, with or without customer research? Or experts deciding, or a process involving users or multiple stakeholders in agreeing a definition? (Gaster and Squires 2003).

23.4.2 Standards and Measurement

A key principle in improving quality is moving from definitions, which may be useful for giving personnel a general orientation, to specifying quality for a particular service. This is particularly important when contracting services. As with definition, there are content and process issues: What should be the content of the specification of quality for everyday action and monitoring, and how should these specifications be made?

Standards are operational definitions of the intended level of service. Measurement is the assessment of the level of service achieved. One approach is to take standards developed externally and set them for the service in question, with or without modification. Another is to find out from users what is important to them and convert this into specifications of what the service must deliver if it is to satisfy users. A combined approach is to take specified standards and consult with users to assess which standards are most important and which levels are wanted by them.

Measurement of quality is a challenge in services: what is quality varies between users and is often difficult for them to articulate. Routine measurement is economically and practically difficult. Different measurement systems have been developed, although many are useful for only for research rather than everyday purposes (Nelson and Batalden 1992). Traditionally standards for "inputs" have been specified and measured: Is certain equipment accessible? How many personnel does the service employ, and with what qualifications and experience? Whilst relatively easy and low cost, it is generally accepted that standards and measures also need to be developed for process aspects of the service—such as waiting times at different points, and outcomes, which includes user satisfaction.

One user satisfaction research tool which is sometimes used in public services is the SERVQUAL measurement system. It is based on assessing users expectations of elements of service, and then asking users to assess their experience on the same elements and comparing the gaps (Parasuraman et al. 1988; Babakus and Mangold 1992). Examples are the use of SERVQUAL in Scotland across a range of council services (Wisniewski 2001), and in North Lanarkshire Council UK to improve both process management and strategic planning (Brysland and Curry 2001).

23.4.3 Evaluation

Quality evaluation (often termed "quality assessment") requires defined standards and ways to measure performance against the standards. Quality evaluation is comparing the level achieved by a service with either the standard intended, or with levels of similar services, or with the same service at another time. (Øvretveit 2002).

Quality evaluation of public services and contracted private services is increasingly undertaken by higher governmental levels or organizations to which govern-

Table 23.1 Quality Standards and Measurement Framework

	Inputs. The right amount and quality of:	Process. Activities of giving a service:	Outcomes. Change in users' experience, and use of resources that can be attributed to the service's actions.
User or Client Quality: What users say they want, or what is necessary in inputs, process, or outcomes to give users what they want.	e.g., Well-qualified and experienced personnel. Clean and attractive buildings and facilities.	e.g., Polite and friendly treatment by personnel. The right amount of information at each stage of the service. Quick service when required.	e.g., User satisfaction.
Professional Quality: Professionals' views about whether the service meets users' needs, whether staff correctly select and carry out procedures which are believed to be necessary to meet user's needs.	e.g., Well trained and cooperative colleagues. The right patients are referred. Sufficient information about patients is provided. The right equipment. Access to efficient support services.	e.g., Correct assessment of user needs. Correct choice of intervention. Compliance with procedures. Fast support services. Good inter-professional communication.	e.g., Good professional outcome. No negative outcomes.
Management Quality: The most efficient and productive use of resources to meet client needs within limits and directive set by higher authorities.	e.g., Sufficient resources. Good external services and information.	e.g., No waste, error or delays. Compliance with higher-level regulations.	e.g., Lowest costs per user, fewest resources consumed.

Source: Donabedian 1980; Øvretveit 1992a

> **Box 23.2 Examples of a study using SERVQUAL in the public sector: A comparison of public and private hospital care service quality in Malta**
>
> The study used the SERVQUAL model to compare and contrast Malta's public and private hospital care service quality. One questionnaire measured patient pre-admission expectations for public and private hospital service quality. It also determined the weighted importance given to the different service quality indicators. The second questionnaire measured patient perceptions of provided service quality. The findings were that private hospitals are expected to offer a higher quality service, particularly in the "hotel services," but it was the public sector that was exceeding its patients' expectations by the wider margin.
>
> *Source*: Camilleri and O'Callaghan 1998

ment assigns the task, or by services to identify areas for action or for advertising. A common approach is external quality assurance (or "audit" in the UK) where external assessors visit the service and assess the service against explicit standards. Examples of external assessment systems are the EFQM model (EFQM 1992; ISO 9000; ISO 2003), the UK and Swedish educational quality standards assessment system, and a system designed specifically for public services (Harwick and Russell 1993).

One issue is whether quality evaluation should be voluntary or mandatory. Accreditation is often used as a requirement to be met before public and/or private services can receive public funds. Another related issue is the balance of emphasis in evaluation between assessment for improvement, and assessment for inspection or "policing."

23.5 APPROACHES TO QUALITY

Public services have used different approaches to improving quality. Any one service might use one or a combination of the following overlapping approaches: customer or user based approach; the legal approach; accreditation; standards-based; organization-wide approaches; and safety and risk management methods.

23.5.1 Customer or User Approaches

The aim of these approaches are to give service users a better experience and to improve "customer satisfaction." A number of methods from service industries have been applied successfully for measuring user perceptions of service (Parasuraman et al. 1988; Øvretveit 1992*b*) and for developing a "user focus" or "listening to the customer": surveys, focus groups, complaints analysis, customer contact reports, suggestion boxes or forms, and "mystery shoppers."

Using these methods also means changing employees' attitudes toward being more customer friendly and changing service organization to provide a more individualized service. These methods have been combined with ideas about user involvement and community participation which have a longer history in public services (Gaster and Squires 2003). The approach can include:

- Surveys of users to discover what they like and do not like about services, deciding priorities for action from these surveys, and using problem solving methods to improve services from the users perspective.
- A national or local statement about what users have a right to expect from the public service.
- Community participation at each level, giving feedback about quality, working with providers to make improvements, and helping with or carrying out service-related interventions.

23.5.2 Legal Approach

This involves the introduction of laws requiring certain standards, or the granting of explicit rights or "guarantees" to service users. These rights or service promises may or may not be backed-up by legal sanctions or procedures for challenging decisions—usually there is an "escape clause" which recognizes what is feasible with available resources. Some countries have introduced "ombudsmen" schemes which give user of public services a route for raising concerns about services, and in some cases for seeking redress (Fallberg and Øvretveit 2003).

Apart from user rights, laws may be introduced to regulate professionals on quality criteria (e.g., prohibit practice by the unlicensed), to require professionals to take part in quality activities, to require providing organizations to meet certain standards thought to ensure quality or to have in place quality systems. The legal approach may also involve laws requiring the provider to meet standards of an external assessment or certification body, and to submit for inspection at regular intervals. For example, the central Norwegian government regularly inspects health service providers for compliance with quality regulations and many European countries have external health provider assessment systems (Shaw 2000).

23.5.3 Quality Assessment, Regulation and Accreditation

Accreditation is a certification by an external body that a provider has met certain and can be voluntary and compulsory. It has been used mostly for educational and health services, and for contracted-out supply services.

It uses systems for awarding certificates of competence for practitioners or facilities, for licensing practitioners or facilities to operate, and for accrediting facilities to show the level of quality they have achieved. There are five methods: self-assessment, peer review, certification, licensing, and accreditation (Scrivens 1995). The advantages can be to reduce the harm to service user from incompetent professionals and dangerous services. The disadvantages are that it can be unpopular with many practitioners and services, takes time and bureaucracy to implement, and that the resources might be better used for other actions to improve quality.

23.5.4 Standards-Based Approach

In this approach a service will set standards for quality—for inputs (e.g., number of staff or for equipment), processes (e.g., waiting times), outcomes (e.g., user satisfaction, error rates), or for all three (Ellis and Whittington 1993). Most approaches under the name of "audit" or "quality assurance" are of this type. Personnel are helped to follow standards through training, job aids, and supervision. Where standards are not followed, this is documented and supervisors and managers have responsibility for taking corrective action. In addition, standards are defined for management activities and service performance. There are three phases to carrying out a standards-based approach:

- develop standards which will ensure effective and safe care and which are feasible given the resources available;
- implement standards: communicate and supervise the standards, and document where standards are not met;
- take corrective action where practice falls below standards using problem solving methods.

The practical advantages of this approach are reported to be that it is easy to understand and can be implemented through an existing management structure, with advice and support. Disadvantages are that the management and supervision structure might not be strong enough to communicate and uphold standards, or there may not be the resources for supervision or for effective action if practice is below standard. It has been observed that showing care to be below standard when nothing can be done can damage morale.

23.5.5 Organization-Wide and Team Project Approaches

This category describes approaches where top management introduces an organization-wide strategy or assessment system to improve quality. There are different systems and approaches. The ISO 9000 standards for a quality system are used by some public services to create a quality assurance system which covers all aspects of quality (ISO 2003; Sweeney and Heaton 2000). This approach has been described as "write what you should do, do as you write, write when you don't do right." For use in public services this approach has been criticized as being overly concerned with documentation and involving too many technical terms originating from quality assurance in manufacturing. However it is increasingly used in more technical or product-oriented services and has been adapted for use in some other services too.

ISO 9000 has in recent years incorporated Total Quality Management (TQM) ideas including process improvement, but other systems are more explicitly TQM based and are used for organization-wide quality approaches. The Baldrige framework was developed in the US by drawing on TQM ideas and has been successfully adapted for public services (Harwick and Russell 1993). The European version—the EFQM model—is increasingly used in European public services, and for a variety of purposes (EFQM 1992).

Box 23.3 Example: Self-assessment of all the health centers of the Basque public health service through the European Model of Total Quality Management (EFQM)

The Basque Country Public Health Service moved from considering quality as an attribute of patient care to thinking that all management can be subject to improvement. The general management team promoted self-assessment of all 26 health centers using the European Quality Model. The strategy was assisted by the Basque Country Government, which encouraged total quality management in companies. The results were identifying different improvement areas and carrying out improvement actions. The study also considered the benefits, challenges, and future work to extend the use of the EFQM model.

Source: Arcelay et al. 1999

Total quality management is defined and interpreted in a number of ways, but generally inviolves a comprehensive strategy of organizational and attitude change for enabling staff to learn and use quality methods in order to reduce costs and meet the requirements of patients and other "customers." Since 1990, TQM methods have been applied in a number of hospitals, clinics and health organizations in Europe (Øvretveit 2000). However, most hospitals and health organizations still do not use TQM methods. TQM means many things to many people, but there is a common agreement that it involves team-based process improvement projects and a customer orientation across the organization. The approach has not been easy to implement. Some of the problems and lessons from the European experience are noted later.

TQM is usually used synonymously with continuous quality improvement (CQI), but some authors define CQI as more about small quality teams carrying out projects using quality methods to improve their service. The project-based improvement approach is to set up quality problem-solving teams which work on specific problems using simple methods ("quality tools") which they have been trained to use. This started in public services in the late 1980s with "quality circles" which died out, in part because they often did not use quality methods (Robinson 1984). More recently, project teams using continuous improvement methods have become a widespread quality improvement approach in public services.

The advantages of a small project team approach are that it allows some units to quickly solve priority quality problems. It can benefit users if users' problems are selected by the team. It can also improve personnel morale and pride and develop professionals' abilities to work in teams. The disadvantages are that this approach only impacts a few problem areas, and teams need to spend time learning the methods before producing results. Experience shows that regular facilitation and management support is needed for the teams to be successful otherwise the training and time spent by the team is wasted.

23.5.6 Approaches: Summary

Often a service will initially focus on one approach, and then introduce another approach "on top of", or as a new program. An organization can combine approaches but it needs to recognized that there is a limited capacity to cope with change, and new concepts can confuse or discredit a quality program. Some take the view that there is a philosophical difference between approaches focused on standard setting and inspection and those which concentrate on teams working to make improvements to processes—the former being more suited to hierarchical bureaucracies, and the latter introducing a different approach to management, motivation and thinking about organization.

23.6 Do Quality Methods "Work" in Public Services?

There is some evidence of projects which have made improvements in some units but little evidence of results from large organization-wide programs (Joss 1995), Shortell et al. 1998), Blumenthal and Kilo 1998). It appears that the more successful programs have been where one approach has been sensitively tailored to the organization and applied consistently over a number of years (Øvretveit 2003). More fruitful scientific questions are: What exactly did this organization do? What was their experience? Is there any evidence of results for different parties? Are there lessons for other organizations?

A number of problems have been reported in using TQM and many other quality approaches in public services. The economics of quality in public services has been one hurdle (Joss 1995). Quality programs have to compete with other investments, such as information technology or equipment, which appear to have a lower risk and can be funded from capital budgets. The returns for organization-wide programs and for some projects are uncertain—the evidence of success is mixed.

There is management resistance towards empowering employees and to taking personnel away from operations for training or working in quality teams. Workers or professionals resist the changes involved, such as teamworking or learning new methods and language, and many do not believe that these methods are the best way to improve quality and fear a loss of autonomy or job security.

Managers and professionals find that reforms and frequent changes in public services do not allow them time to concentrate on long-term projects. Sustaining continuous improvement has been difficult where there are no market competition incentives to do so, or where quality measurement is poor and has not given feedback of the results of people's efforts.

23.7 QUALITY RESEARCH

Several themes and subjects have been addressed by research, and there are a number of discussions of the applicability of private sector quality methods in the public sector and reports of experiences and issues in adapting them (Sanderson 1996; Pollitt et al. 1992; Gaster and Squires 2003). Some research considers implementation approaches and strategies (e.g., Gaster 1996 in UK local government; Morgan and Murgatroyd 1994 in education in the USA and UK; Joss and Kogan 1995 in the UK National Health Service). Some research has compared public and private service quality (hospital care, Camilleri and O'Callaghan 1998; Redman et al. 1995; Black et al. 2001). There are also many case reports of experiences in specific services, for example, local government services (in the UK, Farrell and Ho 1995; in the USA, Osborne and Gaebler 1992), public leisure services (Leigh 2003), government purchasing agencies (Erridge et al. 1998), and public ultilities (Navaratam and Harris 1994).

Most research into quality in the public sector has consisted of studies to examine users' wants and service experience, descriptive or results studies of quality programs, or theoretical and conceptual studies. Many reports of results are by consultants or those leading quality programs, and even the research literature shows a publication bias towards positive results. There are methodological problems in evaluating quality initiatives (Walshe and Freeman 2002; Øvretveit and Gustaffson 2003), including issues about which criteria to use to assess success and results. It is difficult to generalize from one country or organization to another, largely because the context of the initiative appears to be important for success. These methodological problems cast doubt on some of the generalized positive claims made for quality methods by many studies, especially concerning "quality programs."

A quality program (QP) is the planned activities carried out by an organization or service system to prove and improve the quality of the service. This category covers a range of interventions which are more complex than a single quality team improvement project. QPs include programs for a whole organization (e.g., a total quality management program), for teams from many organizations (e.g., a "collaborative" program), for external reviews of organizations (e.g., a quality accreditation program), for practice in many organizations (e.g., a practice guidelines program), and for a national or regional quality initiative or a strategy which itself could include any or all of the above.

One study noted twenty-five separate quality programs in the UK's NHS up to 1996 (Taylor 1996), and there have been more since. Many countries are embarking on accreditation programs in the absence of research evidence that this is the best use of resources for the problem and situation, or of evidence about the effectiveness of different systems and about different ways to implement them (Shaw 2001). These programs consume considerable resources yet little is known of their effectiveness or relative cost-effectiveness.

Hospital quality programs have been the most studied. The general picture that emerges from reviews of this research is of the limitations of the studies which have been done and that few healthcare organizations appear "successfully" to have implemented a quality program (Biglow and Arndt 1995; Motwani et al. 1996; Shortell et al. 1998; Blumenthal and Kilo 1998; Øvretveit 2003). Little is known about whether the programs have been sustained or of any long-term results. Few studies describe or compare different types of hospital quality programs. Many studies rely on self-reports by quality specialists or senior managers, and survey them once, retrospectively. Few other types of quality improvement programs have been systematically studied or evaluated. As regards accreditation, managers have reported that organizations which received low scores ("probation") on the US Joint Commission for Accreditation of Healthcare Organizations assessment were given high scores three years after, but had not made substantive changes (Blumenthal and Kilo 1998). There are some studies describing or assessing the validity or value of the many comparative quality assessment systems in health and in education (Thompson et al. 1997); CHQCP 1995; Rosenthal and Harper 1994), but few studies of external evaluation processes (NIST 1990; EFQM 1992; ISO 2003), or of national or regional quality strategies.

A stream of research which is growing is about how different organizations can coordinate to ensure quality services for specific user groups. Some of this research considers the role of public purchasing or funding organizations as coordinators of other public or mixed ownership services (Mays et al. 2001), and some examines how local "partnerships" with many organizations can be developed, for example, for care of older people (Haydon 2003).

There is clearly a need for more evaluations and other types of studies of quality programs which answer the questions of decision makers, and also build theory about large scale interventions to complex public service organizations.

23.8 THE CHALLENGE OF IMPROVING PUBLIC SECTOR QUALITY

The literature shows mixed evidence of "results" with quality methods, although most studies consider a narrow set of results over the short term. There is, however, more discussion about how to adapt and apply quality methods to public services and of the reasons why improving quality in public services is difficult. Most discussions take the view that quality improvement ideas have usefully concentrated attention on how to make public services more responsive to their users in increasingly consumerist western societies.

It should be noted that quality methods are not an unqualified success in their birthplace: manufacturing industry. Technical quality control and assurance is widespread, but many larger organization-wide and transformational programs like TQM have either failed or shown mixed results (Biglow and Arndt 2000). Most of the public sector provides services and not manufactured products: it is inherently more difficult to define, measure, control, and improve services than physical products. The workers' role and relationships with customers is critical for quality. Further, standardization to reduce variation is not always what is needed—rather, systems and training to enable an appropriate flexible response to the individual client's needs, and different types of accountability in public services are often in conflict with this "service imperative."

Another reason why a simple transfer of quality methods to public services is not possible is because there is often not a simple individual customer for these services. The primary beneficiary of education is the student, but there are also other important "customers": parents, industry, and society. A related issue is that customer wants and expectations should not be the only objective: many public services are professional services where users may not know their own needs. What a badly informed patient wants may kill him or her. In addition quality may only be revealed some time after service consumption: examples are child care, education, and public health programs.

Improving quality has been the greatest challenge in education and healthcare, for a variety of reasons, including multiple objectives, multiple beneficiaries, and professionals' traditional "ownership" of quality and their individual focus and resistance to management-imposed and organization- or system-based quality methods (Donnelly 1999).

A number of commentators note that public sector workers lack the employment incentives to improve quality that are experienced by private sector employees in competitive markets. Poor quality does not threaten jobs or the organization's survival in the same way. An influential US publication in the early 1990s saw this as a fundamental obstacle: Osborne and Gaebler (1992) proposed that their first strategy, "listening to the voice of the customer," would not work unless customers have a choice of provider, and their choice influences the resources which the provider gets. In addition, there must be major programs to transform the bureaucracies management, culture, and systems.

Box 23.4 Differences between private industry and public services which are relevant when adapting quality methods

Private industry	Public services
Simple customer-purchaser	Many "customers," most of whom are not purchasers
Employees know that losing customers means losing their job	Personnel do not see a clear link between fewer clients and loss of jobs
Customer wants are the priority	Client needs are important (in health, reducing suffering is the aim)
Satisfaction all important	
Often a simple service/product	Sometimes a complex multi-professional service combining technical and caring elements
Employees not in separate "tribes"	Occupational power and politics—quality is political
Links between input, process and outputs knowable and predictable	Less predictable links between inputs, processes and outcomes
Simple performance measures of success.	Performance complex, difficult to measure and multifaceted

Most discussion about the challenges of quality improvement has been in education and health, where there is a complex customer, multiple objectives and largely semi-professional and multi-professional work forces. In healthcare, administration has traditionally had a weaker management role than in manufacturing industry. In recent years professionals have felt their independence and power threatened, and the idea that management should take a strong role in leading quality is not welcomed.

TQM has faced particular challenges in healthcare and education, promising much but delivering little. The theory is that TQM programs are management led, but also that the manager's role is to empower employees to improve quality. Thus the manager's role changes from command and control to one of supporting and facilitating employees and teams. This theory of management is not just a theory of a new role for managers, but also a theory of how all employees assume responsibilities for managing the care process—not only are scientific methods "democratized," so is management. Managers have to adopt a new role to introduce the methods; then, as employees take more control of the care process, the role of managers changes again. This has not been understood or, where it has, managers have found change difficult.

Box 23.5 Some differences between private industry and public health services which are relevant when adapting quality methods

Private industry	Public health care
Front-line work often low discretion	Doctors have and need a large degree of autonomy
Often professional managers, and a single line management structure	Management competence not well developed, and multiple professional management structures
Management can direct without reference to higher political bodies: change can be fast	Highly politicized
Top–down directed change programs are possible	Change requires doctors' and others willing cooperation to be successful

---

In summary, the literature suggests that quality methods could improve users' experience of public services in certain situations. To apply the methods more fully and gain benefit from them, the greatest challenges faced by public services are reported to be:

- fully engaging professionals in the more organization and process improvement approach, especially doctors in health services;
- developing managers to take on a quality leadership role;

- developing low-cost and relevant data systems to measure quality and give feedback about the results of quality changes;
- finding effective ways to address the larger quality problems which involve cross-professional and cross-agency working issues.

23.9 CURRENT ISSUES AND FUTURE TRENDS

Over the last ten years there has been a clash of two different quality paradigms: between the standards/inspection-based approaches and the newer continuous quality process improvement approaches. Whilst it is unfair to characterize the former as the "police and punish" method, inspection approaches do tend to be based on the assumption that highlighting employees' divergence from standards is itself enough to produce quality improvement. This approach is not effective if employees do not believe in the standards, if they fear the consequences of being shown to be below standard, or if they do not have the skills or power to make changes. The newer CQI approach is based on the idea that employees are prisoners of the systems in which they work, and are condemned to produce poor quality unless they use proven methods to understand and change the systems. This approach is thought to work when there is already a climate of trust, and the skills and time to use the methods. It also demands a change of the traditional bureaucratic control hierarchies in public services. Both may be are necessary: public services must have standards, inspection and regulation of quality, and indeed this may be a necessary precondition for CQI methods. Yet there is a tension and incompatibility between these approaches which is increasingly recognized.

A second and related issue is whether quality performance information should be made public, or only disclosed to and used internally by the service. In education this debate has been won by those supporting publication—schools and higher education in many western countries publish comparative reports (e.g., QAA 1996 in the UK). Publication is strongly opposed in public healthcare systems. That quality must be measured is rarely disputed by the experts, although which are the best measures will always be contentious issue. If the measures are generally agreed to be adequate, and also allow comparisons, then would publicizing these data produce faster and more significant quality improvements than only releasing the data internally? Publicizing information is the trend—in healthcare the question is now becoming, what right do governments or others have to withhold data and prevent patients from protecting themselves?

The future of quality in public services is likely to be shaped by a number of external factors, as well as internal influences arising from the growing quality movement within these services (Box 23.6).

23.10 CONCLUSIONS

The purpose of quality methods is presented as being to help a service do what it is meant to do: to meet users' needs in a humane and safe way with respect for the person, and to do so without waste and errors. But public services also have other objectives, and a variety of users and stakeholders. Income is often not dependent on pleasing service users, who often do not have a choice of provider. Introducing quality methods entails significant changes: in workers understanding that their interests are advanced by meeting customer's wants; workers learning and using quality methods to analyze and change work organization; and in the role of management and of the balance of responsibility and control over work organization between management and workers.

Some writers and chief executives have presented quality methods as being the way to carry out a total transformation of public services. This contrasts with the more limited aims of many public service managers: to provide the same service, only a bit better—so long as there are extra resources. Others take the view that quality methods can make resources go further, and that quality concepts can keep a focus on service users.

In professional public services, these methods do not radically alter power relations when used by individual professions and for profession-specific quality improvement. Standards-based approaches also can be readily absorbed into a hierarchical bureaucracy. However, with the increasing complexity of service organization and contracting-out, worker or professional quality regulation and improvement alone may be insufficient in public services.

In healthcare and many other public services, the main problems appear to be getting professions to work together to improve quality and to work with management to change service systems or systems of care. And it is here that professional interests and politics cut across what is often presented as the common purpose of giving the best service to the user. The different definitions and interpretations of quality which are one cause of the confusion may not be accidental—they serve to maintain professional boundaries and autonomy: language may be the professions' last defense. There are some within public service unions and the professions who see quality methods as a further onslaught by management to control and direct, or as a "Trojan horse" containing the "soldiers"

Box 23.6 External and internal influences on quality in public services in the future

External influences

- demands from funders and the public for information about quality
- pressures to assess and report on the quality of public service purchasing organizations
- continual pressure on finance, which will force consideration of the costs of poor quality and of the expected return on investment in quality projects and programs
- a pressure for greater accountability for quality performance and internal systems to ensure quality
- new information technology, making data capture and analysis for quality improvement quicker, less expensive, and allowing comparisons, but also leading to a demand for new skills in quality measurement and interpretation
- rising user expectations, as people compare the quality of public services with other services, as they become better able to judge and insist on better quality, together with the growth of power and sophistication of user's associations
- more litigation and less willingness to give the public services the benefit of the doubt
- from some quarters, a pressure to ensure quality for the poor, vulnerable and voiceless, in part articulated through a movement for user's and citizen's rights,
- more regional requirements for basic standards of quality, for quality assurance, (and in Europe, for harmonization of public service users rights)
- increasing competition between public services and the private sector
- methods to ensure inter-organizational quality and continuity of service: increasing fragmentation of services and other changes will lead to assessing and improving the quality of episodes of service for users

Internal influences

- an emerging "quality industry" and an occupation of quality specialists and inspectors, with their own interests and also increased capabilities to facilitate projects and manage information
- a greater understanding of which are the more effective quality methods for which services and of how to achieve change, leading to better selection and management of quality projects
- a more realistic approach to organization-wide quality programs and greater sophistication in adapting the ideas to particular services
- accreditation schemes for different public and private services are likely to become an established part of public services
- an increasing recognition and understanding of the role of managers, and of the need to address inter-service and inter-departmental quality problems
- new approaches to working with service users to enable them to meet their own needs

of cost control. Their history in public services certainly shows the potential of some methods to add more bureaucracy, and for management and others to "intrude" into the workers' discretion and relations with users. Yet it also shows the potential for professions to use quality methods to uphold professional values and to reassert principles which have declined in importance in "the business of public service."

REFERENCES

ANDERSON, C., CASSIDY, B., and RIVENBURGH, P. (1991), "Implementing Continuous Quality Improvement (CQI), in Hospitals: Lessons Learned from the International Quality Study," *Quality Assurance in Health Care* 3(3): 141–6.

ARCELAY, A., SÁNCHEZ, E., HERNÁNDEZ, L., INCLÁN, G., BACIGALUPE, M., LETONA, J., GONZÁLEZ, R., and MARTÍNEZ-CONDE, A. (1999), "Self-Assessment of All the Health Centres of a Public Health Service through the European Model of Total Quality Management (EFQM)," *International Journal of Health Care Quality Assurance* 12(2): 54–9.

ATHOS, A., and PASCALE, R. (1981), *The Art of Japanese Management*, New York: Simon and Schuster.

BABAKUS, E., and MANGOLD, W. G. (1992), "Adapting the SERVQUAL Scale to Hospital Services: An Empirical Investigation," *Health Services Research* 26(6): 767–86.

BIGELOW, B., and ARNDT, M. (1995), "Total Quality Management: Field of Dreams," *Health Care Management Review* 20(4): 15–25.

—— —— (2000), "The More things Change the More they Stay the Same," *Health Care Management Review* 25(1): 65–72.

BLACK, S., BRIGGS, S., and KEOGH, W. (2001), "Service Quality Performance Measurement in Public/Private Sectors," *Managerial Auditing Journal* 16(7): 29–39.

BLUMENTHAL, D., and KILO, C. (1998), "A Report Card on Continuous Quality Improvement," *The Millbank Quarterly* 76: 625–48.

BOUCKAERT, G., and POLLITT, C. (eds.) (1995), *Quality Improvement in European Public Services*, London: Sage.

BRYSLAND, A., and CURRY, A. (2001), "Service Improvements in Public Services Using SERVQUAL," *Managing Service Quality* 11(6): 389–401.

BSI (1990), "Quality Management and Quality system Elements: Draft Guideline for Services," British Standards Institution, Milton Keynes. Definition from BS 4778, 1987.

BURNS, J. (1978), *Leadership*, New York: Harper and Row.

CAMILLERI, D., and O'CALLAGHAN, M. (1998), "A Comparison of Public and Private Hospital Care Service Quality in Malta," *International Journal of Health Care Quality Assurance* 11(4): 127–33.

CHQCP (1995), "Summary Report from the Cleveland Health Quality Choice Program," *Quality Management in Health Care* 3(3): 78–90.

CROSBY, P. (1979), *Quality is Free*, New York: Mentor.

DEMING, W. (1986), *Out of the Crisis*, Cambridge, MA.: MIT Press.

DONABEDIAN, A. (1980), *Exploration in Quality Assessment and Monitoring*. 1: *Definition of Quality and Approaches to its Assessment*, Ann Arbor: Health Administration Press, University of Michigan.

DONNELLY, M. (1999), "Making the Difference: Quality Strategy in the Public Sector," *Managing Service Quality* 9(1): 47–52

Editorial, *Quality and Safety in Health Care* (2002), 11: 110–11

EFQM (1992), "The European Quality Award 1992," Brussels: European Foundation for Quality Management.

ELLIS, R., and WHITTINGTON, D. (1993), *Quality Assurance in Health Care: A Handbook*, London: Edward Arnold.

ERRIDGE, E., FEE, R., and McILROY, J. (1998), "Public Sector Quality Initiatives: Political Project or Legitimate Goal?" *International Journal of Public Sector Management* 11(5): 341–53.

FALLBERG, L., and ØVRETVEIT, J. (2003), "Introduction to Patient Ombudsmen Schemes in Europe," in S. Mackenney and L. Fallberg (eds.), *Protecting Patient's Rights?* Oxford: Radcliffe Medical Press, ch. 1.

FARRELL, C., and HO, S. (1996), "Managing Quality in a UK Local Authority: the Leicester Experience," *Managing Service Quality* 6(5): 38–44.

FERLIE, E., ASHBURNE, L., FITZGERALD, L., and PETTIGREW, A. (1996), *The New Public Management in Action* Oxford: Oxford University Press.

GASTER, L. (1996), "Quality Services in Local Government," *The Journal of Management Development* 15(2): 78–94.

—— and SQUIRES, A. (2003), *Providing Quality in the Public Sector*, Maidenhead: Open University Press.

GODFREY, A., BERWICK, D., and ROESSNER, J. (1992), "Can Quality Management Really Work in Health Care?" *Quality Progress* 25(4): 23–8.

GUMMESSON, E. (1987), *Quality: The Ericsson Approach*, Stockholm: Ericsson.

HARWICK, T., and RUSSELL, M. (1993), "Quality Criteria for Public Service: A Working Model," *International Journal of Service Industry Management* 4(2): 29–39.

HAYDON, C. (2003), "Quality Issues in Partnership Working," in Gaster and Squires 2003: 155–72.

HUGHES, O. (2003), *Public Management and Administration*, London: Palgrave.

INTERNATIONAL STANDARDS ORGANIZATION (2003), ISO 9001, *The Standard Companion*, Geneva: ISO.

JOSS, R. (1995), "Costing Non-Conformance at an NHS Hospital: A Pilot Study," in G. Bouckaert and C. Pollitt (eds.), *Quality improvement in European Public Services*, London: Sage.

—— and KOGAN, M. (1995), *Advancing Quality*, Milton Keynes: Open University Press.

JURAN, J. M. (ed.)(1995), *A History of Managing for Quality: The Evolution, Trends, and Future Directions of Managing for Quality*, New York: McGraw-Hill.

—— and GRYNA, F. M. (1980), *Quality Planning and Analysis*, New Delhi: McGraw-Hill.

LEIGH, R. (2003), "Comitted to Quality: The Use of Quality Schemes in UK Public Leisure Services," *Managing Service Quality* 13(3): 28–38.

MAXWELL, R. (1984), "Quality Assessment in Health," *British Medical Journal* 288: 1470–2.

MAYS, N., WYKE, S., MALBON, G., and GOODWIN, N. (eds.) (2001), *The Purchasing of Health Care by Primary Care Organizations: An Evaluation and Guide to Future Policy*, Buckingham: Open University Press.

MORGAN, C., and MURGATROYD, S. (1994), *Total Quality Management in the Public Sector*, Milton Keynes: Open University Press.

MOTWANI, J., SOWER, V., and BRASIER, L. (1996), "Implementing TQM in the Health Care Sector," *Health Care Management Review* 21(1): 73–82.

NAVARATNAM, K., and HARRIS, B. (1994), "Customer Service in an Australian Quality Award Winning Public Sector Service Industry," *International Journal of Public Sector Management* 7(2): 42–9.

NELSON, E. C., and BATALDEN, P. B. (1992), "Patient-Based Quality Measurement Systems," *Quality Management in Health Care* 2: 18–30.

NIST (1990), *The Malcum Baldridge National Quality Award 1990 Application Guidelines*, Gaithersburg, MD: National Institute of Standards and Technology.

NORMAN, R. (1984), *Service Management: Strategy and Leadership in Service Businesses*, London: Wiley.

OSBORNE, D., and GAEBLER, T. (1992), *Reinventing Government—How the Entrepreneurial Spirit is Transforming the Public Sector*, Reading, MA: Addison Wesley.

ØVRETVEIT, J (1992a), *Health Service Quality*, Oxford: Blackwell Scientific Press.

—— (1992b), "Towards Market-Focused Measures of Customer/Purchaser Perceptions," *Quality Forum, Institute of Quality Assurance*, London, 19(3): 21–4.

—— (2000), "Total Quality Management in Europe," *International Journal of Health Care Quality Assurance* 13(2): 74–9.

—— (2002), *Action Evaluation of Health Programmes and Change: A Handbook for a User Focused Approach*, Oxford: Radcliffe Medical Press.

—— (2003), "What is the Best Strategy for Improving Quality and Safety of Hospitals: A Review and Synthesis of the Evidence," WHO, Copenhagen. (http://www.euro.who.int/eprise/main/WHO/Progs/HEN/Syntheses/20030820_1)

—— and GUSTAFSON D. (2003), "Evaluation of Quality Improvement Programmes" *British Medical Journal* 326: 759–61.

PARASURAMAN, A., et al. (1988), "SERVQUAL: A Multiple Item Scale for Measuring Consumer Perceptions of Service Quality," *Journal of Retailing*, Spring: 12–40.

PFEFFER, N., and COOTE, A. (1991), "Is Quality Good for You?" *Social Policy Paper* 5, London: Institute for Public Policy Research.

POLLITT, C. (1990), "Doing Business in the Temple," *Public Administration* 68(4): 435–52.

—— et al. (1992), "Considering Quality," Centre for the Evaluation of Public Policy and Practice, London: Brunel University.

QAA (1996), "Assessing the Quality of Education," The Quality Assurance Agency for Higher Education (UK), Assessment Process, http://www.qaa.ac.uk/revreps/subjrev/assessingquality.htm

REDMAN, T., MATHEWS, B., WILKINSON, A., and SNAPE, E. (1995), "Quality Management in Services: Is the Public Sector Keeping Pace?" *International Journal of Public Sector Management* 8(7): 21–34.

ROBINSON, R. (1984), *Quality Circles: A Practical Guide*, London: Gower Press.

—— and LE GRAND, J. (1995), "Contracting and the Purchaser–Provider Split," in R. Saltman, and C. von Otter (eds.), *Implementing Planned Markets in Healthcare*, Milton Keynes: Open University Press, 113–33.

ROSENTHAL, G., and HARPER, D. (1994), "Cleveland Health Quality Choice," *The Joint Commission Journal on Quality Improvement* 2(8): 425–42.

SANDERSON, I. (1996), "Evaluation, Learning and the Effectiveness of Public Services: Towards a Quality of Public Service Model," *International Journal of Public Sector Management* 9(5): 90–108.

SCRIVENS, E. (1995), *Accreditation*, Milton Keynes: Open University Press.

SHAW, C. (2000), "External Quality Mechanisms for Health Care: Summary of the ExPeRT Project on Visitatie, Accreditation, EFQM and ISO Assessment in European Union Countries," *International Journal of Quality in Health Care* 12: 169–75.

—— (2001), "External Assessment of Health Care," *British Medical Journal* 322: 851–4

SCHONBERGER (1982), *Japanese Manufacturing Techniques*, New York: Free Press.

SHORTELL, S., BENNET, C., BYCK, G. (1998), "Assessing the Impact of Continuous Quality Improvement on Clinical Practice: What Will it Take to Accelerate Progress?" *The Millbank Quarterly* 76: 593–624.

SWEENEY, J., and HEATON, C. (2000), "Interpretations and Variations of ISO 9000 in Acute Health Care," *International Journal for Quality in Health Care* 12: 203–9.

TAYLOR, D. (1996), "Quality and Professionalism in Health Care: A Review of Current Initiatives in the NHS," *British Medical Journal* 312: 626–9.

THOMPSON, R., MCELROY, H., and KAZANDJIAN, V. (1997), "Maryland Hospital Quality Indicator Project in the UK," *Quality in Health Care* 6(1): 49–55.

WALSHE, K., and FREEMAN, T. (2002), "Effectiveness of Quality Improvement: Learning from Evaluations," *Quality and Safety in Health Care* 11: 85–7.

WISNIEWSKI, M. (2001), "Using SERVQUAL to Assess Customer Satisfaction with Public Sector Services," *Managing Service Quality* 11(6): 380–8.

ZEITHAML, V. A., PARASURAMAN, A., and BERRY, L. L. (1990), *Delivering Service Quality*, London: Macmillan.

CHAPTER 24

BUDGET AND ACCOUNTING REFORMS

IRENE S. RUBIN

JOANNE KELLY

PUBLIC budgeting reform around the world has ranged from minor to dramatic over the past decade. The more dramatic changes include moving from simple line-item budgeting under a centralized government bureaucracy to adopting program and performance budgeting, performance contracts, more entrepreneurial management, contracting or leasing with the private sector, output and outcome measurement, accounting changes, and fiscal decentralization. These reforms impact the rules and processes of budget formulation, authorization, implementation, and reporting as well as public expenditure management more broadly, including the way public services are delivered. Widespread use of the term New Public Management (NPM) to describe many of these initiatives has created a veneer of sameness, but actual reforms have addressed local problems and reflect local politics, history, and culture, as well as previous reform efforts and pressures from international organizations. This variety of possibilities contributes to a complex story, one that does not lend itself to a few summary statements.

This chapter examines what reforms have been proposed, what they are intended to accomplish, and how they are working out. The result of our survey and analysis is somewhat messy if informative. The amount and quality of information available in different countries varies enormously. Failed reforms have often been ignored by researchers, biasing the existing reports in a positive direction. Reforms have been in place for different amounts of time in different countries, and some have been only partly implemented, adding to the difficulty of comparing them. Finally, the large number of countries engaged in such reforms has led to some selectivity in the presentation, making the results less than neat. This essay then represents an interim report on an ongoing set of processes in a limited number of countries, based on the literature and on first-hand observations offered by scholars and practitioners in a number of countries.

24.1 ELEMENTS OF BUDGET REFORMS

The last decade has been marked by a number of budget and accounting reforms, each with different aims. The list that we focus on in this chapter includes output or outcome budgeting, accrual accounting and budgeting, fiscal decentralization, and expenditure prioritization and cutback schemes to help balance budgets.[1] Some of these reforms, when packaged in particular bundles and used for a particular set of purposes, have been associated with the New Public Management, but they need not be. Elements of output budgeting clearly build on early performance budgeting reforms, for example. Countries can adopt performance budgeting without any of the managerialist ideology or public choice philosophy that accompanies NPM.

24.1.1 Output and Outcome budgeting

Some of the most dramatic reform efforts are intended to shift the basis of budgetary control from detailed line-items to measurable goals for output and outcomes. Normally, this shift is accompanied by the introduction of "performance contracts" that set out either the results (outcome) or the amount and quality of services (the output) to be provided for a given lump sum appropriation. Program administrators are then held accountable for delivering those contracted results, and future appropriation levels are, at least theoretically, decided on the basis of this performance. The goals of government programs have to be articulated clearly, performance measures have to be developed and monitored, and this information needs to influence budget decision making.

This set of reforms is intended to give program managers the flexibility to use public resources in a way that ensures policies are delivered efficiently and effectively. Part of the goal is to shift the role of central budget actors—legislators, ministers, and central agencies—from inappropriate micro management (input controls) to the consideration of policy goals and implications. Performance measurement, with its contractual and entrepreneurial elements, is intended to increase transparency and accountability of government. Incorporating output and outcome performance information into the budget process is intended to help weed out ineffective programs that are wasting money by not achieving their goals, or not achieving them to their maximum possible levels.

The budgetary role of legislators is likely to be affected by the introduction of these reforms. If legislators have little or no role in setting the performance goals, prioritizing them, or evaluating them, they lose pre-controls and gain little or no power or influence in return. If they lack the staff to do the initial analysis or to receive and analyze performance reports, they may be disempowered in a less visible fashion. A second potential problem is that holding administrators accountable for results (over which they may have minimal control), may be difficult or impossible, with the added complexity that the agency being judged is also the one producing the information on outputs and outcomes. The accuracy and transparency of reporting may become critical.

24.1.2 Accounting Reforms

Accrual accounting and budgeting reforms are argued to increase the transparency of public asset usage, and thereby improve both government accountability and the efficiency of resource allocation.[2] Accrual accounting reforms impact at several levels including the extension of departmental and government-wide accounting to include balance sheets and statements of assets and liabilities; development of a fully costed public asset registry; and the full costing of government programs. Accrual budgeting reforms use this information about public spending to change the decision making and the basis of budgetary control. While accrual accounting for the public sector has been widely adopted, accrual budgeting has been adopted only by a small number of countries. In some countries these reforms replace cash-based accounting and budgeting, in others accrual information is seen to complement or extend the existing cash-based system.

Advocates of this reform argue that full accrual accounting improves the efficiency of resource allocation and usage by clarifying how much the government is really spending on programs (JCPAA 2002). Without this information it is difficult to know whether a program is too expensive or whether an agency is spending too little on purchasing (or repairing) capital assets. Measuring changes over time in the value of government assets and liabilities might identify places where government agencies or programs have unfunded capital requirements or are drawing down their capital reserves, and hence either need a transfusion of funds or are headed for major financial problems. Others argue that better accounting for

capital assets also allows program managers to estimate a return on public investments. The underlying notion is that if the value of capital assets is made clearer,
estimates of program costs will be more accurate, and the ability to prioritize and
reduce investments that engender lower rates of return will be enhanced.

Some governments have adopted, or are considering this reform as part of a
broader set of public sector reforms. If one assumes that competition between the
public and private sector will be continuous in an effort to benchmark the cost of
government services or to facilitate competitive tendering, then public and private
sector costing models must be comparable. Carlin and Guthrie (2000) have argued
that accrual budgeting in Australia and New Zealand was designed to support the
system of performance measurement and outcomes based budgeting by clarifying
the cost of achieving desired outputs and outcomes over time.

24.1.3 Fiscal Decentralization

Fiscal decentralization means granting taxing powers to local or regional governments, giving them untied grants to run their own services, or a combination of
both. It is the logical concomitant to political decentralization, bringing government closer to the people. When political institutions have been decentralized,
some form of fiscal decentralization is required to allow local governments and
their citizens to choose projects, develop priorities, and implement goals. Local
governments are expected in this model to know better than national governments
what the needs of the local population are, and hence fiscal decentralization is
supposed to create a more efficient distribution of revenue. These two reasons,
implementing democracy and improving economic development expenditure, are
the ones most commonly used to support fiscal decentralization. A third argument
sometimes offered is that governments should raise revenue in the same proportion as they spend money. If the national government spends 50 percent of the
money, it should raise 50 percent of the revenue. The same is true for local
governments. Creating such a match would eliminate intergovernmental payments, which are often gamed, and presumably would help curtail spending,
because the demand for services would be offset by the reluctance, or impossibility,
of raising more taxes at that level of government. In particular, the World Bank
has been concerned that uncontrolled local government spending can unbalance
national budgets.

Fiscal decentralization efforts bring with them fears that inexperienced local
officials will misspend money, especially when there are few rules or traditions to
prevent corruption or brokerage spending. A second difficulty in implementation
is that local governments may have few resources to tax, especially if the population
is poor, so that continued subvention from the national government is necessary.
Formula allocations may be devised, with the intent of equalizing spending across

the country, among poorer and richer districts, but negotiated funding may eat at the edges of these formulae and lessen their impact. Getting the balance correct between national and local levels and preventing excessive gaming of the system or inappropriate responses to built-in incentives is difficult. National governments may find themselves strapped for funds compared to the functions they have to perform. Moreover, local governments may be difficult to control directly, creating avenues for the build up of debt.

24.1.4 Budget Balancing: Prioritization, Cutbacks, and Tax Reforms

Countries aiming to balance the pressure of budgetary imbalance with major policy agendas are attempting some combination of prioritization, spending caps, cutbacks, and tax reforms. Efforts may include getting control of increases in pension costs or health benefits, improved productivity programs, reducing the size of government employment, or controlling capital expenditures. Some countries are working with balanced budget laws while others are following the European Union model (under the Growth and Stability Pact) that allows for countercyclical spending. Medium term spending limits and caps have been introduced in some countries to manage the level of deficits and debt.

Prioritization may use a formal expenditure examination, along the lines of a zero-based budget, with emphasis on cost benefit comparisons, especially for capital projects or it may involve more explicit policy making on the part of the elected officials. Tax reforms may reduce taxation on businesses or the rich in an effort to stimulate the economy, increase taxation to help balance the budget, or shift from one source of revenue to another, in an effort to adapt to a changing economy. Different countries have adopted different sets of changes, and within countries, there has sometimes been a shift from one pattern to another, such as from increased taxation to balance the budget to reducing taxes on the wealthy or the opposite.

24.2 BUDGET AND ACCOUNTING REFORMS IN SELECTED COUNTRIES

The selection of countries presented here is somewhat eclectic. The idea is to present a range, including large countries and small, the core NPM countries and European countries that have not followed the NPM pattern very closely, and countries in transition to democracy and to market economies. Within these constraints, we chose countries based on what we knew first hand and what we could gather from other first hand accounts. The resultant story shows continual learning, adaptation, and change, regardless of whether the country is an exemplar of NPM such as New Zealand or the UK (Barzelay 2001), or one of the many countries in transition to a freer market economy.

24.2.1 New Zealand

The public sector in New Zealand has undergone two distinct phases of budgetary reform (Pallot 1996; NZ Treasury 2002). The first set of reforms began in late 1980s. In 1987, the New Zealand Treasury published arguments on the causes of and solutions to the country's economic woes. The proposed reforms drew on an economic, largely public choice, rationale and were aimed at reducing the size and cost of the public sector by reshaping the incentive structure underpinning public institutions. This meant increasing freedom over inputs, separating out the purchasers and providers of public services, clarifying and strengthening accountability for outputs, and introducing contracting out and privatization. In 1989, legislation was introduced that required fiscal objectives to be clearly stated and reported against and required that annual budgets be developed within the context of these pre-stated fiscal policy objectives. Although the individual elements of this first reform phase were implemented gradually, the fact that they were based on the Treasury "blue print" gave them an overall coherence. This first phase of reform became iconic of the budgeting and accounting reforms of the NPM.

The second stage of budgeting reform in New Zealand began in the late 1990s. These adaptations were partially due to the limitations and problems emerging from the earlier reforms, but were also the result of changes in the political and economic environment. Overall, this second group of reforms was more oriented to consideration of what should be done rather than how it should be done. The focus was more on strategic planning at the government-wide, rather than agency, level. The fiscal management objectives shifted from deficit reduction to the perceived need to impose stricter rules for ongoing fiscal discipline under conditions of budgetary surpluses and coalition governments.

The New Zealand experience suggests some hyperbole in claims that accrual accounting will radically improve transparency and result in better accountability mechanisms. Larry Jones (2003) summarized criticisms of the way accrual accounting was implemented in New Zealand: the valuations required by accrual accounting were made out of sight, were nearly invisible, and were often biased against departments and service provision capability. In an online discussion of NPM reforms, June Pallot and Susan Newberry (2001) argued that the accrual estimates intended to improve the comparability of public and private sector costings were manipulated in some cases to the advantage of the private sector. Newberry (2003: 77–8) reported a series of implementing regulations that led to overestimates of capital costs and to the erosion of departmental capital rather than its maintenance. She noted that under the regulations, departments have to calculate both depreciation and a fee on capital as part of their program delivery costs (the latter is considered as a substitution for taxes, interest, and dividends). The rate of the capital charge and the asset valuation are intentionally calculated high. These higher costs make it more likely that private sector alternatives will be adopted. Jones, cited above, argues that government officials acknowledge the problems but claim they were not intentional. If true, then the accrual reforms have had an unintentional effect of making government look more expensive than the private sector and more expensive than it is.

By far the most fundamental problem to emerge from the New Zealand experiment with devolution and decentralization is a gradual reduction in the capacity of government to address questions of cross-government policy development and coordination in anything but an *ad hoc* manner. As the reforms progressed, agencies increasingly saw themselves as independent entities each considering only their own program goals and outputs, with too little concern for the whole. As a result the reforms had the opposite effect of that intended: agencies became less controllable by and less responsive to the policy concerns of public officials. These criticisms were repeated in a recent OECD report (2002) which underscored that the reforms may create more efficient agencies, but are not particularly good about selecting priorities and allocating to them (also see Campos and Pradham 1996). In addition, the fact that agencies are measured on their achievement of outputs, not outcomes, means there is little incentive or capacity to evaluate whether programs are achieving their objectives.

Efforts to address these problems began in the mid-1990s and continue at the time of writing this chapter. Initially government ministers were required to set out government-wide priorities and policies and then contract with agencies to carry them out. Yet these adjustments did not resolve the lack of coherence and strategic capacity within the bureaucracy or at the center of government. In recognition of these problems the government commenced a Review of the Center project in late 2001 (State Services Commission 2001). This project is primarily an attempt by the Treasury and the State Services Commission to rebalance the forces that have moved deliberative capacity to individual line agencies and ministers. Various review exercises have been introduced including "circuit-breaker" teams and Value for Money (VFM) exercises in an effort to review existing programs. These more recent versions attempt to restore a government-wide policy focus to the bureaucracy by forming cross agency networks and teams to work on difficult problems. Some observers report little demonstrable progress as a result of these efforts. The focus on outputs rather than outcomes continues to be a problem, with increasing emphasis on trying to shift from outputs to outcomes, including a discussion of whether to change the vote and appropriation structures to promote the more results-focused, outcome-based budgeting (State Services Commission, 2002; NZ Treasury 2002).

Finally, changes in both the economic and political environment of New Zealand have undermined some of the earlier strategies for promoting fiscal discipline. While the restraint objective remains, the government is looking to different tools. Electoral reform in 1997 moved NZ to proportional representation and in doing so introduced the reality of coalition governments. Efforts to restrict likely spending pressures saw the introduction of a mechanism known as "fiscal provisioning," essentially a pre-stated and fixed limit on total new spending over the parliamentary term of three years. This has proved to be a difficult instrument to manage politically. During the second cycle of operation, most of this money was spent during the first two years of government and the framework proved incapable of limiting the spending intentions of a coalition government facing six consecutive budget surpluses and an impending election. These difficulties led Treasury to introduce the "new fiscal management" approach in December 2002. The accompanying documentation claims to make the "fiscal limits more flexible": it is too early to know what this means in practice.

24.2.2 Australia

The most substantive budget reforms to be introduced in Australia over the past decade are associated with the introduction of accrual outcome budgeting. The government used accrual accounting to estimate the full cost of delivering government programs (Kelly 2001). In addition, the bottom line budgetary balance was recalculated to reflect accrual accounting principles and to include a consolidated statement of assets and liabilities for the federal government. Second, budget documentation and processes were redesigned to ensure that outcomes became the primary basis for parliamentary control and, theoretically at least, the focus of cabinet decisions of resource allocation. The decision to focus on outcomes rather than outputs reflected an attempt to avoid many of the problems experienced in New Zealand. Information on agency outputs and input consumption continues to be provided in the detailed budget statement and the annual report of each department and agency, so that questions of efficiency and economy can be examined.

While Australia was aware of problems in the accuracy, transparency, and equity of the accrual costing methodology, little was done to address them and several problems quickly emerged. The methodology for moving from cash to accrual costing was based on the status quo program estimates, which meant that existing inaccuracies were incorporated into the new figures. A second problem related to the usability and transparency of the accrual information. Cabinet ministers and parliamentarians were equally flummoxed by the new information and recommended that the cash based information be reinstated in the interests of simplicity and comparability over time.

Relatedly, many program analysts lacked sufficient grounding in accounting theory to understand the new figures and were replaced as least in the short term by financial accountants. This move threatened to undermine both the credibility and relevance of recommendations made by the budget office to the cabinet in the annual budget negotiations. This issue appears to have been recognized and has at least partially been addressed in a recent recruitment drive. Finally, the agency, or perhaps minister, dealing with the budget and reforms (Department of Finance), and the agency responsible for fiscal and taxation policy (Treasury) had different needs. The latter required more cash-based information and published reports with the accrual information buried in the middle. When accrual reporting resulted in deficits, cash figures were conveniently used to suggest a surplus position; when a new Goods and Services Tax was introduced, the government used accrual accounting arguments to justify a decision to remove all mention of this revenue from the government books (Australian National Audit Office 2001, 2002a). While the government is aware of these issues many remain unresolved, primarily for political reasons.

Similarly, the outcome system is proving difficult for both parliament and cabinet. It is unclear how to apportion either funding or responsibility in respect to outcomes that are to be achieved by more than one agency. This has seriously undermined claims of improved accountability and the usefulness of performance reports for decision makers. Both the Auditor General and the relevant parliamentary committees have suggested that the portfolio budget statements in which output and outcome information is found are "at too great a level of generality to be useful" (Australian National Audit Office 2002b; JCPAA 2002). Aggregate data for the whole of government performance is not collected together and published, and trend data on performance is not adequately presented. In addition, the Australian Auditor-General recently discussed the problems of integrating the issues of conformance (in the sense of traditional public sector values of equity, equality, ethics) with performance (in the more managerial sense) (Barrett 2000). DOFA sought to address this problem by encouraging agencies to monitor and report against a range of performance indicators that cover conformance as well as performance.

While advocates suggest these are largely implementation issues that will be resolved in time, some comparative research suggests some weaknesses may be inherent to the output system as currently designed. Carlin and Guthrie (2000), for example, compared output-based budgeting reforms as introduced in New Zealand and Australia and conclude that neither has achieved the promised results. Their study identified the following difficulties common to both countries: "a lack of rigour in the definition and measurement of outputs, a lack of clarity and measurability in the choice of outcomes, and an almost total lack of reflexive feedback performance measurement systems to provide vital feedback as to the impact of purchased outputs on policy driven outcomes." Similarly, they argue that despite claims of radical reform, the budget documentation presented to parliamentarians remains largely unchanged from documentation prepared along traditional "input" lines. As a result, they challenge the notion that internal management processes had fundamentally changed as a result of the adoption of new systems in the guise of OBB budgeting (Carlin and Guthrie 2000). In respect to Australia more specifically, Carlin and Guthrie note that the adoption of different reforms and different rules of calculation in the different states and at the national level has led to confusion in intergovernmental transfers, and that ironically, one way of creating more uniformity is to return to cash-based systems. The issue has only recently become important as cross-jurisdictional performance measures come into play as a basis for national allocation of resources to the states.

24.2.3 United Kingdom

The British government has engaged in a flurry of budgetary and accounting reform since the election of Tony Blair's New Labour government in 1997.[3] These reforms were intended to fundamentally re-engineer the system of expenditure management operating in the UK—they "seemingly tore up the rule book" as Colin Talbot recently noted (Talbot 2001). During the election campaign Labour promised to stay within pre-established expenditure limits and to undertake a comprehensive spending review (CSR) if elected. The CSR was intended to be used as the basis of cross-departmental reallocation to "correct" departmental expenditure trend lines. Within a few years, it had been adapted to form the basis of a three year expenditure and performance management cycle.

A series of adjustments to the fiscal and budgetary framework underpinned the expenditure management reforms. Two golden rules of fiscal policy were established during the election which limited government debt to "reasonable levels" and forbade government borrowing for anything other than capital investment. The 1998 budget introduced a Code of Fiscal Stability which requires Treasury to articulate statements of fiscal objectives and to report each year on progress toward these objectives. The fiscal and debt reduction strategy included an aggregate limit for total managed expenditures (TME) and this limit provided the basis for a three-year expenditure management cycle. TME was divided into two roughly equal categories: annually managed expenditure (AME) and departmental expenditure limits (DEL). AME included the more volatile statutory expenditures including social security and interest repayments and, as the name suggests, continued to be managed on an annual basis as part of the budget process. In contrast, the DEL established aggregate departmental spending budgets that are allocated on the basis of the spending reviews and fixed for three years.

This system is intended to shift the focus of budget negotiations from the size of annual increments to questions of policy continuation, effectiveness, and appropriateness. In return for three-year fixed budgets and greater year-end flexibility, spending departments are required to sign up for three-year performance contracts. Initially this consisted of a Departmental Investment Strategy, and a Performance Service Agreement. The latter states desired outcomes, establishes specific output targets, and provides specific managerial and process targets. Talbot (2001) argued that this "seemed like a revolution—government departments breaking free of the shackles of annularity for most of their spending programmes and held to account by tough contract-like performance targets. Departmental managers would be able to engage in real strategic planning and management, focused on delivery."

Yet maintaining a three-year budgetary cycle has proved difficult. By 2000, the timespan between spending reviews was shortened to two years. The primary driver behind this change appears to have been the Treasury's desire to improve the quality of performance indicators set out in the PSAs. The department also wanted to extend the spending reviews to analyze and develop policies that cut across departmental boundaries. A second driver appears to have been the large proportion of departmental budgets being carried forward in each year. The monetary policy wonks were concerned that it would create a cash management problem; the government and media were concerned that government programs were not being implemented. The latter issue grew in significance as the general election loomed.

The notion of fixed budgets has been further undermined by increasingly regular policy announcements and by top-ups to departmental budgets, initially at budget time and then throughout the year. Treasury officials argue that this additional money does not undermine budgetary discipline because the limit set for total managed expenditures (TME) is not violated. At the level of aggregate expenditures this is correct. For various reasons, including better than expected economic performance and overly cautious economic assumptions, spending in the AME envelope is regularly lower than predicted in the budget documents. In most instances the money allocated to departments is a transfer from the AME envelope into the DEL envelope. But the psychological impact of these continual cash injections is that ministers and officials see an ongoing game of incremental budgeting that operates outside the constraints of either an annual budget round or the spending reviews. A relatively good fiscal environment has enabled the Treasury to manage these pressures over the short term. It will be interesting to see how the system responds when economic conditions worsen.

The performance management system has also been adapted since its inception. The first set of PSAs included performance indicators that were too numerous (over 400), varied in quality and were largely inadequate at measuring performance. The more generous commentators called them a good start. Spending Review 2000 successfully consolidated the outcome indicators (from 400 to 200). But this shift made the outcome targets so general and amorphous that they could not be split among the specific functions within a department (Talbot 2001). Efforts to develop appropriate output and service delivery indicators have seen a proliferation of additional documents. Service Delivery Agreements (SDA) were introduced during Spending Review 2000 in an effort to clarify output targets and performance indicators. This grew to include a set of explanatory notes and, following Spending Review 2002, an additional document was devised that required departments to set out their plans and strategies for achieving the stated targets and indicators. There is also continual frustration that output indicators are little more than business measures and provide little feed back on the achievement of government policies.

Monitoring departmental performance has proved to be both politically and technically complicated. Initially, primary responsibility for monitoring performance within the executive lay with the Spending Teams in Treasury and it was assumed that departments would self-report during the three-year period, and then through the next round of spending reviews. But as the targets gained a higher profile they became politically sensitive. The Cabinet Office quickly became more involved and the Prime Minister established his own Delivery Unit. In theory the Prime Minister's Unit focused on the six main themes of the government, leaving the Treasury to focus on the remaining areas. In practice there was considerable overlap and something of a turf war erupted between the agencies and ministers responsible for monitoring agency performance. Also worrying is the fact that there is little evidence to show that the new system has improved the capacity of Parliament to monitor public sector performance (NAO 2001; House of Commons 1999, 2000).

24.2.4 Sweden

As in other countries, reform in Sweden has occurred in phases with different emphases. The huge deficits of the late 1980s were the primary impetus for the first round of budgetary reform. These early reforms included the abolition of all open ended permanent appropriations (Blondal 2001), and the introduction of a top down three-year budget plan in which parliament first approved total spending levels, and then allocated the total to specific programs and agencies. The reforms also resulted in a more integrated budget that brought off-budget programs into the process of annual budget deliberations. Accrual accounting (but not budgeting) was adopted in 1993 for agencies that had businesslike operations rather than for general government. More recently, the government has proposed to shift to accrual budgeting. Results-oriented budgeting was officially adopted for all state organizations from 1988 (Pollitt and Bouckaert 2000: 265) but the effect was limited to controlling expenditures rather than looking at results. One group of researchers concluded that:

the reform was a success in that line-item budgeting was abandoned for comprehensive cost frames to agencies. But developing performance indicators has not been a high priority task. (Molander, Nilsson, and Schick 2002: 150)

The focus of reform shifted to performance management as the fiscal crisis subsided in the mid-1990s. On 20 November 1997, the Government asked the Ministry of Finance to create the prerequisites for more effective management and follow-up of central government operations (Regeringskansliet 2000: 2). The so-called VESTA project (or the performance budgeting project) sought to increase the use of performance information in the political decision making process with the aim of improving effectiveness, efficiency, quality, and flexibility of central government public services. Sweden has had a separation of responsibility for policy formulation and program delivery for a long time; the new system sought to build on this separation by focusing ministries on questions of policy objectives, while giving agencies more flexibility to use the resources as they saw fit. Immediately after Parliament approves the budget, a performance-type contract, known as Letters of Instruction, are drawn up between the policy ministries and service delivery agencies (Scheers, Sterck, and Van Reeth, 2002).

Yet implementing the new system of performance management has proved problematic and many of the problems are similar to those experienced elsewhere. Letters of Instruction varied in content from very detailed to very vague and general. The more specific letters seem to have been written by the agencies themselves rather than the ministries, creating the impression that the ministries have not gained control over outcomes (Blöndal 2001). Another recent study reported that the letters of instruction were negotiated between the ministry and the agencies, rather than set as instruction by the ministry (Scheers, Sterck and Van Reeth 2002). Blöndal also noted that some people were critical of the letters of instruction because the letters substituted a contractual approach for the traditional approach characterized by dialogue, informality, and flexibility. If the letters of instruction were carried out by the ministries in the detailed manner originally envisioned, the transaction costs would be enormous, and the benefits would probably not be worth the costs. One interviewee summarized by telling Blöndal that it was a golden age for public administration in Sweden because the input controls had been relaxed but the output and outcome controls were not effective.

24.2.5 The United States

Reform in the United States has been marked with different emphases at different times and sometimes has taken U-turns. For example, the period from 1993 to 1998 was dominated by budget discipline, in terms of top–down budgeting with controls over aggregate totals and subtotals, capping discretionary spending and requiring explicit offsets for revenue decreases and entitlement increases. The Budget Reform Act was passed in 1990, and renewed in 1993. The goal was to reach budgetary balance and budget deficits were all but eliminated by 1998. By 2002, however, those budget rules lapsed and while top–down budgeting remained, its effectiveness was swamped by tax reductions without offset requirements. This resulted in a rapid restoration of budget deficits that reached historic highs in 2003.

Throughout the 1990s the US attempted, but largely failed, to introduce an expenditure management system with fewer input controls in exchange for performance contracts. Unable to reduce input controls, the Clinton administration shifted to trying to create Performance Based Organizations (PBOs) which reflected the Next Steps model in the UK. A number of agencies that produced their own revenues and could operate in a business like manner were nominated for PBO status. Yet this initiative was limited in implementation and by the end of 2000 only three PBOs had been created: one in the Education department, one in the Commerce department, and one in the Federal Aviation Administration. In 2001 the Bush administration nominated the State Department's Foreign Building Operations Office as a "Results-based Organization."

The reluctance of Congress to loosen input controls and stop micro-managing the PBOs has proved to be a major impediment to implementing even this small scoped reform. For example, the Patent and Trademark office had been promised that it could retain any fee income that it earned in exchange for more hiring and the elimination of its backlog of cases. Yet several years after the creation of this PBO there is still (or again) a huge backlog of cases and the waiting time for getting patents is long. Reportedly, there are plans to hire more staff but Congress has instructed the agency to solve its problems by increased efficiency not by adding staff. Unless Congress agrees to the terms of the PBO agreement it is unlikely to achieve any of the promised efficiencies.

In 2000, the Bush administration introduced the Performance Assessment Rating Tool (PART) which established a set of simple summary performance measures for each department. Under this system, government departments were assessed as having a red, yellow, or green light performance ranking: most were labeled failures. In response to significant criticisms, the Office of Management and Budget announced a refinement which involved twenty questions each agency must answer. Agencies are also required to provide back up evidence for their answers. Based on the answers, the agencies are ranked as well managed or not or insufficient information. Most of the agencies have been unable to get to green. The new system pays scant if any attention to prior efforts or improvements, and gives more credit to those whose goals are clear and easily measurable.

The president's proposed budget generally suggested increases for the agencies whose performance was rated successful, (very few) and much smaller increases or decreases when compared to inflation, for programs whose summary performance was deemed unsatisfactory. These proposals need to be passed by Congress and signed by the president to become law, but in the second year of the program there is little evidence that the budget office or most of the agencies have drawn their appropriators into the discourse shaped by these performance reports. Appropriators still make judgments on a wide range of evidence, of which the formal PART evaluations are not yet included. As of 2003, Congress has made little use of the scores in their deliberations (Gruber 2003).

Opinions differ widely on how well the new performance budget system is working or whether it is a retreat or an advance from the prior system of program evaluation. It differs from its predecessor in terms of being a forced integration with the budget, and in terms of its simplicity. The central budget office and some of the agency budgeters claim that the system has improved the dialogue between the agencies and the central budget office and helped to identify and improve management problems. There have been concerns that the linkage between the performance reports and budget allocation is too simplistic, (poor reports equal budget cuts) and, more importantly, that departments' performance information is so limited that they are unable to produce performance reports.

A second concern is whether they hold the agencies accountable for matters over which they have little or no control. For example, one question asks the agencies to state their goal or goals in clear language, and describe how they would achieve these goals. Since agencies do not typically give themselves goals, if there are unstated goals in their founding legislation because there was disagreement about those goals, or if the goals are contradictory, the agency would be marked as having poor performance because its performance is not easy to measure. Agencies like the Forest Service, that have radically different constituencies pulling toward either public forest preservation or opening forests to industry, would experience reduced funding. Such an outcome is not likely to achieve better management, though it may make an agency hesitate to report on goals different from the current administration, regardless of its legal mission.

A senior congressional staffer (who asked not to be identified) summarized his observations about the PART process as more proactively linking performance and budgeting than the former system, the Government Performance and Results Act. He felt that PART information on performance could be useful in budgeting, but that it was probably more useful so far in calling attention to management issues in need of resolution. He noted that OMB was claiming that addressing some of these issues was a major success of the evaluation process so far. He was concerned, however, that linking performance and budgeting too closely could be problematic, because it increased pressures to distort information provided by the agencies, and to rely too exclusively on the performance summaries in terms of prioritization criteria. Other factors need to be considered besides performance, such as equity and the importance of the problem being addressed, and too mechanical a reliance on performance is likely to result in cuts for poor performance where increases to improve performance are warranted.

The model of increased freedom over inputs in exchange for more accountability for outputs has not made major inroads in the United States. Some agencies have been granted more freedom from controls, but with minimal requirements for transparency or performance reporting or contracts; other agencies have increased performance reporting, which is now linked at least loosely to the budget allocations, but they have not been granted much if any additional flexibility over inputs.

The national government has rejected accrual budgeting. The federal government has made reporting for loans more accrual based, but there is no capital budget. There is a shadow budget for out-years but it has no binding effect, changes each year, and appears to have little impact on the budgetary choices of decision makers. Social security and health care both have severe problems in the out-years, but the government has so far generally been unable to deal with these longer term problems, even when it was running surpluses. This outcome makes it questionable whether there would be many advantages from a more accrual-based budget.

24.2.6 Japan

Japan is experiencing major financial problems, with huge annual deficits and continuing deflation, a banking crisis that has lasted for years, and an aging population that is contributing to a pension and health care crisis. In an effort to stimulate the economy, the government has engaged in repeated rounds of tax reductions and major capital spending. These efforts have not had striking economic success but have contributed to the deficits; the focus on cyclical economic problems has done little to address structural problems within the economy. In an about face in 2001, the government acknowledged that this strategy was not working, and argued for spending reductions to be followed eventually by some tax increases. The government promulgated a plan to address some if not all the major problems. These plans, though adopted by the cabinet in preparation for the annual budget, have been vague in places, and the pace of fiscal reforms has been slow. For the last three years, the financial reform plans have gone from relatively bold, if not detailed and concrete, to more vague. News stories report opposition to the plans in the ministries and a determined political party opposition.

The plans for cutback have three major components: addressing the social security, pension, and health care crises that are pending; revising the process and dollar amounts of public infrastructure investment; and engaging in complete revision of the central/local government financial relationship focusing on fiscal decentralization.

The health insurance issue was addressed by increasing healthcare premiums and making provisions for co-payments, but other key issues are still pending, such as a provision that would make many drugs available over the counter. Some progress has also been reported in reductions in infrastructure spending, (Asahi.com June 28, 2003). Some of those gains came from dismantling government corporations; the government has been able to proceed with a program to dismantle or privatize 62 special or government sanctioned corporations (Sasaki and Hirai 2003). One of the major proposals was to privatize the government corporation that deals with road building, but this proposal ran into major opposition (Notomi 2002). Other reforms were aimed at changing the way public infrastructure programs are funded, and thereby reducing the cost to government. The Japanese government used to lend money to agencies for capital projects using as resources pension reserves and postal savings, but these dedicated sources may have made more money available than was necessary, and created no incentives for reducing the size or expense of projects. Under the reforms, the government now has to borrow through bonding on the market, and the real costs of lending that money for infrastructure are made clearer by including subsidy costs in budget reports. Rather than fixed rates of interest regardless of duration, the new program charges more for longer term borrowing. The program thus mimics the market and makes the real costs of capital construction much clearer. In addition, the postal savings and the pension systems are free to invest in the market and possibly get higher returns.

Recently, attention has been on efforts to restructure the financial relationship between the national and local governments. The government argued that local governments spend much of the public's tax money, that they run deficits and borrow too much, and that federal subsidies encourage this behavior. The financial reform plan calls for scaling back the local government's functions to the minimum, reducing the federal subsidy, and allowing the local governments to raise more taxes. The goal is to create a better match between the level of government at which services are provided and the level of government where taxes are raised, so that the public will ask for less if it knows it will have to pay for it. This reform is still in progress, with specifics of reductions in national subsidies yet to be agreed upon and major opposition to specific proposals. The proposals are controversial in part because although the local governments will have greater autonomy over revenue, they will receive in total only about 80 percent as much as they do under the current system (Nakata 2003). Though not highlighted in the reform proposals, one approach to cutting back expenditures has been to consolidate local governments, to create scale economies and better services for the more remote areas at lower costs.

Deregulation and letting market incentives work have figured in these reforms, but there has been relatively less attention to output and outcome budgeting, with relaxed input controls. There has been some, if limited, effort to "corporatize," but it is too soon to know or even guess at how successful these efforts have been. The universities have been converted to next step agencies, and are busy drawing up goals and performance measures (Notomi 2002). The postal service has been corporatized as well. The corporatization of the universities envisions more authority to the top administrators over their faculty and staff, granting more discretion to the universities, but less to the faculty. The universities are required to draw up a mid range plan, with measurable goals (the techniques for which have not yet been worked out), and ministerial approval of the universities' goals. The expectation is that the minister will approve the universities' plans, but is not constrained to do so without making changes. The faculty are no longer government employees.

There may be pressure for closure of some institutions as student numbers fall—there have already been amalgamations with more expected—and there could be some privatization of organizations. Funding is likely to be increasingly based on the "quality" of universities as established through evaluations by the soon to be independent National Institute for Academic Degrees and a newly established National University Evaluation Committee within MEXT [Ministry of Education, Culture, Sports, Science and Technology], although the exact content of these evaluations and their impact still remains somewhat unclear. Competition between providers is also likely to become a greater part of funding, although there have been considerable moves in this direction already. (Goldfinch, 2004)

The reforms assume that major changes are necessary, that faculty stand in the way of those changes, and top level business administrators with more authority can create the necessary changes, whatever they are. This part of the reforms is more managerialist than market oriented. How closely the universities will have to adhere to ministerial goals is unclear, and the universities have been looking to the ministry for answers on how to structure their new business processes. The techniques to be used for evaluation and the link between that evaluation and future budgets have not yet been worked out. It is possible as a result that the universities will end up with very little additional autonomy in exchange for their performance evaluations.

Note that what is not part of this set of reforms are accrual accounting and budgeting and the accompanying contracting for service delivery.

24.2.7 China

Many of the budget and accounting reforms adopted in China are intended to provide a transition from government ownership and a planned economy to a more market orientation. They reflect concern for spending control and budgetary balance, in part because of China's new membership in the World Trade Organization. The steps it has taken also include efforts to comply with financial donors such as the Asian Development Bank, which is pressing for improvements in auditing, and to help attract foreign capital.

The reforms suggest the pervasiveness of ideas about best practices in government budgeting and accounting techniques. One observer summarized the reforms as in progress, with enormous potential:

China still has a long way to go. A systematic effort at institutionalizing the adoption of the budget in a democratic, transparent way would be a very significant step in institution innovation and capacity building in the Chinese government system. The effect of such an effort cannot be overestimated in promoting democracy, transparency and efficiency of Chinese public finance; and as a by-product, the budget as a tool will be exerting huge influence in curbing rampant corruption that is now an almost incurable tumour in the government machinery. (Hou 2003)

The first reform efforts focused on reconstructing the taxation relationship between the national government and the provincial and local governments. While sometimes referred to as fiscal decentralization, these reforms were primarily intended to rationalize both the level of taxation and the formulas for distributing funds to the provincial and local levels. At times, these formulas have resulted in so much of the revenues distributed to the provinces that the national government was unable to fund necessary services and projects without running into deficits (Hou 2003; Jin and Zou 2003). These recent changes were introduced with the dual objectives of balancing the national government budget, and making spending on economic development more efficient and effective.

A second effort has been focused on accountability and what is called departmental budgeting. Previously only aggregate spending levels for the national and provincial governments were presented to the legislature by the national government, and four different agencies had the authority to allocate revenue to departments, which they often did at different times of the year. Therefore even agencies were unaware of their share of the budget pie, or how much money was going to be available throughout the year. The departmental budgeting initiative has enormous potential for improving accountability, transparency, and financial management. Reforms to introduce department budgets were initially introduced at the national level, and have now been extended to the provincial level. Departmental budgeting also consolidates the different revenue sources each department receives including extra-budgetary funds. At the same time, the format of the budget presentation was changed to include much more useful information. Major projects are to be described, in what is the core of a capital budget. Equally important, departmental budgets are more timely and have more authority (Lou 2002: 52–80).

A third reform thrust during the 1990s saw a move to either corporatize or privatize some of the state owned enterprises, many of which have not operated efficiently. Compared to eastern European countries, privatization in China has been slow. However a substantial proportion of the state owned enterprises have been altered so that they receive much of their capital from selling shares on a market with outside ownership, rather than inside ownership. Despite an influx of capital to SOEs and these newer collectively owned companies, it is not yet clear that the reform has improved performance compared to the private sector (Zhang, 2001).

Finally, the Chinese government is encouraging zero-based budgeting reforms at the local level in some provinces to reduce the lock in effect of base budgets and incrementalism (Ma 2002; Lou 2002: 52–80). There is as yet little information on how well this is working but it is not surprising to hear initial reports that suggest getting past the expected base budgets to some kind of target based on need has been difficult.

24.2.8 South Africa

The transition from apartheid in South Africa involves building a democratic regime while also trying to recover from generations of economic and political repression. The budget reforms are intended to support the creation of a democratic government that the people control by building a more transparent government and by decentralizing revenues to follow political decentralization. The latter is complicated by the fact that the poorest areas have the most need for public services and projects, and the least ability to raise their own revenue. At the same time, the country must generate sufficient funds to facilitate economic development and ameliorate poverty. The result has been an emphasis on privatization, in essence selling off assets to gain money for development, and compliance with international banking regimes to enable the country to continue borrowing on an international market. This view suggests that the primary reform objectives should be budget balance, moderation in the amount of borrowing, reduction in the amount of corruption, and predictability of the budget.

Observers report that South Africa has enjoyed considerable success in budget and financial management reforms, more than they expected, but they caution that the reforms should be seen as ongoing. Reforms include a medium-term expenditure framework, regular reports with reasonably reliable information for decision makers, and moves to develop a capacity for performance and compliance auditing. Budget transparency has been aided by a more inclusive and consolidated budget and auditing coverage. Extra budget activities have standardized accounting and reporting requirements and while observers report some loopholes, they suggest that compliance is generally good. The Public Finance Management Act of 1999 (PFMA) "sets standard budgeting and reporting requirement for all listed institutions and tasks the accounting authorities of public entities to provide annual reports, financial statements and auditors' reports... also enables the Auditor General to audit any of these institutions" (Barberton 2002).

Reorganizing intergovernmental relations at different levels of government has been a major element of the reform, as the old apartheid divisions into black and white were dissolved and a single system created. Functions were assigned to each level of government in accordance with spillovers, so that functions that affect regions or the whole country were assigned to those regions or the national state, and functions with narrower groups of beneficiaries, such as water production, were assigned to the local level. The national government collected some taxes, such as the VAT and corporate and personal income taxes, and the local government collected property taxes. To compensate for the inability of some very poor areas to collect taxes and provide basic services, the national government created a series of grants.

Evaluations of this element of the reform have been mixed and suggest that fiscal decentralization may be a double edged sword. One observer described "this ambitious policy agenda has resulted in a new intergovernmental system that has become an example of best practices for many developing and transition economies in terms of both the process of implementation and the outcome" (Ahmad 2003). However, others argue that work still needs to be done (Barberton 2002). While there is much more and better information available to the public on the budget, the intergovernmental financial flows are complex and not generally understood, so that citizens do not understand budgets or feel they control them. The OECD country report also expresses a less optimistic view noting that eighty percent of total spending is "channeled through provinces and local governments which have so far proved to be inefficient and unaccountable." As a result, there is significant underspending. While the OECD applauds efforts to "strengthen managerial capacity building programmes, upgrade information systems and enhance financial management training," they warn that it "will take some time before the absorption capacity of the local entities improves" (OECD 2003).

Budgeting reforms are likely to continue in South Africa for the foreseeable future. There is still considerable unpredictability in the budget process and this is the focus of work intended to clarify the use of contingency funds and emergency spending, and also the role of the legislature in amending the budget. Revenue projections have uniformly been below actuals since 1998 (Van der Westhuizen and Zyl 2002) despite the fact that privatization has been somewhat slower than predicted (OECD 2003).

The reforms also get a qualified approval from the Public Service Accountability Monitor, a non profit funded by the Ford Foundation located at Rhodes University. The accountability monitor ploughs through public documents such as budgets, auditor's reports, and plans, to answer a series of questions about the quality of financial management and the agencies' achievement of performance goals. While the answers vary from agency to agency, and they find many strengths, they also find systematic weaknesses, from missing needs assessments to lack of performance contracts, to inability to explain where all the staff are that they have hired (PSAM 2003). In short, the reforms in South Africa are ongoing.

24.3 CONCLUSION

So, what can we conclude from the lessons and questions raised by this somewhat haphazard survey of budget and accounting reforms? Certainly there is a story of ongoing change and adaptation. New Zealand, Australia, and the UK may be seen as leaders in the field of public budgeting but these countries continue to struggle with problems that many claim the NPM resolves. Over time the initial reforms have been adapted and in some instances abandoned, yet other countries continue to examine the experiences of New Zealand, Australia, and the UK looking for reform ideas that apply to their own setting. This active search, combined with adoption of one or several features of the reforms has created an image that the New Public Management is a worldwide phenomenon, somewhere between a fad or style and an exemplar of globalization.

In fact more detailed studies show that differences in institutions, financial conditions, legal structures, and historical dynamics have led to very large differences in what reforms are adopted, even when they look similar on the surface. Very few countries have adopted the whole package of budgetary reforms, some emphasizing one aspect or another, or ignoring particular components. Sometimes countries have adopted initiatives piecemeal, in an experimental fashion, and then abandoned the effort, or have taken the reforms in a new direction. Reforms have been adopted differentially, emphasis placed on different elements; they have evolved differently in the countries that have adopted them; they have been abandoned in places, in others they accomplish different goals than intended initially; and they have sometimes set in motion unintended consequences such as increases in the legislative role to compensate for the overwhelmingly administrative or executive branch focus of some of the reforms.

Countries are learning from each other's experiences, and sometimes do the same thing for different reasons. In the early 1980s Australia and Sweden learned from the managerialist approach to public management being developed in Canada and Britain. New Zealand then built on these experiences, analyzed their problems through the lens of public choice theory and came up with a new model that incorporated some of the previous reform elements but gave them a different ideology. Since the mid-1980s, Canada has seemed to drop out of this master class, while Australia and Britain moved to adopt their own versions of the reforms implemented in New Zealand. Other countries have studied these reforms, added their own particular interpretation and while they seem to be implementing very similar changes this is often done to achieve different objectives or for purely symbolic reasons. In some countries, for example, privatization is justified in the interests of efficiency; in other countries sales have occurred to produce one-time revenues, which may be used well or badly; sometimes privatization occurs in a country because it is required by external authorities such as the international lending agencies or the EU. Often the implementers disagree with both public choice ideology and the belief that the private sector or competition can keep costs down. Yet they are implementing reforms initially steeped in that ethos and designed to achieve particular ends. This is particularly important for the countries that are in transition to democracy, a market economy, or even both. These countries have a very different set of problems than those who are established market economies. Our survey reiterates the warnings of many recent comparative studies that reforms designed for one set of conditions may not work well or long in other countries.

Experience also suggests that the fundamental tradeoff between increased accountability for outputs and outcomes and decentralization of control over inputs is a complex formula on the ground and one that is often incompletely realized. The tension between responsibility for outputs and for outcomes played out differently in each country. After working to link departmental outcomes and outputs, countries often get stymied (at least temporarily) by policy outcomes that cross the responsibility of several different programs or departments. It is not clear how agencies can be held responsible for achieving policy outcomes to which they contribute only a small portion, with not only other programs but other elements of the economy and nature playing a part. Agencies can only formulate goals that they influence substantially, but those may not be the ones the decision makers are interested in, for a basic disconnect. It is probably not surprising that political decision makers have often expressed puzzlement at the new documents developed by officials, and found their needs are not addressed. The ambiguities in accrual accounting only exaggerate these difficulties, and shift some control to accountants who make technical decisions on costing. It is also significant that many of these reforms were designed in countries with Westminster-style parliamentary systems. When compared to multiparty cabinets or the presidential systems, Westminster has a built-in level of non transparency that means accountability reforms are not accountability to the public, but to the policy demands of particular coalitions of elected and appointed public officials. Accountability and transparency then are not overlapping and parallel concepts. It appears that structure makes a difference—much more research is needed to explain what that difference is.

A final and related set of issues revolves around the question of controlling the bureaucracy and taking away its policy prerogatives. Reforms based on principal-agent theory are designed to make the agents (typically the bureaucracy) obey the principal (either ministers or the legislature). Yet accidents of history and the evolution of institutional and political structures in each country have created a different balance of power between principals and agents. Changing this balance of power therefore has a very different meaning and impact in each country; it also raises questions about why the bureaucracy would try to implement reforms that are designed to undermine its power. We have to ask whether the real issues are in fact a principal-agent problem; is this the major issue that needs to be dealt with? Presidents, cabinet ministers and the legislature will always want more control over the bureaucracy; want it to be a neutral tool to carry out their policy will. We need to ask whether and why this was really a problem in the first place: was the bureaucracy not carrying out the policy will of the administration? Or had the administration not formulated a coherent policy agenda, or could not afford the agenda it had worked out? Just taking power away from the bureaucracy is unlikely to be a useful strategy, unless there is a problem of bureaucratic account-ability, and very few if any of the countries adopting these reforms have shown that as the central problem they needed to solve.

Part of the reason for some of the reforms, then, is because they seem to give elected officials more policy control, more policy tools. Bureaucrats accept the reforms, because this is what they are normally trained to do, carry out the policies of the government. They may be upset or demoralized to play a lesser and more mechanical role in policy development, but they do it. To the extent that input controls are lessened and they gain a longer term certainty about revenues, their lives are simplified. This deal, this exchange, however, is not always carried out, and flexibility to reallocate within a ministry results in reduced predictability of resources for the managers actually running the program. The question is flex-ibility for whom? at what level? Experiences in some of the fore-running countries such as New Zealand, Sweden, Australia, and the UK show that bureaucrats are actively involved in articulating the outputs or outcomes they will be contracted to deliver. This may provide a firmer basis for holding the agent accountable but it does little to improve the policy setting capacity of the so called principal. Nor can the bureaucracy be treated as a singular entity. In most of the countries examined the central budget office either designed or acted as the primary advocate for the budgetary reforms. The budget office has a vested interest in designing mechanisms to reduce pressure on the public purse. Typically, they have common academic backgrounds in either economics or, more recently, accounting and organizations such as the public management group with the OECD provide a forum for sharing ideas. Clearly ideas are not enough and it is not an accident that reform seems to have been most prevalent and radical in countries where bureaucratic control over the public purse is centralized in a strong central budget office (Wanna et al. 2000).

In the end we must conclude that NPM seems to have settled into the public administration landscape as one model that has strengths and weaknesses just like all other approaches. Elements can operate individually (as they have in the past) or come together as part of a broader public sector management ethos. The fact that recent history has seen so many countries in transition, facing unprecedented fiscal pressures, or/and attempting to (re)build governance structures has provided a spawning ground for these ideas. As we learn more about the techniques, there is less credence for the argument that this is indeed best practice for everyone (if anyone); it is not a panacea. An enduring impact of the NPM experiment has been to open the options for public policy design by widening the vision of what is possible or ethical in many countries. But as Sharon Sutherland wrote about Canada in the early 1990s, "every reform is its own problem" (Sutherland 1991).

Notes

1. Jim Brumby offers a different but overlapping set of recent reforms for OECD countries: a shift to multi-year budgeting, top down budgeting techniques, reduced input controls, output based accountability schemes, and accrual accounting and budgeting (Brumby 1999). Any list of current reforms is likely to be somewhat arbitrary, depending on the countries looked at, and the degree of detail or level of analysis.
2. For discussion of the features of accrual budgeting and distinction with cash budgeting see Chan and Chen (2002).
3. During this period the UK also introduced accrual based budgeting under the guise of Resource Accounting and Budgeting. The decision not to appropriate cash funds for non-cash expenses (such as depreciation costs) is the primary difference between the UK, and Australia and New Zealand.

References

AHMAD, J. (2003), "Creating Incentives for Fiscal Discipline in the New South Africa," in J. A. Rodden, G. S. Eskeland, and J. Litvak (eds.), *Fiscal Decentralization and the Challenge of Hard Budget Constraints*, Cambridge, MA: MIT Press.

ASAHI. COM (English) (2003), Editorial: "Boneless Reforms," The Asahi Shimbun, June 27 (IHT/Asahi: June 28, 2003). http://www.asahi.com/english/op-ed/K2003062800298.html

AUSTRALIAN NATIONAL AUDIT OFFICE (2001), *Audits of the Financial Statements of Commonwealth Entities for period ended 30 June 2001: Summary Report*, Audit Report 29 of 2001–2 Financial Statement Audit, Commonwealth of Australia, Canberra.

—— (2002*a*), *Audits of the Financial Statements of Commonwealth Entities for period ended 30 June 2002: Summary Report*, Audit Report 25 of 2002–03, Financial Statement Audit, Commonwealth of Australia, Canberra.

—— (2002*b*), "Performance Information in Portfolio Budget Statements: Better Practices Guide," Commonwealth of Australia, Canberra.

BARRETT, P. J. (2000), *Managing Compliance for Assurance and Performance: Setting the Course - Integrating Conformance with Performance*, presented on 7 September at a seminar for Department of Finance and Administration, Attorney-General's Departments and the Australian Competition and Consumer Commission, Canberra.

BARBERTON, C. (2002), *South Africa*, IDASA's [Institute for Democracy in South Africa] Budget Information Service. This is a summary of the South Africa chapter in Alta Folsch (ed.), *Budget Transparency and Participation, Five African Cases*, accessed on the web 6/26/03, http://www.internationalbudget.org/resources/SAFRICA.pdf.

BARZELAY, M. (2001), *The New Public Management: Improving Research and Policy Dialogue*, University of California Press.

BLÖNDAL, JÓN R. (2001), "Budgeting in Sweden," *OECD Journal On Budgeting* 1: 27–57.

BRUMBY, J. (1999), "Budget Reform in OECD Countries", chapter 16 in S. Schiavo-Camp and D. Tommasi (eds.), *Managing Government Expenditure*, Asian Development Bank, Manila, Philippines. on line at http://www.adb.org/Documents/manuals/Govt_Expenditure (accessed February 2003).

CAMPOS, E., and PRADHAM, S. (1996), "Budgetary Institutions and Expenditure Outcomes," World Bank Policy Research Working Paper 1646, September 1996.

CARLIN, T. M., and GUTHRIE, J. (2000), "A Review of Australian and New Zealand Experiences with Accrual Output Based Budgeting," a paper presented at the third Bi-annual Conference of the International Public Management Network (IPMN) Sydney, Australia 4–6 March.

CHAN, J., and CHEN, X. (eds.) (2002), *Models Of Public Budgeting And Accounting Reform. OECD, Journal on Budgeting* 2 supplement 1.

GOLDFINCH, S. F. (2004), "National University Reform and the National University Corporation Model in Japan: Lessons from Higher Education Reform in New Zealand", *Journal of Finance and Management in Colleges and Universities* 2004 (1), 231–61.

GRUBER, A. (2003), "OMB Ratings have Little Impact on Hill Budget Decisions," *Government Executive,* June 13 (accessed on line at www.govexec.com, June 20).

HOU, Y. (2003), "Governmental Budgeting in China 1950–2000: A Brief Survey," draft manuscript.

HOUSE OF COMMONS (1999), "Public Service Agreements: Report, Proceedings of the Committee, Minutes of Evidence and Appendices," Seventh Report of the Treasury Committee, Report HC378. http://www.publications.parliament.uk/pa/cm199899/cmselect/cmtreasy/cmtreasy.htm (accessed 1 August 2003).

—— (2000), "Spending Review 2000," Ninth Report of the Treasury Committee, Report HC485, http://www.publications.parliament.uk/pa/cm199900/cmselect/cmtreasy/485/48502.htm (accessed August 1, 2003).

JING, J., and ZOU, H. (2003), "Soft Budget Constraints and Local Government in China," in J. Rodden, G. Eskeland, and J. Litvak (eds.), *Fiscal Decentralization and the Challenge of Hard Budget Constraints*, Cambridge, MA: MIT Press, 289–324.

JOINT COMMITTEE ON PUBLIC ACCOUNTS AND AUDIT (JCPAA) (2002), *Report 388: Review of the Accrual Budget Documentation*, Parliamentary Paper: 297/2002, tabled 19 June 2002 in the House of Representatives and Senate.

JONES, L. (2003), "Reform Implementation in New Zealand," International Public Management Network Lists, *IPMN Newsletter* no. 2.

KELLY, J. (2001), "Accrual-Based Budgeting in Australia: Getting behind the Myth to Learn Some Lessons", *Financial Management Institute Journal* 12(3/4): 17–22.

LOU, J. (2002), "Governmental Budgeting And Accounting Reform In China," in *Models of Public Budgeting and Accounting Reform, OECD Journal on Budgeting* 2 supplement 1: 52–80.

MA, J. (2002), Public Administration Department, Zhongshan university, Guangzhou province, China, email correspondence with Irene Rubin 20 December.

MOLANDER, P., NILSSON, J.-E., and SCHICK, A. (2002), "Does Anyone Govern? The Relationship Between the Government Office and the Agencies in Sweden," Report from the SNS Constitutional Project (Swedish Center for Business and Policy Studies). On the

Web at http://www.const.sns.se/english/publications/doesanyone.pdf (accessed August 2 2003).

NAKATA, H. (2003), "Economic Reform Package Unveiled to Mixed Reviews," *The Japan Times Online*, Friday, June 27. On line at http://www.japantimes.co.jp/ (accessed June 28 2003).

NATIONAL AUDIT OFFICE (NAO) (2001), "Measuring the Performance of Government Departments," Report by the Comptroller and Auditor General HC301, tabled March 22 HMSO, London.

NEWBERRY, S. (2003), "New Zealand's Responsibility Budgeting and Accounting System and Its Strategic Objective: A Comment on Jones and Thompson," *International Public Management Review* 6(1): 75–82.

NOTOMI, I. (2002), Professor at Saga University, Economics Department, Japan, email correspondence with Irene Rubin.

NZ Treasury. (2002), "Review of the Centre Paper Four: Departmental Accountability & Reporting Arrangements," http://www.ssc.govt.nz/display/document.asp?NavID=105& DocID=2762 (accessed 3 August 2003).

OECD (1999), "Budgeting and Management in Canada," prepared for 20th Annual Meeting of Senior Budget Officials, Paris, 3–4 June.

—— (2002), *OECD Economic Surveys: New Zealand*, by Pietro Catte and Dave Rae under the supervision of Peter Jarrett (May), Paris: OECD.

—— (2003), *African Economic Outlook*, Paris: OECD.

PALLOT, J. (1996), "Newer Than New: Public Management: Financial Management And Collective Strategizing In New Zealand," *The International Public Management Journal* 1(1).

—— and NEWBERRY, S. (2001), On line discussion in IPMN Symposium On Performance Budgeting and The Politics Of Reform, *International Public Management Review* electronic Journal at http://www.ipmr.net Volume 2 Issue 2.

POLLITT, C., and BOUCKAERT, G. (2000), *Public Management Reform–A Comparative Analysis*, Oxford: Oxford University Press.

PUBLIC SERVICE ACCOUNTABILITY MONITOR (PSAM) (2003), on the web at http://perf.p-sam. ru.ac.za/pmwsindex.asp (accessed June 26 2003).

REGERINGSKANSLIET (2000), *Financial Management for Effectiveness and Transparency*, Regeringskansliet, Stockholm: Ministry of Finance.

SASAKI, T., and HIRAI, H. (2003), "Latest Basic Reform plan 'boneless,'" *Daily Yomiuri On-Line*, http://www.yomiuri.co.jp/index-e.htm (accessed June 28 2003).

SCHEERS, B., STERCK, M., and VAN REETH, W. (2002), "Modernizing Financial Management and Policy Cycles: Building Blocks for a Comparative Research," Paper presented at the Study Group on Public Finance and Management, Conference of the European Group of Public Administration:"*The European administrative space: governance in diversity*", Potsdam, September 4–7.

STATE SERVICES COMMISSION. (2001), "Report of the Advisory Group on the Review of the Centre," presented to the Ministers of State Services and Finance, November, http://www.ssc.govt.nz/display/document.asp?NavID=105&DocID=2429 (accessed 3 August 2003).

STATE SERVICES COMMISSION (2002), "Managing for Outcomes: Guidance for Departments," prepared by the Steering Group Managing for Outcomes Roll-out. 16 August, pdf available at http://www.ssc.govt.nz/display/document.asp?NavID=208&DocID=2511 (accessed 3 August 2003).

SUTHERLAND, S. L. (1991), "Responsible Government and Ministerial Responsibility: Every Reform is its Own Problem," *Canadian Journal of Political Science* 24(1): 91–120.

TALBOT, C. (2001), "Government by Performance Based Budgeting?" ASPA Online Columns, August 31, http://216.149.125.141/publications/COLUMNS/archives/2001/Aug/talbot0831.html (accessed August 2 2003).

VAN DER WESTHUIZEN, C., and VAN ZYL, A. (2002), "How Credible Are National Treasury's Revenue Projections?", IDASA, Budget Brief no. 120. On line at http://www.idasa.org.za/pdf/986.pdf (accessed on June 26 2003).

WANNA, J., KELLY, J., and FORSTER, J. (2000), *Managing Public Expenditure in Australia*, Sydney: Allen and Unwin.

ZHANG, L. (2001), "The Impact of Post-1993 Financial Reform on Chinese Enterprises: The Case of Shanghai," presented at the Conference on Financial Sector Reform in China, University College London, September 11–13.

CHAPTER 25

NGOS AND CONTRACTING

STEVEN RATHGEB SMITH

THROUGHOUT the world, governments have been restructuring their public services due to several trends including fiscal pressure, globalization, changing ideas regarding public management, citizen pressure for improved service quality and efficiency, and new demands for inclusion by previously excluded groups and individuals (Kettl 1998; Behn 2001). A central component of this transformation of the public services in many countries has been a substantial increase in government contracting with nonprofit and for-profit organizations to provide needed public services. Governments now routinely contract for many essential public services: sanitation, maintenance, transportation, healthcare, and social services. This chapter focuses on one major part of this overall trend toward contracting: the emergence in the last forty years of widespread contracting between the public sector and non-governmental organizations (NGOs). These organizations play critical roles in the delivery of a wide array of services including: humanitarian assistance, mental health, workforce development, community and economic development, childcare, emergency assistance, child protection, drug treatment, and home healthcare.

NGOs are particularly attractive to governments in the current political environment. As part of the New Public Management (NPM), governments are pressed to cut costs and be more responsive and flexible in the provision of services. Citizens are also demanding greater voice in the administration and implementation of services. Thus, NGOs with their community connections, volunteer participation and greater program flexibility seem to be a particularly good strategy to achieve multiple contemporary public management objectives. NGOs for their part are attracted to providing government services under contract by the possibility of additional resources and the potential to have a wider impact on pressing social problems.

The basic argument of this chapter is that the emergent role of NGOs as providers of public services has created new and complicated public management dilemmas. While nonprofits may offer the opportunity for quick program start-up, lower service costs, and program innovation, the politics of government contracting with NGOs can undermine and greatly reduce these potential benefits. Indeed, competitive tendering for NGO services can introduce a host of unforeseen and unwanted incentives into the government–NGO relationship that can reduce the distinctiveness of NGOs and mute their political voice. Further, the rising importance of NGOs may have profound and enduring effects on citizenship rights. Government and NGOs need to work together to reform and manage the increasingly complicated relationship. Both sides need to approach a contracting relationship as a social contract requires ongoing investment, resources, and accountability.

In terms of structure, Section 25.1 provides an overview and historical perspective on government contracting with NGOs; Section 25.2 offers a conceptual framework to understand the relationship between government and NGOs in the contracting relationship. Next, Section 25.3 is focused on the management and policy challenges posed by contracting, while Section 25.4 details the implications for citizenship of the greater reliance on NGOs for public service delivery. Finally, Section 25.5 discusses contracting in the context of current trends in public management and the implications of these trends on the users of public services and the citizenry more generally.

25.1 Trends in Government–NGO Contracting

Before proceeding further, it is useful to discuss the nettlesome definitional issues posed by this chapter. NGOs is a term that has come into wide usage in the last twenty-five years. Hulme and Edwards (1997) use the term to refer to "intermediary organizations engaged in funding or offering other forms of support to communities and other organizations that seek to promote development" (p. 21). They make a distinction between NGOs and grassroots organizations (GROs) that rely upon a membership. Examples include neighborhood associations, social clubs, and many types of self-help groups. In the literature, GROs are also called community-based organizations (CBOs) to distinguish them from larger more professionalized organizations. This distinction between NGOs and CBOs/GROs is particularly common in field of development. In this context, NGOs refer to a wide variety of intermediary service organizations that are nonprofit but do not have a membership base in the community.

Other scholars define NGOs more broadly, to include any nonprofit organization including membership and service-based organizations (Lindenberg and Bryant 2001; Simmons 1997). Distinctions are then made between different types of NGOs such as development NGOs (DNGOs); northern NGOs such as Save the Children and CARE based in northern OECD countries and southern NGOs with headquarters in southern, generally poorer countries (see also: Lewis and Wallace 2000; Edwards and Fowler 2002; Fowler 1997, 2000). Transnational NGOs involved in advocacy such as Amnesty International, Greenpeace, and the World Wildlife Fund have received worldwide attention particularly in connection with controversial policy issues such as global warming, debt relief, land mines, and free trade (Simmons 1997; Keck and Sikkink 1998). In the United States, the term nonprofit is generally used to refer to intermediary voluntary organizations providing services to the citizenry with NGO referring to nonprofit organizations that have a non-US focus. In the UK, a similar distinction exists between voluntary organizations and NGOs (see Harris and Rochester 2001).

For purposes of this chapter, we will use the term NGO to refer to a broad and diverse range of nonprofit organizations including large transnational organizations such as CARE as well as local nonprofit organizations providing services to the homeless. This usage of NGO fits well given the international focus of the chapter. Moreover, as Simmons (1997) notes, the definition of a NGO is less important than focusing on what they do.

25.1.1 Historical Perspectives on NGOs and Contracting

Government funding of NGOs has a long history in many countries. In the United States, some of the oldest NGOs in the country such as Massachusetts General Hospital and Harvard University received government funding in the colonial period (Smith and Lipsky 1993; Salamon 1987). In many continental European countries including the Netherlands and Germany, NGOs have received substantial public funding since at least the nineteenth century (Burger and Veldeer 2001; James 1987). But these continental countries tend to be the exceptions. In the United States and many other countries, public funding of NGOs remained very restricted and limited throughout the nineteenth and into the twentieth century (Smith and Lipsky 1993). As a result, the government–nonprofit relationship was quite informal and little accountability for the expenditure of public funds existed, partly because the amount of money was quite small.

But the growth of the welfare state in advanced industrial countries in the mid to late twentieth century brought important changes to the government–NGO relationship. In the US, Australia, New Zealand, Canada, and western Europe, the increasing scale of the welfare state meant a sharp increase in public funding of NGOs. In these countries, NGOs grew in tandem with the growth of the state (Smith and Lipsky 1993; Lundstrom and Svedberg 2003; Gutch 1992; James 1987). To be sure, differences existed. In the UK and Sweden for instance, most public social welfare services were delivered by local government with NGOs supplementing statutory provision and filling specific service niches (Gutch 1992; Lundstrom and Svedberg 2003). In the Netherlands and Germany, most social welfare services were actually provided by NGOs with public funds (Burger and Veldeer 2001; Bode 2003). In the US, the situation was quite different. Public social welfare services were provided primarily by local government and were quite limited in nature. And the voluntary sector was quite small and narrow in scope. In the 1960s, public funding of NGOs grew sharply with the growth of the national government's role in social policy.

The shifts to formal contracting between NGOs and government began in the 1970s and then quickened in pace and extensiveness in the 1980s and 1990s. Fiscal pressure in many countries prompted governments to explore ways to reduce public spending and the growth of statutory services. Contracting with NGOs offered the hope of lower costs. Also, conservative governments came to power in the UK, US, New Zealand, and elsewhere. These governments were skeptical of public services and more supportive of market approaches. Consequently, public agencies (usually local government in countries such as the UK, Australia, and New Zealand) were pushed to transform their role into one of a purchaser and enabler rather than a direct provider of services (Gutch 1992; Considine 2000). This shift to the enabler role fit with the emergence of the "New Public Management" (NPM) movement that stressed "steering rather than rowing" for public agencies (Osborne and Gaebler 1993).

A good example of this shift is the Netherlands. Since the nineteenth century, the Dutch government has supported NGOs with a extensive subsidies and grants. Beginning in the 1990s, though, the Dutch government implemented "marktwerking", which entails the introduction of market forces to the relationship between government and NGOs. This policy includes formal competitive bidding and competition among NGOs and for-profit firms for government contracts (Burger and Veldheer 2001). To varying extents, this shift in policy is evident in many other countries such as UK (Kirkpatrick, Kitchener, and Whipp 2001; Gutch 1992); the US (Smith and Lipsky 1993; Gronbjerg 1993); Finland (Simonen and Kovlainen 1998); and Australia and New Zealand (Considine 2000). In these countries, this change to formal contracting has entailed greater receptivity to government contracting with for-profit service agencies especially for services such as long-term care and childcare.

In many countries such as the UK and US, the shift to contracting did not represent "privatization" of previously public services. Instead, contracting represented the creation of entirely new services, often in response to new social movements such as the women's movement. For instance, in the US, UK, and Canada, domestic violence programs are provided by NGOs under government contract (Smith and Lipsky 1993; Smith and Freinkel 1988; Brown and Troutt 2004). Many other examples exist including immigrant assistance and AIDS services.

The political attractiveness of contracting and the use of contracting as a quick way to respond to new needs is evident in the growth of contracting among governments and large multinational NGOs such as Save the Children, CARE, and Oxfam. These NGOs receive hundreds of millions of dollars in contracts to provide humanitarian relief and development programs. Many countries in the developing world also have contracts with locally based NGOs for a variety of important services (Hulme and Edwards 1997). The extent of contracting in the developing world has exploded in the last twenty years due to the changing character of foreign aid; recurring crises, wars, and natural disasters; and political liberalization allowing the growth of the NGOs.

Government contracting with NGOs throughout the world has also been influenced by another tenet of NPM which stresses empowerment, decentralization, and greater responsiveness to citizens (see Hood 1991; Behn 2001). NGOs are often a favored vehicle for government to respond to the needs and concerns of neighborhoods, immigrant groups, and social movements. In the developing world, locally based NGOs are especially attractive to public (and private funders) because of the corruption and rigidity in many public agencies

One additional trend is evident in the relationship between government and NGOs. In the last ten years, many countries have implemented new consumer subsidies as a strategy to provide needed public services. For example, many countries offer vouchers for childcare that parents can use to pay any eligible provider (Besharov and Samari 2000; Simonen and Kovalainen 1998). Many countries have increasingly employed housing vouchers to help the poor and disabled afford adequate housing (Priemus 2000). While vouchers for childcare and housing are not specifically earmarked for NGOs, they have had important direct and indirect effects on government–NGO relationship. In general, vouchers encourage greater competition among service agencies and increase the uncertainty on receiving payments from government.

25.2 CONCEPTUAL FRAMEWORK

NGOs, as providers of public services, present a number of management challenges for public sector administrators as well as nonprofit staff and volunteers. These challenges and possible remedies can be usefully examined through the lens of four key conceptual frameworks: principal–agent theory; nonprofits as representatives of a community of interest; the "contracting regime"; and institutional theory.

Contracting between government and NGOs has received widespread attention from scholars (see Smith and Lipsky 1993; Gronbjerg 1993; Gutch 1992; DeHoog and Salamon 2002; Hartogs and Weber 1978; Kramer 1983). This government–NGO contracting relationship has important, unique characteristics that distinguish it from other types of contracting (such as contracting for garbage collection or water). First, the services—such as residential care for the chronic mentally ill or community development—are complex and the outcomes are uncertain and often contested. Second, services such as home care, counseling, hospice care, and workforce development are typically very labor intensive, thus it can be difficult to achieve productivity gains and/or significantly reduce costs. Third, the users of many NGO services may be unable or unwilling to exercise their own voice to register complaints with services; user or citizen feedback is often quite limited as a measure of performance. Fourth, NGOs are typically undercapitalized, especially compared to for-profit firms contracting for other public services such as garbage collection. NGOs often have problems with cash flow and may be unable to adequately invest in their capital infrastructure. Undercapitalization places NGOs in a politically vulnerable position vis-à-vis government.

The complexity of NGO services and the difficulty of performance assessment create complicated principal–agent problems that affect government and NGOs. As noted by Pratt and Zeckhauser (1985), Donahue (1989), and others, many public management dilemmas can be characterized as principal–agent issues whereupon government as the principal is using an agent, in this case NGOs, to achieve particular goals and objectives. Hansmann (1980) noted nonprofits reflect the problems of "information asymmetry" that arise because of the complications inherent in evaluating the quality of nonprofit programs. He argues that donors might prefer to give to a nonprofit organization rather than a for-profit because they can be assured—due to the prohibition against using donor funds for personal gain—that the money will be used to support the programmatic purposes of the organization. In a similar vein, government officials might prefer nonprofits because they can "trust" that they will use the funds appropriately.

This principal–agent perspective usefully helps to explain the increasing formalization of the contracting process, including more detailed contracts and greater expectations on performance. As government contracting of NGOs expands, public officials face greater pressure to ensure the appropriate accountability for the expenditure of public funds, especially given the many demands on public funds. Government needs to "rationalize" its programs and formalization, particularly through increased regulation, is often a preferred strategy (Brown 1983). Regulation is a strategy to increase the compliance of the agent with the wishes of the principal, especially by tying the public payments under contracts to the attainment of specific performance measures. (For example, many workforce development agencies will only receive public contract payments if they meet specific government performance targets on job placement.)

This principal–agent issue is inherently challenging to resolve because of the different norms that guide public and nonprofit organizations. James Q. Wilson (1967) once observed that organizations are guided by five critical imperatives: equity, efficiency, responsiveness, fiscal integrity, and accountability. But NGOs and government weigh these criteria differently. NGOs are typically created by "communities" of people interested in a particular problem or cause such as community development, homelessness, or juvenile delinquency. Thus, the volunteers and staff of an NGO view the first priority as being responsive to this community, however it is defined by the NGO (Smith and Lipsky 1993). A community mental health center may regard its primary responsibility as serving people with mental health problems in a defined geographic area. Or a halfway house for youth may regard its primary constituency as at risk youth who have not been involved in serious criminal activity.

The primacy placed on responsiveness can lead to conflict with government because government places greater emphasis on equity as a guiding norm. Government officials face the challenge of justifying their allocation decisions given that the demand for government funding and services inevitably exceeds demand. Consequently, government officials are pressured to develop equitable and fair standards to guide their allocation decisions. These standards are evident in many government social and health programs that have strict standards of eligibility based on income or severity of illness.

The differences in guiding norms between government and nonprofit organizations creates two vexing public management dilemmas. First, NGOs tend to be more accepting of client difficulties and situations. They are also more likely to be interested in serving a client rather than evaluating the specific effectiveness of the service. By contrast, government cannot be so accepting and increasingly is focused on outcomes and extensive eligibility documentation. Second, NGOs—due to their emphasis on responsiveness to a specific community of interest—may reject clients who are regarded as incompatible with their mission. For example, faith-based NGOs might reject individuals who do not embrace their particular faith. Or NGOs might reject clients with chronic mental illness because the NGO regards its mission as serving people with less serious mental disorders. In both types of dilemmas, government and NGOs may clash over the appropriate boundary between government and NGO responsibility, especially if government is providing most of the funding for the NGO program.

While this difference in norms creates predictable challenges in the government–NGO relationship, the character of this relationship can vary significantly across countries. For instance, Sweden tends to rely upon public sector provision and much less on NGOs whereas the Netherlands, Germany, the UK and the United

States have a substantially bigger NGO sector with a more extensive role in providing public services under contract. Salamon and Anheier (1998) contend that the variation across countries in the size of the nonprofit sector can be explained by a social origins theory that classifies advanced industrial countries into four different regime categories: social democratic, corporatist, liberal, and statist. A social democratic regime such as Sweden will have a large public sector and a relatively small NGO sector. Liberal countries such as the US will have an extensive NGO sector and a very modest public sector. Underpinning this social origins/regime model is the argument that historical forces in particular countries such as the strength of the working class have had a profound and enduring impact on the size and scope of the government and NGO sectors (also, Moore 1966; Esping-Anderson 1990).

The special importance of historical forces in shaping the role of NGO in society is reflected in the work of scholars such as Hall (1987) and James (1987) who argue for the critical role of organized religion in the formation and development of NGOs. For instance, James (1987) argues that the NGO sector will be larger in countries with diverse religious denominations and groups because religious entrepreneurs compete for adherents by creating nonprofit educational and social organizations as a strategy to increase their membership. Moreover, James (1987), Hall (1987), Alber (1995) and Morgan (2002) and others argue that religious politics matters as much if not more than class politics on the development of NGOs, especially in terms of their place in public service delivery and political advocacy.

The prevalence of NGOs and their political strength will also be greatly influenced by the legal frameworks governing their formation In the US, for example, it is relatively easy to form a NGO while in many other countries such as Japan and China, individuals seeking to create an NGO need to undertake complicated registration and incorporation processes.

These differences among countries are especially significant for the NGO–government relationship because government and NGOs tend to create, over time, a set of norms, or "contracting regime" to govern their relationship (Smith and Lipsky 1993). Many contract relationships tend to be characterized by stability where the two parties settle upon a common set of assumptions to guide the relationship. These assumptions can change of course, especially in times of political or budgetary crisis. Further, the character of the contracting regime will be contingent on the institutional dynamics of the government–NGO relationship in different countries (Considine 2000; Burger and Dekker 2001).

In short, insight into cross-national differences in the government–NGOs is gained from institutional theory. As it relates to our understanding of NGOs, the institutional perspective suggests that the prevalence and vitality of NGOs is the product of the political, legal and institutional environment (Smith 2002; Woolcock and Narayan 2000). Proponents of institutional theory stress that NGOs represent the choices of individuals shaped by the prevailing institutions. Weak and ineffective governments, a lack of public funding or appropriate tax incentives and regulations, and poor public leadership will profoundly affect the development of NGOs. For example, France has historically relied upon public sector service delivery with a minor role for NGOs. But the Decentralization Act of 1982 encouraged the growth of nonprofit organizations and the use of nonprofits to provide public services by local authorities (Archambault 2001). Judith Tendler (1997) concluded that the central government was crucial to the formation and sustainability of NGOs and that positive relationships between government officials and NGO staff were essential to NGO effectiveness.

The work of Tendler (1997), Woolcock and Narayan (2000), Evans (1996) and many other scholars underscores the "embedded" nature of many government–NGO relationships, even in situations of formal contracting (Granovetter 1985; Flynn and Williams 1997). Many contracts do not operate on a traditional competitive basis but instead depend upon networks of trust and cooperation. Contracts are often relational and thus are long-term even in instances where competitive bidding is required (Smith and Smyth 1996). This "relational contracting" does not preclude differences of opinion or outright conflict but it does underscore the stability of many contracting arrangements (Deakin and Michie 1997; Ring and Van de Ven 1992).

To be sure, government support of NGOs can take different forms than relational contracting. Increasingly, for instance, governments provide financial support to NGOs through a variety of policy tools, including tax credits, vouchers and tax-exempt bonds (Salamon 2002; Smith and Ingram 2002). Government can also provide a variety of in-kind subsidies including free rent and technical assistance help. From the perspective of the NGO manager, the diversification of policy tools creates added complexity and greater uncertainty in funding since the stable contracting regime are less likely in situations of voucher payments and tax credits tied to consumers of service such as tax credits for childcare.

25.3 PUBLIC MANAGEMENT AND THE GROWTH OF NGOS: CHALLENGES AND INNOVATIONS

As noted, the prevalence of NGOs and the emergent role in providing important public services (with and without public funds) is a worldwide phenomenon. But this growth presents complex management dilemmas for policymakers and public administrators as well as NGO staff and volunteers. These key challenges are:

assessing performance; governance; sustainability and infrastructure support; and collaboration and cooperation. In each of these areas, innovative practices are being developed to improve NGO performance.

25.3.1 Assessing Performance

The principal rationale for the increasing utilization of NGOs to provide services lies in the following assumptions: (1) the monopoly of direct service provision by public agencies should be broken (or at least greatly diminished), thus service providers (i.e., NGOs) will be more responsive to users; (2) competition among NGOs for public contracts introduces more efficiency into the service system; and (3) the roots of many NGOs in local communities offers greater opportunities for citizen participation in the development and implementation of services, particularly among heretofore socially excluded groups. Important related assumptions are: (1) a market comprised of a sufficient number of competing NGOs exists, or can be created through changes in government regulations and funding incentives; and (2) service providers are self-interested and thus would be willing to compete for more government contracts and funding (Flynn and Williams 1997; Lewis and Glennerster 1996; Pollitt 1990; Smith and Lipsky 1993).

The ability of a market among NGOs to "work" is based on another crucial assumption: the ability of public managers to assess provider performance. But in the absence of clear-cut performance measures, public managers often resort to two strategies: (1) they rely on the reputation of the providers; and (2) they try to tie reimbursement and funding to the attainment of certain specified performance measures. Regarding the former, the reliance on reputation frequently means that public managers choose NGOs with whom they have a good working relationship. The second point reflects the greater formalization of the government–NGO relationship and the pressure on public managers to demonstrate proper accountability for public funds, despite the difficulty of achieving agreement on performance measures.

25.3.1.1 *The Perils of Competitive Tendering*
The difficulties of performance evaluation—rooted in part in the principal–agent problem—are a major reason for the potential of counter-productive effects from competitive tendering. Relational contracting based on trust reflects the information problems involved in contracting for difficult-to-evaluate services. The hallmarks of competitive tendering are: formal requests for proposals; short-term contracts; and choice among providers for contracts. But competitive tendering is directly contrary to the precepts of relational contracting. Further, competitive

tendering can actually fuel dysfunctional behavior by government and NGOs that may be directly contrary to the goals of effective performance. NGOs may rationally react to competitive tendering with actions that are unexpected and unwanted from an overall public management perspective but entirely expected given the incentives facing NGOs.

For instance, Cooley and Ron (2002) documented how competitive bidding for humanitarian assistance contracts in Goma, a town in the Democratic Republic of Congo created powerful disincentives for a well-known and respected aid agency, Refugee Help, to protest the diversion of aid to militants and war criminals. The presence of multiple aid agencies competing for short-term contracts produced an environment where aid agencies including Refugee Help were very cautious about public statements and actions for fear of disrupting their existing contracts or potential contracts.

Short-term contracts and competitive tendering can also be inadvisable because they tend to encourage an under-investment in organizational capacity that can be directly counter to effective service. Competitive tendering coupled with short term contracts tends to squeeze cross-subsidies from contracts and making it difficult for many nonprofits, especially smaller nonprofits to generate surpluses and sufficiently fund their capacity needs such as information and monitoring systems. (Milward and Provan (1995) concluded that effectiveness in local community mental health service networks was directly related to the stability of the network.)

25.3.1.2 *Comparing Sectors*

Evaluating the relative performance of NGOs, for-profit and public organizations can be a methodologically difficult task because many NGOs do not serve the same type of clients as comparable for-profit or public organizations. Further, many service organizations are essentially hybrid organizations. A nonprofit healthcare organization may have a for-profit subsidiary or a NGO may receive all of its revenue from government. Nonetheless, research on differences across sectors points to the following issues for public managers to consider. First, Donahue (1989) concluded that the cost savings from contracting out job training services to NGOs was largely due to lower labor costs (because of low unionization), rather than the inherent efficiency of contracting agencies. Second, many funders are increasingly concerned that the proliferation of NGOs has led to higher costs than would otherwise be the case due to the overlap in the service responsibilities. (Many funders in the US are even taking the lead in pushing NGOs to merge and consolidate their operations.)

But, efficiency is not the only relevant goal of public policy. One could legitimately argue that many services provided by NGOs are worthwhile and needed even if they cost more than comparable public and for-profit programs. For instance, community residential programs for the developmentally disabled are more expensive than the large institutional facilities that warehoused the developmentally disabled for decades. But appropriate community living is a vast improvement in the quality of life and opportunities of the disabled.

Indeed, NGOs are also regarded by many policymakers as offering superior program quality. Weisbrod (1989) concluded that the best nursing homes tended to be nonprofit and the worst nursing homes were for-profit, with a large middle with many mediocre nonprofit and for-profit homes. But Schlesinger (1998) found that differences among nonprofit and for-profit healthcare organizations diminished greatly as the competitiveness of the local market increased; competition precipitated organizational isomorphism due to the need to compete for clients and patients.

Program quality also raises the issue of trust and accountability. The relative trustworthiness of NGOs has emerged as an important public policy concern as the scale of funding has grown and competition between for-profit agencies and NGOs has intensified. To this point, Gray (1991) argues that nonprofit healthcare organizations are inherently more trustworthy than for-profit hospitals and thus have a greater incentive to invest in the development and maintenance of quality of care. Again, experience suggests this basic point to be valid except in situations of multiple principals and multiple agents—i.e., many potential donors and many potential agencies to receive the funds. In these instances, NGOs may have an incentive to be less than completely forthright or "trustworthy."

One other valued trait of NGOs which is often mentioned in public discourse is the belief in the inherent flexibility and innovativeness of NGOs. The argument is typically framed as a contrast between large public agencies with rigid rules and regulations, and nimble, smaller NGOs whose capacity for innovation is similar to a for-profit start-up. But an examination of the role of NGOs in policy and program innovation reveals a more complicated picture. Many NGOs face significant obstacles to developing and sustaining program innovation. Unlike for-profit organizations, NGOs cannot tap investors for financing; as a result, they face limitations on their ability to fund innovative projects. Further, nonprofits are often very risk averse, especially when faced with multiple potential donors and many potential competitors (Kramer 1983). As a result, government funding is actually very important to the adoption and sustainability of innovative program models among nonprofit service agencies (Kramer 1983; Osborne 1998).

However, a paradox exists here as well. While government can promote innovation within NGOs, over time, government regulations and policies tend to reduce the heterogeneity of NGOs within a given field. So for example, residential child welfare programs for foster children will tend to become more homogeneous even among programs that were originally quite innovative and distinctive (see Lynn 2002; Smith and Lipsky 1993).

25.3.2 Governance

NGOs are at the center of the debate on democracy and social capital building (Putnam 1993, 2000). Through their ability to bring citizens together for a common purpose, many scholars and policymakers view NGOs as central to creating a more vibrant civil society, especially among newly democratizing countries such as in eastern and central Europe. But the capacity of NGOs to effectively build social capital hinges in part on their governance and the links between their boards of directors and executives and their communities. For many NGOs, these links are problematic, creating broader management and policy concerns for both public managers and nonprofit staff.

Unlike for-profit organizations, NGOs have no shareholders or members *per se*. Instead, most NGOs, especially those providing services to the public, have self-elected, volunteer boards of directors with no members whatsoever. This governance structure creates ambiguity and a lack of clarity regarding who exactly are the owners of nonprofit organizations (Oster 1995). Some people might argue that NGOs by virtue of their tax exemptions are actually owned by society as a whole. Others suggest that NGOs are really owned by the board which is legally liable for the financial and programmatic performance of the organization. In instances of extensive government funding of NGOs, many policymakers and public managers regard NGOs as an extension of government since NGOs by accepting government funds are relinquishing at least some of their private autonomy. And recently, a lot of attention has focused on the users of NGOs services and the need for their participation in organizational governance in a meaningful way.

In short, NGOs have many potential stakeholders and the proper mix of stakeholders in governance role is matter of legitimate debate, setting up inherent conflicts on accountability and management. How much control should government have? How do NGOs preserve their autonomy? What is the role of users and the local community? These questions and others provoke sometimes passionate, active efforts by stakeholders to press their position.

Resolving these questions is further complicated by the inherent problems of boards of directors as vehicles of governance. Board members are volunteers and legally prohibited from sharing in the profits of the organization (due to the non-distribution constraint). Thus, their ownership stake in the organization is quite attenuated (Steinberg 1987; Stone 1987; Ben-Ner and Van Hoomissen 1991). Thus, NGOs board members may not aggressively monitor the performance of NGOs and/or defer to the executive director and his or her staff on key organizational decisions.

Contracting with government creates further confusion and role conflict for the board. If government is purchasing the services of a NGO, then the implication is that government as the purchaser is in a position to control the services of the NGO. Typically, contracts are negotiated by public managers and NGO staff, effectively cutting out the board from a critical component of the NGO's operation. Government contracting rules can be very complicated so the process of contracting can have the effect of distancing the board from the agency's operations. These pressures can push board members into a focus on fundraising rather than program (Harris 2001).

Thus, in an era of expanded contracting and public responsibilities, NGOs' boards are challenged to find a guiding vision that continues to engage board members. NGOs need to create new strategies for them to connect to their communities. For example, many grassroots NGOs have been devising new models to engage community members in the ongoing activities of the organization, including the governance (Crosby 2003; Ryan, Chait, and Taylor 2003).

25.3.3 Sustainability and Infrastructure Support

Perhaps no subject is more widely discussed among public managers, private funders, and nonprofit staff than sustainability and infrastructure concerns. Funders and NGOs across the world are now collectively worrying and puzzling on how to nurture and support the hundreds of thousands of NGOs upon whom the public sector depends for vital and important public services. A disproportionate amount of the growth in NGOs around the world has been in smaller, community-based organizations. Typically, these organizations are undercapitalized and may at least initially lack sophisticated boards and professional staff with extensive management experience. Yet, these organizations are directly delivering very complicated and difficult services with high expectations on performance.

The capacity problems of NGOs have an enormous impact on their role in society and public service delivery. Undercapitalization and board difficulties tend to make NGOs much more susceptible to donor pressure, especially from government or large private funders. Undercapitalized NGOs are likely to operate on the edge of financial survival, creating enduring challenges in attracting and keeping qualified staff. Financially strapped NGOs are at risk for mission drift and assuming service responsibilities that may not be in the best long-term interests of the agency and its users.

Yet, technical assistance to enhance NGO capacity requires an ongoing and long-term commitment from funders. Too often, technical assistance is in the form of short-term consulting advice that does not really help NGOs address their long-term capacity problems. The widespread attention accorded to venture philanthropy (Letts, Ryan, and Grossman 1999) and restructuring the relationship of funders to their grantees, especially community organizations is a recognition that technical assistance to NGOs needs to be reinvented if NGOs are to be able to provide effective, quality services. Many funders are now experimenting with new models of technical assistance and support, especially through third-party intermediary organizations. These new organizations have the potential to help build the long-term capacity of NGOs to provide effective, quality programs.

A more general but oft-overlooked point related to sustainability and capacity building is that effective and sustainable NGOs tend to have positive and supportive relationships with government, especially local government. Milward and Provan (1995) concluded that effective community mental health networks had supportive and stable relationships with government. Tendler (1997) in her study of NGOs in Brazil found a direct relationship to the quality of federal and local government support and the effectiveness and sustainability of local NGOs. Shortell et al. (2002) found that effectiveness of community based health partnerships depended upon a stable and supportive relationship with local government. In short, NGO performance should not be conceptualized as an isolated organizational phenomenon but instead it depends very directly on the quality of government support and leadership.

25.3.4 Collaboration and Cooperation

The appeal of NGOs stems in part from their ability to be flexible, innovative, and responsive to the needs of a community or client group. This appeal has helped promote the dramatic increase in NGOs throughout the world. But one consequence has been a fragmentation of service, creating high transaction costs for many users of NGOs programs. Also, fragmentation can lead over time to overlapping missions as NGOs compete for new funds and programs.

For these reasons, many funders are challenging NGOs to become more collaborative and demonstrate active efforts to cooperate with other NGOs, government, and the private for-profit sector. But important obstacles to collaboration and cooperation exist. First, undercapitalization creates uncertainty among NGOs, complicating the task of cooperation since many NGOs may fear that cooperation may reduce their future revenue opportunities. Second, competitive tendering with multiple bidders creates concern that cooperation could undermine the long-term future of the organization. Third, the ambiguity of ownership creates complications for collaboration or even mergers of separate organizations because many potential stakeholders can lay claim to the mantle of representing the NGO's interest. (The absence of clear-cut performance metrics in NGOs exacerbates this situation since many potential measures can be used to evaluate organizational performance, especially if an NGO is addressing a long-term and/or complex social problem.) Fourth, collaboration and cooperation among different organizations can entail substantial transaction costs in terms of staff time and resources. Public and private donors rarely provide adequate compensation for these costs. Consequently, serious financial disincentives for collaboration may exist that are very difficult for NGOs to resolve unless they are very large and can cross-subsidize the costs of collaboration.

To overcome these obstacles to cooperation, funders should provide incentives for collaboration and financial support. In the case of mergers, funders will most likely need to take on a sustained role in facilitating the merger. And public managers may need to rethink their approach to the contracting process. Instead of short-term contracts and outcome measures, public managers may want to offer longer contracts (with the appropriate level of accountability) as well as help with their capital situation. These initiatives would enhance the overall feelings of security by NGOs and create an environment that is more likely to promote collaboration.

25.4 NGOs, Citizenship and Democracy

The rise of NGOs as an instrument of public policy has put public managers and NGOs squarely in the middle of contemporary debates on citizenship and democracy. There are two basic streams of thought in this debate: (1) the de Tocquevillian perspective on the value of NGOs as vehicles for citizen participation and representation; and (2) the perspective of T. H. Marshall and others on role of the state and NGOs in fostering citizenship rights. In both cases, the debate about the role of NGOs is inextricably linked with the ongoing restructuring of the state around the world. This section explores these two different streams of thought with particular emphasis on the public management and policy implications.

Alexis de Tocqueville (1956) argued that voluntary associations were essential to democracy because they provided an opportunity for people to come together to express their views. This de Tocquevillian perspective was articulated more recently by Berger and Neuhaus (1977) who argued that voluntary associations (including the church) are important "mediating institutions" between the state and the individual; as such, they are critical to protecting individual freedom since they serve as a bulwark against the state. This perspective suggests that local democracy can be fostered by supporting local community based NGOs —a position represented in many policy initiatives such as the Bush administration's push for greater use of faith-based organizations and the political decentralization of countries such as Australia and New Zealand.

The recent work of Robert Putnam on social capital also calls attention to community-based NGOs. Putnam (1993) concluded that voluntary associations such as sports clubs and PTA chapters build social ties in the local community, creating "social capital" that helps facilitate collective action, improve the effectiveness of government, and spur economic and community development. Given Putnam's work, NGOs have an obvious attractiveness as vehicles for rebuilding communities and promoting greater community solidarity and participation. Indeed, many recent programmatic initiatives in the US and elsewhere are designed to promote social capital building by creating incentives for the establishment and strengthening of social networks. For instance, the Blair administration in the UK has a major community revitalization program in disadvantaged areas around the country that requires the partnership of many different public agencies, NGOs, and private businesses. In the US, many different public agencies and private funders have sponsored Comprehensive Community Initiatives (CCIs) that seek to address difficult social problems such as drug abuse, crime and economic revitalization through multi-party collaborations, typically with a NGO in a lead role (Connell et al. 1995).

The ability of NGOs to empower local citizens, promote user involvement, and build social capital varies enormously. Nonetheless, several important trends and challenges are apparent. First, NGOs serve a very valuable role as vehicles for social movements to pressure government, private organizations and individual citizens to change their policies and viewpoints. Yet, social movement NGOs can encounter organizational challenges over time, partly because of the strong ideological commitment of the staff and volunteers in these organizations. Many social movement NGOs depend upon private grants and donations in their early years. But as the initial grants begin to decline, government grants and contracts are often an attractive option for funding. Typically, government contracts require these NGOs to reorient themselves from advocacy to service delivery. This shift presents very complicated management challenges including balancing professionalization with the desire to keep the strong ideological orientation of the organization. The desire to successfully balance these sometimes competing dynamics is producing very novel structural innovations in NGOs (Saidel and Fletcher 2003).

Second, the ability of NGOs to effectively promote empowerment and participation is affected by organizational characteristics of NGOs. Many community organizations emerge through the dedication and passion of a group of people committed to solving a social problem. But these individuals may not have extensive connections to their communities. And, the challenges of starting and sustaining new community organizations mean that these NGOs may have great difficulty attracting and keeping staff and volunteers and establishing ongoing community connections. (In this sense, NGOs—which provide a service or advocate for a particular cause—are substantively different than voluntary associations such as sports clubs or choral societies that feature prominently in Putnam's research.)

Third, NGOs may be reluctant to actively participate in the political process (including the mobilization of community members) due to concerns about the reaction of government. This concern most directly affects NGOs which receive direct government funds. But governments also regulate the tax-exempt privileges of NGOs so the staff and volunteers of NGOs may be worried that political advocacy may somehow jeopardize their tax exempt status. This is a special concern in newly democratizing countries where NGOs are less established and the government imposes often onerous regulations upon them. But it is a concern in the US and other countries where overly aggressive political action has been known to invite an audit or intensive scrutiny of an NGO's activities (Berry 2003).

Given the great differences among NGOs and the dynamism of the government–NGO relationship, it is not possible to really "solve" these political challenges. To an extent, education of government and NGO staff will help since many NGO staff and volunteers are not well versed in the laws and regulations governing political activities. Model agreements between government and NGOs such as "The Compact" in the UK may assuage concerns on both sides and promote greater cooperation (Plowden 2003). Government can provide incentives for NGOs to reach out to their communities and build new social networks. Indeed, government should approach its involvement with NGOs as a political development issue that requires a long-term commitment to building the civic infrastructure of a local community.

The political role of NGOs has another citizenship dimension. T. H. Marshall (1964), the British sociologist, argued over fifty years ago that full citizenship hinged on the availability of political, civil, and social rights. Political rights are voting and free and unfettered elections. Civil rights include freedom of speech and association. And social rights are the availability of social benefits such as public education, adequate income maintenance, and social services such as childcare and job training. To Marshall and other scholars of his generation, the public sector was the primary guarantor of citizenship rights; they tended to look askance upon NGOs and the voluntary sector. To them, voluntary organizations did not have the resources or overall capacity to ensure the equitable and comprehensive provision of social rights. NGOs as providers of public services represent an implicit rejection of this Marshallian perspective. NGOs offer the possibility of greater flexibility and responsiveness and allow public managers to shift the risk of service delivery from to the NGO sector.

This shift away from the Marshallian position means that many citizenship rights may become more contingent. First, NGOs—due to their focus on responsiveness—do not have the same commitment to equity as government. Second, the use of NGOs, especially through contracts, introduces an unexpected and sometimes complex entity into public service provision, possibly undermining service access and hence social rights and citizenship. With NGOs, accountability and governance is ambiguous. Consequently, a dissatisfied service user may not know who is in charge. And, by introducing another layer into public service delivery, contracting with NGOs may discourage people from using services or voicing complaints about the lack of quality services (Smith 1993; Smith and Ingram 2002). Third, the use of NGOs raises the question about the discretion of front-line workers and the principal–agent problem inherent in the government–NGO relationship. Indeed, the concern that contracting with NGOs may reduce access for at least some people can lead government to demand ever higher levels of accountability on the part of NGOs.

As with many management and policy issues, a trade-off exists: government can promote user and citizen participation through NGOs (albeit imperfectly) but government is then at risk that NGO discretion may undermine the equitable provision of important public services. Given the trends around the world in public service delivery, this fear has some important foundation.

25.5 LOOKING TO THE FUTURE

The role of NGOs in public policy and public service delivery is likely to remain one of the most central issues in public management in the coming years. Almost every major public policy issue around the world—e.g., humanitarian assistance and relief, immigrant and refugee assistance, job training, community regeneration, and childcare—involve NGOs. The capacity of NGOs to meet public expectations will help define whether or not many governments succeed in satisfactorily addressing urgent public problems.

Moreover, the interaction of NGOs with the citizenry will, in a very important and meaningful way, define their citizenship rights. NGOs control access to many critical services. But this effect on citizenship goes well beyond the direct access to services. Marshall (1964) envisioned the political and civil rights would precede the granting of social rights. But throughout the world today, many groups are pushing for access to social rights as a way of gaining political and civil rights and hence full citizenship. In continental Europe, many immigrant groups have been eligible for social benefits for years but have been unable to obtain political citizenship. Now, they are using the access to social benefits as a partial justification for their argument for broader citizenship rights. In the US, gay couples have successfully won the right to have foster children in many states; the resulting legitimacy has been leveraged for other political battles for gay rights. And, the political resistance to the Bush administration's Faith-Based Initiative is premised in part on the concern that advances in protecting workers and clients from discrimination will be eroded, thus setting a very dangerous precedent.

The political debate on NGOs reflects, to an extent, the unrealistic expectations of both the Left and the Right on the potential of NGOs. The Left hopes NGOs will push the state to change and help previously excluded groups achieve full citizenship rights through political empowerment and access to social benefits. But this perspective neglects the resource problems of NGOs as well as their inherent governance challenges. The Right hopes that NGOs will shrink the role of the state in society and shift responsibility for solving social problems to the community and the individual. Yet, this view fails to take into consideration the capacity problems of NGOs and their dependence on the public sector to provide broadly available services.

In general, NGOs are likely to be more effective in providing services and representing their community when public and private funders invest in these organizations as a long-term strategy and conceptualize their relationship with NGOs as a social contract whereupon government and nonprofits recognize that each side needs help and support from the other. Through this approach, issues of disagreement can be discussed and possibly resolved to mutual satisfaction. Absent this approach, disappointment with NGO performance is likely to rise, overshadowing the many positive contributions of NGOs to their community and society at large. Over time, this disappointment could undermine the prevailing legitimacy of NGOs as providers of public services. This outcome would be particularly unfortunate at time when NGOs are being called upon to build and rebuild civil society throughout the world.

REFERENCES

ALBER, J. (1995), "A Framework for the Comparative Study of Social Services," *Journal of European Social Policy* 5(2): 131–49.

ARCHAMBAULT, E. (2001), "Historical Roots of the Nonprofit Sector in France," *Nonprofit and Voluntary Sector Quarterly* 30(2): 204–20.

BEHN, R. D. (2001), *Rethinking Democratic Accountability*, Washington, DC: Brookings.

BEN-NER, A., and VAN HOOMISSEN, T. (1991), "Nonprofit Organizations in a Mixed Economy: A Demand And Supply Analysis," *Annals of Public and Cooperative Economics* 62(4): 519–50.

BERGER, P., and NEUHAUS, R. J. (1977), *To Empower People*, Washington, DC: American Enterprise Institute.

BERRY, J. M. (2003), *A Voice for Nonprofits*, Washington, DC: Brookings.

BESHAROV, D. J., and SAMARI, N. (2000), "Child Care Vouchers and Cash Payments," in C. E. Steuerle et al. (eds.), *Vouchers and the Provision of Public Services*, Washington, DC: Brookings, 195–223.

BODE, I. (2003), "Flexible Response in Changing Environments: The German Third Sector Model in Transition," *Nonprofit and Voluntary Sector Quarterly* 32(2): 190–210.

BROWN, L., and TROUTT, E. (2004), "Funding Relations Between Nonprofits and Government," *Nonprofit and Voluntary Sector Quarterly* 33(1): 5–27.

BROWN, L. D. (1983), *New Policies, New Politics*, Washington, DC: Brookings.

BURGER, A., and DEKKER, P. (2001), *The Nonprofit Sector in the Netherlands*, The Hague: Social and Cultural Planning Bureau.

—— and VELDEER, V. (2001), "The Growth of the Nonprofit Sector in the Netherlands," *Nonprofit and Voluntary Sector Quarterly* 30(2): 221–46.

CONNELL, J. P. et al. (1995), *New Approaches to Evaluating Community Initiatives*, Washington, DC: Aspen Institute.

CONSIDINE, M. (2000), "Contract Regimes and Reflexive Governance: Comparing Employment Service Reforms in the United Kingdom, the Netherlands, New Zealand and Australia," *Public Administration* 78(3): 613–38.

COOLEY, A., and JAMES, R. (2002), "The NGO Scramble: Organizational Insecurity and the Political Economy of Transnational Action," *International Security* 27(1): 5–39.

CROSBY, A. (2003), "Community Purpose Means Community Involvement," *The Nonprofit Quarterly* 10(3): 24–8.

DEAKIN, S., and MICHIE, J. (eds.) (1997), *Contracts, Co-operation, and Competition*. New York: Oxford University Press.

DeHOOG, R. H., and SALAMON, L. M. (2002), "Purchase of Service Contracting," in L. M. Salamon (ed.), *The Tools of Government*, New York: Oxford University Press, 319–39.

DE TOCQUEVILLE, A. (1956), *Democracy in America*, New York: Plume

DONAHUE, J. D. (1989), *The Privatization Decision*, New York: Basic Books.

EDWARDS, M., and FOWLER, A. (2002), *The Earthscan Reader on NGO Management*, London: Earthscan.

ESPING-ANDERSON, G. (1990), *The Three Worlds of Welfare Capitalism*, Princeton, NJ: Princeton University Press.

EVANS, P. B. (1996), "Government Action, Social Capital and Development: Reviewing the Evidence of Synergy," *World Development*, 24(6): 1119–32.

FLYNN, R., and WILLIAMS, G. (eds.) (1997), *Contracting for Health: Quasi-Markets and the National Health Service*, New York: Oxford University Press.

FOWLER, A. (1997), *Striking a Balance*, London: Earthscan.

—— (2000), *The Virtuous Spiral*, London: Earthscan.

GRANOVETTER, M. (1985), "Economic Action and Social Structure: The Problem of Embeddedness," *American Journal of Sociology* 913: 481–510.

GRAY, B. (1991), *The Profit Motive and Patient Care*, Cambridge, MA: Harvard University Press.

GRONBJERG, K. (1993), *Understanding Nonprofit Funding*, San Francisco: Jossey-Bass.

GUTCH, R. (1992: *Contracting Lessons from the US*, London: National Council of Voluntary Organisations.

HALL, P. D. (1987), "A Historical Overview of the Private Nonprofit Sector," in W W. POWELL (ed.), *The Nonprofit Sector: A Research Handbook*, New Haven: Yale University Press, 3–26.

HANSMANN, H. (1980), "A Role of Nonprofit Enterprise," *Yale Law Journal* 89: 835–901.

HARRIS, M. (2001), "Boards: Just Subsidiaries of the State?" in Harris and Rochester 2001: 171–84.

—— and ROCHESTER, C. (eds.) (2001), *Voluntary Organisations and Social Policy in Britain*, London: Palgrave.

HARTOGS, N., and WEBER, J. (1978), *The Impact of Government Funding on the Management of Voluntary Agencies*, New York: United Way.

HOOD, C. (1991), "A Public Management for All Seasons?", *Public Administration* 69: 3–19.

HULME, D., and EDWARDS, M. (1997), *NGOs, States, and Donors: Too Close For Comfort?* New York: St. Martin's Press.

JAMES, E. (1987), "The Nonprofit Sector in Comparative Perspective," in W. W. Powell (ed.), *The Nonprofit Sector: A Research Handbook*, New Haven: Yale University Press, 397–415.

KECK, M., and SIKKINK, K. (1998), *Activists Without Borders*, Ithaca, NY: Cornell University Press.

KETTL, D. (1998), "The Global Revolution in Public Management: Driving Themes, Missing Links," *Journal of Policy Analysis and Management* 16(3): 446–62.

KIRKPATRICK, I., KITCHENER, M., and WHIPP, R. (2001), "'Out of Sight, Out of Mind': Assessing the Impact of Markets for Children's Residential Care," *Public Administration* 79(1): 49–71.

KRAMER, R. (1983), *Voluntary Agencies and the Welfare State*, Berkeley: University of California Press.

LETTS, C., RYAN, W., and GROSSMAN, A. (1999), *High Performing Nonprofit Organizations.* San Francisco: Jossey Bass.

LEWIS, D., and WALLACE, T. (eds.) (2000), *New Roles and Relevance: Development NGOs and the Challenge of Change*, Bloomfield, CT: Kumarian Press.

LEWIS, J., and GLENNERSTER, H. (1996), *Implementing the New Community Care*, Buckingham: Open University Press.

LINDENBERG, M., and BRYANT, C. (2001), *Going Global: Transforming Relief and Development NGOs*, Hartford, CT: Kumarian Press.

LUNDSTROM, T., and SVEDBERG, L. (2003), "The Voluntary Sector in a Social Democratic State—The Case of Sweden," *Journal of Social Policy*, 32(2): 1–22.

LYNN, L. E., JR. (2002), "Social Services and the State: The Public Appropriation of Private Charity," *Social Service Review* 76(1): 58–82.

MARSHALL, T. H. (1964), "Citizenship and Social Class," in *Class, Citizenship and Social Development: Essays*, New York: Doubleday, 71–134.

MILWARD, B., and PROVAN, K. (1995), "A Preliminary Theory of Interorganizational Network Effectiveness: A Comparative Study of Four Community Mental Health Systems," *Administrative Science Quarterly* 40: 1–33.

MOORE, B. (1966), *Social Origins of Dictatorship and Democracy: Lord and Peasant in the Making of the Modern World*, Boston: Beacon Press.

MORGAN, K. J. (2002), "Forging the Frontiers Between State, Church and Family: Religious Cleavages and the Origins of Early Childhood Education and Care Policies in France, Sweden and Germany," *Politics and Society* 30(1): 113–48.

OSBORNE, S. (1998), *Voluntary Organisations and Innovation in Public Services*, London: Routledge.

OSBORNE, D., and GAEBLER, T. (1993), *Reinventing Government*, New York: Plume.

OSTER, S. (1995), *Strategic Management in Nonprofit Organizations*, New York: Oxford University Press.

PLOWDEN, W. (2003), "The Compact: Attempts to Regulate Relationships Between Government and the Voluntary Sector in England," *Nonprofit and Voluntary Sector Quarterly* 32(3): 415–31.

POLLITT, C. (1990), *Managerialism and the Public Service: The Anglo-American Experience*, Oxford: Basil Blackwell.

PRATT, J., and ZECKHAUSER, R. (eds.) (1985), *Principals and Agents: The Structure of Business*, Boston: Harvard Business School Press.

PRIEMUS, H. (2000), "Housing Vouchers: A Contribution from Abroad," in C. E. STEUERLE et al. (eds.), *Vouchers and the Provision of Public Services*, Washington, DC: Brookings, 176–94.

PUTNAM, R. D. (1993), *Making Democracy Work*, Princeton, NJ: Princeton University Press.

—— (2000), *Bowling Alone: The Collapse and Revival of American Community*, New York: Simon and Schuster.

RING, P. S., and VAN DE VEN, A. H. (1992), "Structuring Cooperative Relationships Between Organizations," *Strategic Management Journal* 13(7): 483–98.

RYAN, W. P., CHAIT, R., and TAYLOR, B. E. (2003), "Problem Boards or Board Problem?", *The Nonprofit Quarterly* 10(2): 49–53.

SAIDEL, J., and FLETCHER, K. (2003), "Governance Futures Case Studies," *The Nonprofit Quarterly* 10(3): 34–54.

SALAMON, L. M. (1987), "Partners in Public Service: The Scope and Theory of Government–Nonprofit Relations," in W. W. Powell (ed.), *The Nonprofit Sector: A Research Handbook*. New Haven: Yale University Press, 99–117.

—— (ed.) (2002), *The Tools of Government*, New York: Oxford University Press.

—— and Helmut K. Anheier. (1998), "Social Origins of Civil Society: Explaining the Nonprofit Sector Cross-Nationally," *Voluntas* 9(3): 213–48.

SCHLESINGER, M. (1998), "Mismeasuring the Consequences of Ownership: External Influences and the Comparative Performance of Public, For-Profit, and Private Non-profit Organizations," in W. W. POWELL and E. S. Clemens (ed.), *Public Action and Private Good*, New Haven: Yale University Press, 85–113.

SHORTELL, S. M. et al. (2002), "Evaluating Partnerships for Community Health Improvement: Tracking the Footprints," *Journal of Health Politics, Policy and Law* 27(1): 49–91.

SIMMONS, P. J. (1997), "Learning to Live with NGOs," *Foreign Policy* (Fall): 82–96.

SIMONEN, L., and KOVALAINEN, A. (1998), "Paradoxes of Social Care Restructuring: The Finnish Case," in J. Lewis (ed.), *Gender, Social Care and Welfare State Restructuring in Europe*, Aldershot: Ashgate, 229–56.

SMITH, S. R. (1993), "The New Politics of Contracting: Citizenship and the Nonprofit Role," in H. Ingram and S. R. Smith (eds.), *Public Policy for Democracy*, Washington, DC: Brookings, 163–97.

—— (2002), "Social Services," in L. M. Salamon (ed.), *The State of Nonprofit America*, Washington, DC: Brookings, 149–86.

—— and INGRAM, H. (2002), "Implications of Choice of Policy Tools for Democracy, Civic Capital and Citizenship," in Salamon 2002: 565–84.

—— and LIPSKY, M. (1993), *Nonprofits for Hire: The Welfare State in the Age of Contracting*, Cambridge, MA: Harvard University Press.

—— and FREINKEL, S. (1988), *Adjusting the Balance: Federal Policy and Victim Services*, Westport, CT: Greenwood Press.

—— and SMYTH, J. (1996), "Contracting for Services in a Decentralized System," *Journal of Public Administration Research and Theory* 6(2): 277–296.

STEINBERG, R. (1987), "Nonprofit Organizations and the Market," in W. W. POWELL (ed.), *The Nonprofit Sector: A Research Handbook*, 118–39.

STONE, M. M. (1987), "Nonprofit Boards of Directors: Beyond the Governance Function," in W. W. Powell (ed.), *The Nonprofit Sector: A Research Handbook*, 141–53.

TENDLER, J. (1997), *Good Government in the Tropics*, Baltimore: Johns Hopkins University Press.

WEISBROD, B. A. (1989), *The Nonprofit Economy*, Cambridge, MA: Harvard University Press.

WILSON, J. Q. (1967), "The Bureaucracy Problem," *The Public Interest* 6: 3–9.

—— (1973: *Political Organizations*, New York: Basic Books.

WOOLCOCK, M., and NARAYAN, D. (2000), "Social Capital: Implications for Development Theory, Research and Policy," *The World Bank Research Observer* 15(2): 225–49.

CHAPTER 26

EVALUATION AND PUBLIC MANAGEMENT

PETER DAHLER-LARSEN

26.1 INTRODUCTION

WE LIVE in a time when most social arrangements, and definitely those managed by the public sector, can be questioned. Evaluation is a set of approaches, models, and methods, which help organize this sort of questioning. It is "assisted sense-making" (Mark, Henry, and Julnes 2000), which, by way of "artificially" constructed methods and procedures, helps construct data which indicate whether particular activities are good or good enough, whatever that means in particular contexts. Whether it should mean, as it often but far from always does, that the particular activities lead to certain expected outcomes, specified and measured in particular ways, is of course in itself often a point of contention.

During the years, all western and many other countries have experienced a virtual wave of evaluation activities. Evaluation is now a distinct field with its own professional societies, journals, conferences, training courses, consulting companies, and institutions.

To a large extent, the public sector itself attempts to organize evaluation. This is true whether relatively independent evaluation institutions are created, or particular branches of the public sector establish their own internal evaluation offices, or external consulting services are bought. Thus, the public sector seems to both demand the potentially critical feedback from evaluation, and also seeks to organize it and not rarely, to influence or control its form, shape, timing, and utilization.

Some regimes of governance and some ideologies of public management do so more explicitly, directly and strictly than others. New Public Management (NPM), for instance, advocates a strong focus on "outcomes" of public policies and defines an important role for evaluation with respect to monitoring "outcomes" as an integrated part of this managerial regime.

As we shall see, however, evaluation as such cannot be reduced to this one role and function. The term "evaluation" encompasses a rich and dynamic set of approaches some of which are interesting counterpoints to the idea of a "happy marriage" between evaluation and new public management.

The dual relation between evaluation and public management is reflected both in the content and in the design of this chapter. I will move between the two, showing where they are in alignment, and where they are not.

In the first part of the chapter, I will describe the evaluation wave, which has hit most western countries during the last decade or two. I shall show that different explanations of the current interest in evaluation are possible, and that each type of explanation leads to different views on evaluation and different expectations about its promises and pitfalls.

Next, I will present different approaches to evaluation. With the risk of unduly reducing the complexity of the field, I will argue that goal-oriented evaluation, theory-based evaluation, and responsive/participatory approaches to evaluation are useful labels to identify significant and often competing schools of thought in evaluation. Within each set of approaches, I will look at main principles, legitimacy, practical focus, relevance for public management, and main critical points.

26.2 THE "EVALUATION WAVE"

Conceptually evaluation is a systematic or careful assessment of the merit, worth, and value of administration, output, and outcome of government interventions, which is intended to play a role in future, practical action situations (Vedung 1997: 3).

Evaluation is part and parcel of a larger cultural wave consisting also of audit, inspection, and quality assurance, which together constitute "a huge and unavoidable social experiment which is conspicuously cross-sectional and transnational" (Power 1997: xv).

A total overview of all manifestations of evaluation on all levels of analysis is thus not within reach. The following is a brief collection of observations of particular aspects of the evaluation wave.

In a survey of twenty-one countries most of them were found to have "a mature evaluation culture as an integrated element in its political and administrative system" (Furubo and Sandahl 2001: 6).

Evaluation nourishes an industry of conferences, courses, and consultants. In a sample of consultants, those reporting on growing markets outnumbered those reporting on declining markets by twelve to one (Leeuw, Toulemonde, and Brouwers 1999). The number of journals and books in the field also testify to the growing interest in evaluation.

At closer inspection, evaluation is not characterized by undifferentiated intensity and growth. While programs and institutions in education, social services, and foreign aid are frequent objects of evaluation, a study found that some policy areas and institutions such as defense, law, churches (Hansen 2003), infrastructure, and again (surprise!), defense (Derlien and Rist 2001: 452) are still quite resistant to evaluation.

Differences between countries exist. Among the later adopters of evaluation, a sizeable group of countries have developed their evaluation culture during the 1990s (Furubo and Sandahl 2001: 11). In some of these countries evidence exists of an intense evaluation activity measured in terms of the number of evaluation reports (Hansen 2003). In early-adopting countries some report about a decline in funding and manpower for program evaluation on the federal level in, e.g., the US (Shadish, Cook, and Leviton, 1991: 27) and Canada (Derlien and Rist 2001: 451). Even so, the Canadian Evaluation Society, for example, reports on a continued growth in members from 1071 to 1922 over the last ten years.[1]

This may be because a stagnation in evaluation on the national level in countries which adopted evaluation early is more than compensated for by increased evaluation in other levels of government, in NGOs, in substantive disciplines, and in consulting companies (Derlien and Rist 2001: 454; Shadish, Cook, and Leviton, 1991: 27).

Perhaps the most fascinating aspect of the evaluation wave is its remarkable ability to trancend borders and cross contexts. It is now international and global (Chelimsky 1997). According to an estimate based on an Internet search, the number of evaluation societies around the globe has increased ten times since 1984, and doubled since 1999.[2]

Along with these quantitative indicators, a qualitative solidification characterizes the evaluation wave.

Evaluation becomes mandated by management recipes, monitoring systems, and legislation. Evaluation embodies itself structurally in internal evaluation units, external inspectorates and evaluation centers. The trend today is to "build evaluation capacity" and to "mainstream" evaluation, as suggested by the themes of some of the more recent conferences of the American Evaluation Association. Evaluation is to an increasing extent integrated with performance measurement systems and other forms of NPM-oriented monitoring (Furubo, Rist, and Sandahl 2001). Under these circumstances, the number of evaluation reports does not describe the full magnitude of the evaluation wave, because singular studies are being supplemented with and to some extent replaced by ongoing streams of evaluative knowledge (Rist and Stame, forthcoming). With institutionalization, evaluation becomes a taken-for-granted phenomenon, which needs no further justification.

This situation is a good occasion to reflect and ask the fundamental question why we have the evaluation wave.

Many, if not most of the narratives about the origins of evaluation take their starting point in a particular context of policy making in the United States in the 1960s (Pawson and Tilley 1997: 2; Shadish, Cook, and Leviton 1991: 22). Some find the decisive factors in combination of the Great Society Legislation (not an insignificant label for the ideology of the time), an optimistic belief in the value of social science for societal problem-solving (Patton 1997: 7–10) and a struggle between different branches of the governmental structure for knowledge-based arguments for policy making (Shadish, Cook, and Leviton 1991: 22).

This situation in the United States in the 1960s gave birth to evaluation as we know it as a large-scale government-funded activity (Weiss 1998: 12). It prepared the ground for important experiences, ideas, textbooks, and subsequent evaluation debates which helped constitute evaluation as a distinct field. However, evaluation inscribed itself in a long history of the application of social science to the description and remediation of social problems. It also built on methodologies of testing in education and psychology, which are accounted for as an earlier "generation" of evaluation by some observers (Guba and Lincoln 1989).

While evaluation in the US has played a decisive role for the construction of evaluation as a distinct field, and continues to be the largest and most influential evaluation community in the world, evaluation in the rest of the world cannot be reduced to an extension or repetition of the American experience. Later adopters do evaluation for different reasons (Furubo, Rist, and Sandahl 2001). While evaluation is becoming international, it is also becoming "indigenous," meaning that "evaluators in different countries around the world are developing their own infrastructures to support their endeavours as well as their own preferred theoretical and methodological approaches" (Chelimsky 1997: xi–xii).

Still, according to one simple and general view, evaluation can be largely understood as the response to a demand for increased efficiency in the public sector. Given increasing expectations to services on the one hand and demands to cut costs and taxes on the other, evaluation has grown out of a need to base practices and decision-making more clearly on evidence, and focus more on outcomes and effectiveness, as resources become scarcer.

Thus, evaluation emerges because it is needed. Although perhaps logically appealing, this functionally oriented explanation suffers from two deficiencies. First, the evaluation wave began in a period of growth (1960s) before the more recent focus on outcomes and efficiency in the public sector (1980s). Second, although advocates of functionalist explanations tend to bravely assume that a function is taken care of because it has to be, no further study required, it is not easy to demonstrate that evaluation actually does increase efficiency.

Evaluations are often not used according to official expectations, and when they are, very few lead to the termination of programs, as most lead to only minor adjustments of ongoing activities (Dahler-Larsen 2000). At the same time, evaluations are costly, but do not reveal how costly (Hansen 2003).

Other explanations of the evaluation wave do not take a starting point in costs, efficiency, and the like, but in ideology. Since neo-liberal doctrines about free choice, competition, and the market as a model for all social interaction has invaded the public sector, evaluation and its allies—quantification, performance measurement, and mistrust—have moved forward.

However, the "invasion" of "private sector ideology" into the public realm would probably not have occurred if there had not already been a weakening of some of the more traditional beliefs supporting the modern (welfare) state. Evaluation is not only resulting in but also resulting from decreasing trust between citizens and politicians, between politicians and service-providers, as well as between professionals and citizens. Although the market- and outcome-oriented ideology has helped promote evaluation, it far from fully explains how the social and political setting of the public sector has allowed this movement to occur.

Another obvious weakness of explaining the evaluation wave as an epiphenomenon of one particular ideology is that the field is in fact rich, varied, multifaceted, and full of internal debates between different value positions. Along with NPM paraphernalia, evaluation also encompasses recipes for personal and professional reflection, learning-oriented dialogue, and deliberative democracy.

Therefore, some observers take the broadest possible cultural and institutional view on the evaluation wave. Scott (1995) suggests that all institutionalization rests on regulative, cognitive, and normative pillars. So does the institutionalization of evaluation. Not only is evaluation often obligatory in governmental and organizational regimes; it is also carried and maintained by cognitive scripts, methodologies and ways of thinking about "programs," "activities," and "outcomes." Last but not least, to an increasing extent social norms and expectations take evaluation for granted, not questioning its instrumental function in each and every case, but prescribing evaluation as proper thing to do for modern organizations like ours and for professional people like us in a time like this (March and Olsen 1995).

Because of the broadness of this cultural trend, some observers attribute the evaluation wave to a general diagnosis of modern society, such as reflexive modernization (Beck 1994). In a reflexively modern society, a broad belief in progress has been replaced by doubt, value controversies, and concerns about side effects. These phenomena multiply with increased societal complexity. In addition, as tradition becomes less relevant, and as technologies advance, it becomes more obvious that most social arrangements are contingent, i.e., they can be rearranged. This adds pressure on socially coordinating agencies—they must constantly document their activities and justify their decisions.

Older forms of societal coordination, such as "plans", become obsolete. Instead, various agencies in complex governmental systems sensitize themselves to the social and functional repercussions of their own functioning through a number of feedback loops such as evaluation. In many policy areas, such as primary education, there are several agencies and evaluation centers, each trying to promote "evidence" and "transparency." The roles of "observers," "controllers," "quality developers," etc., have become segregated as various evaluative activities are anchored in different loci in a highly differentiated structuration of the public sector.

How to organize all these evaluative activities is far from evident. Since evaluative feedback loops are part of reflexive modernization too, they are difficult to manage and keep in place. It is difficult to predetermine limits for which issues they can take up. For example, an agency can order a particular piece of applied research based on a particular methodology, hoping that the results will help settle a particular issue and clarify the premises of a particular policy decision. Yet, "research" is itself a self-examining and self-critical endeavor, which applies its own questioning towards itself (Beck 1994). Alternative "experts" may therefore criticize not only the delivered piece of applied research (for its approach or quality), but also the agency for having ordered that type of research rather than another one which would have highlighted other issues, perhaps more pressing ones. Under reflexive modernization, the form and nature of evaluative information are contingent, too.

Evaluation and contingency are mutually reinforcing. Only contingent social phenomena can be evaluated (social services, but not national anthems). Once evaluation takes place, however, contingency increases, because it is difficult to predict which practices become problematized as a result of evaluation. This form of contingency is even doubled when the evaluation process itself becomes contested.

The evaluation wave is thus both a product of and a contribution to a particular societal and cultural form. This form of explanation of the evaluation wave comes with both a functional and a symbolic emphasis. Evaluation is functionally superior to, say, plans when it comes to sensitizing authorities to critique and social side effects. Evaluation is also a symbolically legitimate procedure in an era characterized by reflexivity, doubt, and lack of belief in general progress.

Notice how the symbolically oriented views on evaluation invite quite a different view on the role of evaluation in societies and organizations: Managers spend time setting up monitoring systems, negotiating the content and function of such systems, preparing themselves for evaluation, defending their evaluation data publicly, etc. A new wave of evaluation activities focuses again on procedures, including inspection, accreditation, and self-evaluation (Sahlin-Andersson 2004). Still, all these and other "rituals of verification" (Power 1997) are imposed everywhere in the name of "effectiveness," "outcome-orientation," and "deregulation."

Paying attention to the cultural affinity between evaluation and reflexive modernization helps us understand how evaluation can become a legitimate and taken-for-granted organizational ritual, the virtues of which sometimes lie in its congruence with dominant cultural patterns, not in its effects on better outcomes, better policies, or more sophisticated decisions. Evaluation may as well just create a very superficial form of legitimacy or simply more uncertainty (Stehr 2001).

Evidently, a broad cultural and symbolic view of evaluation has limitations, too. For example, it mostly ignores power and interest in struggles about evaluation. In addition, it does not explain most variations in the quantity and form of evaluations across nations and sectors (except the fact that evaluation is more intense in modern, reflexive areas of life such as health and teaching than in traditional institutions such as courts, churches, militaries and royal families).

Over time, the evaluation wave has had a remarkable ability to interact productively with various fashions and longer trends in the history of ideas. The debates about paradigms within social science, and the quantitative–qualitative debate, have not only been neatly reflected in the evaluation field, but have also helped the field move forward. In recent years, the movement towards evidence-based practices has both intensified the search for empirical underpinnings of professional practices and stimulated the evaluation field to discuss the different ways "evidence" can be produced under different knowledge regimes, sometimes in direct competition with the natural science epistemology and experimental methodology known from "evidence-based medicine".

In addition, our account of the evaluation wave should not overlook the importance of active organizational and personal actors in the promotion of evaluation. For example, The European Union (Derlien and Rist 2001: 451) and other international organizations such as the OECD have played a significant role in both executing evaluations (such as international reading tests) and in establishing mandatory regimes for evaluation across nations.

Furthermore, several of the leading scholars in the field of evaluation have played the role of salesmen, missionaries, educators, or advocates. They have carried an enthusiastic belief in the value of evaluation along with various "brands" in evaluation, supported by commitments to various methodological paradigms, notions of democracy, and personal careers. Evaluation centers and consultants also sell the need for evaluation along with evaluation. Thus, the evaluation wave is self-promoting.

None of the above factors in isolation explain more than a small fraction of the evaluation wave. Together, they do not amount to a total "explanation." The point is rather to suggest that the evaluation wave has many sources. It is a composite rather than a monolithic phenomenon. It cannot be reduced to one functional response to one functional demand, nor to one particular ideology. Instead, it operates at several levels of analysis and freely combines functional and symbolic aspects.

As an implication, evaluation as a field incorporates a number of interesting tensions. For example, there is a tension between the alleged focus on effectiveness and the fact that the effectiveness of evaluation itself hardly needs to be demonstrated. There is a tension between particular regimes of evaluation (including, say, performance indicators) and the broader cultural claim to the contingency and fragility of practically every social construction (Stehr 2001), including systems which monitor performance indicators. Not the least through meta-evaluation, the field reflects quite a lot on its own development. More often than not, a critical discussion of existing evaluation practices has led to new models and approaches within the field, thus keeping "the evaluation wave" both dynamic and diverse.

In the following section, we will take a closer look at three different schools of thought within the field of evaluation.

26.3 APPROACHES IN EVALUATION

Remember evaluation is a systematic or careful assessment of the merit, worth, and value of administration, output, and outcome of government interventions, which is intended to play a role in future, practical action situations (Vedung 1997: 3). This definition reveals the four core dimensions in any conceptual work with evaluation:

1. A knowledge dimension ("systematic" assessment). Together with scientific practice, evaluation shares a concern for the systematic production of knowledge and a foundation in ontology, epistemology, and methodology. While not all evaluators are always explicit about their fundamental choices on these levels of knowledge production, many work in contexts where they have to defend the claims they make about the validity, reliability, generalizability and trustworthiness of the knowledge produced.

2. A value dimension ("assessment of merit, worth, and value"). Obviously, different values and standards lead to different evaluations. Evaluators must thus justify the framework of values on which they base evaluative judgments.

3. A utilization dimension ("intended to play a role in future, practical action situations"). According to the definition, evaluations are not always utilized. But they are produced with that intention in mind. Different evaluators serve different masters and have different types of utilization in mind, often only their favorite types (Shadish, Cook, and Leviton 1991: 54), although actual use takes a number of forms in different time frames (Kirkhart 2000; Weiss 1998).

4. An evaluand ("administration, output, and outcome of public activities"). Evaluators must be clear about the definition of their evaluands. Although logically obvious, this rule may be complicated to follow, because different stakeholders may hold different views about what the defining feature of the evaluand is or should be in a given setting. Programs also change and learn over time, before, during, and after an evaluation.

Along these four dimensions, different evaluators take different standpoints in different situations, but not every time from scratch. Their typical standpoints tend to coalesce with a number of schools of thought, models, or approaches. In the following, I will use the term "approach" to denote a principled way to focus an evaluation based on thoughtful responses to the fundamental questions raised above. In principle, a coherent approach to evaluation takes well-articulated positions along each of the four dimensions above. However, some approaches to evaluation are anchored more clearly and explicitly in some dimensions rather than others.

The four-dimensional framework is useful because it helps sort out many of the controversies which occur when evaluation takes place. Sometimes an evaluation proceeds rigorously and consistently based on taking a clear position on each of the four dimensions. Still, it may be severely criticized because some people hold a different view about one of the conceptual dimensions underlying the evaluation, say, the value framework which helps define the evaluation criteria or the expected use or purpose of the evaluation. It is useful to distinguish such cases of fundamental disagreements about values and purposes from cases of inconsistent evaluation. Both occur frequently, but they are of not of the same nature.

In the following, I will present three approaches to evaluation, each taking its own position along the core dimensions of evaluation theory. Clearly, the three approaches are not exhaustive, and clearly, each approach in fact comprises a plethora of evaluation practices. Nevertheless, the three approaches are based on fundamentally different principles, and they do represent main currents in the field of evaluation.

Within each approach, I will look at main principles, legitimacy, practical focus, relevance for public management, and main critical points. I will be a bit meticulous in the conceptual definition of each approach to distinguish it as clearly as possible from the other ones. Furthermore, I intend to show that the strict ideal-typical requirements of a particular evaluation approach are often not met in practice by all evaluations which seek legitimacy from it and appear to comply with it. As we will see in the following section, this trick is often played in goal-oriented approaches.

26.3.1 Goal-oriented Approaches

In goal-oriented evaluation, activities are evaluated on the bases of whether they help achieve formally stated goals. More often than not, this school of thought takes for granted that it is meaningful to talk about public activities such as programs in terms of "inputs", "processes", "outputs", and "outcomes." Outcomes are most often seen as the ultimate justification of an activity. Programs are, in this light, merely tools, even expendable tools, which help us achieve certain outcomes. When the evaluator is considering the construction or selection of specific outcome measures, she starts with the programs' official goals (Weiss 1998: 117). In fact, program goals are only one way of understanding a program (Weiss 1998: 51), *but in goal-oriented evaluation approaches, they constitute the only legitimate source of criteria for judging the program*. In other words, if a particular value, criteria or standard cannot be demonstrably rooted in an official statement about program goals, it can safely be left out of an evaluation of that program.

The beauty of this simple principle should not be underestimated; many is the situation in which evaluators are torn between different value positions when evaluating a program, and sometimes, more or less knowingly, find their own values interfering in the game. Goal-oriented evaluation claims to offer a way out of this misery (Vedung 1997: 43). All that is needed is for the evaluator to describe official program goals thoroughly and from here deduce specific outcome measures. Why should program goals be a legitimate source of evaluation criteria? The answer lies in a relatively simple theory of representative democracy. An officially legitimate goal is rooted in a statement authorized somewhere in the parliamentary chain of command, which extends, in an unbroken fashion, from program staff to program managers, to top administrative executives, to politicians, to the ultimate source of power in a representative democracy, the people (Vedung 1997). This normative justification is all that the goal-oriented evaluator needs to accept. The evaluator can then base an evaluation on criteria deduced from program goals, irregardless of sympathy with the goals, or belief in the program's ability to fulfill them.

Since goals are rooted in the top of the political-administrative system, some argue that goal-oriented approaches are elitist in their orientation, but this is clearly a misunderstanding, argue their advocates (Vedung 1997: 42). It is quite an important role for evaluation to identify gaps between what politicians promise and what the public institutions actually deliver. In this capacity the evaluator may criticize a ruling elite, not legitimize it. Goal-oriented evaluation does not say that goals are met, it checks *if* they are met.

To maintain the legitimacy of an evaluation, however, evaluators working on the basis of the goal-oriented model must make sure that their outcome measures remain safely and explicitly anchored in official goals. If not, the evaluation loses its normative and intellectual foundation.

26.3.1.1 *The Relevance of Goal-oriented Approaches to Public Management*

Goal-oriented approaches are inherently relevant to public management as an integrated part of the chain of command in a representative democracy. Public managers are thus accountable to the higher echelons of the political-administrative system, and next, public managers themselves exercise control of the operational levels of service delivery. In both instances, formal goals specified on different levels provide the relevant criteria.

In recent years, in addition to these formalistic considerations, the dominant managerial discourses, such as those known from New Public Management, have advocated a shift in focus from rules and procedures to outcomes (Dunleavy and Hood 1994). This often involves redesigning organizational structures and steering mechanisms. Organizations are viewed as a chain of low-trust principal-agent relationships regulated by a network of contracts linking incentives to performance; in principle, contracts can be terminated and consumers can choose another provider. This should create incentives for providers to keep contracts and increase efficiency (Dunleavy and Hood 1994).

Within the framework of NPM, outcomes should therefore be measured regularly. In this spirit, a whole movement in evaluation focusing on "performance indicators" has evolved. The idea is to establish monitoring systems, which constantly makes it possible to hold service producers accountable for their results. Every aspect of service-providing organizations—structures, cultures, and practices—should thus be oriented towards measurable outcomes.

26.3.1.2 *Critical Points*

I will mention five critical points (*a–e*) of goal-based evaluation approaches—and evaluations taking place in their name.

(*a*) Causality is often not attended to. Although outcomes are, in principle, "effects" of public activities, most goal-oriented evaluations do not carefully attend to the complicated methodological problem of how to specify causal links between interventions and effects. This is especially true of performance indicator systems, which some evaluators suggest should be supplemented with ad-hoc in-depth evaluations, which map causal relations (de Lancer-Julnes 2004). Even so, an unquestionable identification of causal links is one of the most difficult endeavors the social sciences can take on.

Without a serious solution to the problem of causal attribution, however, performance indicator systems hold various institutions, or public employees, responsible for a set of outcomes in a relatively random and thus unfair way. A tough rhetoric on "accountability" only conceals, but does not ameliorate, this problem.

In a similar vein, a rhetoric of accountability sometimes confuses responsibility for amelioration of public ills. For instance, in a caricature of policy making, which is not far from a real example, operational units of a policy-making structure are politically required to develop a set of actions plans, which effectively secure the removal of a particular social problem. When the implementation of the plans is evaluated, the operational units are, of course, to blame if the problem still exists. But a good theory of how to solve a complex problem does not emerge out of the blue just because someone is held accountable for the solution.

(*b*) Goal-based approaches are not in themselves helpful in making recommendations about how to improve performance. Goal-based evaluations deliver descriptive statements about whether goals are met, but since they are often weak on causal attribution, they are difficult to use in a formative way. Without quality development, quality measurement has limited practical value.

Summative evaluation (which offers judgment but no proposals about improvement) does have its virtues and it is not, as some of its enemies argue, generally useless or unethical (Scriven 1991). Yet, since most decision-making situations do not deal with major policy changes or termination of programs (Shadish, Cook, and Leviton 1991: 54), but with incremental improvement of services on a more or less ongoing basis; and since most commissioners of evaluation do seek formative advice, the value of goal-based evaluative information oriented solely towards summative purposes is somewhat overrated.

(*c*) Side effects are ignored in goal-oriented approaches (Vedung 1997). Outcome measures are anchored in stated political goals, which, per definition, concern intended and positive effects. In a time when it is acknowledged that most social problems are multidimensional and interlinked, and when most adequate interventions are organized as cooperative networks in relatively complex governance structures, it is somewhat paradoxical that one of the dominant steering regimes of our time recommends an intensified exclusive focus on narrowly defined outcomes. However, with uncertain technologies, complex organizations, and crowded policy spaces, most public interventions have a number of side effects on other interventions as well as on the lives of citizens (Beck 1994).

Michael Scriven (1973) has suggested goal-free evaluation as a way to capture positive and negative effects of programs with reference to the needs of recipients, not to formal goals. Since the term is negatively defined, it is not intuitively appealing (Shadish, Cook, and Leviton 1991: 114).

(*d*) Strict monitoring of outcomes often leads to a serious change in the activities under evaluation. "Outcomes" is not an evident concept, but often obfuscates or redefines what it claims to measure. For example, for some time, the care for the elderly was an integrated and legitimate part of the welfare activities in Denmark. When an intense wave of "outcome-orientation" became manifest, the care was then expected to have "effects." Care not leading to "outcomes" had difficulty in justifying itself, and duty-oriented values among some professionals were made less welcome than a utility-oriented way of thinking. Although coined in an innocent optimistic voice, an outcome-orientation thus has serious hidden effects on our way of thinking about common problems in the public sphere.

"Constitutive effects" is a conceptual term which describes changing social realities that emerge when human beings react to outcome measures as if they were goals in themselves. The content of work may be influenced, for example, as teachers adopt the practice of "teaching to the test" (Weiss 1998). The timing and rhythm of practices may also be affected when outcome measures include a time-line. Last, but not least, the social identities and relations of professionals and clients, and others involved in public activities, may be affected. Outcome measures draw distinctions between the normal and the abnormal, the desirable and the undesirable, the over-achievers and the under-achievers. Evaluation attaches corresponding social labels to human beings. The old sociological dictum that definitions of situations are real in their consequences is confirmed when sanctions are imposed on low-scoring schools in league tables and on children failing to pass evaluative tests. Good clients in public services may be "creamed." Low-performing pupils may be given less attention or transferred to other institutions.

An alleged focus on "outcomes" may thus have somewhat paradoxical effects. Evaluation literature has coined the term "performance paradox" (van Thiel and Leeuw 2002) to describe situations in which more outcome measurement leads to everything but better performance. These phenomena are also, by some, described as "goal displacements" and "unintended effects of evaluation". The limitations of these two concepts are exactly their starting point in goals and intentions, as if these are well defined and known, which they are often not.

(*e*) Outcome measures do not often meet the requirements of a genuinely goal-oriented approach.

In many policy areas relevant to the modern welfare state, especially the "people-oriented" areas such as teaching, social work, mental health, counseling, etc., the nature of work makes it difficult to specify clear and relevant outcome measures, and general political goals are, for good reasons, abstractions like "renewal," "higher quality," "service improvements," and the like. Goals in official statements are often hazy, ambiguous, hard to pin down, or inconsistent. This is sometimes because different political fractions can come together to form a majority only if the proposal which they accept remains unclear in its intent.

Sometimes standardized outcome measures are imposed later in a political process, not because they improve quality, but because standardized activity is more easily monitored and controlled (Stake 2004: 227) or gives an appearance of control (Brunsson 1989).

In some international evaluations of educational quality, international organizations set their own criteria based on a particular vision of the qualifications needed in the future. In some international reading tests, items tend to be selected chosen which perform especially well in terms of the statistical distribution of the results. None of these criteria have much to do with official, nationally accepted political goals.

Yet, particular operationalized definitions of "outcomes" emerge, often because they are required as a part of the evaluation process. Sometimes particular outcome measures are chosen because they are measurable or fashionable or because the consultant doing the evaluation has some routine in handling similar measures from an earlier study, and perhaps provides a ready-made computer program or survey-technology which matches so remarkably with the outcome measures at hand. In other situations, a particular outcome measure is chosen for no particular reason, there just has to be some measure.

For example, in a Danish legislation about educational counseling for youth, it was a stated political goal not to have too many students dropping out of their studies. A consulting company was hired to produce a handbook guiding local counseling offices through an evaluation of their efforts. The handbook suggested specific outcome measures in terms of statistical drop-out rates. Although this outcome measure may be in line with the spirit of the legislation, it constitutes in a subtle way a distinction between successful and unsuccessful counseling which is not mandated in the legislation.

In a careful analysis, it is thus often impossible to justify a particular set of outcome measures in given political goals. This fundamental evaluation problem is often remedied by building a set of outcome measures into, say, a policy document or a contract between a public authority and a service provider. Quality is then politically defined as better test scores or another such set of outcomes. However, then the relation between politics and evaluation methodology is confusing, if not reversed.

What appears as "a goal-oriented approach to evaluation" is in fact often political goal-setting disguised under a dense fog of measurement jargon. On top of that, taking the paradoxical effects of outcome measurement into account, it becomes less credible that NPM supported by outcome-oriented evaluation in fact secures an increased focus on "outcomes." Then the concept of outcomes loses some of its blue-eyed quality.

26.3.2 Theory-based Approaches

Theory-based evaluation views a particular activity under evaluation as rooted in a more general set of assumptions. These assumptions, often called "program theory," explain why activities like these at hand can plausibly lead to a stipulated outcome, and what else is likely to happen. Theory-based approaches include Chen's (1990) theory-driven evaluation, Pawson and Tilley's (1997) realistic evaluation and a number of practical ways to systematically connect means–ends relationships in program activities (such as log-frame analysis).

It is not prohibitive for evaluation if no program theory is made explicit by the policy architect—very often, it is not. The evaluator can "reconstruct" the program theory as part of the evaluation. In doing so, some evaluators use official documents, or field observations, while Patton (1997) focuses on a dialogue with the intended users of the evaluation and Chen (1990) prefers linking evaluation with social science theory. Each of these ways leads to different types of theory and to different characteristics of the feedback provided by evaluation.

Yet, basing an evaluation on a program theory generally leads to a number of advantages, which distinguish this approach clearly from goal-based approaches.

First, theory-based evaluation is in a position to provide a firm empirical foundation for recommendations. Since it focuses on how and why the program works (Weiss 1998: 60), a theory-based evaluation pinpoints at which link in a larger causal chain repair work is needed. Furthermore, only theory-based evaluation can distinguish those situations where imperfect implementation calls for remedial action from situations where it is better to terminate a program because its underlying theory is flawed. The latter is logically the case if all program activities were carried out as prescribed, but the expected results did not appear. Although it is not always possible in practice to differentiate clearly between the two situations, "implementation failure" and "theory failure", the distinction is extremely useful, not the least because their action implications are entirely different. The first suggests spending more resources on improved implementation, the second recommends in principle a quick termination of all program activities based on the same theory.

Second, theory-based evaluation offers a way to qualify outcome measures. Indicators are too often developed in a theoretical vacuum (Cave et al. 1997: 151). A particular outcome measure is qualified only to the extent that a plausible theory can be developed to explain why this particular outcome can be expected as a result of the specific activities under evaluation. Theory-based evaluation thus has a critical edge against holding institutions and professionals accountable for outcome measures which are not under their influence, carelessly selected, or just generally amorphous. We have no theory which explains, say, how one hour of counseling per month for youngsters leads to a greatly improved quality of life in the target group. Instead, activities and outcomes should be carefully aligned and operate on roughly the same level of abstraction.

Third, theory-based evaluation allows a qualified integration of side effects into the evaluative inquiry. Many theories explicitly predict side effects; others provide a general model which the evaluator can use to formulate case-specific hypotheses about side effects.

Fourth, theory-based evaluation allows knowledge to be accumulated over several evaluations (Pawson 2002). Program theories are a medium in which lessons learned over time and across contexts are stored. Comparisons are useful. Looking at a mechanism applied in different contexts leads to broader conclusions about program theories than evaluations focusing on only one policy area. For this reason, much meta-evaluation should look at mechanisms across contexts rather than net effects within one policy domain (Pawson 2002).

A final note is that theory-oriented evaluation often entangles itself in technical jargon and in controversies about causal attribution. It should not be forgotten, however, that the beauty of the approach lies not in its technicalities, but in its critical thinking. Theories can, in contradistinction to dogma, be discussed and tested. So can the "theories", explicit or not, of public authorities who carry out public policies. The value of theory-based evaluation lies in its contribution to open, critical and democratic discussions of the assumptions on which policies are based. This contribution, it should be maintained, is not just an opinion, but systematically constructed knowledge based on the methods of scientific work. One of the best explanations of the renewed interest in theory-based approaches in recent years (e.g. Pawson and Tilley 1997) is probably that these approaches have revitalized the scientific element in evaluation.

26.3.2.1 *The Relevance to Public Management*

Advocates of theory-based evaluation argue that it is clearly in the interest of public managers to base any program change on empirical evidence, to rely on qualified outcome measures only, to show attention to side effects, and to learn lessons over time and across contexts. Public management has a role to play as a knowledgeable counterpart in dialogue with policy architects.

Theory-based evaluation also offers a way forward for public managers who wish to not only manage and monitor professionals, but also to cooperate with them. Good theory-based evaluation invites those with substantial insights, including professionals, to outline a relevant program theory, select realistic outcome measures, and do evaluation continuously as an integrated part of a reflexive professional practice.

However, the actual dissemination of theory-based evaluation in managerial circles is remarkably limited. The construction of "theory" is often viewed as a superfluous academic pastime. In addition, in most practical contexts, politicians and public managers work under specific pressures which together provide an unfavorable climate for theory-based evaluation. To signal optimism and legitimacy, responsible decision makers often maintain a commitment to already-approved policies. Theorizing is threatening, because it questions the underpinnings of public policy making, if not the very infallibility of authority. Public managers are under pressure to demonstrate positive outcomes narrowly within their own policy domain and organizational jurisdiction. This leads to an over-emphasis of organization-specific goals and on the perceived uniqueness of each intervention. Less attention is paid to what can be learned from other similar interventions across policy domains. Learning processes are also tampered by another feature characteristic of the daily life of managers—the pressure to focus on the next immediate decision.

26.3.2.2 Critical Points

Other opponents of theory-based evaluation argue that it takes a disproportionate amount of time, is not always necessary, and confusingly assumes that it is the responsibility of the evaluator to construct explanations of public activities (Stufflebeam 2001).

Another controversial point is that some theory-based evaluators assume that there is *a* program theory. However, different stakeholders hold different assumptions, and different approaches to theory-constructions lead to quite different theories. Thus, the evaluator does not "reconstruct" a theory, but organizes a process, which allows a particular theoretical construct to emerge. The roles played in and the rules applied to this process influence the contours of the theory or theories which emerge (Gargani 2002). This should be openly admitted and described as a part of a theory-based evaluation. If so, the multiplicity of theories can be handled within the evaluation model as such (Weiss 1998: 61).

A perhaps more fundamental critique is that theory-based evaluations are not always based on a correct understanding of the relation between causal thinking on the one hand and normative and political thinking on the other. Theory-based evaluation was born in an era with high expectations about the possibility of reducing politics to social engineering; and still today, political choices are often concealed under the rhetoric of "variables," "contexts," and statistical "evidence." For example, theory-based evaluation can demonstrate that a particular intervention works under some contextual conditions but not others. In the latter case, the program theory is thus "incorrect." However, "contextual conditions" are not just different geographical entities as is most often thought, but also social constructions—institutional settings, social structures, incentive structures, and cultural values—which can be changed over time within a particular policy setting. As a corollary, an "incorrect" program theory can become correct under the circumstances (Dahler-Larsen 2001). Obviously, what *should* be changed is a political and normative question; but to a large extent, the same is true about statements about what *can* be changed. Most social orders base themselves on a number of ideological doctrines about what can and what cannot be changed. Theory-based evaluation should not unknowingly conceal normative statements under a technical-methodological vocabulary.

Perhaps the most profound critique of evaluations based on program theory comes from philosophers who view a given practice as more complex than a theory of it formalized from a point of view exterior to that practice. Practice, such as the practice of teaching, is sensitive to the specificities of time, situation, and person. It incorporates complex ethical judgments and ongoing evaluation, although often not based on an explicit criteriology (Schwandt 2002). An explicit program theory is thus largely a reduction of practice, not a representation of its nature.

26.3.3 Responsive and Participatory Approaches

Responsive and participatory approaches encompass a range of different ways of doing evaluation with a number of different justifications along all components of evaluation theory: values, knowledge, utilization, and the evaluand.

A common denominator among these approaches, however, is denial of the relevance of exterior constructs, be they formal "goals," "outcomes," or "theories," to a particular local evaluation situation. Instead, in responsive and participatory approaches, an immersion into a case context, a dialogue with local stakeholders, and/or a sharing of responsibility for the evaluation with local people opens the evaluation towards the complexities of the local setting, identification of local criteria, and an evaluation process which sometimes benefits the involved partners both directly and indirectly.

For example, Robert Stake believes that the very concept of quality is relative to human subjectivity; thus, the quality of work at a particular school cannot be separated from the questions and concerns most pressing under the local circumstances. Stake coined the term "responsive evaluation" as a reaction against "preordinate" evaluation (with a priori selection and final measurement of a few outcome criteria) (Stake 2004: 95). Responsive evaluation favors the case study as an appropriate methodological way into the uniqueness of a local setting. "Issues" are selected not in advance, but as a result of preliminary study, interviews, and, very important, observation. Issues constitute the main conceptual framework of a responsive evaluation. Issues are per definition contested. The primary concern in responsive evaluation is the understanding of goodness in relation to the issues, not to produce goodness or to advocate any particular position on how to resolve the issues (Stake 2004: 89).

Responsive evaluation is not participatory evaluation, but participatory evaluation often involves some degree of responsiveness (Stake 2004: 101).

In participatory evaluation, again an umbrella term for different approaches, various participants are invited to share responsibility for the evaluation process.

In its ideal form, writes Greene (1997: 174), "participatory evaluation intention-ally involves all legitimate stakeholder interests in a collaborative, dialogic inquiry process that enables the construction of contextually meaningful knowledge, that engenders the personal and structural capacity to act on that knowledge and that seeks action that contributes to democratizing social change."

Evaluators engage in participatory evaluation for a variety of reasons. Therefore, the fundamental dimensions in participatory evaluation neatly captured by Greene, the "contextually meaningful knowledge," the "capacity to act," and the "social change" are in fact emphasized very differently by practicing participatory evaluation in different ways. Participatory evaluation approaches differ as to how many stakeholders are involved, how deep the involvement is and how much control of the evaluation process they take (Cousins and Earl 1995).

In one variant, utilization-focused evaluation (Patton 1997), participation among intended users is crucial because it helps make the evaluation relevant and promotes ownership of evaluation results, which again strengthens utilization. Others have a broader definition of the usefulness of evaluation, such as organiza-tional learning or the building of evaluation capacity. In these situations, a broader set of participants are often involved. To enhance utilization, not only on individ-ual, but also on organizational and institutional levels, this strand of participatory evaluation often seeks the authorization of the whole evaluation process by power holders (Greene 1997: 176), for instance managers with position power or a coalition of influential reform zealots.

Others anchor their approach to participatory evaluation, not in the utilization dimension of evaluation theory, but more in a particular value position.

In fourth generation evaluation (Guba and Lincoln 1989), all relevant stake-holders have a voice in the exchange of views, issues, and concerns about a program. The evaluator's role is to moderate the negotiation between the different constructions held by stakeholders. The approach is called "constructivist," but it is a very peculiar form of constructivism with no advanced element of interpretation or theorizing. Instead, all constructions, including those of the evaluator, are relativized. An orientation is provided not by a knowledge claim, but by a value claim: There should be extraordinary attention to groups who are especially underprivileged.

Underprivileged groups are also in focus in empowerment evaluation (Fetter-man 1994). Here the explicit purpose of evaluation is the empowerment of a particular group as it takes charge not only of its own evaluation process, but also in a broader sense of its own destiny.

Democratic deliberative evaluation is a recipe for evaluation, which prescribes a particular set of principles, inclusion, dialogue and deliberation, for the evaluation process. Deliberation helps facilitate a nonviolent approach to social tensions, it facilitates mutual recognition and respect between various stakeholders, and it allows each participant to adjust his or her views as a result of the exchange of viewpoints and arguments. The idea is that if evaluation has a role to play in a democracy, the evaluation process itself must be of a democratic nature (House and Howe 2000). Evaluation is a countermeasure against fundamentalism and intolerance and itself a democratic exercise.

Quite characteristically, deliberative democratic evaluation, as well as a number of the other participatory approaches, finds the quality of evaluation in an exemplary process as much as in specific results.

Taken together, participatory evaluation thus incorporates these two tendencies, one anchored mostly in concerns for utilization, the other one anchored mostly in values connected to transformative democratic processes. Participatory evaluation faces the tensions between these two concerns in practical evaluation, too (Greene 1997: 181).

However, it is not often acknowledged that participatory evaluation can be anchored in a third way, namely in the knowledge dimension in evaluation theory. More specifically, participatory evaluation can be a road to the specific life-world knowledge (typifications, habits, inhibitions, norms, rules, practices) which characterizes particular groups of users, clients, citizens etc., of relevance to a public activity. An attention to the needs, views, and norms of these groups can lead to more user-friendly services or more effective policies, or both (Dahlberg and Vedung 2001).

To do this, the whole evaluation design should not just reflect what public managers want to know, but rather what participants have to say to describe their perspective on public activities. To communicate about their world, they must speak in their own words. To create a forum, where this is possible, calls for qualitative methods and at least some degree of a participatory approach.

26.3.3.1 The Relevance of Participatory Evaluation to Public Management

Participatory evaluation is useful in situations where a coordinated approach to evaluation is called for in a complex political or organizational setting with many stakeholders with different views.

Participatory evaluation is also useful for public managers who want a richer and more nuanced feedback from clients, customers and users than merely the exit option, which is typically offered by most market-inspired and NPM-oriented ways of organizing services. Through participatory evaluation, it becomes clear that clients, customers, and users of services often hold problem definitions and evaluation criteria which differ starkly from those of professionals and managers. The life-worlds of public managers and of clients are often entirely segregated. Large organizations, both bureaucratic and market-oriented ones, talk much more than they listen. An attentive participatory evaluation directed towards the views of citizens and clients is one of the few ways through which this bias in modern organizational life can be compensated.

Openness towards clients, users, and citizens sometimes leads to an explication of deeper conflicts of both values and interests around a public activity. Some public managers hesitate to embark on participatory evaluation because they fear that it will be too painful and unproductive to reveal contradictory expectations to public policies among stakeholders. Other public managers find that evaluations which allow clients and citizens to speak in their own terms about public services provide a fine way to stay in touch with lived reality and to remind themselves of the justifications for public activities, which actually do rest outside of the managerial circles of public organizations!

The more explicit political agendas in some variants of participatory evaluation are sometimes in conflict with managerial priorities, and most public managers are hesitant to negotiate away their proportion of control over an evaluation process. This is not only because public managers seek to protect their own interests, but also because they have obligations prescribed by the hierarchical control structures of representative democracy. This aspect of public management is only rudimentarily dealt with, if not bluntly ignored, by many of the participatory approaches with a value-base in alternative visions of democracy.

26.3.3.2 Critical Points

Since responsive and participatory approaches include a variety of different ideas, not all critical points are relevant to all approaches.

The utilization-oriented strand of participatory evaluation is criticized for its lack of philosophical foundation and for its tendency to more or less quietly team up with those in power in order to secure utilization. In addition, if utilization is given absolute priority, evaluation is doomed to occupy itself with small adjustments rather than major reforms or social transformations.

The political agendas in many of the other variants of participatory evaluation are sometimes criticized, not only for confusing evaluation and advocacy, but also for a lack of a theory of representative democracy—the type of democracy, which participatory evaluators rarely endorse. Admittedly, dialogue, deliberation, and respect for underprivileged groups are respectable values, but at what point should the standards and criteria authorized by a representative democracy not be adhered to? When is it legitimate not to respect representative democracy? Can it be assumed that representative democracy safely takes care of itself, and is present when needed, while evaluators focus on values anchored in alternative notions of democracy?

Both the utilization-oriented and the value-oriented camps in participatory evaluation are criticized for sacrificing evaluation as a unique and distinct undertaking, which has much to do with the maintenance of a relatively independent and competent evaluative glance.

Instead, participatory evaluators invest most of their energy in activities, which may be related to evaluation but are not specific for evaluation, such as process management, organizational learning and development, deliberation, negotiation, or advocacy. In many variants of participatory evaluation (but not in responsive evaluation), the responsibility for evaluation is thus partly or fully handed over to partners who often lack competence in evaluation and/or have a number of motives for avoiding or obstructing relatively objective evaluation.

To share control of the evaluation process is a more controversial matter than most participatory evaluators will admit. Although evaluators believe that they "share" control of the evaluation process with stakeholders, do stakeholders feel that they assume control correspondingly? Do all stakeholders have the same sense about the locus of control? If evaluations are open-ended, complex processes, which initial promises can a responsible evaluator on ethical grounds make about the way the evaluation affects the various groups in later stages of the process? Clearly, some participatory evaluators, such as those committed to democratic deliberative evaluation, seek to establish a consensus on procedural ground rules among all participants at an early stage of the evaluation. Too often, the good *intentions* of participatory-friendly evaluators are stated early on as a moral guarantee of the quality of the entire evaluation process.

The best participatory evaluators analyze the tensions in these approaches (Greene 1997) and report on both successes and failures of participatory evaluation processes (Cousins and Earl (1995).

26.4 CONCLUDING REMARK

Evaluation is a field with vitality and diversity. It encompasses a number of different approaches each seeking responses to somewhat different problems. Parts of the field of evaluation are in clear alignment with the dominant doctrines of public management focusing on outcomes, performance, and the like. Other parts of the field of evaluation see it as their mission to deliver forms of knowledge and organizational feedback, which are richer, more nuanced, more learning-oriented, more theory-oriented, or more oriented towards transformative social change than that, which is in demand by the dominant management discourses.

So far, the field of evaluation has thrived on, rather than suffered from, its different schools of thought, the tension between theory and practice, and the many dashed expectations about how much evaluation can do for the world.

Notes

1. http://www.evaluationcanada.ca/site.cgi?s=1&ss=2&_lang= Most recent figure is from 2003.

2. An Internet search in November, 2004, identified 83 such associations, societies, or networks plus three "under construction." All of them included the term "evaluation" in either English, German, Spanish, French, Italian, or Scandinavian languages, and all of them were geographically defined, and not sector-specific. International, national, regional organizations as well as chapters of national associations were included. Organizations represented only by one persons e-mail address were not included. The method used was to start with well-known international associations and from there exploit all links to other organizations until dead-ends and repetitions occurred. Obviously, this method is linguistically biased, ignores organizations not having links to other organizations or not on the Internet, and overrates web-based organizations with no members and no activities. Of all the organizations found, 45 informed about which year they were founded. Most of the strong growth in recent years has taken place in Europe and Africa.

References

BECK, U. (1994), "The Reinvention of Politics: Towards a Theory of Reflexive Moderniza-tion," in U. Beck, A. Giddens, and S. Lash (eds.), *Reflexive Modernization*. Stanford: Stanford University Press, 1–55.

BRUNSSON, N. (1989), *The Organization of Hypocrisy. Talk, Decisions and Actions in Organizations*, Chichester: John Wiley & Sons.

CAVE, M., HANNEY, S. HENKEL, M., and KOGAN, M. (1997), *The Use of Performance Indicators in Higher Education*. London: Jessica Kingsley.

CHELIMSKY, E. (1997), "Preface," in E. Chelimsky and W. R. Shadish (eds.), *Evaluation for the 21st Century*. Thousand Oaks, CA: Sage, xi–xiii.

CHEN, H. (1990), *Theory-Driven Evaluation*, Beverly Hills: Sage.

COUSINS, B., and EARL, L. (1995), "Participatory Evaluation in Education: What do we Know? Where do we Go?", in B. Cousins and L. Earl (eds.), *Participatory Evaluation in Education*, London: Routledge Falmer, 159–80.

DAHLBERG, M., and VEDUNG, E. (2001), *Demokrati och brukarutvärdering*, Lund: Studentlitteratur.

DAHLER-LARSEN, P. (2000), "Surviving the Routinization of Evaluation: the Administrative Use of Evaluation in Danish Municipalities," *Administration and Society* 32(1): 70–92.

—— (2001), "From Programme Theory to Constructivism: On Tragic, Magic and Competing Programmes," *Evaluation* 7(3): 331–49.

DE LANCER-JULNES, P. (2004), *Using performance measurement information for government accountability and performance improvement*. Paper presented at the European Evaluation Society conference in Berlin, 30 Sept.–2 Oct.

DERLIEN, H.-U., and RIST, R. C. (2001), "Policy Evaluation in International Comparison," in J.-E. Furubo, R. C. Rist, and R. Sandahl (eds.), *International Atlas of Evaluation*, New Brunswick: Transaction Publishers, 439–55.

DUNLEAVY, P., and HOOD, C. (1994), "From Old Public Administration to New Public Management," *Public Money and Management* (July-September), 9–16.

FETTERMAN, D. (1994), "Empowerment Evaluation," *Evaluation Practice* 15: 1–16.

FURUBO, J.-E., and SANDAHL, R. (2001), "A Diffusion Perspective on Global Developments in Evaluation," in J.-E. Furubo, R. C. Rist, and R. Sandahl (eds.), *International Atlas of Evaluation*, New Brunswick: Transaction Publishers, 1–23.

—— RIST, R. C., and SANDAHL, R. (eds.) (2001), *International Atlas of Evaluation*, New Brunswick: Transaction Publishers.

GARGANI, J. (2002), *The Challenge of Evaluating Theory-Based Evaluation*. Paper presented at the Annual Meeting of the American Evaluation Association, St. Louis, MO, November 7.

GREENE, J. (1997), "Participatory Evaluation," in L. Mabry (volume ed.), *Evaluation and the Postmodern Dilemma*, in R. Stake (series ed.), *Advances in Program Evaluation*, vol. 3, London: JAI Press, 41–59.

GUBA, E., and LINCOLN, Y. (1989), *Fourth Generation Evaluation*, Newbury Park, CA: Sage.

HANSEN, H. F. (2003), *Evaluering i Staten*, Copenhagen: Samfundslitteratur.

HOUSE, E., and HOWE, K. R. (2000), "Deliberative Democratic Evaluation," in K. Ryan and L. DeStefano (eds.), *New Directions for Evaluation* (85), 3–12.

KIRKHART, K. E. (2000), "Reconceptualizing Evaluation Use: An Integrated Theory of Influence," in K. Ryan and L. DeStefano (eds.), *New Directions for Evaluation* (88): 5–23.

LEEUW, F., TOULEMONDE, J., and BROUWERS, A. (1999), "Evaluation Activities in Europe: A Quick Scan of the Market," *Evaluation* 5(4): 487–96.

MARCH, J. and OLSEN, J. P. (1995), *Democratic Governance*, New York: The Free Press.

MARK, M. M., HENRY, G. T., and JULNES, G. (2000), *Evaluation. An Integrated Framework for Understanding, Guiding, and Improving Public and Nonprofit Policies and Programs*, San Francisco: Jossey-Bass.

PATTON, M.Q. (1997), *Utilization-focused evaluation*, 3rd edn., Thousand Oaks, CA: Sage.

PAWSON, R. (2002), "Evidence-based Policy: The Promise of 'Realist Synthesis,'" *Evaluation* 8(3), 340–58.

—— and TILLEY, N. (1997), *Realistic Evaluation*, London: Sage.

POWER, M. (1997), *The Audit Society: Rituals of Verification*, Oxford: Oxford University Press.

RIST, R. C., and STAME, N. (eds.) (forthcoming), *From Studies to Streams*, New Brunswick: Transaction Publishers.

SAHLIN-ANDERSSON, K. (2004), Presentation at the conference of the Swedish Evaluation Society in Stockholm in May.

SCHWANDT, T. (2002), *Evaluation Practice Reconsidered*, New York: Peter Lang.

SCOTT, W.R. (1995), *Institutions and Organizations*, Thousand Oaks, CA: Sage.

SCRIVEN, M. (1973), "Goal-free Evaluation," in E. R. House (ed.), *School Evaluation: the Politics and Process*, Berkeley: McCutchan, 319–28.

—— (1991), "Beyond Formative and Summative Evaluation," in M. W. McLaughlin and D. C. Philips (eds.), *Evaluation and Education: At Quarter Century*, Chicago: Chicago University Press, 18–64.

SHADISH, W. R., COOK, T. D., and LEVITON, L. C. (1991), *Foundations of Program Evaluation*, Newbury Park, CA: Sage.

STAKE, R. E. (2004), *Standards-based and Responsive Evaluation*, Thousand Oaks, CA: Sage.

STEHR, N. (2001), *The Fragility of Modern Societies. Knowledge and Risk in the Information Age*, London: Sage.

STUFFLEBEAM, D. (2001), "Evaluation Models," *New Directions for Evaluation* (89), 1–106.

VAN THIEL, S., and LEEUW, F. (2002), "The Performance Paradox in the Public Sector," *Public Performance and Management Review* 25(3): 267–81.

VEDUNG, E. (1997), *Public Policy and Program Evaluation*, 2nd edn., Lund: Studentlitteratur.

WEISS, C. (1998), *Evaluation*, 2nd edn., Upper Saddle River: Prentice Hall.

SECTION V

NATIONAL AND INTERNATIONAL COMPARISONS

CHAPTER 27

INTERNATIONAL PUBLIC MANAGEMENT

DAVID MATHIASEN

Good government is not a luxury—it is a vital necessity for development.

World Bank Development Report 1997

We all tend to think of our problems as unique, or specific to national history, culture or ideology. The fact is that many—probably over 50—countries are engaged in moving toward sustainable democracies after an authoritarian rule of one sort or another.

Randall Baker, *Transitions from Authoritarianism*

27.1 "INVISIBLE INFRASTRUCTURE" GOES GLOBAL

The rapid growth of international public management during the past two decades has gone largely unnoticed. Public sector institutions across the globe have been changing management practices, often using new (to them) approaches adopted from other countries. International institutions have been assembling knowledge about public management systems, developing guidelines for adopting them and fielding advisory teams to apply them to individual county circumstances. Profit-making consulting firms and non-governmental organizations (NGOs) have built up substantial rosters of advisors on public management practice and stand ready to dispatch them to almost any part of the world, in some cases under conditions of hardship or danger. Thousands of documents on improving public management exist in file drawers and on computer disks around the world. Most are unanalysed and many ignored.

Box 27.1 International public management can include:

- management systems used by multilateral institutions such as the International Monetary Fund (IMF) and the International Bank for Reconstruction and Development (the World Bank) to govern themselves;
- public management systems in individual countries that are developed in response to external forces, such as the globalization of the world economy, and the need to accommodate multilateral institutions; and,
- the movement of public management practices from one national political/social system to another.

All of these are important; however, this chapter covers primarily the third, which is by far the most extensive aspect of contemporary international public management.

The precise number of "experts" participating in these developments is unknown, and by and large they do not know each other. But the number is most certainly large, and their existence reflects political, economic, and social changes across the globe. The political forces have been the break-up of the former Soviet Union and the emergence of new democracies. On the economic front, the big change has been globalization. This has pushed countries interested in participating in a world market economy toward the kinds of public institutions that are necessary for efficient and stable international trade and financial policies. The social pressures have included specific concerns about corruption and transparency and more general ones about democratization, civil society and the development of nongovernmental institutions.

These pressures alone do not explain why public management has become internationalized. This has happened in part because of real or perceived needs for reform. Rebellion against earlier authoritarian political systems, dissatisfaction and distrust of outdated public management systems in mature democracies, and the need for public management to meet the challenge of rapidly changing world economic conditions—all of these created pressure for reform. *The key, however, lies in the belief that it is both possible and desirable to transfer public management concepts and practices from one political and social setting to another.* As the OECD put it, "The main impact of the reform period [of the past two decades] was to change a long-standing view that public administration was unique to an individual country, and unique as a discipline" (OECD 2002).

The academic literature has focused particular attention on new concepts of public management—often associated with the "New Public Management" (NPM). These new concepts carry with them the notion that many systems of public management are candidates for reform, and that the concepts and practices themselves are generic in nature and thus transferable. Literature on this reflects an unusually productive collaboration between academics and practitioners.

Part of the NPM debate has revolved around a concept of an international convergence, that is, the notion that public management reform is moving the field to a standard set of practices (Osborne and McLaughlin, 2002). There is an implicit "invisible hand" aspect to convergence theories. One notion seems to be that there is an "Anglo" conspiracy network, or at least a consensus process among Westminster-based governments. The Americans are sometimes lumped in. The reasons for this are unclear, since the American reform efforts have been largely unconnected with those in the Westminster countries, and on the face of it the presidential system of government, along with the high degree of regional and local autonomy under the US federal system, makes it hard to see an American connection to Westminster-based reforms.

A conspiracy engineered by the OECD and the IFIs is sometimes mentioned but hard to imagine (McCourt, 2002). For its part, the OECD is explicit about its agenda:

- budgeting and financial management process;
- civil service system;
- public transparency and accountability;
- decision-rights between central agencies and departments;
- creation and closure of organizations;
- use of private sector providers; and,
- devolution of decision-making to agencies, authorities and other governmental bodies (2002).

Moreover, NPM is a patchwork of practices, many of which existed before the broader concept was articulated.[1] Convergence has probably fulfilled its usefulness as a fruitful basis for discussion.

It is international public management *in its entirety* that has largely gone unnoticed. In particular areas of concern there is a different story.

- International lending countries and institutions highlight their support for measures to improve the public management capacity of client countries to manage development programs.

Box 27.2 Abbreviations

ADB	Asian Development Bank
ADB; AfDB (internet)	African Development Bank
CAPAM	Commonwealth Association for Public Administration and Management
EU	European Union
IDB	Inter-American Development Bank
IFI; IFIs	International Financial Institution(s)
IIAS	International Institute of Administrative Sciences
IMF	International Monetary Fund
IPMN	International Public Management Network
NGOs	Non-governmental Organizations
NPM	New Public Management
OECD	Organization for International Cooperation and Development
OECD–GOV	Public Governance and Territorial Development Directorate of the OECD
OECD–PUMA	Public Management Service of the OECD
OEEC	Organization for European Economic Cooperation
SIGMA	Support for Improvement in Governance and Management in Central and Eastern European Countries, part of the OECD's Public Management Service,
TQM	Total Quality Management
World Bank; IBRD	International Bank For Reconstruction And Development

- The international finance community stresses the importance of national institutions that can manage the robust regulatory systems that are necessary to deal with international trade and capital flows.
- The OECD works with its member countries to facilitate the exchange of public management practice among wealthy industrialized countries and to establish standards for management effectiveness.
- Those that favor expanded free trade emphasize the importance of public institutions that foster efficient (and honest) market economies.
- Former communist countries recognize that their inherited public management systems are incompatible with the responsiveness and transparency that are inherent in democratic systems.
- Countries such as Spain, Portugal, and South Africa have restructured their public management systems as part of post-authoritarian reforms.

In all of these cases public management reform has meant using concepts and models developed from beyond the boundaries of the country involved.

27.2 FORCES BEHIND
INTERNATIONALIZATION

The overall pattern has remained unidentified and un-analyzed partly because pressure for change came from a variety of sources. Six major sources can be specified:

- economic globalization of trade and capital movements, and the newfound concern by international assistance organizations about effective public management;
- contemporaneous national fiscal problems;
- discontent about the size, effectiveness, and cost of government;
- the need for transformed public management in post-Soviet and other previously authoritarian countries;
- interest by nongovernmental organizations and public interest groups in "democratization," and by scholars and practitioners in "subsidiarity"; and,
- Total Quality Management as an international phenomenon.

27.2.1 Economic Globalization and the Need for "Invisible Infrastructure"

To be successful, globalization of the world economy requires more than new international economic policies. It also requires effective supporting institutions. A case in point is the economic collapse of Mexico, which led in 1995 to emergency international financial support. This was followed in 1997–9 by fiscal crises in Southeast Asia and Brazil. These crises were for the most part triggered by unstable short-term capital movements. The IMF, the World Bank, and countries involved in debt restructuring concluded that a major underlying cause was institutional failure. They stressed the need for more effective public management as critical in the long term to avoid recurring crises. During the Mexican crisis the term "invisible infrastructure" was first used (by the US Undersecretary of the Treasury) to characterize the institutional underpinning needed by market economies participating in the global economy (Stiglitz 2002).

27.2.2 National Fiscal Problems

The longer-term causes of fiscal stress and budget deficits in the OECD countries resulted in major part from the expansion of government entitlement programs during the 1970s, in some cases extending into the 1980s. These problems were exacerbated by the recession of the early 1990s (OECD 1996*b*).

This issue became "internationalized" because what was first seen as a case-by-case problem became recognized as one that was shared. The parliamentary secretary of the United Kingdom linked fiscal stress to management reform by quoting the New Zealand physicist Lord Rutherford, who said when faced with budgetary problems "we have no more money, now we must think" (Wilits in OECD 1996*a*). Citing a number of sources, Jones and Kettl (2003) have observed that fiscal stress has "increased the cry for less costly or less expensive government." In 1995 the OECD Public Management Service (PUMA) reported that "The costs of not pursuing public sector management reform are high, and will be reflected in declining international competitiveness and stagnating national economic and social prosperity" (OECD 1995*a*: 10).

27.2.3 Citizen Discontent

Jones and Kettl have observed:

Over the past three decades, criticism about government performance has surfaced across the world from all points of the political spectrum. Critics have alleged that governments are inefficient, ineffective, too large, too costly, overly bureaucratic, overburdened by unnecessary rules, unresponsive to public wants and needs, secretive, undemocratic, invasive into the private rights of citizens, self-serving, and failing in the provision of either the quantity or quality of services deserved by the taxpaying public. (2003: 1)

An earlier validation at the political level of these concerns came out of a 1996 OECD ministerial symposium at which the Chair stated, "Delegates reported that government itself is being criticized in many of their countries as being wasteful, expensive, and unresponsive to the demands of the citizen" (OECD 1996*a*: 40). Numerous country studies contain similar statements.

27.2.4 Post-Soviet and Other Previously Authoritarian Countries

The relationship between political and public management systems was never clearer then during the transformations of Spain, Portugal, South Africa, and the former Soviet Bloc. As these countries moved away from authoritarianism, which most did, they recognized that their inherited public management systems were incompatible with the responsiveness and transparency that are inherent in democratic systems. Civil service needed to replace service to the state; political parties could no longer control bureaucracies; transparency needed to replace state security. Those countries that wanted to develop open market economies and participate in globalization found that effective governance was a prerequisite to achieving these goals.

Baker indicates:

when democracy arrived, as it did in a rush, it was not as a result of decades of indigenous struggle and reform, but more often as a result of sudden disappearance or departure of a General Franco, Salazar, or Stroessner, or the remarkable revelation of the fragilities of regimes of intimidation.... Instead of the indigenous evolution of public institutions over time, these countries now confronted the urgent need for a transition in order to build the foundations of democracy in short order and through very unstable and dangerous times. (Baker 2002: 4)

27.2.5 Democratization and Subsidiarity

Democratization and subsidiarity require effective public management, although this is not always stated explicitly. The democratization movement can trace its historical roots to American colonialism and foreign intervention (Carothers 1999: 19). It gained renewed support in the late 1980s and early 1990s in connection with the post-Cold War concern for "civil society." There are various definitions of this term, but they all relate to that aspect of society that excludes private sector business activity on the one hand and activity of the formal political structure on the other.

Subsidiarity also focuses on the importance of local government. It has to do with the issue, often discussed as part of new public management reforms, of which level of government is the most desirable or effective to carry out a public purpose or activity. In a glossary of public management terms, the OECD's Public Management Service defines it as follows:

A paper on this subject by the Council of Europe states "subsidiarity is a fashionable idea today, although its meaning remains unclear. It is not a term with a limited technical meaning applying to governmental structures. Rather, it conveys a political philosophy, which is the constant search for a decision-making level as close to the citizen as possible. For some, this also implies that the political power in a society rests inherently with the individual not the state. (OECD 1996a: 44)

Subsidiarity is found in European and Canadian discussions of governance, but is rarely part of the US vocabulary.

27.2.6 Total Quality Management

Total Quality Management is important because of its close association with the international New Public Management (NPM) reform movement, about which more below. It is based on ideas that originated but were ignored in United States. TQM was first developed and widely adopted in Japan as a result of the missionary activity of two Americans, W. Edwards Deming and Joseph M. Juran. Deming was a government statistician with a Ph.D. in physics from Yale University. Duran was an engineer who advocated making quality control an integral part of management leadership, identifying quality as the means to lower costs and increase consumer satisfaction. Deming is often viewed as the contributor of statistical measurement techniques to TQM, but in fact he, with other TQM pioneers, advocated management concepts that went well beyond this.

In many respects these concepts closely resemble those of the new public management (Walton 1986). For example, both TQM and NPM emphasize the importance of the final production worker or service provider. In case of NPM this is part of a broader concept of decentralization, and a clear delineation of responsibility and accountability (by contract if necessary) between the various layers of the bureaucracy. TQM reflects Deming's belief that quality is in the hands of the line worker but that management is always responsible for outcomes. Similarly, both stress quantitative measures of output and quality. For NPM quantitative measures are the complement of delegation and decentralization in the sense that they provide management with objective measures of service delivery or other outputs. In Deming's original model of TQM, quantitative measures are used, among other things, to establish realistic quality goals and to identify best practices.[2]

One can reasonably ask whether TQM was a driver behind the internationalization or a response to it. In reality it is both; certainly it was a response to citizen discontent. It is included here as a driver because it preceded the new public management reform movement and was already internationalized before moving to the public sector. It provided a rational way of escaping what had been previously thought of as an inevitable trade-off between cost and quality. As public sector managers looked for ways to "do more with less" and improve the quality of service delivery, TQM was a readily available source of promising techniques. (Morgan, Murgatroyd 1994; Savoie 1994; Berry, Chackerian, and Wechsler in Frederickson and Johnson 1999).

27.3 RESPONSE TO THE SIX DRIVERS

International public management is a self-organizing phenomenon, although within it leadership organizations are readily apparent. Despite the lack of any overall strategy, plan, or rationale, there have been major conceptual and practical responses to the pressures for new or improved public management.

Box 27.3 Selected developments fostering international public management reform

---

1989 The crumbling of the Soviet Union, which resulted in the prospect and actuality of entry of new members to the EU, and thereby stimulated major efforts at improving public governance.

1989 The creation within the OECD of the Public Management Service.

1992 The publication of the best-selling and often cited *Reinventing Government: How the Entrepreneurial Spirit Is Transforming the Public Sector*, which was on The New York Times list of the fifteen best selling books in the United States for two months, sold 340,000 hardback and paperback copies in English, and was published in nineteen foreign language editions. (Osborne and Gaebler 1992).

1994 The agreement by the 54 Commonwealth nations to form the Commonwealth Association for Public Administration and Management. The inaugural conference of the Association in October 1994 resulted in a report entitled "Government in Transition: a New Paradigm in Public Administration," which was a version of NPM (Borins 1994).

1997 The World Bank publication of *World Development Report 1997: The State in a Changing World*.

1999 The hosting by American vice president Al Gore of a 45-nation, two-day "Global Forum on Reinventing Government," which relied heavily on experiences of non-US countries.

- *New Approaches* to public management have evolved.
- *International Institutions* have intensified their commitment to public management.
- *Prototypes* of public management systems have been developed.

All of these responses explore the potential for public management to apply across national boundaries and cultural differences.

27.3.1 Approaches to International Public Management

Five approaches to international public management span the interests of the researcher to the needs of the practitioner:

- systems and models;
- descriptive analysis, including comparative country studies, case studies and best practices;

- traditional sub-disciplines, such as budgeting and financial management, human resource management, and program implementation;
- international regulatory activities; and
- New Public Management.

27.3.1.1 *Systems and Models*

NPM has been a rich source of what has been called "alternative idea systems" (Ferlie et al. 1996). Systems and models compete in number with definitions of NPM. Ferlie et al. identify four models, which they analyse in terms of characteristics rather than countries, although they include extensive country-based supporting detail.

A different methodological approach supports *Collision and Collusion* (Wedel 1998). She is interested in relationships, in particular those among the foreign aid-giving mature democracies and the former Communist countries of Central Europe, Russia, and Ukraine. She developed a database using a large number of personal interviews and drew upon anthropology to reach her conclusions. This approach, which combines features of standard quantitative research and case studies, is of some interest to international public management, since it focuses on the largely ignored process by which public management and public policy concepts are transferred from one cultural/political environment to another.

Jann looks at administrative reform in terms of the "new steering model" (NSM), which he (and others) see as a German counterpart to NPM. He describes a number of distinguishing characteristics (relative to NPM) indicating that "the movement originated from below," i.e. from local, not central, governments and was pushed by practitioners, not academics and think tanks. It was not part of a simple political strategy to "roll back the state," (European Group of Public Administration, Kickert 1997: 85). Many of these characteristics can be found in other countries, such as Portugal, Brazil, and, at the local level, the United States.

Eilsberger sees the German experience with reform from the point of view of a transition of the former German Democratic Republic, which he suggests is at least partly transferable. Despite "several reservations," he states, "It is safe to say that the German model may be of some relevance, especially in the case of countries that reunite after having been divided by the iron curtain. One thinks South Korea, Vietnam, or Communist China and Formosa" (Baker 2002: 97). Here the term "model" has a different meaning from that of Ferlie et al., above. It would be possible to substitute "experience" or "approach" without significantly altering the meaning. Another approach to transition from an authoritarian regime was the incremental process used in Spain (see Baker 2002).

27.3.1.2 Descriptive Analysis

International public management scholarship is not based *only* on clearly articulated models from which follow hypotheses that can be subject to rigorous analysis. It encompasses both research and practice. It may be descriptive, or consist of case studies. It has many roots: traditional public administration; various reform practices in individual countries; institutional, welfare, market and macroeconomics; and total quality management (TQM) and other private sector management innovations.

As early as 1931 one can find comparative *descriptions* covering sixty-four countries, but limited to their governing systems (Mallory 1931). However, contemporary public management is more comprehensive, spanning traditional public administration, business administration, institutional economics, public choice theory, agency theory, transaction cost economics and organizational behavior, among others (OECD 1999b). This evolution of public management has coincided with the evolution of international public management.

A recent attempt to identify where reform efforts have taken place in 123 countries can be found in *Globalization and Public Administration Reform*. This effort identifies the reasons for undertaking reforms and some of their common elements, but it also shows some of the problems of analysis using many countries. The data are based on a survey, but neither the structure nor the methodology of the survey is described. The article includes a cautionary note, "Determining the extent to which *self reports* of governmental reform efforts are true is a project in itself" with the obvious problem of bias in the data source (emphasis added). The analytical portions of the article rest on anecdotal examples (Kamark 2000: 251).

Important scholarly studies include Pollitt and Bouckaert, *Public Management Reform: A Comparative Analysis* (2000); Aucoin, *The New Public Management: Canada in Comparative Perspective* (1995); Savoie, *Thatcher, Reagan, Mulroney: In Search of a New Bureaucracy* (1994), which covers bureaucratic reform in Canada, the United Kingdom, and the United States; Lane (1997), which covers thirteen individual countries plus the Nordic and Central and European countries as groupings; and Baker, *Transition from Authoritarianism* (2002), which covers ten countries.

More analytical works involve fewer countries. These include a five-country study by the Government of Finland (1997) and an OECD background paper for a symposium (1999b).

Many other comparative public management studies exist, necessarily limited in the number of countries examined. For example, the OECD's Public Management Directorate (usually cited as PUMA, now OECD GOV) published descriptive materials covering its member countries (OECD 1993; rev. 1997). SIGMA, part of PUMA, covered eleven former communist countries of central and eastern Europe in "Public Management Profiles" (OECD 1995b).

27.3.1.3 *Traditional Public Management Sub-disciplines*

Specialties, such as regulation, taxation, budgeting and financial management, auditing, organizational structures, program evaluation, and human resource development have gone international. Professional organizations in these fields, easily recognisable at the national level, now form globe-spanning networks.

The internationalization of academic sub-disciplines has been both a bottom–up and top–down process. The former takes place when experts come together for scholarly inquiry (how are these issues handled in other countries?), or professional necessity (audit and accounting procedures need to be standardized). The latter takes place when an issue such as transparency or corruption becomes of international concern, resulting in an international organization reaching out and often forming national chapters or affiliates.

The resulting entities may be little more than informal networks of academics and and/or practitioners, often held together by no more than a professional journal and periodic conferences. Alternatively, the result may be a specialized international organization at the centre of a network of national organizations, which spends money and employs staff.

Box 27.4 Representative international networks of public management sub-disciplines

---

International Federation of Accountants, with 159 member organizations in 118 countries
International Organization of Supreme Audit Institutions, which facilitates the exchange of experience among members.
European Supreme Audit Institutions, a grouping of 45 Supreme External Control Institutions on the European continent.
Civil Service Reform Virtual Network (ACSR-VNet), sponsored by the Administrative and Civil Service Thematic
Group of the World Bank, CAPAM, IIAS, and OECD GOV and SIGMA, is an information sharing, global virtual network focused on administrative and civil service reform.
OECD Senior Budget Officials group, Parliamentary Budget Officials group, and Financial Management and Accountability Officials group, three networks that provide a means for officials from the OECD's 30 member countries to discuss, develop, and perfect institutional arrangements, processes, and instruments.
Transparency International, a global anti-corruption movement with national chapters, active in more than 90 countries worldwide. TI also monitors the implementation of the OECD Convention on combating bribery.

Continued

Box 27.4 Continued

The International Institute of Public Ethics: an Australia-based international professional association for practitioners and scholars working in the field of Public Sector Ethics, part of a network of organizations including the OECD, Transparency International, government agencies such as the US Office of Government Ethics, various anti-corruption commissions, international organizations of ombudsmen, internal auditors, auditors-general, inspectors-general, and university-based specialist research units.

CIVITAS International, a worldwide non-governmental organization for civic education, composed of individuals, non-governmental associations, governmental institutions and international organizations.

International Institute for Democracy and Electoral Assistance, an inter-governmental organization with member states from all continents, which promotes stronger democratic institutions, dialogue among academics, policy-makers and practitioners, practical tools to help improve democratic processes, and transparency, accountability, and efficiency in election management.

27.3.1.4 *International Regulatory Activities*

A different kind of international public management is carried out by special purpose organizations that coordinate regulatory activities. From a conventional perspective, these organizations seem to have little to do with management and a great deal to do with the policies of specific activities such as the postal service, telecommunications, air traffic control, police and public safety, fisheries, immigration, atomic energy, and health. However, regulation has become a central management issue. It was a major part of New Zealand reforms. In the United States the Office of Information and Regulatory Affairs is located in the White House Office of Management and Budget. The OECD has highlighted it as a major area of concentration within public management. With globalization the process of harmonizing regulatory practice among countries has become both more important and more intense. As a result, the organizations sponsoring harmonizing efforts are involved in activities of significant management concern to participating countries.

27.3.1.5 *The Special Case of NPM*

New public management (NPM) now has many parents, ranging from "Next Steps" in Prime Minister Thatcher's government in the United Kingdom, to the Labour Party reforms in Australia and New Zealand in the 1980s, to concepts borrowed from Total Quality Management. It is easy to gain the impression that international public management and NPM are the same. This is to some extent no more than a reflection of the reality that many scholars working internationally have focused on NPM and NPM issues. But in addition there is some confusion of public management reform *in general* with NPM. This confusion comes about in part because NPM has no standard definition, although definitions overlap. It is also sometimes assumed that public management reform and NPM are similar or identical. For example, the reforms advocated by the OECD overlap substantially with characteristics usually attributed to NPM, so it is hardly surprising that the two are sometimes considered the same (see, for example, Sahlin-Andersson 2002).

However, reform has and is taking place in countries without regard to either NPM or the OECD. Concepts such as subsidiarity, transparency, and regulatory reform, as well as practical application of reform in countries such as Spain and Portugal, predate NPM. Moreover, NPM is relevant marginally, if at all, to many newly emerging democracies whose needs are basic. In these countries, eliminating corruption is more important than sorting out purchaser-provider relationships, financial auditing is more important than quantifying performance management, and accurate and honest cash accounting is more important than accrual accounting.

For many countries, public management reform is approached as a means for meeting domestic needs, the requirements of international lending institutions, the standards of international financial markets, or the practices of the European Community. Whether the resulting reform proposals are NPM or have a close association with NPM is not, for them, a significant issue.

Therefore, while NPM has dominated the international discourse in recent years, much more has been going on. Some critics indicate that the diversity and proliferation of reform ideas can themselves become a problem. Lane states, "Public sector reform has become one of those things that no government can do without." As a result, "The tendency towards a garbage-can process is reinforced by the competition among politicians for offering various proposals for public sector reform" (1997: 14).

NPM itself has come in for considerable criticism. This can be, perhaps unfairly, characterized along the following lines. First, critics say, it is just another passing fad. Moreover, they say, careful reading of public administration reveals that new public management cannot be correctly characterized as public administration. Even if it can be characterized as overlapping with public administration, it is simply a rearrangement of old ideas. Even if it is more than a new mixture of old ideas, the concept is unsound not least because it rests on no clear theoretical basis. Finally, in this line of criticism, even if it were supported by theory, it is in conflict with basic concepts of constitutional law, the responsible execution of statutes, and the proper distinction between the functions of the private and public sectors.

This is not the place to revisit those arguments, but they can be found in Lynn (1992, 1997), Moe (1997*a*, 1997*b*, 1994), Frederickson (1994; 1996), and Denhardt (1996). Despite the misgivings, there are many who embrace NPM and others who simply ignore the arguments.

27.3.1.6 *Results and Uses*

For public management as a whole, application of professional findings to the real word of practice presents a number of difficulties. Careful analysis based on a consistent framework is necessarily limited to one or a few countries unless carried out by institutions such as the OECD. One interesting approach was that used by the Finnish Ministry of Finance, mentioned above. In addition to the five country studies, the work included the results of a set of standardized questions put to each of the governments. The limits of such self-reporting in terms of objectivity and completeness are well known. Nevertheless, this seems to be an under-appreciated effort.

A kind of non-quantitative meta-analysis is an alternative that probably requires more small-scale studies than are now available. It would also require some thought on the question of "What is the question?" Hill and Lynn report on the results of such an effort, reviewing more than 800 studies of "governance research" in more than seventy academic journals (2004). They state that "most of these findings are contingent: few if any generic management principles are directly confirmed. Furthermore, our review indicates than governance can matter" (p. 8).

The international community already believes that governance matters. The word "contingent" is of central importance to those who are concerned with management techniques that are transferable. No one is naïve enough to believe that all techniques are transferable to all settings. This leads to the question "contingent on what?"

This question is being addressed in an unsystematic way by some combination of individual or group expert experience and feedback and collective judgment. Individual and group experience has grown out of the hundreds of consulting missions related to public management. With the fall of the Berlin Wall in November of 1989 the number of such missions increased greatly as former Soviet Bloc countries tried to restructure their governments and aid donors opened their pocketbooks (Wedel 1998). The trend continued, fueled by the Mexican financial crisis of 1995 and the Asian financial crises of 1997–9, and further stimulated by the World Bank's dramatic policy statement on the importance of governance to development in 1997. It is reasonable to assume that expert consultants know a lot more then they did in 1990, and the consulting groups have been able to build up practices with considerable depth of knowledge.

Collective judgment derives from organized efforts, particularly by the World Bank and the OECD, to bring together groups to evaluate reform efforts or develop best practices. This process results in reports, staff papers, and guidelines, many of which are available to the public. The most tangible and systematic results are related to the prototypes of public management practices discussed below.

In addition to the IFIs and the OECD, there are single-purpose international organizations that are devoted exclusively to public management. They are quite small when compared to the IFIs and the OECD.

The International Public Management Network (IPMN) is a relatively new stand-alone organization. In addition to research conferences, it produces both an electronic and a conventional journal. The Commonwealth Association for Public Administration and Management (CAPAM) is also a single purpose organization, with participation by "individuals and organizations [from the Commonwealth countries] having an interest in the practice, study, and improvement of public management" (Borins 1994).

The International Institute of Administrative Sciences (IIAS) has existed for over seventy years (since 1930). Its focus is on "How governance is done and how it could be done better" (IIAS website). Although it has ninety member states and national sections, its limited budget (€1 million) restricts its scope to publishing the International Review of Administrative Sciences (in English, French, and Arabic) and some books, and to sponsoring three conferences a year.

None of these plays an important role in the systematic development of public management. Is there a lesson in this? Public Management at the international level has—*with one important exception*—been promoted largely by institutions that have as their primary mission economic development and globalization, not management for its own sake.

The exception is not an international institution, a think tank, a professional association, or a network. It is NPM, which has been the major mechanism driving the internationalization of public management scholarship. This makes some sense. From its inception it was associated with several countries—more were added as time passed. It was also assumed to be transferable, where and to what degree unspecified, although it was sometimes characterized as an Anglo or Anglo-American phenomenon. It was associated by some with the OECD, although that organization carefully avoided using the term.

Any doubt as to its importance as a vehicle for discussion of international public management can be eliminated by reference to the recent compendium of articles in *New Public Management* (McLaughlin, Osborne, and Ferlie 2002), which considers NPM in the context of a broad range of countries and international organizations. Further evidence can be found throughout the latest edition of *Public Management and Administration: An Introduction*. In this basic textbook NPM is not presented as novel or exotic. Rather it supplants the "traditional model of administration, derived from Weber, Wilson and Taylor..." (Hughes 2003: 3).

27.3.2 Institutional Development

The most significant institutional development in international public management has been the unexpected and unplanned evolution of economic development institutions as conduits of public management knowledge and experience. No specific date or event can properly capture the significance of this. The most important of these are the World Bank and the OECD.

The Bank and the Fund were established July 22, 1944, in the aftermath of the Second World War at the International Monetary and Financial Conference, Bretton Woods, New Hampshire, USA. The original primary mission of the Bank was to provide financial resources for post-Second World War Reconstruction. The role of the IMF was to stabilize the international monetary system by providing balance-of-payments support to countries facing external financial pressures.

The OECD has emerged as the leading international organization in the development of tools for the transfer of public management practice. The IFIs have more money than the OECD and support a broader array of public management technical assistance missions and projects, but do so as part of their overall lending and development efforts. The OECD's Public Management Directorate (usually cited as PUMA, now OECD GOV) is focused entirely on knowledge exchange and development.

The forerunner of the OECD, the Organization for European Economic Co-operation (OEEC), was formed to administer American and Canadian aid under the Marshall Plan for reconstruction of Europe after the Second World War. It sought to harmonize, to the extent possible, economic and social policies. As part of that effort, it developed an extensive database, with emphasis on economics, of the member countries, becoming what we would now call a "knowledge organization." The OECD took over from the OEEC in 1961 to maintain and develop its policy coordination and knowledge development functions.

At its inception, the OECD conducted technical assistance activities in some of its member countries. As these activities were phased out, the OECD experimented with conferences and publications on aspects of public management, beginning with public budgeting. This work expanded and, in 1989, was formalized as the "Public Management Service" (PUMA) of the OECD.

After the fall of the Berlin Wall, PUMA used its accumulated experience to assist emerging market economies in central and eastern Europe in making their transition from centrally planned to market systems. To do so it established SIGMA (Support for Improvement in Governance and Management in central and eastern European Countries) as a subsidiary organization.

The public management program was recently reorganized into the new Public Governance and Territorial Development Directorate (GOV). According to the OECD website, it "assists countries in adapting their public sector governance arrangements to the changing needs of society. The Directorate supports mutual

---

Box 27.5 IFI public management activities

IFI	Activities (past and prospective)
Asian Development Bank	Projects designed to increase governance quality through Policy measures, project components, or technical assistance.
Inter-American Development Bank	Country studies on modernization of the State and strengthening of civil society. Dialogue with recipient countries.
IMF	Policy advice, financial support and technical assistance to help countries ensure the rule of law, improve the efficiency and accountability of their public sectors, and reduce corruption.
World Bank	Country Assistance Strategies that diagnose country governance situations. Increased lending for governance and institution building. Analytic work and external learning and knowledge sharing.
African Development Bank	Advocacy of good governance in policy dialogues and consultations with regional member countries.

---

learning and peer review amongst countries on key organizational, structural and territorial development issues" (http://www.OECD.GOV 2004).

27.3.3 Prototypes of Public Management Practices

Templates or prototypes for public management processes and operation are commonplace in national public management systems, and essential where consistency is required of subordinate governmental units. For the first time they have been designed to be adaptable across countries. They are a natural outcome of international public management.

Templates or prototypes provide instructions and guidelines for public management systems. They are foundations for "how to" presentations or publications: "how to establish a government corporation," how to modernize a municipal budget system," "how to use performance measures." With the continued use of international technical assistance programs in public management, prototypes are being more fully developed, and "how to" guidelines are continuing to increase in size and number.

Before these were developed, knowledge transfer was primarily a face-to-face exchange from one technician to another, or a team to a client. What the recipient country heard was largely determined by the individuals involved. In management areas where there is a high degree of consensus, this may not be a problem. However, there are often several ways of carrying out public management functions, each with its own national tradition and philosophy. In a perfect world one might advocate making all the alternatives available, with the understanding that the recipient country would use what was likely to be the most effective within its own national context. This is impractical.

Prototypes have been formulated by expert teams, largely under the aegis of international institutions. In the case of the OECD, the organization uses its own country membership to establish a set of guidelines. In many cases these are explicitly endorsed by the membership. The World Bank places a greater stress on the use of staff to develop prototypes, but using feedback from country experience as part of the process.

The approaches listed in Table 27.1 are explicitly designed in the context of international public management. They are generic in that they are not limited in

Table 27.1 Public management templates and guidelines

Area	Source	Description
Taxation	World Bank	A comprehensive diagnostic framework for revenue administration.
	OECD	The principles of good tax administration.
Regulation	OECD	Guidelines to enhance the performance, cost-effectiveness, or legal quality of regulations and related government formalities.
Corruption	OECD	An analysis of common trends and good practices and a comprehensive database of integrity measures in OECD countries.
Transparency	World Bank	Code of good practices to provide information on monetary and fiscal policies to the public in a clear and timely manner.
	IMF	Code and manual on fiscal transparency practices to provide public information about the structure and functions of government, fiscal policy intentions, public sector accounts, and fiscal projections
Public Expenditure Management	World Bank	A framework for attaining sound budget performance and guidance on the key elements of a well-performing public expenditure management framework (PEMF).

their applicability to a specific setting. This is illustrated with a highly condensed example based on the World Bank's Public Expenditure Management Framework. This illustrates only the broad structure of a highly detailed database, which includes tool kits, manuals, instructions for assessing a country's public expenditure system, reports of over 50 country experiences using this framework between 2000 and 2003, and training.

Box 27.6 Public expenditure management framework

Level 1: Macro Policies—Meet National Economic Goals and Ensure That Cash Balances Will Be Available to Pay Bills

> "If you do not get the macroeconomic policy right nothing else matters."
> Gramme Scott, former Secretary of Finance, New Zealand

Purpose of macro policy:

- Control public sector debt
- Establish tax and other receipts policies
- Set expenditure limits ("Top-down budgeting targets")
- **Ensure future cash balances will be available to meet commitments**

Macro Policies Lead to:

- Top–down expenditure limits

Macro policies are concerned with:

- National Saving Rates
- Balance of Payments
- Overall Investment
- Inflation

Macro Policies are NOT Concerned with:

- **Strategic Allocation of Funds by Sector, (Health, Education, National Security, etc.)**

Level 2: Strategic Choices: Set National Strategic Objectives and Enforce Budget Discipline (Requires Bottom–up Budgeting)

Spending Ministers submit requests to budget office based on:

- National Needs
- Policy Analysis
- Cost/Benefit, Cost Effectiveness Analysis
- Program Evaluations
- Performance Measures
- Political Considerations

Continued

Box 27.6 Continued

Budget Office:

- Makes initial broad allocations to spending ministries
- May require specific decrements and increments to a current budget level
- Provides guidance on the content and format of budget requests to be submitted by spending agencies
- Reviews Requests
- Presents Options to Political Decision Makers
- Prepares Budget

Reconciliation of Top–down limits and bottom–up requirements
Problem:

- Spending Ministries Requests Exceed Top-Down Spending Limits by Large Amounts
- Budget Office Allocations to Meet Top-Down Spending Limits are Unacceptable to Spending Ministries.

Solution:

- **Budget Office Must Manage a Process that Permits Senior Policy Makers to Reconcile Requests with Spending Limits.**

For this Process to be Effective, Spending Agencies May Appeal Ministry of Finance Budget Allocations To Political Leadership.
However:

- Ministry of Finance must be an "Honest Broker"
- Everyone must accept the need for Fiscal Discipline and therefore top–down Expenditure Limits
- **Reallocations must be a zero-sum game**

Level 3: Execution, Performance and Accountability: Operating Units Approve Payments for Goods, Services, Grants, etc.
Budget Office:

- Reviews budget laws
- Allocates funds to spending ministries
- Informs ministries of earmarking, restrictions or other special conditions that affect the use of funds

Spending Agencies Commit (or Obligate) Funds by :

- Signing contracts
- Hiring staff
- Making grants
- Purchasing goods and services
- Manage programs, administer contracts, negotiate agreements with third parties and monitor results
- Maintain internal accounting control systems
- Approve cash payments

27.4 INTERNATIONAL PUBLIC MANAGEMENT AT THE TURN OF THE CENTURY

Today governance has moved alongside economics as a major world preoccupation. Many of the conditions that characterize international public management today are similar to those that applied to development economics in the 1960s. The ascendancy of economics to a privileged position began in the 1950s, when the industrialized countries began to undertake one of the most ambitious tasks in history: to promote economic growth and reduce poverty in the Third World. The reconstruction of the post-Second World War economies of Europe and Japan was well underway. But the world was hardly calm. Third World counties, many of which were in—or about to be in—a post-colonial stage of development, appeared restive, unstable, or destitute. After decades of conflict, China had become communist. Economic development gained support because it could be viewed as humanitarian, enlightened self-interest, or a key factor in fighting the cold war by different groups all at the same time. The World Bank and the IMF shifted their attention away from reconstruction and toward development. An astonishing number of countries undertook bilateral foreign aid programs. The OECD took on a major role as a foreign aid policy clearinghouse and coordinator.

In this environment, economic development policy was a driving force, and economists were to the foreign aid establishment what doctors were to the World Health Organization. Economic development has made enormous strides with the emergence of Southeast Asia, China, India, and much of Latin America as economic growth centres. Many former communist states are finally achieving prosperity. Yet the world is still hardly calm. Global terrorism and ethnic strife have replaced the cold war as major international concerns. Newly found prosperity has not brought with it automatic social and political stability, nor has it brought an end to rampant corruption. In this new environment economic policy alone is insufficient. Public management now competes for the kind of attention once given almost entirely to economics.

At the turn of the century, however, the public management community faces conditions quite different from those of the economic community in the 1950s. Consider three overlapping areas of international public management: academia, supporting institutions, and practitioners.

- Academic research and teaching of international public management has not gained the leading edge status that development economics did.
- Supporting institutions are less committed. The IFIs are the largest source of funds that public management draws on, but it is a newcomer to their portfolio

of activities, and the economists are still in charge. The large foundations have mostly left the international field.

- The practitioners have less coherence than the economists developed. Few are likely to use professional titles equivalent to "development economist" or "international economist" on their résumés, not least because comparable titles do not exist.

There is a substantial amount of excellent thought and research from the academic community, but, except for NPM, no major debates have developed comparable to the great economic development debates over import substitution vs. export development, basic industry vs. agriculture and small-scale manufacturing, or central planning vs. free markets.

Hill and Lynn (2004) state, "An important objective of governance research is to identify the determinants of governmental performance in order to inform administrative reform, public policy design, and public management practice." In international public management it is not a major stretch to go further: the objectives are to find out which practices are transferable and effective and under what circumstances. An economic equivalent of Hill and Lynn might be: "An important objective of economic research is to identify the determinants of economic performance in order to inform structural adjustment (macro policy), public policy design, and income distribution policies." However, there are as yet no public management equivalents of macroeconomic variables (national savings, investment, net exports, and the money supply), efficient markets and income distribution.

This brings us to the institutions, which are trying to learn and teach simultaneously, with some sense of urgency. The IFIs and the OECD have incorporated public management into the mainstream of their activities and sponsored major efforts at developing public management prototypes with a view to the all-important issue of transferability. In so doing they have relied more on expert opinion and experience than on theory.

The OECD approach combines gathering experience from its members with establishing standards to which it members may wish to conform, or, in some cases such as corruption and regulation, are expected to conform. The feedback from country members to the OECD secretariat provides a constant reality check on the work of its experts. The OECD is a consensus organization, so the inevitable compromises involved in developing OECD doctrine are unlikely to please anyone completely. However, individual products are often surprisingly clear and forceful. The OECD has made its material much more accessible and has expanded its reach, both by adding new members and by developing relationships with non-member countries, notably China, Russia, and Brazil.

Moreover, it has reached a new, more confident, stage of development, consolidating its earlier, often experimental experience into a more clearly defined set of functions: budgeting and financial management process, the civil service, public transparency and accountability, powers of departments vis-à-vis central agencies, creation and closure of organizations, use of private sector service providers, and devolution or centralization of decision-making power. The OECD view is that while "these levers can indeed change behavior; they need to be operated judiciously with a clear sense of the problem being addressed, and an understanding of their dynamic, longer-term, and cultural consequences" (2002).

27.5 The Future of International Public Management

Like many human endeavors, international public management is largely self-organizing. Whatever centralized organization takes place is limited to a few international organizations and perhaps a government that may, from time to time, engage in a systematic effort at public management reform. Centrally managed international efforts can be found in operational organizations ranging from those that provide emergency refugee assistance to those that regulate telecommunications, but they are unlikely candidates to provide leadership for public management. Centralized leadership might be provided by the international organizations that are currently involved in public management or by one or more major private foundations. This was the institutional basis for the remarkable development and adoption of new technology that was a major component of the agricultural green revolution. However, the coordinated political support that was behind the green revolution shows no signs of emerging in support of public management.

An alternative could be to take advantage of the existing debate over NPM in a more organized way. The multiple definitions of NPM can invite confusion, but the extent of their reach covers most of public management and touches on many practices and the reasons behind them. Devolution of responsibility, for example, can promote debate on subsidiarity, total quality management, or the applicability of institutional economic theory and concepts of economic efficiency. NPM's use of quantitative techniques and performance measures can similarly be discussed in terms of TQM, principal/agent theory or an essential element of output and outcome measures in the public resource allocation process.

The controversy over NPM can also be seen as an asset. The vigorous debates among the proponents and detractors have provided a remarkably useful opportunity—it would be an overstatement to say focus—for discussion of public management values and techniques. It has been international in scope from the beginning. Moe's (and many others') vigorous and extensive criticism of NPM serves as a useful restatement of traditional public administration values in the context of twenty-first-century governance. NPM proponents have similarly been challenged to justify NPM concepts not purely on the basis of "In Search of Excellence" inductive observation of what works, but in terms of principles that explain why what works, works.

NPM involves change and therefore provides a useful existing basis for international public management dialogue on the key question: what is transferable and under what conditions. This question requires addressing a criticism that goes beyond NPM: that public management in general suffers from the implicit assumption that states ought "to develop into states on the European-Atlantic model" (Finer 1997: 5).

The "what is transferable" question has been part of the debate since the beginning of NPM because of its international nature. The "under what conditions" question applies to the political and cultural context in which change takes place. To some extent the cross-sectional nature of most research—looking at different systems at a given point in time—is limiting in this respect because it tends to subordinate consideration of the roots of current systems. Moreover, there is little consideration of how public management systems may have been influenced by worldwide phenomena, such as the emergence of Islamic law, the Napoleonic code, and the French and Marxist Revolutions. The interdisciplinary nature of the "under what conditions" inquiry has been recognized as the relationship of public management to governance has evolved. How to conduct this type of research is less clear, however.

Of course, those who support current reforms can argue that they are *not* based on Finer's "European-Atlantic model," which, he says, reflects the incorrect assumption that "the state originated only at the end of the Middle Ages in Europe" (1997: 5). Rather, they may argue, reforms represent best practices, and are based on what is required to participate effectively in the global economy. They reflect "a wealth of cross country experience on a wide range of issues" (World Bank 1997: 14–15).

Nevertheless, Finer's point is well taken. Most of the people in the world do not live in societies whose political roots go back to the Middle Ages in Europe. The problems involved in developing new western-style democracies in their countries are evident from the daily press reports. Western technical assistance practitioners working at the ground level refer to the need to understand and take into account the social and political context of the countries in which they are working. So does the World Bank: "There is no unique model for change" (1997: 15). Pollitt (2002) cautions,

What works and what does not tends to be heavily context-dependent. That is to say, a technique or organizational structure that succeeds in one place may fail in another. There is no set of general tools that can be transferred from one jurisdiction to another, all around the world, with confidence that they will work well every time. This means we have to look carefully at contexts, and at the "terms of trade" each time we are thinking of borrowing a good management idea from somewhere else.

Thus, there needs to be an open and honest recognition of the difficulties and frustrations that reformers face in countries with non-European antecedents. The incompatibility of fundamentalist Islamic or communist ideas of governance with those of the West highlight the essential truth that modern constitutional democracies are not the result of a natural evolution, but in fact represent a set of competing social values and political systems.

NOTES

1. In the United States, for example, the idea of contracting out can be explicitly traced to the administration of President Eisenhower, and accrual accounting, a central aspect of the New Zealand reforms, was recommended by the 1967 Commission on Budget Concepts, although it was the one recommendation that was discarded. Devolution and decentralization have been discussed and practiced in at least some of the Nordic countries from the beginning of modern public management. Performance measurement relating programs or activities to outputs goes back at least as far as the Program Planning Budgeting System in the United States. While the PPBS as a structured budget decision-making system organized in the 1960s is seen, quite rightly, as a failure that was abandoned, the cost/benefit and cost/effectiveness logic that were the essence of PPBS not only survived but is heavily embedded in public policy decisions today.

2. This deserves more consideration than is possible here, since there is no obvious reason for the observed similarities. NPM and TQM are neither management structures nor management "solutions." Both are principles or approaches that emphasize the need for continuous change. In this important sense, both are best seen as processes, rather than theories or static solutions.

REFERENCES

AUCOIN, P. (1995), *The New Public Management: Canada in Comparative Perspective*, Montreal: Institute for Research on Public Policy.

BAKER, R. (ed.) (2002), *Transitions from Authoritarianism*, Westport, CT: Praeger.

BORINS, S. (1994), *Government in Transition*, Toronto: Commonwealth Association for Public Administration and Management.

CAROTHERS, T. (1999), *Aiding Democracy Abroad*, Washington, DC: Carnegie Endowment for International Peace.

DENHARDT, R. B. (1996), "Public Administration, Public Service & Democratic Citizenship," *Delaware Public Affairs Report* 3, University of Delaware Graduate College of Urban Affairs and Public Policy.

EUROPEAN GROUP OF PUBLIC ADMINISTRATION (1997), *Public Management and Administrative Reform in Western Europe*, ed. W. J. M. Kickert, Cheltenham: Edward Elgar.

FERLIE, E., ASHBURNER, L., FITZGERALD, L., and PETTIGREW, A. (1996), *The New Public Management in Action*, Oxford: Oxford University Press.

FINER, S. E. (1997), *The History of Government*, Oxford: Oxford University Press.

FREDERICKSON, H. G. (1994), Paper prepared for a meeting of the National Academy of Public Administration.

—— (1996), *The Spirit of Public Administration*, San Francisco: Jossey-Bass.

—— and JOHNSTON, J. (eds.) (1999), *Public Management Reform and Innovation* Tuscaloosa: University of Alabama Press.

HILL, C. J., and LYNN, L. E., JR. (2004), "Governance and Public Management, an Introduction," *Journal of Policy Analysis and Management* 23(1): 3–11.

HUGHES, O. (2003), *Public Management and Administration*, 3rd edn., New York: Palgrave Macmillan.

JONES, L. R., and KETTL, D. F., "Assessing the Public Management Reform in an International Context," *International Public Management Review* 4(1): electronic journal, at http://www.ipmr.net.

KAMARCK, E. C. (2000), "Globalisation and Public Administrative Reform," in J. S. Nye and J. D. Donahue, *Governance in a Globalizing World* Cambridge, MA; *Visions of Governance for the 21st Century*, Washington, DC: Brookings Institution Press.

LANE, J. (ed.) (1992), *Public Sector Reform: Rationale, Trends and Problems*, London: Sage.

LYNN, L. E., JR. (1992), *Management without Managers: the False Promise of Administrative Reform*, Working Paper Series: 92–3 Chicago: The Irving P. Harris Graduate School of Public Policy Studies.

—— (1997), "The New Public Management as an International Phenomenon: A Skeptical View," in L. R. Jones, K. Schedler, and S. W. Wade (eds.), *Advances In International Comparative Management*, Suppl. 3 of *Advances in International Comparative Management*, JAI Press,.

MCCOURT, W. (2002), "New Public Management in Developing Countries," in McLaughlin, Osborne and Ferlie 2002: 227–42.

MCLAUGHLIN, K., OSBORNE, S., FERLIE, E. (eds.) (2002), *New Public Management*, London: Routledge.

MALLORY, W. (ed.) (1931), *Political Handbook of the World*, New Haven: Yale University Press.

MOE, R. C. (1994), "The 'Reinventing Government' Exercise: Misinterpreting the Problem, Misjudging the Consequences," *Public Administration Review* 54(2): 111–22.

—— (1997a), *Ethics Administration Confronts the New Public Management*, Washington, DC: Congressional Research Service.

—— (1997b), "The Importance of Public Law," in R. Cooper (ed.), *Handbook of Public Law and Administration* San Francisco: Jossey-Bass, 41–57.

MORGAN, C. and MURGATROYD, S. (1994), *Total Quality Management in the Public Sector*, Philadelphia: Open University Press.

ORGANISATION FOR ECONOMIC COOPERATION AND DEVELOPMENT (1993; 1997), *Public Management: OECD Country Profiles*, Paris: OECD.

—— (1995a), *Governance in Transition: Public Management Reforms in OECD Countries* Paris: OECD

—— (1995b), SIGMA Support for Improvement in Governance and Management in Central and Eastern European Countries, *Public Management Profiles*" Paris: OECD.

ORGANISATION FOR ECONOMIC COOPERATION AND DEVELOPMENT (1996a), *Ministerial Symposium on the Future of Public Services* Paris: OECD.

—— (1996b), "Managing Structural Deficit Reduction," *Public Management Srvice Occasional Papers* 11, Paris: OECD.

—— (1999a), *A Synthesis of Reform Experiences in Nine OECD Countries: Government Roles and Functions, and Public Management* Paris, OECD.

—— (1999b), *Government of The Future: Getting From Here To There*, PUMA/SGF 99 Paris: OECD.

—— (2002), "Public Sector Modernization, a New Agenda," GOV/PUMA 2002, Paris.

OSBORNE, D., and GAEBLER, T. (1992), *Reinventing Government*, Reading, MA: Addison-Wesley.

OSBORNE, S., and MCLAUGHLIN, K. (2002), "The New Public Management in Context," in McLaughlin, Osborne, and Ferlie.

POLLITT, C., and BOUCKAERT, G. (2000), *Public Management Reform: A Comparative Analysis* Oxford: Oxford University Press.

SAHLIN-ANDERSSON, K. (2002), "National, International, and Transactional Contsrtuctions of New Public Management," in T Christensen and P. Lægreid, *New Public Management*, Aldershot: Ashgate.

SAVOIE, D. J. (1994), *Thatcher, Reagan, Mulroney: In Search of a New Bureaucracy*, Toronto: University of Toronto Press.

STIGLITZ, J. (2002), *Globalisation and Its Discontents*, New York: W.W. Norton.

WALTON, M. (1986), *The Deming Management Method*, New York: Putnam.

WEDEL, J. (1998), *Collision and Collusion* New York: St. Martin's Press.

WORLD BANK (1997), *World Development Report 1997: The State in a Changing World*, World Bank: Oxford University Press.

CHAPTER 28

....

MANAGEMENT CONSULTANCY

....

DENIS SAINT MARTIN

28.1 INTRODUCTION

....

MANAGEMENT consultants have become increasingly visible players in the process of public sector reform over the last twenty years. While in the 1960s attempts at restructuring government were carried out largely as an internal matter, in the 1980s and 1990s reform efforts in various OECD countries often included the participation of management consultants from the private sector. Global consulting firms are also involved in redesigning bureaucracies in developing countries, often as part of the conditions of "structural adjustment loans" provided by international financial institutions (Dolowitz 2000: 18). Over the past years, a growing number of scholars have underlined the role of management consultants in developing the ideas that are part of the New Public Management (NPM) (Christensen 2003; Perl and White 2002). Some have written about the "new cult of the management consultant" in government (Smith 1994: 130), and described consultants as "intellectual mercenaries" (Leys 1999) or "hired guns" that "politicians can use to bypass reluctant civil servants" (Bakvis 1997: 106), while others have coined the term "consultocracy" (Hood and Jackson: 1991: 224) to underline the growing influence of consultants in the public management process. In Australia, a study goes as far as saying that consultants "reoriented the nation's social policy framework" (Martin 1998), while in France, a former Minister of Industry claimed that a minister arriving at a cabinet meeting with a report from McKinsey or the Boston Consulting Group is like "Moïse redescendant de la montagne avec les Tables de la loi" (Le Monde 1999).

What accounts for the growing importance of management consultants in the public policy process? This is the key question explored in this chapter. To do so, I rely on historical–institutionalist theories emphasizing the interactions between processes of state formation (and transformation) and social knowledge (Hall 1989; Rueschemeyer and Skocpol 1996). The approach used is both historical and comparative, looking at the role of consultants in public service reforms in various European and North American countries, and at how governments have used consultants since at least the 1960s with the Planning, Programming, and Budgeting System (PPBS) movement, whereas in the 1980s it was more linked to the "audit explosion" (Power 1997) and more recently, to e-Government (Dunleavy et al. 2001). Whether the growing presence of consultants in government is the result of politicians who want to broaden their sources of policy advice, or of the lobbying efforts of consulting firms seeking to expand their activities in the public sector, is an open question. But like the dynamics of demand and supply in the economy we know that the two go together. Accordingly, the chapter is organized into two major sections, the first looking at the demand for consultants in public service reform. The second looks at the supply side of the equation. The conclusion discusses the effects of the growing use of consultants in the public sector on the government and the consulting industry.

28.2 THE DEMAND FOR MANAGEMENT CONSULTANCY IN GOVERNMENT

Management consultancy is an industry largely dominated by US-based firms. The United States represents more than half of the world market for consulting services, estimated to be around $119 billion in 2003 (Kennedy Information 2003). And as the available evidence suggests, consultants have always been more actively involved in the policy process in Washington than in any other national capitals in the developed world (GAO 1992; Guttman and Willner 1976; Heinz et al. 1993). These are two basic facts that cannot be ignored in any discussion of the role of consultants in government. Taken together, they also account for a great deal of all the talk about the "Americanization" of both public and business management practices (Bissessar 2002; Djelic 1998; Locke 1996). Various observers have underlined, for instance, the impact of *In Search of Excellence* by Peters and Waterman (two McKinsey consultants at the time) on public sector reform in various countries (Aucoin 1990), or the influence of *Reinventing Government* by Osborne and Gaebler (1992), described in the British press as the "two management 'fixers' who have achieved cult status in the United States and whose ideas could help transform Britain's public sector" (Holman 1997: 9). As Pollitt once wrote, "management consultants have contributed important ideas" to British public service reform, but as he noted, the traffic has been largely one way: "it is American management ideas and American management gurus that have seized the attention of UK politicians and public officials" (1996: 84–5). But before looking at how consultants seek to seize the attention of public officials, the following section investigates the demand for management consultancy in government and focuses on three types of factor: public sector size, the organization of the policy advisory system, and the impact of politics on how, over the years, decision makers have framed the use of consultants in government.

28.2.1 Public Sector Size

All things being equal, a larger public sector is likely to consume more consulting services than a smaller one. Of course, size in itself does not automatically generate demand. But as what might be called a "structural" factor, size is generally correlated to organizational complexity and issues of coordination and control, all of which are likely to exercise pressures on managers to seek help in finding appropriate solutions (Kipping and Engwall 2002). This, at least, is the explanation that policy makers provided in the 1960s, arguing that outside expertise was needed to help public managers face the new organizational challenges created by the growth of the modern welfare state (Fry 1993). A larger public sector also provides more opportunities for suppliers of consulting services as there are more 'organizational doors' on which consultants can knock in trying to promote and sell their products. But as Table 28.1 indicates, that hypothesis is not supported by empirical evidence.

The demand for consulting services, as measured by the revenues coming from public sector work, is not higher in countries that have a larger state sector. There is a positive relation between the two variables only in the case of Canada, while France and Britain represent two radically opposite scenarios. There is no comparable data for the American consulting industry, but the available evidence (Gross 2001) suggests a situation not unlike that of Britain (i.e., smaller public sector and greater share of consulting revenues from government). In fact, it is also possible that the hypothesis works the other way around: that a smaller public sector consumes more consulting services because more work is contracted-out to private sector suppliers, whereas a larger public sector will tend to rely more on in-house staff. But whatever the direction of the causal connection, the link between public sector size and the demand for consulting services is not as simple as one might have expected.

Table 28.1. Public sector size and revenues share of consulting industry from public
sector work in 2000

	France	Germany	Britain	Italy	Spain	Canada
Share of public employment To total employment	24	15	14	15	15	18
Share of revenues derived From public sector work	8	7	13	6	4	13

Source: European Federation of Management Consulting Associations (FEACO) 2000, *Survey of the European Management Consultancy Market*; OECD, 2001. *Highlights of Public Sector Pay and Employment Trends.*

28.2.2 The Openness of the Policy Advisory System

To make policy, politicians rely heavily on the advice of experts (Hall 1989). In some states, this advice comes primarily from an echelon of permanent civil servants who have a virtual monopoly on access both to official information and to the ultimate decision makers. In others, a new administration can bring its own advisers and consult widely with outside experts. This is the case of the US, where the practice of recruiting "inners and outers" (MacKenzie 1987), a legacy of the spoils system, allows each newly elected President to appoint a large number of outsiders to senior civil service positions (Heclo 1977). One of the key factors driving the demand for management consulting services in government is thus largely institutional in nature: the organization of the policy advisory system.

In the US, the greater openness of the policy advisory system has given birth to a wide range of external sources of advice in Washington: private foundations, non-profit research organizations, think tanks, management consulting firms and various professional associations. By contrast, in parliamentary systems, policy advisory systems have traditionally been much less open than in the US (Plowden 1987). In such systems, recruitment into government is generally less flexible, governed by strict guidelines emphasizing conformity to established civil service norms (Campbell and Wilson 1995). The consequence of this is that the demand for external sources of advice has, traditionally, been more limited, thus making management consultants much less present in the policy process.

28.2.3 The Effect of Politics

In his comparative analysis of policy advice and the public service, John Halligan noted that in many countries, there has been over the years "a tendency to bring in more outsiders" (1995: 146). This tendency—which has contributed to the demand for consultancy in government—is largely a political creation, in the sense that it is politicians who have decided to transform policy making institutions and make them more open to outside sources of advice. From the 1960s to now, political leaders and policy makers have framed the use of consultants in government in at least three different ways, each of which is discussed in the following pages: (1): consultants as rational planners; (2) as "cost-cutters" and the apostles of the NPM, and (3) as partners in governance.

28.2.3.1 *Rational Planning and Technocratic Politics in the 1960s*

In the 1960s, at a time when Keynesianism was still influential and faith in the capacity of the social sciences to help solve public problems was high, decision makers in government were looking for new ways to strengthen and rationalize the interventions of the state in society and the economy. This was the era of "rational management" (Aucoin 1986), of the PPBS and the beginning of the so-called "policy analysis industry" (Pal 1992: 66). The goal was to make the management of the modern welfare state more "scientific" and professional (Fischer 1990). For instance, in Britain, the 1966 Fulton Committee on the Civil Service complained that, "too few civil servants are skilled managers" (Fulton 1968: 12). It sought to open up the civil service and argued that it was too closed: "there is not enough awareness of how the world outside Whitehall works" (p. 12). Fulton encouraged the "free flow of men, ideas and knowledge" between the civil service and the world of industry and research (p. 13).

In Canada, the 1962 Royal Commission on Government Organization argued in favor of "letting the managers manage" (Canada 1962). To professionalize government management, Glassco saw the need to learn from the private sector. As a result of Glassco and Fulton, both the Canadian and British governments became more open to the use of external consultants. In 1968, the Treasury, with the support of the British Institute of Management Consultants (IMC), established a register of management consultants that departments were required to consult before using external consulting services (Archer 1968). In 1970, the Civil Service Department began to develop a secondment programme between Whitehall and large consulting firms. In a speech to the IMC in 1971, Prime Minister Heath noted that, "the practice has grown of seconding management consultants to work alongside civil servants" (Civil Service Department 1972: 5). He added that, "consultants [were] playing a valuable role in improving the quality of central government management." In Canada, some have argued that, "the practice of using external consultants was given a significant boost by the Royal Commission on Government Organization" (Mellett 1988: 22).

The requirement to evaluate policy more systematically, which came out of the new budget cycle imposed by PPBS, opened a lucrative market for management consulting firms (Pattenaude 1979). As is well known, PPBS is largely based on systems theory, which itself became a booming business in the 1960s. As one

American critic noted: "Taught in universities, bought by private business and government agencies, and sold by a cadre of experts, systems analysis is a commodity commanding high prices and ready acceptance at home and abroad" (Hoos 1972: 1–2).

In the early 1970s, it was estimated that the American government was spending "billions of dollars" in subcontracting to consulting firms work "concerned with policy formation, organizational models and even the recruitment of Federal executives" (Nader 1976: p. x). The title of a book published in 1976 by two American lawyers is evocative: *The Shadow Government: The Government's Multi-Billion Dollar Giveaway of its Decision Making Powers to Private Management Consultants, 'Experts', and Think Tanks.*

In parliamentary regimes, the growing demand for evaluation and policy analysis generated by PPBS or similar types of rational management systems led to the creation, within government, of small policy units, often located a the center of the executive machinery (Prince 1983). These units, such as the CPRS in Britain or the Priority Review Staff (PRS) known as the "policy think tank" created by Australian Prime Minister Whitlam in 1973 (Hawker, Smith, and Weller 1979: 116), were generally staffed by a mix of civil servants, academics and management consultants (Plowden 1991: 229). This practice became sufficiently widespread that analysts began to talk about the "presidentialization" of the executive in parliamentary systems, in reference to both the American practice of recruiting inners and outers, and growing centralization of power around the Prime Minister (Jones 1991).

Thus, already by the mid-1970s, the policy advisory systems of governments in many countries became more open than before. One indication of such openness was the growth of think tanks (Stone 1996). "Once regarded as a peculiarly American phenomenon," writes Halligan, "the think tank was taken up in other countries" in the 1970s and 1980s (1995: 153). A second indication is that there was, as one observer noted, "an exponential growth in the use of consultants by the public sector and a concomitant growth in the size of the consulting industry" (Pattenaude 1979: 203).

28.2.3.2 *The new public management and "conviction politics" in the 1980s*

In the 1970s, as governments were consolidating their own, internal, policy making capacities, and as the fiscal crisis led to cutbacks in public expenditures, the use of consultants in the public sector became less important than it had been in the previous years (Wilding 1976: 69). But that changed in the 1980s when, as a result of the influence of public choice theory and the rise of the New Right, governments, seeking to improve efficiency, increased their reliance on outside consultants as a way to transfer business management ideas and practices into the public sector (Saint Martin 2004).

In Britain, if in the year following Mrs. Thatcher election the government was spending about £6 million on consulting services, by the end of her tenure as Prime Minister in 1990, this amount had grown to £246 million. In Canada, when the Conservative government was in power, spending on consultancy went from $56 million in 1984 to almost $190 million in 1993. In Australia, during the Hawke–Keating Labor government, expenditure on consultancies rose from $91 million in 1987 to $342 million in 1993 (Howard 1996: 70). In Australia, the increase was so significant that it led to an inquiry by a parliamentary committee on the engagement of consultants by government departments (Parliament of the Commonwealth of Australia 1990). Growth in expenditures on consultants in New Zealand also led to an investigation by the Comptroller and Auditor General in 1994 (NZ Audit Office 1994). In that same year, the Efficiency Unit in Britain issued a study on the use of external consultants. It noted that, "Over the past ten years the Government has substantially increased its use of external consultants" (Efficiency Unit 1994: 19).

The release of that study, which showed that government spending on external consultancy increased "nearly fourfold" between 1985 and 1990 (Efficiency Unit 1994: 46), created a political backlash as civil service unions, the media and Labour MPs denounced what they saw as a too cozy relationship between consultants and the Tories (Willman 1994). It has thus been argued that "the era of Conservative government since 1979 has certainly been the age of management consultancy" (Beale 1994: 13), and that "the rise of management consultants was one of the distinctive features of the Thatcher years" (Smith and Young 1996: 137).

In the case of Britain, it is true that there is a connection between the rise of consultants in government and the fact that the Tories were in power throughout the 1980s and until the mid-1990s. It is also true that, one year after the election of New Labour, the Management Consultancies Association (MCA), the trade association that represents the interests of the consulting industry in Britain, reported the end of the "dramatic rise in public sector revenues" of the past fifteen years (MCA 1998: 3). As Table 28.2 indicates, although in 1990 over 30 percent of revenues for MCA members came from the public sector, that figure fell to just 15 percent in 1999 and 10 percent in 2000. But a close look at Table 28.2 also shows that the most important reduction in spending came under the Tories in 1995, thus suggesting a close link to the 1994 Efficiency Unit report, which was described in the press as evidence of "waste of resources" (Willman 1994).

28.2.3.3 Governance and the politics of pragmatism in the new millennium

Starting in the mid-1990s, after almost two decades of focussing on reforming the *management* of government, decision makers began to worry more about the *policy* side of the governing process (Peters 1996). To use Osborne and Gaebler's distinction (1992), over the past few years the focus of reform seems to have shifted

Table 28.2 Management consultancies association (MCA) revenues from public sector (percent of total)

Year	%
1980	14%
1985	24%
1990	31%
1991	28%
1992	26%
1993	27%
1994	29%
1995	17%
1996	15%
1997	21%
1998	21%
1999	15%
2000	10%
2001	13%

Source: Management Consultancies Association, Annual Reports.

from *rowing* to *steering*. After coming to power, the Blair government issued a White Paper on *Modernising Government* (1999). The document argued that whereas earlier management reforms brought improved productivity and better value for money, they paid little attention to the policy process. It underlined in particular the problem of ensuring that policies are devised and delivered in a consistent and effective way across institutional boundaries to address issues that cannot be tackled on a departmental basis—the need for what came to be called "joined-up" policies—against a background of increasing separation between policy and delivery, and more diverse and decentralized delivery arrangements (Williams 1999: 452). Similarly, in Canada, once the government had solved its deficit problem, the focus of reform in the mid-1990s shifted to building policy capacity and horizontal management (Bakvis 2000).

Largely inspired by the new politics of the "third way" developed by Clinton, Blair, Schröeder, and other leaders located at the center of the political spectrum, these reforms were designed to make government more "intelligent" and better able to meet the needs of the people (Giddens 1998). Whereas the political right of the 1980s was anti-statist or anti-bureaucratic, the politics of the *neu mitte* in the late 1990s was more pragmatic, and less inclined to denigrate the role of the public sector (Newman 2001). The new focus was on "partnerships" with either the private or voluntary sectors. As Neil Williams observed in the case of Britain, modernizing the policy process has meant a "greater role for outsiders" (1999: 456) as a way to ensure that a wider range of viewpoints, knowledge and experience is brought to bear on policy. It is in this context that management consultants redefined themselves in the late 1990s as "partners in governance." As one can read on the website of Accenture, the world's leading consulting firm, "Citizens now expect government to be more like the 24x7 world of the private sector—more efficient, and always aligned with the people it serves. And government needs a partner who will help improve the way it serves citizens . . . Accenture is that partner."

Being a partner means that consultancy is no longer simply about providing advices to a client organization that is then alone responsible for subsequently deciding whether to implement the consultants' recommendations. In 1986, the International Labour Office defined a consultant as an expert detached from the employing organization (Kubr 1986). But now, with the growth of "outsourcing consultancy," consultants are more involved in service delivery and less detached from their clients than in the past. "Outsourcing consultancy"—which has become in the past few years the fastest growth sector for consultants—is when an organization assigns whole business or administrative function to a consulting firm (Tewksbury 1999). In Britain, a survey of users of consulting services found in 2001 that 96 percent of clients said that they wanted "some form of relationship with their consultancy firm rather than keeping them at arms length. There is no doubt that consultants are increasingly seen as partners rather than suppliers" (MCA 2001: 4). The quick intervention is less the norm and the trend today is for large firms to have long-term contracts, such as the six-year contract between PwC and the UK Ministry of Defence and the ten-year contract with the Home Office covering immigration programs and services (Huntington 2001). Consultants are keen to take up large contracts because this is a way of protecting their business from the up and down of the economy.

"Outsourcing consultancy" is especially strong in the field of information technology (IT). Consulting firms have become increasingly active in the development of e-Government, promoting the use of IT as a tool to transcend organizational boundaries and make government more "joined up" (Fountain 2001). Some have described e-Government as the "new paradigm" of public sector reform (Accenture) and according to Patrick Dunleavy and his colleague, it has "overtaken and superseded" the NPM whose time, they argue, is now "over" (Dunleavy and Margetts 2000: 1). Whether e-Government is different from the NPM is still an open question. But like the NPM whose emergence in the 1980s increased public spending on consulting services, e-Government is also becoming a fast growing market for management consultancies. In Europe, the e-Europe Action Plan first adopted by the European Union in 2000 is driving the demand for information technologies in the public sector. Research indicates that e-Government spending by governments in western Europe was around US$2.3 billion in 20003 (IDC 2002).

In the United States, it is estimated that federal, state, and local spending on e-Government will be at around $6 billion in 2005 (CIBER 2003). Moreover, in the US, the use of information technology (IT) in government has taken a new, more security-oriented direction following the events of September 11 2001 and the creation of the Homeland Security Department. Consulting firms in Washington are now involved in providing the technology that could help, in the words of the Head of the Public Sector Branch of Bearing Point (formerly KPMG Consulting), "mitigate the risk of exposing valuable information to our enemies" (Bearing Point 2002). Consultants see the global war against terrorism as a growing market where governments across the world are expected to spend an estimate $550 billion on homeland security (Reuters 2003).

28.3 THE SUPPLY OF CONSULTING SERVICES TO GOVERNMENT

From rational planners and technocrats, to advocates of the NPM, to partners in governance and in the global fight against terrorism, what stands out from the above discussion is that management consultants are highly adaptable creatures, able to transform themselves to seize the opportunities opened by the political context of the moment. In this sense, management consultancy, as a business, is more opportunistic than ideological.

Formally, it is decision makers in government that are seeking the help of consultants in changing the way the public sector is managed. But they would not be likely to do this if management consultancy, as a field of activity, was non-existent or only weakly developed. Obviously, the mere existence and degree of development of management consultancy is likely to affect the extent to which states can use the services of management consultants in reforming their bureaucracies.

In looking at the supply side of the relationship between consultants and government, the following section focuses on three factors: the development and size of the consulting industry, the marketing strategies that consultants use to promote their products, and the lobbying efforts they deploy to build networks of contacts with policy makers in government.

28.3.1 Industry Size

Until recently, management consultancy has been a booming industry, with broadly similar growth patterns between the private and public sectors (Rassam

Table 28.3 Global management consulting market

(billion US$)	1996	1997	1998	1999	2000	2001	2002
	51	62	73	89	102	112	119

Source: Kennedy Information 2003.

1998). In 2002, the size of the global market for consulting services was estimated to be around US$119 billion. The United States alone account for at least half of the global consulting marketplace (Gross 2001), compared to about 40 percent for Europe.

For the first time in more than three decades, global consulting revenues are expected to decline in 2003. According to Kennedy Information (KI), a research organization that gathers information and conducts analysis on the management consulting industry, "indications are that 2003 will be a very difficult year for the consulting profession." Among the factors that KI identifies as contributing to this trend are "the various accounting scandals that erupted during 2002."

28.3.1.1 *The Link with Accountancy*

Management consulting has both an engineering and accounting background. It first emerged in the US in the early 1900 with Frederick Taylor and his "scientific management" approach to the work process (Rassam and Oates 1991). Most of the early American practitioners described themselves as "industrial engineers." But management consulting only started to establish itself as a multi-billion dollar industry in the 1960s when the large international accounting firms moved into consultancy (Stevens 1991). These firms, which were then known as the "Big Eight" included Arthur Andersen, Coopers & Lybrand, Ernst & Whinney, Arthur Young, KPMG Peat Marwick, Deloitte, Haskins & Sells, Touche Ross, and Price Waterhouse.

In moving into management consulting, accountants improved its image considerably. Accountants brought with them a certain aura of respectability, seriousness, and professionalism. Contrary to the industrial engineers, the involvement of accountants in management consulting was not seen as that of an "intruder or snoop" in the operations of a company, since accountants had already developed an organized relationship with their audit clients (Mellett 1988: 5). As the auditors to blue chip North American and European businesses and industries, many of the Big Eight firms had earned a reputation for being the world's premiere accountants. The prestige coming with this reputation helped the Big Eight to become the world leaders in management consulting services (Hanlon 1994). In 1998, the "Big Eight," which, following a series of mergers had then become the "Big Five," shared global revenues of US$25 billion, representing almost 35 percent of the world market (Industry Week 2000).

Thus, in moving into management consulting, accountants had a head start since they already knew their audit clients and were party to their business secrets. At the same time, however, they faced potential conflicts of interests between their roles as certified public accountant and management consultant. This is exactly what happened in 2002, when it was found that Arthur Andersen had broken the law by shredding Enron Corp. documents while Enron, a client of Andersen, was under investigation by the US government for hiding debts and concealing its imminent collapse from creditors and investors (Glater 2002). The fact that over half of the US$52 million Andersen earned from Enron in 2000 came from consulting fees, led observers in the US and politicians in Congress to argue that this might have played a role in Andersen's "decision not to expose Enron's ongoing lies" (Hastings 2002).

Fearing that the US Securities and Exchange Commission might weaken the self-regulatory practices of the accounting profession and intervene to make it illegal for accountants to provide consulting work to their audit clients, the Big Five sold their consulting arms. For instance, KPMG Consulting became Bearing Point, while Ernst & Young sold its consulting business to Cap Gemini in 2000 and IBM bought PricewaterhouseCoopers' consulting arm in 2002 for US$3.5 billion.

In a number of European countries, including Portugal, Italy, and France, it is illegal for accountants to provide consulting and auditing services to the same client (Ridyard and De Bolle 1992: 67). This is one of the key reasons why management consulting is not as developed there as it is in countries like Britain and Germany. As Figure 28.1 indicates, Britain has the largest management consulting market in Europe.

Thus supply, understood in terms of market or industry size, varies significantly from one country or region to another. When supply is weak demand is also weak, and different levels of development of the management consulting industry partly explain some of the cross-national variations noted earlier in the use of consultants by governments.

28.3.2 Management Consultants as Fashion Setters

The consulting industry is generally divided between the large accountancy-based firms and the so-called "strategy consultancies" such as McKinsey, Mercer, Booz-Allen, and Towers Perrin. Unlike the accounting firms, which specialize in financial management and information technology (IT) consulting, these firms focus more on strategic advice, including marketing, brand management, and organizational development, especially business-process re-engineering (Rassam 1998: 13). It is estimated that large strategy consultancies such as McKinsey spends US$50–100 million a year on research. McKinsey also publishes a review (the McKinsey Quarterly), and has produced fifty-four books on management since 1980

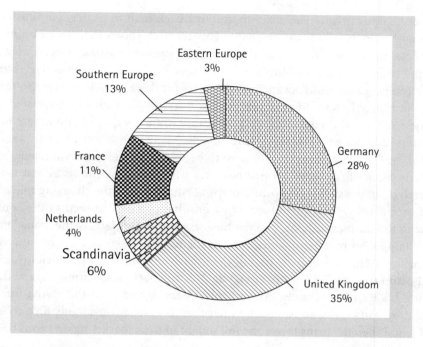

Fig. 28.1 European consultancy revenue breakdown by country/region, 2003

Source: Kennedy information, 2003a

(*The Economist* 1995: 57). The most famous book produced by two consultants from McKinsey is the best-selling *In Search of Excellence* by Peters and Waterman (1982). This book, which sold more than five million copies, has been described as one of the "most influential" sources of ideas in the development of the NPM (Aucoin 1990: 117).

For large consultancies such as McKinsey, Booz Allen, Gemini, and Arthur D. Little, one of the key instruments for disseminating ideas is the publication of articles or books, which has become a favored marketing tactic in the firms' attempts to increase their share of the market (Dwyer and Harding 1996). The book is a tool of the consultant. As one can read in a "how to" manual on management consulting, "a book can create wide exposure, immediate credibility and generate revenue" (Blumberg 1994: 46). For instance, since its publication in 1993, *Re-Engineering the Corporation* by Champy and Hammer has sold nearly two million copies worldwide. Subsequently, the consulting firm that employed the two authors, increased its annual revenues from US$70 million the year preceding publication, to more than $160 million the year after (*The Economist* 1995: 57).

Organizational sociologists interested in the study of management innovations have argued that management consulting firms are "fashion-setting organizations" whose missions involve the creation and/or dissemination of new administrative ideas and models (Abrahamson 1996). This research shows that new administrative ideas do not become fashionable by direct popular demand. Instead, "fashion setters" such as consulting firms and business mass media, play active roles in developing organizations' awareness and tastes for these models in order to render them fashionable and to prompt their diffusion. Abrahamson suggested that business schools and consulting firms, because of their expertise, dominate in the selection of fashionable management models. Many of the consultancies that are part of the "strategy" category are keen to be seen at the forefront of management thinking. Some firms have formed alliances with business schools by sponsoring research on issues such as the future shape of companies of the changing role of the chief executives (Wooldridge 1997: 17). Consultants are often seen as the conduit between the business schools and the business world. It is largely the management consultants who transfer new ideas from the academic world out onto the commercial one. This is especially true of the American-owned consultancies (McKinsey, Boston Consulting Group, etc.), which have always had strong links with the leading US business schools (Rassam and Oates 1991: 23). In the search for new groundbreaking ideas, consultancies offer their brightest consultants time to write books, and then the firms throw the full weight of their marketing divisions behind the final products.

Consultancies arrange for such books to be serialized in magazines, advertised in newspapers, and endorsed by well-known business persons or even by the President of the United States. On the front cover of Osborne and Gaebler's *Reinventing Government*, a best-seller written by two management consultants, there is a quotation from Bill Clinton saying that this book "should be read by every elected official in America." *Reinventing Government* was a major source of NPM ideas across the world in the 1990s, with Osborne and Gaebler giving speeches to senior government officials in places such as Ottawa, London, Italy, Japan, Canberra, and Turkey (Saint-Martin 2001: 587).

A common practice among the 'strategies', and increasingly also among the accounting firms, is to buy large quantities of books written by their employees to pass along to clients as 'gifts'. This practice provides consulting firms with a means by which they can have their ideas come to the attention of those they want to influence. For example, in 1991 Coopers & Lybrand published *Excellence in Government* which advocated the application of Total Quality Management (TQM) in government. In the introduction, the authors wrote:

We hope this book will help promote TQM in government, because we see it as the best way to improve public services... To this end we are giving copies of *Excellence in Government* to Members of Congress, the President, federal cabinet secretaries, the heads of major independent agencies, and the governors of all states... We address the last chapter of the book to them: they must lead the way to government excellence. (Carr and Littman 1991: 1)

Throughout the 1980s, Peat Marwick (which later became KPMG) in Britain organized seminars for civil servants and consultants involved in the process of bureaucratic reform and published books advocating the adoption of "a more managerial approach in government which is seeking to learn from (and where appropriate to emulate) some of the culture and, attitudes and values of the private sector" (Peat Marwick 1986: 14). These publications included: *Financial Management in the Public Sector: A Review 1979–1984*; *Management Information and Control in Whitehall*; *Developing the FMI: Changes in Process and Culture*; *Policy Management and Policy Assessment.*

In Australia, throughout the late 1980s and early 1990s, publications aimed at civil servants, such as the *Australia Journal of Public Administration*, were filled with advertising by management consulting firms. In Canada, KPMG created in 1995 the KPMG Centre for Government Foundation, which launched a joint venture with the Institute of Public Administration of Canada, the main professional body for academics and civil servants, to research "Alternative Service Delivery" mechanisms (Lindquist and Sica 1995).

28.3.3 Lobbying Strategies

As the demand for consultancy in government became more important in countries like Britain, Canada, or Australia, most consulting firms, as well as the trade association that represents their interests, began in the 1980s to develop various institutions and practices designed at building networks of contacts with government officials.

In Britain, following the introduction of Mrs. Thatcher's "Efficiency Strategy" in 1980, it was noted that, "the Management Consultancies Association (MCA) moved swiftly to consolidate its position by developing its network of contacts within the civil service" (Smith and Young 1996: 142). In the early 1980s, the MCA created within its organization a "Public Sector Working Party" (PSWP) to develop a more coordinated strategy for promoting management consulting to government. According to the MCA, "the Group dealing with the public sector has established close links with departments employing management consultancy services with the intention not only of establishing a better understanding within Whitehall of the services that we can offer, but of equal importance, ensuring that our membership is aware of the needs and constraints faced by Ministries" (MCA 1989: 4). The PSWP is made of various "subgroups" one of which is directly linked to the Cabinet Office and whose role is to make sure, in the words of the MCA Director, that there is "a regular dialogue between the MCA and members of Cabinet and with senior officials" (MCA 1995: 3).

Following its creation, the PSWP began to organize a number of events to facilitate the exchange of ideas between Whitehall officials and consultants.

Each year, the MCA runs half-day seminars for civil servants on management reform and on the use of consultants in the public sector. In the past, such seminars were sometimes attended by no less than 200 civil servants (MCA 1995: 3). The MCA's Public Sector Working Party also holds a series of meetings (four or five a year) attended by member firms and Permanent Secretaries. The purpose of such meetings is to receive an authoritative update on activities within a particular sector of government. As written in the letters sent by the MCA to the senior officials invited to speak to the PSWP, the goal is to see "how consultants can act as advisers and partners in helping the Civil Service to face future management challenges." These meetings are supplemented by a series of small monthly lunches consisting of senior staff from member firms and policy makers. For the MCA, these luncheons "provided an ideal 'off the record' opportunity for wide ranging discussions on subjects of particular interest to both guests and hosts" (MCA 1996: 5). In the past, the MCA guests included the head of the Policy Unit, senior Treasury officials, and members of the Efficiency Unit and of the Cabinet Office.

Following the example of their business association, MCA member-firms began in the 1980s to organize various lobbying activities targeted at Whitehall officials and created "Government Services Divisions" within their organizational structures. These divisions are often made up of "former bureaucrats and others with public sector expertise [who] have been hired to develop a rapport with civil servants and to sell the firms' many and varied services" (Bakvis 1997: 109).

As the government became a more important client, management consultants increasingly sought to get inside knowledge and to obtain information on Whitehall's current and future plan for management reforms. In this search for information, MPs became important assets in helping to secure valuable Whitehall contacts. In 1988 Tim Smith, a Tory MP and consultant to Price Waterhouse, asked no less than eighteen government department parliamentary questions for detailed information on management consulting. The answers disclosed the nature of the contracts, the successful companies, their assignments and the government expenditures involved (Halloran and Hollingworth 1994: 198).

In Britain, some have also noted the "revolving door" between government and management consulting firms by pointing to the fact, for instance, that before becoming minister, Margaret Hodge worked at PricewaterhouseCoopers and that Patricia Hewitt was research director at Andersen (Simms 2002: 34). Large consultancies also offer some of their staff for free on secondment to various government departments. An investigation by *The Observer* in 2000, which led to the "staff-for favours row" (Barnett 2000), found that firms like Pricewaterhouse-Coopers and Ernst & Young, which had donated staff free to departments, had subsequently won lucrative government contracts. One consultant to the Treasury quoted in the *Observer* article said: "I did work on policy issues and got amazing access... It is now much easier for me to ring up Treasury officials and get the information I need" (reported in Barnett 2000).

Table 28.4 Political contributions in the US by the Big Five: Election year 2000

Organization	Amount	Democrats (per cent)	Republicans (per cent)
Ernst and Young	$2,361,186	42	57
Deloitte & Touche	$1,691,661	29	71
PwC	$1,678,811	25	75
Arthur Anderson	$1,210,664	27	73
KPMG LLP	$1,055,039	30	69

In the United States, financial contributions to parties and candidates for Congress are common practice among the large consulting firms. In the 2000 election cycle, the "Big Five" donated $8 million to the two major political parties: 61 percent to the Republicans and 38 percent to the Democrats.

In the aftermath of the Enron scandal, observers of the American political scene uncovered the fact that "very few politicians in Washington haven't been on the receiving end of Arthur Andersen" (Center for Responsive Politics 2002). Andersen was the fifth biggest donor to Bush's White House run, contributing nearly $146,000 via its employees and political action committee (PAC). Since 1989, Andersen has contributed more than $5 million in soft money, PAC and individual contributions to federal candidates and parties, more than two-thirds to Republicans. It is also reported that more than half of the current members of the House of Representatives were recipients of Andersen cash over the last decade. In the Senate, 94 of the chamber's 100 members reported Andersen contributions since 1989 (Center for Responsive Politics 2002).

Finally, at the European level, national associations of management consulting firms are regrouped in an organization called the FEACO: the European Federation of Management Consulting Associations based in Brussels. The FEACO presents itself as the "united voice" of consultants, promoting the "the interests of management consultants with various international organizations by maintaining close contacts with European institutions, such as the European Commission" (FEACO 2001: 3). The FEACO is organized into various committees, one of which is the European Community Institutions Committee (ECIC). That committee became very active following publication of the White Paper on Reforming the Commission in 2000 (FEACO 2000b). Led by Neil Kinnock, the reform exercise is based on four guiding principles: efficiency, accountability, service, and transparency (Metcalfe 2000). Soon after the introduction of the White Paper, members of the ECIC met to develop their "action plan" for 2000. In that document, one can read that,

The main objective of the ECIC should be to monitor, influence and provide input into the modernization of the European Commission . . . The ECIC should maintain close contacts with key persons in the European Commission...and maintain close contacts with the European Parliament by inviting MEPS to lunches and organize meetings with them, to help them better understand the role of consultants and their contribution to the improvement of the efficient management of all EU activities. (FEACO 2000*a*)

28.4 CONCLUSION

This broad comparative overview has mainly focused on the relationships between consultants and governments and reviewed some of the reasons why this link has been closer in some countries than in others. In places where the supply and demand for consultancy has been stronger, what impact is this "liaison" having on each of the two partners in the relationship?

In terms of the impact on government, the opinions seem to be quite contradictory. On the one hand, public officials and consultants argue that the use of consultants in the policy process is a way of strengthening the policy capacities of governments by mobilizing expertise that is often unavailable internally. Also, consultants are seen as providing flexibility: they are brought in at the discretion of the department or body concerned, and they can be selected according to specific needs. But on the other hand, critics are suggesting that consultants are weakening the capacities of government because they are possibly usurping policy functions. Consultants, along with other external advisers, would be part of a "shadow government" (Guttman and Willner 1976) that has effectively taken the policy-making function away from elected officials and bureaucrats. This view is partly linked to the "hollowing out" of the state thesis, which argues that because of globalization, the state is "being eroded or eaten away" (Rhodes 1994: 138).

As is often the case with such debates, the reality probably lies between these two positions. Policy capacity concerns the intellectual dimension of governance (Bakvis 2000). It is a tricky concept, encompassing both staffing issues and organizational matters. It is difficult to measure precisely whether consultants are solidifying or undermining policy capacity. It is likely that no broad generalization can be made, and that consultants can either strengthen or weaken policy capacity, depending on the particular case one is studying. But one thing that seems more certain is that consultants are contributing to expand the *political capacities* of decision makers in government. Observers and critics often look at consultants as manipulators who are seeking to influence policy makers to make more money. But what about the opposite scenario? Consultants allow policy makers to diffuse blame and provide a layer of protection from attack on proposed policies by political adversaries (Martin 1998).

Concerning the impact on consultants, their growing use in the policy process in the past twenty years has made government a better—or at least, a more knowledgeable—buyer of consulting services. Various reports, either from government agencies or audit offices, have highlighted ways of improving value for money in the engagement of external consultants. Today, the consulting industry faces more administrative procedures and rules when doing business with government for public sector contracts (Jarrett 1998).

And finally, one paradoxical development in the relationship between consultants and government is what can be called the "think tank-ization" of management consultancy: the idea that large consulting firms are becoming more and more like think tanks. The paradox is that if consultants have contributed to the "privatization" of government, facilitating the introduction of business management practices in the public sector, their more or less intimate relationship with government has transformed them into somewhat less "private" and more "public" actors. In the past ten years or so, a number of large consulting firms have developed not-for-profit research institutes that produce research on key public policy issues. These include PricewaterhouseCoopers (now IBM) Endowment for The Business of Government or the KPMG Centre for Government Foundation created in 1995 in Canada, and the publication of journals such as the McKinsey Quarterly or Accenture's *Outlook*. Whether this new, more visible, policy advocacy role is simply a public relation strategy designed to show that consulting firms are good "corporate citizens" who care about the collectivity, is an open question. But the fact is that in developing closer interactions with government, management consultancy is no longer what it was thirty years ago.

REFERENCES

ABRAHAMSON, E. (1996), "Management Fashion," *Academy of Management Review* 21(1): 254–85.

ARCHER, J. N. (1968), "Management Consultants in Government," *O&M Bulletin* 23(1): 23–33.

AUCOIN, P. (1986), "Organizational Change in the Machinery of Canadian Government: From Rational Management to Brokerage Politics," *Canadian Journal of Political Science* 19(2): 3–27.

—— (1990), "Administrative reform in Public Management: Paradigms, Principles, Paradoxes and Pendulums," *Governance* 3(2): 115–37.

Audit Office (1994), "Employment of Consultants by Government Departments," In *Report of the Comptroller and Auditor General: Third Report for 1994)*, Wellington.

BAKVIS, H. (1997), "Advising the Executive: Think Tanks, Consultants, Political Staff and Kitchen Cabinet," in P. Weller, H. Bakvis, and R. A. W. Rhodes (eds), *The Hollow Crown: Countervailing Trends in Core Executives*, London: Macmillan, 84–125.

BAKVIS, H. (2000), "Rebuilding Policy capacity in the Era of the Fiscal Dividend," *Governance* 193(1): 71–104.

BARNETT, A. (2000), "Staff for Favours Row Hits Treasury," *The Observer*, June 25, http://www.guardian.co.uk/Archive/Article/0,4273,4033309,00.html

BEALE, D. (1994), *Driven by Nissan? A Critical Guide of New Management Techniques*, London: Lawrence & Wishart.

BearingPoint. (2002), Homeland Security Testimonials. Statement of S. Daniel Johnson, Executive Vice-President, Public Services, Committee on House Government Reform. http://www.bearingpoint.com/about_us/features/home_sec_testimony.html

BISSESSAR, A.-M. (2002), "Globalization, Domestic Politics and the Introduction of New Public Management in the Commonwealth Caribbean," *International Review of Administrative Sciences* 68(1): 113–25.

BLUMBERG, D. F. (1994), "Marketing Consulting Services Using Public Relations Strategies," *Journal of Management Consulting* 8(1): 42–8.

BLUNSDON, B. J. (2002), "Beneath Fashion: Why is there a Market for Management Consulting Services?" Paper presented at the Professional Service Firms Workshop, University of Alberta, Edmonton, Canada, August.

CAMPBELL, C., and WILSON, G. K. (1995), *The End of Whitehall: Death of a Paradigm?*, Oxford: Basil Blackwell.

CANADA (1962), The Royal Commission on Government Organization. *Volume 1: Management of the Public Service*. Ottawa: The Queen's Printer.

CARR, D. K., and LITTMAN, I. D. (1991), *Excellence in Government*, Washington, DC: Coopers & Lybrand.

Centre for Responsive Politics (2002), Enron and Andersen. http://www.opensecrets.org/news/enron/index.asp

CHRISTENSEN, M. (2003), "The Big Six Consulting Firms: Creating a New Market or Meeting a Public Policy Need?", *Australasian Journal of Business & Social Inquiry* 1(1): 24–32.

CIBER (2003), *Overview of Sate Government Solutions Provided by CIBER*. http://ciber.com/services_solutions/other_services/egovt/images/CIBER-SGS-Overview.pdf

Civil Service Department. (1972), *CSD News* 3(2) February.

DJELIC, M.-L. (1998), *Exporting the American Model: The Postwar Transformation of American Business*, Oxford: Oxford University Press.

DOLOWITZ, D. P. (2000), *Policy Transfer and British Social Policy*, Buckingham: Open University Press.

DUNLEAVY, P., and MARGETTS, H. (2000), The Advent of Digital Government: Public Bureaucracies and the State in the Internet Age. Paper prepared for delivery at the 2000 Annual Meeting of the American Political Science Association, Washington, September 4.

—— et al. (2001), Policy Learning and Public Sector it: Contractual and Egovernment Change. Paper prepared for delivery at the 2001 Annual Meeting of the American Political Science Association, San Francisco, August 30–September 2.

DWYER, A., and HARDING, F. (1996), "Using Ideas to Increase the Marketability of Your Firm," *Journal of Management Consulting* 9(2): 56–61.

Efficiency Unit (1994), *The Government' s Use of External Consultants. An Efficiency Unit Scrutiny*, London: HMSO.

FEACO (2000*a*), *ECIC Action Plan 2000*.http://www.feaco.org/ECICAction2000.pdf

—— (2000*b*), *Newsletter*, Winter, Issue 1), http://www.feaco.org/downloads/2000_3–4.pdf

—— (2001), *Survey of European Management Consultancy Market*, Brussels.

FISCHER, F. (1990), *Technocracy and the Politics of Expertise*, Newbury Park, CA.: Sage.

FOUNTAIN, J. E. (2001), *Building the Virtual State. Information Technology and Institutional Change*, Washington, DC: Brookings Institution.

FRY, G. K. (1993), *Reforming the Civil Service: The Fulton Committee on Home Civil Service*, Edinburgh: Edinburgh University Press.

FULTON, Lord. (1968), *The Civil Service. Volume 1), Report of the Committee 1966–68)*, Cmnd. 3638), London: HMSO.

GAO (General Accounting Office) (1992), *Government Contractors: Are Service Contractors Performing Inherently Governmental Functions?* Washington, DC: United States General Accounting Office.

GIDDENS, A. (1998), *The Third Way: the Renewal of Social Democracy*, Cambridge: Polity Press.

GLATER, J. D. (2002), "Longtime Clients Leave Arthur Andersen," *The New York Times*, March 16, p. 1 and B3.

GROSS, A. C. (2001) *Overview of the U.S. Management Consulting Industry*. University of Colorado, unpublished paper, http://www.assoconsult.org/download/articoli/overview.pdf

GUTTMAN, D., and WILLNER, B. (1976), *The Shadow Government: The Government's Multi-Billion Dollar Giveaway of its Decision-Making Powers to Private Management Consultants, "Experts," and Think Tanks*, New York: Pantheon Books.

HALL, P. A. (ed). (1989), *The Political Power of Economic Ideas*, Princeton: Princeton University Press.

HALLIGAN J. (1995), "Policy Advice and the Public Service," in B. G. Peters and D. J. Savoie (eds), *Governance in a Changing Environment*, Montreal and Kingston: McGill-Queen's University Press, 138–72.

HALLORAN, P., and HOLLINGWORTH, M. (1994), *A Bit on the Side: Politicians and Who Pays Them? An Insider's Guide*, London: Simon & Schuster.

HANLON, G. (1994), *The Commercialization of Accountancy*, London: Macmillan.

HASTINGS, A. L. (2002), *The Need for Auditor Independence*. US House of Representatives, http://www.house.gov/alceehastings/op_eds/oped_auditor_indep.html

HAWKER, G. et al. (1979), *Politics and Policy in Australia*, University of Queensland Press.

HECLO, H. A. (1977), *A Government of Strangers: Executive Politics in Washington*. Washington, DC: Brookings Institution.

HEINZ, J. P. et al. (1993), *The Hollow Core: Private Interests in National Policy-Making*, Cambridge, MA: Harvard University Press.

HOLMAN, K. (1997), "Day of the Gurus," *The Guardian*, November 12, p. 9.

HOOD, C., and JACKSON, M. (1991), *Administrative Argument*, Aldershot: Dartmouth.

HOOS, I. (1972), *Systems Analysis in Public Policy: A Critique*, Berkeley: University of California Press.

HOWARD, M. (1996), "A Growth Industry? Use of Consultants Reported by Commonwealth Departments, 1974–1994," *Canberra Bulletin of Public Administration* 80 (Sept.): 62–74.

HUNTINGTON, M. (2001), "Careers: Public Sector—Working in the Public Eye," *Management Consultancy*, March 12.

IDC (2002), Survey—IT Purchasing Patterns in Western European Public Sector: IDC # PP08J. http://www.idcresearch.com/getdoc.jhtml?containerId=PP08J

Industry Week (2000), *Global Manufacturers' Resource Guide. Top Consulting Firms.* http://www.industryweek.com/iwinprint/data/chart6–2.html

JARRETT, M. C. (1998), "Consultancy in the Public Sector," in P. Sadler (ed), *Management Consultancy: A Handbook of Best Practices*, London: Kogan, 369–83.

JONES, G. W. (1991), "Presidentialization in a Parliamentary System?", in C. Campbell and M. J. Wyszomirski (eds.), *Executive Leadership in Anglo-American Systems*, Pittsburgh: University of Pittsburgh Press, 111–38.

Kennedy Information (2003*a*), *Competing in the European Consulting Market.* http://www.consultingcentral.com/reports/euro_2003_exec_summ.pdf

—— (2003*b*), The Global Consulting Marketplace 2003: Key Data, Forecasts & Trends. Kennedy Information Inc. http://www.consultingcentral.com/reports/doc_GlobalMC2003execsumm.pdf

KIPPING, M., and ENGWALL, L. (2002), *Management Consulting: Emergence and Dynamics of a Knowledge Industry*, Oxford: Oxford University Press.

KUBR, M. (1986), *Management Consulting: A Guide to the Profession*, Geneva: International Labour Office.

LE MONDE (1999), "Les cabinets de conseil, les géo-maîtres du monde," Economic Section, January 19, pp. i–iii.

LEYS, C. (1999), "Intellectual Mercenaries and the Public Interest: Management Consultants and the NHS," *Policy & Politics* 27(4): 447–65.

LINDQUIST, E., and SICA, T. (1995), *Canadian Governments and the Search for Alternative Program Delivery and Financing*, Toronto: KPMG Centre for Government Foundation and Institute of Public Administration of Canada.

LOCKE, R. R. (1996), *The Collapse of the American Management Mystique*, Oxford: Oxford University Press.

MACKENZIE, G. C. (1987), *The In and Outers: Presidential Appointees and Transient Government in Washington.* Baltimore: John Hopkins Press.

MARTIN, J. F. (1998), *Reorienting a Nation: Consultants and Australian Public Policy*, Aldershot: Ashgate.

MCA (1989), *President's Statement and Annual Report*, London: Management Consultancies Association.

—— (1995), *President's Statement and Annual Report*, London.

—— (1996), *President's Statement and Annual Report*, London.

—— (1998), *President's Statement and Annual Report*, London.

—— (2001), *President's Statement and Annual Report*, London.

MELLETT, E. B. (1988), *From Stopwatch to Strategy: A History of the First Twenty-Five Years of the Canadian Association of Management Consultants*, Toronto: CAMC.

METCALFE, L. (2000), "Reforming the Commission: Will Organisational Efficiency Produce Effective Governance?" *Journal of Common Market Studies* 38(5): 817–41.

NADER, R. (1976), "Introduction," in D. Guttman and B. Willner. *The Shadow Government: The Government's Multi-Billion Dollar Giveaway of its Decision-Making Powers to Private Management Consultants, "Experts," and Think Tanks*, New York: Pantheon Books.

NEWMAN, J. (2001), *Modernising Governance: New Labour, Policy and Society*, London: Sage.

OSBORNE, D., and GAEBLER, T. (1992), *Reinventing Government: How the Entrepreneurial Spirit is Transforming the Public Sector*, New York: Plume.

PAL, L. A. (1992), *Public Policy Analysis: An Introduction*, 2nd edn., Scarborough: Nelson Canada.

PARLIAMENT OF THE COMMONWEALTH OF AUSTRALIA (1990), *Engagement of External Consultants by Commonwealth Departments*. Report 302, Joint Committee of Public Accounts. Canberra: Australian Government Publishing Service.

PATTENAUDE, R. L. (1979), "Consultants in the Public Sector" *Public Administration Review* (May/June): 203–5.

PEAT, M. (1986), *Current Issues in Public Sector Management*, London.

PERL, A., and WHITE, D. J. (2002), "The Changing Role of Consultants in Canadian Policy Analysis," *Policy, Organisation & Society* 21(4): 49–73.

PETERS, B. G. (1996), *The Policy Capacity of Government*. Ottawa: Canadian Centre for Management Development. Research Paper no.18.

PLOWDEN, W. (ed.) (1987), *Advising the Rulers*, Oxford: Basil Blackwell.

—— (1991), "Providing Countervailing Analysis and Advice in a Career-Dominated Bureaucratic System," in C. Campbell and M. J. Wyszomirski (eds.), *Executive Leadership in Anglo-American Systems*, Pittsburgh: University of Pittsburgh Press, 219–48.

POLLITT, C. (1996), "Antistatist Reforms and New Administrative Directions: Public Administration in the United Kingdom," *Public Administration Review* 56(1): 81–7.

PRINCE, M. (1983), *Policy Advice and Organizational Survival: Policy Planning and Research Units in British Government*, Aldershot, Hampshire: Gower.

POWER, M. (1997), *The Audit Society*, Oxford: Oxford University Press.

RASSAM, C. (1998), "The Management Consulting Industry' in P. Sadler (ed.), *Management Consultancy: A Handbook for Best Practice*, London: Kogan Page, 3–29.

—— and OATES, D. (1991), *Management Consultancy: The Inside Story*, London: Mercury.

Reuters (2003), "Governments around the world will spend an estimated $550 billion on homeland security in 2003," Washington, July 7), http://www.world-am.com/body_03–04–2.html

RHODES, R. A. W. (1994), "The Hollowing Out of the State," *Political Quarterly* 65(2): 138–51.

RIDYARD, D., and DE BOLLE, J. (1992), *Competition in European Accounting: A Study of the EC Audit and Consulting Sectors*, Dublin: Lafferty Publications.

RUESCHEMEYER, D., and Skcopol, T. (1996), *States, Social Knowledge, and the Origins of Modern Social Policies*, Princeton: Princeton University Press.

SAINT MARTIN, D. (2001), "When Industrial Policy Shapes Public Sector Reform: TQM in Britain and France," *West European Politics* 24(4): 105–24.

—— (2004), *Building the New Managerialist State: Consultants and the Politics of Public Sector Reform in Comparative Perspective*, 2nd edn., Oxford: Oxford University Press.

SIMMS, A. (2002), *Five Brothers: The Rise and Nemesis of the Big Bean Counters*, London: New Economics Foundation.

SMITH, T. (1994), "Post-Modern Politics and the Case for Constitutional Renewal," *Political Quarterly* 65(2): 128–38.

—— and YOUNG, A. (1996), *The Fixers: Crisis Management in British Politics*, Aldershot: Dartmouth.

STEVENS, M. (1991), *The Big Six: The Selling Out of America's Top Accounting Firms*, New York: Simon & Schuster.

STONE, D. (1996), *Capturing the Political Imagination: Think Tanks and the Policy Process*, London: Frank Cass.

TEWKSBURY, H. (1999), "Survey: Public Sector—Public Sector Go-Slow," *Management Consultancy*, February 11.

The Economist (1995), "Manufacturing Best-Sellers: A Scam Over a "Best-Selling' Business Book Shows How Obsessed Management Consultancies Have Become with Producing the Next Big Idea," August 5, p. 57.

WILDING, R. W. L. (1976), "The Use of Management Consultants in Government Departments," *Management Services in Government* 31(2): 60–70.

WILLIAMS, N. (1999), "Modernising Government: Policy-Making within Whitehall," *Political Quarterly*, pp. 452–9.

WILLMAN, J. (1994), "Con Artists or Cost-Cutters? Do Whitehall's Outside Consultants Provide Value for Money?" *Financial Times Week-End*, April 30, p. 7.

WOOLDRIDGE, A. (1997), "Trimming the Fat: A Survey of Management Consultancy," *The Economist*, March 22, pp.1–22.

CHAPTER 29

CHANGE AND CONTINUITY IN THE CONTINENTAL TRADITION OF PUBLIC MANAGEMENT

ISABELLA PROELLER
KUNO SCHEDLER

29.1 INTRODUCTION

CONTINENTAL European traditions of public administration and public management are generally characterized as distinct, even opposite models to those prevailing in Anglo-Saxon countries. This difference seems to be rooted in different notions of the state, legal systems, and historical settings which lead to specific features in terms of role, structure, and functioning of the state and its administration. Within continental Europe, the public administration models of France and Germany have a prominent role. This stems from the continuity they have shown over the last two centuries, their influence on other countries mainly due to conquest and war, and the close resemblance both administrative systems have to the Weberian bureaucratic model. For this latter reason, France and Germany are often referred to as examples of "classical" public administration (Heady 1996). The term "classical" applies since their performance procedures, established with modernity, have persisted throughout times of political instability and change right up to the present day. Public administration has represented stability in periods of political rupture and has shouldered the burden of public action during political instability (König 2001: 14; König and Beck 1997: 15). Even though Germany and France are often referred to as examples of continental European public administration, it would be a grave oversimplification to reduce heterogeneity of European countries and administrations to French and German examples (for an overview on continental European public administration and public management see Heady 1996; Rowat 1988; Lüder and Jones 2003; Brovetto 1996; Farnham et al. 1996; Naschold 1996; Kickert 1997; Pollitt and Bouckaert 2000; Lane 1997; Flynn and Strehl 1996; Olsen and Peters 1996; Ziller 1993; Rugge 2003). Although the basic mechanisms and principles are comparable, structure, functioning and implementation can differ vastly.

The specific traditions of French and German administrative systems are also evident in recent and current reform trajectories. Even though current reform issues show certain similarities across Western Europe—mainly with regard to reactions to financial crisis, lack of flexibility and waning public acceptance of administrative procedures—national approaches strongly reflect the specific characteristics of each particular country. Thus, although France and Germany share and build on a set of common or similar premises due to their common historic roots, mutual influences, and their origins in Roman law tradition, the specific characteristics of the public administration of each of the two countries should not be overlooked or underestimated.

The aim of this chapter is to characterize French and German public administration and management, outline their specific reform trajectories and indicate the influence both systems have had abroad. We will begin by highlighting some characteristic traditions of the German and French systems. This will be followed by an overview of important reform trajectories in each country, which will highlight factors that have shaped the national administrative systems. The final section will focus on the influence of Germany and France on foreign public administrations.

29.2 THE STARTING POINT: STATE AND RULE OF LAW

Continental European political thought is strongly founded on the idea of the "State." This perspective, which is rooted in Roman Law tradition, views the state as a separate legal entity ("moral being"), which is granted certain competencies by constitution and which acts through "organs" (such as parliament, government, agencies, etc.) (Dyson 1980; Wollmann 2000*a*; Johnson 2000; Ridley 2000). Anglo-Saxon political thinking, embedded in Common Law tradition, has never really adopted the term "State" as a concept for the expression of the methods and structure of government and the political organization of society (Johnson 2000: 27). Instead, it is oriented towards institutions, ranging, for instance in the British case, from Parliament or the Crown to other institutions such as local councils. In the continental European tradition, which originates from the eighteenth-century Absolutist State, the state is still seen as a realm that is conceptually, legally and institutionally distinct from society and the private sector. Anglo-Saxon civil society tradition (for civil society tradition in Anglo-Saxon countries see Heady 1996: 236) has taken a more pragmatic view of government by seeing it as instrumental, if not ancillary, to the needs of society and economy (for western European state traditions in detail see Dyson 1980).

A typical feature of both the French and the German systems lies in the tradition of rule of law and strict limitation of administrative and state action to a legal basis. A focus on abstract legal norms and codified law is the primary medium for controlling administrative action. Both countries are considered to have a "legalistic administrative culture" (Schröter and Wollmann 1997: 177). At the time of its emergence in the 18th century, German administrative legal development—as in many other continental European countries—drew heavily on French experience (Wollmann 2000*a*: 7). It should be noted that the legal orientation of present-day administrative practice stems from different sources, and the different routes and traits of this tradition should not be overlooked. In France, law has traditionally been considered as an incorporation of public interest (*volonté générale*) and refers to the ideas of sovereignty of the people and the nation state (*l'état-nation*). In Germany, the idea of rule of law (*Rechtsstaat*) has prevailed according to codification seen as protection of citizens against bureaucracy—formerly against monarchic authorities, and today against unjustified constraints of human rights (Schröter and Wollmann 1997; Wollmann 2000*a*:7).

According to the principle of rule of law, every state action has to be tied to a legal basis. In both countries this has led to the formation of large bodies of administrative—as opposed to private—law, to regulate the citizen/state and inner-state relations. In conjunction with the typical notion of the state—as outlined above—in which the state has its own legal personality, everything done in its name is a legal act. This underlines the notion that the state—and supposedly not individuals—acts in its name. The importance of administrative law for daily procedures and actions in the administration has been accompanied by a self-standing system of administrative courts. These administrative courts are completely separate from civil or criminal courts and deal in particular with complaints and appeals against public actions. The existence of a large body of special administrative law with specialized courts and the specific law-orientated notion of the state contribute to the prevailing differentiation between state and society into two spheres or legal systems (Wollmann 2000a; Jann 2003). This is one of the most important reasons why private sector style management techniques were virtually ignored by administrations both in France and Germany for decades. In Germany, the concept of the Rechtsstaat (judicial state, legal state, or state of rule of law) has a strong impact on the administrative system (Klages and Löffler 1995: 374; Pollitt and Bouckaert 2000: 238). Application of law and compliance with rule has traditionally been seen as the functional core of public administration. The production of legally correct administrative acts has often been given priority over more managerial aspects like efficiency and effectiveness (Wollmann 2001: 159).

The advance of legalism and codification in the realm of public administration have led to a strong representation of legal training and the legal profession in the public service. In Germany, the term *Juristenmonopol* ("lawyer monopoly") has been coined due to the fact that higher civil servants have typically studied law (Wollmann 1997: 84). On the federal and state levels (Germany) an overwhelming majority of civil servants are lawyers, while on a local level lawyers tend to be the exception (Klages and Löffler 1995: 374). In France, two of the most important *grands corps* are considered as lawyers *grands corps* and—in line with philosophical orientation—as "bastions" of public service ideals (Clark 1998: 103; Jobert 1989: 386).

It should be stressed that a rule-oriented administrative culture may be interpreted as impeding radical reforms of an administrative system, especially on the federal level, where it is strongly anchored. A picture of administration as solely an apparatus for applying rules does not correspond to reality. First, legal propositions are generally prepared by the administration—often by the same people who will subsequently bring them into force. Second, public administration has always been engaged in negotiation and the weighing up of interests and cooperation, and this tendency is on the increase. Even where it is possible to apply law, negotiation still takes place (Ellwein 1994; Jann 1999: 537).

In the context of Germany, Wagener claims that rule orientation and rule of law have even become fictitious for a further reason, namely that of overregulation. As the norms are not "known" in their entirety, a time-consuming search for the relevant norms is often required. This results in pragmatic rule reduction, which is normally pursued by the specialized administrations themselves, who use this to decide which rules are to be applied (Wagener 1979: 244). Although there have been some reform initiatives and commissions that aim to tackle "law and administration simplification", no relevant progress can be noted in this regard.

The traditional, authoritarian notion of the state—as standing above society—no longer fully captures today's reality (Jann 2003: 100). Nevertheless, its effects are still shown in today's administration and explain some of the peculiarities of continental European public administration. Discourse about state traditions in modern-day Germany follows competing narratives and Leitbilder, promoting a more cooperative, activating role of the state (Jann 1999, 2003).

29.3 FRANCO–GERMAN ADMINISTRATIVE SYSTEMS AND THEIR CHARACTERISTICS

Notions of State of legalism account for a large degree of the differing characteristics of continental European administrative systems and make their mark on every aspect of administration and public management. They represent a common and combining feature of continental European administrative systems. In the following, three structural aspects are addressed which further characterize continental European administrations and reveal significant differences between the French and German systems.

29.3.1 French Centralism vs. German Federalism

The most obvious difference between France and Germany lies in their basic structural principle. Whereas in France most of the political and administrative control is concentrated in Paris (centralism), the German tradition is based on a complicated sharing of responsibilities and rights among the different levels of state (federalism). Historically, the French state-centered structure, which shaped institutional development well into the 1980s, dates back to Napoleon's recentralization policy in the aftermath of post-revolutionary decentralization initiatives. Germany's federal system has its traces in the long absence of a nation state and the multitude of (quasi-) sovereign states and principalities.

France had long been known for its centralized polity, and its administrative system has been considered to be an archetype of the centralized nation-state serving as example for the construction of hierarchical administration, centralized under government and organized according to a uniform state concept. Even autonomous responsibilities of local self-administration were administratively carried out by state administration directed by the prefect (Wollmann n.d.: 4). However, critical examination reveals the situation to be considerably more complicated than the "ideal" impression that is sometimes given (Mény 1988: 274). Furthermore, since the decentralization reforms of 1982, the tendency appears to have been reversed (Nakano 2000: 97). According to Clark, it is generally agreed that the territorial reforms of the 1980s strengthened local government as an institution. Elected political leaders, particularly mayors of larger cities, now have more policy autonomy than they did prior to the reforms (Clark 2000a: 31).

The institutional setting in Germany strongly reflects the country's federal character and is characterized as a "decentralized" system (Katzenstein 1987: 15; Becker 1989; König and Siedentopf 2001). The division of the German Republic into the Federal Republic and its constituent states, as well as the important role given to local self-government, has to be seen in light of the historical importance and prerogatives of state bureaucracies at the time of Bismarck. The federalist compromise, which safeguarded interests of territorial bureaucracies, accounts to a large degree for the particular system of federalism in Germany, which has been labeled as "administrative-executive federalism" (*Exekutivföderalismus*) and refers to the peculiarity that almost all federal legislation is executed by state and local administrations, meaning that the federal level, accordingly, has very limited executive administrative capacity (Lehmbruch 2000: 88). Power is widely dispersed in Germany's federal systems and prescribes an administrative structure that permits an overall system of political administration with a graded and diversified distribution of functions and responsibilities at the middle and lower levels of administration. The major elements of organizational structure granted by constitution are federalism and two tiers of local government (Siedentopf 1988b).

The local level of administration plays an important role in the provision of services to citizens and is one of the main interfaces between public administration and citizens. Local autonomy of municipalities accounts for an enormous variety of approaches in terms of various aspects. Autonomy in Germany includes a limited power to determine tax levels for local businesses. The local level has proven to be a creative innovator and promoter of reforms in Germany. The reform movement, internationally referred to as New Public Management (NPM), began on the local level and has developed from there to the upper federal levels (Röber 1996: 174; Reichard 2003).

29.3.2 Hierarchy

Inspired by analogy to the organization of an army (Hattenhauer 1993: 99), the hierarchic structure in both countries stands for effective control by top officials and politicians as well as for efficient execution of orders throughout the whole organization. The principle of hierarchy in the Weberian model therefore includes a fixed structure and order of administrative agencies which provides supervisory and control agencies and the right to appeal from subordinated to higher agencies. Hierarchical organization reflects federalist and centralist structures of the political system. In France, ideas of *bonapartisme* and centralism used to focus on Paris and the central government. A famous quote by Bonaparte states that he was more worried about what could happen in Paris than in the rest of France. Decision-making powers of the state apparatus have been highly centralized, which is often referred to as legacy of Jacobinism (Attarça and Nioche 1996: 88). The French hierarchical conception therefore included, for example, submitting local matters to a central structure controlled by Paris. It also stresses the personal responsibility of ministers for all actions of their administration as well as the institution of the *préféct* or commissioner as a regional representative of central government. Members of the cabinet observe actions of the subordinated ministries and coordinate between them (cf. Suleiman 1974: 222). Germany also follows the principle of responsibility of ministers and the hierarchical, pyramid-like structure of ministries (König 2001: 21; Heady 1996: 221). Administrative institutions were transferred from France to Germany during the emergence of modern administrative law and therefore show some resemblance (König 1995: 350). Due to the federalist structure of Germany, different hierarchical structures of federal, state and local governments coexist and vary between states and local governments. The staffs of ministers are considerably smaller than in France. Features of hierarchical organization and structure have been very stable and resistant to reform in the Federal Republic. Nevertheless, a silent change and trend towards "dehierarchization" and "autonomization" (*Entbürokratisierung und Verselbständigung*) has recently become apparent. These developments cannot generally be attributed to specific motivated reform programs, but have rather emerged as an accumulation of typical German incrementalist adoptions and patterns of change (Jann 1999: 533). In the last few decades, hierarchy has lost its primary role in German administration. As Scharpf and Mayntz stated, policy formulation and implementation no longer occurs in a top–down hierarchical manner, but rather within complex negotiating systems—at most "in the shadow of hierarchy" (Scharpf 1993; Mayntz 1996). In this context, administration no longer receives its premises only by law, but reacts and responds to external influence (Jann 1999: 538).

References to cultural aspects could prove to be helpful for understanding and analyzing the actual implications of current trends. In his classic study of national cultures, Hofstede (1980) found that France and Germany are similar with respect to individualism, but show significant differences in the dimensions of power distance, masculinity, and avoidance of uncertainty. For power distance, France scores in the upper tier, while Germany is in the lower tier. The scores for masculinity are exactly the opposite of this. In the dimension of uncertainty avoidance, France lies in the upper tier and Germany in the middle tier. The high score of France for power distance and avoidance of uncertainty generally points to a greater acceptance of control and obedience as well as to greater preference for clear instruction, standards, written rules and more ritual behavior. The high masculinity index for Germany, on the other hand, points to a greater importance of careers and higher task-orientated motivation (Jann 2000: 339).

29.3.3 Civil Service

Public bureaucracy in Germany and France builds on a professional and highly specialized work force, which has traces—in line with other western European countries—in the historically based emergence of a distinct, classical profession (Chapman 1959). The status of civil servants is legally codified by (often even constitutional) law and differs from ordinary working relationships through special privileges, rights and duties. Bureaucrats in Germany and France consider themselves as public officials rather than public servants.

In order to understand the French Civil Service, it is necessary to appreciate the significance and role of the *corps*. Firstly, being a French senior civil servant automatically entails being a member of a corps. Corps are by purpose organized via a variety of resorts and members show a high degree of mobility (Siedentopf and Speer 2001: 51). The *grands corps* (great corps) embrace all senior civil servant positions (Owen 2000: 57). There are some 1,800 different corps spread across four occupational categories (Mény 1988: 286; Escoube 1971). The corps system has particular implications for the management of the civil service, in that individual careers do not depend on one's hierarchical superior in the ministry but on the organizational requirements of the corps. Within the corps, it is customary for careers to be managed impersonally, on the basis of seniority rather than performance (Stevens 1988; see also Clark 1998: 99).

Admission to one of the *grands corps* is preceded by education in one of the *grandes écoles*, such as the *École Nationale d'Administration* (ENA). The strength of the *grandes écoles* resides in their role as selecting machines, enforced by strict entry and final exams. The great majority of the administration's elite have been trained in one of them. According to Suleiman's research, former students consider themselves "generalist" rather than specialists, and point out that this general education has made them able to adapt to all types of situation. (Suleiman 1979; Mény 1988: 285). The syllabus at specialized institutions like ENA is considered law-oriented and conservative, although it has been modified in recent years and now also covers issues like contemporary management techniques, information systems and performance evaluation (Owen 2000: 59). Still, Rouban argues "that the very idea of management, with its Anglo-American sound, has never seduced higher civil servants (especially those coming from the *grands corps*) and that they would help more to renew political control over public administration than to rationalize day-to-day administrative action" (Rouban 1997: 142).

Unlike the classic Anglo-American image of an impartial public administration, in France the influence of the *grands corps* and senior civil servants extends well beyond the sphere of public administration. The senior civil service has also "colonized" the political sphere, the public economic sector and even the private sector (Mény 1988: 286). The practice of network-based assignment of positions in other sectors is called *pantouflage* (Suleiman 1979: 179). The quality of members of a corps is so highly appreciated that they are found in significant numbers outside their corp's original field, such as occupying positions in a nationalized industry (Owen 2000: 57). Hoffmann-Martinot reports that a generation of politicians has come into office who frequently come from the public sector. Thus, their know-how and time resources are sufficient to modify the previous politician-adminis-trator balance in their favor since the homogeneity and stability of corps implies that the same corps and people remain after political shifts (Hoffmann-Martinot 2002). Guyomarch states that "strong intellectual sympathy" for administration can be noted on the political side (Guyomarch 1999: 183). The French civil servants see themselves as political persons (Wilsford 2001). In contrast to the Anglo-Saxon view, the French have always recognized that the dichotomy between politics and administration is artificial and that administrators have actually made policies all along (Martin 1987). This politicization of the administration triggers some de-ontological difficulties in an already complex relationship and leads to the inter-locking of public administration with the political system at all levels of government (Jean-Pierre 1999: 87–99; Ashford 1982: 188).

With regard to Germany, "one of the most characteristic elements of German public services is the enormous scope of the 'Beamten', comprising not only persons having 'state authority' but also every judge, teacher, university professor, postman, or train driver" (Stammen and Wessels 1996: 131). Reflecting structural differences in Germany, the vast majority of civil servants are associated to the *Länder* and local governments (90 percent). Civil service is codified by federal framework law and therefore no major difference exists between levels of govern-ment. Recruitment of personnel is not centrally organized but is delegated to the lower levels and institutions. In actual fact only about 30 percent of public sector employees are employed with special status as civil servants. The rest qualify as either public employees or public workers (Schröter and Wollmann 1997: 182). However, in many relevant aspects, regulations for civil servants and other public employees have been brought in line with one another (Siedentopf 1981: 332). *Beamten* continue to characterize the German bureaucracy, even though they are no longer given the special deference and respect they enjoyed in the past. Public administration in Germany is not very well respected and appreciated either by citizens or politicians, or even by itself (Klages 2001: 442; Jann 1999: 534). Employ-ment as a public agent is generally sought for reasons of job security and security in old age rather than for interesting tasks or ambitions regarding position or income (Heady 1996: 224; Jann 1999: 535).

Civil servants, and accordingly predominately jurists, have taken a crucial role in the process of public sector reform. Not surprisingly, reforms have not aimed—beyond rhetorical and conceptual statements—to significantly change the basic structures and principles of civil service in Germany. In this regard it should also be noted that main reform initiatives were launched by local government while vast aspects of civil service are codified on the federal level.

29.3.4 Comparison of French and German Classical Administration

French and German public administrative systems—in line with their the continental European siblings—are classified as Weberian models of administration. As outlined above, they share common elements and characteristics like the legalistic-orientated culture, civil service, and structure as well as the dominant role played by civil servants with respect to administrative matters, policy formulation and policy implementation. In broader terms, both administrations and systems used to be and still are highly "traditional" and "self-referencing", meaning that reflections and judgements about the structure, performance, duty, etc., of the state have always (implicitly or explicitly) been based on the countries' own philosophers—such as Montesquieu and Rousseau for France, or Hegel, Stein and Kant for Germany—and the referring purpose and role of public administration within the state (like central control or adoption of law). This has led to high degree of self-confidence and a deeply rooted belief in the high performance of public service in line with its philosophical traditions. Pursuit of general interest and accordance with law are given a much higher priority within the system than objectives of efficiency and effectiveness more recently highlighted in international debate. Of course, the Zeitgeist has reached both countries and managerial aspects are now receiving greater attention and leading to a critical questioning of existing practices. However, reform discourse, for example in Germany, is still largely shaped by legal and constitutional reasoning (Johnson 1997: 177).

French and German public administration also differ in some important respects, not least in terms of the centralized and decentralized structure in the respective countries. To characterize their distinction, Cassese has identified two models of the Weberian administration besides the Anglo-Saxon one. He describes the German model as "dominated by legalism, rigidity and administrative planning" and the French as characterized by "the rigidity of the structures and the flexibility of the bureaucracy" (Cassese 1987: 12). The difference can be derived from varying ideological bases of rule of law and state conception in the two countries.

29.4 DEVELOPMENT TRAJECTORIES

In this section, main reform trajectories affecting administrative structures and procedures and their modernization in France and Germany will be discussed. With the exception of the French territorial decentralization reforms, which are important as a precursor for subsequent reforms and are included due to their significant impact on the structure of French administration, reforms addressed in this section share a managerial orientation and may be regarded as national efforts of NPM.

29.4.1 France: A Modernizing State

In the last 20 years, a number of reform programs have been launched by successive governments to modernize the structures and methods of public administration in France. Central government is the key player in the realm of reform initiatives. Even though local governments have received more room to maneuver as a consequence of the territorial decentralization in the 1980s, very little is known about reform agendas on the local level besides those initiated by central government.

Modernization of public administration is identified with the program of public service renewal launched in 1989, which has been consolidated by subsequent governments through various larger and smaller reform programs such as the Reform of the State (Clark 2000a: 30). All these reforms have to be placed in the broader context of the preceding territorial reforms.

Territorial reforms of the early 1980s gave more power to the authorities of local government and changed the relationship between them and the State's field services. Principal measures were (Mény 1988: 278): transfer of powers of the regional and department executives from the prefects to the chairmen of the regional and department councils; the prefect (now Commissioner) has become simply a representative of the State, responsible for coordinating the field services; prefectoral supervision of the communes and departments has been removed and replaced by the jurisdictional control of the regional administrative courts and the financial control of the new regional audit offices; local authority personnel have been awarded a new statute, comparable to that of civil servants; regional assemblies (from 1986 onwards) are elected by universal suffrage; responsibilities of local authorities have been redefined and extended, assigning local management to the communes, social services to the departments and responsibility for economic development to the regions.

The territorial reforms were embedded in a rhetoric of "rupture" between past and upcoming policy proclaiming a fundamental redirection and reorientation of policy. In fact, though, Defferre—himself an experienced local politician—adopted a pragmatic approach that was not revolutionarily different from previous initiatives (Mabileau 1997: 342). Policy outcomes have been significantly determined by elite coalitions (see Nakano 2000). The reforms have strengthened local government as an institution. Increased capacity of local governments following these reforms is considered as main catalyst for the restructuring of local state apparatus, which is the main theme of the following reforms (Clark 2000a: 31; also Verpeaux 2002: 15).

In 1989, the "renewal of the state", followed by a number of decrees in its aftermath, was proclaimed. It included four objectives (Guyomarch 1999: 173; Clark 2000a: 30; Serieyx 1994):

- Strengthening of human resource management, staff training and appraisal programs, and internal communications
- Devolution of executive management form the central ministries to their territorial field services on the local (department) level and closer to the user
- Introduction of policy and performance evaluation into government
- Enhancement of responsiveness to the users by improvement of quality, prioritizing accessibility, user information and simplification of procedures.

To devolve executive management, so-called responsibility centers were set up with pluri-annual contracts fixing targets and resources (Ryckeboer 1996; Postif 1997: 218). Further, special committees, councils and funds were entrusted with the development of performance evaluation throughout the civil service. In the same period, training programs and syllabi at institutions like the ENA were updated. The end of the Socialist reforms, in 1992, was marked by two measures. A law on deconcentration was passed by parliament, which generalized experiences of responsibility centers. By the same legislation, a "charter of deconcentration" was passed according to which every administrative decision had to be taken at the level closest to the users. The second measure was the adoption of a Charter of Public Service. It has been pointed out that the French charters were not set up with the intention of "British customer-style empowerment." The French charters are more to be seen as a reassertion of the Republican value of equality and are therefore largely concerned with principles of legality and due process (Clark 2000a: 32).

The "Reforms of the state and the public service" focused on the contractualization of relations between central ministries and their territorial field services, confining the ministries to policy setting, resource allocation, monitoring and evaluation functions. The new government initialized its reform program with a circular stating five policy goals (Guyomarch 1999: 175):

- Redefine the tasks of the State and the field of action of public services
- Take into account the needs and expectations of citizens (charters; simplification of contacts, etc.)

- The central state should take on a regulatory function. Central ministries to be transformed into holdings, limited to the functions of policy setting, resource allocation, monitoring and evaluation.
- Delegate all operational tasks, all non-regulatory responsibilities performed by central administration.
- Renovate public management according to modern management principles

Prime Minister Jean-Pierre Raffarin has also set a focus on decentralization policy in his reforms. As a very symbolic step, the first article of the French constitution was newly redacted and now states that "the organization of the republic is decentralized". It is argued that the old description of France as "one and indivisible" nowadays has to be taken in a more relative sense (Verpeaux 2002, Hoffmann-Martinot 2002).

How do these reforms relate to others in the Anglo-Saxon world? The aforementioned reforms are characterized by an enormous degree of continuity despite political shifts during the time they were made. The political and administrative impacts have been described as substantial (Clark 2000*b*: 31; Rouban 1997: 151; Wollmann 2002: 38). In addition, more flexible and businesslike forms of internal management and service delivery can be discerned. However, legalistic tradition still defines the scope and speed of many aspects of administrative reform due to the fact that national law regulates many important aspects, especially with respect to the civil service. Managerial delegation with regard to appointment, promotion and pay has therefore been limited. Most importantly, recent reforms have had considerable symbolic significance in signalling a changing role of the central state and a shift of orientation towards modern public management and towards the international reform debate (Clark 2000*b*).

29.4.2 Persisting Incrementalism in Germany

Public management reforms in the Germany began in the late 1980s. The term that is used the most frequently with regard to German public management and public administration reforms seems to be *incrementalism* (for public administration and management reforms in Germany see Wollmann 2000*b*; Benz and Goetz 1996; Reichard 2003; Seibel 2001). Reform efforts have not overcome traditional structural and institutional settings, and the traditional primacy of legalism and rule-bound bureaucracy have remained largely unchanged while fostering more managerial flexibility and methods in the existing administrative system. The stability of basic structures should not be mistaken as implying a lack of reform efforts or an absence of any effects of reform. The qualitative orientation of reforms has experienced substantial redirection in the last decade in line with international NPM ideas, but the scope and pace of actual reforms rather followed a step-by-step strategy. In contrast to France and in line with the federal, decentralized structures, public administration modernization in Germany is a "bottom–up" process. While there are hardly any effective public management reforms at the federal level (Naschold et al. 1999: 13), at least some states have been engaging in reforms. The actual reform motors and entrepreneurs are local governments. Since each level of government within the federal system has pursued its own autonomous reform initiatives, significant differences in speed and substance of modernization have been revealed.

On the federal level, two administrative reform programs of the last decade can be distinguished.

- In 1995, after 15 years in office, the conservative-liberal government set up an independent reform commission entitled "Lean State" (*Schlanker Staat*). The commission produced reports, but practical effects were limited to the privatization of federal rail and postal systems.
- After coming into power in 1996, the red-green government coined the *Leitbild* of the "activating state" (*Aktivierender Staat*) for their approach to state modernization. This builds on the idea of a "new division of responsibilities between state and society" and—not following neo-liberal ideas—strongly emphases ideas of subsidiarity and empowerment. Not until 1999 was a public sector reform program developed which included the introduction of modern management (like cost accounting, performance agreements, benchmarking) into federal administration. As yet, although pilot projects have been testing some efficiency measures and instruments, reform activities along NPM lines seen at federal level have been very limited (Jann and Reichard 2001).

By 2000, almost all states had taken measures towards NPM, including concepts such as one-line budgeting, cost accounting, and management control systems. Reforms of the preceding decades (see Wollmann 2000*b*; Seibel 2001) produced ambiguous results, while most managerial reforms rather contributed to maintain the status quo and followed bureaucratic lines (Reichard 2003: 348). Since the 1990s, three reform waves have been observed:

- Local government levels had to be constructed and transformed in the aftermath of reunification. The transformation of East German local government followed the same pattern as on the state level and consisted in the adoption of West German models and concepts (see Reichard and Röber 1993).
- Strengthening of direct democratic elements by local constitutional reforms. In the early 1990s, all German Länder subsequently changed their local charter by providing for directly elected mayors (which was previously only the case in two states) and some even adopted provisions for recall of mayors, and direct democratic elements (Wollmann 2001: 163, 2000*b*: 929; Bogumil 2001: 174).
- Public management reforms labelled under the German NPM-style variant *Neues Steuerungsmodell* (new steering model) (NSM).

Since the 1990s, a number of German municipalities have started to engage in management-like reforms (see Reichard 2003: 353). A variety of modernization strategies have emerged within administrations initially largely isolated from academia, consultancy, or international reform discourse (Klages and Löffler 1995: 375). In its first years of use, NSM focused rather on technical instruments concerned with strengthening accountability and cost efficiency by integrating responsibilities for resources and policy issues that had formerly been separated (Reichard 2003: 353; Bogumil 2001: 137). Around 1998, a second phase of NSM reforms was revealed, which extended the conceptual framework with additional elements. While the first phase rather focused on instruments driven by hard facts, emphasis was now widened to soft elements. Experiments with quality management, human resource management and competition were included in the range of NSM modernization strategies.

How do these developments relate to the Anglo-Saxon experiences? Even though reforms have been pursued for over ten years now, there is still very little in the way of reliable and precise empirical data and evaluations of the actual impact and effects of reforms (cf. Jaedicke et al. 2000). Surveys reveal that the reform wave has swept across almost all municipalities—indeed 92 percent of municipalities claimed to be engaged in reforms in 2000 (Grömig 2001; for preceding years Grömig and Thielen 1996; Grömig and Gruner 1998). However, the scope and substance of reforms have varied widely (Wollmann 2001: 162). In general, the basic legalistic culture in Germany has never been jeopardised by the reforms, and not infrequently bureaucracy has swallowed up the new public management together with its instruments. The result of bureaucratizing new public management instruments has at times been even more regulation and bureaucracy.

29.5 INFLUENCE ABROAD

Since France and Germany are considered as reference examples of classical public administrations, it is interesting to explore the influence of French and German administrative systems and reform trajectories beyond their national boundaries and ask how characteristics of the two countries apply to other national administrative systems. First, traces of French and German influence within other continental European countries are explored. Further, the European Union will be addressed as an arena of influence. This will include a consideration of classical administrative traits in the administration of the European Union itself, as well as the transformation of public administrations in central and eastern Europe. Finally, the impact that classical administrative systems have had outside of Europe, namely in former colonies, will be discussed.

29.5.1 Western Continental Europe

Continental European countries show a great deal of variety and diversity with respect to their political and administrative systems. Path dependency needs to be taken into account when addressing commonalities and explaining differences between countries. Federal countries reveal significant differences regarding the role, task and interlocking of federal levels (see Hesse and Sharpe 1991; Page 1991) Within this diversity, all continental European governments and administrations correspond in two very relevant aspects. They are commonly attributed with the Weberian model of administration and are characterized by legalism and the existence of a specially trained, professional public service (Siedentopf 1988a: 340). Even in countries with no explicit Roman law tradition like the Scandinavian countries, the idea of rule of law is deeply rooted (Schröter 2001: 431).

French ideas and administrative settings had been very influential over time throughout Continental Europe. First, there has been a vast reception of French administrative structures by what is often referred to as the *Napoleonic factor*. During France's period of expansion, Napoleon imposed the French model of administration in the countries he conquered. The persistence of Napoleonic administration is explained by its modernity at the time and the lack of alternatives. Spain, for example, adopted an administrative system described as "perhaps the most Napoleonic one" outside of France, with characteristics such as centralism and hierarchy, administrative law, equality before the law and entrance to the civil service based on merit examinations (Beltrán 1988: 256). French traits have since diluted in Spain, particularly with regard to centralism, and Spain is nowadays considered as having a quasi-federal administration. Descendants of the French *préfet* are found in many European countries, such as the Queen's commissars in the Netherlands, or in Belgium and Spain. Division of executive powers and responsibility of ministers for their administration is further considered as a typically French, Napoleonic feature of administrative systems. Its influence has evolved as far as Nordic states like Denmark and Norway. However, the prominent French feature of elite corps structures has experienced only limited reception in continental Europe and remains largely unique to the French system, although it has had some influence on the Spanish administration (see Beltrán 1988: 267). Competitive entry examinations are today practiced by all EU member states, with the exception of Germany and the Netherlands (Ziller 1998). Probably the most influential, yet least obvious, is the model function of Napoleonic legal codes in various countries. Not only have vast parts of Europe been ruled for many years under Napoleonic legislation, it has also served as a framework for legal systems, for example in Germany and Switzerland.

In the last decades, French elite formation practice has been used as inspiration in various continental European states. Following the reference model of the École Nationale de l'Administration (ENA), specialized schools for higher civil service and elite formation have been established. Siblings of the ENA are now found in Germany (Deutsche Hochschule für Verwaltungswissenschaften Speyer), Spain (Instituto Nacional de Administracion Publica—INAP), Portugal (Instituto Nacional de Administraçao—INA), Italy (Scuola Superiore della Pubblica Amministrazione della Presidenza del Consiglio dei Ministri—SSPA), to name just a few.

Far less account is given in the literature and in general perception to the German influence on other countries. An obvious reason for this might be the lack of a comparable Napoleonic factor: German occupation, where it took place, never had an ideal-driven ambition to install a certain political system as was the case with the revolutionary Napoleon. Reference to the German model is generally made in the context of a state of civil servants, and the conception as *Rechtsstaat* (state of rule of law) is accompanied by the dominance of lawyers in the public sector. The civil service in Norway and Sweden was built up in close resemblance to the German example, but over the course of time has developed in different directions and has undergone public service reforms that have placed public civil servants almost on a par with private employees. Nowadays, Sweden's civil service system is categorized as an "open" system more in line with that of Great Britain and the Netherlands than with "closed" systems like those of Germany and France (Auer et al. 1996: 131; Holmgren 1988; Mac Donald 1988; Lundquist 1988: 166).

29.5.2 The European Union

The European Union is of interest for two phases of continental European administrative systems. First, national administrative systems had an influence on the shape of the European administrative system. Second, the latter has in turn influenced national public administration systems and has led to some changes in them. We will begin by concentrating on the first phase and limit the second aspect to the effects on administrations in central and eastern European Countries. (For effects on western European countries see Romentsch and Wessels 1996; Page and Wouters 1995; Harmsen 1999; Knill 2002; Hix and Goetz 2000.)

France is often cited as having had substantial influence on the European Union and its administrative structures (for European administration see Coombes 1970; Cassese 1987; Page 1997). Leaving aside the political ambitions and positions of France and other member states (see Guyomarch et al. 1998), in terms of the current shape and status of European administration, a number of important elements point to a dilution of elements generally attributed to the French system. The European Union was set up in line with Republican ideas and follows the French perspective of general interest. In this tradition, administration is to defend the general interest not only based upon its legal basis, but also in terms of its provision of counterweight political forces. As empirical research shows, the notion of benevolent technocrats has nowadays come to be seen as somewhat outdated by most European top officials. Nevertheless, a shared belief in the duty to "construct Europe," if necessary against resistance, is widespread (Hooghe 1999: 358). European administration is a law-based system, and key legal texts are the *statut du personnel* and the Financial Regulation. This embedding in a solid legal framework stems from national, particularly French, traditions of identifying administration with a durable "state" and not with a particular ruler. By supporters of republican ideals, the *statut* is seen as a symbol for the support of the idea that there is a "European" interest above that of the various "rulers" and that EU officials are its defenders (Stevens 2002: 5). The structure of the Commission, with cabinets and organization in general directories, strongly resembles the French regime. French roots are also found in the civil service system with regard to its entrance and career criteria based on competition, the career logic, the ranks and the non-automatic attribution of a position.

Administration of the European Community can be characterized as more continental European, referring to the fact that its set-up is more in line with the idea of an administrative, working state than with the ideas of civic culture traditions (König 2001: 15; Siedentopf 1997: 338). From the beginning, administrative structures, such as civil service regulations and internal organization, have been influenced by member states, and especially by France and its tradition. Nevertheless, the initial French influence is increasingly waning due to the enlargement of the Union, reforms, and cultural diffusion within its administration.

Recently, a new arena for possible traits showing the influence of continental European administrative traditions has opened up in central and eastern European countries (CEE). Following the breakdown of the former communist regimes, countries have been faced with the rebuilding and transformation of their administrative structures. Due to aspirations to join the EU, the requirements and recommendations of the Union in this regard have gained top priority. European influence on the administrative systems of central and eastern European countries cannot be denied, and continental European systems in particular seem to be considered as reference models. To explain this orientation, aside from prerequisites set up by the EU, it has been argued that the capacity building and trajectories of these countries have historical kinship with continental Europe countries, not least Germany, rather than with the Anglo-Saxon world (Wollmann 2001: 167). Intentions and efforts clearly focus on establishing a more Weberian model of bureaucracy than on more managerial alternatives as proclaimed under the NPM credo (Fournier 1998: 113). Orientation and knowledge of existing European models is predominant and reference to different national features such as the *Rechtsstaat*, *l'état de droit, estato di diritto*, is explicitly cited. Institutions and structures often represent a blend of continental European examples, as shown, for example, by the Polish civil service (see Czaputowicz 2002). Another very concrete channel of influence emerges from the various advisory programs such as the OECD Sigma program. Financed by the EU, Sigma supports the administration of candidate countries in their preparations for successful entry into the Union by assessing reform progress in terms of good European practice and assisting in building institutions to meet European standards, etc. Besides financial resources, Western experts also consult or advise the CEE administration. CEE administrators receive training from partner institutions in Western Europe. Programs such as these foster and catalyse West–East influence on CEE countries.

29.5.3 Former Colonies

In the context of continental European influence on administrative systems abroad, it is also important to consider the footprints left in former colonial countries by their colonial European power. With regard to the French and German impact in former colonies, it can be stated that the French influence has been much more persistent than the German one. The reasons for this lie in the duration of colonial power and its aspirations for assimilation. Due to the limited duration and succession of German colonial power, its influence was largely displaced by succeeding powers. Thus, for example, Tanzania, which was formerly a German colony, under British protectorate after the Second World War, adopted a common law-based legal system after independence. As Heady summarizes, "a country that was formerly a colony almost certainly will resemble the parent administratively, even though independence was forcibly won and political apron stings have been cut" (Heady 1996: 318). French colonial policy was influenced by republican principles. As the republic was a single, indivisible one, the colonies were an intrinsic part of it, and should be assimilated to it in every aspect (Fieldhouse 1966: 308), including administrative structures. Remainders of French bureaucratic traits have carried over to the successor states after gaining independence, so that in many former French colonies such as Algeria, Tunisia, or Morocco, remainders of the French *préfet* structure can still be discerned. In addition, the national legal system generally reflects former colonial influence, meaning that most of the former French colonies have a Roman law-based, legal system.

29.6 Conclusion

Analysis of the public administration and public management reforms in Continental Europe of roughly the last twenty years reveals that they are simultaneously characterized by change and continuity (Kickert 1997; Pollitt and Bouckaert 2000).

All countries have engaged in efforts for change by means of modernization and reform initiatives. The scope, focus, and speed of reforms vary widely between countries. Continental European countries in the sample used by Pollitt and Bouckaert have been grouped as maintainer (federal Germany) and as modernizers (France, the Netherlands, Sweden, and Finland) (Pollitt and Bouckaert 2000: 93), while reform efforts include areas such as finance, personnel, organization, and performance measurement. Reforms show a certain extent of similarity across continental European countries, largely attributed to the universal spread of socio-economic problems and the political context accompanied by the dispersion of a (at times deceptive) common terminology of the New Public Management wave. Despite common traditions in continental European administrations and the internationality of NPM ideas, it is obvious that reform contents are rather chosen in response to particular actual problems faced by the polity (Schedler and Proeller 2002) than in terms of the dissemination of a new managerialist model. The diversity of reform trajectories points to "path dependency" as an important explanation variable, highlighting the extent to which institutional legacies of the past are inextricably linked with the politics of change (Clark 2000a: 36; Wollmann 2000a: 20). As a consequence, path dependency also leads to the preservation of national characteristics of administrative systems. For example, the strong representation of civil servants in French and German parliaments makes it more difficult to adopt legislative measures perceived as disadvantageous or hostile to the interests of public officials, with the result that such measures are found more rarely in the two countries. In consequence, path dependency preserves account for the continuation of national administrative traditions and characteristics. However, it does not prevent radical modernization and restructuring, as is shown by the examples of French territorial reforms.

References

ASHFORD, D. (1982), *British Dogmatism and French Pragmatism*. London, George Allen & Unwin.

ATTARÇA, M., and NIOCHE, J. (1996), "The Political and Administrative Institutions of France," in Brovetto 1996: 87–124.

AUER, A., DEMNKE, C. et al. (1996), *Civil Service in the Europe of Fifteen*. EIPA. Mastricht.

BECKER, B. (1989), *Öffentliche Verwaltung*. Percha am Starnberger See, Schulz.

BELTRÁN, M. (1988), "Spain," in Rowat 1988: 255–72.

BENZ, A., and GOETZ, K. H. (eds.) (1996), *A New German Public Sector? Reform, Adaptation and Stability*, Aldershot: Dartmouth.

BOGUMIL, J. (2001), *Modernisierung lokaler Politik. Kommunale Entscheidungsprozesse im Spannungsfeld zwischen Parteienwettbewerb, Verhandlungszwängen und Ökonomisierung*, Baden-Baden: Nomos.

BROVETTO, R. (ed.) (1996), *European Government a Guide through Diversity*, Atti e monografie. Milano, Edizioni Giuridiche Economiche Aziendali dell'Universitá Bocconi e Giuffrè Editori.

CASSESE, S. (1987), *The European Administration*, Brussels, International Institute of Administrative Science.

CHAPMAN, B. (1959), *The Profession of Government: The Public Service in Europe*, Westport, CT: Greenwood Press.

CLARK, D. (1998), "The Modernization of the French Civil Service: Crisis, Change and Continuity," *Public Administration*, 76, (Spring): 97–115.

—— (2000*a*), "Public Service Reform: A Comparative West European Perspective," *West European Politics* 23(3): 25–44.

—— (2000*b*), "Public Service Reform: A Comparative West European Perspective," *West European Politics* 23(3): 25–44.

COOMBES, D. (1970), *Politics and bureaucracy in the European Community: A Portrait of the Commission of the E.E.C.*, London: Allen & Unwin.

CZAPUTOWICZ, J. (2002), "From Co-operation to Integration—the case of Poland," in F. v. d. Berg, G. Jenei, and L. T. Leloup (eds.), *East–West Co-operation in Public Sector Reform*, Amsterdam: IOS Press, 81–93.

DYSON, K. (1980), *The State Tradition in Western Europe*, Oxford: Robertson.

ELLWEIN, T. (1994), *Das Dilemma der Verwaltung Verwaltungsstruktur und Verwaltungsreformen in Deutschland*, Mannheim: Bibliographisches Institut.

ESCOUBE, P. (1971), *Les Grands Corps de l'Etat*, Paris: Presses Universitaire de France.

FARNHAM, D., HORTON, S. et al. (eds.) (1996), *The New Public Managers in Europe: Public Servants in Transition*, Houndmills: Macmillan.

FIELDHOUSE, D. K. (1966), *The Colonial Empires from the 18th Century*, New York: Dell Publishing.

FLYNN, N., and STREHL, F. (1996), *Public Sector Management in Europe*, London: Prentice-Hall.

FOURNIER, J. (1998), "Administrative Reform in the Commission Opinions Concerning the Accession of the Central and Eastern European Countries to the European Union," in Sigma (ed.), *Preparing Administration for the European Administrative Space*, Sigma papers 23, Paris: Sigma/OECD, 110–18.

GRÖMIG, E. (2001), "Reform der Verwaltungen vor allem wegen Finanzkrise und überholter Strukturen," *Der Städtetag* 3: 11–18.

—— and GRUNER, M. (1998), "Reform in den Rathäusern," *Der Städtetag* 8: 312–16.

—— and THIELEN, H. (1996), "Städte auf dem Reformweg," *Der Städtetag* 9: 596–600.

GUYOMARCH, A. (1999), "'Public Service', 'Public Management' and the 'Modernization' of French Public Administration," *Public Administration* 77(1): 171–93.

—— MACHIN, H. et al. (1998), *France and the European Union*, New York: St. Martin's Press.

HARMSEN, R. (1999), "The Europeanization of National Administrations: A Comparative Study of France and the Netherlands," *Governance* 12(1): 81–113.

HATTENHAUER, H. (1993), *Geschichte des deutschen Beamtentums*, Köln: Heymann.

HEADY, F. (1996), *Public Administration: A Comparative Perspective*, New York: Dekker.

HESSE, J. J., and SHARPE, L. J. (1991), "Conclusions," in J. J. Hesse (ed.), *Local Goverment and Urban Affairs in International Perspective*, Baden-Baden, Nomos, 603–21.

HIX, S., and GOETZ, K. H. (2000), "Introduction: European Integration and National Political Systems," *West European Politics* (special issue): 1–26.

HOFFMANN-MARTINOT, V. (2002), *The French Republic, One and Divisible?* Paper presented at the Conference "Reforming local government: closing the gap between democracy and efficiency," University of Stuttgart.

HOFSTEDE, G. (1980), *Culture's Consequence:. International Differences in Work-Related Values*, London, Sage.

HOLMGREN, K. (1988), "Sweden," in Rowat 1988: 147–56.

HOOGHE, L. (1999), "Images of Europe: Orientations to European Integration among Senior Officials of the Commission," *British Journal of Political Science* 29: 345–67.

JAEDICKE, W., THRUN, T. et al. (2000), *Modernisierung der Kommunalverwaltung Evaluierungsstudie zur Verwaltungsmodernisierung im Bereich Planen, Bauen und Umwelt*, Stuttgart: Kohlhammer.

JANN, W. (1999), "Zur Entwicklung der öffentlichen Verwaltung," in T. Ellwein and E. Holtmann (eds.), *50 Jahre Bundesrepublik Deutschland: Rahmenbedingungen— Entwicklungen— Perspektiven*, Opladen: Westdeutscher Verlag, 520–43.

—— (2000), "Verwaltungskulturen im Vergleich," *Die Verwaltung*: 325–49.

—— (2003), "State, Administration and Governance in Germany: Competing Traditions and Dominant Narratives," *Public Administration* 81(1): 95–118.

—— and REICHARD, C. (2001), "Best Practice in Central Government Modernization," *Inernational Journal of Political Studies* (3): 93–111.

JEAN-PIERRE, D. (1999), *La Déontologie de l'administration*, Paris: PUF.

JOBERT, B. (1989), "The Normative Frameworks of Public Policy," *Policy Studies* 37(3): 376–86.

JOHNSON, N. (1997), "Über den Begriff des Staates aus vergleichender Sicht," in R. Morsey, H. Quaritsch, and H. Siedentopf (eds.), *Staat, Politik, Verwaltung in Europa*, Berlin: Duncker & Humblot, 167–80.

—— (2000), "State and Society in Britain: Some Contrasts with German Experience," in H. Wollmann and E. Schröter (eds.), *Comparing Public Sector Reform in Britain and Germany: Key Traditions and Trends of Modernisation*, Aldershot: Ashgate, 27–46.

KATZENSTEIN, J. (1987), *Policy and Politics in West Germany: The Growth of a Semi-Sovereign State*, Philadelphia: Temple University Press.

KICKERT, W. J. M. (ed.) (1997), *Public Management and Administrative Reform in Western Europe*, Cheltenham: Elgar.

KLAGES, H. (2001), "The Situation of the German Civil Service, in König and Siedentopf 2001: 441–55.

—— and LÖFFLER, E. (1995), "Administrative Modernization in Germany: A Big Qualitative Jump in Small Steps," *International Review of Administrative Science* 61: 373–83.

KNILL, C. (2002), *The Europeanisation of National Administration*, Cambridge: Cambrigde University Press.

KÖNIG, K. (1995), "'Neue' Verwaltung oder Verwaltungsmodernisierung: Verwaltungspolitik in den 90er Jahren," *Die öffentliche Verwaltung* 48(9): 349–58.

—— (2001), Public Administration in the Unified Germany, in K. König and H. Siedentopf (eds.), *Public administration in Germany*, Baden-Baden: Nomos, 13–31.

—— and BECK, J. (1997), *Modernisierung von Staat und Verwaltung*, Baden-Baden: Nomos Verlagsgesellschaft.

—— and SIEDENTOPF, H. (2001), *Public Administration in Germany*, Baden-Baden: Nomos.

LANE, J.-E. (ed.) (1997), *Public Sector Reform: Rationale, Trends and Problems*, London: Sage.

LEHMBRUCH, G. (2000), The Institutional Framework: Federalism and Decentralisation in Germany, in H. Wollmann and E. Schröter (eds.), *Comparing Public Sector Reform in Britain and Germany: Key Traditions and Trends of Modernisation*, Aldershot: Ashgate, 85–106.

LÜDER, K., and JONES, R. (eds.) (2003), *Reforming Governmental Accounting and Budgeting in Europe*, Frankfurt a. M.: Fachverlag Moderne Wirtschaft.

LUNDQUIST, L. (1988), "A Comparative Overview," in Rowat, 1988: 157–68.

MABILEAU, A. (1997), "Les genies invisible du local," *Revue française d'administration publique* 47: 340–75.

MAC DONALD, D. (1988), "Norway," in Rowat 1988: 103–16.

MARTIN, D. W. (1987), "Déjà vu: French antecedents of American public administration," *Public Administration Review* (July/August): 297–303.

MAYNTZ, R. (1996), "Politische Steuerung: Aufstieg, Niedergang und Transformation einer Theorie," in K. v. Beyme and C. Offe (eds.), *Politische Theorien in der Ära der Transformation*. Opladen: Leske & Budrich, 148–68.

MÉNY, Y. (1988), "France," in Rowat 1988: 273–92.

NAKANO, K. (2000), "The Role of Ideology and Elite Networks in the Decentralisation Reforms in 1980s France," *West European Politics* 23(3): 97–114.

NASCHOLD, F. (1996), *New Frontiers in Public Sector Management Trends and Issues in State and Local Government in Europe*, Berlin: de Gruyter.

—— JANN, W. et al. (1999), *Innovation, Effektivität, Nachhaltigkeit. Internationale Erfahrungen zentralstaatlicher Verwaltungsreformen*, Berlin: Edition Sigma.

OLSEN, J., and PETERS, B. G., (eds.) (1996), *Lessons from Experience*, Oslo: Scandinavian University Press.

OWEN, B. (2000), "France," in J. A. Chandler (ed.), *Comparative Public Administration*, London: Routledge, 50–74.

PAGE, E. (1991), *Localism and Centralism in Europe*, Oxford, Oxford University Press.

—— (1997), *People who Run Europe*, Oxford, Oxford University Press.

—— and WOUTERS, L. (1995), "The Europeanization of the National Bureaucracies?" in J. Pierre (ed.), *Bureaucracy in the Modern State: An Introduction to Comparative Public Administration*, Aldershot: Edward Elgar, 185–204.

POLLITT, C., and BOUCKAERT, G. (2000), *Public Management Reform a Comparative Analysis*, Oxford: Oxford University Press.

POSTIF, T. (1997), "Public Sector Reform in France, in Lane 1997: 209–24.

REICHARD, C. (2003), "Local Public Management Reforms in Germany," *Public Administration* 81(2): 345–63.

—— and Röber, M. (1993), "Was kommt nach der Einheit? Die öffentlichen Verwaltung in der ehemaligen DDR zwischen Blaupause und Reform," in G. J. Glaessner (ed.), *Der lange Weg zur Einheit*, Berlin: Dietz, 215–45.

RIDLEY, F. F. (2000), "The Public Service in Britain: From Administrative to Managerial Culture," in H. Wollmann and E. Schröter (eds.), *Comparing Public Sector Reform in Britain and Germany: Key Traditions and Trends of Modernisation*, Aldershot: Ashgate, 132–49.

RÖBER, M. (1996), "Germany," in D. Farnham, S. Horton, J. Barlow, and A. Hondeghem (eds.), *New Public Managers in Europe: Public Servants in Transition*, London: Houndsmill, Macmillan: 169–93.

ROMENTSCH, D., and WESSELS, W. (eds.) (1996), *The European Union and Member States: Towars Institutional Fusion?* Manchester: Manchester University Press.

ROUBAN, L. (1997), The administrative modernisation policy in France, in Kickert 1997: 141–56.

ROWAT, D. C. (1988), *Public Administration in Developed Democracies: A Comparative Study*, New York: Marcel Dekker.

RUGGE, F. (2003), "Administrative Traditions in Western Europe," in B. G. Peters and J. Pierre (eds.), *Handbook of Public Administration*, London: Sage, 177–89.

RYCKEBOER, V. (1996), *Centre de responsabilité*, Paris: Direction Générale de la Fonction Publique.

SCHARPF, F. W. (1993), "Versuch über Demokratie im verhandelnden Staat," in R. Czada and M. Schmidt (eds.), *Verhandlungsdemokratie, Interessenvermittlung, Regierbarkeit*, Opladen: Leske & Budrich, 25–50.

SCHEDLER, K., and PROELLER, I. (2002), "The New Public Management: A perspective from mainland Europe," in K. McLaughlin, S. Osborne, and E. Ferlie (eds.), *New Public Management: Current Trends and Future Prospects*, London: Routledge, 163–80.

SCHRÖTER, E. (2001), "Staats-und Verwaltungsreformen in Europa: Internationale Trends und nationale Profile," in: Schröter, E. (Hrsg.): Empirische Policy-und Verwaltungs-forschung. Lokale, nationale und internationale Perspektiven. Festschrift für Hellmut Wollmann. Opladen: Leske & Budrich, 431–437.

—— and WOLLMANN, H. (1997), "Verwaltung—Öffentlicher Dienst," in Picht, R. et al.. (ed.), *Fremde Freunde. Deutsche und Franzosen vor dem 21. Jahrhundert*, München: Piper, 175–85.

SEIBEL, W. (2001), "Administrative Reforms," in König and Siedentopf 2001: 73–89.

SERIEYX, H. (1994), *L'Etat dans tous ses projects: Un bilan des project de service dans l'administration*, Paris: La Documentation Française.

SIEDENTOPF, H. (1981), Der öffentliche Dienst, in K. König, ed. (1981), *Öffentliche Verwaltung in der Bundesrepublik Deutschland*. Baden-Baden, Nomos: 321–335.

—— (1988a), "A Comparative Overview," in Rowat 1988a: 339–53.

—— (1988b), "Western Germany," in Rowat 1988: 315–38.

—— (1997), "Der öffentliche Dienst in Europa," in R. Morsey, H. Quaritsch, and H. Siedentopf (eds.), *Staat, Politik, Verwaltung in Europa. Gedächtnisschrift für Roman Schnur*, Berlin: Duncker & Humblot, 327–51.

—— and SPEER, B. (2001), "Verwaltungssystem und -kulturen im Frankreich am Beispiel der Entstehung, Umsetzung und Anwendung von Gemeinschaftsrecht," in H. Siedentopf (ed.), *Modernisierug von Staat und Verwaltung*, Speyer: Deutsche Hochschule für Verwaltungswissenschaften, 48–62.

STAMMEN, T., and WESSELS, W. (1996), "The Public Administration System of the Federal Republic of Germany," in Brovetto (ed.), *European Government. A Guide through Diversity*, Milan: EGEA, 128–38.

STEVENS, A. (1988), "The Mitterand Government and the French Civil Service," in J. Howorth and G. Ross (eds.), *Contemporary France*, 2, London: Pinter.

—— (2002), *Europeanisation and the Administration of the EU: a Comparative Perspective*. Queen's Papers on Europeanisation 04/2002, Institute of European Studies, Queen's University of Belfast.

SULEIMAN, E. (1974), *Politics, Power, and Bureaucracy in France: The Adminsitrative*, Princeton: Princeton University Press.

—— (1979), *Les Elites en France. Grands Corps et Grandes Ecoles*, Paris: Seuil.

VERPEAUX, M. (2002), *Les Collectivités locales en France*, Paris: La Documentation Française.

WAGENER, F. (1979), "Der öffentliche Dienst im Staat der Gegenwart," *Veröffentlichungen der Vereinigung der Deutschen Staatsrechtslehrer* (37): 215–36.

WILSFORD, D. (2001), "Running the Bureaucratic State," in A. Farazmand (ed.), *Handbook of Comparative and Devolopment Public Administration*, New York: Marcel Dekker, 963–75.

WOLLMANN, H. (1997), "Modernization of the Public Sector and Public Administration in the Federal Republic of Germany—(Mostly) A Story of Fragmented Incrementalism," in M. Maramatsu and F. Naschold (eds.), *State and Administration in Japan and Germany*, Berlin: de Guyter, 79–101.

—— (2000*a*), "Comparing Institutional Development in Britain and Germany: (Persistant) Divergence or (Progressive) Convergence?" in H. Wollmann and E. Schröter (eds.), *Comparing Public Sector Reform in Britain and Germany: Key Traditions and Trends of Modernisation*, Aldershot: Ashgate, 1–26.

—— (2000*b*), "Local Government Modernization in Germany: between Incrementalism and Reform Waves," *Public Administration* 78(4): 915–36.

—— (2001), "Germany's Trajectory of Public Sector Modernisation: Continuities and Discontinuities," *Policy & Politics* 29(2): 151–69.

—— (2002), "Verwaltungspolitische Reformdiskurse und -verläufe im internationalen Vergleich," in K. König (ed.), *Zum Stand der Verwaltungsforschung*, Baden-Baden: Nomos

—— (n.d.), "Local Government Systems ('path-dependent') Divergence or ('Globalizing') Convergence? The U.K., France and Germany as (comparative) Cases in Point," Berlin.

ZILLER, J. (1993), *Administrations comparées*, Paris: Montchrestien.

—— (1998), "EU Integration and Civil Service Reform," in Sigma (ed.), *Preparing Administration for the European Administrative Space*, Sigma papers 23, Paris: Sigma/OECD, 136–54.

CHAPTER 30

AFTERWORD

EWAN FERLIE

LAURENCE E. LYNN, JR.

CHRISTOPHER POLLITT

30.1 INTRODUCTION

NATURALLY, these final words by the editors cannot for long remain final. The strange mixture of disciplines, concerns, and *instrumentaria* that is the field of public management constantly moves on. Nor can we realistically aspire to offer a clinching summary of what has gone before: the preceding chapters are too numerous and too rich to be reduced to a few bullet points or a seven-step program. What may be more appropriate and feasible, however, is to explore in very general terms what this mass of material tells us about the current coordinates of the field. What do the efforts of our many distinguished contributors show about the view or views which academic public management takes of itself?

We will therefore first take note of what seem to be the main contemporary preoccupations in terms of substance and theme. Then, second, we will review—lightly and quickly—the positions which have been here been taken in respect of five more enduring and fundamental questions. These are:

1. What are the boundaries of "public?"
2. What are the boundaries of "management?"
3. What are the appropriate epistemological frameworks or paradigms within which the work of the field should be carried forward?

4. What particular disciplines and theories are in play?
5. How do scholars in the field handle the distinction between the descriptive, the prescriptive and the normative dimensions of their work?

30.2 SUBSTANCE AND THEMES

Naturally, we as editors bear responsibility for the selection of chapter titles (see the Introduction for an account of our intentions). Within broad chapter titles, however, we gave contributors considerable leeway as to how they interpreted the subject. Several interesting points seem to emerge from their collective and individual exercise of this discretion.

To begin with, it does seem that the "New Public Management," two decades after its christening, continues to exert widespread fascination. Many more chapters position themselves mainly or partly in relation to NPM themes and controversies than in relation to, say, "governance" or "networks" (although the latter two subjects do appear fairly frequently). At least 10 of the 29 substantive chapters are centrally framed by or focused upon the NPM agenda. It is an exaggeration—but only a small one—to say that the *Handbook* has spontaneously developed an NPM center of gravity. By now the NPM may be middle-aged rather than new, but it is still the center of attention for many academics—and for many practitioners too (Hood and Peters, 2004; Pollitt, 2003).

Does this mean that the predictions of (among others) Osborne and Gaebler that there would be a global convergence on NPM/"re-invention" practices are confirmed (Osborne and Gaebler 1992: 328)? Certainly the global reach of these ideas has been impressive. Nevertheless, the arguments presented here suggest a less imperial conclusion. A number of contributors stress how, while the broad ideas and slogans may travel widely, each country makes its own translation or adaptation of the NPM package (e.g., Dingwall and Strangleman; Ferlie and Geraghty; Ingraham; Lynn; Proeller and Schendler; Rubin and Kelly). Constitutional differences, patterns of institutions, administrative cultures and economic circumstances are some of the principal sources of variation. What is more, in some significant cases, NPM ideas have not just been adapted, they have been consciously rejected, or backed away from after initial adoption. Commentators should also be careful to distinguish between different levels of penetration: that NPM ideas are much debated among the chattering classes does not mean that they can necessarily command the backing of authoritative political elites, and that they have achieved the status of white papers or ministerial speeches does not (as any student of our subject knows) mean that they will be put into practice by rank-and-file public officials (Pollitt 2002).

We should also ask whether the NPM has a single stable identity, or whether it is just a portmanteau concept? Many different definitions have been offered in the literature (see, *inter alia*, Ferlie et al. 1996; Hood 1991; Kettl 2000; Lane 2000; Pollitt 2003). Within these covers, also, we find (*inter alia*) Hood treating the NPM as an ideology or religion, while Vining and Weimar stress that at its core lie a set of economic doctrines and Bertelli sees it as a vehicle through which contracts become central to national administrative law. Clearly, it is possible fruitfully to regard the NPM from a variety of perspectives, but this is not the only threat to the coherence of the NPM debate. For it is also the case that NPM doctrines, whether regarded as religious, economic, legal, or simply managerial, contain tensions and paradoxes among themselves (Hood and Peters 2004; Pollitt and Bouckaert 2004). Hood points to paradoxes and anomalies. Mathiasen notes that the NPM "has many parents." Meier and Hill speak of two "wings" of NPM, one of which seeks to eliminate government and another which seeks to liberate managers from red tape and political interference. Power writes that the NPM is neither unitary nor very clearly defined.

One danger here is that *all* contemporary public management reform will be thought of as "NPM," a lack of discrimination that deprives the original title of any specific meaning. None of our contributors fall into this trap, but in the wider literature it occasionally happens. This error leads observers to overlook or under-estimate the mass of reforms which go forward without any of the characteristic NPM labels. There are budgeting reforms which are not in any sense performance budgeting and which have little to do with the NPM doctrine. There are accounting and auditing reforms and HRM reforms and public participation reforms which are similarly distant from NPM thinking.

Finally, even if the NPM remains the center of academic gravity in our field, what else is there in the solar system of public management? The short answer is plain from this *Handbook*—the lasting fundamentals. Issues of constitutions, legalism and juridification, democracy, bureaucracy, accountability, ethics, centralization, and the public interest. For many of these topics the NPM gives a new twist to an ongoing debate, but that is all. Then there are new topics, such as networks, virtual organizations and governance, topics where the NPM features as either just one perspective among several (virtual organizations) or as the previous, now-too-narrow way of thinking (networks, governance).

30.3 THE FIVE FUNDAMENTAL QUESTIONS

Additional insights to the nature of the field can be gained by interrogating the foregoing chapters with each of the five fundamental questions posed at the beginning of this chapter. Whilst we did not specifically ask most of our contributors to reflect on these issues they arguably constitute the key meta-issues for the field. In a sense, therefore, they are always present. Thus we will now examine a set of theoretical, epistemological (and in some cases normative) preferences which have been revealed during the process of addressing the more specific issues about which we asked our distinguished contributors to write.

30.3.1 What are the Boundaries of the "Public?"

It has become a commonplace that the boundaries between the public sector, the private sector, and civil society are becoming less clear-cut and more ambiguous (see, e.g., the chapters by Skelcher, Klijn, Frederickson, and Smith). The consequences of the growing interconnections between hitherto more sharply differentiated spheres of society are both numerous and profound. Indeed, some of them strike at the very heart of our notions of the public domain, and demand far more research and debate than we have yet afforded them. Four cases will have to suffice to illustrate this point. First, Bertelli notes (p. ooo) that the NPM trend to more and more contractualization of hitherto hierarchical relationships "places administrative law in something of a disequilibrium" (although he remains optimistic about the long-run ability of the courts to rectify imbalances). Second, Dobel wonders how "to extend the ethos and values [of the public sector] across networks of partners and contractors" (p. ooo). Third, Bovens acknowledges that "the increasing use of private companies in the provision of public services and the privatization of public organizations raise questions about the public accountability of private managers" (p. ooo). Fourth, Smith notes how many major public policy issues now involve NGOs, and how these bodies may even, *de facto*, define citizenship rights (p. ooo). These are hardly trivial matters. The traditional public sector was defined to a considerable extent by its distinctive laws, ethics, patterns of accountability, and definition of citizenship rights. If all four dimensions are now shifting under the impact of new approaches to management—along with new systems of public accounting (Rubin and Kelly) and of human resource management (Ingraham)—then the normative foundations of the liberal democratic state are in question. Many "public" services will henceforth be delivered under a different legal framework, by private sector or NGO employees operating in a different ethical climate, spending money under more commercial accounting systems, and with reduced political accountability. Already, it is estimated that the US Federal government retains four times as many people through grants and contracts as through direct employment (Light 1999, cited in Skelcher's chapter).

Boundaries are less marked in a second sense also. One "public sector" is less insulated from another than used to be the case. Mathiasen makes the case for the internationalization of public management thinking and advice, and lists many international organizations which have grown up to promote and feed upon this global traffic. Many other chapters add to his testimony on this point, including Dobel (who remarks on the apparent recent international consensus on fundamental administrative values), Skelcher (who records an upsurge of interests in PPPs in Australasia, Scandinavia, the UK, and the USA) and Vining and Weimer (who mention the international reach of economics-based forms of reasoning concerning the design public sector organizations).

30.3.2 What are the Boundaries of Management?

It has to be said that this question is not much discussed within these covers. Most of what can be said must be inferred from reading between the lines. In some ways this is a surprising omission, which leaves several rather important questions hanging in the air. For example, who are the public officials who are *not* managers? How do we characterize them? How are they different? What are their relations with managers like? Have the boundaries between managers and non-managers been changing? If there were ever to be a second edition of this handbook the future editors might well consider commissioning a chapter aimed specifically at such issues.

A far more common preoccupation has been the differences between *public* management and *private* management. On this issue, most of our contributors seem in broad agreement that there *are* such differences and that they are significant. Rainey and Chun produce a finely nuanced account and signal the need for a contingency approach to the complexities of multidimensional difference. But they nevertheless read the literature as pointing towards appreciable differences in respect of formalization, rule intensity, the valuation of financial incentives, levels of altruism, and so on. Lynn puts it more succinctly:

there is widespread professional acknowledgement that constitutions, collective goods production, and electoral institutions create distinctive managerial challenges that justify a separate field. (p. 000)

Bertelli (law), Dobel (ethics), Bovens (accountability), and Meier (bureaucracy) are among the other contributors who also clearly see enduring differences between public and private management (whilst not denying the existence of ambiguous border zones).

Finally, it is the chapter by Lynn that brings the two sets of boundary issues together, as he attempts to define the field of public management. This is seen as encompassing "the organizational structures, managerial practices, and institutionalized values by which officials enact the will of sovereign authority, whether that authority is prince, parliament or civil society" (p. 000).

30.3.3 What are the Preferred Epistemological Frameworks?

Most of our contributors simply get on with their business, without feeling any need to dig up their own epistemological foundations. Nevertheless, we can plainly see a number of different assumptions in action. Perhaps the biggest divergence is between those who largely rely on positivistic assumptions of a researchable external reality and those who, by contrast, adopt a more constructivist stance. Take, for example, our two opening chapters. In Chapter 1, Christopher Hood treats public management as a belief system, a secular religion or movement that is perhaps best understood through efforts culturally and historically to situate and interpret an ever-shifting kaleidoscope of doctrines and catchecisms. In Chapter 2, however, Hal Rainey carefully reviews a large body of research which has, by and large, conceived the task of comparing public and private as an empirical question of looking for externally existing patterns of similarity and/or difference. Both camps are well represented in the remainder of the book. Both contain within themselves many degrees and nuances, and neither term should be used (as each sometimes is) as a catch-all intellectual dismissal.

Within the second group, the social constructivists, another significant epistemological frontier divides those who have taken the "argumentative turn" from those who have not. "What if our language does not simply mirror or picture the world, but instead profoundly shapes our view of it in the first place?" asked Fischer and Forester (1993: 1). While some of our contributors hover uneasily at or near the frontier between these two positions, others are clearly on one side or the other. Looking over the *Handbook* as a whole, one might be tempted to see this divide as, in part, a transatlantic one. Most of the American contributors (Rainey and Chun, Bertelli, Mathiasen, Weimer, Meier and Hill, Rubin and Kelly, Ingraham, and Smith) ignore or stop short of the "argumentative turn." Equally, most of those contributors who actively embrace a more constructivist/constitutive view of language are European (Hood, Bovens, Bogason, Dingwall and Strangleman, Power, and Dahler-Larson). Now of course there are representatives of both camps in the academic public management communities on either side of the ocean (as Bogason's chapter, among others, makes clear) but perhaps the "balance of power" between the two perspectives is indeed different on either Atlantic shore. The problem, perhaps, is that the different camps often seem to rest content with internal conversations, conducted in their own associations and journals, and not to invest much effort in constructive dialogue with the other groups.

30.3.4 What Disciplines and Theories are in Play?

Public management, like public administration, may be "a subject matter in search of a discipline" (Waldo 1968: 2) but it is certainly not short of theories. The evidence between these covers indicates that the field resembles a kind of theoretical car-boot sale. Anything and everything—from pre-modern to post-modern, from public choice to discourse analysis to regime theory to chaos theory—is in use somewhere or other. It would seem that the "decades of heterodoxy" referred to by Lynn (p. ooo) as following upon the seminal works by Dahl, Simon, and Waldo during the 1940s have yet to reach any consensual terminus.

The contributing disciplines are equally diverse. Anthropologists, accountants, economists, lawyers, organization theorists, political scientists, and sociologists are among those who have made notable inputs to the public management literature of the past decade or so. Waldo was right, though one might add that few are now even bothering to look for disciplinary unity. Whether this rich variety is a source of weakness or of strength is a debatable question. It could be argued that diversity fosters adaptability and the kind of three-dimensional vision that comes from multiple perspectives. On the other hand it could equally well be pointed out that the Tower of Babel was not the best place to seek clear understandings.

One interesting point that emerges almost from a side door during the exercise of these different theories and disciplines is that the field remains embarrassingly short of ambitious, large-scale empirical work. (Some post modernist theorists may question the very concept of "empirical research", but most of our contributors, and most of the wider public management community still assert that it should play a central role.) In a substantial number of chapters authors refer to the lack of decisive research (among them Rainey and Chun, Mathiasen, Meier and Hill, Klijn, Øvretveit, Ferlie and Talbot). In part this is no doubt due to the genuine difficulties of organizing and financing such inquiries. Anyone who has tried to conduct large-scale fieldwork in many organizations (and especially in many countries and languages) will testify to the fact that such projects are major management challenges in themselves. Yet the paucity of such studies perhaps goes beyond practical barriers and speaks to a certain failure of imagination, ambition, and cooperative inclination among our community.

30.3.5 How Are Normative/Prescriptive/Descriptive Distinctions Handled?

Looking over the *Handbook*'s many chapters, it seems clear that the field of public management is thoroughly suffused with normative and prescriptive issues. This is no dry science, limiting itself to value-free description and analysis. Indeed, some of the central concepts of the field are irredeemably value-laden: public accountability, public service ethics, public service traditions, quality, and, most recently, "good governance."

Beyond this, it is very common indeed for public management scholars, even when writing academic material, to move into prescriptive mode (many of them, of course, go further and become advisers or consultants as well as academics). Thus (to take just a few local examples) Skelcher's chapter not only describes public private partnerships, but indulges in some searching for ways of reducing the risks and lowering the barriers. Pollitt's analysis of decentralization includes a tentative identification of some of the conditions that may be conducive to or antipathetic to efficiency gains. Klijn examines networks as, *inter alia*, a form of prescriptive theory. Øvretveit tries to pin down those factors which help make quality improvement techniques effective. Smith points to factors which make the use of NGOs more or less risky in the delivery of public policies. And so on. If the aforementioned second edition of this handbook were ever to see the light there would be a strong case for adding a chapter on public management academics as advisers and consultants. These roles are both commonplace and yet at the same time fraught with complex power relationships, theoretical challenges, and ethical issues.

30.4 FINAL THOUGHTS

It is perhaps remarkable that public management/public administration, a field periodically condemned as atheoretical, confused, over-dependent on contradictory and proverb-like statements, or just plain boring, should even qualify for the status of an Oxford *Handbook*. However, a kinder reading of the offerings we have assembled would find this elevation less surprising. This more sympathetic critic might note that ours is an academic arena that contains several species of topic. There are long-standing debates on foundational issues, where some degree of cumulation of knowledge can be detected (for example in relation to accountability, bureaucracy, or budgeting). There are technical issues where academic study may lead to innovations in techniques and methods (such as HRM, quality improvement, or contracting-out). And there are also the green shoots of emerging new topics and theories (as in the debates on consultancy and virtual organizations articulated in the chapters by Saint-Martin and Margetts). The garden of public management is certainly untidy, and its borders are frequently vague, but it is nonetheless a fertile territory, in some parts of which careful cultivation over the years has born considerable fruit. The modern-day ecologist might compliment it on its biodiversity!

The foundational strength of this field comes from the unceasing relevance of its core subject matter. The (alleged) "rolling back of the state" and "end of big government" have come and gone without any discernable lessening in the intensity of public debate concerning law and order, the provision of healthcare, education, and social security, the regulation of public utilities, and a host of other public management-type issues. To these have been added more international concerns, including terrorism, climate change, environmental protection, immigration, and the role of international and supranational organizations, such as the United Nations and the European Commission. Indeed, there is a sense in which, as public trust in political leaders and bold ideological programs has dwindled, public management has come to bear an *increased* load of attention and expectation. Many political leaders have fostered this increasing prominence by announcing programs of administrative reform and claiming that they will be better than their opponents at the business of *managing* the state. In some instances they have attempted to displace political crises onto the administrative machinery—not necessarily solving the political crisis but certainly helping to foster citizen anxiety about public services. Indeed, possession of some program of public management reform (preferably with a catchy title like Reinventing Government, the Citizen's Charter, Copernicus, or *Een Andere Overheid*) seems to have become a *sine qua non* for political parties aspiring to government. This was not the case fifty years ago.

Thus we are confident that public management as a field of study will not disappear. It may change its name, and its disciplinary recruiting grounds. Having (in some countries, but not others) moved its academic base from law to political science departments to business and professional schools, it may move again. It may be studied by professors who profess all manner of disciplinary allegiances, from computer studies to development economics to social anthropology. In this unpredictable future the NPM may come to be regarded as a form of late twentieth-century cargo cult, and earlier fashions for administrative durability and continuity may come around again. But, whatever future academic formations evolve, we believe that there will remain a need for periodic stock-taking of the field of public management. We have been honored to have the responsibility for shaping this particular early twenty-first century version.

REFERENCES

FERLIE, E., PETTIGREW, A., ASHBURNER, L., and FITZGERALD, L. (1996), *The New Public Management in Action*, Oxford: Oxford University Press.

FISCHER, F., and FORESTER, J. (eds.) (1993), *The Argumentative Turn in Policy Analysis and Planning*, London: University College Press.

HOOD, C. (1991), "A Public Management for all Seasons," *Public Administration* 69(1): 3–19.

—— and PETERS, G. B. (2004), "The Middle Aging of New Public Management: into the age of paradox?" *Journal of Public Administration Research and Theory* 14(3): 267–82.

KETTL, D. (2000), *The Global Public Management Revolution: A Report on the Transformation of Governance*, Washington, DC.: Brookings Institution.

LANE, J.-E. (2000), *New Public Management*, London: Routledge.

Osborne, D., and Gaebler, T. (1992), *Reinventing Government: How the Entrepreneurial Spirit is Transforming the Public Sector*, Reading, MA: Addison Wesley.

Pollitt, C. (2002), "Clarifying Convergence: Striking Similarities and Durable Differences in Public Management Reform," *Public Management Review*, 4(1): 471–92.

—— (2003), *The Essential Public Manager*, Maidenhead and Philadelphia: Open University Press/McGraw Hill.

—— and Bouckaert, G. (2004) *Public Management Reform: A Comparative Analysis*, 2nd edn., Oxford: Oxford University Press.

Waldo, R. (1968), "The Scope of the Theory of Public Administration," in J. C. Charlesworth (ed.), *The Theory and Practice of Public Administration*, Philadelphia: American Academy of Political and Social Science/American Society for Public Administration.

AUTHOR INDEX

INDEX